中国式现代化与丝路发展

Chinese Modernization and Development of Silk Road

张翼 孙壮志 张志强 等著
Zhang Yi　Sun Zhuangzhi　Zhang Zhiqiang　et al.

中国社会科学出版社

图书在版编目（CIP）数据

中国式现代化与丝路发展/张翼等著. —北京：中国社会科学出版社，2023.10
ISBN 978-7-5227-2610-6

Ⅰ.①中⋯ Ⅱ.①张⋯ Ⅲ.①现代化建设—研究—中国 Ⅳ.①D61

中国国家版本馆 CIP 数据核字（2023）第 178401 号

出 版 人	赵剑英
责任编辑	乔镜蕚
责任校对	闫　萃
责任印制	王　超

出　　版	中国社会科学出版社
社　　址	北京鼓楼西大街甲 158 号
邮　　编	100720
网　　址	http://www.csspw.cn
发 行 部	010-84083685
门 市 部	010-84029450
经　　销	新华书店及其他书店
印　　刷	北京明恒达印务有限公司
装　　订	廊坊市广阳区广增装订厂
版　　次	2023 年 10 月第 1 版
印　　次	2023 年 10 月第 1 次印刷
开　　本	710×1000　1/16
印　　张	32.25
字　　数	502 千字
定　　价	168.00 元

凡购买中国社会科学出版社图书，如有质量问题请与本社营销中心联系调换
电话：010-84083683
版权所有　侵权必究

前　　言

　　2023年是"一带一路"倡议提出十周年，十年来丝路沿线国家守望相助，共同绘就了精谨细腻的丝路发展工笔画。中国共产党第二十次全国代表大会，擘画了以中国式现代化全面推进中华民族伟大复兴的宏伟蓝图。中国式现代化的成功拓展和推进，为世界发展带来了新的机遇。中国式现代化是人口规模巨大的现代化，是全体人民共同富裕的现代化，是物质文明和精神文明相协调的现代化，是人与自然和谐共生的现代化，是走和平发展道路的现代化。中国式现代化既有各国现代化的共同特征，更有基于自己国情的鲜明特色。新中国成立特别是改革开放以来，中国用几十年时间走完西方发达国家几百年走过的工业化历程，创造了经济快速发展和社会长期稳定的奇迹，为中华民族伟大复兴开辟了广阔前景。

　　中国发展的成功经验成为世界关注的研究现象。在"一带一路"倡议提出十周年之际，为更好地讲好中国式现代化的故事，增进"一带一路"沿线国家更好地感知中国、理解中国，推动海外中国学的发展。社会发展战略研究院组织了不同学科的学者和格鲁吉亚学者，一起完成了这本共述丝路友好的学术著作。著作分别从中国式现代化与现代化发展的中国经验、中国式现代化与中国发展主动性、中国式现代化与中国社会发展经验、中国式现代化与中国经济发展经验、中国式现代化与中格丝路发展新机遇五个方面展开，如同一幅精谨细腻的丝路工笔画，涉及中国式现代化与现代化话语体系的构建、现代化视域下的"一带一路"建设与欧亚地区治理、世界百年未有之大变局与人类文明新形态、中国式现代化与中国全球治理新主张、中国式现代化与人民现代化美好生活的构建，以及"一带一路"倡议和格鲁吉亚的前景、中国式现代化和社会发展对格鲁吉亚的影响等内容。著作主题内容丰富，聚焦学术前沿，是一部凝聚中国与格鲁吉亚两国学者共同学术经验的力作。自中国社会科学院在格鲁吉亚设立中国研究中心以来，中国研究中心始终响应"一带一路"倡议，增进"一带一路"民心相通，开展"一带一路"学术研究，努力搭建中格高水平学术交流平台。在中国驻格鲁吉亚大使馆支持和参与下，社会发展战略研究院发挥中国研究中心平台优势，2019年与格鲁吉亚理工大学在格鲁吉亚举办新中国成立七十周年图片展及相关国际学术研讨会。2021年与格鲁吉亚理工大学等机构合作举办"百年中国社会发展与社会变迁"国际学术研讨会。2022年与格鲁吉亚第比利斯国立大学等机构共同举办"'一带一路'：中国式现代化与社会发展经验"国际研讨会。这些高端学术活动的举办，增进了中格双方学者的学术交流，对于促进中格双方学者在"各美其美，美美与共"中加强文明交流互鉴，共同讲好发展中国家走向现代化的故事，发挥了桥梁和纽带作用。

今天，中国新的发展蓝图徐徐展开。格鲁吉亚在国家建设事业中不断取得新成就。中格两国建交30年来，无论国际和地区形势如何变化，中格双方始终相互尊重、平等相待，将两国关系保持在健康稳定发展的轨道上。

实现第二个百年奋斗目标是中国人民共同的追求和梦想。中国式现代化属于中国，也属于世界。格鲁吉亚也发挥自身优势，在走向现代化过程中，不断取得新的发展成绩。现代化是各国人民的共同期待和目标，但每个国家都应结合自身实际作出路径选择。当前，世界之变、时代之变、历史之变加速演进，各国都在思考未来之路。中格双方学者通力协作、共同努力，完成这一学术著作，在交流互鉴中践行"一带一路"倡议共建共享精神和全球文明倡议，在学术合作中构建人类命运共同体，将为两国人民增进相互了解、相互借鉴，做出新的贡献。

著　者
二零二三年八月于北京

Foreword

The year 2023 marks the tenth anniversary of the proposal of the Belt and Road Initiative (BRI). Over the past decade, BRI participants have helped each other and contributed to their common prosperous development, just like an architect refining the blueprint. The 20th National Congress of the Communist Party of China drew up a grand blueprint for advancing the rejuvenation of the Chinese nation on all fronts through a Chinese path to modernization. The successful practice of Chinese modernization has brought about new opportunities for global development. Chinese modernization is the modernization of a huge population, the modernization of common prosperity for all, the modernization of material and cultural-ethical advancement, the modernization of harmony between humanity and nature, and the modernization of peaceful development. It not only shares common characteristics with the modernization of other countries, but also boasts unique features based on its own national conditions. Since the founding of the Republic of China in 1949, especially since the reform and opening up, China has completed a process of industrialization that took developed countries several centuries in the space of mere decades, bringing about the two miracles of rapid economic growth and enduring social stability. This opens up broad prospects for the great rejuvenation of the Chinese nation.

Consequently, China's successful experience of development has become a research object of worldwide concern. On the occasion of the tenth anniversary of the proposal of the BRI, National Institute of Social Development (NISD) has organized scholars from various disciplines from Chinese Academy of Social

Sciences (CASS) and Georgian scholars to complete this book on the friendship among BRI participants. The aim is to better tell stories of Chinese modernization, enhance the BRI participants' understanding of China, and boost the development of China Studies overseas. This book involves four aspects: Chinese modernization and China's related experience; Chinese modernization and initiative for China's development; Chinese modernization and China's experience of social development; Chinese modernization and China's experience of economic development; and Chinese path to modernization and new opportunities for the development of the China-Georgia BRI cooperation. Just like an architect refining the blueprint, it touches on topics of Chinese modernization and the construction of discourse systems for modernization, the building of the BRI and the governance in the Eurasian region from the perspective of modernization. It also covers Chinese modernization and China's new propositions on global governance, Chinese modernization and the building of people's better modern life, profound changes unseen in a century and new models for human civilization, prospects for the BRI and Georgia, and impacts of Chinese modernization and social development on Georgia, among others. This book, with rich content and cutting-edge academic results, represents a masterpiece and the crystallization of the academic experience of Chinese and Georgian scholars.

Since the establishment of the China Research Center in Georgia by CASS, the center has always been responding to the BRI, promoting people-to-people connectivity among BRI-related, conducting BRI-related studies, and striving to provide a platform for high level academic exchanges between China and Georgia. In 2019, with the support and participation of the Embassy of the People's Republic of China in Georgia, NISD fully leveraged the advantages of the Center and held a picture exhibition on the occasion of the 70th anniversary of the founding of the People's Republic of China/as well as related international academic seminars, together with Georgia Institute of Technology in Georgia. In 2021, it held an international academic seminar under the theme "China's Social Development and Vicissitudes over the Past Century" in cooperation with Georgia Institute of Technology and other institutes. In 2022, it held an international seminar themed "BRI: Chinese Modernization and China's Experience of Social Development" together with Ivane Javakhishvili Tbilisi State University and other institutes. Such high-end academic events have facilitated academic exchanges among scholars from China and Georgia, and served as a bridge in promoting inter-civilization exchanges and mutual learning between the two sides. They have also helped to better tell the stories of developing countries marching towards modernization, as both sides proper respectively and together.

Today, China is entering a new era for development, and Georgia has continuously made new achievements in terms of national development. Since China and Georgia established diplomatic ties three decades ago, both sides have treated each other with mutual respect as equals, thus keeping their relations on a track of healthy and stable development.

The second centenary goal of building China into a great modern socialist country in all respects is a dream shared by all Chinese people. Chinese modernization belongs to both China and the world. Georgia has also given play to its strengths and delivered new development outcomes while marching towards modernization. Modernization represents a common expectation and goal for people in all countries, but each country should work out its own pathway based on its own national conditions. Today, as our world, our times, and history are changing rapidly, all countries are thinking about their paths forward. Chinese and Georgian scholars have completed this book through joint efforts, staying true to the principle of cooperation for shared benefits under the BRI and practiced the Global Civilization Initiative. They have built a community with a shared future for mankind through academic cooperation, thus making new contributions to mutual understanding and mutual learning between the peoples of both sides.

Authors
In Beijing
August 2023

目 录

第一编 中国式现代化与现代化发展的中国经验

中国式现代化与现代化话语体系的构建 …………………… 张　翼（3）
现代化视域下的"一带一路"建设与欧亚地区治理 ……… 孙壮志（20）
在世界百年未有之大变局中创造人类文明新形态 ………… 张志强（30）

第二编 中国式现代化与中国发展主动性

中国式现代化与中国全球治理新主张 ……………………… 欧阳向英（43）
中国式现代化新进程与发展战略的主动性 ………………… 景向辉（55）

第三编 中国式现代化与中国社会发展经验

中国式现代化与教育强国建设 ……………………………… 孙兆阳（77）
中国式现代化与人民美好生活的构建 ……………………… 马　峰（90）
中国式现代化与城市老龄友好型社区建设 ………………… 戈艳霞（99）

第四编 中国式现代化与中国经济发展经验

中国式现代化与中国房产税收政策模拟分析 ……………… 娄　峰（119）
中国式现代化作为文明新形态的理论阐释 ………………… 刘洪愧（137）

第五编　中国式现代化与中格丝路发展新机遇

中国现代化进程中的教育国际合作与交流 …………… 卢雨菁（159）
中国"一带一路"倡议和格鲁吉亚的前景 …… 塔玛尔·多尔巴拉（170）
历史和当代背景下的格鲁吉亚与中国关系 …… 纳娜·格拉什维利（178）
从古至今：格鲁吉亚人眼中的中国 ………………………… 奥　塔（186）
中国式现代化和社会发展对格鲁吉亚的
　　影响 ……………………………………… 塔玛尔·巴达舒里（198）

CONTENTS

Chapter 1 Chinese Modernization and the Chinese Experience of Modernization Development

Chinese Modernization and the Formation of its Modernization
    Discourse System ·· Zhang Yi (209)
Enhancing the Belt and Road Cooperation and the Eurasian Governance
    from the Perspective of Modernization ··············· Sun Zhuangzhi (233)
Creating a New Form of Human Civilization in the Profound World
    Changes Unseen in a Century ····················· Zhang Zhiqiang (248)

Chapter 2 Chinese Modernization and New Initiative for China's Development

Chinese Modernization and China's New Proposition for Global
    Governance ··· Ouyang Xiangying (267)
New Process of Chinese Modernization and Initiative of Development
    Strategy ·· Jing Xianghui (286)

Chapter 3 Chinese Modernization and Chinese Experience of Social Development

Chinese Modernization and China's Efforts to Build a Strong Education
    System ·· Sun Zhaoyang (319)

Chinese Modernization and People's Better Life .... Ma Feng (341)
Chinese Modernization and China's Efforts to Build Urban
    Aging-friendly Communities .... Ge Yanxia (355)

Chapter 4　Chinese Modernization and Chinese Experience of Economic Development

Simulation Analysis of Chinese Modernization and China's Real
    Estate Tax Policy .... Lou Feng (385)
Theoretical Elucidation of the Chinese Modernization as a New
    Model for Human Advancement .... Liu Hongkui (409)

Chapter 5　Chinese Path to Modernization and New Opportunities for the Development of the China-Georgia BRI Cooperation

International Cooperation and Exchange in Education in the Process
    of Chinese Modernization: Taking Georgia as an
    Example .... Lu Yujing (439)
The Belt and Road Initiative and Perspectives of
    Georgia .... Tamar Dolbaia (457)
Georgia-China Relations in Historical and Contemporary
Context .... Nana Gelashvili (466)
China in the Eyes of Georgian People: From Antiquity to the
Present Times .... Otari Tchigladze (477)
The Impact of Chinese Modernization and Social Development
    on Georgia .... Tamar Patashuri (491)

第一编

中国式现代化与现代化发展的中国经验

中国式现代化与现代化话语体系的构建

张 翼[*]

一 现代化、西方中心主义与欧美现代化话语

现代化[①]是农业社会向工业社会转变以来的人类发展进程，其主要表现为科技创新驱动所引发的生产方式、分配方式、交换方式、消费方式和社会组织方式的一系列变迁以及由此推动的整个社会结构的转型过程[②]。现代化大体可以划分为两个阶段：第一阶段，从农业社会向工业社会的转型——由大机器发明引起的工业革命所带来的社会结构转型；第二阶段，从工业社会向后工业社会的转型——由信息技术引起的人工智能革命所带来的社会结构转型[③]。当然，如果细化人类社会的最新转型趋

---

[*] 张翼，中国社会科学院社会发展战略研究院研究员、院长。

[①] 什么是现代化理论？这个问题在学界长期争论不休。自20世纪50年代已降，现代化研究经历了"经典现代化理论""后现代化理论"和"新现代化理论"三个时期。在不同阶段，学术界讨论的重心有所不同。第一时期聚焦于"二战"之后逐步独立的发展中国家的现代化上，第二时期聚焦于对第一时期现代化理论的反思上，第三时期聚焦于科技进步与社会风险防范上。参见何传启《如何成为一个现代化国家》，《世界科技研究与发展》2018年第1期，第5—16页。

[②] 以过程的视角解释现代化，就使现代化与发展紧密联系在一起。参见［美］吉尔伯特·罗兹曼主编《中国的现代化》，国家社会科学基金"比较现代化"课题组译，江苏人民出版社1995年版，第4页。

[③] 奈斯比特在《大趋势》一书中，充分肯定了丹尼尔·贝尔在《后工业社会的来临》一书中的判断，将工业社会之后的社会称为"信息社会"，并认为信息社会彻底改变了社会结构。

势,还可以构建出第三阶段或第四阶段的现代化理论假说①。在后工业化的不断演进中,当前社会实践与理论研究的焦点已逐渐转移到互联网、人工智能、大数据、区块链和元宇宙等引发的人类向"数字社会"(digital society)或"人机共生社会"(Human-Robot Co-Existence Society)的转型问题上②。

因为现代化率先发轫于英法,故从参照系角度,西方学界经常将西欧地区发生的这种变迁称为"内生现代化"(modernization from within),而将受西欧影响而衍生的其他国家和地区的变迁称为"外生现代化"(modernization from without)。在早期阶段,内生性与先发性(早发)联系在一起,外生性与后发性密切相关。所以,在西方学界,将早发与内生结合,建构出"早发内生性现代化"和"后发外生性现代化"概念。第二次世界大战之后,在全球化影响下,世界各国加强了政治、经济、社会、文化与生态文明的全方位交流,这就使各地的现代化,在内生性中交织外生性,外生性中嵌套内生性。但在路径依赖与话语霸权意义上,大多数发展中国家被赋予了较强的"后发外生性"特征。

还因为"现代"具有与"传统"相比较而发生的变迁性,故而,如将农业社会视为现代社会的参照,则现代化就具有西方先发意义的"成熟"的工业化特征。因此,为研究现代化而形成的所谓古典现代化理论,便以西方资本主义的缘起与发展过程为基础而构建了"传统—现代"的理论分析框架,并在话语霸权的作用下,国际上将西欧和北美等国建构为"现代""先进""理性""民主""世俗化"等,而将广大发展中国家建构为"传统""落后"与"蒙昧"等,从而形成由西方学者言说的"西方中心主义"或"欧洲中心主义"——这既为西方知识界建构"西

---

① 罗荣渠在讨论现代化的阶段性问题时,就将其概括为"三次现代化浪潮",第一次发生于1780—1860年,由工业革命所推动。第二次发生于"19世纪下半叶至20世纪初,主要由"电与钢铁"所推动。第三次现代化发生于"20世纪下半叶",主要由石油能源、人工合成材料、微电子技术、人工智能等推动。见罗荣渠《现代化新论》,华东师范大学出版社2013年版,第108—113页。

② 在万物互联背景下,将来发展的趋势,还会强化人机物三位一体社会(a tri-world of people, computers, and things)的特征。

方的东方学"打下了实践基础，也在话语指称中奠定了西方的现代化理论基础，并通过教育与知识的非对称传播，以及各类学科对东方社会的跟踪研究，将"西方书写的东方"体系化，然后再渗透进发展中国家的学术体系，形成以西方为中心的对东方社会的解释力。这种"话语霸权"，既在殖民地和半殖民地时期强化了西方对东方的"解释力"，也在后殖民主义时期强化了西方对发展中国家的意识形态控制[①]。随着第二次世界大战的结束，伴随经济中心从欧洲向美国的转移，又逐渐生成了以"美国中心主义"为基础的现代化知识体系——即所谓的盎格鲁-萨克逊现代化知识体系。因为英国王室本身具有来自"诺曼"的基因，故有人还会加上"诺曼"而丰富其内涵。也因为现代化被赋予西方式意义的"发展与进步"色彩，所以，以现代化为时代表征而形成的现代哲学社会科学，就具有先发意义的西方式"初创—成熟"路径依赖关系。

西方在近代迅速推进生产力革命的同时，也催生了资本主义生产关系。资产阶级发展的每一阶段，都伴随着其对政治上层建筑的相应改造。13世纪英国的大宪章限制了封建王权。都铎王朝形成以新教为主的君主专制国家——在这个意义上，生产力的发展同时推进了君主专制上层建筑与宗教上层建筑的改革。肇始于1640年的英国资产阶级革命，最终使克伦威尔将查理一世送上断头台。1688—1689年的光荣革命确立了君主立宪制，以资产阶级统治稳定了工业革命成果，形成国王"统而不治"的基本格局。1832年议会改革保障了工业资产阶级的选举权。1837年的《人民宪章》运动，废除了议会候选人的财产资格限制条件，为年满21岁的城市男子赋予选举权与匿名投票权。1884年的议会改革最终赋予所有成年男子以选举权。

在法国，路易十五的穷兵黩武、持续发生的通货膨胀、接连不断的自然灾害激发了第一阶层、第二阶层和第三阶层之间的矛盾。启蒙运动调动了经济上业已取得统治地位的资产阶级的革命热情，其联合和利用工人阶级和农民阶级，发起了举世闻名的1789年"大革命"，通过了

---

① [美]萨义德：《东方学》，王宇根译，生活·读书·新知三联书店1999年版，第16页。

《人权宣言》(宣布人们生来而且始终自由平等),建立了法兰西第一共和国,将路易十六送上了断头台,最后以"雾月政变"巩固了革命成果,颁布了《拿破仑民法典》,传播了民主自由思想,树立了"天赋人权、三权分立、社会契约、私有财产神圣不可侵犯、法律面前人人平等"的政治理念。按照托克维尔的解释,大革命既是对旧制度之教权的革命,也是对王权的革命——但在暴力指向上直接打碎了王权。因为封建专制政府——中央集权制政府——"只有一个行政实体,被置于法兰西王国中央,全国的行政管理制度都由它来制定;几乎全部的国内事务都只由一个大臣统领;各省一切具体事务也都由一个代理人掌管;没有附属行政机构或事先获准方可行动的机构;特别法院审理与政府有关的所有案件并庇护所有政府官员。"[1] 所以,在政府作为取向与人民预期愈拉愈远时,人民便将所有愤恨集中到中央政府那里——这使大革命此起彼伏、持续不断、惨烈推进、直到彻底打碎封建专制统治。

从整个现代化的历史可以看出,在其改变传统社会生产力与生产关系的同时,也迫使上层建筑随经济基础的变化而不断变化,由此不断推动政府转型、宗教转型和社会转型:推动政府从封建贵族地主专制转型为资产阶级统治,并将宗教永久置于国家的威权之下,从而在资本主义经济的发展中逐步形成繁荣的工业社会。因此,在西方历史上,现代化不是和平发展的结果,而是在旧制度的瓦砾上,伴随血与火的洗礼而进行的上层建筑改造。不管是英国,还是法国,他们都通过一系列旷日持久的暴力或非暴力革命(光荣革命),才建立起了不同于封建时代的资产阶级国家。在完成国内经济基础与上层建筑的配置任务后,就开始了源源不断地对外扩张,将美洲、亚洲和非洲沦为殖民地。由此也在西方现代化的话语体系中,建构出了宗主国与殖民地国之间的话语关系,甚至于也惨无人道地推进了"黑奴贸易"[2]。资本主义现代化的发展,更造成

---

[1] [法]托克维尔:《旧制度与大革命》,李焰明译,译林出版社 2018 年版,第 2 编第 5 章。
[2] 马克思曾经说,当我们把自己的目光从资产阶级文明的故乡转向殖民地的时候,资产阶级文明的极端虚伪和它的野蛮本性就赤裸裸地呈现在我们面前,因为它在故乡还装出一副很体面的样子,而一到殖民地它就丝毫不加掩饰了。

了第一次世界大战和第二次世界大战,最终以夺取千百万无辜者的生命而开启了其下一旅程。

正如马克思和恩格斯在《共产党宣言》里所说的那样,"美洲的发现、绕过非洲的航行,给新兴的资产阶级开辟了新天地。东印度和中国的市场、美洲的殖民化、对殖民地的贸易、交换手段和一般的商品的增加,使商业、航海业和工业空前高涨,因而使正在崩溃的封建社会内部的革命因素迅速发展"——这预示资本所到之处(即使以殖民地方式推进的资本主义),都以资本之现代逻辑修改其所席卷之地的社会发展和社会转型逻辑。

总之,西方的现代化实践,从萌芽到开花结果,书写了文艺复兴、大航海与发现新大陆、启蒙运动与人本主义、重视科学技术、推进宗教改革等话语,奠定了西方现代科学与现代哲学社会科学的基础[①]。在对国家的建构中,又以"人权平等""私有财产神圣不可侵犯"与"三权分立"等制度设计,搭建起了资本主义的上层建筑大厦,并发展出市民社会,由此推进人类进入工业社会和后工业社会。宗教改革将人从神的代言者罗马教廷那里解放出来,转变为因信取义的"勤勉"劳动者,使其顺应"命定"的安排而合理地积累财富与投资取利——由此建构了宗教上层建筑与资本主义制度的适应性[②]。政治上层建筑的革命打破了君权神授与权力的血缘继承性,以现代政党制度为基础建立起代议制政府,限制了权力的滥用,鼓励了市场竞争。市民社会的出现,既在政府与家庭的宽广地带建立了酒馆、咖啡馆、俱乐部、博物馆、影剧院等公共领域,也以书报刊行的方式保障了民意的表达。凡此一切,都拓展了个体的社会活动空间,解放了生产力——不断累积为西方的"现代性"。因此,在

[①] 在牛顿的经典力学发表之后,欧洲于17世纪末和18世纪初,逐渐将这些"规律"植入社会意识形态与日常生活。这使人们在看待自然现象时,不再寄托于神的解释,而接受科学的解释。

[②] 虽然托克维尔认为反宗教并非大革命本身的特征,但反宗教运动却贯穿法国大革命的始终——"法国大革命早期的一个步骤就是向教会发起攻击,源自大革命的种种激情中,最先点燃和最后熄灭的便是反宗教狂热。"——见[法]托克维尔《旧制度与大革命》,李焰明译,译林出版社2018年版,第3章。

马克思和恩格斯看来，资产阶级既在其不到一百年的阶级统治中创造了比过去一切世代还要多的生产力，但同时也在每个毛孔都释放着血与肮脏的东西。

二 现代化与现代化的反思性话语

众所周知，社会学与其他哲学社会科学一样，自其初创时期开始，就以西方为背景建构现代化话语体系。奠基了西方社会学的主要人物，基本以"传统—现代"的叙事模式描述社会发展的宏观过程。孔德基于"神学阶段—形而上学阶段—实证阶段"而构建了"军事时期—法权时期—工业时期"论；梅因建构了"身份社会—契约社会"论；斯宾塞建构了"军事社会—工业社会"论；滕尼斯建构了"社区—社会"论；托克维尔建构了"贵族制—民主制"论；涂尔干建构了"机械团结—有机团结"论；齐美尔建构了"自然经济社会与货币经济社会"论；舍勒建构了"休戚与共社会与竞争社会"论；韦伯不仅建构了"传统资本主义—理性资本主义经济"①论，还建构了"传统型统治—克里斯马统治—法理型统治"②论；帕森斯建构了"特殊主义—普遍主义"论和"传统社会—现代社会"模式变量论；经济学家刘易斯建构了传统经济部门与现代经济部门论，这个论述被社会学广泛采用，罗斯托的"起飞说"等，也成为社会学家讨论社会与经济发展过程的基本话语。应该说，如上所述的这些理论，基本都以西方现代化实践为参照，深入讨论了西方现代

---

① 或者传统资本主义与理性资本主义。在韦伯看来，新教伦理、理性主义、私有财产、政教分离与市场等的结合，推动了欧洲资本主义对封建主义的替代。但韦伯的这种认识，恰与宗教的世俗化、个人主义的出现等理论形成张力。韦伯认为，加尔文教是在强化其宗教教义与宗教组织生活的过程中形成资本主义精神的。理性资本主义是加尔文教徒运用宗教禁欲主义驾驭世俗行为——在禁欲的同时，将经济行为与职业生活视为天职的结果。这里要问：在加尔文教那里，解决了理性主义与宗教主义的冲突吗？

② 彼得·伯克（Peter Burke）在《历史学与社会理论》一书中曾经指出，"克里斯玛"这一概念（charisma，源于教会史专家鲁道夫·索姆对早期教会"克里斯玛式组织"的相关讨论，韦伯在其论述中将其世俗化，赋予其以更普遍的适用性。[英]彼得·伯克：《历史学与社会理论》，李康译，上海人民出版社2019年版。

化、同时也涉及了非西方的现代化问题。

尤其要说明的是——自孔德以来的社会学基本范式，也天然具有帕森斯意义的西方现代性特征①。广被引用的韦伯宗教社会学，就以欧美中心论构造其理论大厦。为在理论上回答为什么西方会发展出理性（或现代）资本主义，而在农业社会取得辉煌成就的东方却没有发展出理性资本主义的问题，其以传统资本主义定义历史上曾经存在过的各种资本生产与经商现象，然后以理性资本主义定义加尔文教促动形成的资本主义精神。韦伯力图说明，在新教伦理与理性资本主义具有某种亲和性——因为东方的各种宗教不能形成理性资本主义精神，故其会重复传统而在发展道路上步履维艰——言下之意，没有理性资本主义精神的浇灌，东方很难形成现代资本主义的丰厚土壤②。这就给西方的东方学得出了一个暗含韦伯意义的"合理化"结论：东方社会的现代化（或除欧美之外其他社会的现代化），需要借助西方文化的推动才能进行。虽然韦伯自己并不是一个一元决定论社会学家，其表述有时显现着矛盾性地"似是而非"③，其欧美中心论④的叙事风格，的确存在许多对"他者"（包括中国）的误读问题⑤。如果不论上述误读，则毋庸置疑的是，在韦伯的笔下，自路德以来发生的一系列基督教改革，以及西欧各国的宗教的本土化运动，推动了宗教意识形态的现代化进程，解决了宗教与资本主义发

---

① 帕森斯认为，现代西方社会的发展（即现代化）在人类史上具有普遍意义，它不是随机的，而是具有导向性的，尽管这并不排除现代化实际包含不同的社会形态。

② 自20世纪40年代以来中国部分学人讨论的"儒家资本主义"或"新儒家资本主义"对此进行了回应。

③ 韦伯在其《关于"资本主义精神"的反批评的结束语》中说：认为资本主义经济制度和资本主义"精神"仅仅产生于宗教改革是"荒谬的"。他接着又说，宗教—心理因素只是在众多其他的，尤其是自然—地理"条件"的背景下才能直接促进资本主义的发展……我的研究仅仅是一种与新兴的现代资本主义相适应的道德"生活方式"的发展……因此，如果有人"高估了我的讨论范围"，这不是我的错。见［德］韦伯《新教伦理与资本主义精神》，闫克译，上海人民出版社2018年版，第467—468页。

④ 苏国勋：《韦伯关于中国文化论述的再思考》，《社会学研究》2011年第4期。

⑤ 关于这一点，中外社会学家都有反思。在布朗大学社会学系执教的罗伯特·马什（Robert M. Marsh）发表于《美国社会学杂志》的文章，就命名为《韦伯对中国传统法律的误读》（Weber's Misunderstanding of Chinese Traditional Law）》。实际上，要全面理解韦伯的洞见，需要回到韦伯本身，即其自称是一个"经济的民族主义者"。

展的相适应问题，以宗教伦理赋予了教徒以积累财富的道德合理性，在现代化与宗教活动之间构筑起自洽的理论相关性话语。

另外，需要指出的是，西方学者对东方社会的误读，非独发生在韦伯身上，其他社会科学也充满了对非西方社会的歧视性。第二次世界大战之后走向独立的发展中国家，通过移植而新建的现代化话语，就不免带有以西方解释东方的特性。在实践上，发展中国家的最大渴望，即是通过向西方学习以跟上或者赶上世界发展水平。西方的现代化理论为发展中国家开出的药方，无不先入为主地打上"现代化即西方化""西方化即美国化"的政治烙印。有些著述还会将现代化特意建构为仅仅是对发展中国家发展学说的研究。绝大多数发展中国家"全盘西化"的实践，因为"不服水土"而遭受重大挫折[1]。而挫折的主要原因，经常会被西方解释为"不彻底的现代化"或"不完全的现代化"——此类话语的逻辑是：唯有经过西方式自由民主制度的上层建筑改造，或者经由长期的殖民过程，发展中国家才能顺利步入现代化正途。但发展中国家西方化的结果，非但没有迎来预期的繁荣，反倒强化了宗主国对原殖民地国家的政治与经济渗透——以所谓"自由"的理念，建造了"实然"的不平等，形成了新的"买办"，解构了发展中国家的经济民族主义与学术民族主义。这激发了学术界对古典现代化理论"二分模式"与"西化模式"的批判性思考，发展出著名的"依附理论"和"世界体系理论"[2]。

在依附理论[3]看来，发展中国家现代化受阻的主要原因，不在于自己的不努力，也不在于自己的国情不符合西方资本主义的政治与经济逻辑，

---

[1] ［美］亨廷顿：《变动社会中的政治秩序》，王冠华等译，上海人民出版社2021年版。在其第一章——"政治秩序和政治衰朽"之"政治差距"部分，就详细讨论过此类问题。

[2] 先有现代化事实，后有现代化研究。有关现代化的理论研究，起源于20世纪50年代和60年代。"二战"之后，在讨论原殖民地半殖民地国家在独立自主之后的发展问题时，提出了"现代化"（modernization）这一概念。因为最初将现代化简单解释为"西方化"，把"西方化"简单解释为"美国化"，故后来的现代化理论，才着重从批判原初理论出发，围绕"依附论"和"世界体系理论"展开争论。

[3] 虽然依附论在其发展过程中，有"激进主义依附论""改良主义依附论"和"正统主流依附论"等，但其反思的主题均聚焦于发展中国家与发达国家的关系问题上，其理论基础奠基在马克思主义与经济民族主义的结合上。

而在于宗主国将原殖民地国家沦为能源或原材料供给国的那种依附结构，以及借此而建成的贸易与国际分工体系——将广大发展中国家置于资源出口的依赖型位置，形成资本主义体系中的不平等交换关系，使宗主国拿走大部分利润，而给依附国留下贫穷①。一句话，发达国家通过其制定的世界贸易规则，建构了不平等的"谈判"机制，长期使殖民地或原殖民地国家处于"依附"状态，这引发了学界对弗兰克所说的"欠发展的发展"（the development of underdevelopment）"的广泛热议。虽然大多数学者只将依附理论用于对非洲与美洲的研究，但如果考察西欧与东欧在16—17世纪的发展史就会发现，在西欧城市化迅速发展与农奴制衰落的过程中，在东欧或"中东欧"却不仅出现了城市的衰落现象，而且还伴之以农奴制的复归——这在某种程度上也显示着中心国的发展依赖于边缘国实然的"欠发展"。

应该说，世界体系理论是依附理论的升级版——在世界资本主义体系打造的"中心国""半边缘国"或"边缘国"的结构体系中，资本会长期向"中心国"集中。"中心国"的发展往往伴随着"边缘国"的衰落。在"中心国"随竞争而从一个国家转移到另外一个国家后，金融资本也会随之而向新的"中心国"转移。这会源源不断地拉大"中心国"与"半边缘国"或"边缘国"之间的发展差距②。如果将地球村的经济与政治布局理解为基于地缘关系而形成的空间结构，则沃勒斯坦的理论就具有很强的话语解释力。正因为如此，印度的德赛才说："现代西方学者使用这一概念（指现代化）时所带的价值观偏见和意识形态语调，对正确理解几十年来人类社会所发生的变革过程已经造成某种危险后果"③。

---

① 埃及的阿明甚至于拒斥将世界各国分类为"发达国家"和"欠发达国家"。在他看来，此种分类逻辑暗含了这样一种设定："只存在一种发展形式，只有一条通向进步与普遍福利的道路"。阿明：《依附性发展》，载［美］亨廷顿等《现代化：理论与历史经验的再探讨》，上海译文出版社1993年版，第77页。

② ［日］富永健一：《"现代化理论"今日之课题——关于非西方后发展社会发展理论的探讨》，载［美］塞缪尔·亨廷顿等《现代化：理论与历史经验的再探讨》，上海译文出版社1993年版，第133页。

③ ［印］德赛：《重新评价现代化概念》，载［美］亨廷顿等《现代化：理论与历史经验的再探讨》，上海译文出版社1993年版，第27页。

埃及的阿明也质问说，我们到底是在发展还是在西化?①"中心国""半边缘国"和"边缘国"之间的经济与社会发展差距，往往也会造成学术发展差距，形成葛兰西意义的宗主国对原殖民地国家和地区的霸权，形成布尔迪厄意义的"符号暴力"（symbolic violence）——那些居于统治地位的国家，往往将自己的文化强加于从属国，并迫使从属国人民认为这些输入的文化是所谓"合法文化"，而将自己民族国家的文化视为"不合法的文化"。

事实上，即使是在西方国家，法国的现代化就与英国不同。德国的现代化，就与英法截然不同。美国的现代化，更是在独立战争和南北战争之后才步入正途，形成后来居上之势。西方国家上层建筑的建构模式，也存在君主立宪制、民主共和制和联邦制等区别。在现代化发展过程中，赶超性在西方广泛存在：比如美国与德国对英国与法国的赶超，也比如日本和韩国对西欧其他国家的赶超，还比如20世纪中后期亚洲四小龙的崛起等，就在不同时代创造了不同的现代化模式。这使广大发展中国家认识到，抛却现代化的"应然"不论，在现代化的"实然"案例中，既找不到因循"全盘西化"而成功的标本，也很难发现挖断自身文化之根而新起炉灶的模板。

在发展中国家反思西方现代化话语体系的同时，伴随西方社会从工业社会向后工业社会的深层推进，西方学术界也掀起了对其自身所建构的"现代化"的反思性批评，由此发展出"后现代性"话语。应该说，"后现代性"讨论的时段，交汇于工业现代性的濒临终结与后现代大门的徐徐开启之际。在研究对象上，其以"后现代社会的事物"代替"现代社会的事物"。在理论建构上，其以非理性主义挑战理性主义，以相对主义质疑宏大叙事，以理性主义和非理性主义的统一重塑"完整的人"，从而回归到马克思所说的"人就是人的最高本质"，并以萨特意义的存在主

---

① ［埃及］阿明：《依附性发展》，载［美］亨廷顿等《现代化：理论与历史经验的再探讨》，上海译文出版社1993年版，第99页。

义对抗理性主义①，以"后工业化社会的理想型"替代"工业社会的理想型"，以风险社会对抗工业社会的极致发展。在贝克看来，还可能是现代化的中断和现代风险分配的失衡，以及工业社会家庭模式的解体。后现代性认知体系对事物的解读，也是以后现代科学发现的不确定性对抗现代科学主义的所谓确定性。

在人类社会秩序的建构上，西方的后现代性也掀起了对各类"权威"话语及其解释力的解构运动。不断发生的新科技革命，在对原有以工业社会为基础而建构的学科体系及其所奉圭臬的再反思中，形成了对工业主义制度体系的怀疑，并以后工业社会的学科体系替代工业社会的学科体系，借此掀起对工业社会和农业社会所形成的一系列"科学发现""学科界限""事物运行规律"和"主观之外的客观性"的深刻反思。当然，其中也包括了对新社会形态与新社会体系的建构性探索。应该说，至今为止，后现代性还没有最终形成所谓的"后现代性的后现代性"——没有建构出如工业社会那样的"社会准则"，也没有形成共识意义的后现代研究方法。

三 现代化与中国现代化话语的本土化

绝大多数学者倾向于认为，自 1840 年鸦片战争开始，中国原有社会演进逻辑被外敌入侵所改写。在来自海洋的西方工业文明的撞击下，古老的农业文明分崩离析，并一步步沦为殖民地和半殖民地。为拯救国家危亡，为实现民族复兴，中国人民奋起反抗，仁人志士奔走呐喊，力图从器物、制度到文化各方面求取新路。历经太平天国运动、洋务运动、戊戌变法、义和团运动、辛亥革命、二次革命等，引进过各种主义和思潮，尝试过民主共和制、君主立宪制、议会制和总统制，救国方案轮番出台，均以失败告终。工业虽有发展，但限于零星城市。帝制虽已推翻，

---

① 威廉·巴雷特在《非理性的人》中曾经说，技术是理性主义的一种物质化身，因为它源于科学；官僚政治是理性主义的另一种化身，因为它旨在对社会生活进行理性的控制和安排。[美] 威廉·巴雷特：《非理性的人》，段德智译，上海译文出版社 2012 年版，第 11 章。

但国家四分五裂、人民积贫积弱。历史一再证明，统治阶级不可能在上层建筑的旧船上仅仅通过修补漏洞就能适应时代的风吹浪打。一个没有经过深入改造的、本质上仍然体现着封建主义内核的上层建筑外壳，很难整合举国之力以推动国家的现代化转型①。

中国的知识界，在放眼向洋看世界中，力图"师夷长技以制夷"（师夷长技以自强），形成以"中学为体、西学为用"为宗旨的学术框架，建构自己的实践体系和知识体系。但旧制度的桎梏深重抑制着现代化的经济基础与理论意识形态，封建社会的经济基础也很难生长出现代性社会结构。现代社会结构的发生学，只有经由现代思想的传播并通过打碎旧有的桎梏才得以确立。在十月革命炮声的洗礼中成立的中国共产党，最终将中国革命顺利导入现代化之列。历经长期艰苦卓绝的奋斗，党领导人民取得新民主主义革命的伟大胜利，结束了一盘散沙的政治局面，将全中国人民组织了起来，从而形成有史以来最为磅礴的现代化推力。中华人民共和国的成立，实现了中国从几千年封建专制向人民民主的伟大飞跃，为中华民族伟大复兴创造了根本社会条件，为中国式现代化建设奠定了根本政治前提和制度基础。

新中国的成立，在国民经济恢复中迅速医治了战争创伤、同时废除了封建土地制度，完成了农村土地改革，建立了城乡基层政权，倡导男女平等，颁布《婚姻法》，保障婚姻自主，焕发了人民的政治参与积极性——总而言之，新中国建立了一个完全有别于传统旧中国的新经济基础与新社会结构。随后进行的工业化、进行的"对农业手工业和资本主义工商业的社会主义改造"等，完成了新民主主义革命向社会主义的过

---

① 李鸿章晚年曾说："我办了一辈子的事，练兵也，海军也，都是纸糊的老虎，何尝能实在放手办理？不过勉强涂饰，虚有其表，不揭破犹可敷衍一时。如一间破屋，由裱糊匠东补西贴，居然成一净室，虽明知为纸片糊裱，然究竟决不定里面是何等材料，既有小小风雨，打成几个窟窿，随时补葺，亦可支吾对付……"由此可见，洋务运动，实际只在办经济的洋务，但因为没有对腐朽的封建王朝的本质改造，其很难将外在的西学内化为内在的现代化实践。如果洋务运动的失败只惊醒了精英的话，那么，北洋水师的覆没，则惊醒了举国之人。郑观应在其《盛世危言》中，曾经引用德国首相俾斯麦的评论说："昔同治初年，德相俾斯麦语人曰：'三十年后，日本其兴，中国其弱乎？日人之游欧洲者，讨论学业讲学管制，归而行之。中人之游欧洲者，询问船炮之利，某厂价格之廉，购而用之。强弱之源，其在此乎？'"

渡，奠定了国家的工业基础。可以说，中国的工业化，拒斥了西方各国的殖民地之路，开创了独立自主的现代化实践过程，摒弃了"依附性发展"的战略模式，创造了政府驱动发展的东方式经验。在社会主义建设时期，以"四个现代化"建设——即现代农业、现代工业、现代国防和现代科学技术的建设过程中，形成了独立的比较完整的工业体系和国民经济体系。

1978年以来，中国通过对生产关系的不断完善以使其适应生产力迅速发展的需要。国家治理体系和治理能力的现代化推进，通过对上层建筑的改革促进经济基础的顺利发展，创造了世所罕见的经济快速发展奇迹和社会长期稳定两大奇迹。中国社会实现了从计划经济向市场经济、从农业社会向工业社会，从全面建设小康社会向全面建成小康社会再向全面建设社会主义现代化国家的伟大飞跃。中国社会学人在亲身参与中国和平崛起的整个实践过程中，推动了社会学的中国化和时代化，围绕社会形态的重塑而研究社会结构、社会关系、社会变迁、社会行为方式和社会心理的转型过程，由此逐步搭建了中国特色的社会主义社会学现代化话语体系[①]。

中国式现代化的有力推进，提升了劳动生产率，畅通了社会流动渠道，拉动劳动力人口源源不断从农业部门进入工业部门和服务业部门，优化了三次产业的从业人员结构——这使第三产业从业人员占比大大超过第二产业和第一产业。第七次人口普查表明，流动人口规模已达4.9亿，这预示中国已从定居社会转变为迁居社会。中国社会学曾经以"农民工"这一具有乡土情结的创新性概念发展了原有社会学的社会流动理论和人口迁移理论，丰富了基于城镇化而推动的社会结构变迁所引发的城乡关系假说。农民工既代表了从农村迁居到城市的务工经商群体，也反映了中国农民转化为中国工人和城市市民的社会转型过程，更代表了中国产业工人崛起的时代特征。截至2021年年底，中国已将占总人口64.7%的9亿多人口导入城镇社会，加速了现代城市文明的进程。

千百年来，中国都是一个典型的农民农村农业和农地社会。中华人

[①] 张翼：《扎根中国实践构建中国特色社会主义社会学》，《光明日报》2021年9月14日。

民共和国成立之后短短几十年的赶超型发展，使中国走过了西方发达国家几百年的现代化之路。进入新时代以来，在城镇化的促动之下，中国社会流动的大潮已从农民变农民工阶段推进到农民工变城市市民阶段。现在，除个别超大城市之外，绝大多数大城市和中小城市已放开落户限制，一方面将农民从土地上解放出来，另一方面又以自愿的土地流转形成机械化农业的农地聚合基础，形成现代化的职业农民群体，创造了农民、农业、农村和农地的同步现代化新发展格局。

在农民工大规模进城的同时，工业化和后工业化的拉力、也使中国迅速将中等收入群体的规模扩大到4亿—5亿多人口，在消费侧奠定了"双循环"战略的社会结构基础。新时代大力推进的精准扶贫战略，在中国有史以来第一次消除了农村绝对贫困现象，极大程度改善了村落社会的基本面貌。在全面建设社会主义现代化国家的新征程中，中国必将从世界第二大经济体转化为第一大经济体，也必将从中高收入国家逐步转化为高收入国家。在扎实推进共同富裕过程中，中国的收入结构、城乡结构、人力资源结构和社会阶层结构将更加优化。中国这个世界第一人口大国的现代化进程，不仅会增加国内14亿多人民的现代文明成色，而且还将彻底改变世界人口分享现代化成果的比重结构，继续为发展中国家的现代化创造更为辉煌的中国方案，贡献更为管用的中国智慧。

中国式现代化的成功推进为中国社会学的现代化话语创新奠定了实践基础。社会学界的理论建构提炼了标识性和专业化核心概念。有关农村社会结构与城镇社会结构变迁的研究、有关农民工从业职业与行业的研究、有关市民化与迁移和留守问题的研究、有关社会既充满活力又良序善治问题的研究、有关城乡融合发展与乡村振兴问题的研究、有关家庭小型化与家庭结构变迁问题的研究、有关城镇基层社会转型问题的研究、有关扩大中等收入群体与中产阶层问题的研究、有关职业分流与收入分配问题的研究、有关社会心理与积极向上社会心态建设问题的研究、有关社会转型与消费升级问题的研究等，都极大程度丰富了中国特色社会主义社会学的现代话语，为世界社会学贡献了中国社会学人的理论创新，激发了世界社会学界研究中国社会发展问题的兴趣①。中国社会学人也以"后西方社会学""新发展社会学""社会运行学""关系社会学"等方式，或者以"中国人解释中国社会"的方式终结了西方的东方学对中国社会的误读，在守正创新中提升了中国社会学的话语权。

从"四个现代化"到小康社会再到全面建设小康社会和全面建成小康社会的实践过程，书写了改革开放以来中国现代化的强劲发展趋势。如果说有关"小康社会"的话语及其形成的理论体系构成了中国特色社会主义社会学在前一时期的发展主题的话，那么，"共同富裕"社会及与此相关的理论体系必将成为今后三十年社会学的标识性概念。从小康社会到共同富裕社会的宏大叙事，既统领了中国特色社会主义社会学的历史进路，也涵括了中国特色社会主义社会学的未来方向。在解释发展中国家的现代化转型时，不管是世界市场理论还是依附理论和后现代理论等，都有与生俱来的重大缺陷，都不能完全解释中国的崛起动因。而唯有基于中国历史与中国实践而构造的小康社会理论与共同富裕社会理论，才是社会学基本原理与中国社会实践有机结合的产物。因此，由小康社会与共同富裕社会所浓缩的社会学的发展学说，既是中国社会发展经验的高度总结，也是中国社会学理论创新的元叙事和元话语。

党的二十大报告对中国式现代化作出了高度概括。中国式现代化是中国共产党领导的社会主义现代化，既有各国现代化的共同特征（比如科技化、工业化、城镇化、宗教世俗化等），更有基于自己国情的中国特色。中国式现代化的本质要求是坚持中国共产党的领导，坚持中国特色社会主义，实现高质量发展，发展全过程人民民主，丰富人民精神世界，实现全体人民共同富裕，促进人与自然和谐共生，推动构建人类命运共同体，创造人类文明新形态。中国式现代化的重大原则是坚持和加强党的全面领导，坚持中国特色社会主义道路，坚持以人民为中心的发展思想，坚持深化改革开放，坚持发扬斗争精神。中国式现代化总的战略安排是两步走，即将最近五年构想为打下坚实基础的"关键时期"，到2035

---

① 这部分内容参见张翼《扎根中国实践构建中国特色社会主义社会学》，《光明日报》2021年9月14日。

年基本实现现代化，完成"第一步走"任务，到 21 世纪中叶建成富强民主文明和谐美丽的社会主义现代化强国，完成"第二步走"任务。与此同时，坚持以中国式现代化推进中华民族的伟大复兴。中国式现代化不同于西方式现代化。我们有基于中国实际国情的现代化特征：第一是人口规模巨大的现代化，第二是全体人民共同富裕的现代化，第三是物质文明和精神文明相协调的现代化，第四是人与自然和谐共生的现代化，第五是走和平发展道路的现代化。这些表述进一步丰富了中国式现代化的话语体系。

在全面建成小康社会之后，中国式现代化就成为整个国家工作的重心。为让全体人民分享到经济社会发展成果，就需要扎实推进共同富裕，使之呈现一个动态的向前发展过程。中国式现代化建设中的共同富裕，绝不是所谓的"同时富裕、同步富裕、同等富裕"，也不是整齐划一的平均主义、不是吃大锅饭，更不是新的劫富济贫，而会沿着从局部到整体、从量变到质变的发展方向逻辑展开。对共同富裕社会的建设，既要注意激发社会活力，又要防止收入差距的拉大。改革开放 40 多年得出的一个重要经验，就是必须坚持公有制为主体、多种所有制经济共同发展，必须坚持按劳分配为主体、多种分配方式并存，必须坚持社会主义市场经济体制这三个基本经济制度。在鼓励勤劳致富、重视一次分配和二次分配的基础上，开发三次分配的潜力。当然，伴随人口老龄化程度的持续加深，还必须继续建立健全多层次的社会保障体系，并使其发挥维护代内公平和代际公平的作用。只有使这些标识性概念与共同富裕一起形成系列话语，才能显示出强大社会影响力，并通过其对社会政策的建构，服务于社会主义现代化国家的建设。

总之，中国式现代化所锻造的社会大转型，是世界第一人口大国从农业社会向工业社会的大转型，是政府驱动发展与民间首创精神密切结合的社会大转型，是消除了农村绝对贫困、防止了城市贫民窟与社会撕裂的社会大转型。中国在社会转型中，疏通了社会流通渠道，消解了社会张力，凝聚了人心，形成了较好的社会整合格局。如果说中国已经成功谱写了一曲人口大国的工业化、城镇化、理性化、世俗化的现代化歌谣的话，那么，在工业社会向网络社会和数字社会迅速转型过程中，社会学界还需紧跟形势变化，把脉科技进步趋势，继续以法治化为基础，继续畅通社会流动渠道，继续回答时代之问，继续如费孝通先生所倡导的那样，构建"为现代化服务的社会学"（sociology for modernization）话语。可以自豪地说，当前正在构建的中国式现代化话语，既基于中国的现代化实践，又借鉴了人类文明成果（包括西方现代化实践与理论的优秀成果），还吸纳了具有 5000 年悠久历史的中华优秀传统文化，必将为人类文明新形态的创新持续做出社会学应有的全新贡献。

现代化视域下的"一带一路"建设与欧亚地区治理

孙壮志[*]

中国国家主席习近平2013年提出的共建"一带一路"重要倡议，目的在于推动区域国家实现共同发展，是当代国际关系中一种创新的合作理念与模式。随着中国国内的社会经济发展进入新阶段，提倡创新发展、绿色发展，重视社会的稳定与安全，实现国家治理体系和治理能力的现代化，也影响到对外合作的重点方向。中国式现代化受到世界各国特别是欧亚国家的关注和推崇，相互学习、取长补短，实现共同发展，为中国与欧亚国家的合作提供了一个现实的路径选择。正如习近平主席在2023年3月在中国共产党与世界政党高层对话会上的讲话中强调的，要携手推进全球治理体系改革和建设，推动国际秩序朝着更加公正合理的方向发展，在不断促进权利公平、机会公平、规则公平的努力中推进人类社会现代化[①]。这样的理念和实践，借助"一带一路"重要倡议的推进，在欧亚地区体现出特殊的重要性与号召力。

一 欧亚国家现代化改革的路径选择

1991年苏联解体后获得独立的欧亚国家，30多年来在建构政治经济

---

[*] 孙壮志，中国社会科学院俄罗斯东欧中亚研究所研究员、所长。
[①] 习近平：《携手同行现代化之路——在中国共产党与世界政党高层对话会上的主旨讲话》，《人民日报》2023年3月16日。

新体制的过程中也积极推动现代化改革，探索符合本国实际的发展道路，努力实现经济和社会的进步，取得了不小的成就，但也遭遇很多难题和挫折，走了不少弯路。现代化对于这些年轻国家来说是一个新的课题，路径选择上呈现一些共同的特征。

（一）欧亚国家现代化进程的基本特征

从政治来说是实现形式上的"西方化"与内容上的"主体民族化"。一个是模仿西方的体制，建立了议会，实行多党制；另一个是提高主体民族的地位，强调建设单一制的民主国家，努力增强新的民族国家的凝聚力和自豪感。实际上这是两种相互矛盾的政策取向，最终只能是形式上接受西方的体制，更多还是保留或者恢复传统的执政方式；

从经济来说就是推动大规模"私有化"与面向社会的"市场化"。从一系列指标来看，这些国家在苏联时期已经实现了工业化、城市化，建立了比较完善的社会保障体系，发达程度高于邻近的发展中国家，属于"第一世界"国家的组成部分。独立后传统经济联系中断，遭遇巨大的危机，出现逆工业化、逆城市化的趋势，开始了艰难的经济转型，但遇到的困难很多，至今还在努力之中；

社会领域出现了"重新城市化"与人口的年轻化。独立后多数欧亚国家都出现大规模对外移民的现象，一些国家出现城市人口减少，农村人口比例上升。因本国就业压力很大，对外劳务输出增多，社会流动性增大，贫困问题突出。中亚、南亚国家出生率高，人口增长迅速，结构发生很大变化。基层管理弱化，更多依靠非政府组织和居民自治，造成社会与政府的疏离现象；

文化领域强调"本土化"与"世俗化"。欧亚国家在逐步实现"去俄罗斯化"和向西方开放的同时，试图解决意识形态"真空"的问题。但是促进传统文化回归、鼓励宗教传播，又带来极端主义的新挑战，影响到国家的世俗体制。

（二）现代化难题与民族国家建构

可以看出，欧亚国家寻求现代化的过程中呈现比较矛盾的现象，同一个时间段在这些国家集中出现,导致"现代化"和"现代性"发生冲突。现代化是一个进步的过程,任何国家都难回避这个过程,特别是在全球化的背景下,但也容易引发各种结构性的调整,不同利益集团之间的争斗升级,需要不断进行调整、平衡,上层建筑要适应经济基础,解决不好可能发生动乱。在亨廷顿看来,现代性是稳定的,现代化是不稳定的,欧亚国家已经具备了某种"现代性",也不排除与世界经济接轨,向更先进的文化学习,但无论是体制转型还是选择的发展模式,都是不稳定的。

从社会政治领域来说,遇到的困难更多,国家的现代化带来了更多不确定因素。第一是单一制民族国家的确立根基不稳。欧亚国家都是多民族国家,苏联时期成立了民族自治实体,欧亚国家试图改变,引发了民族甚至是国家间冲突;第二是宗教文化传统与世俗政治体制难以兼容。为了提升国家认同和政权的合法性,鼓励宗教文化的复兴,导致出现宗教政治组织,在中亚甚至出现伊斯兰政治化的问题,威胁到国家的政治稳定[1];第三是超级总统制带来的权力交接风险。多数国家选择了强有力的总统制,领导人巩固政权后大都长期执政,有独特的政治冲突;第四是政治多元带来的规则"失序":有的国家为了解决权力过于集中的问题,也为了平衡不同利益群体的政治诉求,实行了议会制,往往是受到欧洲政治文化的影响;第五是社会管理体系的重构:苏联时期形成的社会保障制度和基层管理方式难以为继,开始实行基层的"自治",但有的国家又不断加强对社会的管控,依靠强力部门或者传统方式;第六是外部压力下的主权安全与政权安全。欧亚国家与俄罗斯都有千丝万缕的联系,俄罗斯也希望保持自己的全方位影响,西方也试图在欧亚推动"民主化",对这些国家不断施压。

(三)现代化道路的选择是巨大的考验

现在国际上关于现代化的标准,一般是经济或者社会标准,例如人

---

[1] Виктория Панфилова:Ташкент снижает риск исламизации ——Узбекистан по новой Конституции становится светским государством,12.03.2023,https://www.ng.ru/cis/2023-03-12/5_8677_uzbekistan.html.

均产值、城市人口比例、受教育水平、人均寿命等，但要实现这些目标，需要提升的是治理能力和治理水平。欧亚国家在苏联时期已经达到或者接近了这些指标，但随着苏联的解体，出现了一个回归"起点"的过程，经济、社会的状况回到了发展中国家的水平，而且呈现了与其他发展中国家类似的特征。在这种情况下，一方面要完成民族国家构建的任务，另一方面又要实现根植于具体国情和文化冲突的现代化；苏联时期是简单"移植"的，经常水土不服，不平衡、不平等的问题比较突出，独立后建构民族国家的过程中这些与"现代性"背道而驰的因素越来越多，阻滞了国家的开放及融入国际体系，造成经济和社会发展的相对滞后。而执政当局关心的政治权力的归属使政治问题往往处于优先的位置。这种发展的"脱节"引发了社会矛盾越来越尖锐，社会不满情绪日益累积。

新独立国家的民族问题既有过去遗留下来的，又有在现代民族国家建设过程中新产生的，非常复杂，加上特殊背景下社会问题越来越尖锐，分化愈来愈严重，不断出现矛盾冲突。民族问题涉及政治权利、经济待遇、文化教育、社会支持等各个方面，这是发达国家也很难处理成功，对于这些仅仅独立30多年，甚至国家发展方向都没有最终确定的年轻共和国来说，更是一个巨大的挑战。对欧亚地区的一体化机制来说，除了解决经贸合作的问题外，还要协调现代化的政策①，因为现代化对于这些国家来说是非常紧迫的任务，各国在国家建构和经济改革方面已经做出了不同的选择。

二 共建"一带一路"与解决治理难题

"一带一路"倡议不仅能够促进跨国、跨地区合作，而且能够有助于提升地区和国家的治理水平。2016年6月习近平主席在乌兹别克斯坦议会演讲时就进一步推进"一带一路"建设提出建议，强调中国愿同伙伴

---

① На городском завтраке РСМД обсудили перспективы развития ЕАЭС, 2 марта 2023, https：//russiancouncil. ru/news/na － gorodskom － zavtrake － rsmd － obsudili － perspektivy － razvitiya － eaes/? sphrase_id = 96866744.

国家携手努力，推动各国政府、企业、社会机构、民间团体开展形式多样的互利合作，增强企业自主参与意愿，吸收社会资本参与合作项目，[①]有利于突破治理困境，解决治理赤字。习近平主席还提出"四个着力"的合作思路，作为对经贸合作的重要补充和支撑，这一思路对完善地区治理体系，帮助各国提升治理能力具有重要作用。

（一）"绿色丝绸之路"主要是沿线国家深化环保合作，践行绿色发展理念，加大生态环境保护力度。"一带一路"的沿线地区，特别是欧亚大陆的腹地是生态环境比较脆弱的地带，自然灾害频发，需要协同应对，防范环境恶化和气候风险。还可以帮助欧亚国家积极发展绿色产业和新能源，开拓新的绿色产品、技术、服务贸易种类，提高经济效率水平和综合竞争力。

（二）"健康丝绸之路"就是促进沿线国家深化医疗卫生合作，加强在传染病疫情通报、疾病防控、医疗救援、传统医药领域互利合作。欧亚国家卫生保健的涵盖率比较有限，贫困化的问题比较突出，流行性疾病经常发生，威胁着当地居民的身体健康。新冠疫情暴发后，中方的倡议对地区国家开展抗疫合作、共同打造卫生健康共同体起到了引领作用。中国还向很多欧亚国家提供抗疫物资和疫苗，在上合组织框架内与中亚国家在药物研发方面开展合作。

（三）"智力丝绸之路"就是要深化沿线国家的人才培养合作，中方倡议成立"一带一路"职业技术合作联盟，培养培训各类专业人才。推进"一带一路"倡议，人才的培养与储备是关键和保障。一方面，各国在人才队伍、科技能力建设等方面存在差异，人才短缺的问题不同程度存在。另一方面，各国教育特色鲜明、资源丰富、互补性强，合作空间巨大。

（四）"和平丝绸之路"包括沿线国家深化安保合作，践行共同、综合、合作、可持续的亚洲安全观，推动构建具有亚洲特色的安全治理模式，应对"一带一路"建设过程中面临的风险和挑战。欧亚地区既面临

---

① 习近平：《携手共创丝绸之路新辉煌——在乌兹别克斯坦最高会议立法院的演讲》，《光明日报》2016年6月23日。

传统的安全威胁，如军事冲突、边界争端，也有范围更广的非传统安全挑战，如恐怖主义、极端主义、分裂主义、跨国犯罪，以及紧迫的能源安全、金融安全、粮食安全、网络信息安全等。

对于发展中国家来说，现代化是一个艰难的"赶超"过程，不是一个自然而然的结果，也不是可以依靠发达国家的施舍可以实现的，需要一个国家从上到下形成合力，需要系统的谋划与长期的努力。现代化不是只有西方一种现成的模式，不能仅仅关注经济的增长，还要兼顾社会的发展与公平，这也是中国式现代化的宝贵经验。正如习近平主席所强调的，一个国家走向现代化，既要遵循现代化一般规律，更要符合本国实际，具有本国特色。中国式现代化既有各国现代化的共同特征，更有基于自己国情的鲜明特色。中国式现代化是人口规模巨大的现代化、是全体人民共同富裕的现代化、是物质文明和精神文明相协调的现代化、是人与自然和谐共生的现代化、是走和平发展道路的现代化[1]。这对"一带一路"参与国，特别是与中国有着密切政治、经济和文化联系的欧亚国家来说，都具有重要的启发意义和借鉴价值。通过共同建设"一带一路"，可以分享现代化建设的经验，也可以明确现代化的重点方向，更可以携手在各个领域以合作促发展，以更加广阔时空的合作为现代化开辟良好的前景。

欧亚国家在现代化的过程中，形式上模仿西方，特别是20世纪90年代的政治经济转型，都是在西方指导下确定了基本的规划，结果遭到了失败，特别是经济上代价惨重。近些年多数欧亚国家开始根据国情重新设计自己的行政管理体制，经济上希望发挥自己的优势，重视学习西方之外发展中国家的治理经验。无论是托卡耶夫总统提出的"新哈萨克斯坦"战略，还是乌兹别克斯坦总统米尔济约耶夫推动的宪法改革，都是要根据自身国情实现政治和社会的现代化，同时广泛借鉴世界上的各种成功经验。正如古代的"丝绸之路"既是贸易之路，也是文化之路一样，现在的"一带一路"同样承载着治理理念和治理模式上交流互鉴的新使

---

[1] 《习近平在学习贯彻党的二十大精神研讨班开班式上发表重要讲话强调　正确理解和大力推进中国式现代化》，《人民日报》2023年2月8日。

命，为各国的现代化提供支持和帮助，中国式现代化具有独特的示范意义，有助于避免类似于欧亚国家这样的"后发者"走更多弯路。

三 以互联互通促进完善地区治理体系

"一带一路"建设的一个特点是多层次、多主体，能够促进不同国家、不同区域多边合作机制间的协调与合作，同时也可以借助双边和多边机制的支持，相辅相成，实现地区治理能力的整体提升。习近平主席在博鳌亚洲论坛2021年年会开幕式上的主旨演讲中明确提出，将同各方继续高质量共建"一带一路"，践行共商共建共享原则，弘扬开放、绿色、廉洁理念，努力实现高标准、惠民生、可持续目标。中方将同各方携手，加强基础设施"硬联通"以及规则标准"软联通"。世界银行有关报告认为，到2030年，共建"一带一路"有望帮助全球760万人摆脱极端贫困、3200万人摆脱中度贫困。将本着开放包容精神，同愿意参与的各相关方共同努力，把"一带一路"建成"减贫之路"、"增长之路"[①]。

（一）"一带一路"为地区国家的发展开启机遇之窗

"一带一路"倡议，就是要以经济、文化的互联互通为着力点，促进生产要素自由便利流动和民间的友好往来，实现互利共赢，赋予复兴"丝绸之路"以更多的时代内涵。中国领导人又提出"廉洁丝绸之路""数字丝绸之路"等新理念，不断充实合作的内涵，实际上都同完善地区国家的政治和经济治理有关，完善现代化管理体系，有助于欧亚国家改变不合理的产业结构，推进廉洁政治建设，从而改善本国的营商环境，提升国际竞争力。更加契合地区发展的共同需求，为地区各国实现优势互补开启了新的机遇之窗。

地处欧亚地区的哈萨克斯坦是"一带一路"的首倡之地，该地区各国也是"一带一路"的积极参与者。欧亚各国之间也有着密切的社会联

---

① 习近平：《同舟共济克时艰，命运与共创未来——在博鳌亚洲论坛2021年年会开幕式上的视频主旨演讲》，《光明日报》2021年4月21日。

系，虽然文化多元，但跨境民族众多，地区合作拥有地缘和制度优势。完善地区治理体系，要求各种多边机制能够相互配合，和睦共处，开展合作。要完善欧亚地区治理，首先应该增强地区国家的互信，尊重彼此的制度和文化差异；其次要形成相互依存、共同发展的稳定关系，利用具有战略性质的双边和多边合作，提升地区国家间合作的水平；最后是确定公认的规则和制度框架，形成各种推动多边合作的有效机制。中国领导人提出要打造上合组织命运共同体，深耕成员国民间友好的土壤，形成各个重点方向的多边合作机制和伙伴关系网络，丰富合作的内涵，为构建相互尊重、平等互利、开放包容的新型国际关系发挥引领和示范作用。地区治理能否取得成功的重要标志之一，在于多边合作能否真正造福各国人民，能否真正实现地区国家的共同繁荣。

（二）"一带一路"有助于现代化与地区治理的良性互动

地区治理包括几个要点：一是地区的整体性，发挥地缘优势；二是相互依存性，地区国家经济上具有互补性、安全上面临共同的威胁；三是民众的亲近感，能够相互尊重各自的文化传统；四是机制和平台的作用，有多边机制发挥保障与协调作用。"一带一路"建设在欧亚地区的推进显然有助于在上述方面形成地区的合作，促进区域化进程。地区治理与一般多边合作的区别在于，不仅仅是政治与安全层面的合作，而是要着眼于地区的长期稳定与共同发展，需要有政府部门、民间组织和社会团体的共同参与，特别是要加强社会领域和地方层面的互动，形成一种"立体的"合作模式。欧亚腹地的地区治理具有独特的特征，目标同样是政治、经济、文化在各个层次上的相互接近甚至相互融合，但在国家之间实现一体化又面临非常复杂的问题。

"一带一路"是中国贡献给全球最重要的公共外交产品，当前的最重要任务是使经济和人文交往打破人为壁垒，实现互联互通，既包括基础设施的"硬联通"，也包括规则制度的"软联通"。正如习近平主席2014年11月在加强互联互通伙伴关系对话会上的重要讲话中强调的，我们要建设的互联互通，应该是基础设施、制度规章、人员交流三位一体，应该是政策沟通、设施联通、贸易畅通、资金融通、民心相通五大领域齐头并进。这是全方位、立体化、网络状的大联通，是生机勃勃、群策群力的开放系统。如果将"一带一路"比喻为亚洲腾飞的两只翅膀，那么互联互通就是两只翅膀的血脉经络①。在建议当中习近平主席欢迎其他国家搭乘中国发展的列车，以经济走廊为依托建立互联互通的基本框架，以交通基础设施为突破实现互联互通的早期收获，优先部署中国同邻国的铁路、公路项目。中国与欧亚国家正在打造"新亚欧大陆桥"等经济走廊，正在筹划建设中国—吉尔吉斯斯坦—乌兹别克斯坦铁路，都有助于区域国家的互联互通。

（三）"一带一路"有助于增进各国民生福祉

西方现代化理论认为，现代化是一个历史过程，包括从传统经济向现代经济、传统社会向现代社会、传统政治向现代政治、传统文明向现代文明的转变等。基于现代西方主要发达国家的发展经验而生的现代化发展模式，被学界称为"早发内生型现代化发展模式"，与后发国家所实施的"后发外生型现代化发展模式"相对。虽然西方学者也承认有些社会的现代化并没有成功，而向现代化迈进的国家的情况也是千差万别，但他们普遍认为，现代化不成功和差异性只是暂时的现象，而现代化中的各种差异都将在现代化完成的时候消失。因此，实现了现代化的国家势必具有一些西方发达国家的特征：市场经济、经济增长、民主政治、城市化等。在西方的现代化模式中，标榜的价值观实际上是以资本为中心，以发达国家的利益为中心，发展中国家只能处于从属地位。

中国式现代化与西方的现代化完全不同，首先就是坚守人民至上理念，突出现代化方向的人民性。现代化道路最终能否走得通、行得稳，关键要看是否坚持以人民为中心。有数据显示，2013—2019 年"一带一路"为相关国家创造了 20 多万个就业岗位，中国与 30 多个国家签署经贸协议，有力促进了参与国家的经济发展和民生改善。随着乌克兰危机的不断升级，全球经济发展进入一个非常困难的时期，无论是供应链、

---

① 《习近平主持加强互联互通伙伴关系对话会并发表重要讲话　倡导深化互联互通伙伴关系　加强"一带一路"务实合作》，《光明日报》2014 年 11 月 9 日。

产业链的断裂，还是能源和粮食的短缺甚至危机，不断高企的通货膨胀让地区经济治理的重要性日益提升。在欧亚地区，上海合作组织、欧亚经济联盟等区域组织都越来越关注贸易和投资合作，把推动成员国经济现代化，增加本币结算、抵御外部风险等问题提上日程，欧亚经济联盟成员国贸易中本币结算的比例已经达到75%[1]，体现出新形势下欧亚地区治理的方向正在发生明显变化。

---

[1] Сара Шаймерденова：Итоги саммита ВЕЭС и председательство России в ЕАЭС в 2023 году，21 декабря 2022，https：//russiancouncil. ru/blogs/CIS – NSO – MGIMO/itogi – sammita – vees – i – predsedatelstvo – rossii – v – eaes – v – 2023 – godu/？sphrase_id = 96866744.

在世界百年未有之大变局中创造人类文明新形态

张志强[*]

中华民族伟大复兴不仅推动了世界百年未有之大变局的演变,而且向人类示范了一种新的文明形态。这个新文明形态就是中华文明的新形态。中华文明新形态是中国在克服资本主义现代文明的内在矛盾和根本危机中走出的一条新道路,它向人类昭示了一种人类文明新形态的可能性。世界百年未有之大变局在一定意义上意味着一种文明原理的变局,意味着对于任何具体社会和古老文明选择自身现代化道路的主体性赋权。世界百年未有之大变局向全人类昭示了人类文明的未来前景,这个前景就是由中华文明新形态所显示的一种大格局的人类文明新形态,一种由不同文明传统创造出的不同的现代社会形态所共同构成的人类命运共同体,一种美美与共、不齐而齐的人类新文明。

习近平总书记在党的十九届五中全会上指出,全党要统筹中华民族伟大复兴战略全局和世界百年未有之大变局。这是我们党谋划工作的基本出发点。

全面把握和统筹两个大局,就需要深刻认识两个大局的内在关联。世界百年未有之大变局的突出特点是中华民族伟大复兴所带动的现代世界文明格局的大变化。中华民族伟大复兴的历史进程与世界历史格局大

---

[*] 张志强,中国社会科学院哲学研究所研究员、所长。

调整的历史过程同步，同时也同步于世界文明格局的大调整，同步于现代世界构造原理及其所代表的文明价值的大调整。

中华民族伟大复兴既是推动世界百年未有之大变局的力量，也是百年来世界历史内在变动的结果。在一定意义上，我们可以说，中华民族从近代以来国家蒙辱、人民蒙难、文明蒙尘的悲惨境遇，经过百年奋斗逐渐走向民族复兴，逐渐重铸中华文明新辉煌的历史进程，是运用马克思主义基本原理，利用资本主义所开启的世界历史进程中的内在矛盾和根本危机，在中国共产党的领导下，通过社会主义的方式，一方面克服资本主义的矛盾和危机，另一方面则一步步实现了中国的现代化，一步步实现了中华民族伟大复兴，一步步激活了中华文明的内在力量，一步步促进了中华文明的现代转化。正是在这个意义上，中华民族伟大复兴不仅推动了世界百年未有之大变局，也向人类示范了一种新的文明形态，一种古老文明实现现代化的形态。这个新文明形态就是中华文明新形态。中华文明新形态是人类在克服资本主义现代文明的内在矛盾和根本危机中走出的一条新道路，它向人类昭示了一种新的文明可能性，一种人类文明新形态的可能性。

一 在世界百年未有之大变局中开创的中国式现代化道路，为人类示范了一种新文明形态

习近平总书记在"七一"讲话中向世人宣告："我们坚持和发展中国特色社会主义，推动物质文明、政治文明、精神文明、社会文明、生态文明协调发展，创造了中国式现代化新道路，创造了人类文明新形态。"[①]

深入理解习近平总书记"两个创造"论断，必须深刻把握住"两个创造"的创造主体，必须充分认识到"两个创造"是中国共产党领导全体中国人民经过百年奋斗实现的创造结果。

深入理解习近平总书记"两个创造"论断，就要深刻认识"两个创

---

① 习近平：《在庆祝中国共产党成立100周年大会上的讲话》，人民出版社2021年版，第13—14页。

造"之间的关系，要充分认识到中国式现代化道路是中国共产党经过百年奋斗、艰苦探索出的一条古老文明实现全面现代化的道路，一条殖民地半殖民地实现独立解放的道路，一条发展中国家实现富强文明的道路，一条克服并超越资本主义内在危机和固有矛盾的道路。我们更要认识到，中国共产党领导中国人民创造的中国式现代化道路，为人类开辟了一条超越和克服西方现代文明内在危机的新道路，也为人类文明永续发展，提供了一个可资借鉴的人类文明新形态，一个新的现代文明形态。

"中国式现代化道路"的提法着眼于对中国共产党历史探索的经验总结，"人类文明新形态"的提法则放眼于人类未来，向世人展示中国式现代化道路的世界历史意义和人类文明史意义。"中国式现代化道路"是从中国出发提供的"人类文明新形态"的具体内容，"人类文明新形态"则是立足于全人类的未来，宣示中国式现代化道路的全人类共同价值。

中国共产党经过百年奋斗创造的中国式现代化道路，让接近世界人口 1/5 的中国人民历史性地摆脱绝对贫困、实现全面小康并将进一步建成社会主义现代化强国，创造了人类文明史上的伟大奇迹，它必将作为一种人类文明新形态，一种新的现代文明，深刻影响世界历史发展进程和人类文明发展方向。

1. 中国式现代化道路作为一种人类文明新形态的伟大意义，在于它改变了 1500 年以来西方列强所主导的现代世界形成和演进的现代化逻辑。

马克思说过："各民族的原始封闭状态由于日益完善的生产方式、交往以及因交往而自然形成的不同民族之间的分工消灭得越是彻底，历史也就越是成为世界历史。"[①] 资本主义的"世界历史性存在"是历史成为世界历史的前提条件，正是资本主义生产方式打破了民族之间的自然分工，通过资本的扩张过程逐渐形成了一个边缘依附中心的世界体系。换言之，资本主义的扩张正是民族历史成为世界历史的动力所在。但是，正如马克思所指出的，资本主义扩张尽管带来一个人类相互依存的统一的世界，但在打破了地域局限和人身束缚的同时，并没有真正带来人的彻底解放，而是用商品交换的表面平等掩盖了人对人的奴役关系，用世

[①]《马克思恩格斯文集》第 1 卷，人民出版社 2009 年版，第 540 页。

界市场一体化掩盖了中心对边缘的权力宰制关系，用发展繁荣的幻象掩盖了社会内部的两极分化，用极度解放的生产力掩盖了人对自然的过度压榨。更为重要的是，资本主义扩张带来的现代化，为西方之外的古老文明设置了一个吊诡性的处境，要么顺应这种现代化而从自身文明传统中连根拔起，要么固守自身文明传统而被时代抛弃。文明传统成为这种现代化的对立物，这种现代化让人沦落为从文明土壤中拔根的孤绝个体。

中国式现代化道路是中国共产党领导中国人民经过艰苦摸索创造出的一种新的现代化逻辑，创造出的一种新的现代文明。第一，作为中国式的现代化，它必须能够与西方世界的现代化一样，极大解放生产力。中国共产党领导中国人民通过对各种现代化经验的创造性学习，对各种现代化教训的总结性转化，在社会主义革命和建设时期，建立起独立的比较完整的工业体系和国民经济体系，奠定了工业化的基础。在改革开放和社会主义现代化建设新时期，确立社会主义市场经济的体制机制，充分发挥市场在资源配置中的决定性作用，促进了科技创新，提高了劳动生产率。中国式现代化，充分运用社会化大生产实现了中国社会生产力的极大发展。第二，作为中国式的现代化，在解放社会生产力的同时不仅带来了经济长期发展，更带来了社会长期稳定。"两大奇迹"的同时发生，从根本上摆脱了两者不能兼得的发展中国家的发展悖论，用几十年的时间快速跨越了西方现代化几百年所走过的道路。第三，作为中国式的现代化，是克服了资本主义生产资料私人所有与社会化大生产之间内在矛盾的现代化。资本主义的现代化在极大解放生产力的同时，并没有创造出全体人民共享的社会福祉，而是进一步分化了社会。中国式现代化则是以全体人民共同富裕为目标的社会主义现代化，兼顾了效率与公平。第四，作为中国式的现代化，经历了从人定胜天到天人和谐的发展模式，确立了以人类永续发展为目标、以人与自然和谐共生为原则的可持续发展观，让发展最终落实为人类文明程度的整体提升。第五，作为中国式的现代化，在尊重个人价值的前提下，更加注重个人利益与集体利益的协调，确立起立足世界看待个人、立足整体安顿个人的价值观，从而把人的全面发展与社会的全面进步结合起来，从根本上克服了封闭在狭隘自我内部的个人主义价值观，超越了资本主义社会人与人之间的关系，从而确立起了中国式现代化的文化理想。

中国式现代化之所以取得成功，关键在于中国共产党的领导。中国共产党领导是中国特色社会主义最本质的特征。中国共产党的集中统一领导与以人民为中心的价值观相结合，使得政治具有了以人民至上的价值导引经济、社会、文化、生态诸领域发展的能力。正是基于中国共产党的领导，中国式现代化才创造出了不同于西方现代化的政治模式。正是基于中国共产党的领导，政治、经济、社会、文化、生态诸领域协调发展的中国式现代化才可能确立。正是基于中国共产党的领导，中国才能在通过革命获得政治独立前提下，通过社会主义建设与改革开放获得经济独立，摆脱对西方主导的世界体系的依附地位，并将最终赢得彻底的文化独立，最终迎来中华民族伟大复兴，最终全面建成社会主义现代化强国。中国式现代化，不仅给发展中国家示范了一条新的现代化道路，改变了西式现代化的逻辑，更为重要的在于，它重塑了世界历史的面貌，为人类提供了一个可资借鉴和选择的文明新形态。

2. 中国式现代化道路作为一种人类文明新形态的伟大意义，在于它以中国特色社会主义道路、理论、制度、文化，重新为世界社会主义运动注入了活力、提供了方向。

马克思和恩格斯运用唯物史观深刻揭示了资本主义社会的内在矛盾，并指出资本主义的"世界历史性存在"不会使人获得彻底解放。正是伴随着资本主义扩张的世界历史进程，世界社会主义运动应运而生，它是批判、克服并超越资本主义内在危机的另一种世界历史运动。世界社会主义运动旨在提供一条超越资本主义的现代化道路，旨在创造一个体现人类文明共同体基本价值关怀的现代文明形态，建立一种不同于资本主义的现代社会形态。为了克服生产资料的私人所有与现代社会化大生产之间的矛盾，从根本上避免社会生产的无政府状态，解决公平与效率无法兼顾的矛盾，就必须为社会生产确立价值目标。立足人民立场的社会主义，用满足全体人民的生存发展需要来规定、调整和导引社会化大生产，从而达致生产与需求相匹配，实现社会主义价值对社会化大生产的驾驭。因此，只有社会主义，才是与现代社会化大生产相适应的社会形态，社会主义与现代社会化大生产之间最终可以取得目的与手段的一致。

如果说，现代化是对生产力的极大解放的话，那么社会主义的价值理想可以让解放的生产力更大程度地造福全人类，消除不平等，而资本主义则让解放的生产力遵循资本逐利的动机，不断制造社会分化。这是社会主义现代化与资本主义现代化的根本不同。

世界社会主义运动经历了曲折而艰辛的探索过程，在探索社会主义现代化的进程中留下了许多历史经验和教训。中国特色社会主义区分了市场机制与资本主义的关系，充分发挥市场在资源配置中的决定性作用，破除高度集中计划体制的僵化弊端，同时坚持更好发挥政府作用。在社会主义的价值目标、体制机制和市场经济之间形成良性互动，建立起独特有效的社会主义市场经济体制。中国式现代化道路就是以社会主义的价值理想来导引现代社会化大生产从而实现现代化的典范，为世界社会主义运动开辟了一条新路。中国式现代化道路就是社会主义现代化的成功之路，其根本特征在于，能够在社会主义体制机制中纳入市场经济，能够在共同富裕的目标下不牺牲发展效率，能够在坚持社会主义公平理想的前提下充分解放生产力，能够在融入国际经济体系的过程中始终保持国家主权独立。中国式现代化道路能够成功的关键，在于坚持中国共产党的全面领导，在于中国共产党对经济社会发展的价值导引和政治治理，在于中国共产党能够始终代表最广大人民根本利益，没有任何自己特殊的利益，从来不代表任何利益集团、任何权势团体、任何特权阶层的利益，始终坚持为人民服务。只有在中国共产党的领导下，现代化的发展才会形成国家社会整体发展的效应，现代化才会造福全体人民。

3. 中国式现代化道路作为一种人类文明新形态的伟大意义，在于它激活了中华文明的内在力量，充分实现了中华文明的现代化，创造了中华文明新形态。

钱穆先生曾说："希腊乃西方历史之播种者，中国乃东方历史之栽根者。播种者新种散布，旧种凋零。栽根者枝叶日茂，根盘日大。"[①] 西方文明尽管作为文明是连续的，但其文明的主体早已散开，不再以一个统一的政治主体面目出现，而中华文明始终以大一统的政治体作为主体，

---

① 钱穆：《政学私言》，九州出版社2011年版，第256页。

凝聚不散、根深叶茂。5000多年连续发展不间断的历史，广土众民凝聚而成的大规模政治体，多元一体、和而不同的一统秩序，是中华文明的突出特点。连续性、规模性和一统性是中华文明的伟大成就。中华文明之所以生生不息，正在于中华文明始终具有能够不断适应环境、迎接内外挑战的历史主动精神。正是这种历史主动精神，让中华文明能够"承蔽通变""穷变通久"，能够"承百代之流而会乎当今之变"。这种历史主动精神，正是经史合一的"通史"精神。正是这种精神让中华文明能够一次次走出困境，通过不断从实际出发、因应时势的创造，开辟出中华文明的新境界。中华文明长期存续的奥秘，就要从孕育这种历史主动精神的基因中去寻找。也正是这种精神，让中华文明在近代遭遇困难挑战时，能够逐步克服制约中华文明发展的瓶颈问题，让中华文明重新焕发生机。

中国式现代化道路的成功开辟和人类文明新形态的创造，最为深刻也最为生动地体现了中华文明的内在生命力。中国共产党深刻把握住中华文明的历史主动精神，以实事求是的方法论态度，创造性地运用马克思主义，将马克思主义与中国历史实际和文明实际深度结合，充分激活了中华文明的内在力量，领导中国人民创造出了中国式现代化道路，创造出了人类文明新形态。

中国式现代化道路具有深远的中国史意义。一方面，它昭示了中国式现代化道路的深厚中华文明根基，增强了集中统一的政治权威，以人民至上的核心价值导引经济、社会诸领域发展的结构功能，凝聚起中华民族共同体意识，塑造了天人和谐共生的地球生命共同体理念，构建了天下一家的人类命运共同体理念，确立了"和而不同""不齐而齐"的和平发展、和谐共享的世界秩序观念。另一方面，中国式现代化创造性地解决了民本理想虽然高远但无法突破帝制家天下的制约、权力虽然高度集中但缺乏广泛基础、国家规模虽然广大但人民却一盘散沙缺乏组织、小农经济虽然发达但发展却陷入内卷等一系列难题，创造出了具有深厚基础的人民民主政治，将党的领导以民主集中的方式建立在广泛社会基础之上，通过引入积极向上的团体生活组织起了人民，以社会化的大生产突破了小农经济的内卷化。中国式现代化道路的中国史意义还在于向我们更深刻地揭示了与具体实际相结合的道理。道路的开辟必须建立在实事求是地认识国情，尊重客观历史条件上。实际上，"文明土壤"作为"国性"是更为根本、更为基础的"国情"，与"文明实际"相结合，是与具体实际相结合的进一步深化。

中国式现代化道路具有深远的世界历史意义。它向世界昭示了一种现代文明形态，这种现代文明形态不再是一种与传统断裂的、从文明土壤中拔根的新文明，而是从古老文明中不断创造出来的古今一贯、新旧相续的新文明。正是在这个意义上，中国式现代化道路作为中华文明的新形态，向世界昭示了一条古老文明的新生之路，昭示了一种熔旧铸新而非弃旧逐新的人类文明新形态。正是在这个意义上，当今世界"东升西降"的趋势，其实质内涵正是古老文明复兴的趋势，而我们正在经历的世界百年未有之大变局，也正是东方古老文明通过全面学习现代文明成果，全面继承古老文明的丰厚积累，经过不懈艰苦奋斗，最终带来的世界变局。

中国式现代化道路以中华文明为根基，以现代化为历史使命，以社会主义为价值理想，通过在世界百年未有之大变局中创造人类文明新形态。中国共产党百年奋斗，熔铸为一条世界现代化的新道路，创造出一种人类文明的新形态。这条道路是中国共产党领导中国人民经历千辛万苦、百死千难摸索出来的，今后也必将牢牢掌握历史主动，独立自主地沿着这条道路走下去！

二 中国式现代化道路所开创的人类文明新形态，昭示了世界百年未有之大变局的实质和目标

作为资本主义全球扩张的世界历史进程，是现代世界形成的根本动力。"现代"成为一个具有特定历史内涵的规范性概念，标志着一种与前现代迥然不同的社会状态。在经典社会理论家那里，"社会"的出现本身就是对现代性的刻画：只有在现代，才出现了与前现代的"共同体"不同的"社会"。"社会"意味着一种由抽象化的功能系统整合而成的人类组织状态，这种人类组织状态不同于由具体的价值规范进行有机整合的

"共同体"。"社会"是理性化的产物，是工具理性扩张的结果，但同时也伴随着一系列与工具理性匹配的价值理性的运作方式，瓦解了以具体价值规范进行整合的"共同体"。作为理性化产物的"现代社会"，从根本上说是一种彻底"反传统"的"社会"，"反共同体"的社会，反对统一价值规范整合的社会。一般意义上的"现代化"，就是资本主义的生产方式、理性化的抽象社会相结合构成的一种世界历史进程，其所到之处，必定会瓦解任何固有文明共同体，创造出一种"普世性"的人类文明。更为值得关注的是，从现代社会的抽象性特质，形成了一种抽象社会与具体社会的对立关系，以理性化的系统整合为特征的抽象社会是现代社会，而以传统价值观实现有机整合的共同体，则是前现代社会。现代化的过程，就是一种普世性的抽象社会的普及过程，就是对任何具体社会的瓦解过程。不过，问题在于，抽象社会的形成，作为一种理性化的产物，实际上是程序化的功能与抽象性价值以及自我伦理实践的复杂运作的产物，这一复杂运作恰恰出自于具体社会的历史条件。正如韦伯所指出的，作为现代社会诞生地的西欧，正是新教伦理构成了资本主义精神的伦理条件。这说明，理性化的现代是西欧文明的独特产物。因此，它的普世化，实际上不过是帝国主义暴力手段的推广结果。大多数非西欧国家对理性化的模仿之所以是不成功的，就是忽略了现代性的特定历史条件。

  中国式现代化道路的示范性意义就在于从根本上突破了对现代社会的抽象模仿，从具体社会的具体文明历史条件出发，实现了一种生产力极大释放、人的全面发展和社会全面和谐的现代化。中国式现代化道路所开创出的人类文明新形态，与西欧文明所开创出的所谓现代文明形态的根本不同在于，它扎根于具体社会的文明土壤，利用具体社会长期积淀的文明历史条件，积极借鉴与吸收人类文明一切有益成果，主动开创出的新文明。作为一种人类新文明，它是从旧文明中生长出来的新文明，而不是否定旧文明的新文明，是新旧文明连续生长的结果，而不是与旧文明断裂的结果。中国式现代化是古老文明的现代化，而不是消灭古老文明的现代化。在我们看来，这是中国式现代化的独特价值。正是基于此，中国式现代化所开创的人类文明新形态，才会对于任何其他古老文明立足自身具体社会实现的现代化具有重要的示范性意义。

中国式现代化道路所开创的人类文明新形态，是从中国的具体文明历史条件下创造出来的人类新文明，是中华优秀传统文化的创造性转化和创新性发展，这种新文明不会将自身抽象化为一种普世价值而形成一种文明的霸权，而是以自身的独特道路向人类昭示一种从各自文明土壤和具体社会中成功创造转化出自己的现代社会的典范。世界百年未有之大变局在一定意义上就意味着这样一种文明原理的变局。世界百年未有之大变局意味着对于任何具体社会和古老文明选择自身现代化道路的主体性赋权，让那些既想实现现代化又想保持主体性即自身独立性的国家、民族和其他文明体深刻认识到，必须结合自身具体社会的历史和文明条件，才有可能真正实现现代化，只有如此才能从根本上改变跟随西方现代化道路亦步亦趋、人云亦云的无主体状态。世界百年未有之大变局向全人类昭示了一种人类文明的未来前景，这个前景就是由中华文明的新形态显示的一种大格局的人类文明新形态，一种由不同文明传统创造出的不同的现代社会形态所共同构成的人类命运共同体，一个美美与共、不齐而齐的人类新文明。

中国式现代化道路所开创的人类文明新形态，在一定意义上也阐明了一个重要的道理：社会形态的演化，必须是扎根于具体社会的文明历史条件实现的演化，其中人的主体性就表现在努力将时代需要与文明历史条件紧密结合起来以促进自身社会的演化上。在这个意义上，所谓的社会形态的演化，从根本上说都是文明的演化。文明的演化，是文明自身根据新的时代条件不断激活自身内在力量和核心价值的过程。文明的演化正是文明的成长，文明在演化中不断生长，生生不息。社会形态的演化不过是文明演化的具体内容。正是在这个意义上，中国式现代化所实现的中国社会的现代演化，具有了中华文明更化的意义，也正因此具有了为人类文明示范新形态的伟大意义。

中国共产党百年奋斗历程，是中华文明内在生命力的根本展现。中华文明经由中国共产党的伟大斗争，终于化生出自己的现代形态。中国共产党的伟大斗争就是通过中华文明新形态的开创，向人类展示了一种新的人类文明的可能性，一种新的世界历史进程的方向和目标。习近平总书记在"七一"讲话中庄严宣告:"中华民族拥有5000多年历史演进中形成的灿烂文明,中国共产党拥有百年奋斗实践和70多年执政兴国经验,我们积极学习借鉴人类文明的一切成果,欢迎一切有益的建议和善意的批评,但我们绝不接受'教师爷'般颐指气使的说教!中国共产党和中国人民将在自己选择的道路上昂首阔步走下去,把中国发展进步的命运牢牢掌握在自己手中!"[①] 我们从百年党史中汲取的正是这样一种掌握自身命运和历史主动的力量,正是这样一种着眼全人类的、改变世界历史进程的气魄,正是这样一种从人类文明根基中开创新价值、新文明的胸怀!

[①] 习近平:《在庆祝中国共产党成立100周年大会上的讲话》,人民出版社2021年版,第13—14页。

第二编

中国式现代化与中国发展主动性

中国式现代化与中国全球治理新主张

欧阳向英[*]

在中国共产党第二十次全国代表大会上,习近平总书记向世界各国呼吁:"中国提出了全球发展倡议、全球安全倡议,愿同国际社会一道努力落实。"[①] "两个倡议"既包括中国作为世界最大的发展中国家提出的全球发展新主张,也包括中国作为负责任大国提出的全球安全新倡议,反映了中国在应对全球"四大赤字"上的新理念和新举措。

一 "两个倡议"的时代背景

维护世界和平、促进共同发展是中国外交政策的宗旨,而统筹中华民族伟大复兴战略全局和世界百年未有之大变局是党在新时代的战略重心。从国际看,新冠疫情全球大流行,推动世界百年未有之大变局加速演进。一方面,国际力量对比深刻调整,人类命运共同体理念深入人心;另一方面,经济全球化遭遇逆流,单边主义、保护主义、霸权主义对世界和平与发展构成威胁,和平赤字、发展赤字、安全赤字、治理赤字仍在扩大,乌克兰危机推高了世界经济中的通胀风险和不确定性。从国内看,以中国式现代化全面推进中华民族伟大复兴正处在关键期。一方面,

---

[*] 欧阳向英,中国社会科学院世界经济与政治研究所研究员。
[①] 习近平:《高举中国特色社会主义伟大旗帜 为全面建设社会主义现代化国家而团结奋斗——在中国共产党第二十次全国代表大会上的报告》,《人民日报》2022年10月26日。

贯彻新发展理念，推进高质量发展，推动构建新发展格局，实施供给侧结构性改革，制定一系列具有全局性意义的区域重大战略，使中国经济实力实现历史性跃升；另一方面，发展不平衡不充分的问题依然存在，人与自然和谐共生有待进一步优化，共同富裕有待进一步扎实推进。总的来说，世界之变、时代之变、历史之变正在以前所未有的方式展开。这个基本判断是完全正确的。

后疫情时代，世界经济和安全形势错综复杂，充满变数。主要表现在：

第一，发达国家"高利率抑通胀"和"债务高企"存在逻辑冲突。以美国为首的西方发达国家债务居高不下，以往通过多种形式的货币宽松政策，包括美联储的QE（量化宽松）、OT（扭转操作）和欧洲央行的OMT（直接货币交易计划）进行稀释，旨在增加经济体内的流动性，激励企业投资，提振消费欲望，拉动经济增长和创造就业机会。然而，在乌克兰危机推高全球通胀后，美国采取了提高利率以抑制通胀的措施，但一方面高利率增加了偿债成本，另一方面国际资本加速回流进一步推高通胀[1]。美国经济政策顾此失彼的原因在于脱实向虚已成痼疾，单靠货币政策只能延缓危机，难以扭转2023年后进入衰退的风险。

第二，大宗商品市场剧烈波动助推世界动荡变革。乌克兰危机爆发后，能源价格剧烈波动，全球稀有金属和原材料价格快速攀升，导致全球供应链和产业链可能局部调整。由于俄罗斯和乌克兰两国占全球谷物出口的三分之一以上，危机使粮食出口一度中断，全球粮食供应出现短缺。联合国成立了"全球粮食、能源和金融危机应对小组"，以应对可能引爆的全球性粮荒。自黑海粮食倡议实施以来，至2022年10月15日，已有341艘货船驶离乌南部港口，乌已出口750万吨农产品。由于极端天气和新冠疫情等原因，目前约3.45亿人受到饥饿影响，而全球约9.24亿

---

[1] 截至2022年10月，美国联邦债务规模已超31万亿美元，距离31.4万亿美元的债务"红线"仅剩2500亿美元。同时，海外投资净流入美国累计金额已超过2021年全年的总流入额11114亿美元，创下自1978年有数据以来的新高。

人面临严重粮食不安全状况[①]。

第三,贸易保护主义成为大国政治和经济领域斗争的融汇点。目前,国际贸易不平衡持续存在,全球经常账户失衡格局未见明显改善。美国出台《2022年芯片和科学法案》等,催生新一轮贸易保护主义,并有导致全球价值链断裂的风险。值得注意的是,美国芯片法案授权资金总额高达2800亿美元,通过对单一产业给予高额补贴的办法发展美国国内半导体制造业,却向WTO(世界贸易组织)投诉中国在高级材料、金属行业、纺织品、轻工业、专用化学品、医疗产品、计算机硬件、建筑材料等方面给予出口企业补贴,双标做法十分明显。其实,中国加入世贸组织以来,严格遵守世贸组织《补贴和反补贴措施协定》的各项义务,全面取消了协定下的禁止性补贴,这是有据可查的,而美国以国内法取代国际法,用保护主义和霸权主义破坏了国际贸易关系和基本准则。

第四,地区安全危机对世界局势产生消极影响。正如耿爽大使在乌克兰问题紧急特别联大上的发言指出:乌克兰危机已持续八个月之久,日益呈现长期化、扩大化、复杂化的态势,其外溢影响持续向经济民生领域扩散,给本已动荡不安的世界带来更多不稳定性和不确定性,令人深感忧虑。此外,阿富汗、利比亚、中亚等国局势变化也造成诸多区域的不稳定。

二 时代变局对中国的影响

外部环境的不确定性增加,对中国的发展既是挑战,又是机遇。

首先,全球增长重心转移,发达国家与发展中国家实力对比发生显著改变,是世界经济环境最重要的变化之一。现在,新兴经济体和低收入国家占全球GDP权重的一半以上,未来5年内整个新兴经济体在全球贸易中的比重还会不断上升,预计对全球GDP增长贡献率在2/3左右。这导致整个世界需求结构的巨大变化,而这一变化将为增长带来从量变

[①] 刘燕春子:《全球气候变化风险加剧 能源与粮食安全何去何从》,中国金融新闻网,https://www.financialnews.com.cn/hq/cj/202210/t20221025_257863.html,2022年10月25日。

到质变的真实含义。相比发达国家的财政警戒，新兴经济体有更好的财政空间，一是总体债务水平比较低，二是赤字水平比较低，实施财政政策和货币政策的空间很大。随着世界经济力量对比的巨大变化，发展中国家和发达国家在规则制定权上的博弈将更加激烈。通过制定水平更高、执行更严的国际规则，新兴经济体与发展中国家一道，谋求互利共赢。中国有能力促进全球包容性发展，让更多的发展中国家分享到中国发展的果实。

其次，长期经济增长归根到底取决于劳动生产率的提高，而实现劳动生产率提高不外乎三个主要途径：一是技术进步；二是贸易扩大化；三是制度创新。现阶段，制度创新和技术进步尤为重要，因为好的制度安排和技术进步与要素流动密切相关，从而为劳动生产率的提高释放出空间。党和人民历经百年奋斗和积累，探索出中国特色社会主义道路，这是中国社会最大的共识，也是中国最大的制度优势。目前，我国经济社会发展基本面趋好，国内市场潜力巨大，科技创新能力增强，人力资源丰富，生产要素综合优势明显，但仍存在贯彻新发展理念、构建新发展格局的迫切任务。制度创新就是在坚持中国共产党领导、坚持中国特色社会主义制度前提下，不断完善中国特色社会主义理论体系，坚决破除一切束缚生产力发展的体制机制，并建立适应经济—社会发展新阶段要求的体制机制。必须完整、准确、全面贯彻新发展理念，坚持社会主义市场经济改革方向，坚持高水平对外开放，加快构建以国内大循环为主体、国内国际双循环相互促进的新发展格局。要构建高水平社会主义市场经济体制，坚持和完善社会主义基本经济制度，毫不动摇巩固和发展公有制经济，毫不动摇鼓励、支持、引导非公有制经济发展，充分发挥市场在资源配置中的决定性作用，更好发挥政府作用。这是中国赢得经济竞赛的制度保障。

最后，中国面临的根本问题还是国家建设和国内发展，以中国式现代化全面推进中华民族伟大复兴。中华民族伟大复兴的标志是全面复兴，所以中国式现代化也应是包括经济、科技、政治、法律、文化、社会、安全和国防等各个方面在内的国家治理体系现代化。在决胜"十四五"、奔向2035远景目标的过程中，最主要的抓手有：经济上加快构建新发展格局，着力推动高质量发展；科技上实施科教兴国战略，强化现代化建设人才支撑；政治上发展全过程人民民主，保障人民当家作主；法治上坚持全面依法治国，推进法治中国建设；文化上推进自信自强，铸就社会主义文化新辉煌；社会上增进民生福祉，提高人民生活品质；安全上推进国家安全体系和能力现代化，坚决维护国家安全和社会稳定；国防上实现建军一百年奋斗目标，开创国防和军队现代化新局面。特别要强调的是，"坚持党的全面领导是坚持和发展中国特色社会主义的必由之路，中国特色社会主义是实现中华民族伟大复兴的必由之路，团结奋斗是中国人民创造历史伟业的必由之路，贯彻新发展理念是新时代我国发展壮大的必由之路，全面从严治党是党永葆生机活力、走好新的赶考之路的必由之路。"[①] 这是我们在长期实践中得出的至关紧要的规律性认识，也是中国迎来战略胜利的根本原因。

世界的发展离不开中国，中国的发展也离不开世界。新发展格局不仅要求我们勠力同心，建设好我们的家园，也要求我们逆风而上，驾驭时代的惊涛骇浪，在国际社会开拓更广泛的发展空间。

三 "两个倡议"的理念与与内涵

当前，人类社会面临前所未有的挑战，主要原因是国际社会三大突出矛盾没有得到有效解决。这三大突出矛盾是：全球发展不平衡，全球治理缺位，国际安全呈现结构性紧张。西方发达国家利用自身领先发展的优势获得的不平等贸易条件占有落后国家更多经济利益和资源的商业、政治、科技以及文化活动仍在持续，推动世界经济发展水平两极分化，富者愈富，贫者愈贫，发展差距日益拉大。民族矛盾、种族矛盾、社会矛盾并存，特别是大国利益博弈可能激化大国矛盾，甚至引发激烈冲突。许多经济落后国家被一定程度上阻挡和隔离在全球大市场之外，进出口贸易和国际经济合作缺乏竞争优势，国际收支面临严重赤字的困境，基

[①] 习近平：《高举中国特色社会主义伟大旗帜　为全面建设社会主义现代化国家而团结奋斗——在中国共产党第二十次全国代表大会上的报告》，《人民日报》2022年10月26日。

础设施落后，教育、医疗、体育等公共服务严重不足，经济过度依靠农业和采矿业，国民收入偏低。同时，发达经济体日益偏向服务化、虚拟化、空心化，出现增长疲软和不可持续的局面。全球经济的不均衡发展带来全球范围内不同社会阶层之间的不均衡发展。在一些落后地区贫困与饥饿仍威胁着人们，全球仍然有7亿多人口生活在极端贫困之中。对很多家庭而言，拥有温暖住房、充足食物和稳定工作还是一种奢望。这是当今世界面临的最大挑战，也是一些国家社会动荡的重要原因。21世纪以来，随着贫富分化在不同阶级、不同族群、不同国家间日益加剧，收入不均等已成为全球经济治理关注的核心问题之一。

在现有的全球治理机制中，发达国家掌握着主要话语权。正如习近平主席所指出的："过去数十年，国际经济力量对比深刻演变，而全球治理体系未能反映新格局，代表性和包容性很不够。"[①] 尽管近几十年来，国际经济力量格局发生了重大改变，新兴市场国家和发展中国家对全球经济增长的贡献率已经达到80%，但这种变化在现有全球治理机制中并没有得到及时的反映，全球治理结构不能很好地代表广大发展中国家的利益与诉求。发展中国家群体性崛起，必然呼唤全球治理体系进行相应的调整和变革，在国际利益分配格局中取得更优位势。后疫情时代，在全球经济放缓的大势下，不同经济体以四个层次拉开了距离：第一层次是继续维持中高速增长的新兴市场国家和发展中国家，如中国和印度；第二层次是缓慢增长或负增长的发达经济体，其中尤以英国和日本为代表，经济减速趋势较为明显；第三层次是陷入"中等收入陷阱"的一些国家和地区；第四层次是经济落后国家和地区，在疫情等综合影响下进入衰退状态。各国发展不均衡和国际地位不平等，是国际安全受到威胁的根本原因。近年来，在多个国际场合，中国国家领导人提出新的全球治理观，旨在改变全球治理原有的模式和方法，为经济发展与世界和平开出"药方"。

中国的全球治理观是带有浓厚"问题意识"的，也经历了一个与时

[①] 习近平：《共担时代责任 共促全球发展——在世界经济论坛2017年年会开幕式上的主旨演讲》，《人民日报》2017年1月17日。

俱进的过程，这完全符合马克思主义唯物辩证法。2015年10月12日，中共中央政治局专门就"全球治理格局和全球治理体制"进行集体学习。习近平发表重要讲话，系统阐明了中国引领全球治理体制改革的新理念。他强调，中国参与全球治理的根本目的，就是服从服务于实现"两个一百年"奋斗目标、实现中华民族伟大复兴的"中国梦"。要审时度势，努力抓住机遇，妥善应对挑战，统筹国内国际两个大局，推动全球治理体制向着"更加公正合理"方向发展，为中国发展和世界和平创造更加有利的条件。2017年，习近平出席达沃斯经济论坛开幕式发表主旨演讲，其中关于全球治理的新主张引起世界舆论高度关注。习近平提出："我们一要坚持创新驱动，打造富有活力的增长模式。二要坚持协同联动，打造开放共赢的合作模式。三要坚持与时俱进，打造公正合理的治理模式。四要坚持公平包容，打造平衡普惠的发展模式。"[①] 2019年，在中法全球治理论坛闭幕式上，习近平主席指出，我们要坚持共商共建共享的全球治理观，坚持全球事务由各国人民商量着办，积极推进全球治理规则民主化。2022年1月，在世界经济论坛视频会议演讲中，习近平主席强调，"要以公平正义为理念引领全球治理体系变革，维护以世界贸易组织为核心的多边贸易体制，在充分协商基础上，为人工智能、数字经济等打造各方普遍接受、行之有效的规则，为科技创新营造开放、公正、非歧视的有利环境，推动经济全球化朝着更加开放、包容、普惠、平衡、共赢的方向发展，让世界经济活力充分迸发出来"[②]。在党的二十大报告中，习近平总书记再次强调，"中国积极参与全球治理体系改革和建设，坚持真正的多边主义，推进国际关系民主化，推动全球治理朝着更加公正合理的方向发展"，[③] 并呼吁国际社会一道落实全球发展倡议和全球安全倡议，弘扬和平、发展、公平、正义、民主、自由的全人类共同价值，同世界人民携手开创人类更加美好的未来。习近平主席关于全球治理思想

[①] 习近平：《共担时代责任 共促全球发展——在世界经济论坛2017年年会开幕式上的主旨演讲》，《人民日报》2017年1月17日。
[②] 《习近平谈治国理政》（第四卷），外文出版社2022年版，第485页。
[③] 习近平：《高举中国特色社会主义伟大旗帜 为全面建设社会主义现代化国家而团结奋斗——在中国共产党第二十次全国代表大会上的报告》，《人民日报》2022年10月26日。

的阐述是新时代中国特色社会主义思想的有机组成部分,在我国对外交往中起着重要的指导作用。

独立自主与开放共赢是国际经济关系的基本准则。前者强调的是经济主权上的独立与完整,而后者是操作层面的策略,两者并不矛盾。马克思和恩格斯早就说过,竞争是实际的贸易自由,而保护关税在竞争中只是治标的办法,是贸易自由范围内的防卫手段。要发展壮大,必须主动顺应经济全球化的潮流。坚持国际关系民主化和不干涉别国内政是国际政治关系的基本准则。国际关系民主化的核心是国家不分大小,一律平等,但在当下的国际政治实践中还远远做不到这一点,多数国际组织都是大国俱乐部。不干涉别国内政有两条含义,一是我们不干涉别国内政,二是也不允许外国干涉我们的内政,这是世界各国得以和平共处的法宝。中国处理国际关系不看社会制度,而是从国家自身的战略利益出发,既着眼于自身长远的战略利益,同时也尊重对方的利益,不计较历史恩怨,不计较社会制度和意识形态的差别,并且国家不分大小强弱都相互尊重,平等相待,这些都应成为国际政治关系的基本准则。保卫世界和平和反对霸权主义是国际安全关系的基本准则。世界和平不可分割,制止战争、维护和平的斗争也相互联系、不可分割,这是国际安全关系的特点。营造人类命运共同体,建立以互信、互利、平等、合作为核心的新安全观,实现有效裁军和军备控制,强化在国际和地区事务中的协调与合作,强调维护联合国权威和公认的国际准则,成为防止冲突和战争的可靠前提。习主席的国家安全观强调与邻为善、以邻为伴,倡导求同存异,而不是你死我活,已经有越来越多的国家形成共识。只有以合作谋和平、以合作促安全,才能实现世界的和平稳定与中国的长治久安。在国际安全问题上,中国将积极承担更多国际责任,同世界各国共同维护人类良知和国际公理,在世界和地区事务中主持公道、伸张正义,更加积极有为地参与热点问题的解决,通过平等协商处理矛盾和分歧,以最大的诚意和耐心,坚持对话解决分歧。

作为负责任的大国,中国努力为维护世界发展与和平贡献更多公共产品,突出表现就是"两个倡议"。全球发展倡议是 2021 年 9 月 21 日习近平主席在第七十六届联合国大会上提出的。主要包括六项内容:一是坚持发展优先,将发展置于全球宏观政策框架的突出位置,加强主要经济体政策协调,保持连续性、稳定性、可持续性,构建更加平等均衡的全球发展伙伴关系;二是坚持以人民为中心,在发展中保障和改善民生,保护和促进人权,做到发展为了人民、发展依靠人民、发展成果由人民共享,不断增强民众的幸福感、获得感、安全感,实现人的全面发展;三是坚持普惠包容,关注发展中国家特殊需求,通过缓债、发展援助等方式支持发展中国家尤其是困难特别大的脆弱国家,着力解决国家间和各国内部发展不平衡、不充分问题;四是坚持创新驱动,抓住新一轮科技革命和产业变革的历史性机遇,加速科技成果向现实生产力转化,打造开放、公平、公正、非歧视的科技发展环境,挖掘疫后经济增长新动能,携手实现跨越发展;五是坚持人与自然和谐共生,完善全球环境治理,积极应对气候变化,构建人与自然生命共同体;六是坚持行动导向,加大发展资源投入,重点推进减贫、粮食安全、抗疫和疫苗、发展筹资、气候变化和绿色发展、工业化、数字经济、互联互通等领域合作,加快落实联合国 2030 年可持续发展议程,构建全球发展命运共同体。全球安全倡议是 2022 年 4 月 21 日习近平主席在博鳌亚洲论坛年会开幕式上首次提出的,旨在剧烈动荡变革的国际形势下发出构建人类安全共同体的中国声音。主要内容有六项:一是坚持共同、综合、合作、可持续的安全观,共同维护世界和平和安全;二是坚持尊重各国主权、领土完整,不干涉别国内政,尊重各国人民自主选择的发展道路和社会制度;三是坚持遵守联合国宪章宗旨和原则,摒弃冷战思维,反对单边主义,不搞集团政治和阵营对抗;四是坚持重视各国合理安全关切,秉持安全不可分割原则,构建均衡、有效、可持续的安全架构,反对把本国安全建立在他国不安全的基础之上;五是坚持通过对话协商以和平方式解决国家间的分歧和争端,支持一切有利于和平解决危机的努力,不能搞双重标准,反对滥用单边制裁和"长臂管辖";六是坚持统筹维护传统领域和非传统领域安全,共同应对地区争端和恐怖主义、气候变化、网络安全、生物安全等全球性问题。

"两个倡议"反映了中国对和平与发展的最新最深入的思考,回答的是中国之问、世界之问、人民之问、时代之问,是新时代中国处理国际问题的重要原则，也希望得到其他国家的认同和支持，共同创造人类更美好的明天。

四 "两个倡议"的世界意义

新发展理念告诉我们，增长与发展是两个相关联却不完全等同的概念。在经济领域，增长通常表示一个国家经济总量和均量的增加，而发展不仅包括数量的增加，也包括经济过程的整体进步。经济增长不等于经济发展，而经济发展也不等于发展。基于一切生产和社会活动都应服务于人类自身，而人类发展主要体现在人的各种能力的提高上，所以发展理应包含人的全面发展和自由解放。

人类发展主要受到人口—资源—环境失衡的制约。现在，全球有10亿左右的人口每天平均收入不足1.25美元，还有10亿人口营养不良。根据美国国家情报委员会的预测，到2030年，由于经济发展、个人收入提高，极端贫困人口的数量将会下降约50%，但如果全球经济出现长期萧条，到2030年，那么减贫50%的目标就只能完成一半。到2030年，传染疾病造成的死亡预计将会减少30%，而非传染性疾病导致死亡的人数将增多。到21世纪中叶，根据人口与社会学家的预测，全球人口可能超过80亿，主要增长来自亚非发展中国家，人类将面临传统疾病及其变异传播、不可再生能源枯竭、环境承载力濒于极限的威胁。国际社会迫切需要实现人口—资源—环境全面协调可持续发展，这有赖于人类创造新的发展模式，从传统的以自然为征服对象的发展观中解放出来。

资源与环境问题涉及发展中国家的贫困问题，而发展中国家的贫困问题又与不公正、不合理的国际政治经济秩序有密切的联系。现存的国际秩序大多是在"二战"后由西方国家主导建立的。发展中国家在脱离西方殖民体系取得独立后，旧的国际垂直分工体系和经济结构并未相应改变，这种状况恶化了发展中国家谋求发展的条件，制约着发展中国家保护资源和环境的努力。国际社会要谋求人类可持续发展，首先要设法解决发展中国家的贫困问题，使发展中国家尽量摆脱对环境资源的依赖，而要做到这一点，就必须改变不公正、不合理的国际政治经济旧秩序。

目前，单边主义、保护主义、霸凌行径愈演愈烈，和平赤字、发展赤字、安全赤字、治理赤字有增无减，本来就非中性的国际制度在以美国为首的西方发达国家推动下继续向既得利益者倾斜。中国推动"一带一路"、亚投行、金砖银行等顶层设计，旨在统筹国际国内两个市场、两种资源，同时打造富有活力的增长模式、开放共赢的合作模式、公正合理的治理模式和平衡普惠的发展模式，以解决世界经济发展动力不足和分配不均的难题，理应得到国际社会的广泛认同。借助高新技术垄断和国际体系把持，西方国家不会迅速衰落。发展中国家与发达国家，一方推动权力平等，一方努力捍卫霸权，博弈和斗争在所难免。中国需要团结世界大多数发展中国家，寻求共同利益，付诸一致行动，齐心协力推动国际政治经济秩序创新。

全球发展倡议不仅是中国基于新时代经济运行规律总结出来的指导思想，也是中国对联合国2030可持续发展议程的应对之策，对世界发展模式是个贡献。作为地球村的一员，任何国家在追求自身发展的同时，必须兼顾其他国家的发展，不能将自己的发展建立在损害他国利益的基础上。对于发展中国家和不发达国家来说，必须要做到全面协调，努力满足人民群众多层次的需求，也要协调好各个方面的发展，做到统筹兼顾。随着中国特色社会主义实践的不断深入，中国的发展模式必将引领中华民族走向伟大复兴。到那时，中国的发展观对各国探索更科学、更文明的发展道路，对人类探索一般社会发展规律，乃至对世界社会主义运动的复兴必将做出更大贡献，从而彰显出更重大、更深远的世界影响。

全球安全倡议应成为解决地区武装冲突的纽带和共识。21世纪以来，全球局部战争和武装冲突并不少，据统计每年平均几十起，但是没有任何一场战争像乌克兰危机这样，造成世界性和全局性的影响。

美元作为国际货币，是支撑美国霸权的工具，但其基础是国家信用。现在看来，美国的国家信用不可高估，尤其在政治和军事对立的情况下，信用不再是美国的第一选项。印度前中央银行行长拉詹在 Project Syndicate 的专栏中指出，在冻结了俄罗斯中央银行的外汇储备之后，中国、印度和许多其他国家会为它们的外汇储备感到担忧。他进一步指出，由于具有像欧元和美元那样具有流动性的储备货币屈指可数，许多政府将不得不对诸如公司跨境借贷之类的活动加以限制。破坏美元信用将反噬美国自身，美元神话破灭的后果恐怕是美国难以承受的。

乌克兰危机日益变得凶险，其对世界和平与发展带来的冲击不可低估。抱守冷战思维、推行集团政治、制造阵营对抗、追求绝对安全不会带来和平，不符合任何人的利益。随着新冠疫情负面影响在美国和其他国家日益凸显，世界愈发需要团结合作、共克时艰。任何强调本国绝对安全，突出意识形态分歧，胁迫他国选边站队，制造孤立打压，推行脱钩断链的行为，都是不负责任的。应该深刻汲取历史教训，相互尊重主权和领土完整，共同维护以联合国为核心的国际体系，以国际法为基础的国际秩序，共同推进世界的和平与发展。

今天我们面临的全球性问题，既有地区战争与冲突的控制问题，又有国际经济和政治秩序的重构问题，还有宗教和文化的多样性问题，错综复杂，各种利益诉求和价值理念交织在一起。"一带一路"倡议，它不局限于一国一地，而是构建经济和命运共同体。随着实践的不断发展，中国的发展经验必将引发各国人民的关注和思考，焕发更大的生机活力。到那时，"两个倡议"对各国探索更科学、更文明的发展道路，对人类的和平与幸福必将做出更大贡献，从而彰显出更重大、更深远的世界意义。

中国式现代化新进程与发展战略的主动性

景向辉[*]

战略问题极端重要,是古今中外治国理政需要运筹谋划的头等大事。战略主动问题则是决定军事斗争成败、国家政权安危存亡不可不察的"死生之地、存亡之道"[①]。战略主动问题直接关乎自主权,是战略思维的核心内容。在一定程度上,战略思维能力的高低也是衡量人类文明发展程度的重要标尺。纵观人类社会发展史,中华民族在源远流长的历史文化中对战略问题进行了持久深入的探索与总结,并在此基础上形成了高度发达、博大精深、独具魅力的战略思想、战略思维,有力地创造、守护、延续和发展了中华文明文脉与中华民族血脉。中华民族的战略思想、战略思维,在中华优秀传统文化尤其是兵学思想中拥有浩如烟海的丰厚资源,成为中国共产党百年奋斗实践和70多年执政兴国经验与智慧的植根沃土与重要理论之源,也成为伟大建党精神的重要思想之源,更成为做中国人的志气、骨气、底气的重要文化与心理之源。中华民族的战略思想、战略思维在世界范围内具有持久广泛深远的学术影响力和思想穿透力。世界范围内包括欧美国家一直经久不衰的孙子文化现象,就是有力的证明。在当前"两个大局"的时代背景下,思考和研究百年中国共

---

[*] 景向辉,中国社会科学院信息情报研究院副研究员。
[①] 《孙子》,上海古籍出版社2013年版,第1页。

产党党史尤其是新时代以来中国共产党关于战略主动问题的思考与实践，具有特殊重要的意义。

"战略"一词是中国共产党第二十次全国代表大会报告中出现的高频词。"牢牢把握战略主动"也是贯穿报告全文的一条思维主线。中国共产党第二十次全国代表大会报告在谈到党的十九大以来极不寻常、极不平凡的五年工作时明确指出，"面对'台独'势力分裂活动和外部势力干涉台湾事务的严重挑衅，我们坚决开展反分裂、反干涉重大斗争，展示了我们维护国家主权和领土完整、反对'台独'的坚强决心和强大能力，进一步掌握了实现祖国完全统一的战略主动，进一步巩固了国际社会坚持一个中国的格局。"[1] "面对国际局势急剧变化，特别是面对外部讹诈、遏制、封锁、极限施压，我们坚持国家利益为重、国内政治优先，保持战略定力，发扬斗争精神，展示不畏强权的坚定意志，在斗争中维护国家尊严和核心利益，牢牢掌握了我国发展和安全主动权。"[2] 正是由于牢牢掌握了我国发展和安全主动权，新时代十年来，我们才经历和办成了"对党和人民事业具有重大现实意义和深远历史意义的三件大事：一是迎来中国共产党成立一百周年，二是中国特色社会主义进入新时代，三是完成脱贫攻坚、全面建成小康社会的历史任务，实现第一个百年奋斗目标。这是中国共产党和中国人民团结奋斗赢得的历史性胜利，是彪炳中华民族发展史册的历史性胜利，也是对世界具有深远影响的历史性胜利。"[3] 由此取得的新时代十年的伟大变革，"在党史、新中国史、改革开放史、社会主义发展史、中华民族发展史上具有里程碑意义。"[4] 报告在第十三部分"坚持和完善'一国两制'，推进祖国统一"时指出，"解决台湾问题、实现祖国完全统一，是党矢志不渝的历史任务，是全体中华

---

[1] 习近平：《高举中国特色社会主义伟大旗帜　为全面建设社会主义现代化国家而团结奋斗——在中国共产党第二十次全国代表大会上的报告》，《人民日报》2022年10月26日。

[2] 习近平：《高举中国特色社会主义伟大旗帜　为全面建设社会主义现代化国家而团结奋斗——在中国共产党第二十次全国代表大会上的报告》，《人民日报》2022年10月26日。

[3] 习近平：《高举中国特色社会主义伟大旗帜　为全面建设社会主义现代化国家而团结奋斗——在中国共产党第二十次全国代表大会上的报告》，《人民日报》2022年10月26日。

[4] 习近平：《高举中国特色社会主义伟大旗帜　为全面建设社会主义现代化国家而团结奋斗——在中国共产党第二十次全国代表大会上的报告》，《人民日报》2022年10月26日。

儿女的共同愿望,是实现中华民族伟大复兴的必然要求。坚持贯彻新时代党解决台湾问题的总体方略,牢牢把握两岸关系主导权和主动权,坚定不移推进祖国统一大业。"①

一 牢牢把握战略主动是中国共产党战略思维的精髓

"牢牢把握战略主动"也是贯穿百年党史的一条思维主线,贯穿中国共产党十九届六中全会《中共中央关于党的百年奋斗重大成就和历史经验的决议》的一条重要主线。习近平总书记在省部级主要领导干部学习贯彻党的十九届六中全会精神专题研讨班上发表的重要讲话着重强调指出,"战略问题是一个政党、一个国家的根本性问题。战略上判断得准确,战略上谋划得科学,战略上赢得主动,党和人民事业就大有希望。一百年来,党总是能够在重大历史关头从战略上认识、分析、判断面临的重大历史课题,制定正确的政治战略策略,这是党战胜无数风险挑战、不断从胜利走向胜利的有力保证。"②"这次全会决议对百年奋斗历程中党高度重视战略策略问题、不断提出科学的战略策略作了全面总结。注重分析和总结党在百年奋斗历程中对战略策略的研究和把握,是贯穿全会决议的一个重要内容,我们一定要深入学习、全面领会。"③ 关于党的十九届六中全会《中共中央关于党的百年奋斗重大成就和历史经验的决议》,习近平总书记本人的重要解读就有多次,这几次解读从不同的方面加以强调,每次均有所深化。一个是关于《中共中央关于党的百年奋斗重大成就和历史经验的决议》起草情况的说明,习近平总书记谈了关于党的十九届六中全会议题的三点考虑。第二个就是习近平总书记在党的

---

① 习近平:《高举中国特色社会主义伟大旗帜 为全面建设社会主义现代化国家而团结奋斗——在中国共产党第二十次全国代表大会上的报告》,《人民日报》2022 年 10 月 26 日。

② 《习近平在省部级主要领导干部学习贯彻党的十九届六中全会精神专题研讨班开班式上发表重要讲话强调 继续把党史总结学习教育宣传引向深入 更好把握和运用党的百年奋斗历史经验》,《人民日报》2022 年 1 月 12 日。

③ 《习近平在省部级主要领导干部学习贯彻党的十九届六中全会精神专题研讨班开班式上发表重要讲话强调 继续把党史总结学习教育宣传引向深入 更好把握和运用党的百年奋斗历史经验》,《人民日报》2022 年 1 月 12 日。

十九届六中全会第二次全体会议上的重要讲话,这里面明确提到中央召开党的十九届六中全会是郑重的战略性决策,《中共中央关于党的百年奋斗重大成就和历史经验的决议》的政治性、理论性、战略性和指导性都很强等一系列重要观点。第三个就是习近平总书记在省部级主要领导干部学习贯彻党的十九届六中全会精神的专题研讨班上的重要讲话。这个讲话从五个方面对《中共中央关于党的百年奋斗重大成就和历史经验的决议》中百年奋斗历程中的重大历史经验做了系统梳理,战略策略问题是其中的一个重要方面。此次重要讲话与习近平总书记2014年在纪念邓小平同志诞辰110周年座谈会的讲话里关于学习邓小平同志高瞻远瞩的战略思维的重要论述一脉相承,针对战略问题、战略主动问题、如何研究和把握战略策略等问题作出了一系列重要论述。如何从理论上对百年党史中这一条重大历史经验进行深入总结和阐释,对理论界而言是一个重大的理论命题。

  对战略主动问题的深刻洞察与把握,是中国共产党战略思维的精髓,体现了中国共产党人非凡的气魄、智慧与胆识。毛泽东说:"主动权是一个极端重要的事情。主动权,就是'高屋建瓴'、'势如破竹'。这件事来自实事求是……"[①] 回顾百年党史的浴血奋斗与艰辛探索,始终牢牢把握战略主动是中国共产党团结带领中国人民敢打必胜、战无不胜、始终立于不败之地的重要法宝,也是中国共产党把中国发展进步的命运牢牢掌握在自己手中,团结带领中国人民努力奋进的重要方法论。牢牢把握战略主动是毛泽东思想的鲜明特征。毛泽东是举世公认的伟大的战略家和军事理论家。在革命、建设的不同历史时期,在中国共产党领导军事斗争、领导社会主义革命与建设工作、领导宣传思想文化工作、观察与分析国内国际形势等不同的领域,毛泽东对战略问题尤其是战略主动问题均有过系统论述,集中体现在抗日战争时期所作的《抗日游击战争的战略问题》《论持久战》《统一战线中的独立自主问题》《战争和战略问题》等经典名篇中。毛泽东军事思想中的战略进攻思想、"你打你的,我打我的"等重要战略指导思想,究其根本均是如何夺取战略主动的问题,他

[①] 《毛泽东文集》第8卷,人民出版社1999年版,第197页。

对这一问题的深谋远虑与鲜活运用，已经成为中国人民乃至人类文明的宝贵财富。习近平总书记在省部级主要领导干部学习贯彻党的十九届六中全会精神专题研讨班上发表的重要讲话着重引用了毛泽东的一段话说明什么是战略领导艺术，他在讲话中指出，"战略是从全局、长远、大势上作出判断和决策。毛泽东同志很形象地说过这个问题，他说：'坐在指挥台上，如果什么也看不见，就不能叫领导。坐在指挥台上，只看见地平线上已经出现的大量的普遍的东西，那是平平常常的，也不能算领导。只有当着还没有出现大量的明显的东西的时候，当桅杆顶刚刚露出的时候，就能看出这是要发展成为大量的普遍的东西，并能掌握住它，这才叫领导。'毛泽东同志讲的这种领导，就是战略领导。"① 他还详细列举了两个事例，一个是日本发动全面侵华战争后，毛泽东同志在 1938 年发表《论持久战》一文科学地回答了"这场战争能不能胜利？怎样争取胜利？"这个问题，从而使全国人民对抗战的进程和前途有了清晰的认识，极大坚定了全国军民坚持抗战的信心。另一个是，1945 年党的七大期间讨论抗战胜利后党的发展前途时，毛泽东强调东北对于中国革命的最近将来的前途极其重要的战略意义，"如果我们把现有的一切根据地都丢了，只要我们有了东北，那末中国革命就有了巩固的基础。当然，其他根据地没有丢，我们又有了东北，中国革命的基础就更巩固了。"习近平总书记指出，"这是多么富有远见的战略决断！后来的发展也证明这个战略决断对解放战争胜利发挥了多么重要的作用。"②

　　牢牢把握战略主动是贯穿习近平新时代中国特色社会主义思想的一条重要主线。在关乎党治国理政全局的各个方面，无论是在事关全局的系统性深层次变革的重大问题上，还是在防范化解重大风险的底线思维上，习近平总书记都高度重视牢牢把握战略主动这个关键问题。可以说，党的十八大以来，中国共产党团结带领全国人民之所以能够创造新时代的伟大成就，实现中华民族复兴伟业之所以能够进入不可逆转的历史进程，很重要的一个方面，就在于我们党始终牢牢把握了战略主动这个关

---

① 习近平：《更好把握和运用党的百年奋斗历史经验》，《求是》2022 年第 13 期。
② 习近平：《更好把握和运用党的百年奋斗历史经验》，《求是》2022 年第 13 期。

键问题。习近平总书记在省部级主要领导干部学习贯彻党的十九届六中全会精神专题研讨班上发表的重要讲话指出,"我们是一个大党,领导的是一个大国,进行的是伟大的事业,绝不能犯战略性错误。小的方面有看不到的,出现这样那样的失误,是难以完全避免的,这样的失误牵涉的是一点一事的问题,影响面不大,纠正起来也比较容易。如果在战略上出现了偏差,那后果将是很严重的,付出的代价将会很大。党在早期有过惨痛的教训。……所以,我一直强调,领导干部要善于进行战略思维,善于从战略上看问题、想问题。"[①] 在谈到战略和策略辩证统一的关系时,习近平总书记强调指出,"正确的战略需要正确的策略来落实。要取得各方面斗争的胜利,我们不仅要有战略谋划,有坚定斗志,还要有策略、有智慧、有方法。策略是在战略指导下为战略服务的。战略和策略是辩证统一的关系,把战略的坚定性和策略的灵活性结合起来,站位要高,做事要实,既要把方向、抓大事、谋长远,又要抓准抓好工作的切入点和着力点,既要算大账总账,又要算小账细账。如果没有足够的战略定力和策略活力,就容易出现患得患失、摇摆不定、进退失据的问题,就会错失发展机遇。"[②]

在事关发展全局的重大战略任务上强调要牢牢把握战略主动。习近平总书记指出:"一个党要立于不败之地,必须立于时代潮头,紧扣新的历史特点,科学谋划全局,牢牢把握战略主动,坚定不移实现我们的战略目标。"[③]"在新的长征路上,我们要立足世情国情党情,统筹国内国际两个大局,统筹党和国家事业发展全局,协调推进各项事业发展,抓住战略重点,实现关键突破,赢得战略主动,防范系统性风险,避免颠覆性危机,维护好发展全局。"[④]"坚持创新发展,是我们分析近代以来世界发展历程特别是总结我国改革开放成功实践得出的结论,是我们应对发展环境变化、增强发展动力、把握发展主动权,更好引领新常态的根本

---

① 习近平:《更好把握和运用党的百年奋斗历史经验》,《求是》2022 年第 13 期。
② 习近平:《更好把握和运用党的百年奋斗历史经验》,《求是》2022 年第 13 期。
③ 《习近平在纪念红军长征胜利 80 周年大会上的讲话》,《人民日报》2016 年 10 月 22 日。
④ 《习近平在纪念红军长征胜利 80 周年大会上的讲话》,《人民日报》2016 年 10 月 22 日。

之策。"① 在党的十九大报告中谈到全面增强党的执政本领时，习近平强调："增强驾驭风险本领，健全各方面风险防控机制，善于处理各种复杂矛盾，勇于战胜前进道路上的各种艰难险阻，牢牢把握工作主动权。"② 对于国家安全、国防和军队建设工作，他强调："中央国家安全委员会成立4年来……国家安全工作得到全面加强，牢牢掌握了维护国家安全的全局性主动。"③ "解决军事政策制度深层次矛盾和问题，全面释放深化国防和军队改革效能，开创强军事业新局面，掌握军事竞争和战争主动权，迫切需要适应形势任务发展要求，对军事政策制度进行系统、深入改革。"④

习近平总书记高度重视加快构建新发展格局，多次强调"加快构建新发展格局，是我们把握未来发展主动权的战略举措"⑤。针对这一问题，2021年1月11日，习近平总书记意味深长地引用了毛泽东同志1936年在谈到指导军事斗争时的一段话，认为这段话至今都对我们有启示意义。毛泽东说："无论处于怎样复杂、严重、惨苦的环境，军事指导者首先需要的是独立自主地组织和使用自己的力量。被敌逼迫到被动地位的事是常有的，重要的是要迅速地恢复主动地位。如果不能恢复到这种地位，下文就是失败。主动地位不是空想的，而是具体的，物质的。"⑥ 习近平总书记引用这段话，表现出大国领袖立足"两个大局"对时与势的深刻洞察，体现了——"确保中华民族伟大复兴进程不被迟滞甚至中断"——深沉的忧患意识；同时也有力地彰显了——"没有任何人能打倒我们、卡死我们！"——击水中流、迎难而上的顽强的革命意志与鲜明的斗争精神。

---

① 习近平：《深入理解新发展理念》，《求是》2019年第10期。
② 《中国共产党第十九次全国代表大会文件汇编》，人民出版社2017年版，第55页。
③ 《习近平谈治国理政》（第三卷），外文出版社2020年版，第217页。
④ 《习近平出席中央军委政策制度改革工作会议并发表重要讲话》，《人民日报》2018年11月15日。
⑤ 《统筹指导构建新发展格局推进种业振兴推动青藏高原生态环境保护和可持续发展》，《人民日报》2021年7月10日。
⑥ 习近平：《把握新发展阶段，贯彻新发展理念，构建新发展格局》，《求是》2021年第9期。

在抓好党的意识形态工作、着力防范化解重大风险等方面强调要牢牢把握战略主动。习近平总书记深刻指出："坚持团结稳定鼓劲、正面宣传为主，是宣传思想工作必须遵循的重要方针……在事关大是大非和政治原则问题上，必须增强主动性、掌握主动权、打好主动仗，帮助干部群众划清是非界限、澄清模糊认识。"①"根据形势发展需要，我看要把网上舆论工作作为宣传思想工作的重中之重来抓……必须正视这个事实，加大力量投入，尽快掌握这个舆论战场上的主动权，不能被边缘化了。"②"要牢牢把握舆论主动权和主导权，让互联网成为构筑各民族共有精神家园、铸牢中华民族共同体意识的最大增量。"③ 在坚持底线思维，着力防范化解重大风险的问题上，习近平总书记强调，必须始终保持高度警惕，"既要有防范风险的先手，也要有应对和化解风险挑战的高招；既要打好防范和抵御风险的有准备之战，也要打好化险为夷、转危为机的战略主动战"④。在加快实施创新驱动发展战略、加快推动经济发展方式转变上，他强调必须增强紧迫感，"紧紧抓住机遇，及时确立发展战略，全面增强自主创新能力，掌握新一轮全球科技竞争的战略主动"⑤。习近平总书记在省部级主要领导干部学习贯彻党的十九届六中全会精神专题研讨班上发表的重要讲话指出，"各地区各部门确定工作思路、工作部署、政策措施，要自觉同党的理论和路线方针政策对标对表、及时校准偏差，党中央作出的战略决策必须无条件执行，确保不偏向、不变通、不走样。各地区各部门在贯彻党中央战略决策时应该根据本地区本部门的实际制定策略，这是必须的。同时也要注意，大家提出的各种策略，有的可能是符合中央战略的，有的则可能是偏离中央战略的。这就要注意及时总结评估，偏离了的要赶紧调整。"⑥

---

① 《习近平谈治国理政》（第一卷），外文出版社2018年版，第155页。
② 《习近平关于总体国家安全观论述摘编》，中央文献出版社2018年版，第103、104页。
③ 《习近平谈治国理政》（第三卷），外文出版社2020年版，第301页。
④ 《习近平谈治国理政》（第三卷），外文出版社2020年版，第73页。
⑤ 《习近平主持召开中央财经领导小组第七次会议》，《人民日报》2014年8月19日。
⑥ 习近平：《更好把握和运用党的百年奋斗历史经验》，《求是》2022年第13期。

二　牢牢把握战略主动就是要牢牢掌握历史主动

历史是一面镜子，鉴古知今，学史明智。从逻辑与本质上看，历史、现实和未来互为规定，相互贯通，只有对重大历史问题保持清醒认识与准确把握，才能够形成历史主动。掌握历史主动是赢得现实主动与未来主动的基本前提。习近平总书记指出："中国共产党坚持马克思主义基本原理，坚持实事求是，从中国实际出发，洞察时代大势，把握历史主动，进行艰辛探索，不断推进马克思主义中国化时代化，指导中国人民不断推进伟大社会革命。"① 他在会见中国共产党成立100周年庆祝活动筹办工作各方面代表时的重要讲话中强调，"要深入总结百年党史正反两方面经验，在历史智慧的学习运用中提升历史自觉、把握历史主动"②。习近平总书记关于把握历史主动的重要论断，为我们深刻认识和把握中国共产党的百年历史提供了根本遵循。

掌握历史主动必须清醒认识和把握历史发展规律和大势。"用兵任势也。"③ 把握历史大势、掌握历史主动是中国共产党创造百年辉煌的重要经验④。习近平总书记强调："100年来，中国共产党坚持中国人民和世界各国人民命运与共，在世界大局和时代潮流中把握中国发展的前进方向、促进各国共同发展繁荣。"⑤ "历史发展有其规律，但人在其中不是完全消极被动的。只要把握住历史发展大势，抓住历史变革时机，奋发有为，锐意进取，人类社会就能更好前进。"⑥ 在党史学习教育动员大会上的重要讲话中，习近平总书记强调，要"进一步把握历史发展规律和大

---

① 习近平：《在庆祝中国共产党成立100周年大会上的讲话》，人民出版社2021年版，第12—13页。
② 《习近平亲切会见庆祝活动筹办工作各方面代表》，《人民日报》2021年7月14日。
③ 《孙子》，上海古籍出版社2013年版，第57页。
④ 参见曲青山《把握历史大势掌握历史主动》，《求是》2021年第11期。
⑤ 习近平：《加强政党合作共谋人民幸福——在中国共产党与世界政党领导人峰会上的主旨讲话》，《人民日报》2021年7月7日。
⑥ 《庆祝改革开放40周年大会在京隆重举行习近平发表重要讲话》，《人民日报》2018年12月19日。

势,始终掌握党和国家事业发展的历史主动"①。"我们要以史为鉴、开创未来,在全面建设社会主义现代化国家新征程上继续担当历史使命,掌握历史主动,不断把中华民族伟大复兴的历史伟业推向前进。"②

在谈到经济全球化进程、新时代科技创新及干部队伍建设等问题时,习近平强调:"经济全球化是历史大势,促成了贸易大繁荣、投资大便利、人员大流动、技术大发展。"③"我们要顺应大势、结合国情,正确选择融入经济全球化的路径和节奏。"④"党的十八大以来,我们总结我国科技事业发展实践,观察大势,谋划全局,深化改革,全面发力,推动我国科技事业发生历史性变革、取得历史性成就。"⑤"党的十九大以来……我们坚持党对科技事业的全面领导,观大势、谋全局、抓根本,形成高效的组织动员体系和统筹协调的科技资源配置模式。"⑥"党的政治建设落实到干部队伍建设上,就要不断提高各级领导干部特别是高级干部把握方向、把握大势、把握全局的能力,辨别政治是非、保持政治定力、驾驭政治局面、防范政治风险的能力。"⑦"要在自我革新上求突破,深刻把握时代发展大势,坚决破除一切不合时宜的思想观念和体制机制弊端。"⑧在谈到防范化解重大风险是各级党委、政府和领导干部的政治职责时,他强调,要强化风险意识,常观大势、常思大局,科学预见形势发展走势和隐藏其中的风险挑战,做到未雨绸缪⑨。

在谈到努力开创中国特色大国外交新局面时,习近平总书记着重强调:"把握国际形势要树立正确的历史观、大局观、角色观。所谓正确历

---

① 习近平:《在党史学习教育动员大会上的讲话》,《求是》2021年第7期。
② 习近平:《在纪念辛亥革命110周年大会上的讲话》,《人民日报》2021年10月10日。
③ 习近平:《共同构建人类命运共同体》,《求是》2021年第1期。
④ 习近平:《共担时代责任,共促全球发展》,《求是》2020年第24期。
⑤ 《习近平出席中国科学院第十九次院士大会、中国工程院第十四次院士大会开幕会并发表重要讲话》,《人民日报》2018年5月29日。
⑥ 《习近平出席中国科学院第十九次院士大会、中国工程院第十四次院士大会开幕会并发表重要讲话》,《人民日报》2018年5月29日。
⑦ 《习近平谈治国理政》(第三卷),外文出版社2020年版,第97页。
⑧ 习近平:《牢记初心使命,推进自我革命》,《求是》2019年第15期。
⑨ 参见《习近平在省部级主要领导干部坚持底线思维着力防范化解重大风险专题研讨班开班式上发表重要讲话》,《人民日报》2019年1月22日。

史观，就是不仅要看现在国际形势什么样，而且要端起历史望远镜回顾过去、总结历史规律，展望未来、把握历史前进大势。"① 在谈到携手构建人类命运共同体时，他强调："当前，世界格局在变，发展格局在变，各个政党都要顺应时代发展潮流、把握人类进步大势、顺应人民共同期待，把自身发展同国家、民族、人类的发展紧密结合在一起。"② "金砖国家要顺应历史大势，把握发展机遇，合力克服挑战，为构建新型国际关系、构建人类命运共同体发挥建设性作用。"③ "我们应该把握时代大势，客观认识世界发展变化，以负责任、合规矩的方式应对新情况新挑战。"④ "面向未来，我们应该把握大势、顺应潮流，努力把亚洲人民对美好生活的向往变成现实。"⑤ 做好党的意识形态工作，把握大势、掌握主动权更为重要。习近平总书记多次就这一紧要问题作出重要论述。"宣传思想工作一定要把围绕中心、服务大局作为基本职责，胸怀大局、把握大势、着眼大事，找准工作切入点和着力点，做到因势而谋、应势而动、顺势而为。"⑥ "要不断提升中华文化影响力，把握大势、区分对象、精准施策，主动宣介新时代中国特色社会主义思想，主动讲好中国共产党治国理政的故事、中国人民奋斗圆梦的故事、中国坚持和平发展合作共赢的故事，让世界更好了解中国。"⑦

掌握历史主动必须树立大历史观。大历史观重在历史眼光、历史思维、历史自觉。习近平总书记多次论及大历史观这一重要问题。不同于西方大历史观，习近平总书记所论述的大历史观是以历史唯物主义为指导，从历史的阶段性与连续性、民族性与世界性、前进性与曲折性辩证

---

① 《习近平谈治国理政》（第三卷），外文出版社 2020 年版，第 427 页。
② 《习近平出席中国共产党与世界政党高层对话会开幕式并发表主旨讲话》，《人民日报》2017 年 12 月 2 日。
③ 《习近平出席金砖国家领导人第十次会晤并发表重要讲话》，《人民日报》2018 年 7 月 27 日。
④ 《同舟共济创造美好未来》，《人民日报》2018 年 11 月 18 日。
⑤ 《习近平出席亚洲文明对话大会开幕式并发表主旨演讲》，《人民日报》2019 年 5 月 16 日。
⑥ 《习近平谈治国理政》（第一卷），外文出版社 2018 年版，第 153 页。
⑦ 《习近平谈治国理政》（第三卷），外文出版社 2020 年版，第 314 页。

统一的视角出发,全程、全方位、全局地看待历史与现实,实现了对历史唯物主义的创新性发展①。

习近平强调:"以数千年大历史观之,变革和开放总体上是中国的历史常态。中华民族以改革开放的姿态继续走向未来,有着深远的历史渊源、深厚的文化根基。"②"要教育引导全党胸怀中华民族伟大复兴战略全局和世界百年未有之大变局,树立大历史观,从历史长河、时代大潮、全球风云中分析演变机理、探究历史规律,提出因应的战略策略,增强工作的系统性、预见性、创造性。"③ 要"多从人类发展大潮流、世界变化大格局、中国发展大历史来认识和把握党的基本路线,深刻领会为什么基本路线要长期坚持"④。"在 5000 多年文明发展中孕育的中华优秀传统文化,在党和人民伟大斗争中孕育的革命文化和社会主义先进文化,积淀着中华民族最深层的精神追求,代表着中华民族独特的精神标识。"⑤ "中国特色社会主义不是从天上掉下来的,而是在改革开放 40 年的伟大实践中得来的,是在中华人民共和国成立近 70 年的持续探索中得来的,是在我们党领导人民进行伟大社会革命 97 年的实践中得来的,是在近代以来中华民族由衰到盛 170 多年的历史进程中得来的,是对中华文明 5000 多年的传承发展中得来的,是党和人民历经千辛万苦、付出各种代价取得的宝贵成果。得到这个成果极不容易。"⑥ 习近平指出:"中华民族 5000 多年的文明史,中国人民近代以来 170 多年的斗争史,中国共产党 90 多年的奋斗史,中华人民共和国 60 多年的发展史,都是人民书写的历

---

① 金梦、周良书:《习近平大历史观对历史唯物主义的创新性发展》,《理论视野》2020 年第 6 期。
② 《庆祝改革开放 40 周年大会在京隆重举行习近平发表重要讲话》,《人民日报》2018 年 12 月 19 日。
③ 习近平:《在党史学习教育动员大会上的讲话》,《求是》2021 年第 7 期。
④ 《中共中央政治局召开民主生活会强调树牢"四个意识"坚定"四个自信"坚决做到"两个维护"勇于担当作为以求真务实作风把党中央决策部署落到实处》,《人民日报》2018 年 12 月 27 日。
⑤ 习近平:《在庆祝中国共产党成立 95 周年大会上的讲话》,《求是》2021 年第 8 期。
⑥ 《习近平谈治国理政》(第三卷),外文出版社 2020 年版,第 70 页。

史。"①"历史是最好的老师。思政课教师的历史视野中，要有5000多年中华文明史，要有500多年世界社会主义史，要有中国人民近代以来170多年斗争史，要有中国共产党近100年的奋斗史，要有中华人民共和国70年的发展史，要有改革开放40多年的实践史，要有新时代中国特色社会主义取得的历史性成就、发生的历史性变革，通过生动、深入、具体的纵横比较，把一些道理讲明白、讲清楚。"②他强调："中国共产党领导中国人民取得的伟大胜利，使具有5000多年文明历史的中华民族全面迈向现代化，让中华文明在现代化进程中焕发出新的蓬勃生机；使具有500年历史的社会主义主张在世界上人口最多的国家成功开辟出具有高度现实性和可行性的正确道路，让科学社会主义在21世纪焕发出新的蓬勃生机；使具有60多年历史的新中国建设取得举世瞩目的成就，中国这个世界上最大的发展中国家在短短30多年里摆脱贫困并跃升为世界第二大经济体，彻底摆脱被开除球籍的危险，创造了人类社会发展史上惊天动地的发展奇迹，使中华民族焕发出新的蓬勃生机。"③

习近平总书记对如何跳出历史周期率、自觉纠正超越历史阶段的错误观念等重大问题的深入思考，都体现了大历史观的深邃眼光。他系统回顾了我国历史上封建王朝兴衰更替难以摆脱的宿命，总结了我们党执政正反两方面的经验以及世界上一些社会主义国家和政党演变的教训，认为只要马克思主义执政党不出问题，社会主义国家就出不了大问题，我们就能够跳出"其兴也勃焉，其亡也忽焉"的历史周期率④。他引用邓小平同志的话说："巩固和发展社会主义制度，还需要一个很长的历史阶段，需要我们几代人、十几代人甚至几十代人坚持不懈地努力奋斗。几十代人，那是多么长啊！从孔老夫子到现在也不过七十几代人。这样看问题，充分说明了我们中国共产党人政治上的清醒。"⑤

---

① 《纪念毛泽东诞辰120周年座谈会举行 习近平发表重要讲话》，《人民日报》2013年12月27日。
② 习近平：《以史为镜、以史明志 知史爱党、知史爱国》，《求是》2021年第12期。
③ 习近平：《在庆祝中国共产党成立95周年大会上的讲话》，《求是》2021年第8期。
④ 参见习近平《推进党的建设新的伟大工程要一以贯之》，《求是》2019年第19期。
⑤ 习近平：《关于坚持和发展中国特色社会主义的几个问题》，《求是》2019年第7期。

三 牢牢把握战略主动就是要牢牢把握理论创新的战略主动

持久深入的理论创新能力，是衡量一个政党、一种制度是否具有生命活力，是否具备时代先进性与坚强领导力的重要标志。对于马克思主义政党而言，理论建设与创新更是其始终保持旺盛的战斗力和立于不败之地的重要法宝。中国共产党作为百年大党能够始终保持风华正茂、生机盎然，一个重要原因在于不断进行理论创新，积极引导和推动党的各项事业开创新局面，夺取新胜利。党的十八大以来，以习近平同志为核心的党中央在推进中国特色社会主义建设实践的进程中高度重视理论创新问题，紧密结合新时代特点和实践要求，不断深化对共产党执政规律、社会主义建设规律、人类社会发展规律的认识，进行不懈的理论探索，提出了一系列原创性的思想理论观点，有力推动了党的理论创新，有力推动了马克思主义中国化的新进展，取得了一系列重大理论创新成果[1]。习近平总书记指出："中国共产党之所以能够历经艰难困苦而不断发展壮大，很重要的一个原因就是我们党始终重视思想建党、理论强党，使全党始终保持统一的思想、坚定的意志、协调的行动、强大的战斗力。"[2] "新时代中国特色社会主义思想和基本方略，不是从天上掉下来的，不是主观臆想出来的，而是党的十八大以来，在新中国成立特别是改革开放以来我们党推进理论创新和实践创新的基础上，全党全国各族人民进行艰辛理论探索的成果，是全党全国各族人民创新创造的智慧结晶。"[3] "我们党的历史，就是一部不断推进马克思主义中国化的历史，就是一部不断推进理论创新、进行理论创造的历史。"[4] 在理论概括上牢牢把握主动。

---

[1] 参见中共中央党校报刊社"四情"调查课题组《为当代中国马克思主义增添真理力量——领导干部看新时代党的理论创新成果》，《理论视野》2018年第1期。
[2] 《纪念马克思诞辰200周年大会在京举行 习近平发表重要讲话》，《人民日报》2018年5月5日。
[3] 《习近平谈治国理政》（第三卷），外文出版社2020年版，第63页。
[4] 习近平：《在党史学习教育动员大会上的讲话》，《求是》2021年第7期。

善于提炼标识性概念，能够对一些重大理论与实践问题作出及时准确的理论概括，这是在理论创新上掌握战略主动的重要方法。习近平总书记强调："我们要在迅速变化的时代中赢得主动，要在新的伟大斗争中赢得胜利，就要在坚持马克思主义基本原理的基础上……在理论上不断拓展新视野、作出新概括。"①"要善于提炼标识性概念，打造易于为国际社会所理解和接受的新概念、新范畴、新表述，引导国际学术界展开研究和讨论。"②党的十八大以来，习近平总书记牢牢把握战略主动权，在运筹"两个大局"方面，概括提出了构建人类命运共同体、"一带一路"倡议等一系列原创性理论谋划与中国方案，在国际上引起了热烈反响，并切实惠及世界范围内广大民众；在党的建设领域，概括提出了初心使命、自我革命、"政治三力"即"政治判断力、政治领悟力、政治执行力"等一系列重大理论命题，构成习近平新时代中国特色社会主义思想的重要内容；在治国理政领域概括提出并全面系统阐述了"国之大者"、重要战略机遇期、战略定力、统筹发展和安全、"三新一高"即"把握新发展阶段，贯彻新发展理念，构建新发展格局，实现高质量发展"等一系列理论概括和重大原则。

这些具有标识性概念的理论概括与重大判断相互贯通、一以贯之，在习近平新时代中国特色社会主义思想的科学体系中具有提纲挈领的标志性意义，发挥了强有力的理论引领作用。习近平总书记多次总结党的历史上尤其是党的十八大以来的诸多重要理论概括与论断。他说："理论源于实践，又用来指导实践。改革开放以来，我们及时总结新的生动实践，不断推进理论创新，在发展理念、所有制、分配体制、政府职能、市场机制、宏观调控、产业结构、企业治理结构、民生保障、社会治理等重大问题上提出了许多重要论断……这些理论成果，不仅有力指导了我国经济发展实践，而且开拓了马克思主义政治经济学新境界。"③他系

---

① 《习近平在省部级主要领导干部"学习习近平总书记重要讲话精神，迎接党的十九大"专题研讨班开班式上发表重要讲话强调　高举中国特色社会主义伟大旗帜　为决胜全面小康社会实现中国梦而奋斗》，《人民日报》2017年7月28日。
② 习近平：《在哲学社会科学工作座谈会上的讲话》，《人民日报》2016年5月19日。
③ 习近平：《正确认识和把握中长期经济社会发展重大问题》，《求是》2021年第2期。

统总结回顾了党的十八大以来，我们党对经济形势进行科学判断，对发展理念和思路作出及时调整，对经济社会发展提出的坚持以人民为中心的发展思想、不再简单以国内生产总值增长率论英雄、我国经济处于"三期叠加"时期等十三个方面的重大理论和理念[1]。习近平总书记还强调，这十三个重大理论和理念中新发展理念是最重要、最主要的。全党必须完整、准确、全面贯彻新发展理念。

在理论武装上牢牢把握主动。党的创新理论只有真正武装头脑掌握群众，才能够成为真正有力的斗争武器。马克思在《〈黑格尔法哲学批判〉导言》中有一句名言："理论只要说服人，就能掌握群众；而理论只要彻底，就能说服人。所谓彻底，就是抓住事物的根本。而人的根本就是人本身。"[2] 习近平总书记强调，要炼就"金刚不坏之身"，"必须用科学理论武装头脑，不断培植我们的精神家园。要把系统掌握马克思主义基本理论作为看家本领"[3]。"理论修养是干部综合素质的核心，理论上的成熟是政治上成熟的基础，政治上的坚定源于理论上的清醒。从一定意义上说，掌握马克思主义理论的深度，决定着政治敏感的程度、思维视野的广度、思想境界的高度。"[4] "要深化党的创新理论学习教育，推动理想信念教育常态化制度化……促进全体人民在思想上精神上紧紧团结在一起。"[5] "要深入学习党的创新理论，加强党史学习教育，同时学习新中国史、改革开放史、社会主义发展史，不断提高政治判断力、政治领悟力、政治执行力。"[6] 坚持和发展中国特色社会主义，必须高度重视理论的作用，"理论创新每前进一步，理论武装就要跟进一步……要把学习贯

---

[1] 参见习近平《把握新发展阶段，贯彻新发展理念，构建新发展格局》，《求是》2021年第9期。

[2] 《马克思恩格斯文集》（第一卷），人民出版社2009年版，第11页。

[3] 习近平：《胸怀大局把握大势着眼大事努力把宣传思想工作做得更好》，《人民日报》2013年8月21日。

[4] 《中共中央政治局召开专题民主生活会 中共中央总书记习近平主持会议并发表重要讲话》，《人民日报》2015年12月27日。

[5] 《习近平主持召开教育文化卫生体育领域专家代表座谈会强调 全面推进教育文化卫生体育事业发展 不断增强人民群众获得感幸福感安全感》，《人民日报》2020年9月23日。

[6] 《习近平春节前夕赴贵州看望慰问各族干部群众》，《人民日报》2021年2月6日。

彻党的创新理论作为思想武装的重中之重"①。

在加强意识形态工作的制度建设上牢牢把握主动。习近平总书记强调:"一个政权的瓦解往往是从思想领域开始的,政治动荡、政权更迭可能在一夜之间发生,但思想演化是个长期过程。思想防线被攻破了,其他防线就很难守住。我们必须把意识形态工作的领导权、管理权、话语权牢牢掌握在手中,任何时候都不能旁落,否则就要犯无可挽回的历史性错误。"② 党的十九届四中全会审议通过的《中共中央关于坚持和完善中国特色社会主义制度推进国家治理体系和治理能力现代化若干重大问题的决定》,强调坚持马克思主义在意识形态领域指导地位的根本制度,并作出一系列重大部署。这是我们党第一次把马克思主义在意识形态领域的指导地位作为一项根本制度明确提出来,是关系党和国家事业长远发展、关系我国文化前进方向和发展道路的重大制度创新,集中体现了我们党在领导文化建设长期实践中积累的成功经验和形成的方针原则,充分反映了以习近平同志为核心的党中央对社会主义文化建设规律的认识进入了一个新的境界③。

习近平总书记强调:"制度优势是一个政党、一个国家的最大优势。"④ "相比过去,新时代改革开放具有许多新的内涵和特点,其中很重要的一点就是制度建设分量更重……相应地建章立制、构建体系的任务更重。"⑤ 针对这一重大问题,党的十八大以来,以习近平同志为核心的党中央高度重视制度治党、依规治党,把加强党内法规制度建设作为全面从严治党的长远之策、根本之策,作为事关党长期执政、国家长治久

---

① 习近平:《在"不忘初心、牢记使命"主题教育总结大会上的讲话》,《求是》2020年第13期。
② 《习近平关于总体国家安全观论述摘编》,中央文献出版社2013年版,第100页。
③ 参见黄坤明《坚持马克思主义在意识形态领域指导地位的根本制度》,《人民日报》2019年11月20日。
④ 习近平:《在"不忘初心、牢记使命"主题教育总结大会上的讲话》,《求是》2020年第13期。
⑤ 《中共中央关于坚持和完善中国特色社会主义制度 推进国家治理体系和治理能力现代化若干重大问题的决定》,人民出版社2019年版,第49页。

安的重大战略任务，摆在突出位置部署推进，取得历史性成就①。

如面对新的形势和任务，党的十八届六中全会分析了全面从严治党形势，审议通过了《关于新形势下党内政治生活的若干准则》和《中国共产党党内监督条例》②。《关于新形势下党内政治生活的若干准则》指出："健全党内重大思想理论问题分析研究和情况通报制度，强化互联网思想理论引导，把深层次思想理论问题讲清楚，帮助党员、干部站稳政治立场，分清是非界限，坚决抵制错误思想侵蚀。"③ 这是在制度建设的层面贯彻落实党加强对宣传思想工作全面领导的重要内容。建立意识形态工作责任制，是加强党对意识形态工作全面领导的重大举措，也是坚持马克思主义在意识形态领域指导地位这一根本制度的重要体现。党的十八大以来，党的意识形态工作责任制进一步得到深入贯彻落实，意识形态专项专题巡视效果不断显现。中共中央办公厅颁布的《党委（党组）意识形态工作责任制实施办法》指出，要强化党管宣传、党管意识形态，牢牢掌握意识形态工作的领导权主动权。此外，《中国共产党党委（党组）理论学习中心组学习规则》，对党委（党组）理论学习中心组学习的性质定位原则、内容形式要求、组织管理考核等方面均作出明确规定。这部专门的党内法规对于推动理论武装工作深入开展，提高领导干部的理论水平和工作能力，加强领导班子思想政治建设，具有十分重要的意义④。

主峰浮水面，一柱钉波心。习近平总书记在党的十九大报告中强调指出，1921 年中国共产党应运而生，"从此，中国人民谋求民族独立、人民解放和国家富强、人民幸福的斗争就有了主心骨，中国人民就从精神上由被动转为主动"⑤。"夫为国之道，恃贤与民。""英雄者，国之干；

---

① 参见中共中央办公厅法规局《开辟新时代依规治党新境界——党的十八大以来党内法规制度建设成就综述》，《人民日报》2021 年 6 月 17 日。

② 参见习近平《在党的十八届六中全会第二次全体会议上的讲话（节选）》，《求是》2017 年第 1 期。

③ 《中国共产党党内重要法规汇编》，党建读物出版社 2019 年版，第 43 页。

④ 《中办印发〈中国共产党党委（党组）理论学习中心组学习规则〉》，《人民日报》2017 年 3 月 31 日。

⑤ 《习近平谈治国理政》（第三卷），外文出版社 2020 年版，第 10—11 页。

庶民者，国之本。得其干，收其本，则政行而无怨。"① 习近平总书记强调，"江山就是人民、人民就是江山，打江山、守江山，守的是人民的心。中国共产党根基在人民、血脉在人民、力量在人民。"② "我将无我，不负人民。"③ 从根本上而言，全心全意为人民服务，着力践行以人民为中心的发展思想，这是中国共产党人最大的战略主动。这也是部分西方政客及各种敌对势力最为忌惮之处，也是其妄想把中国共产党同中国人民分割开来、对立起来的卑劣企图不能得逞的最大缘由。"是故兵有不战，有必战，夫不战者在我，必战者在敌。"④ 中国共产党人历来有不信邪、不怕鬼、不当软骨头的风骨、气节、胆魄⑤。中国共产党只要能够紧紧依靠人民，牢牢把握战略主动，中国特色社会主义这艘巨轮在中华民族伟大复兴的历史征程中就必将能够行稳致远。

---

① 《六韬·三略译注》，上海古籍出版社 2012 年版，第 117、118 页。
② 习近平：《在庆祝中国共产党成立 100 周年大会上的讲话》，人民出版社 2021 年版，第 11 页。
③ 《习近平谈治国理政》（第三卷），外文出版社 2020 年版，第 144 页。
④ 《唐太宗李卫公问对》，《武经七书（下）》，中华书局 2007 年版，第 611 页。
⑤ 《习近平在中央党校（国家行政学院）中青年干部培训班开班式上发表重要讲话强调 信念坚定对党忠诚实事求是担当作为 努力成为可堪大用能担重任的栋梁之才》，《人民日报》2021 年 9 月 2 日。

第三编

中国式现代化与中国社会发展经验

中国式现代化与教育强国建设

孙兆阳[*]

教育兴则国家兴，教育强则国家强。教育事业为我国经济增长、社会发展、人民富裕、国家富强、安定团结的中国特色社会主义现代化建设过程中起到重要作用。习近平总书记在党的二十大报告中指出："我们要坚持教育优先发展、科技自立自强、人才引领驱动，加快建设教育强国、科技强国、人才强国，坚持为党育人、为国育才，全面提高人才自主培养质量，着力造就拔尖创新人才，聚天下英才而用之。"[①] 党的十八大以来，以习近平同志为核心的党中央高瞻远瞩，以破除万难的勇气，锐意推进全面深化改革，大力促进教育公平、调整教育结构、提高教育质量，我国教育事业取得新的巨大成就。习近平总书记统揽国内国际两个大局，从党和国家事业发展全局的战略高度，科学回答了事关教育现代化和教育创新发展的一系列重大理论和实践问题，对教育工作做出一系列重大决策部署，先后提出并实施了科教兴国战略、人才强国战略和创新驱动发展战略，将教育放在优先发展的战略位置上，深化改革我国教育体制机制障碍，我国教育迈进世界中上行列，正在走出一条中国式现代化教育强国的道路。

---

[*] 孙兆阳，中国社会科学院大学副教授、国际教育学院副院长。
[①] 习近平：《高举中国特色社会主义伟大旗帜　为全面建设社会主义现代化国家而团结奋斗——在中国共产党第二十次全国代表大会上的报告》，《人民日报》2022年10月26日。

一　迈向教育强国，新时代教育事业发展新成就

党的十八大以来，习近平总书记统筹国际国内两个大局，从党和国家事业发展全局的战略高度，科学回答了"培养什么人、怎样培养人、为谁培养人"这一根本问题，提出了关于教育发展的系列重要论述。教育系统认真贯彻落实习近平新时代中国特色社会主义思想，坚持以习近平总书记关于教育发展的重要论述为指导，扎实推进思想政治教育改革创新，取得了一系列重大成就。

（一）全面坚持党的领导的管理体制

在长期的实践中，我国教育管理逐步建立了中央领导、地方负责、分级管理的体制，教育改革也基本上采取自上而下的路径，这是与我国政治体制和治理结构相适应的。在管理体制上，我国政府通过法律政策、人事组织、评估拨款等途径，对各级教育管理体制、发展规模、速度、区域布局、办学方式、学科设置等实施全面统筹，形成了政府主导下的行政管理模式[1]。同时，每一时期的教育改革都是政府根据核心任务提出改革目标和设想，确定改革内容和进程，各级政府负责落实这些目标和设想，其政策制定、政策实施、效果评价、保障机制等方面都是从中央到地方、政府到学校、学校到教师分级传递执行[2]。政府主导、运动式的政策对教育事业的快速扩展具有积极作用。

政府主导教育模式有利于在短期内迅速形成合力，实现教育数量的快速发展，但如果缺乏党的正确指导，缺少市场调节和社会力量参与，容易导致行政管理和主观决策过强，出现专家与社会监督缺位现象[3]。党

---

[1] 赵俊芳：《中国高等教育改革发展六十年的历程与经验》，《中国高教研究》2009年第10期。

[2] 石中英、张夏青：《30年教育改革的中国经验》，《北京师范大学学报》（社会科学版）2008年第5期。

[3] 储朝晖：《中国教育六十年发展的启示》，《河北师范大学学报》（教育科学版）2014年第2期。

中央不断推进我国教育领域综合改革,强调党对教育的全面领导,逐步取消对学校的直接行政管理,鼓励、引导社会力量投资办学,扩大社会资源投入,重视运用立法、拨款、规划、信息服务、政策指导和必要的行政手段进行宏观管理。建立起中央、省、市、县四级财政分担机制,按照经济发展水平、学校隶属关系等因素实行资金合理分担。

从教育投入上看,2012年以来连续十年我国财政性教育经费支出占GDP比例在4%以上,国家财政性教育经费十年累计支出33.5万亿元,年均增长率达9.4%,高于同期8.9%的GDP年均名义增幅和6.9%的一般公共预算收入年均增幅;从2011年到2021年,全国教育经费总投入从2.4万亿增加到5.8万亿,国家财政性教育经费从不到2万亿增加到4.6万亿,全国一般公共预算教育支出从1.6万亿增加到3.7万亿,全国非财政教育经费从不到6000亿增加到1.2万亿,均实现了翻番;中央对地方教育转移支付资金80%以上用于中西部地区,原"三区三州"等深度贫困地区的财政性教育经费年均增速达到12.2%,超过全国平均水平2.8个百分点,全国学生资助金额累计超过2万亿元,各级教育阶段的"建档立卡"等家庭经济特别困难的学生得到优先资助,真正解决了学生因家庭经济困难而失学的问题[①]。大量的教育投资改善了教师特别是基层教师的收入水平,提高了办学条件标准,促进了教育总体水平的提升。

(二) 高等教育从大众化到普及化

当前,我国经济社会发展面临着人口红利逐渐消失、经济增速放缓、社会发展转型矛盾多发等多重因素叠加影响,传统经济增长方式难以为继,高等教育是实现高质量发展最大的红利、最重要的牵引力。"高等教育发展水平是一个国家发展水平和发展潜力的重要标志。世界各国都把办好大学、培养人才作为实现国家发展、增加综合国力的战略举措。"[②]

---

① 《"教育这十年""1+1"系列发布会第十五场:介绍从数据看党的十八大以来我国教育改革发展成效》,教育部,http://www.moe.gov.cn/fbh/live/2022/54875/twwd/202209/t20220927_665276.html,2022年9月27日。

② 习近平:《在全国高校思想政治工作会议上的讲话》,2016年12月7日,载《习近平关于社会主义社会建设论述摘编》,中央文献出版社2017年版,第60页。

1999年开始的高等教育扩张为我国迅速成为高等教育大国，实现高等教育大众化贡献巨大。根据现代高等教育理论，高等教育毛入学率低于15%属于精英教育，大于15%并小于50%属于大众化教育，高于50%属于普及化教育①。2019年，我国高等教育毛入学率达到51.6%，已完成大众化阶段，并开始向普及化发展。

高等教育要有规模，更要有质量，"规模能力上去了，质量也要上去。要深入研究教育体制、教学体制、教师管理等问题，着力把教育质量搞上去。"② 为了增强高等教育综合实力和国际竞争力，实现从人力资源大国向人才强国的转变，国家采取一系列措施加快高等教育强国建设。2015年8月18日，中央深改组审议通过《统筹推进世界一流大学和一流学科建设总体方案》，对新时期高等教育建设作出新部署。2016年6月23日，教育部宣布《关于继续实施"985工程"建设项目的意见》等382份规范性文件失效，正式宣告停止"211""985"以及重点、优势学科建设工程。2017年1月，教育部等三部委印发《统筹推进世界一流大学和一流学科建设实施办法（暂行）》，9月公布首批世界一流大学建设高校42所，一流学科建设高校95所，双一流建设学科465个。习近平总书记在党的十九大报告中提出"加快一流大学和一流学科建设，实现高等教育内涵式发展"要求，我国高等教育事业走向新的征程。在进一步完善"双一流"评审标准基础上，2022年公布147所"双一流"建设高校和建设学科名单。

习近平总书记高度重视高等教育发展，十年来先后20余次到高校视察并发表重要讲话，20余次给高教领域的师生回信，为高等教育改革发展指明了前进方向，提供了根本遵循。高等教育在制度创新、人才培养、学科建设等方面都取得突出成绩。党中央、国务院出台一系列政策文件，落实党的十八大提出的"推动高等教育内涵式发展"和党的十九大提出的"实现高等教育内涵式发展"；建成世界最大规模的高等教育体系，在

---

① ［美］马丁·特罗：《从精英向大众高等教育转变中的问题》，王香丽译，《外国高等教育资料》1999年第1期。

② 习近平：《在中央财经领导小组第十三次会议上的讲话》，2016年5月16日，载《习近平关于社会主义社会建设论述摘编》，中央文献出版社2017年版，第55页。

学总人数达到4430万人，2012年至2021年，毛入学率从30%提高到57.8%，提高了27.8个百分点，我国接受高等教育的人口达到2.4亿，新增劳动力平均受教育年限达到13.8年，劳动力素质结构发生了重大变化；形成了慕课与在线教育发展的中国范式，截至2022年2月底，我国上线慕课数量超过5.25万门，注册用户达3.7亿，已经有超过3.3亿人次在校大学生获得慕课学分，慕课数量和应用规模均居世界第一，形成了一整套包括理念、技术、标准、方法、评价等在内的慕课发展的中国范式；持续深化高校创新创业教育改革，成功举办了7届中国国际"互联网+"大学生创新创业大赛，累计吸引五大洲120多个国家和地区的603万个团队、2533万名大学生参赛，大赛累计直接创造就业岗位75万个，间接提供就业岗位516万个；新工科、新医科、新农科、新文科建设从教育思想、发展理念、质量标准、技术方法、质量评价等人才培养范式方面进行全方位的改革；主动融入国家战略和行业发展，对接新发展格局调整优化学科专业布局，共有265种新专业纳入本科专业目录，新增本科专业点1.7万个，撤销或停招1万个，人才培养对新技术新产业新业态的适应度明显增强[1]。

（三）加速教育对外开放和国际化发展

教育国际合作与交流一直是我国教育体系的组成部分，从早期的留苏到改革开放后的留英留美，再到吸引发展中国家学生来学习，中国逐渐成为世界上最大的留学输出国和亚洲最大、世界第三的留学目的国。2013年10月，习近平总书记在欧美同学会成立100周年庆祝大会上，提出"支持留学、鼓励回国、来去自由、发挥作用"的新时期留学工作方针，推动新时期留学工作高速发展。习近平总书记统筹考虑国内国际两个大局，相继提出了构建人类命运共同体、全球发展倡议等重要号召，并指出，"推进教育现代化，要坚持对外开放不动摇，加强同世界各国的

---

[1]《"教育这十年""1+1"系列发布会第二场：介绍党的十八大以来我国高等教育改革发展成效》，教育部，http://www.moe.gov.cn/fbh/live/2022/54453/twwd/202205/t20220517_628181.html，2022年5月17日。

互容、互鉴、互通"①。2016年4月,中办、国办印发《关于做好新时期教育对外开放工作的若干意见》,这是新中国成立以来第一份全面指导我国教育对外开放事业的纲领性文件,提出"丰富中外人文交流,促进民心相通",推动我国教育对外开放加速发展。

党的十八大以来,习近平总书记在一系列国际国内重大场合宣示扩大教育对外开放,多次作出重要指示批示,饱含深情给海外学子、留学归国人员、在华外国留学生、外国中小学生回信,为教育对外开放指明了方向,提供了根本遵循。十年来,我国同181个建交国普遍开展了教育合作与交流,与159个国家和地区合作举办了孔子学院(孔子课堂),与58个国家和地区签署了学历学位互认协议;超过八成出国留学生选择回国发展;2020—2021学年,在册国际学生来自195个国家和地区,学历生占比达76%,比2012年提高了35个百分点;教育部共举办中外高级别人文交流机制会议37场,签署300多项合作协议,达成近3000项具体合作成果;引导高校通过国际合作与交流推进"双一流"建设,于2018年启动国际产学研用合作会议以来,累计吸引70多个国家超过1.4万名专家学者参会,开展部门间和专家"一对一"科研合作2300多项,中外导师联合培养研究生4000多人;深入实施共建"一带一路"教育行动,加强同共建国家教育领域互联互通,建设了23个鲁班工坊;成立"中国—东盟职业教育联合会",设立中国上海合作组织经贸学院,启动"未来非洲—中非职业教育合作计划",深化中国—中东欧教育交流合作;成功举办世界职业教育发展大会,积极筹办世界数字教育大会,搭建全球性高端教育合作平台,为全球教育治理贡献智慧和力量②。

二 建设教育强国,奋力推进中国式现代化

习近平总书记指出,"我国是人口大国,要从人口大国迈向人才强

---

① 《习近平谈治国理政》(第三卷),外文出版社2020年版,第351页。
② 《"教育这十年""1+1"系列发布会第十三场:介绍党的十八大以来教育国际合作交流情况》,教育部,http://www.moe.gov.cn/fbh/live/2022/54849/twwd/202209/t20220920_663141.html,2022年9月20日。

国,实现中华民族伟大复兴,教育的地位和作用不可忽视。"① 要想在21世纪竞争中取得优势,实现中华民族伟大复兴,我国必须重视教育发展,加快建设教育强国,在加强学校教育、正规教育的同时,也必须从建设终身学习型社会着手,全面、系统、可持续地提升人力资本水平,为全面建设社会主义现代化强国提供坚实基础和助力。

(一) 坚持教育优先发展

习近平总书记科学运用马克思主义立场、观点和方法,对教育的本质、价值和目的进行系统分析,聚焦教育优先发展提出了一系列新观点新论断,成为全面指导教育事业改革发展的政治宣言、思想武器和行动纲领。② 坚持教育优先发展的战略定位为我国教育工作指明了发展方向。实现这一过程的指导原则为,"坚持以人民为中心发展教育,加快建设高质量教育体系,发展素质教育,促进教育公平。"③

第一,明确教育是"国之大计、党之大计"。改革开放以来,我国对教育的战略地位表述经历了"首要位置""优先发展""科教兴国""国计民生"等提法,习近平总书记对教育的性质、内涵和外延进行充分思考,创造性地作出教育是"国之大计、党之大计"的高度概括④。这一论述第一次将教育发展与党和国家的战略需求联系起来,标志着我们党对教育发展规律的认识达到了新的历史高度。这一论述是针对教育事业发展的顶层设计,要求从党和国家事业发展全局的高度,把党的教育方针贯穿教育工作的全过程。坚持用党的理想信念凝聚人,坚持用中华民族伟大复兴历史使命激励人,坚持用习近平新时代中国特色社会主义思想教育人,引导广大青少年继承党的精神谱系、弘扬社会主义核心价值观。

---

① 习近平:《在全国高校思想政治工作会议上的讲话》,2016年12月7日,载《习近平关于社会主义社会建设论述摘编》,中央文献出版社2017年版,第60页。
② 马晓强等:《坚持优先发展教育事业——习近平总书记关于教育的重要论述学习研究之九》,《教育研究》2022年第9期。
③ 习近平:《高举中国特色社会主义伟大旗帜 为全面建设社会主义现代化国家而团结奋斗——在中国共产党第二十次全国代表大会上的报告》,《人民日报》2022年10月26日。
④ 习近平:《坚持中国特色社会主义教育发展道路 培养德智体美劳全面发展的社会主义建设者和接班人——在全国教育大会上的讲话》,《人民日报》2018年9月11日。

第二，教育要从投入优先到全局优先。在较长一段时间内，我国教育优先发展战略等同于教育投入的增加，对提高教育质量、促进教育公平的要求落实还不充分，教育发展战略的内涵还不够丰富。习近平总书记在全国教育大会上指出："坚持把优先发展教育事业作为推动党和国家各项事业发展的重要先手棋，不断使教育同党和国家事业发展要求相适应、同人民群众期待相契合、同我国综合国力和国际地位相匹配。"[①] 这就意味着，教育优先发展战略不是片面的静态的考虑其在党和国家各项事业中排序问题，而是要坚持系统思维和战略思维，把教育作为全局和整体中的决定因子，以获得全局和整体的胜利。

第三，坚持教育是筑基民生的根本立场。党的十二大第一次将教育列入国家发展战略，主要目的是重视教育发展，培养更多有知识有文化的劳动者，从而提高经济劳动生产率，促进经济增长。改革开放四十年见证了大量优质劳动力带来"人口红利"，促进经济增长的奇迹。随着经济社会发展，人们的需求也发生改变，教育也不是简单为了服务经济。习近平总书记在党的十九大报告中宣布，我国社会主要矛盾已经转化为人民日益增长的美好生活需要和不平衡不充分的发展之间的矛盾。这一转化要求教育不能仅重视数量规模的增长，而应当转向促进教育公平与质量提升，不断推动教育事业发展成果惠及全体人民。

第四，坚持教育的国际视野。习近平总书记关于教育优先发展的重要论述具备全球视野，以面向世界和共同繁荣的胸怀作为实践宗旨，充分体现了大国的自信与担当。习近平总书记指出："当今时代，世界各国人民的命运更加紧密地联系在一起，各国青年应该通过教育树立世界眼光、增强合作意识，共同开创人类社会美好未来。"[②] 习近平总书记先后提出构建人类命运共同体倡议、全球发展倡议，我国教育与世界联系更加紧密，积极参与联合国"教育第一"全球倡议行动，牵头开展"一带一路"国际教育交流与合作，为"一带一路"倡议实施提供优质服务、

---

① 习近平：《坚持中国特色社会主义教育发展道路 培养德智体美劳全面发展的社会主义建设者和接班人——在全国教育大会上的讲话》，《人民日报》2018年9月11日。
② 习近平：《致首届清华大学苏世民书院开学典礼的贺信》，《人民日报》2016年9月11日。

智力支撑和人才保障，为发展中国家人民提供更多优质教育机会，体现了大国担当和国际胸襟。

（二）加快建设高质量教育体系

基础教育是提高民族素质的奠基工程，是立德树人的事业，在国民教育体系中处于基础性、先导性地位。习近平总书记站在实现中华民族伟大复兴的政治立场，对新时代我国基础教育的战略定位、使命任务与发展方略作出了高屋建瓴的擘画。① 习近平总书记指出，"加快义务教育优质均衡发展和城乡一体化，优化区域教育资源配置，强化学前教育、特殊教育普惠发展，坚持高中阶段学校多样化发展，完善覆盖全学段学生资助体系。"②

第一，培养社会主义建设者和接班人。习近平总书记反复强调和解读"中国特色""中国精神"，不断突出社会主义建设者和接班人的"中国人"意识。我国正处于全面建设社会主义现代化国家、全面推进中华民族伟大复兴关键时期，突出社会主义建设者和接班人的"中国人"意识，有助于夯实少年儿童文化自信、价值自信的心理根基，筑牢中华民族共同体意识，有效确立文化身份认同。习近平总书记强调中小学生要了解中华优秀传统文化和中国历史，这些"是我们在世界文化激荡中站稳脚跟的坚实根基"③。要从背诵优秀古诗词、练习毛笔字、阅读史书中，深入了解中华文化和中国历史，特别是党史、国史、改革开放史、社会主义发展史，强化"中国人"意识，主动做社会主义建设者和接班人。

第二，适应新时代对全面发展的人的要求。努力构建德智体美劳全面培养的教育体系是对"怎么培养人"问题的根本解答。德智体美劳全面培养，既是中国共产党人对马克思"全面发展的人"的中国化理论诠

---

① 牛楠森、李红恩：《基础教育是全社会的事业——习近平总书记关于教育的重要论述学习研究之八》，《教育研究》2022 年第 8 期。
② 习近平：《高举中国特色社会主义伟大旗帜　为全面建设社会主义现代化国家而团结奋斗——在中国共产党第二十次全国代表大会上的报告》，《人民日报》2022 年 10 月 26 日。
③ 习近平：《在文艺工作座谈会上的讲话》，《人民日报》2015 年 10 月 15 日。

释，也是我国教育智慧的结晶。习近平总书记根据现代生产对全面发展的人的客观要求提出"在学生中弘扬劳动精神"，"要努力构建德智体美劳全面培养的教育体系"①。新时代的青少年肩负着实现中国式现代化和中华民族伟大复兴的重任，只有具备德智体美劳全面发展的能力才能够适应时代的要求和呼声，"孩子们才能成长为心灵丰盈、人格健全、精神饱满、能力全面的新时代栋梁，担当起民族复兴的历史重任。"②

第三，突出基础教育的公益属性。党的十八大以来，基础教育的公益属性取向愈加鲜明，习近平总书记指出，"坚持党对义务教育的全面领导，坚持社会主义办学方向"，"各级党委和政府要坚持国家举办义务教育，确保义务教育公益属性，办好办强公办义务教育"③。社会主义国家属性决定着国家是学校的主要投资者，国家承担主要的举办责任，这保证了学校系统的公益性，也决定了学校所担负的主体责任。学校不仅要促进每一名学生发展，还要发挥引导和规范发展的作用，预防狭隘的功利主义和精致的利己主义倾向，激励和赋能于学生担当民族复兴大任④。要继续强调基础教育的公益属性和学校主体责任，体现我国社会主义国家性质，应对我国家庭结构和生活方式变化，加速使教育成果更多公平惠及全体人民。

第四，明确基础教育是全社会的共同责任。家庭、学校、社会协同配合是我国基础教育政策一贯坚持的精神，是对人才培育培养规律的科学把握。习近平总书记提出构建育人全链条新理念，提出培养德智体美劳全面发展的社会主义建设者和接班人，其实现需要全社会共担重任、共同协作，家庭和社会要"主动配合学校教育，以良好的家庭氛围和社会风气巩固学校教育成果"⑤。"深化教育领域综合改革，加强教材建设和

---

① 习近平:《坚持中国特色社会主义教育发展道路 培养德智体美劳全面发展的社会主义建设者和接班人——在全国教育大会上的讲话》,《人民日报》2018年9月11日。

② 习近平:《"德智体美劳"：字字千金促"全面发展"》,新华社《学习快评》,http://www.xinhuanet.com/video/2021-09/15/c_1211371286.htm, 2021年9月15日。

③ 习近平:《推动更深层次改革实行更高水平开放 为构建新发展格局提供强大动力——在中央全面深化改革委员会第十五次会议上的讲话》,《人民日报》2020年9月2日。

④ 石中英:《公共教育学》,北京师范大学出版社2008年版,第12—21页。

⑤ 《习近平总书记教育重要论述讲义》,高等教育出版社2020年版,第51页。

管理，完善学校管理和教育评价体系，健全学校家庭社会育人机制。"①家校社协同育人的大教育格局需要社会各界、各群体、各组织的协同配合，德智体美劳全面教育的执行和落实都需要多主体、多层次、多方面的合作。

（三）加快建设中国特色、世界一流的大学

习近平总书记综合研判世界高等教育的发展趋势和我国社会主义高等教育发展的本质要求，准确分析高等教育改革发展中存在的难点、堵点、痛点，紧紧抓住高等教育办学规律和高层次人才培养规律，夯实新时代高等教育改革发展的理论基石②。在党的二十大报告中，习近平总书记指出，"加强基础学科、新兴学科、交叉学科建设，加快建设中国特色、世界一流的大学和优势学科"③，为实现高等教育高质量发展提供行动指南。

第一，坚持党对高等教育的全面领导。党是新时代我国高等教育事业发展的领导核心，是确保党的教育方针政策贯彻落实、实现高等教育现代化发展的根本政治保障。我国的社会主义制度性质决定，必须坚持和加强党对高等教育事业的全面领导。习近平总书记指出，"办好我国高等教育，必须坚持党的领导，牢牢掌握党对高校工作的领导权，使高校成为坚持党的领导的坚强阵地。"④ 坚持党对高等教育的全面领导，要完善党对教育工作的领导体制和工作机制，准确理解和贯彻党委领导下的校长负责制；推动高校党的建设和事业发展的深度融合，确保党的各项政治原则、政治标准、政治要求贯彻落实到办学治校和教书育人的各要素、各环节、全流程。

---

① 习近平：《高举中国特色社会主义伟大旗帜　为全面建设社会主义现代化国家而团结奋斗——在中国共产党第二十次全国代表大会上的报告》，《人民日报》2022年10月26日。
② 罗建平、桂庆平：《扎根中国大地 加快建设中国特色社会主义大学——习近平总书记关于教育的重要论述学习研究之六》，《教育研究》2022年第6期。
③ 习近平：《高举中国特色社会主义伟大旗帜　为全面建设社会主义现代化国家而团结奋斗——在中国共产党第二十次全国代表大会上的报告》，《人民日报》2022年10月26日。
④ 《习近平谈治国理政》（第二卷），外文出版社2017年版，第379页。

第二,坚持走中国特色的高等教育发展道路。扎根中国大地办大学、走中国特色发展道路,是习近平总书记对我国高等教育发展所提出的殷切期望。中国特色高等教育的核心特征就是,"传承红色基因,扎根中国大地办大学,走出一条建设中国特色、世界一流大学的新路。"[1] 坚持走中国特色高等教育发展道路,要辩证看待中国与世界的关系,坚持高水平的教育对外开放,坚持"引进来、走出去"的发展战略,加大高等教育领域开展高层次人文交流、项目合作、平台建设力度,积极参与全球教育治理,针对世界高等教育改革发展的共性问题,提供中国方案,发出中国声音,贡献中国智慧,为广大发展中国家实现高等教育现代化提供新思路。

第三,加快建设高等教育强国。习近平总书记坚持把高等教育发展和民族复兴、国家富强统筹考虑、全盘谋划,凸显高等教育在教育强国战略中的重要地位,赋予高等教育新的时代责任和历史使命。高等教育要服务于民族复兴和国家富强的伟大使命,要"为人民服务,为中国共产党治国理政服务,为巩固和发展中国特色社会主义制度服务,为改革开放和社会主义现代化建设服务"[2]。只有坚持建设社会主义使命,高等教育才能真正成为中华民族伟大复兴的动力。高等教育体系是一个有机整体,办大学要坚持系统性思维,要启动"双一流"建设,集中打造优质高校群体,又要支持不同地区、不同层次和类型高校差异化发展,共同促进高等教育整体的发展。要把人才培养作为高校的核心工作,缓解总体教育水平和资源配置不平衡,加快构建世界一流、中国特色的高等教育发展理论,提高服务国家战略和区域发展的能力水平。

第四,坚持高等教育内涵式发展。党的十八大提出,"推动高等教育内涵发展"。党的十九大明确要求,"实现高等教育内涵式发展"。从"推动"到"实现",体现出实现目标的坚定意志。内涵式发展的本质要求在于提供公平而有质量的教育,加大优质资源向中西部地区、革命老

---

[1] 习近平:《坚持党的领导传承红色基因扎根中国大地 走出一条建设中国特色世界一流大学新路——在中国人民大学师生代表座谈会上的讲话》,《人民日报》2022年4月26日。
[2] 《习近平谈治国理政》(第二卷),外文出版社2017年版,第377页。

区、少数民族地区、边疆地区倾斜的政策力度，努力缩小高等教育资源在校际、区域、群体中的差距，让人人都能享受更加公平的高等教育。提升本科教育质量是内涵式发展的必由之路。本科教育是整个高等教育的基础，要牢固确立人才培养在高校工作中的中心地位，坚持以本为本，推进"四个回归"。[1]

党的二十大报告将教育与科技、人才一并部署，强调实施科教兴国战略，体现了习近平总书记教育是党之大计、国之大计的根本战略思想，突出了教育是关乎人民生活幸福，更是关乎党和国家事业发展全局的事业，突出了教育在社会主义现代化建设中的战略支撑作用，以及在科教兴国中的基础性、战略性地位。我们要按照习近平总书记关于教育的系列重要论述，按照党的二十大关于教育的重要指示精神，坚持科教兴国战略，坚持教育优先发展。要优化教育资源配置，促进教育公平；要面向经济社会发展需求，努力培养经济社会急需的高质量人才；要优化调整教育结构，提高教育发展重心；要深化课程教学改革，转变育人方式；要推进教育数字化、信息化，全面赋能教育；要统筹学校家庭社会教育，加强家校社协同育人。我们要更好地发挥教育的基础性人才培养功能，坚持以人民为中心的教育理念，坚持培养德智体美劳全面发展的社会主义建设者和接班人，为全面建设社会主义现代化国家、全面推进中华民族伟大复兴贡献出更大的力量。

---

[1] 陈宝生：《坚持以本为本推进四个回归　建设中国特色、世界水平的一流本科教育》，《时事报告（党委中心组学习）》2018年第5期。

中国式现代化与人民
美好生活的构建

马　峰[*]

习近平总书记所作的党的二十大报告擘画了我国全面建设社会主义现代化国家时期发展的宏伟蓝图,以中国式现代化全面推进中华民族伟大复兴。习近平总书记强调:"党的二十大报告明确概括了中国式现代化是人口规模巨大的现代化、是全体人民共同富裕的现代化、是物质文明和精神文明相协调的现代化、是人与自然和谐共生的现代化、是走和平发展道路的现代化这5个方面的中国特色,深刻揭示了中国式现代化的科学内涵。这既是理论概括,也是实践要求,为全面建成社会主义现代化强国、实现中华民族伟大复兴指明了一条康庄大道。"[①] 党的二十大报告在提出到二〇三五年我国发展的总体目标时,指出:"人民生活更加幸福美好,居民人均可支配收入再上新台阶,中等收入群体比重明显提高,基本公共服务实现均等化,农村基本具备现代生活条件,社会保持长期稳定,人的全面发展、全体人民共同富裕取得更为明显的实质性进展。"[②] 人民对美好生活的向往就是我们的奋斗目标,在实现中华民族伟大复兴

---

[*] 马峰,中国社会科学院社会发展战略研究院副研究员。
[①] 《习近平在学习贯彻党的二十大精神研讨班开班式上发表重要讲话强调　正确理解和大力推进中国式现代化》,《人民日报》2023年2月8日。
[②] 习近平:《高举中国特色社会主义伟大旗帜　为全面建设社会主义现代化国家而团结奋斗——在中国共产党第二十次全国代表大会上的报告》,《人民日报》2022年10月26日。

的征程上,党的二十大报告指出:"我们坚持把实现人民对美好生活的向往作为现代化建设的出发点和落脚点。"①

一　增进民生福祉,提高人民生活品质

党的二十大报告指出:"增进民生福祉,提高人民生活品质。""必须坚持在发展中保障和改善民生,鼓励共同奋斗创造美好生活,不断实现人民对美好生活的向往。"②

一个国家走向现代化,既要遵循现代化一般规律,更要符合本国实际,具有本国特色。新中国成立特别是改革开放以来,我们用几十年时间走完西方发达国家几百年走过的工业化历程,创造了经济快速发展和社会长期稳定的奇迹,为中华民族伟大复兴开辟了广阔前景。党的十八大以来,中国特色社会主义进入新时代,明确坚持和发展中国特色社会主义,总任务是实现社会主义现代化和中华民族伟大复兴,在全面建成小康社会的基础上,分两步走在21世纪中叶建成富强民主文明和谐美丽的社会主义现代化强国。在新中国成立特别是改革开放以来长期探索和实践基础上,经过党的十八大以来在理论和实践上的创新突破的历史表明,只有中国式现代化发展道路,才能让人民生活全方位改善,才能让人民生活美好,才能让人民的幸福生活得到根本的保障。

党的十八大以来,我们贯彻新发展理念,坚持高质量发展,深化供给侧结构性改革,加快构建新发展格局,举全国之力打赢了脱贫攻坚战,历史性解决了绝对贫困问题,如期全面建成小康社会,开创了中华民族有史以来未曾有过的经济社会全面进步、全体人民共同受惠的好时代,为实现第二个百年奋斗目标、实现中华民族伟大复兴奠定了更为坚实的物质基础。人民生活全方位改善。在幼有所育、学有所教、劳有所得、病有所医、老有所养、住有所居、弱有所扶上持续用力,人民生活全方

---

① 习近平:《高举中国特色社会主义伟大旗帜　为全面建设社会主义现代化国家而团结奋斗——在中国共产党第二十次全国代表大会上的报告》,《人民日报》2022年10月26日。

② 习近平:《高举中国特色社会主义伟大旗帜　为全面建设社会主义现代化国家而团结奋斗——在中国共产党第二十次全国代表大会上的报告》,《人民日报》2022年10月26日。

位改善。人均预期寿命增长到78.2岁。居民人均可支配收入从16500元增加到35100元。城镇新增就业年均1300万人以上。建成世界上规模最大的教育体系、社会保障体系、医疗卫生体系，教育普及水平实现历史性跨越，基本养老保险覆盖14000万人，基本医疗保险参保率稳定在95%。及时调整生育政策。改造棚户区住房4200多万套，改造农村危房2400多万户，城乡居民住房条件明显改善。互联网上网人数达13000万人。人民群众获得感、幸福感、安全感更加充实、更有保障、更可持续，共同富裕取得新成效①。

党的十八大以来，人民生活水平和质量取得了历史性进步、全方位跃升，党和人民胜利实现第一个百年奋斗目标，在中华大地上全面建成了小康社会。随着居民收入和消费水平的提高，家庭耐用消费品持续升级换代，基本公共服务均等化的推进，公共设施覆盖率的提高，城乡居民生活环境全方位改善。着力改善民生，健全社会保障体系。当前，我国多层次社会保障体系加快完善，社会保障网织密兜牢，建成世界规模最大的社会保障体系。2021年末，全国基本养老保险、基本医疗保险覆盖人数分别达10.3亿人、13.6亿人；参加失业、工伤、生育保险人数分别比2012年增加7733万人、9277万人、8323万人。基本住房保障得到加强。2015—2021年，全国开工改造各类棚户区3100多万套。2021年，全国保障性租赁住房开工建设和筹集94万套②。社会保障体系是人民生活的安全网和社会运行的稳定器。健全覆盖全民、统筹城乡、公平统一、安全规范、可持续的多层次社会保障体系。统筹发展与安全，加强社会保障基金规范管理，守住社会基金安全底线。立足当前、着眼长远，确保各项社会保险基金收支平衡，制度长期稳定运行，促进社会保障事业高质量可持续发展，有效应对老龄化对社会制度的可持续发展带来的挑战。

---

① 习近平：《高举中国特色社会主义伟大旗帜　为全面建设社会主义现代化国家而团结奋斗——在中国共产党第二十次全国代表大会上的报告》，《人民日报》2022年10月26日。
② 《新理念引领新发展　新时代开创新局面——党的十八大以来经济社会发展成就系列报告之一》，国家统计局，http://www.stats.gov.cn/sj/sjjd/202302/t20230202_1896671.html，2022年9月13日。

健康中国战略的全面实施,城乡居民能够享有的医疗公共服务水平逐步提高。医疗服务供给能力显著提升。2021年末,全国医疗卫生机构床位、卫生技术人员分别达945万张、1124万人,分别比2012年末增长65.0%、68.4%。居民健康状况明显改善。人均预期寿命由2010年的74.8岁提高至2021年的78.2岁;婴儿死亡率由2012年的10.3‰下降至5.0‰[①]。人民健康是民族昌盛和国家强盛的重要标志。把保障人民健康放在优先发展的战略位置,完善人民健康促进政策。优化人口发展战略,建立生育支持政策体系。实施积极应对人口老龄化国家战略,发展养老事业和养老产业。深化医药卫生体制改革,促进优质医疗资源扩容和区域均衡布局。深化以公益性为导向的公立医院改革,深入开展健康中国行动和爱国卫生运动,倡导文明健康生活方式。

二 不断实现人民现代化美好生活

在经济发展的基础上,不断提高人民生活水平,是党和国家一切工作的根本目的。发展是党执政兴国的第一要务。我们的发展,始终是为了人民的发展。人民是一切物质财富和精神财富的创造者。我们党的初心和使命就是为人民谋幸福、为民族谋复兴。

中国式现代化是人口规模巨大的现代化。"我国十四亿多人口整体迈进现代化社会,规模超过现有发达国家人口的总和,艰巨性和复杂性前所未有,发展途径和推进方式也必然具有自己的特点。"[②] 在14亿人口规模的基础上实现现代化其难度可想而知,其规模将超过现在发达国家人口的总和,14亿人口进入现代化社会,其本身带来的示范效应是巨大的。如何实现14亿人口规模的现代化,其路径、其方法,每一个步骤,每一个方略,都是中国为人类对更好社会制度的探索提供的中国方案,现代

---

① 《新理念引领新发展 新时代开创新局面——党的十八大以来经济社会发展成就系列报告之一》,国家统计局,http://www.stats.gov.cn/sj/sjjd/202302/t20230202_1896671.html,2022年9月13日。

② 习近平:《高举中国特色社会主义伟大旗帜 为全面建设社会主义现代化国家而团结奋斗——在中国共产党第二十次全国代表大会上的报告》,《人民日报》2022年10月26日。

化的中国方案。因此,"只有坚持以人民为中心的发展思想,坚持发展为了人民、发展依靠人民、发展成果由人民共享,才会有正确的发展观、现代化观。"① 中国的现代化道路是社会主义的道路,中国的现代化是社会主义性质的现代化。作为中国式现代化核心领导进程的中国共产党,没有任何自己的特殊利益,人民至上的人民利益是中国共产党唯一坚持的利益所在。"正因为无私,才能本着彻底的唯物主义精神经常检视自身、常思己过,才能摆脱一切利益集团、权势集团、特权阶层的围猎腐蚀,并向党内被这些集团、团体、阶层所裹挟的人开刀。"② 社会主义制度和党的领导是机制性的结构保障。

此外,中国共产党在百年奋斗的"赶考路"上,不断答好时代出卷人的时代答卷。带领人民创造美好生活,是我们党始终不渝的奋斗目标。我们的人民热爱生活,期盼有更好的教育、更稳定的工作、更满意的收入、更可靠的社会保障、更高水平的医疗卫生服务、更舒适的居住条件、更优美的环境,期盼着孩子们能成长得更好、工作得更好、生活得更好。人民对美好生活的向往,就是我们的奋斗目标。在经济发展的基础上,不断提高人民生活水平,是党和国家一切工作的根本目的。当前,我国社会主要矛盾已经转化为人民日益增长的美好生活需要和不平衡不充分的发展之间的矛盾,发展中的矛盾和问题集中体现在发展质量上。这就要求我们必须把发展质量问题摆在更为突出的位置,着力提升发展质量和效益。而且,我国发展不平衡不充分问题仍比较突出,城乡区域发展和收入分配差距较大,生态环保任重道远,民生保障存在短板,社会治理还有弱项。此外,人民美好生活需要日益广泛,不仅对物质文化生活提出了更高要求,而且在民主、法治、公平、正义、安全、环境等方面的要求日益增长。当前和今后一个时期,我国发展环境面临深刻复杂变化。我国发展虽然仍处于重要战略机遇期,但机遇和挑战都有新的发展变化。对此,我们要统筹中华民族伟大复兴战略全局和世界百年未有之

---

① 习近平:《把握新发展阶段,贯彻新发展理念,构建新发展格局》,《求是》2021 年第 9 期。

② 习近平:《以史为鉴、开创未来 埋头苦干、勇毅前行》,《求是》2022 年第 1 期。

大变局，深刻认识我国社会主要矛盾变化带来的新特征新要求，深刻认识错综复杂的国际环境带来的新矛盾新挑战，立足社会主义初级阶段基本国情，始终把人民利益摆在至高无上的地位，让改革发展成果更多更公平惠及全体人民，让人民群众获得感、幸福感、安全感更加充实、更有保障、更可持续。

人民是历史的创造者，是真正的英雄。我们党从革命、建设到改革开放，始终与人民休戚与共、命运相连，始终与人民团结在一起、奋斗在一起，不断依靠人民创造历史伟业。人民是共和国的坚实根基，是党执政的最大底气。民心是最大的政治。当今世界正经历百年未有之大变局，今后一个时期，我们将面对更多逆风逆水的外部环境。新发展阶段，面对我国发展环境的深刻复杂变化，要紧紧依靠人民，把为人民造福的事情真正办好办实，把老百姓的安危冷暖时刻放在心上，以造福人民为最大政绩，想群众之所想，急群众之所急，让人民生活更加幸福美满；着力解决好人民群众最关心最直接最现实的利益问题，不断提高公共服务均衡化、优质化水平，促进教育、就业、收入、社保、医疗、养老、居住、环境等方面不断取得新进展，改善人民生活品质，提高社会建设水平。

三　扎实推进共同富裕

"中国式现代化是全体人民共同富裕的现代化。共同富裕是中国特色社会主义的本质要求，也是一个长期的历史过程。我们坚持把实现人民对美好生活的向往作为现代化建设的出发点和落脚点，着力维护和促进社会公平正义，着力促进全体人民共同富裕，坚决防止两极分化。"[1] 中国的现代化，是全体人民共同富裕的现代化。到 2035 年，共同富裕要取得更为明显的实质性进展。伟大的发展成就由人民创造，理应由人民共享。

---

[1] 习近平：《高举中国特色社会主义伟大旗帜　为全面建设社会主义现代化国家而团结奋斗——在中国共产党第二十次全国代表大会上的报告》，《人民日报》2022 年 10 月 26 日。

社会主义的本质，是解放生产力，发展生产力，消灭剥削，消除两极分化，最终达到共同富裕。事实证明，发展起来以后的问题不比不发展时少。当前，我国社会结构正在发生深刻变化，互联网深刻改变人类交往方式，社会观念、社会心理、社会行为发生深刻变化。发展过程中，要激发全体人民积极性、主动性、创造性，使人人都有通过辛勤劳动实现自身发展的机会，引导个人发展融入国家富强、民族复兴进程之中。

中国式现代化促进包容、普惠、均衡发展，让全体人民团结发展成为一国实现现代化的可能。共同富裕是社会主义的本质要求，是中国式现代化的重要特征。作为中华民族的主心骨，在涉及人民现实利益的根本问题上，中国共产党不断夯实全国各族人民团结奋斗的经济基础、政治基础，围绕明确奋斗目标形成最牢固的团结。在实现共同富裕的问题上，中国共产党有着清醒的认识，"一些发达国家工业化搞了几百年，但由于社会制度原因，到现在共同富裕问题仍未解决，贫富悬殊问题反而越来越严重。"[①]"我国必须坚决防止两极分化，促进共同富裕，实现社会和谐安定。"[②] 一百年来，中国人民始终紧紧围绕在中国共产党周围，以团结谋发展，以团结谋振兴。可以说，"一百年来，党和人民取得的一切成就都是团结奋斗的结果，团结奋斗是中国共产党和中国人民最显著的精神标识。"[③] 我们全面建成小康社会，全面小康一个都没少，历史性地破解了绝对贫困问题，向着全体人民共同富裕扎实迈进。全面建设社会主义现代化国家的新发展阶段，中国式现代化的优势将会更加有力地发挥出来，自觉主动解决地区差距、城乡差距、收入差距，推动社会全面进步和人的全面发展，促进社会公平正义，发展成果将会更多更公平惠及全体人民[④]。

在共同富裕中推动共享发展。共享是新发展理念的重要一环。促进共享发展，根本目的在于让人民共享人民创造的发展成果。从共享的覆

---

① 习近平：《扎实推动共同富裕》，《求是》2021年第20期。
② 习近平：《扎实推动共同富裕》，《求是》2021年第20期。
③ 习近平：《在二〇二二年春节团拜会上的讲话》，《人民日报》2022年1月31日。
④ 习近平：《把握新发展阶段，贯彻新发展理念，构建新发展格局》，《求是》2021年第9期。

盖面而言，共享是全民共享。共享发展是人人享有、各得其所，不是少数人共享、一部分人共享。从共享的内容而言，共享是全面共享。共享发展就是要共享国家经济、政治、文化、社会、生态各方面建设成果，全面保障人民在各方面的合法权益。从共享的实现途径而言，共享是共建共享。共建才能共享，共建的过程也是共享的过程。从共享发展的推进进程而言，共享是渐进共享。共享发展必将有一个从低级到高级、从不均衡到均衡的过程，即使达到很高的水平也会有差别。

人民走向共享发展、共同富裕的过程中，我们要在全面建成小康社会的基础上，进一步实现好、维护好、发展好最广大人民的根本利益，注重民生、保障民生、改善民生，激发全体人民积极性、主动性、创造性，引导个人发展融入国家富强、民族复兴进程之中。坚持以人民为中心发展思想。以人民为中心的发展思想，体现了我们党全心全意为人民服务的根本宗旨，体现了人民是推动发展的根本力量的唯物史观。要紧紧围绕"发展为了人民，发展依靠人民，发展成果由人民共享"的要求，把增进人民福祉、促进人的全面发展、社会全面进步、朝着共同富裕方向稳步前进，作为经济发展的出发点和落脚点。

党和人民事业是人类进步事业的重要组成部分。中国式现代化道路的创造和开拓，不是中国历史文化母版的简单延续，不是马克思主义经典作家设想模板的简单套用，不是其他国家社会主义实践的再版，也不是国外现代化发展的翻版。它"源自对自身历史和国情的深刻了解，源自对西方现代化道路的深刻总结，源自对其他发展中国家现代化历程的深刻分析，源自对人类追求现代化道路的深刻洞察"[①]。中国式现代化新道路是对西方现代化老路的摒弃和超越，中国的成功为人类带来希望，人类发展为创造美好未来提供可能，也为人类对更好社会制度的探索提供了中国方案。当前百年未有之大变局深刻演化，时代之变和世纪疫情相互叠加，世界进入新的动荡变革期。"人类发展指数30年来首次下降，世界新增1亿多贫困人口，近8亿人生活在饥饿之中，粮食安全、教育、

---

① 马峰：《各美其美 美人之美 美美与共 让人类文明花园百花齐放》，《人民日报》2017年11月5日。

就业、医药卫生等民生领域面临更多困难。一些发展中国家因疫返贫、因疫生乱，发达国家也有很多人陷入生活困境。"① 厄立特里亚总统伊萨亚斯对百年变局中世界与中国的发展，有着深刻的判断和认识，他认为，"中国不仅在自身国家建设和经济发展中取得辉煌成就，也致力于反对霸权主义、构建公正平等的全球秩序，为人类进步事业作出巨大贡献。中国的全球影响正在不断增强。这归功于中国共产党卓越的领导力和中国人民的坚韧不拔。"②

总之，习近平总书记曾经指出"为人民谋幸福、为民族谋复兴，这既是我们党领导现代化建设的出发点和落脚点"③。这科学地回答了中国式现代化建设的精神实质和价值归一，这是中国式现代化道路与西方以资本为中心忽视人民的现代化老路最本质的不同，而这也是在国际社会中国式现代化道路与西方现代化老路给人类社会带来不同发展结果的最本质区分的来源。

---

① 习近平：《坚定信心 勇毅前行 共创后疫情时代美好世界——在2022年世界经济论坛视频会议的演讲》，《人民日报》2022年1月8日。
② 《厄立特里亚总统伊萨亚斯会见王毅》，外交部，https：//www.mfa.gov.cn/web/wjbz_673089/xghd_673097/202201/t20220105_10479198.shtml，2022年1月5日。
③ 习近平：《以史为鉴、开创未来 埋头苦干、勇毅前行》，《求是》2022年第1期。

中国式现代化与城市老龄友好型社区建设

戈艳霞[*]

习近平总书记在党的二十大报告中明确指出,"中国式现代化是人口规模巨大的现代化。我国十四亿多人口整体迈进现代化社会,规模超过现有发达国家人口的总和,艰巨性和复杂性前所未有,发展途径和推进方式也必然具有自己的特点。"[①]当前,人口老龄化已经成为我国人口发展的主要形势,是我国全面建设社会主义现代化国家面临的基本人口国情。积极应对人口老龄化是全面建设社会主义现代化国家的必然要求。党的二十大报告进一步明确指出,要"实施积极应对人口老龄化国家战略,发展养老事业和养老产业,优化孤寡老人服务,推动实现全体老年人享有基本养老服务"[②]。这一重大部署,为我国养老服务发展明确了方向,提供了根本遵循。我们要坚持以人民为中心的发展思想,积极推动实现全体老年人享有基本养老服务。根据目前"9073"(抑或"9064")的养老安排模式规律,"十四五"时期我国约有2.9亿老人在家庭和社区中度过晚年,约占老年人口的97%。这意味着,加强老年友好型社区建

---

[*] 戈艳霞,中国社会科学院社会发展战略研究院副研究员。
[①] 习近平:《高举中国特色社会主义伟大旗帜 为全面建设社会主义现代化国家而团结奋斗——在中国共产党第二十次全国代表大会上的报告》,《人民日报》2022年10月26日。
[②] 习近平:《高举中国特色社会主义伟大旗帜 为全面建设社会主义现代化国家而团结奋斗——在中国共产党第二十次全国代表大会上的报告》,《人民日报》2022年10月26日。

设是积极推动全体老年人享有基本养老服务的有效实践，也是我国积极应对人口老龄化国家战略和健康中国战略的重要举措。

人口老龄化是社会发展的重要趋势，是人类文明进步的重要体现，也是我国今后较长一个时期的基本国情。按照国际通行标准，当一个国家或地区65岁及以上人口占比超过7%时，意味着进入老龄化社会，达到14%为深度老龄化，超过20%则进入超老龄化社会。第七次全国人口普查数据显示，2020年我国65岁及以上老年人口占总人口的比重已高达13.50%。显然，我国已濒临深度老龄化。从政策脉络看，我们党和政府高度重视养老服务体系建设。党的十九大报告提出，积极应对人口老龄化，构建居家为基础、社区为依托、机构为补充、医养相结合的养老服务体系，构建养老、孝老、敬老政策体系和社会环境。党的第十九届五中全会审议通过的《中共中央关于制定国民经济和社会发展第十四个五年规划和二〇三五年远景目标的建议》进一步明确要求完善社区居家养老服务网络，推进公共设施适老化改造，提升服务能力和水平。2020年12月，国家卫生健康委、全国老龄办联合发布《关于开展示范性全国老年友好型社区创建工作的通知》[1]，明确提出探索建立老年友好型社区创建工作模式和长效机制，切实增强老年人的获得感、幸福感、安全感。到2025年，全国建成5000个示范性城乡老年友好型社区；到2035年，全国城乡实现老年友好型社区全覆盖。党的二十大报告进一步强调，实施积极应对人口老龄化国家战略，发展养老事业和养老产业，优化孤寡老人服务，推动实现全体老年人享有基本养老服务。

从工作实践看，尽管近年来我国城市老龄友好型社区建设取得了长足进步，但在应对城市社区居家养老难题上仍存在一些短板和弱项，居住环境适老化程度低、日常生活和医疗健康等社会化服务供给不足、尊老敬老文化氛围淡薄等问题在城市社区仍普遍存在。第四次中国城乡老年人生活状况抽样调查数据显示，超过50%的城市老人认为住房缺乏呼叫和报警设施、无扶手、光线昏暗。其他不适老问题还包括，厕所或浴

---

[1] 相关文件和学者对此类社区的称谓有"老年友好型社区"和"老龄友好型社区"等，我们认为其内涵是一致的。本文使用"老龄友好型社区"概念。

室不好用、门槛绊脚或地面高低不平、地面易滑倒等风险因素[1]。面对老年人日益增长的多样化、多层次、多维度的养老需求，城市社区不适老的问题日益突出，加强城市老龄友好型社区建设成为日益迫切的要求，同时也是政府老龄社会治理的重要工作内容[2][3]。

目前，我国关于老龄友好型社区的研究主要从社会学、经济学、地理学、城市规划以及建筑学等视角出发。例如，于一凡等、郑玲和郑华阐释了老龄友好型社区的概念内涵；[4][5] 胡庭浩和沈山、李小云综述了老龄友好型社区的研究进展与建设实践；[6][7] 窦晓璐等、于一凡和王沁沁总结了国内外老龄友好型社区的建设经验以及对我国的启示；[8][9] 于一凡等、戈艳霞和孙兆阳对老年友好型社区的评价体系进行了研究；[10][11] 伍小兰、

---

[1] 伍小兰、曲嘉瑶：《中国老年宜居环境建设现状、问题与对策研究》，《老龄科学研究》2016年第8期。

[2] 罗兴奇：《居家养老服务的结构困境及优化路径——以上海市为例》，《城市问题》2017年第2期。

[3] 邬樱、李爱群：《北京老旧小区更新改造政策梳理与柔性化策略研究——双重老龄化视角》，《城市发展研究》2022年第5期。

[4] 于一凡、王亮非、管轶群、黄晓靖、崔哲、张立嵘、李昆、金清源、范浩阳、郭驶：《"老年友好城市——面向未来的设计"主题沙龙暨第三届老龄城市研究论坛》，《城市建筑》2018年第21期。

[5] 郑玲、郑华：《"老龄友好型城市"的理论内涵与构建框架——基于扎根理论的分析》，《社会科学战线》2021年第10期。

[6] 胡庭浩、沈山：《老年友好型城市研究进展与建设实践》，《现代城市研究》2014年第9期。

[7] 李小云：《人与环境匹配理论及其对乡村老年宜居环境研究的启示》，《城市发展研究》2020年第7期。

[8] 窦晓璐、约翰·派努斯、冯长春：《城市与积极老龄化：老年友好城市建设的国际经验》，《国际城市规划》2015年第3期。

[9] 于一凡、王沁沁：《健康导向下的老年宜居环境建设——国际研究进展及其启示》，《城市建筑》2018年第21期。

[10] 于一凡、朱霏飓、贾淑颖、郭禹婷、胡玉婷：《老年友好社区的评价体系研究》，《上海城市规划》2020年第6期。

[11] 戈艳霞、孙兆阳：《中国农村老龄友好型社区建设评估与优化研究——一项基于世界卫生组织老龄友好指标体系的考量》，《南京理工大学学报》（社会科学版）2021年第5期。

戈艳霞则从理念、政策和实践等方面对我国老龄友好型社区建设进行研究。①② 还有一些研究关注老年人的家庭结构、居住环境以及周边公共服务供给对老年人健康和幸福感的影响，为推进老龄友好型社区建设提供研究依据。③④ 总体上，我国有关老龄友好型社区的研究日益增多，然而相对于丰富的社区实践以及亟待解决的问题来讲，相关研究支撑仍显滞后。特别是，囿于评价指标体系和数据资料不足，我国老龄友好型社区建设的系统量化评价几乎空白，在很大程度上影响了全社会对老龄友好型社区建设状况的客观全面认识。未来加强老龄友好型社区建设的系统量化评价，将有助于全面把握建设状况并发现短板和弱项，帮助决策者判断实施干预的重点与时序，为高效推进老龄友好型社区建设提供研究依据。

在此背景下，我们依据人境匹配原则，借鉴世界卫生组织老龄友好指标体系，开发出一种信度效度良好的适用于我国城市的老龄友好型社区测量指标体系，并对城市社区的老龄友好程度进行量化评估，分析其建设水平、结构特征及区域差异，旨在分层次和维度量化考察社区与老年人需求之间的匹配状况。在此基础上，针对研究发现的短板和弱项提出改善建议，为高质高效推进城市老龄友好型社区建设、提升老年福祉提供实证依据。

一 人境匹配原则下的老龄友好型社区建设

人—环境研究范式认为，老年是一个受环境深刻影响和塑造的成人

---

① 伍小兰：《我国年龄友好环境的建设现状和发展趋势分析》，《老龄科学研究》2022年第3期。
② 戈艳霞：《老年友好型社区：积极应对人口老龄化国家战略的新落脚点》，《中国社会科学报》2022年1月12日。
③ 赵立志、廖筱萱、王佩玉：《居家养老模式下城市基层医疗设施配置研究——以北京城市副中心为例》，《城市发展研究》2022年第8期。
④ 蒋炜康、孙鹃娟：《居住方式、居住环境与城乡老年人心理健康——一个老年友好社区建设的分析框架》，《城市问题》2022年第1期。

发展阶段[1]。由于与年龄相关的视力减退、活动能力和认知能力丧失对个体与环境之间的关系有直接影响，从而老年人特别容易受到所处环境的影响。换言之，这种研究范式将情境因素视为老年人日常行为和晚年幸福的关键决定因素，非常重视随着人们年龄的增长而加强对人与环境关系的关注和改善。[2][3] 早在 20 世纪 20 年代，芝加哥学派就已证实，破败的市区等人造环境对人类的生存、健康和福利有害[4]。20 世纪三四十年代，德国社会心理学家勒温提出一种新观点，认为行为应该被视为人和环境的共同作用的结果[5]。美国人格研究者默里引入"压力"一词用来表示外部环境力量对个人客观和主观感知的影响[6]。劳顿和纳赫莫夫进一步提出压力—能力模型，认为随着年龄的增长，生理机能的衰老，人和环境之间将处于一种日渐紧张的关系状态[7]。在老年阶段，生活场所可能存在一种影响老年人的能力以及对行为和福祉产生负面影响的环境压力。这种环境压力，既可能来自物理空间及设施的不适老，也可能来自社会支持和养老服务等的不完善。1984 年卡帕等人从人的全面发展的需求出发，提出了一种积极的、有目标导向的应对模式，即人境匹配模型，认

---

[1] Wahl, H. - W., Scheidt, R., & Windley, P. G. eds., *Aging in Context: Socio-physical Environments (Annual Review of Gerontology and Geriatrics, 2003)*, New York: Springer, 2004.

[2] Scheidt, R. J., & Windley, P. G. eds., *Environment and Aging Theory: A Focus on Housing*, Westport, CT: Greenwood Press, 1998.

[3] Wahl, H. - W., "Environmental Influences on Aging and Behavior", in J. E. Birren & K. W. Schaie eds., *Handbook of the Psychology of Aging (5th ed)*, San Diego: Academic Press, 2001, pp. 215 - 237.

[4] Park, R. E., Burgess, E. W., & McKenzie, R. D., *The City*, Chicago: Chicago University Press, 1925.

[5] Lewin, K., *Field Theory in Social Science*, New York: Harper, 1951.

[6] Murray, H. A., *Explorations in Personality: A Clinical and Experimental Study of Fifty Men of College Age*, Oxford: Oxford University Press, 1938.

[7] Lawton, M. P., & Nahemow, L., "Ecology and the Aging Process", in C. Eisdorfer & M. P. Lawton eds., *The Psychology of Adult Development and Aging*, Washington, DC: American Psychological Association, 1973, pp. 619 - 674.

为应该通过利用和改善环境中的资源和支持来满足和平衡个体需求[1]。进一步地,菲利普斯等人将孝道文化价值观纳入模型,提出了具有文化因素的人—境匹配模型[2]。该模型认为,人全面发展所需的环境因素不仅包括物理空间、社会支持,也包括文化价值观念等。这些基于人—环境研究范式的模型共同解释了老年人与其居住生活环境相互作用和适应的复杂方式,证实了营造老龄友好环境的必要性,倡导从老年人的需求出发,调整和改善环境的物质、社会、文化特征,以寻求环境支持与老年人需求之间的最佳平衡状态。

作为老年人生活的主要空间载体,社区环境与老年人能力和需求之间的匹配度直接影响老年人的生活质量。有关社区与老年人的研究早期主要关注建筑环境对老年人的影响,缺乏对社区层面人与环境互动和匹配的关注,特别是当老年人面临越来越多的行动限制和有限的住房选择时,与之相匹配的社区居住环境和社区支持愈发显得重要[3]。近年来,越来越多的学者将人—境匹配理论应用于老龄友好型社区的建设实践中。如沙尔拉赫基于人—境匹配关系提出的建设性老龄化过程模型,认为老龄友好型社区的创建必须提高社区居民终生应对环境变化的能力[4]。尤其当老年人的个体能力出现功能局限时,必须从社区环境因素进行补偿,弥补老年人的功能障碍。这其中不仅包括物理环境,还包括经济状况、家庭和社会环境、住房和社区质量等社会因素,以及文化等影响老龄化

---

[1] Carp, F. M., & Carp, A., "A Complementary/Congruence Model of Well-being or Mental Health for the Community Elderly", in I. Altman, M. P. Lawton, & J. F. Wohlwill eds., *Human Behavior and Environment*: *Vol. 7. Elderly People and the Environment*, New York: Plenum Press, 1984, pp. 279 – 336.

[2] Phillips, D. R., K. H. C. Cheng, A. G. O. Yeh, O. – L. Siu, "Person—Environment (P—E) Fit Models and Psychological Well-Being Among Older Persons in Hong Kong", *Environment and Behavior*, 2010 42 (2), pp. 221 – 242.

[3] Kahana, E., L. Lovegreen, B. Kahana, M. Kahana, "Person, Environment, and Person-Environment Fit as Influences on Residential Satisfaction of Elders", *Environment and Behavior*, 2003, 35 (3), pp. 434 – 453.

[4] Scharlach, A. E., "Aging in Context: Individual and Environmental Pathways to Aging-Friendly Communities: The 2015 Matthew A. Pollack Award Lecture", *The Gerontologist*, 2017, 57 (4), pp. 606 – 618.

的因素。

基于人—境匹配原则,英国、加拿大、美国等主要老龄化国家以及世界卫生组织都提出过老龄友好指标体系。总体来讲,这些老龄友好指标体系涵盖了户外空间环境、交通出行、住房环境、公共服务、社会交往、信息交流、社会融入、尊重包容、生存与发展等多个维度和层次的指标,具备友好宜居社区必需的安全性、健康性、便捷性和舒适性等核心特质。有所不同的是,不同国家的老龄友好指标体系也表现出一定的地域文化差异和指标选取差异。

表1　世界卫生组织及主要老龄化国家的老龄友好指标体系

名称	发布机构	主要维度
老龄友好城市	世界卫生组织	户外空间和建筑、室内住房、交通运输、信息交流、社会参与、技能提升与再就业促进、生活服务与医疗服务、尊重与包容、社会融入
终身住宅、终生社区	英国住房建设部和地方政府	建筑环境、住房、社会联结和归属感、社会融入、创新和跨界别规划
宜居社区	美国退休人员协会	土地利用、交通和活动、住房、合作与交流、公共教育和参与社区规划、领导能力
宜居社区	美国老龄机构协会	空间规划和分区、交通、住房、公共安全、文化与终身学习
长者宜居社区	加拿大卡尔加里大学	活动无障碍、获取信息和服务便利、保持独立和参与活动、被重视和尊重、财务安全、个人安全、社区发展工作
老龄友好型社区	美国老龄倡议项目组	最大限度的独立、促进社会和公民参与、强调基本需求
长者友善社区	中国香港社会服务联会	室外空间和建筑、交通、住所、社会参与、尊重和社会包容、社区参与和就业、信息交流、社区支持与医疗健康
全国示范性老年友好型社区评分细则	中国国家卫生健康委(全国老龄办)	居住环境、出行设施、社区服务、社会参与、孝亲敬老氛围、科技助老、管理保障、特色亮点

资料来源:作者整理。

鉴于以往老龄友好指标体系主要是在欧美发达经济体中发展并得到验证，不宜完全照搬应用于我国老龄友好型社区的相关研究。相较而言，世界卫生组织对发达国家和发展中国家之间的发展差异考虑比较充分，其提出的老龄友好指标体系具有更广泛的适用性。基于前期调研经验[1]，综合考虑我国各地区在人口、经济、社会和文化方面的异质性，我们认为世界卫生组织提出的指标体系在我国的适用范围可能更广泛一些。该指标宗旨与我国倡导的"积极老龄化"和"健康老龄化"总目标相一致，包含了保证和维持老年人群体具有良好的生存质量的物理、社会、文化等方面的核心要素，并且指标的获取和测量都具有较好的可操作性，从而在一定程度上保证了该指标体系在我国具有较好的适用性。

为提高该指标体系与我国国情的适应性，我们对指标体系的权重进行了适当的优化调整。具体方法是采用专家打分法，邀请国家相关职能部门、科研机构以及基层社区老龄工作者和老年人代表对指标体系的权重进行重新赋权[2]。各指标权重取值范围均为0—100分。指标权重系数越低说明指标的重要性越小；系数越高说明指标的重要性越大。最终我们共收到10份完整有效的打分反馈表，再通过加权平均得到一个综合指标权重。指标的综合权重测算结果显示，一级指标物理、社会、文化的权重系数分别为42.30分、33.40分和24.30分。二级指标户外空间、住房、交通出行、技能提升与再就业促进、信息交流、日常生活与医疗健康服务、尊重和包容、社会融入的权重系数分别为13.00分、17.80分、11.50分、8.82分、10.22分、14.36分、11.45分和12.85分。权重赋值结果说明，专家们认为该老龄友好指标体系基本适用于我国，但同时也认为各指标的重要性应有所差异，即在实施干预中存在重点和时序差异。

---

[1] 为做好研究，我们在广州、南京、成都、苏州、南通、佛山等地开展了相关调研工作。

[2] 本研究指标体系的设计得到国家卫生健康委员会、民政部、住房和城乡建设部、中国社会科学院、清华大学等有关专家以及基层社区老龄工作者和老年人代表的宝贵建议，特此感谢。

表2　　　　　　我国城市老龄友好型社区指标体系及权重

一级指标	权重	二级指标	权重	三级指标	权重
物理环境	42.30	户外空间	13.00	道路平整无障碍	4.48
				照明系统完善	3.62
				老年设施齐全	4.90
		住房	17.80	房间出入无障碍	5.86
				室内地面平整无障碍	5.11
				厨房/厕所/浴室对老年人安全友好	6.83
		交通出行	11.50	交通费用的可负担性	2.91
				交通工具适老化	4.29
				交通设施便捷可及	4.30
社会环境	33.40	技能提升与再就业促进	8.82	有就业和参与公益志愿服务的机会	4.45
				有提升技能的机会	4.37
		信息交流	10.22	有获取信息的渠道	5.52
				获取信息的渠道畅通	4.70
		日常生活与医疗健康服务	14.36	可及的初级医疗服务	6.99
				可及的日常生活服务	7.37
文化环境	24.30	尊重和包容	11.45	对老年人的尊重程度	5.58
				对老年人的包容程度	5.87
		社会融入	12.85	有老年人社交活动场所	5.18
				有老年人可参与的社交活动	4.36
				活动费用的可负担性	3.31

资料来源：根据专家打分反馈表整理。

进一步地，我们采用Cronbach α系数方法和Speason相关分析方法对指标体系的信度和效度进行检验，结果也表明该指标具备良好的信度和效度，可作为研究我国城市老龄友好型社区状况的量化工具。接下来，将该指标体系与有关调查数据相结合，即可量化分析我国城市老龄友好型社区的建设状况。测量得分范围为0—100分。测量得分越高说明老龄友好型社区建设距离最优状态越近，与老年人的实际需求越契合；测量得分越低表示老龄友好型社区建设与最优状态越远,与老年人实际需求之间的差距越大。

二 城市老龄友好型社区建设量化分析

(一)基础数据说明

本文主要使用全国人大社会建设委员会和中国社会科学院联合开展的中国人口老龄化与养老工作调查2019年度数据。该调查数据以我国29省、自治区、直辖市(未包括新疆维吾尔自治区和西藏自治区以及港澳台)为抽样框,采用分层等概率抽样方法,抽取8个省份800个社区的8800多个老年人家庭进行调查,收集了老年人日常生活的社区环境、家庭居住环境以及公共服务和文化观念等方面的主客观指标数据。[1][2] 我们还进一步从年龄、性别、省市等维度对数据进行二次加权调整,以降低样本结构性偏差,达到我国城市老龄友好型社区考察的数据要求。除去缺失值、奇异值后,得到一个容量为2772的城市样本数据集。

(一)指标体系的信度和效度检验

我们使用 Cronbach α 系数对指标体系的信度进行检验。一般认为 Cronbach α 系数值最好在0.8以上,0.7—0.8可以接受;分量表的信度系数最好在0.7以上,0.6—0.7还可以接受[3]。结果显示,该指标的总体 Cronbach α 系数为0.93,各分项的 Cronbach α 系数均在0.93以上,说明该指标体系对我国城市地区的整体考察和分项考察结果都具有很好的信度。

---

[1] 张翼:《中国老年人口同居问题研究》,《中国人口科学》2020年第4期。
[2] 孙兆阳、戈艳霞、张博:《居家养老服务供给对老年人养老满意度影响研究——基于8省市调查数据的分析》,《中共中央党校(国家行政学院)学报》2021年第1期。
[3] DeVellis, R. F., *Scale Development Theory and Applications*, London: SAGE, 1991.

表3　城市老龄友好型社区指标体系的Cronbach α系数检验结果

总指标	Cronbach α	一级指标	Cronbach α	二级指标	Cronbach α
老龄友好型社区	0.931	物理环境	0.932	户外空间	0.934
				住房	0.934
				交通出行	0.936
		社会环境	0.933	技能提升与再就业促进	0.939
				信息交流	0.934
				日常生活与医疗健康服务	0.935
		文化环境	0.933	尊重和包容	0.935
				社会融入	0.934

由于本文指标及权重的确定是建立在世界卫生组织和相关专家的实践经验和理论基础之上，从而保证了指标体系具有良好的内容效度。结构效度的检验则需将所有指标和各上级指标做Speason相关分析。结果显示，各级指标分值与其上级指标分值的相关性均较大（0.61—0.94），而与其他指标分值的相关系数较小，说明指标体系具有良好的结构效度[①]。

表4　　　　城市老龄友好型社区指标体系相关矩阵结果

	Ⅰ-0	Ⅰ-1	Ⅰ-2	Ⅰ-3	Ⅱ-1	Ⅱ-2	Ⅱ-3	Ⅱ-4	Ⅱ-5	Ⅱ-6	Ⅱ-7	Ⅱ-8
Ⅰ-0	1.00											
Ⅰ-1	0.88	1.00										
Ⅰ-2	0.85	0.58	1.00									
Ⅰ-3	0.86	0.63	0.63	1.00								
Ⅱ-1	0.77	0.75	0.58	0.78	1.00							
Ⅱ-2	0.70	0.89	0.41	0.43	0.33	1.00						
Ⅱ-3	0.54	0.71	0.37	0.23	0.22	0.53	1.00					
Ⅱ-4	0.35	0.18	0.68	0.18	0.21	0.14	0.04	1.00				
Ⅱ-5	0.73	0.61	0.66	0.63	0.50	0.50	0.38	0.11	1.00			

---

① 一般认为，如果各级指标分值与其上级指标分值的相关性较大，而与其他指标分值的相关系数较小，则说明指标体系具有良好的结构效度。

续表

	Ⅰ-0	Ⅰ-1	Ⅰ-2	Ⅰ-3	Ⅱ-1	Ⅱ-2	Ⅱ-3	Ⅱ-4	Ⅱ-5	Ⅱ-6	Ⅱ-7	Ⅱ-8
Ⅱ-6	0.65	0.42	0.80	0.48	0.47	0.22	0.33	0.20	0.30	1.00		
Ⅱ-7	0.65	0.48	0.45	0.79	0.55	0.35	0.19	0.04	0.36	0.47	1.00	
Ⅱ-8	0.78	0.57	0.59	0.89	0.74	0.38	0.20	0.23	0.66	0.35	0.41	1.00
Ⅲ-1	0.32	0.27	0.23	0.33	0.69	0.09	0.11	0.05	0.15	0.32	0.47	0.13
Ⅲ-2	0.56	0.48	0.51	0.46	0.68	0.27	0.17	0.35	0.28	0.40	0.40	0.38
Ⅲ-3	0.70	0.58	0.50	0.76	0.91	0.29	0.19	0.14	0.51	0.37	0.44	0.78
Ⅲ-4	0.67	0.82	0.40	0.44	0.32	0.94	0.44	0.17	0.46	0.22	0.33	0.40
Ⅲ-5	0.63	0.75	0.38	0.44	0.33	0.88	0.31	0.21	0.38	0.22	0.34	0.39
Ⅲ-6	0.50	0.70	0.26	0.25	0.19	0.75	0.59	0.01	0.42	0.14	0.24	0.19
Ⅲ-7	0.31	0.32	0.27	0.13	0.14	0.16	0.83	0.08	0.17	0.34	0.13	0.19
Ⅲ-8	0.32	0.37	0.32	0.12	0.16	0.14	0.73	0.09	0.14	0.37	0.09	0.11
Ⅲ-9	0.46	0.67	0.22	0.22	0.17	0.63	0.73	0.03	0.41	0.11	0.20	0.18
Ⅲ-10	0.01	0.14	-0.25	0.11	0.10	0.13	-0.07	0.78	0.10	0.06	0.17	0.03
Ⅲ-11	0.58	0.47	0.61	0.43	0.46	0.40	0.16	0.65	0.32	0.40	0.28	0.42
Ⅲ-12	0.63	0.46	0.55	0.66	0.55	0.31	0.21	0.08	0.83	0.26	0.33	0.72
Ⅲ-13	0.54	0.52	0.51	0.33	0.24	0.50	0.42	0.11	0.77	0.21	0.25	0.31
Ⅲ-14	0.29	0.23	0.40	0.12	0.20	0.06	0.38	0.01	0.11	0.61	0.22	0.01
Ⅲ-15	0.62	0.38	0.75	0.52	0.46	0.24	0.17	0.25	0.30	0.87	0.45	0.43
Ⅲ-16	0.40	0.33	0.21	0.50	0.31	0.27	0.15	0.09	0.23	0.24	0.72	0.21
Ⅲ-17	0.63	0.45	0.48	0.75	0.55	0.31	0.17	0.10	0.35	0.49	0.91	0.33
Ⅲ-18	0.70	0.58	0.50	0.76	0.91	0.29	0.19	0.14	0.51	0.37	0.44	0.78
Ⅲ-19	0.37	0.19	0.35	0.44	0.23	0.13	-0.09	0.02	0.63	0.12	0.16	0.63
Ⅲ-20	0.46	0.31	0.34	0.56	0.24	0.32	0.10	0.27	0.28	0.18	0.19	0.69

（三）城市老龄友好型社区建设量化考察结果

1. 全国城市老龄友好型社区建设概况

总体来讲，我国城市老龄友好型社区测量得分的均值为64.02分，距离最优状态（与老年人的实际需求达成平衡状态）还存在一定的差距。标准差为11.57，表明不同社区的老龄友好程度也存在一定的差距。

表5　　　　　我国城市老龄友好型社区量化考察结果

总指标	均值（标准差）	一级指标	均值（标准差）	二级指标	均值（标准差）	样本量
老龄友好型社区	64.02 (11.57)	物理环境	30.96 (4.98)	户外空间	6.03 (2.04)	2772
				住房	15.46 (3.00)	2772
				交通出行	9.46 (1.67)	2772
		社会环境	17.98 (4.45)	技能提升与再就业促进	4.20 (1.92)	2772
				信息交流	4.91 (1.92)	2772
				日常生活与医疗健康服务	8.86 (2.63)	2772
		文化环境	15.09 (4.08)	尊重和包容	7.49 (2.00)	2772
				社会融入	7.59 (2.83)	2772

在一级指标层面，各指标的测量得分存在明显差异。其中，物理环境的测量得分最高，为30.96分（73.19%）[1]；其次是文化环境，测量得分为15.09分（62.10%）；最后是社会环境，测量得分为17.98分（53.83%）。在物理环境的分项指标中，测量得分最高的是住房，为15.46分（86.85%）；其次是交通出行，为9.46分（82.26%）；最后是户外空间，为6.03分（46.38%）。在社会环境的分项指标中，测量得分最高的是日常生活和医疗健康服务，为8.86分（61.70%）；其次是信息交流，为4.91分（48.04%）；最后是技能提升与再就业促进，为4.20分（47.62%）。文化环境方面，测量得分较高的是对老年人尊重和包容，为7.49分（65.41%）；其次是社会融入，为7.59分（59.07%）。

总体而言，我国城市老龄友好型社区建设质量整体不高，距离最优状态仍有一定差距。同时，不同社区之间存在明显的建设差距，反映出我国城市老龄友好型社区建设存在非均衡性。分指标看，各指标的测量得分也有明显的差异，说明老龄友好型社区建设存在结构性短板问题。其中，在一级指标层面，短板最突出的是社会环境，其次是文化环境和物理环境。在物理环境的分项指标中，短板最突出的是户外空间，其次是交通出行和住房。在社会环境的分项指标中，短板最突出的是技能提

---

[1] 括号内的百分数为标准化后的测量得分。

升与再就业促进，其次是信息交流，以及日常生活和医疗健康服务。文化环境方面，短板相对突出的是社会融入，然后是尊重和包容。

2. 城市老龄友好型社区建设的异质性分析

（1）老龄友好型社区建设的区域不均衡格局

本文按照国家统计局的标准将样本划分为东部、中部、西部和东北地区，考察不同区域的城市老龄友好型社区建设状况。样本中的东部地区包括上海市、河北省、山东省和广东省4省区，共计有1745个观测样本；中部地区包括河南省的234个观测样本；西部地区包括四川省和陕西省的513个观测样本；东北地区包括辽宁省的280个观测样本。测算结果显示，各区域城市老龄友好型社区测量得分存在明显的差异。其中，得分最高的是东部地区（66.66分），其次是西部地区（60.76分），然后是中部地区（58.78分），最后是东北地区（57.92分）。分项指标测量结果与总指标测量结果基本一致而略有差异。其中，物理环境测量得分最高的是东部地区（31.88分），其次是中部地区（30.15分）、东北地区（29.57分）和西部地区（28.92分）。社会环境测量得分最高的是东部地区（18.89分），其次是西部地区（16.87分）、中部地区（16.43分）和东北地区（15.57分）。文化环境测量得分最高的是东部地区（15.88分），其次是西部地区（14.96分）、东北地区（12.78分）和中部地区（12.20分）。

表6　　　　　　不同区域城市老龄友好型社区建设状况

地区	总指标	均值（标准差）	一级指标	均值（标准差）	观测样本量
东部	老龄友好型社区	66.66（11.35）	物理环境	31.88（4.70）	1745
			社会环境	18.89（4.57）	1745
			文化环境	15.88（3.89）	1745
中部	老龄友好型社区	58.78（8.80）	物理环境	30.15（4.21）	234
			社会环境	16.43（3.52）	234
			文化环境	12.20（3.23）	234

续表

地区	总指标	均值（标准差）	一级指标	均值（标准差）	观测样本量
西部	老龄友好型社区	60.76（11.45）	物理环境	28.92（5.70）	513
			社会环境	16.87（3.47）	513
			文化环境	14.96（4.25）	513
东北	老龄友好型社区	57.92（9.72）	物理环境	29.57（4.34）	280
			社会环境	15.57（4.27）	280
			文化环境	12.78（3.62）	280

总体看，城市老龄友好型社区建设存在明显的区域差异。整体指标测量结果和分项指标的测量结果都基本表现出"东部较高，西部居中，中部和东北塌陷"的空间格局。这一研究发现与以往研究发现的基本公共服务"中部和东北塌陷"现象具有一致性[1]。[2]

（2）老龄友好型社区建设的城市规模效益分析

进一步地，根据住房和城乡建设部公布的城市规模标准，将样本所在城市划分为超大城市、特大城市、Ⅰ型大城市、Ⅱ型大城市和其他中小城市五类，对不同人口规模的城市老龄友好型社区建设状况进行考察[3]。需要说明的是，该标准统计的是城区常住人口，不涉及县域和农村人口。该指标不仅是衡量城市层级的重要指标，也是判断一个城市修建地铁、医院等基本公共设施的重要门槛之一，还是确定能否"零门槛落户"的主要参考因素。从而，该指标与基本设施和公共服务之间具有较强的相关性，常作为分析城市规模与公共服务供给的划分标准。根据该

---

[1] 安虎森、殷广卫：《中部塌陷：现象及其内在机制推测》，《中南财经政法大学学报》2009年第1期。

[2] 潘文轩：《公共服务"中部塌陷"现象研究：表现、成因与对策》，《湖北社会科学》2012年第4期。周灵灵：《未富先老：中国式养老的路径选择》，载邹东涛主编《改革发展再扬帆》，国家行政学院出版社2013年版。

[3] 根据住房和城乡建设部发布的中国城市规模划分标准，城区常住人口超过1000万的是超大城市；500万—1000万的属于特大城市；300万—500万的属于Ⅰ型大城市；100万—300万的属于Ⅱ型大城市；低于100万的则属于中小城市。根据住房和城乡建设部发布的《2019年城市建设统计年鉴》，目前我国共有6个超大城市，11个特大城市，13个Ⅰ型大城市，超过60个Ⅱ型大城市。

标准对研究样本进行划分，超大城市有两个，分别是上海和广州，共计971个观测样本；特大城市样本有5个，分别是成都、郑州、沈阳、西安和济南，共计308个观测样本；Ⅰ型大城市样本有两个，分别是大连和石家庄，共计136个观测样本；Ⅱ型大城市有18个，主要是省内较发达的市区，共计542个观测样本；其他中小城市有30个，共计815个观测样本。对不同人口规模城市层级的老龄友好型社区建设状况进行测算，结果显示城市人口规模与老龄友好型社区建设状况基本存在正向关系，即人口规模越大，老龄友好型社区建设水平越高；人口规模越小，老龄友好型社区建设水平越低。按照城市人口规模的大小排列，老龄友好型社区测量得分依次为72.23、64.01、68.46、58.25和57.33；分一级指标看，各层级城市老龄友好型社区物理环境的测量得分为33.82、31.05、32.55、28.92和28.60；社会环境的测量得分为20.62、17.23、20.77、16.06和15.91；文化环境的测量得分为17.79、15.73、15.14、13.27和12.83。

表7　　　　不同层级城市的老龄友好型社区建设状况

城市级别	总指标	均值（标准差）	一级指标	均值（标准差）	样本量
超大城市	老龄友好型社区	72.23（8.73）	物理环境	33.82（3.68）	971
			社会环境	20.62（4.07）	971
			文化环境	17.79（2.73）	971
特大城市	老龄友好型社区	64.01（11.48）	物理环境	31.05（5.19）	308
			社会环境	17.23（4.26）	308
			文化环境	15.73（4.29）	308
Ⅰ型大城市	老龄友好型社区	68.46（8.91）	物理环境	32.55（4.02）	136
			社会环境	20.77（4.02）	136
			文化环境	15.14（3.27）	136
Ⅱ型大城市	老龄友好型社区	58.25（10.13）	物理环境	28.92（5.18）	542
			社会环境	16.06（3.36）	542
			文化环境	13.27（3.85）	542
其他中小城市	老龄友好型社区	57.33（9.11）	物理环境	28.6（4.37）	815
			社会环境	15.91（3.75）	815
			文化环境	12.83（3.62）	815

总体而言，随着城市人口规模的增大，城市老龄友好型社区的整体建设水平基本上表现为逐级升高的变化规律；反之，随着城市人口规模的减少，城市老龄友好型社区的整体建设水平逐级下降。各分项指标的变化规律与总体指标变化规律一致。一方面，该变化规律与我国超大城市养老支持体系建设较早且较为完善的事实基本一致。另一方面，这也反映出老龄友好型社区建设可能存在城市规模效益现象，即伴随人口在城市集聚程度的提高，老龄友好型社区建设的投入产出效率可能有所提升。需要说明的是，特大城市老龄友好型社区的测量得分低于Ⅰ型大城市，原因可能是特大城市青年人口流入较多，老龄化速度相对缓慢，养老体系建设需求被压制。Ⅰ型大城市虽然与特大城市一样多为省会城市，但青年人口远不及特大城市多，人口老龄化进程较快，故而在养老体系建设上的速度快于特大城市。

三 结论

"未富先老"是我国人口老龄化进程中的一个重要客观事实，这使得应对老龄化的思想准备不足、服务供给不够、保障结构失衡，而创建老龄友好型社区，有助于提升应对老龄化的机动性和功能性，是老年人顺利实现"原地安老"的必然要求。基于世界卫生组织的老龄友好指标体系，提出一种信度效度良好的适用于我国城市的老龄友好型社区测量指标体系。进一步利用全国大型调查数据，对我国城市社区的老龄友好程度进行量化分析，发现我国城市老龄友好型社区建设的整体水平还不高，距离最优状态尚有较大改善空间，同时结构性短板问题突出，其中短板弱项最突出的是社会环境，其次是文化环境和物理环境。社会环境方面，短板最突出的是技能提升与再就业促进，其次是信息交流以及日常生活和医疗健康服务。文化环境方面，短板较突出的是老年人的社会融入，然后是对老年人的尊重包容；物理环境方面，短板最突出的是户外空间，其次是交通出行和住房。另外，老龄友好型社区建设的区域不均衡性和城市异质性特征明显。区域不均衡总体表现为"东部较高，西部居中，中部和东北塌陷"，即中部地区和东北地区的城市老龄友好型社区建设水平相对较低。城市异质性则表现为城市人口规模越大，老龄友好型社区建设水平越高；反之，城市人口规模越小，老龄友好型社区建设水平越低。

针对我国城市老龄友好型社区建设存在的结构性短板和弱项，需要从以下四个方面推进相关工作。

一是优化老年人的社会环境支持。重点加强老年人技能提升和再就业促进工作，解决老年人再就业面临的技能不足、年龄歧视、渠道不畅，权益难保障等问题。其次，加强老年人信息交流的无障碍化改造，缩小数字鸿沟，为老年人提供便捷的信息服务。再次，完善日常生活和医疗健康服务体系，着力打造更加便捷、更高品质、综合连续的日常生活服务体系，加强老年医疗健康服务网络建设，促进医疗健康资源优化配置，提升医疗健康服务水平等。

二是营造尊老爱老敬老的文化环境。努力营造对老年人尊重和包容的文化环境，积极创造机会引导老年人参与社会活动，增加老年人的社会融入。在全社会弘扬尊老敬老爱老助老的优良传统，为老年人送温暖、办实事、解难事，使广大老年人生活更安康、精神更快乐。

三是优化老年人的物理环境支持。加强室外公共空间、住房、交通出行的适老化改造和无障碍化建设。在室外公共空间增强对老年人行动能力和安全性的考虑，有针对性地展开适老化改造，打造安全、舒适、便利的居住生活环境。加强城市道路、公共交通工具以及客运站场和高速公路服务区等无障碍改造，设置清晰、明显的老年人服务引导标志，推出适老化的健康码方案，提高老年人交通出行的便捷性和安全性等。

此外，针对研究发现的区域不均衡和城市不均衡问题，建议进一步加大对中部和东北地区以及中小城市老龄友好型社区建设的支持力度，优化养老配套设施和资源，鼓励和引进社会力量多方参与，共同促进老龄友好型社区建设水平和质量的持续提升，不断增强老年人的获得感、体验感和满足感。

第四编

中国式现代化与中国经济发展经验

中国式现代化与中国房产税收政策模拟分析

娄　峰[*]

随着近十年来房地产市场的繁荣，中国一直在积极讨论征收房产税或房地产税以稳定房地产市场。党的二十大报告提出，要完善分配制度，坚持按劳分配为主体、多种分配方式并存，坚持多劳多得，鼓励勤劳致富，促进机会公平，增加低收入者收入，扩大中等收入者群体，规范收入分配秩序。其中以房地产为主的财产性收入是增加居民收入不可或缺的渠道。

房产税在许多发达国家相当普遍，并逐渐成为政府提供公共物品（如公立学校、警察系统等）的主要税收来源。目前，中国经济逐渐由注重经济增长速度转向更加注重经济发展质量。财政作为国家治理的基础和重要支柱，财税体制在治国安邦中始终发挥着基础性、制度性、保障性作用，如何更好地发挥房地产税等财税政策，促进我国经济实现高质量发展，完善分配制度，规范收入分配机制等问题成为各界关注的重要话题。

早在 2011 年，房产税改革开始在沪渝两地试点，标志着我国房产税改革正式启动。党的十八届三中全会通过的《中共中央关于全面深化改革若干重大问题的决定》提出要"加快房地产税立法并适时推进改革"，

---

[*] 娄峰，中国社会科学院数量经济与技术经济研究所研究员、经济预测分析研究室主任。

为我国房产税改革提供了法理上的依据。2017年党的十九大召开，明确提出"深化税收制度改革，健全地方税体系"，同时，2018年的政府工作报告提出"稳妥推进房产税立法"。2022年政府工作报告明确提出"做好房地产税、环境保护税立法相关工作"，要求推进房地产税改革需要立法先行，彰显了我国房产税改革正在提速。美国和经合组织等发达国家的经验表明，房地产税在控制房价、抑制某些投机行为方面具有重要作用[1]。因此，一个悬而未决的问题是，如果我国实施房产税，在这一新改革下，各个家庭将受到怎样的影响？他们自掏腰包的钱会因为缴纳新税而增加，会不会使他们的生活变糟？中国的国民经济又会受到何种影响？因此，如何设计合适的房产税改革方案将是这一政策能否成功的关键。本文利用最新的中国投入产出表等数据，构建了包含居民房产税的可计算一般均衡（CGE）模型，模拟分析不同房产税改革政策可能产生的结果。

一　文献综述

目前国内外关于房产税改革的影响研究主要包括以下几个方面。

首先，房产税改革对地方财政的影响：胡洪曙通过构建地方财力缺口测算模型，发现开征房产税不仅不会对地方财力造成难以承受的缺口，而且能为地方政府带来持续稳定收入，进而有效缓解地方政府的财政困难[2]；韦志超和易刚在相关理论基础上进行实证分析发现，只要政府改革措施得当，物业税改革将有助于政府职能转变[3]；财政部课题组认为随着城镇化进程的不断推进，房产税收入将会成为拓宽地方政府财政收入的重要渠道[4]。

---

[1] 况伟大、朱勇、刘江涛：《房产税对房价的影响：来自OECD国家的证据》，《财贸经济》2012年第5期。
[2] 胡洪曙：《开征财产税后的地方财力缺口测算研究》，《财贸经济》2011年第10期。
[3] 韦志超、易刚：《物业税改革与地方公共财政》，《经济研究》2006年第3期。
[4] 《资源税、房产税改革及对地方财政影响分析》课题组：《资源税、房产税改革及对地方财政影响分析》，《财政研究》2013年第7期。

其次，房产税改革对房价的影响：陈多长和踪家峰研究认为房产税会降低住宅资产的长期均衡价格，但是短期内会提高房租、降低住房供给量，同时还会产生效率损失[①]；而朱润喜认为，物业税的征收不会对房价产生明显的抑制作用[②]；畅军锋认为在我国各项社会福利保障制度还不健全不完善的条件下，不宜全面开征房产税。全面开征房产税只会降低人们的幸福感指数，对抑制高房价的作用甚微，但差别化征收房产税，对抑制投机投资房产有作用[③]；Bai ChongEn 等利用上海和重庆两地的数据探讨房产税改革对房价的影响，结果表明，房产税改革使上海平均房价下降了15%，却使重庆平均房价上升了11%[④]。

再次，房产税改革对居民收入分配的影响：詹鹏和李实运用城镇住户调查数据研究发现房产税改革能够有效降低居民收入不平等[⑤]；胡海生等运用可计算一般均衡模型模拟分析了在不同政策方案下，房产税改革对居民收入差距的影响[⑥]；黄潇认为房产税在影响居民收入和财富的同时，还通过转移支付来改善中低收入群体的住房和公共服务，具有调节收入分配的功能[⑦]。相反，夏商末却认为房产税不仅无法对收入分配不公起到调节作用，而且会产生福利损失[⑧]；Lai 和 David 在扩展 Frank 模型的基础上，分析了财产税的福利影响，结果表明，房地产升值会使房产者福利降低，但是如果财产税也降低，对于常住居民来说情况就会变得

---

① 陈多长、踪家峰：《房地产税收与住宅资产价格：理论分析与政策评价》，《财贸研究》2004 年第 1 期。
② 朱润喜：《开征物业税的动因及定位》，《税务研究》2006 年第 9 期。
③ 畅军锋：《房产税试点以来对房价影响之实证分析与探讨》，《经济体制改革》2013 年第 5 期。
④ ChongEn Bai, Qi Li, Min Ouyang, "Property Taxes and Home Prices: A Tale of Two Cities", *Journal of Econometrics*, 2014（1）.
⑤ 詹鹏、李实：《我国居民房产税与收入不平等》，《经济学动态》2015 年第 7 期。
⑥ 胡海生、刘红梅、王克强：《中国房产税改革方案比较研究——基于可计算一般均衡（CGE）的分析》，《财政研究》2012 年第 12 期。
⑦ 黄潇：《房产税调节收入分配的机理、条件与改革方向》，《西部论坛》2014 年第 1 期。
⑧ 夏商末：《房产税能够调节收入分配不公和抑制房价上涨吗》，《税务研究》2011 年第 4 期。

更糟①。

最后，房产税改革对宏观经济的影响：李言、骆永民和伍文中通过构建包含房产税的 DSGE 模型，模拟分析了房产税改革对主要宏观经济变量的影响②③。梁云芳等利用 CGE 模型模拟分析了房地产资本税对房地产业及宏观经济的影响，结果表明，房地产资本税率的提高可以拉动房地产业的发展，而房地产资本税率降低则有利于房地产业的内部结构优化④；Zodrow 认为房产税的征收降低了资本收入，进而对房地产市场和宏观经济产生了一定影响⑤。M. Sullivan 利用城市一般均衡效应模型来研究房产税的效率效应以及分配效应，结果表明，在此次税收政策的改革中，土地所有者是获益的，而普通居民的利益是受损的⑥。

从以往国内外研究文献可以看出，房产税改革是一项系统性工程，其改革效果不仅会影响到某一具体产业部门，还会影响到社会经济系统的方方面面，但回顾以往研究，大多数是围绕某一单一视角分析房产税改革的影响，虽然也有关于房产税改革对国民经济整体影响的研究，但是，此类研究又缺乏对产业部门的微观分析。因此，本文在借鉴以往研究的基础上，构建了包含居民房产税的可计算一般均衡（CGE）模型，从微观、中观、宏观的视角分析房产税改革对我国国民经济的影响。相比以往研究，本文的创新点主要包括：第一，本文基于最新的 2017 年中国投入产出表等数据构建了包含房产税的 CGE 模型。在模型中，将产业部门划分为 26 个部门，可以很好地分析房产税改革在产业层面上的具体

---

① Fu-Chuan Lai, David Merriman, "Housing appreciation (depreciation) and owners welfare", *Journal of Housing Economics*, 2010 (1).

② 李言：《组合式房产税改革的宏观经济效应——兼顾居民用房与商业用房的 DSGE 框架分析》，《经济与管理研究》2019 年第 12 期。

③ 骆永民、伍文中：《房产税改革与房价变动的宏观经济效应——基于 DSGE 模型的数值模拟分析》，《金融研究》2012 年第 5 期。

④ 梁云芳、张同斌、高玲玲：《房地产资本税对房地产业及国民经济影响的实证研究》，《统计研究》2013 年第 5 期。

⑤ Mieszkowski, Peter M, Zodrow, George B, "The New View of The Property Tax: A Reformulation", *Regional Science and Urban Economics*, 1986 (16).

⑥ M. Sullivan, "The general equilibrium effects of the industrial property tax: Incidence and excess burden", *Regional Science and Urban Economics*, 1984 (4).

影响；第二，本文将城镇居民和农村居民按照收入水平分别划分为五类，可以更准确地分析房产税改革对不同收入阶层居民的具体影响，同时，本文还测算了基尼系数，可以用来分析不同的房产税改革政策对我国基尼系数的影响；第三，从理论上，本文基于两阶段模型理论，阐述了征收房产税影响国民经济的理论机制。从实证上，对可能采取的房产税改革方案的影响效果进行测算，得出各项房产税改革方案对国民经济影响的综合效应，弥补了现有研究的不足。

二 理论分析

根据 Jae-Cheol 等人开发的两阶段模型理论[①]，假设商品房的销售仅存在两个时期，并且这两期所有的商品房都是同质的，由于商品房销售只持续两个时期，所以第二个时期是最后一个时期，所以这一时期生产的商品房的经济寿命缩短为一个时期。设 q_t 表示第 t 期建造商品房的产量，Q_t 表示 t 时期商品房的存货量，且有 $Q_t = q_t + q_{t-1}$。在该模型中，厂商决定是否在生产的同时销售或者租赁商品房，设 s_t 为厂商在 t 时期销售的商品房数量，l_t 为厂商在 t 时期租赁的商品房数量，且有 $q_t = s_t + l_t$。设在 t 时期厂商出租和销售商品房的价格分别为 p_{lt} 和 p_{st}，商品房出租的需求函数为 $p_{lt} = p(Q_t)$，当出租商品房的数量为 q 时，收益函数为 $\psi(q) = p(q)q$。

假设对商品房所有者征收房产税，且假设房产税税率 r ($r \geq 0$) 固定不变且为比例税率，则有

$$\hat{\Pi}_{1r} = (1 + r)\Pi_1$$

$$\hat{\Pi}_{2r} = (1 + r)\Pi_2$$

$$c_{1r} = (1 + r)c$$

[①] Kim Jae-Cheol, Kim Min-Young, Chun Se-Hak, "Property tax and its effects on strategic behavior of leasing and selling for a durable-goods monopolist", *International Review of Economics and Finance*, 2014 (1).

其中，Π_1 和 Π_2 分别为第一时期和第二时期的利润函数，c 为商品房的边际生产成本。

由于第二期是最后一个时期，无套利行为的存在，则有

$$(1+r)p_{st} = p_{lt}$$

$$\begin{aligned}\Pi_2 &= \Pi_2(q_2,s_1,l_1:r)\\ &= (1+r)\{p_{s2}s_2 + p_{l2}(l_2+l_1) - rp_{s2}(l_2+l_1) - cq_2\}\\ &= (1+r)p_{s2}s_2 + (1+r)p_{l2}(l_2+l_1) - (1+r)rp_{s2}(l_2+l_1) - (1+r)cq_2\\ &= p_{l2}s_2 + s_2(l_2+l_1) - c_rq_2\\ &= \psi(Q_2) - p(Q_2)s_1 - c_rq_2\end{aligned}$$

由于第二期为最后一期，此时 s_2 和 l_2 无区别，因此假定 $s_2 = l_2$。

在第一期，销售价格与不征税情况下的价格不同。如果消费者购买商品房并使用两期，则必须花费 $(1+r)p_{s1} + \beta rp_{s2}$，另一方面，如果他租赁两个时期的商品房，他需要花费 $p(q_1) + \beta p(Q_2)$。因此，在不存在套利行为的情况下，有

$$(1+r)p_{s1} + \beta rp_{s2} = p(q_1) + \beta p(Q_2)$$

整理可得：$(1+r)p_{s1} = p(q_1) + \dfrac{\beta p(Q_2)}{1+r}$

则有

$$\begin{aligned}\hat{\Pi}_r &= \hat{\Pi}_r(s_1,l_1:r)\\ &= (1+r)(p_{s1}s_1 + p_{l1}l_1 - rp_{s1}l_1 - cq_1 + \beta\hat{\Pi}_{2r})\\ &= \psi(q_1) + \beta p(\hat{Q}_2)\left(\dfrac{q_1}{1+r} + \hat{q}_2\right) - c_r(q_1 + \beta\hat{q}_2)\end{aligned}$$

通过将利润函数与无税情况下的利润函数进行比较，我们发现两者在函数形式上都非常相似，不同的是，第一时期的生产需要在第二时期进行折现 $1+r$。

现在我们讨论房产税对生产和福利的影响，为了便于处理，我们假设边际生产成本 $c=0$，下面考虑两个特定条件。一种是税率足够低时，另一种是需求是线性时。对方程

$$\psi'(Q_2) - \frac{r}{1+r}p'(Q_2)q_1 = c_r$$

$$\psi'(q_1) - \frac{\beta r}{1+r}p(Q_2) = (1-\beta)c_r$$

求微分，则有：

$$D\begin{bmatrix} \dfrac{\partial q_1^*}{\partial r} \\ \dfrac{\partial Q_2^*}{\partial r} \end{bmatrix} = \frac{1}{1+r}\begin{bmatrix} \beta p(Q_2^*) \\ p'(Q_2^*)q_1^* \end{bmatrix}$$

其中，$D = \begin{bmatrix} (1+r)\psi''(q_1^*) & -\beta r p'(Q_2^*) \\ -rp'(Q_2^*) & (1+r)\psi''(Q_2^*) - rq_1^* p''(Q_2^*) \end{bmatrix}$

因此有：

$$\frac{\partial q_1^*}{\partial r} = \frac{1}{1+r} \frac{\begin{vmatrix} \beta p(Q_2^*) & -\beta r p'(Q_2^*) \\ p'(Q_2^*)q_1^* & (1+r)\psi''(Q_2^*) - rq_1^* p''(Q_2^*) \end{vmatrix}}{|D|}$$

$$\frac{\partial Q_2^*}{\partial r} = \frac{1}{1+r} \frac{\begin{vmatrix} (1+r)\psi''(q_1^*) & -\beta r p'(Q_2^*) \\ -rp'(Q_2^*) & p'(Q_2^*)q_1^* \end{vmatrix}}{|D|}$$

通常不可能确定 $\dfrac{\partial q_1^*}{\partial r}$ 和 $\dfrac{\partial Q_2^*}{\partial r}$ 的正负。但是，我们可以在以下特殊情况下预测其符号。在线性需求 [$q(p) = a - bp$] 的情况下，征收房产税会使第1时期的产出吸引力降低，从而导致生产推迟。结果导致租金价格在两个时期内下降，即 $p_1^* > p_2^*$，有：

$$\frac{\partial p_{l1}^*}{\partial r} = -a\beta \frac{(\beta r^2 + 4r + 4)}{h(r)^2} < 0$$

$$\frac{\partial p_{l2}^*}{\partial r} = -a \frac{(4-3\beta)r^2 + 4(2-\beta)r + 4}{h(r)^2} < 0$$

此外，两个时期的销售价格都随着税率的上升而下降。

$$\frac{\partial p_{s1}^*}{\partial r} = -2a\frac{(4-\beta)r^2 + 2(4+3\beta-\beta^2)r + 4(1+2\beta)}{h(r)^2} < 0$$

$$\frac{\partial p_{s2}^*}{\partial r} = -a\frac{(4-\beta)r^2 + 4(4-\beta)r + 12}{h(r)^2} < 0$$

其中，$h(r) \equiv 4(1+r)^2 - \beta r^2 > 0$。

可见，征收房产税不仅会降低租金价格，还会降低销售价格。

征收房产税时，消费者剩余（CS^*）、厂商利润（Π^*）、税收收入（TR^*）和社会福利（SW^*）可以表示为：

$$CS^* = \int_0^{q_1^*} p(q)dq - (p_{s1}^* s_1^* + p_{l1}^* l_1^*) - rp_{s1}^* s_1^*$$

$$+ \beta(\int_0^{Q_2^*} p(q)dq - p_{l2}^*(q_2^* + l_1^*) - rp_{s2}^* s_1^*)$$

$$\Pi^* = (p_{l1}^* q_1^* + \beta p_{l2}^*(\frac{q_1^*}{1+r} + q_2^*))/(1+r)$$

$$TR^* = rp_{s1}^* q_1^* + \beta r p_{s2}^* Q_2^*$$

$$SW^* = \int_0^{q_1^*} p(q)dq + \beta \int_0^{Q_2^*} p(q)dq$$

在线性需求的情况下，征收房产税时，对消费者剩余、厂商利润、税收收入和社会福利的影响表现为：

$$\frac{\partial CS^*}{\partial r} = \frac{a^2 \beta v}{b} \frac{(12-15\beta+4\beta^2)r^3 + (36-35\beta+5\beta^2)r^2}{h(r)^3}$$

$$+ \frac{a^2 \beta v}{b} \frac{12(3-2\beta)r + 4(3-\beta)}{h(r)^3} > 0$$

$$\frac{\partial \Pi^*}{\partial r} = -\frac{a^2}{b}\frac{(4-\beta)r^2 + 2(4+3\beta-\beta^2)r + 4(1+2\beta)}{h(r)^2} < 0$$

$$\frac{\partial TR^*}{\partial r} = \frac{a^2}{b}\frac{(16-16\beta+11\beta^2-4\beta^3)r^4 + (64+4\beta^2-16\beta-4\beta^3)r^3}{h(r)^3}$$

$$+ \frac{a^2}{b}\frac{24(4+2\beta-\beta^2)r^2 + 16(4+5\beta-\beta^2)r + 16(1+2\beta)}{h(r)^3} > 0$$

$$\frac{\partial SW^*}{\partial r} = \frac{a^2 \beta v}{b}\frac{(4-5\beta)r^3 + (12-17\beta-\beta^2)r^2 + 12(1-2\beta)r + 4(1-3\beta)}{h(r)^3}$$

可见，征收房产税使得消费者剩余和税收收入增加，厂商利润减少。尽管征收房产税使得税收增加，但对社会福利的影响却模棱两可。如果 $\beta = 1$，则 $\frac{\partial SW^*}{\partial r} < 0$，并且如果 $\beta \approx 0$，则 $\frac{\partial SW^*}{\partial r} > 0$。此外，对于 β 的某些值，SW^* 可能会先减小后增加。

三 中国居民房产税 CGE 模型设定

（一）社会核算矩阵构建

本文构建的居民房产税社会核算矩阵表（SAM）是在最新的 2017 年投入产出表的基础上，结合《中国统计年鉴》《中国住户调查年鉴》等数据编制完成的。在该 SAM 中，共包括 26 个生产活动部门，分别是：农业、采矿业、制造业、电力、热力、燃气及水的生产和供应业、建筑业、批发、零售、交通运输、仓储和邮政业、住宿、餐饮、电信、广播电视和卫星传输服务业、互联网和相关服务、软件和信息技术服务业、货币金融和其他金融服务、资本市场服务、保险、房地产、租赁、商务服务、科学研究和技术服务业、水利、环境和公共设施管理业、居民服务、修理和其他服务业、教育、卫生和社会工作、文化、体育和娱乐业、公共管理、社会保障和社会组织。居民划分为 10 组，分别是：城镇低收入户、城镇中等偏下户、城镇中等收入户、城镇中等偏上户、城镇高收入户、农村低收入户、农村中等偏下户、农村中等收入户、农村中等偏上户、农村高收入户。税收划分为增值税、营业税、耕地占用税、城市维护建设税、契税、印花税、土地增值税、城镇土地使用税、企业所得税、个人所得税、经营性房产税、居民非经营性房产税、关税、其他税收。此外，还包括企业、政府、投资储蓄、存贷变动、国外等账户。

（二）政策模拟方案设定

为了模拟征收房产税对中国宏观经济和部门经济的具体影响，本文在借鉴以往研究①②③的基础上，并结合房产税在我国实施的可能性，设置了以下八种政策模拟方案：

政策模拟方案一（S1）：对城镇居民的房产征收 2.0% 的房产税；

政策模拟方案二（S2）：对所有居民的房产征收 2.0% 的房产税；

政策模拟方案三（S3）：实施累进制房产税条件下，对城镇居民征收房产税；

政策模拟方案四（S4）：实施累进制房产税条件下，对所有居民征收房产税；

政策模拟方案五（S5）：实施人均免征 20 平方米的条件下，对城镇居民征收房产税；

政策模拟方案六（S6）：实施人均免征 20 平方米的条件下，对所有居民征收房产税；

政策模拟方案七（S7）：实施人均免征额的条件下，对城镇居民征收房产税；

政策模拟方案八（S8）：实施人均免征额的条件下，对所有居民征收房产税；

通过设置政策模拟方案一和方案二，可以清晰地比较出在不考虑其他因素的情况下，仅对城镇居民或所有居民征收房产税将会对国民经济产生何种影响。同时，考虑到现实条件下，我国房产税征收过程中可能存在的种种困难以及可能采取的房产税措施，分别设置了累进制房产税、人均免征面积以及人均免征额条件下的各种政策模拟方案，以便更好地模拟分析不同房产税政策对国民经济产生的影响。

---

① 张平、侯一麟：《房地产税的纳税能力、税负分布及再分配效应》，《经济研究》2016 年第 12 期。

② 李文：《我国房地产税收入数量测算及其充当地方税主体税种的可行性分析》，《财贸经济》2014 年第 9 期。

③ 刘金东、王生发：《新房产税的累进性与充分性测算——基于家户调查数据的微观模拟》，《财经论丛》2015 年第 12 期。

四 模拟结果分析

（一）对宏观经济的影响

表1　　　　房产税改革对主要宏观经济指标的影响　　　（单位:%）

模拟方案	GDP	总产出	总出口	总进口	总投资	居民总消费	政府总消费
S1	-0.118	-0.620	-1.315	-1.443	-1.764	-5.693	18.048
S2	-0.130	-0.739	-1.514	-1.662	-2.380	-5.877	20.371
S3	-0.213	-1.256	-2.636	-2.894	-3.828	-11.301	37.112
S4	-0.233	-1.510	-3.057	-3.356	-5.220	-11.572	42.078
S5	-0.054	-0.279	-0.571	-0.627	-0.865	-2.408	7.990
S6	-0.061	-0.339	-0.669	-0.734	-1.198	-2.455	9.107
S7	-0.107	-0.563	-1.189	-1.305	-1.612	-5.137	16.340
S8	-0.113	-0.621	-1.282	-1.407	-1.932	-5.179	17.418

房产税作为一种对房产持有者（在本文模型中，房产持有者为居民）直接征收的税额，其本质上是一种财产税。房产税的征收增加了居民持有房产的成本，使得居民总消费出现不同程度的减少，同时，现实经济系统中，供需总是相互影响，居民总消费的减少将会对总产出的变化产生不同程度的负面冲击，同时，总产出的减少使得投资者对未来经济发展预期的担忧，造成投资水平的下降。对于总进口和总出口，我国作为制造业大国，每年需要从国外进口大量的原材料，总产出的减少一方面降低了国内对进口原材料的需求，另一方面又减少了国内产品的出口，再加上居民总消费的减少，在一定程度上也降低了对进口品的需求。对于政府部门而言，征收房产税拓宽了政府的税收渠道，增加了政府的财政收入，一定程度上促进了政府总消费的增加。作为宏观经济的重要指标，房产税的征收使得实际GDP出现不同程度的减少，对比八种政策模拟方案的结果可以发现，变化较大的为S3和S4，即实施累进制房产税将会对总体宏观经济产生的负面冲击较大，可能的原因是，随着居民持有

房产面积的增加,居民所承受的房产税的缴税压力也在不断增大,同时,在现实情况中,居民房产价值在居民家庭总资产占有相当大的比例,居民缴税压力的不断增大势必会影响家庭的行为决策,最终影响整个宏观经济的发展。

(二) 对部门产出的影响

表2　　　　　　　　　　对部门产出的影响①　　　　　　（单位:%）

	S1	S2	S3	S4	S5	S6	S7	S8
sector1	-2.122	-2.430	-4.313	-4.885	-0.935	-1.061	-1.921	-2.040
sector2	-1.676	-1.935	-3.341	-3.890	-0.721	-0.848	-1.514	-1.636
sector3	-1.633	-1.889	-3.258	-3.799	-0.703	-0.828	-1.476	-1.595
sector4	-1.684	-1.826	-3.320	-3.618	-0.716	-0.785	-1.520	-1.586
sector5	-1.392	-2.055	-3.153	-4.662	-0.721	-1.079	-1.279	-1.625
sector6	-1.367	-1.596	-2.867	-3.359	-0.630	-0.744	-1.242	-1.352
sector7	-1.710	-1.871	-3.567	-3.897	-0.781	-0.856	-1.553	-1.624
sector8	-0.532	-0.558	-1.110	-1.164	-0.247	-0.261	-0.484	-0.497
sector9	1.781	2.246	3.646	4.638	0.780	1.004	1.611	1.826
sector10	-3.179	-3.103	-6.634	-6.456	-1.450	-1.406	-2.887	-2.844
sector11	-0.976	-0.876	-2.068	-1.855	-0.455	-0.404	-0.888	-0.839
sector12	0.236	0.270	0.408	0.469	0.076	0.088	0.209	0.220
sector13	-1.142	-1.649	-2.600	-3.762	-0.596	-0.872	-1.050	-1.317
sector14	-1.154	-1.223	-2.379	-2.528	-0.521	-0.556	-1.047	-1.081
sector15	-2.173	-2.167	-4.542	-4.496	-0.992	-0.977	-1.973	-1.958
sector16	-4.619	-4.491	-9.610	-9.331	-2.098	-2.028	-4.193	-4.127
sector17	-2.731	-2.881	-5.324	-5.610	-1.144	-1.205	-2.463	-2.520

① 表2中sector1-sector26分别代表:农业、采矿业、制造业、电力、热力、燃气及水的生产和供应业、建筑业、批发、零售、交通运输、仓储和邮政业、住宿、餐饮、电信、广播电视和卫星传输服务业、互联网和相关服务、软件和信息技术服务业、货币金融和其他金融服务、资本市场服务、保险、房地产、租赁、商务服务、科学研究和技术服务业、水利、环境和公共设施管理业、居民服务、修理和其他服务业、教育、卫生和社会工作、文化、体育和娱乐业、公共管理、社会保障和社会组织共26个产业部门。

续表

	S1	S2	S3	S4	S5	S6	S7	S8
sector18	-0.792	-1.091	-1.766	-2.448	-0.403	-0.566	-0.726	-0.884
sector19	-0.735	-0.737	-1.508	-1.516	-0.331	-0.334	-0.667	-0.669
sector20	1.903	1.826	3.725	3.493	0.778	0.715	1.712	1.650
sector21	12.061	13.693	24.973	28.525	5.309	6.089	10.911	11.669
sector22	-2.371	-2.291	-4.955	-4.759	-1.087	-1.039	-2.154	-2.108
sector23	7.808	9.052	16.471	19.167	3.580	4.191	7.091	7.681
sector24	9.314	10.715	18.637	21.657	4.009	4.700	8.414	9.080
sector25	3.907	4.817	8.467	10.437	1.853	2.298	3.558	3.987
sector26	15.816	17.860	32.559	36.924	7.017	7.999	14.322	15.271

从表2可以看出，房产税的征收使得绝大多数部门的产出受到不同程度的负面影响，其中，受到负面影响程度最大的部门是保险业，在八种不同的政策方案下，分别减少4.619%、4.491%、9.610%、9.331%、2.098%、2.028%、4.193%、4.127%；除此之外，房产税的征收也使得一些产业部门的产出增加，主要包括住宿、互联网和相关服务、科学研究和技术服务业、水利。环境和公共设施管理业、教育、卫生和社会工作、文化、体育和娱乐业、公共管理、社会保障和社会组织等，其中，产出增加幅度最大的部门是公共管理、社会保障和社会组织部门，在八种不同的政策方案下，分别增加15.816%、17.860%、32.559%、36.924%、7.017%、7.999%、14.322%、15.271%；对于房地产部门而言，在八种不同的政策方案下，房地产部门产出分别减少2.731%、2.881%、5.324%、5.610%、1.144%、1.205%、2.463%、2.520%，鉴于加征房产税政策增加了居民持有房产的成本，降低了居民对房产的需求意愿，使得房地产市场价格也出现不同程度的下降，分别减少0.284%、0.379%、0.629%、0.850%、0.142%、0.194%、0.260%、0.311%。

(三) 对政府收入的影响

政府财政收入作为国家各项公共事业健康发展的重要保障，在本文构建的中国居民房产税 CGE 模型中，政府财政收入来源主要为各项税收收入，包括增值税、营业税、耕地占用税、城市维护建设税、契税、印花税、土地增值税、城镇土地使用税、企业所得税、个人所得税、经营性房产税、居民非经营性房产税、关税以及其他共 14 种税收。居民非经营性房产税作为政府财政收入的重要组成部分，对居民拥有的居住性房产进行征税，势必会增加政府财政收入。表现为：在八种不同的政策模拟方案下，政府收入分别增加 16.450%、18.538%、33.490%、37.851%、7.327%、8.341%、14.908%、15.877%。其中，增加幅度较大的为 S3 和 S4，即实施累进制房产税情况下，对城镇居民或所有居民征收房产税。原因在于，在保持房产税征收税基不变的前提下，随着居民房产价值的不断增加，居民所缴纳的房产税税额也在不断增加，进而使得在八种政策模拟方案条件下，S3 和 S4 的政府收入增长幅度较大。

（四）对居民可支配收入和基尼系数的影响

表3　　　　　　　　对居民可支配收入和基尼系数的影响

	S1	S2	S3	S4	S5	S6	S7	S8
城镇低收入户/%	-14.548	-14.228	-11.938	-11.270	0.788	0.943	-11.957	-11.808
城镇中等偏下户/%	-9.950	-9.610	-11.202	-10.493	-2.047	-1.882	-8.615	-8.457
城镇中等收入户/%	-8.196	-7.838	-11.594	-10.847	-2.896	-2.723	-7.300	-7.134
城镇中等偏上户/%	-7.387	-7.032	-14.075	-13.334	-3.794	-3.622	-6.780	-6.615
城镇高收入户/%	-6.725	-6.411	-22.513	-21.857	-5.085	-4.933	-6.448	-6.302
农村低收入户/%	0.726	-5.182	1.481	-4.327	0.325	-0.126	0.658	0.435
农村中等偏下户/%	0.691	-2.080	1.409	-1.882	0.309	-0.349	0.626	0.056
农村中等收入户/%	0.617	-1.842	1.260	-2.524	0.276	-0.727	0.560	-0.382
农村中等偏上户/%	0.605	-1.743	1.233	-3.711	0.270	-1.060	0.548	-0.740
农村高收入户/%	0.547	-1.308	1.117	-4.638	0.245	-1.070	0.496	-0.797
基尼系数	-0.012	-0.006	-0.043	-0.033	-0.010	-0.008	-0.012	-0.010

在本文构建的中国居民房产税 CGE 模型中，将城镇居民和农村居民按照收入不同分别划分为五组。从表 4 可以看出，面对不同的房产税征收政策，不同类型的居民所受影响是不同的。由于 S1、S3、S5 和 S7 四种政策模拟方案仅考虑对城镇居民征收房产税，因此农村居民可支配收入并没有受到负面冲击，相反，农村居民可支配收入出现不同程度的增加。可能的原因是模型中包含了政府对农村居民的转移支付，在其他条件不变的情况下，政府财政收入的提高带动了政府对农村居民转移支付的增加，从而使得农村居民的可支配收入出现不同程度的增加。对比 S1 和 S2 的政策模拟结果可以发现，无论是城镇居民还是农村居民，随着居民收入水平的不断提高，征收房产税带来的影响逐渐减小。可能的原因是随着居民收入水平的提高，居民有更多配置家庭资产的选择，从而征收房产税对其可支配收入的影响也逐渐减小。对比 S3 和 S4 的政策模拟结果可以发现，随着居民收入水平的提高，征收累进制房产税对其可支配收入的影响也逐渐增加，其中，S4 的农村低收入户的模拟结果较大，可能的原因是其本身家庭资产就相对较少，征收房产税加重了家庭负担，因而出现征收累进制房产税政策对农村低收入户的可支配收入影响较大的结果。对比 S5 和 S6 的政策模拟结果可以发现，房产税的征收并没有对城镇低收入户的可支配收入产生负面冲击，原因在于 S5 和 S6 实行的人均免征面积条件下征收房产税，由于城镇低收入户人均房产面积较小，实施人均免征面积避免了对城镇低收入户房产税的征收。对比 S7 和 S8 的政策模拟结果可以发现，在实施人均免征额的条件下征收房产税，虽然在一定程度上降低直接征收房产税带来的负面冲击，但并没有从根本上改变征收房产税对城镇低收入户带来的冲击大于城镇高收入户的现象，而对于农村居民而言，达到了预期效果，农村低收入户和中等偏下收入户的可支配收入并没有受到负面影响，农村中等收入户、中等偏上收入户以及高收入户所受影响随着收入水平的提高也逐渐增大。同时，本文还测算了基尼系数指标，在八种不同的政策方案下，基尼系数分别下降 0.012、0.006、0.043、0.033、0.010、0.008、0.012、0.010。可见房产税政策在一定程度上调节了城乡财富收入分配，缩小了居民之间的收入差距，且实施累进制房产税政策对于缩小居民收入差距具有明显的促进效果。

五 结论

本文通过构建中国居民房产税 CGE 模型,模拟分析了房产税改革对我国国民经济的影响。政策模拟结果显示,在宏观经济方面,房产税的征收对实际 GDP、总产出、总出口、总进口、总投资、居民消费产生负面影响,其中,负面影响最为严重的是政策模拟方案四,即实施累进制房产税条件下,对所有居民征收房产税。表现为实际 GDP、总产出、总出口、总进口、总投资、居民消费分别减少 0.233%、1.510%、3.057%、3.356%、5.220%、11.572%。对政府消费产生正面影响,且影响效果随着房产税征收方案的不同呈现明显的差异性,其中,政府消费所受正面影响最大的依然是政策模拟方案四,表现为政府消费提高 42.078%。对比八种政策模拟方案发现,宏观经济指标所受影响较小的模拟方案为 S5 和 S6,即实施人均免征面积的条件下,对城镇居民或者所有居民征收房产税。

在部门产出方面,房产税的征收加大了房产持有者的成本,降低了居民对房产的刚性需求,使得房地产部门的产出减少,同时也使得房地产价格出现不同程度的下降;其中,房地产部门产出和价格所受负面冲击最为严重的为政策模拟方案四,表现为产出和价格分别下降 5.610% 和 0.850%。对比政策模拟方案四的宏观经济指标变化结果,虽然该方案能够有效优化房地产部门的供给侧结构,降低房地产价格,但是对主要宏观经济指标却产生了较大的负面冲击。

在政府收入方面,政府部门作为房产税改革政策的受益者,房产税的征收拓宽了政府财政收入渠道,增加了政府收入。其中政府收入增加最为明显的是政策模拟方案四。表现为政府收入增加 37.851%。政府收入的大幅提高也带动了政府消费的大幅增加,表现为政策模拟方案四中政府消费增加 42.078%。同时,政府支出多用于社会公共事业等领域,表现为政策模拟方案四中公共管理、社会保障和社会组织部门产出增加 36.924%。

在居民可支配收入方面。不同房产税征收方案对居民可支配收入产生的影响具有明显的差异性。对比八种政策模拟方案的结果可以发现，模拟方案 S6 和 S8 对居民的可支配收入影响相对较小，且在一定程度上体现了房产税政策对低收入人群的保护。但是，两种政策模拟方案并没有完全达到对低收入人群的保护，因此有待进行最优的房产税改革政策的组合，以达到既能有效实施房产税改革政策，又能对低收入人群进行适当保护。

在基尼系数变化方面，房产税的征收在一定程度上降低了基尼系数，缩小了城乡财富收入之间的差距。对比八种政策模拟方案结果，政策模拟方案三（即实施累进制房产税条件下，对城镇居民征收房产税）能够有效降低基尼系数，表现为基尼系数下降 0.043，但该政策仅仅是对城镇居民征收房产税，不能体现税收公平的特性。政策模拟四（即实施累进制房产税条件下，对所有居民征收房产税）是仅次于政策模拟三的能够有效降低基尼系数的政策，表现为基尼系数下降 0.033，但该政策虽然能够有效降低基尼系数，但对主要宏观经济指标产生的负面冲击较大。因此应结合 S6 和 S8 的方案设计，做出房产税改革政策最优组合。

根据上述研究结论，提出以下几方面的政策建议：

首先，有序推进我国房产税改革。目前，居民房产税改革仅在沪渝两地进行试点，尚未在全国全面实施。考虑到我国各地区经济社会发展的不同特点，在房产税税率确定方面，应秉持"因地制宜、因地施策"的原则，最大程度地减少房产税征收对居民造成的影响。同时，在征收房产税的过程中，要坚持"以人为本"的原则，充分考虑家庭的支付能力，如对于没有收入来源的老年人和残疾人或者低收入家庭的自住房给予适当的优惠，此时的政策设计可以借鉴美国的"断路器"抵免措施，以免影响居民正常的基本生活需求。

其次，更好地发挥房产税作为调节居民收入分配工具的功能。从模型的政策模拟结果中可以发现，房产税的征收在一定程度上降低了基尼系数，调节了城乡之间的财富收入分配，缩小了城乡收入差距。虽然在本文的政策模拟方案中，各个政策模拟方案或多或少对经济系统产生一定的负面冲击，但并不能因此而否定其政策研究的价值。在未来房产税的实施过程中，可以根据发展阶段的现实情况和特点，采取不同的房产税改革方案组合，以期更好地发挥房产税调节收入分配的功能，促进经济社会平稳健康发展。

再次，不断扩充房产税税基，增加政府房产税收入。现实条件下，居民的房产价值与居民房产所处的地理位置紧密联系，在居民房产总量不变的假设下，提高居民房产的单位价值将会有效地扩充房产税税基。因此，应该借助国家大力实施的"新基建"发展机遇，完善城市郊区及县域地区的基础设施建设，提升该地区的基础设施服务水平，带动该地区的经济社会发展，从而加快该地区房产价值的提升，进而促进房产税税基的扩大和政府房产税收入的增加。

最后，加快推动房产税相关立法程序和房产价值评估等技术性问题的发展进程。随着公众对实施房产税政策的呼声愈加强烈，相关政府部门应及时快速地出台与房产税改革相关的法律法规，使得房产税改革有法可依，有规可循。同时，随着互联网大数据技术的快速发展，应该建立起一套方便快捷的房产价值评估体系，能够及时反映经济社会变化对房产价值的动态影响，快速评估房产税改革政策对房地产业可能产生的影响，进而及时调整房产税改革动向。

中国式现代化作为文明新形态的理论阐释

刘洪愧[*]

文明既是承载一种精神和文化的实体，也意味着一定的发展水平、发展阶段和发展过程，工业革命以来的人类社会发展造就了世界范围内的现代化文明及其基本要素。在此过程中，党领导人民建立社会主义制度，探索出一条符合中国实际、具有中国理论特色的现代化道路。中国式现代化也取得了举世瞩目的成就，在很短时间内完成工业化和信息化并向更加高级的数字化文明转型。任何一种文明都生成于具体的历史过程中，因而中国式现代化的发展历程也构成了一种文明形态。由于中国式现代化发展理论的独特性、发展成就的显著性、发展方向的确定性、以及其对于广大发展中国家摆脱西方现代化道路唯一性束缚的启示性，中国式现代化因而也成为一种世界文明新形态。

一 文明的内涵与现代化的本质

习近平总书记《在庆祝中国共产党成立100周年大会上的讲话》中指出，"我们坚持和发展中国特色社会主义，推动物质文明、政治文明、精神文明、社会文明、生态文明协调发展，创造了中国式现代化新道路，

---

[*] 刘洪愧，中国社会科学院经济研究所副研究员。

创造了人类文明新形态。"① 党带领人民创造中国式现代化道路，归根结底是为了给中国和世界提供一种新的现代化文明形态。

（一）文明的内涵

根据亨廷顿的总结，文明最早是由18世纪法国思想家相对于野蛮状态而提出的一个概念②。之后，美国社会学家沃勒斯坦在其著作《现代世界体系》中认为文明是一种历史的总和，它包括世界观、习俗、物质文化和精神文化等方面的特殊联结③。而著名历史学家汤因比则在其著作《历史研究》中提出，每一种文明都具有其特殊性和历史延续性，包含着不被其他文明所理解的方面④。按照上述界定，文明事实上具有丰富的内涵：

首先，文明是承载一种精神和文化的实体（如民族国家），历史以来以及当今世界有多个这样的实体。西方理论学者尼古拉·丹尼列夫斯基、奎格利、奥斯瓦尔德·斯宾格勒、阿诺德·汤因比、塞缪尔·亨廷顿等都持这一观点。他们对人类发展历史过程中的文明类型进行了归纳和梳理。其中，俄罗斯思想家尼古拉·丹尼列夫斯基在《俄罗斯和欧洲》一书中较早指出了10种单独的文明类型，他在批判欧洲文明的同时，提出了斯拉夫文明的概念。亨廷顿对学者们的观点进行了总结：奎格利认为人类历史上有16个明显的文明类型，汤因比罗列了20个文明，斯宾格勒列举了8个主要文明，麦克尼尔和布罗代尔则分析了人类历史上的9个主要文明。目前，国内外学术界普遍认为人类历史上至少出现了12个主要文明，但是其中7个文明已经不复存在，现存的仅有中华文明、日本文明、印度文明、伊斯兰文明和西方文明⑤。亨廷顿进一步指出，未来世界

---

① 习近平：《在庆祝中国共产党成立100周年大会上的讲话》，《人民日报》2021年7月2日。
② ［美］塞缪尔·亨廷顿：《文明的冲突与世界秩序的重建》（修订版），周琪等译，新华出版社2009年版。
③ ［美］伊曼纽尔·沃勒斯坦：《现代世界体系》，郭方等译，社会科学文献出版社2013年版。
④ ［英］阿诺德·汤因比：《历史研究》，郭小凌等译，上海人民出版社2010年版。
⑤ ［美］塞缪尔·亨廷顿：《文明的冲突与世界秩序的重建》（修订版），周琪等译，新华出版社2009年版。

将不是一种单一的普世文明所主导,而是有许多不同的文明所共存。中国哲学家梁漱溟则将世界分为三种文明类型,即欧洲文明、中国文明和印度文明①。其中,中国文明是所有文明中唯一延续了5000年左右的单一文明。党的十九届六中全会则旗帜鲜明地指出,文明不仅有不同的形态,还有一种单一的人类文明发展方式,这就是"中华民族这个世界上古老而伟大的民族,为人类文明的发展作出了不可磨灭的贡献",创造了"具有五千多年历史的灿烂文明"②。

其次,文明也意味着一定的发展水平或发展阶段。例如,在马克思恩格斯的理论中,文明被暗含为一个更发达的社会状态。恩格斯在《共产主义原理》中指出:"共产主义革命将不仅是一个国家的革命,而将在一切文明国家里,即至少在英国、美国、法国、德国同时发生。"③ 在这里,文明显然意味着更发达的社会实体。事实上,就文明形态或者发展阶段看,人类至少经历了原始文明、农业文明、工业文明,目前正在从工业文明走向后工业文明、信息文明或数字文明时代。对应于每个文明形态,都有与其相适应的生产力、生产关系和上层建筑,从而形成了各种文明形态的差异。

最后,文明也包括多个维度。习近平总书记就明确指出,中国文明新形态包括物质文明、政治文明、精神文明、社会文明、生态文明协调发展。以上几方面是文明的主要维度,当然文明还包括其他维度。

但是需要强调的是,文明的最核心标志仍然是生产力,文明进入更高发展阶段的主要标志也是生产力的升级。这也体现了马克思主义的唯物史观,其中生产力是基础,生产力决定生产关系和上层建筑。

(二) 现代化的本质是一种文明形态

按照上文关于文明的界定,那么18世纪60年代的工业革命以来,人类文明便进入了一个新的发展阶段,即工业文明阶段。学术界也惯用现

---

① 梁漱溟:《中国文化要义》,商务印书馆2021年版。
② 《中共中央关于党的百年奋斗重大成就和历史经验的决议》,《人民日报》2021年11月17日。
③ 《马克思恩格斯全集》(第四卷),人民出版社1958年版,第369页。

代化概念来叙述工业革命以来的文明历程，它主要是指工业化以及其所带动的城市化和社会文化程度的提高。正因如此，现代化的主要内容是工业化，它本质上是一种文明形态。而且从历史的视角看，现代化代表了一个世界性的历史过程，指代人类社会从工业革命以来所经历的一场变革，可以看作代表我们这个历史时代的一种文明形式[1]。从这个角度看，中国式现代化道路也代表一种新的文明形态。这一文明形态以工业化为推动力，促成传统农业社会向现代工业社会进行全球性的转变，并使得经济、政治、文化、思想等各个领域发生深刻变革。

工业革命以来的科学、技术和工程知识的惊人扩张，使得人类以前所未有的方式来改造和利用自然资源和社会环境。在工业化或者说现代化的过程中，西方资本主义文明依靠其生产力优势，开始对劳动者的剩余价值进行残酷剥削，并通过海外扩张和殖民掠夺来推进其工业化和现代化步伐。数据显示，19世纪初期，欧洲及其殖民地占据全球土地的35%，到1878年，这一数字达到67%，1914年达到84%，之后还有所提高；19世纪初期，英国仅有150万平方英里的土地和2000万人口，到20世纪初期，英国占有1100万平方英里土地和3.9亿人口[2]。在其扩张进程中，西方文明对其他文明产生了巨大影响，渗透甚至消灭了许多人类文明（如中美洲文明），其他一些文明不是被征服就是被弱化，从而居于从属地位，如印度文明、伊斯兰文明和中华文明。

到现在为止，现代化工业文明经历了几百年的发展历程，其中西方文明一直占据主导地位。然而，西方文明的扩张并不是因为其文化影响力，而是因为其先进的技术和生产力以及有组织的暴力。西方文明借助工业革命的生产力大力发展军事产业，提高了武器、交通工具、后勤和医疗方面的先发优势，增强了其发动战争的能力，促成了西方的扩张。正如亨廷顿指出的，西方文明的兴起和扩张在很大程度上依赖于有组织地使用武力，而不是通过其思想、价值观或宗教的优越性，西方人已经

---

[1] 罗荣渠：《现代化新论》，北京大学出版社1993年版，第8—15页。
[2] [美] 塞缪尔·亨廷顿：《文明的冲突与世界秩序的重建》（修订版），周琪等译，新华出版社2009年版。

忘记这一事实，但非西方人从未忘记①。

现代化是文明进步的主要标志，非西方国家也在探索现代化的工业道路。但对于选择什么样的现代化发展模式，至今依然困扰着众多发展中国家。经典的现代化理论都是从西方文明进程和实践中提炼现代化的特性，然后把它们作为现代化的标准。甚至于一些学者认为，现代化几乎等同于西方化，欧美发展模式是现代化的唯一模式。但是，非西方国家却在这一模式中屡屡碰壁。根据世界银行统计，在 1960 年的 101 个中等收入经济体中，到 2008 年跨过中等收入陷阱的经济体只有 13 个，其中还包括 5 个西方国家，真正跨过中等收入陷阱的非西方经济体只有新加坡、中国香港、韩国、中国台湾等少数的小型经济体或资源型国家②。对于更多发展中国家而言，西方现代化模式可望而不可即。

（三）中国式现代化同样是一种文明形态

从晚清开始，中国的无数先贤们也一直在探索中国的现代化道路。19 世纪 60 年代的洋务运动可以认为是中国现代化努力的开端，当时的知识分子提出了"中学为体、西学为用"的方针，试图通过结合中国传统文化和西方先进技术来推进中国的现代化。但是由于封建官僚和帝国主义势力的强大，近代以来中国现代化的各种努力和尝试都没有成功。中国共产党成立之后，通过新民主主义革命推翻封建官僚和帝国主义，建立了新中国，为中国的现代化奠定了政治基础。之后，党领导人民通过社会主义改造建立社会主义制度，立足社会主义初级阶段的基本国情探索出一条中国式现代化道路，使得中国基本实现工业化，正在迈向基本建成现代化和全面建成社会主义现代化强国的征程。回顾这一历程，我国完全是和平崛起和复兴的，我国主动参与全球经济体系，依靠自身艰苦奋斗实现了工业化和人民富裕。在这个过程中，中国并没有出现西方那样对其他国家和文明的征服、殖民和掠夺。进一步回顾中国历史也可

---

① ［美］塞缪尔·亨廷顿：《文明的冲突与世界秩序的重建》（修订版），周琪等译，新华出版社 2009 年版。

② 世界银行、国务院发展研究中心联合课题组：《2030 年的中国：建设现代、和谐、有创造力的社会》，中国财政经济出版社 2013 年版。

发现，中华文明及其对周边国家的辐射和影响就从来不是依靠武力扩张，而是主要依赖文化优势以及海纳百川的气度。这就决定了中国式现代化道路的独特属性，因而也是一种文明新形态。而且，中国式现代化道路和人类文明新形态的形成过程也与世界其他文明发展和复兴的步调一致，是在西方文明整体衰落的情况下发生的，是世界多个文明共同发展的一部分。在中国发展的过程中，其他文明并没有式微，反而蓬勃发展，这就体现了中国式现代化道路的世界意义。

中国式现代化道路的成功无疑打破了将现代化等同于西方化的教条主义思维，从而给其他发展中国家的现代化提供新启示和新选择。它说明："通向现代化的道路不止一条，世界上既不存在定于一尊的现代化模式，也不存在放之四海而皆准的现代化标准。"[1] "我国的实践向世界说明了一个道理：治理一个国家，推动一个国家实现现代化，并不只有西方制度模式这一条道，各国完全可以走出自己的道路来。"[2] 可以说，我们用事实宣告了"历史终结论"的破产，宣告了西方制度模式是唯一选择观念的破产。中国式现代化道路也意味着，非西方国家在现代化过程中完全可以保留和发扬自身文化，而不必全盘采用西方价值观。这也正如布罗代尔所批判的，"现代化或单一文明的胜利将导致世界各伟大文明中的历史文化的多元性终结"的看法是幼稚的。

二 中国式现代化文明形态的理论特性

目前的现代化理论大都是对西方国家经验的提炼和概括，而缺乏对中国现代化道路的总结。中国特色现代化和工业化道路的发展理论、发展阶段和发展维度是世界现代化的重要组成部分，有必要认真总结和提炼。结合现代化的理论和中国实际，中国式现代化在发展过程中具有诸多理论特性。

---

[1] 《求是》杂志编辑部：《指引全面建设社会主义现代化国家的纲领性文献》，《小康》2021年第15期。

[2] 《习近平关于社会主义政治建设论述摘编》，中央文献出版社2017年版，第7页。

（一）在党的领导下建立社会主义制度，始终坚持工业化目标

正如上文所阐述的，现代化的基本前提是工业化，但之后逐步增加了新的内容和维度。我们很难想象一个没有实现工业化的现代化国家。马克思和恩格斯在他们的经典文献中也很早就提及大工业创造了现代化的交通工具和现代化的市场，建立了现代化大工业城市这样的话语。大工业首次创造了世界历史，其实也就是创造了现代化的历史。所以说，虽然现代化不等同于工业化，但其基本内容仍然是工业化。据此类推，现代化的实质就是工业化所驱动的社会变迁过程，一个国家要实现现代化，就需要首先完成工业化。这决定了完成社会主义工业化不仅是新中国成立时的首要任务，也是改革开放以来的首要目标，这是中国式现代化道路的核心，也是新中国成立以来党和人民始终追求的目标。

工业化是发达国家强大的主要原因，也是党和国家一以贯之的追求。在新中国成立之前，毛泽东同志在《论联合政府》《论人民民主专政》中就多次强调，在革命战争结束后，必须有步骤地解决工业化问题，将中国从落后的农业国转变为先进的工业国是我们的首要任务，1949年9月政治协商会议通过的《中国人民政治协商会议共同纲领》明确提出，发展新民主主义的人民经济，稳步地变农业国为工业国[①]。但我们那时还是一个人口多、底子薄、经济落后的农业大国，这是新中国工业化的起点。如果按照西方那套传统的工业化理论模式，我们将很难快速将中国建成一个工业化国家，我们必须提出自己的工业化理论和工业化实践道路。因此，形成中国式工业化理论，探索中国式现代化和工业化道路就成为新中国成立以来的努力方向。

因此，新中国成立后，我们进行了社会主义改造，建立社会主义制度，从而建立起工业化和现代化的政治基础。1953年，我们正式提出过渡时期的总路线，即在一个相当长的时期内，逐步实现国家的社会主义工业化，并逐步实现国家对农业、手工业和资本主义工商业的社会主义

---

① 黄群慧：《中国共产党领导社会主义工业化建设及其历史经验》，《中国社会科学》2021年第7期。

改造。1956年，我们基本完成对生产资料私有制的社会主义改造，基本实现生产资料公有制和按劳分配，建立起社会主义经济制度。在此指导思想上，党的八大提出，国内主要矛盾已经不再是工人阶级和资产阶级的矛盾，而是人民对于经济文化迅速发展的需要同当前经济文化不能满足人民需要的状况之间的矛盾，全国人民的主要任务是集中力量发展社会生产力，实现国家工业化。我们也因此提出建设四个现代化：即把我国建设成为一个具有现代农业、现代工业、现代国防和现代科学技术的社会主义强国。

（二）优先发展重工业，但也强调重工业和轻工业协调发展

关于如何进行社会主义工业化，我们改革开放之前的政策是优先发展重工业，这不仅是马克思主义政治经济学的客观规律，也是当时国际政治经济环境的要求。一方面，按照马克思主义的观点，工业化不仅包括新的科学技术及相应的物质生产，还包括用机器设备去装备和改造国民经济的主要部门，如轻工业、农业、交通运输业和服务业。因此第Ⅰ部类生产快于第Ⅱ部类生产是一个客观经济规律，也是一切社会扩大再生产的共同规律。因此，毛泽东同志1956年在《论十大关系》中指出："重工业是我国建设的重点。必须优先发展生产资料的生产，这是已经定了的。"毛泽东同志也指出，"生产资料优先增长的规律，是一切社会扩大再生产的共同规律。资本主义社会如果不是生产资料优先增长，它的社会生产也不能不断增长。"[1]而且，重工业优先发展的观点还可追溯到列宁关于生产资料优先增长的理论，列宁很早就提出第Ⅰ部类优先增长规律，即生产生产资料的生产资料增长最快，生产消费资料的生产资料增长次之，消费资料增长最慢[2]。另一方面，在新中国成立之后的一段时间，我们还必须兼顾发展与安全问题。当时的国际政治形势要求我们快速发展工业，特别是重工业和国防工业。新中国成立初期，我国工业化

---

[1] 《毛泽东文集》（第八卷），人民出版社1999年版，第121页。

[2] 但这也只是问题的一个方面；另一个方面是，当消费资料与生产资料不能形成合理比例时，不仅人民享受不到经济增长本来应该带来的好处，而且会对重工业长期发展产生拖累。

道路有两种选择：第一种是走西方国家工业化道路，即根据市场需求先发展轻工业，等积累大量资本后再发展重工业；第二种是走苏联的工业化道路，即通过国家指导优先发展重工业，在较短时间内快速实现工业化，然后发展轻工业。当时的国际政治形势决定了我们必须快速实现工业化特别是重工业，只有这样才能维持政权稳定，从而在国际社会有立足之地。

当然，我们也重视工业和农业、重工业和轻工业的协调发展问题。例如，1951年，毛泽东同志指出："完成工业化当然不只是重工业和国防工业，一切必要的轻工业都应建设起来。为了完成国家工业化，必须发展农业，并逐步完成农业社会化。"① 1957年，毛泽东同志再次强调："以重工业为中心，优先发展重工业，这一条毫无问题，毫不动摇，但是在这个条件下，必须实行工业与农业同时并举，逐步建立现代化的工业和现代化的农业。"②

（三）在独立自主、自力更生基础上开展对外经济合作

在改革开放之前，我们虽然始终坚持独立自主、自力更生，但是从来不拒绝外部援助，而是努力寻求参与国际经济循环。1956年，毛泽东同志在《要团结一切可以团结的力量》的讲话中指出，"中国现在在经济上文化上还很落后，要取得真正的独立，实现国家的富强和工业现代化，还需要很长的时间，需要各国同志和人民的支持。"③在这一思想指导下，在改革开放之前，我们接受了两次比较大的外国援助，第一次是新中国成立初期苏联等东欧国家援助我国建设了156项重大工程，奠定了新中国工业化的基础；第二次是20世纪70年代以第二世界发达国家为主提供的大型成套设备的引进，弥补了我国轻工业的短板，对解决人们迫切需要的日用物资具有重要作用。

---

① 《毛泽东文集》（第六卷），人民出版社1999年版，第143、207页。
② 《毛泽东文集》（第七卷），人民出版社1999年版，第310页。
③ 《毛泽东文集》（第七卷），人民出版社1999年版，第64页。

(四) 确定并始终立足社会主义初级阶段国情

在改革开放之前,党和国家领导人就认识到我国处于一个不太发达的社会主义阶段。毛泽东同志在 1956 年召开的知识分子问题会议上就提出我国已经进入社会主义、但尚未完成的思想。毛泽东在考虑社会主义建设的时间问题时,就指出"社会主义分成两个阶段,第一个是不发达的社会主义,第二个是比较发达的社会主义"①。改革开放初期,党和国家领导人更是深刻认识到我国社会主义不发达的国情,认识到我国的基础太薄弱。1981 年 6 月,党的十一届六中全会通过《关于建国以来党的若干历史问题的决议》,第一次正式使用社会主义初级阶段的概念,指出:"尽管我们的社会主义制度还是处于初级的阶段,但是毫无疑问,我国已经建立了社会主义制度,进入了社会主义社会,任何否认这个基本事实的观点都是错误的。""当然,我们的社会主义制度由比较不完善到比较完善,必然要经历一个长久的过程。"1982 年 9 月,党的十二大报告再次提出,"我国的社会主义社会现正处在初级发展阶段",并用"物质文明还不发达"对我国社会主义初级阶段国情进行了概括。社会主义初级阶段的主要任务是提高生产力,其主要的方面就是提高工业化水平。

(五) 开创性构建社会主义市场经济体制

立足我国社会主义初级阶段的国情,我们创造性地将社会主义与市场经济相结合,构建了社会主义市场经济体制,不断满足人民生活需要的轻工业的发展,并由此继续推动重工业领域的升级改造,从而创造了中国经济增长奇迹。早在 1979 年,邓小平同志就提出"社会主义也可以搞市场经济"。1981 年的《关于建国以来党的若干历史问题的决议》正式提出"以计划经济为主,市场调节为辅"。1984 年,党的十二届三中全会提出"社会主义经济是公有制基础上的有计划的商品经济"。1987 年,党的十三大提出"社会主义有计划商品经济的体制,应该是计划与市场内在统一的体制"。1992 年,邓小平同志在"南方谈话"中进一步提出

---

① 《毛泽东文集》(第八卷),人民出版社 1999 年版,第 116 页。

要建立社会主义市场经济体制,指出"计划多一点还是市场多一点,不是社会主义与资本主义的本质区别。计划经济不等于社会主义,资本主义也有计划;市场经济不等于资本主义,社会主义也有市场"[①]的重要论断。在此基础上,党的十四大报告正式提出:"我国经济体制改革的目标是建立社会主义市场经济体制"。之后,党的十四届三中全会通过《关于建立社会主义市场经济体制若干问题的决定》。社会主义市场经济体制的确立释放了经济发展的诸多约束,对推动我国工业化快速发展起到了非常重要的作用。它有效发挥了政府"看得见的手"和市场"看不见的手"的双重作用,既可以发挥市场机制对资源配置的调节作用,也可以发挥政府的宏观调控和集中力量办大事的作用,使得我国工业化以前所未有的速度推进。

三　中国式现代化文明的发展成就

中国式现代化首先是成功实现了现代化,然后在工业化基础上,逐步向信息化和数字化转型,从而将现代化推进到新的高度。

(一) 工业化取得了历史性成就

新中国成立之初,我国基本上还是一个传统的农业国,工业化的基础异常薄弱。对此,毛泽东同志在1954年有非常形象的描述:"现在我们能造什么?能造桌子椅子,能造茶碗茶壶,能种粮食,还能磨成面粉,还能造纸,但是,一辆汽车、一架飞机、一辆坦克、一辆拖拉机都不能造"[②]。这就是我们当时的工业化基础,可以说是接近于无。但是经过"一五"计划(1953—1957年),新中国的工业生产体系从无到有地建立起来,具备了工业化的基本框架,已经可以生产包括飞机、汽车、发电设备、重型机器、机床、精密仪表、合金钢等高技术产品。五年间,我

[①]《邓小平关于建设有中国特色社会主义的论述专题摘编》,中央文献出版社1992年版,第98页。

[②]《毛泽东文集》(第六卷),人民出版社1999年版,第329页。

国新增固定资产460亿元，相当于1952年全国固定资产存量的1.9倍。从更加系统的数据来看，表1显示1952—1957年，第二产业增加值由141.8亿元增加到317亿元，第二产业增加值指数增长2.45倍；工业增加值由119.8亿元增加到271亿元，增长126.2%，工业增加值指数增长2.47倍；第二产业和工业占GDP比重从1952年的20.9%和17.6%提高到1957年的29.6%和25.3%。

对于主要的工业产品，表2显示，1957年间的生铁、粗钢和成品钢材的产量分别达到594万吨、535万吨、415万吨。五年间合计粗钢产量达到1656万吨，比1952年增长近4倍，等于旧中国从1900—1948年粗钢总产量的218%。原煤和原油分别达到1.31亿吨和146万吨，比1952年分别增长98%和231.8%。发电量达到193亿度，比1952年增长164.4%。汽车生产工业从无到有建立起来，1957年达到0.79万辆。1957年底，全国铁路通车里程达到29862公里，比1952年增长22%。而且五年内新建铁路33条，恢复铁路3条，新建、修复铁路干线、复线、支线共约一万公里。五年间，产业结构也发生了重要变化，重工业占工业总产值的比重由26.4%提高到48.4%。

此后的1957—1979年，虽然工业发展有所减速或有所起伏，但总体发展势头事实上在整个改革开放之前基本得到了较好的延续。表1显示到1978年，第二产业增加值提高到1745.2亿元，相比1957年增长4.5倍，工业增加值提高到1607亿元，增长4.93倍；第二产业增加值和工业增加值指数分别提高到1525.2和1694，相比1957年增加5.21倍和5.85倍；第二产业和工业占GDP比重则分别提高到47.9%和44.1%，相对发达国家来看，已经达到比较高的水平。表2也显示各主要工业产品在1978年之前都实现了快速增长，相对1957年，棉纱产量增长1.82倍，达到238.2万吨，化学纤维几乎从无到有建立起来；原煤产量增长3.72倍，达到6.18亿吨；原油产量增长70.27%，达到10405万吨；发电量增长12.3倍，达到2566亿度；粗钢产量增加4.94倍，达到3178万吨；乙烯工业从无到有建立，产量达到38万吨；汽车增加17.87倍，达到14.91万辆。

1978年改革开放以来，阻碍工业发展的政策制约因素进一步得到释放，工业开始了更加快速的增长。表1显示，1978—2012年①，第二产业增加值达到235162亿元，增长几乎134倍，工业增加值达到199671亿元，增长123倍。剔除价格因素的第二产业和工业增加值指数也均增长约37倍。但就第二产业和工业占GDP比重来看，则没有继续增加，反而在改革开放初期的20世纪80年代有所下降，但是之后又开始回升，基本保持了较高的比重，并在2006年达到峰值（47.9%），之后又开始下降。这意味着在2006年之后，我国的工业化已经达到高潮，逐渐进入工业化后期。这也与上文的理论分析一致，在改革开放之前，我国以重工业优先发展为目标，促进了重工业和工业相对农业和服务业的更高增速，使得工业占比大幅度上升，一定程度上脱离了经济发展的客观规律和发展阶段。但是在改革开放之后，我国调整了产业发展模式，产业发展更加协调，特别是服务业开始快速发展，在国民经济中的占比逐渐上升。此外，我们采用与我国比较优势更加吻合的发展模式，更加注重轻工业和重工业的协调发展，甚至在某个阶段更加重视发展劳动密集型的轻工业。这在外贸出口领域尤为明显，改革开放初期我国大量的加工贸易出口都属于服装、鞋帽、箱包等轻工业产品。

这一时期的工业化也体现在城市化的快速推进中，从表1可以发现，改革开放之后，城市化进入了快速发展阶段，1978—1998年城市化率几乎增加一倍，每一年增加1个百分点。1998年之后，城市化推进速度再度加快，每年增加多于1个百分点，从1998年的33.35%迅速跃升到2012年的52.57%，城市化率超过50%。

此外1978—2012年，主要的工业产品也大幅度增长（见表2）。其中，化学纤维产量增长幅度非常大，增加将近134倍，且明显高于纱和布的增长幅度，反映出轻工业领域工业化程度的提高。原煤和原油则分别增加将近5倍和1倍，其中原油产量增长相对不高主要是受制于我国石油储量少，从而更多依赖进口。发电量增加18.57倍，反映出强劲的工业生产需求。最能反映工业化生产的生铁、粗钢和成品钢材分别增长约18

---

① 1978—2012年，中国工业化快速发展，在2012年前后达到工业化的顶峰，此后进入工业化后期，经济的服务化趋势更加显著，所以本文主要考察1978—2012年的工业化发展情况。

倍、22 倍和 42 倍,中国逐渐跃升为世界上最大的钢铁生产国。化学工业中使用最多的乙烯则增加 38 倍。此外,汽车产量快速增长,增加 128 倍,达到约 1928 万辆,由于汽车的产业链供应链较长,更加能够反映我国工业综合能力的提高。

总之,新中国成立以来,中国的工业化取得了举世瞩目的成就,建立了世界上最完整的现代工业体系,拥有 39 个大类,191 个中类,525 个小类,成为唯一拥有联合国产业分类中全部工业门类的国家。在 500 多种主要工业产品中,中国有 220 多种产品的产量位居世界第一。其中,原煤、水泥、粗钢、成品钢材、化肥、发电量、电视机等主要工业产品的产量连续多年位居世界第一。2010 年开始,中国就成为世界制造业第一大国,制造业增加值几乎是美国和日本的总和,2011 年以后中国逐渐进入工业化后期[1]。到党的十八大召开,中国事实上已经完成工业化的绝大部分进程。习近平总书记 2018 年《在庆祝改革开放 40 周年大会上的讲话》中则更加精确概括了中国工业化获得的历史性成就:一是"我们用几十年时间走完了发达国家几百年走过的工业化历程",二是"建立了全世界最完整的现代工业体系",三是"我国是世界第二大经济体、制造业第一大国"[2]。《中共中央关于党的百年奋斗重大成就和历史经验的决议》也指出,我国"从积贫积弱、一穷二白到全面小康、繁荣富强,从被动挨打、饱受欺凌到独立自主、坚定自信,仅用几十年时间就走完发达国家几百年走过的工业化历程,创造了经济快速发展和社会长期稳定两大奇迹"[3]。

---

[1] 参见黄群慧《中国共产党领导社会主义工业化建设及其历史经验》,《中国社会科学》2021 年第 7 期。

[2] 习近平:《在庆祝改革开放 40 周年大会上的讲话》,《人民日报》2018 年 12 月 19 日。

[3] 《中共中央关于党的百年奋斗重大成就和历史经验的决议》,《人民日报》2021 年 11 月 17 日。

表 1　　　　　　　1952—2018 年中国工业发展成就

年份	1952	1957	1966	1978	1988	1998	2008	2018
第二产业增加值（亿元）	141.8	317.0	709.5	1745.2	6587.2	39004	149003	235162
工业增加值（亿元）	119.8	271.0	648.6	1607	5777.2	34018	130260	199671
第二产业增加值指数	100.0	245.5	564.0	1525.2	4332.6	13943	38884	58058
工业增加值指数	100.0	247.2	608.9	1694.0	4756.9	15901	45114	65580
第二产业占 GDP 比重（%）	20.9	29.6	37.9	47.9	43.8	46.2	47.4	45.3
工业占 GDP 比重（%）	17.6	25.3	34.6	44.1	38.4	40.3	41.5	38.4
城镇化率（%）	12.46	15.39	17.86	17.92	25.81	33.35	46.99	52.57

数据来源：作者根据《新中国 60 年统计资料汇编》及历年《中国统计年鉴》整理计算得出，下表同。其中第二产业增加值指数和工业增加值指数以 1952＝100 计算。

表 2　　　　　　　1952—2018 年中国主要工业产品增长情况

年份	1952	1957	1966	1978	1988	1998	2008	2012
化学纤维（万吨）	—	0.02	7.58	28.46	130.12	510.00	2415.00	3837.37
纱（万吨）	65.6	84.4	156.5	238.2	465.7	542.0	2123.3	2984
布（亿米）	38.3	50.5	73.1	110.3	187.9	241.0	710.0	848.94
原煤（亿吨）	0.66	1.31	2.52	6.18	9.80	12.50	27.88	36.5
原油（万吨）	44	146	1455	10405	13705	16100	19001	20571.14
发电量（亿千瓦小时）	73	193	825	2566	5452	11670	34669	50210.41
生铁（万吨）	193	594	1334	3479	5704	11864	47067	66354.4
粗钢（万吨）	135	535	1532	3178	5943	11559	50092	72388.22
成品钢材（万吨）	106	415	1035	2208	4689	10737	58488	95577.83
硫酸（万吨）	19.0	63.2	290.9	661.0	1111.3	2171.0	5132.7	7876.63
化肥（万吨）	3.9	15.1	240.9	869.3	1740.2	3010.0	6012.7	6832.1
乙烯（万吨）	—	—	0.54	38.03	123.21	377.30	998.26	1486.8
汽车（万辆）	—	0.79	5.59	14.91	64.47	163.00	934.55	1927.62

（二）工业化和信息化融合发展成效显著

2001 年之后，世界进入信息化阶段，利用信息技术对工业进行改造、从后工业社会向信息化社会转型成为世界各国的重要目标。在这个过程中，信息技术和相应产业不断成长壮大，从而开始了以信息化带动的新型工业化进程。根据 UNCTAD 发布的《数字经济报告 2019》，1992 年全球数据流量才 100GB/天，2002 年达到 100GB/秒，2017 年达到 46600GB/秒，2022 年达到 150700GB/秒；全球 ICT 服务业增加值在 2015 年达到 3.2 万亿美元，占全球 GDP 比重达到 4.3%。近年来，信息化更是发展到高级阶段或者说是数字化阶段。这也使得工业化出现了新的动向，即利用数字化智能化技术对传统工业进行改造，这是奠定未来世界各国工业和制造业国际竞争力的关键所在。

在快速推进工业化进程的同时，中国也密切注意到国际社会工业化的新形势和新动向。为了追赶发达国家利用信息技术对工业行业进行改造的大潮流和生产力发展趋势，我们 2001 年就与时俱进地提出要走新型工业化道路，推动工业化和信息化融合发展。党的十六大报告首次正式提出我国应该走新型工业化道路，要求"坚持以信息化带动工业化，以工业化促进信息化，走出一条科技含量高、经济效益好、资源消耗低、环境污染少、人力资源优势得到充分发挥的发展道路"[①]。新型工业化是相对于传统工业化而言的，更加强调与工业化和信息化的融合。党的十六大以后，我国一直坚持走新型工业化道路，其内涵也结合全面建成小康社会要求逐步丰富。党的十七大报告、十八大报告和十九大报告都强调，坚持走中国特色新型工业化道路，推动信息化和工业化深度融合。党的十九届五中全会提出，到 2035 年基本实现新型工业化、信息化、城镇化、农业现代化，即完成信息科技成果对国民经济主要部门的改造，"十四五"规划进一步重申了这个目标。可以说，在新时代和新发展阶段，我国现代化的新任务就是用信息化和数字化来对国民经济各部门进行改造，这也是世界各国现代化的新目标和新任务。中国式现代化的目标也包括这些内容，但有新的属性和任务。

从我国的发展实践看，2001 年中国的信息技术和信息产业就开始发展，但是还比较滞后。根据国际电信联盟的数据，当时我国互联网接入比例、移动电话使用比例、固定宽带和移动宽带使用比例都处于非常低的水平。2001 年时，中国还在工业化中期，信息化可以说是刚起步，其

---

① 江泽民：《全面建设小康社会，开创中国特色社会主义事业新局面》，《人民日报》2002 年 11 月 18 日。

中互联网使用比例仅1.78%，移动电话使用比例仅6.61%，固定宽带和移动宽带的使用几乎为零。此后，中国提出信息化和工业化融合发展战略，信息化开始加速，到2010年互联网使用比例已经达到34.3%，移动电话已经达到比较高的水平为62.76%，但固定宽带和移动宽带的使用比例仍比较低，分别为9.23%与3.44%。2010年之后，中国信息化进入更快速的发展阶段，到2020年前后，各项指标与发达国家已经相差较小了，如果进一步考虑中国人口基数和农村地区的制约，那么与发达国家基本没有差距，特别是在城市地区甚至优于发达国家。

而且，近20年我国信息基础设施快速发展，到2019年前后，我国已经基本赶上美国、日本和德国的发展水平。根据国家统计局数据，2019年我国各行业中使用计算机的人数比例已经比较高，全部行业达到32%，采矿业、制造业、电热燃气及水生产和供应业分别达到25%、28%和68%。除了建筑业等少数几个行业外，其他的服务业中计算机的使用比例也较高，其中，信息传输、软件和信息技术业的比例最高，达到131%，教育业达到108%。就企业利用互联网网站来看，全部行业的使用比例达到了51%，制造业的使用比例达到67%，其他行业的使用比例都普遍较高。但除了住宿和餐饮业，信息传输、软件和信息技术业以及文化、体育和娱乐业外，其他行业的使用比例都还比较低，制造业的比例仅10.2%，有进一步提高的潜力。可以说，我国已经实现了信息化的初级阶段任务，基本完成一般的信息化通信和传输技术对国民经济各部门的技术改造。

（三）产业数字化改造为中国现代化文明进入新阶段准备了生产力基础

数字技术和数字经济加快发展，为中国现代化向数字化全面转型奠定了物质技术和知识基础。数字化可以说是信息化的高级发展阶段，世界各国正通过数字化技术对传统产业进行改造升级，中国也面临这一任务。在信息化初级阶段的发展基础上，我国开始对国民经济各部门进行信息化的高级阶段改造（即数字化改造）。虽然中国的数字化水平与美国仍还有一些差距，但是由于中国超大规模市场优势，中国的数字经济规模发展已经仅次于美国，其他国家受市场大小的限制，在数字经济方面显然落后于中国和美国。而就数字经济规模、平台企业数量、工业机器人的使用数量、产业数字化程度等指标看，中国几乎与美国并驾齐驱，成为引领全球数字经济发展的主要国家。

虽然我国数字基础设施还处于发展的早期阶段，但是近年也取得了初步的成就。在5G通信方面，我国2020年就实现5G网络基本覆盖全国地级以上城市主城区；2020年，我国新开通5G基站超过60万个，连接的5G终端机器数量超过2亿个；2021年11月，工信部召开的"十四五"信息通信业发展规划会指出我国已建成5G基站超过115万个，占全球的70%以上，5G终端用户达到4.5亿户，占全球的80%以上。2021年11月，工业和信息化部披露我国已建成"5G+工业互联网"项目超过1800个，覆盖22个重点行业领域。2022年1月，工业和信息化部发布的《2021年通信业统计公报》数据显示截至2021年底，我国累计建成并开通5G基站142.5万个，总量占全球的60%以上。在数据中心建设方面，因为大数据和人工智能的广泛应用，互联网龙头企业建成了诸多超大规模数据中心。在工业互联网方面，诸多大型制造业企业都在加快建设行业层面的工业互联网平台，部署与机械装备相互连接的边缘计算网络。在人工智能方面，国内大型互联网企业正在建设人工智能开放平台，在自动驾驶、人脸识别、医疗读片等领域已经实现一定突破。在此基础上，数据也成为一种新的生产要素，2020年4月出台的《中共中央国务院关于构建更加完善的要素市场化配置体制机制的意见》首次将数据作为一种新型生产要素写入文件，提出在农业、工业、交通、教育等领域开发各种数据应用场景。可以预见在不久的将来，随着我国数字基础设施的完善，必将成为我国工业升级和经济数字化转型的重要推动因素。

中国现代化文明形态与世界其他文明也有诸多共同点，吸收并有效利用了世界一切文明的优秀成果，特别是生产力方面的成果。这种文明的共同点也正是其世界意义的体现。但是中国现代化文明形态与其他文明特别是西方文明有明显不同。对此，习近平总书记概括为以下几个方面："我们建设的现代化必须是具有中国特色、符合中国实际的。我国现代化是人口规模巨大的现代化，是全体人民共同富裕的现代化，是物质文明和精神文明相协调的现代化，是人与自然和谐共生的现代化，是走和平发展道路的现代化，这是我国现代化建设必须坚持的方向。"[1]

中国现代化文明形态在和平发展中形成，也追求并有利于世界和平发展。习近平总书记始终强调中国"走和平发展道路的现代化"，并且指出"中国走和平发展道路，不是权宜之计，更不是外交辞令，而是从历史、现实、未来的客观判断中得出的结论，是思想自信和实践自觉的有机统一"[2]。这种和平发展的中国现代化道路为世界发展做出了突出贡献。例如，中国全面脱贫就是对联合国千年发展目标的最大贡献，解决了几亿人的贫困问题。中国对世界经济增长的贡献越来越大。2008年国际金融危机之后，随着中国工业化的快速推进，中国成为全球经济增长最大拉动因素，连续多年对世界经济增长贡献率超过30%。中国推动的共建"一带一路"使得更多发展中国家和内陆国家融入全球经济地理，促进了这些国家的发展，是对世界经济平衡发展的重大贡献。总之，中国现代化文明形态是马克思主义与中华文明深刻结合的产物，它终结了西方现代资本主义文明形态的唯一性和话语霸权，为那些既希望实现工业化又想保持自身独立自主的发展中国家提供了新的选择，为解决人类社会发展问题提供了中华文明的智慧。

---

[1] 习近平：《把握新发展阶段，贯彻新发展理念，构建新发展格局》，《求是》2021年第9期。

[2] 《习近平总书记系列重要讲话读本（2016年版）》，人民出版社2016年版，第263页。

第五编

中国式现代化与中格丝路发展新机遇

中国现代化进程中的教育
国际合作与交流

卢雨菁[*]

党的二十大报告指出："中国式现代化，是中国共产党领导的社会主义现代化，既有各国现代化的共同特征，更有基于自己国情的中国特色。"[①] 在中国式现代化建设进程中，党中央高度重视我国教育事业。党的二十大报告全面擘画了我国教育事业发展蓝图，明确指出："办好人民满意的教育。教育是国之大计、党之大计。"[②] 中国教育国际合作与交流也随着中国式现代化进程不断发展壮大，成为"一带一路"倡议民心相通友好合作的重要方面。展望未来，全面建设社会主义现代化国家时期，随着教育强国战略的推进，我国教育国际合作与交流的深度和广度，也必将进一步提高。

一 中国式现代化与中国教育国际合作发展

改革开放以来，中国高等教育事业蓬勃发展。邓小平1983年提出

---

[*] 卢雨菁，兰州大学外国语学院教授。
[①] 习近平：《高举中国特色社会主义伟大旗帜　为全面建设社会主义现代化国家而团结奋斗——在中国共产党第二十次全国代表大会上的报告》，《人民日报》2022年10月26日。
[②] 习近平：《高举中国特色社会主义伟大旗帜　为全面建设社会主义现代化国家而团结奋斗——在中国共产党第二十次全国代表大会上的报告》，《人民日报》2022年10月26日。

"教育要面向现代化,面向世界,面向未来"的要求,为教育改革指明了方向。中共中央1985年颁布《关于教育体制改革的决定》,提出大学在总结历史和现实经验的同时,要积极借鉴国外大学的办学和改革经验,使大学的国际化加快进行①。

21世纪以来,随着经济发展和国际交流日趋频繁,中国教育国际化日益加深,教育国际合作增强是很多大学的愿景。国家政策、顶层设计推动着国内外大学、学术机构的交流。2009年,中国与东盟国家达成共识,将"双十万学生流动计划"作为深化双方战略合作伙伴关系的倡议之一,即到2020年,东盟来华留学生和中国到东盟的留学生都将达到10万人规模,以增强高等教育领域的国际合作②。这其中也包括中国与格鲁吉亚的交流。

建设世界一流大学与一流学科是中国建设世界高等教育强国与建成创新型国家的重要战略决策。2015年,国务院印发《统筹推进世界一流大学和一流学科建设总体方案》,要提高中国高等教育的竞争力,培养世界一流的教师队伍,实行开放教育,在高等教育阶段需要更多的开放、更多的协作③。

2016年,中央提出深化新时期"教育对外开放"和教育界共建"一带一路"的重大倡议,在世界多极化和全球化趋势下,教育界顺应文化多样和人文沟通,追求构建"人类文明共同体"。

2020年,国家印发《教育部等八部门关于加快和扩大新时代教育对外开放的意见》,推动中国教育以更加开放自信主动的姿态走向世界舞台④。

党的二十大报告也强调"坚持教育优先发展",中央提出深化新时期

---

① 《中共中央关于教育体制改革的决定》,《十二大以来重要文献选编》(中),人民出版社1985年版。
② 《"双十万计划"引发工薪家庭东南亚留学潮》,搜狐出国,http://goabroad.sohu.com/20100902/n274661858.shtml,2010年9月2日。
③ 《国务院印发统筹推进世界一流大学和一流学科建设总体方案》,中华人民共和国中央人民政府,www.gov.cn/zhengce/content/2015-11/05/content_10269.htm,2015年11月5日。
④ 《教育部等八部门印发意见 加快和扩大新时代教育对外开放》,教育部,http://www.moe.gov.cn/jyb_xwfb/s5147/202006/t20200623_467784.html,2020年6月23日。

"教育对外开放"和教育界共建"一带一路"的重大倡议，彰显着教育对于构建"人类文明共同体"的不懈追求[①]。推进教育现代化，要坚持对外开放不动摇，加强同世界各国的互容、互鉴、互通。国际合作与交流在我国教育事业中的地位和作用进一步凸显。

以上概略的时间线，说明中国教育，尤其是中国高等教育国际化始终与中国现代化同步。

二 中国教育布局变化及中外双向留学生变化

教育国际化过程中不可缺少的就是"走出去，请进来"。可以从国际中文教育规模、来华留学生人数、中国出国留学生人数、中国留学生回国创业、双向留学生公费自费比例等方面来分析。

1. 自全球首家孔子学院 2004 年 11 月 21 日在韩国首尔成立，孔子学院给世界各地的汉语学习者提供规范、权威的现代汉语教材；提供了最正规、最主要的汉语教学渠道。孔子学院在很多国家的建立，正是孔子"四海之内皆兄弟""和而不同"以及"君子以文会友，以友辅仁"思想的实践，为发展中国与世界各国的友好关系，增进世界各国人民对中国语言文化的理解，为各国汉语学习者提供方便、优良的学习条件做出了贡献。截至 2022 年，中国同 181 个建交国有教育合作与交流，有 180 多个国家和地区开展中文教学，在 159 个国家和地区合办孔子学院/课堂，81 个国家将中文纳入国民教育体系，与 58 个国家/地区签署学历学位互认协议。在格鲁吉亚的孔子学院也从无到有，由一变三。

2. 中国经济的发展以及了解中华文化后有意深入学习的来华留学生人数增加。改革开放以来，来华留学进入新时期，中国从 1979—2000 年的 22 年里就累计接受了约 39.4 万人次各类来华留学生。中国社会政治稳定，经济建设实现持续高速发展，综合国力和国际地位显著提高，来华

[①] 《党的二十大代表热议——加快实施创新驱动发展战略》，《人民日报》2022 年 10 月 22 日。

留学工作有大发展。来华留学生数量增幅巨大,从1992年的1.4万到1996年的4.1万,5年年均增速逾30%,留学生层次也明显提高。自费留学生人数也大幅度增加,成为来华留学生的主流。到2018年,"共有来自196个国家和地区的492185名各类外国留学人员在全国31个省(区、市)的1004所高等院校学习[1]",其中来自亚洲的留学生295043人,占59.95%〔如果和2004的数据"共有来自178个国家和地区的110844名各类外国留学人员在全国31个省(区、市)的420所高等院校学习"相比,增长趋势更为显著〕。包括美国、法国、俄罗斯、日本、韩国等15个国家的留学生人数数以万计。相比之下,来自格鲁吉亚的留学生仅有几十名,数量和比例有待大幅度提高。

根据我国与有关国家之间的教育交流协议和交流计划,2000年教育部向152个国家提供了中国政府奖学金名额。2000年以来每年有很多留学生和外国学者获得教育部"长城奖学金"(通过联合国教科文组织提供)、"优秀生奖学金""外国汉语教师短期研修奖学金""HSK优胜者奖学金"和"中华文化研究奖学金"等专项奖学金来华学习或从事研究。后来,部分高等学校还有"校长奖学金",部分企业也提供企业奖学金,如腾讯、阿里巴巴等。中国政府奖学金生总体占比12.81%。世界外国留学生教育发展的事实证明,一个国家的经济发展是吸引大量外国留学生的先决条件之一。经济优势代表一个国家的形象,影响一个国家的方方面面。中国经济的发展速度,中国现代化的加速,势必吸引更多外国留学生前来学习交流。[2]

目前看,来自格鲁吉亚的绝大多数留学生是奖学金生,自费留学者数量很少。可以预期,在不远的将来有越来越多的格鲁吉亚学生到中国高校学习。

3. 出国留学和回国创业人数变化

改革开放后,出国留学一直是一种风潮,中国留学生从祖国的四面

---

[1] 《2018年来华留学统计》,教育部,http://www.moe.gov.cn/jyb_xwfb/gzdt_gzdt/s5987/201904/t20190412_377692.html,2019年4月12日。

[2] 《当前我国发展来华留学生教育的意义与优势分析》,《高教探索》2010年第5期。

八方，奔赴世界各个角落，从欧美、澳新，到东南亚，留学生或看重留学国的自然环境，或喜欢当地的人文环境，也由于当地的留学政策比如奖学金、免费医疗等，更多还是因为学科相关、世界名校、学业与就业的关系等。

每年的留学生人数不等，但过去几十年一直呈现上升趋势，统计数据上看，1978 至 2019 年度，各类出国留学人员累计达 656.06 万人，其中 165.62 万人正在国外进行相关阶段的学习或研究；490.44 万人已完成。即使在疫情因素影响下的 2021 年度我国出国留学人员总数为 66.21 万人。其中，国家公派 3.02 万人，单位公派 3.56 万人，自费留学 59.63 万人。

近年来回国创业的留学人员增多对中国经济、教育发展带来一些变化。"2021 年回国创新创业的留学人员首次超过 100 万！"[1] 1978—2019 年各类出国留学人员 650 万人中回国 420 余万人。其中改革开放的前 30 年间，我国公费、自费等各类出国留学生总数达 139 万人，只有 39 万人回国[2]。新冠疫情及国际关系变化等因素加速推动海归回国潮流。2020 年留学生学成回国 77.7 万人，2021 年回国就业学生估计达到 104.9 万人。这也是教育国际化的一个侧面印证。

因疫情出国留学势头有所减缓，但 2021 国际教育高峰论坛发布的《2021 年全国留学报告》[3] 显示，原计划留学的人中，91% 坚持出国留学计划。提升自我能力是意向留学人群的主要目的。拓展国际视野、学习国外先进丰富人生经历、提高外语能力，以及就业前景等方面，是留学生最主要考虑的因素。"在过去的 2021 年，国家全面支持留学，鼓励回国，认为留学生应该来去自由，在未来的祖国发展中发挥重要作用。"[4]

---

[1] 中国国际人才交流大会官网：http：//www.ciep.gov.cn/content/2022 - 11/30/content_25491323.htm，2022 年 11 月 30 日。
[2] 《我国公费、自费等各类留学生回国率不足三成》，晨报，http：//news.sohu.com/20090326/n263011598.shtml，2009 年 3 月 26 日。
[3] 《2021 年度全国留学报告》，搜狐网，https：//www.sohu.com/a/501268719_99945202，2021 年 11 月 15 日。
[4] 《2021 留学大数据公布，留学人数持续增长》，搜狐网，https：//www.sohu.com/a/515785582_543744，2022 年 1 月 13 日。

4. 双向留学生（出国留学人数和来华留学）中自费—公费比例在过去20年一直呈现上升趋势，自费—公费比基本在9∶1。随着中外合作办学和中国高等教育国际化水平提升，中国在2018年前后成为亚洲学生重要留学目的国，且来华留学生中自费生占大多数①。而出国留学的中国学生，在2010年时就已经占全部留学人数的90%以上②，目前，到格鲁吉亚留学的中国学生还比较少，但也实现了由个位数到两位数的突破。

三 中国式现代化进程与中外合作办学、人文交流、科研合作

2017年12月，《关于加强和改进中外人文交流工作的若干意见》实行。《意见》指出，要构建语言互通工作机制，推动我国与世界各国语言互通，开辟多种层次语言文化交流渠道。着力加大汉语国际推广力度，支持更多国家将汉语教学纳入国民教育体系，努力将孔子学院打造成国际一流的语言推广机构。健全国内高校外语学科体系，加快培养非通用语人才，不断提升广大民众的语言交流能力③。

回顾历史，"从1983年中德合作南京建筑职业技术教育中心成立，1986年中美合作南京大学—霍普金斯大学中美文化交流中心成立，这分别是中外合作职教和高教机构诞生的标志，合作办学在探索中起步。"④熊建辉在2019年的文章中将中国的合作办学分为4个阶段：第一，改革开放之初的起步阶段。第二，20世纪90年代经济转型期开始的快速发展阶段，尤其是1995年国家教委颁布的《中外合作办学暂行规定》，为合

---

① 《最新〈中国留学发展报告〉：来华留学生中自费生占大多数》，华商网，http://news.hsw.cn/system/2022/0928/1527086.shtml，2022年9月28日。
② 《90%以上的中国留学生都是自费留学》，留学网，https://m.liuxue86.com/a/207169.html，2011年3月24日。
③ 《中共中央办公厅 国务院办公厅印发〈关于加强和改进中外人文交流工作的若干意见〉》，教育部，www.moe.gov.cn/jyb_xwfb/s6052/moe_838/201712/t20171222_322183.html，2017年12月21日。
④ 《熊建辉：中外合作办学的四大发展阶段》，搜狐网，https://www.sohu.com/a/289917862_380485，2019年1月18日。

作办学提供了直接可遵循的政策依据。合作办学规模迅速扩大，2002年底就已经覆盖整个教育体系。第三，在市场经济大潮中，在中国现代化的进程中，中外合作办学为中国教育国际化发挥了积极作用；千禧年后"入世"，两份重要文件，即2003年国务院颁布的《中华人民共和国中外合作办学条例》，和2004年教育部颁布的《中华人民共和国中外合作办学条例实施办法》推动有法可依、调适发展。第四，伴随着中国教育对外开放从"扩大"迈向"做好"，中外合作办学亦进入转型升级、内涵发展的新时代。经过四十年发展，合作办学拓宽了我国人才培养途径，丰富了国内特别是高等教育资源的供给，同时也以文化交流窗口的形式，服务中外人文交流、促进全面对外开放和社会主义现代化建设，沟通中国与世界的重要途径。

在格鲁吉亚，有德国学校、英国学校、美国学校、芬兰学校等合作盈利的学校，但是没有一所盈利的中国学校。教育合作方面的工作主要集中在两所孔子学院和一所孔子课堂。期望不久的将来，两国教育合作在中小学和高等院校层面均有所突破，院系之间的合作意向逐渐变为实实在在的教学和科研合作。

《关于加强和改进中外人文交流工作的若干意见》指出，要丰富和拓展人文交流的内涵和领域，打造人文交流国际知名品牌。坚持走出去和引进来双向发力，重点支持汉语、中医药、武术、美食、节日民俗以及其他非物质文化遗产等代表性项目走出去，深化中外留学与合作办学，高校和科研机构国际协同创新，文物、美术和音乐展演，大型体育赛事举办和重点体育项目发展等方面的合作。在人文交流各领域形成一批有国际影响力的品牌项目，进一步丰富中外人文交流年度主题。

冯仲平认为，"国之交在于民相亲，民相亲在于心相通……随着中国的快速发展和与外部世界的广泛交往，世界了解中国的愿望日益增加。孔子学院和世界中国学论坛在短短几年间成为品牌项目，中国电视剧在周边及非洲等国家和地区受到追捧……逐年增多的中国出国留学生、游客、企业家，促进了中华文化的海外传播，也带动了世界各地新的持续不断的汉语热、中医热、武术热……"①

在中国经济蓬勃发展，中国式现代化进程不断加速的大背景下，国际合作教育、人文交流汇聚，扩大面向周边国家的教育开放，中国与海外高校间的合作日渐频繁。比如2015年10月，由兰州大学牵头，复旦大学、北京师范大学、俄罗斯乌拉尔国立经济大学等47所中外高校在甘肃敦煌发起成立的"一带一路"高校联盟，发布了《敦煌共识》，倡建高校国际联盟智库，秉承"互联互通、开放包容、协同创新、合作共赢"的理念，共同打造"一带一路"高等教育共同体，推动沿线国家和地区高校之间在教育、科技、文化等领域的全面交流合作，服务沿线国家和地区的经济社会发展。截至2018年，联盟已发展成为拥有178所成员高校、覆盖27个国家和地区、具有较强影响力的"一带一路"沿线高校交流合作新平台。中格学者科研合作、共同参会、学生交换的数量逐年上升。2021年，兰州大学的"中欧丝路审美文化双边论坛"国际会议，语言学前沿问题研究与中文教育"国际学术会议如期举办，孔子学院参与其中。

人文交流格局完善，中外"心联通"更紧。中国和格鲁吉亚高层互访增多，民间往来频繁形成多元互动新格局。中国传媒大学、兰州大学外语学院、郑州大学等中方院校与格方大学和研究机构的互动频繁，为双边关系发展注入了力量。中国搭建全球性高端教育合作平台，为全球教育治理贡献智慧和力量。在与格鲁吉亚的教育往来中，格方很多院校表达了与中方院校合作的愿望，不仅在高校层面，格方的中小学也愿与中国学校建姊妹学校关系互访互学，第比利斯98学校与南京四中的姊妹关系为例证之一。

四 "一带一路"倡议与中格教育合作

中格两国中高层互动日益频繁，对于两国教育、文化、人文交流与

---

① 《中外人文交流的新方向》，搜狐网，https：//www.sohu.com/a/221573212_115423，2018年2月8日。

合作有很大推动作用。

2022年9月22日，驻格鲁吉亚大使周谦出席中共中央对外联络部副部长钱洪山同格鲁吉亚议会教育科学委员会主席、格中友好小组主席阿米拉赫瓦里的视频会晤。格方表示，"格鲁吉亚梦想—民主格鲁吉亚"党高度重视发展两党两国关系，钦佩中共取得的巨大执政成就，愿同中共加强治党治国经验交流，通过党际渠道深化双边政治、经济、人文等各领域合作[1]。23日，周大使拜会格鲁吉亚副总理兼文化、体育和青年事务部部长楚卢基亚尼，双方表示愿以中格建交30周年为契机，深入开展人文合作。周大使回顾了近年中格文化领域交流成果，欢迎格方积极参与"一带一路"框架下的各项文化合作，表示愿在疫情形势缓和后，在互办展览、文艺团组访问表演、电影交流等方面进一步加强合作。格方表示中国是格对外文化交流与合作的重点方向，愿与中方一道创新文化合作方式，推动两国文化交流取得新进展[2]。27日，驻格鲁吉亚大使周谦会见格鲁吉亚议会文化委员会主席博尔克瓦泽，介绍了中国文化立法及文化建设方面的经验成果，回顾了中格文化交流成果，欢迎格方积极参与"一带一路"框架下的各项文化合作。格方表示近年来格中保持高水平文化交流，愿通过具体项目进一步推动两国文化合作。中共二十大后的11月7日，驻格鲁吉亚大使周谦拜会格议会副议长埃努基泽，宣介党的二十大精神，分享中国现代化成就与经验。周大使介绍了二十大报告中关于中国未来发展任务、中国式现代化、全过程人民民主等内容，表示中方将以二十大为契机，继续深化中格各领域务实合作。格方祝贺中共二十大取得圆满成功，赞叹中国发展成就，表示愿与中国共产党就治国理政开展深入交流，广泛借鉴中国式现代化经验。

此前，周大使就中共二十大等接受格媒体中心书面采访，回答了格方关切，表示中国愿同格鲁吉亚在内的世界各国一道，为和平发展尽力，为团结进步担当，为全球治理贡献智慧，携手构建人类命运共同体，共

---

[1] 中华人民共和国驻格鲁吉亚大使馆：《驻格鲁吉亚大使周谦出席中联部副部长钱洪山同格议会教育科学委员会主席、格中友好小组主席阿米拉赫瓦里视频会晤》，http://ge.china-embassy.gov.cn/chn/，2022年9月23日。

[2] 本条及以下相关信息均来自中华人民共和国驻格鲁吉亚大使馆网站。

同开创更加美好的世界。中国政府高度重视在"一带一路"框架下与格方共同推进中间走廊建设。中资企业在格承建了大量的基础设施项目,目前在建的重点项目有 E60 公路、现代化铁路等,很多项目建设已接近尾声,顺利通车后,将显著缩短通行时间,提高格交通运输能力,强化格交通枢纽作用,为中间走廊的发展提供更强大的基础设施支撑。越来越多的中国企业正进入格鲁吉亚市场并积极关注中间走廊建设。

尽管地缘政治环境良好,格鲁吉亚的地理条件却多沟壑、峡谷和几乎无法逾越的山脉,阻碍了该国的交通运输。建设克服地理环境的基础设施需要大量投资,以及知识和经验。中国企业正重塑格鲁吉亚的地理环境,使第比利斯在各种欧亚贸易路线上处于更好的位置。比如,2019年中铁二十三局集团有限公司开始在格鲁吉亚建造全长 22.7 公里的公路,总成本估计约合 4.286 亿美元。这是国际南北运输走廊的一部分。中企在格鲁吉亚的激增将改变该国的交通运输能力[①]。格鲁吉亚驻华大使阿尔赤·卡岚第亚在 2022 年 9 月接受中国网采访时说:"2021 年 12 月开通了从中国(甘肃)到格鲁吉亚的双向直达货运列车。我们希望该线路在双边经贸合作中发挥有益作用,因为这是首次开通从中国(甘肃)至格鲁吉亚首都第比利斯的货运列车。我们正计划着开辟更多线路。"他还说"格鲁吉亚是中国以外第一个举办有关'一带一路'论坛的国家……格鲁吉亚于 2015 年举办了第一届第比利斯丝绸之路国际论坛,加上 2017 年和 2019 年,总共举办了三届。今年,我们计划继续举办论坛,诚邀合作伙伴和中国朋友,格鲁吉亚将为大家提供平台,共商问题,一起探讨'一带一路'倡议框架下有望在格鲁吉亚开展的项目,这也体现出'一带一路'倡议对我们的重要性。[②]"

建交 30 年来,中国与格鲁吉亚始终是相互信任的好朋友,真诚合作的好伙伴,两国彼此尊重,互助合作,中格共建"一带一路"和各领域务实合作不断走深走实。双边贸易额比建交之初的 368 万美元增长了 400

---

① 《埃米尔·阿维达利亚尼:中国在改变格鲁吉亚的地貌》,环球时报,https://mil.news.sina.com.cn/2022-10-11/doc-imqqsmrp2180192.shtml,2022 年 10 月 11 日。

② 《红星何以照耀中国 | 格鲁吉亚驻华大使谈他眼中的"一带一路"》,中国网,https://news.ycwb.com/2022-09/30/content_41079259.htm,2022 年 9 月 30 日。

多倍。2022年1—6月中国是格鲁吉亚第三大贸易伙伴，中方已成为格最大出口市场[1]。做好下一个30年合作规划，秉持相互尊重、平等互利精神，在"一带一路"框架下继续深化两国关系健康、稳定发展，其中教育合作必不能少。中格两个有悠久历史的国家在发展中交流互鉴、互利共赢意义深远。

格鲁吉亚经济中心网记者莉安娜回忆，自己第一次来中国是在2015年，此后多次到访中国各地。她认为，中共二十大不仅是中国政治生活中的大事，也具有国际意义。中国是世界工厂和世界经济的引擎，中国的稳定和繁荣与国际社会的政治、经济气候息息相关[2]。格鲁吉亚与中国在教育方面合作的前景值得展望。

---

[1] 《2022年1—6月中国是格鲁吉亚第三大贸易伙伴》，商务部：http://www.mofcom.gov.cn/article/zwjg/zwxw/zwxwoy/202207/20220703334607.shtml，2022年7月20日。

[2] 《我在中国看二十大——格鲁吉亚记者：中国以开放的姿态面向世界》，新浪网，https://news.sina.com.cn/gov/xlxw/2022-10-20/doc-imqqsmrp3188491.shtml，2022年10月20日。

中国"一带一路"倡议和格鲁吉亚的前景

塔玛尔·多尔巴拉[*]

一 引言

在苏联解体后,欧洲的运输战略为通过发展国际运输走廊来扩大欧洲市场,这被视为转型国家进入欧洲空间的最佳途径之一。对欧盟而言,实现运输多样化,并通过格鲁吉亚和南高加索建立新的运输走廊作为经过俄罗斯的运输走廊的替代方案,这很重要。新的现实改变了格鲁吉亚的地缘战略功能,由于其独特的交通地理位置,格鲁吉亚被纳入"TRACECA"运输走廊,该走廊连接欧洲和亚洲,并为格鲁吉亚提供过境货物。这是格鲁吉亚进行区域合作、确保安全和可持续发展的保障。对我们而言,研究下列问题的可能性是很重要的:通过中国"一带一路"倡议使格鲁吉亚保持过境功能和发展机会,从而参与欧亚大陆重要进程。

二 关于格鲁吉亚过境功能的历史回顾

格鲁吉亚的过境功能对该国发展的重要性和作用始于19世纪。1821年,俄国在格鲁吉亚黑海沿岸开设了库勒维[列杜特-卡列(Redut-

---

[*] 塔玛尔·多尔巴拉,格鲁吉亚第比利斯国立大学教授、社会与政治学院院长。

Kale）] 佛朗哥港，1823 年，开始在敖德萨和列杜特—卡列港口之间开展定期运输。1828 年，《梯弗里斯公报》（Тифлисские ведомости）第六版报道："第比利斯 [旧称梯弗里斯（Tiflis/Тифлисские）] 地理位置优越，靠近伊朗边境因而有机会吸引亚洲商人……拥有黑海港口（尤其是现在我们拥有了里奥尼河河口），这些都为我们与欧洲建立联系提供了有利条件。此外，俄国将有机会向亚洲人销售其产品"。库勒维—第比利斯过境路线有助于欧洲产品在伊朗市场占据主导地位，同时却损害了俄罗斯贸易和工业发展的前景，因为俄罗斯产品价格更高，质量更低。伊朗和格鲁吉亚商人绕过俄罗斯市场前往莱比锡，带去更便宜、更优质的欧洲产品。这就是为什么俄罗斯制造商要请求其政府废除 1821 年制定的优惠政策，该政策最终于 1831 年废除。然而，法国和德国已经掌握了亚洲市场，他们并没有回到俄罗斯市场，而是继续通过土耳其进行贸易。[①]

旧的过境路线通过河流 [里奥尼河－库拉河（Rioni-Mtkvari）] 和陆地系统将黑海与里海相连，享受了长达 10 年的关税和贸易优惠政策，因此，俄罗斯通过将从土耳其至伊朗的路线迁移至外高加索，为欧洲提供了进入伊朗市场的临时途径，从而加强了其在欧洲和东方的政治影响力。从欧洲到伊朗的过境路线由库勒维—第比利斯迁移至特拉佩松德—埃尔祖鲁姆。第比利斯失去了在过境方面的重要地位。格鲁吉亚和外高加索参与世界贸易的第一次尝试以失败告终。

苏联时期，格鲁吉亚实行计划经济框架，其分工由苏联的共同利益所决定。格鲁吉亚独立后，有必要自行决定其在全球政治和经济空间中的作用。格鲁吉亚没有战略性自然资源，但有着优越的交通地理位置，这使其具备战略性过境功能，也成为格鲁吉亚制定外交和国内政策的主要依据。

[①] Janashia, S., *History of Georgia from Ancient Times to the End of 19 – th Century*. Tbilisi, 1943.

三　格鲁吉亚的过境功能和国际运输走廊

当今世界，国际交通走廊分布广泛，形成了一个复杂的技术系统，将各种运输和通信组合在一起，实现了物资、金融和信息的流动与同步。格鲁吉亚凭借其独特的交通地理位置，参与了连接欧亚的运输走廊"TRACECA"。欧洲—高加索—亚洲运输走廊——"TRACECA"是在欧盟的协助下建立的。该项目旨在支持欧亚区域国家实现政治和经济自由，以便这些国家能够参与世界市场并发展地区关系，实现过境路线的多样化。"TRACECA"路线为：中国（连云港）—德鲁日巴过境站—哈萨克斯坦—乌兹别克斯坦—土库曼斯坦—阿塞拜疆—格鲁吉亚—波季港。"TRACECA"在波季分为两条支线。线路1：波季—乌克兰（敖德萨）—乔普（Chop）过境站—斯洛伐克—奥地利。线路2：波季—保加利亚—罗马尼亚—奥地利。

"TRACECA"自1996年开始运营，当时根据《萨拉赫斯协定》，开始将雪佛龙石油从哈萨克斯坦通过铁路运输至巴统港，并从该地通过海运运输至国际市场。为了从格鲁吉亚出口阿塞拜疆石油，修建了巴库—苏普萨管道，这为该走廊带来了"能源"影响力。然而，"TRACECA"对于各成员国的重要程度并不相同。中亚面向俄罗斯和伊朗的走廊，黑海以西则面向泛欧。欧洲只有在极少数情况下才会对穿过中亚的乌克兰—南高加索走廊感兴趣。只有在高加索地区，才会重视该走廊。

格鲁吉亚的交通基础设施和法律基础或多或少地确保了其过境潜力的开发。但管理的分散阻碍了格鲁吉亚对统一的过境政策的细化和实施。格鲁吉亚的关税没有优势。港口服务也遭遇同样的情况。格鲁吉亚的港口费明显高于黑海盆地其他港口。运输基础设施的各参与方以获得短期最大利润为目标。参与国数量众多，且各有打算。走廊沿线国家无法就统一的关税和海关准则达成一致。该走廊采取多式联运，这提高了项目成本，并延长了运输时间。由于格鲁吉亚国内市场规模较小，大部分进出口流量流向南高加索和中亚地区。格鲁吉亚所有类型的运输均参与过境业务。如果按不同的运输类型来看总周转量，我们会发现，公路汽车运输无疑占据最大份额。87%的过境货物针对亚美尼亚和阿塞拜疆通过海运运输，其余针对中亚。

表1　　　　　　　　货物运输（按运输模式）　　　　（单位：百万吨）

运输模式	2006	2007	2008	2009	2010	2011	2012	2013	2014	2015	2016
民用航空	0.017	0.012	0.017	0.012	0.015	0.016	0.016	0.017	0.017	0.015	0.033
公路	27.8	27.5	27.8	28.2	28.5	28.8	29.1	29.4	29.8	30.1	30.4
铁路	21.2	22.2	21.2	17.1	19.9	20.1	20.1	18.2	16.7	14.1	11.9
海港	25.5	18.9	18.6	20.2	22.7	22.1	21.8	21.9	21.3	19.2	17.6
总计	74.5	68.6	67.7	65.5	71.1	48.9	49.2	47.6	46.4	44.2	42.3

资料来源：格鲁吉亚经济和可持续发展部数据。

在波季港的周转量中，过境业务所占份额非常大——2004—2015年，这一比例在48%至55%。进口份额从2004年的20%增长至2015年的36%。出口份额从2004年的25%下降至2014年的16%。导致出口下降的原因是，部分中亚货物转移到了俄罗斯，而格鲁吉亚市场太小，无法弥补损失。该港口专门从事干货物运输，因此，干货物和一般货物的比例很高。巴统港的过境货物份额从2009年的93.9%下降至2015年的85.8%。该港口由哈萨克斯坦管理，专门出口哈萨克斯坦石油。后来，因油价问题，哈萨克斯坦关闭了巴统石油码头，以下国家在进口方面所占份额最大：乌克兰、土耳其、希腊、俄罗斯、意大利、保加利亚。出口方面则是：保加利亚、意大利、土耳其、乌克兰、罗马尼亚、马耳他。

表2　　　　　　海港和海运码头所装卸的货物　　　　　（百万吨）

海港和海运码头的名称	2006	2007	2008	2009	2010	2011	2012	2013	2014	2015	2016
波季港	6.7	7.7	8.0	6.1	7.3	7.2	7.5	7.4	8.6	6.8	6.3
巴统港	13.2	11.2	8.7	7.8	8.0	7.9	7.9	8.3	6.3	5.7	5.6
库勒维海运码头	0.0	0.0	1.3	2.1	3.4	3.3	2.5	2.1	2.1	2.5	1.6
苏普萨海运码头	5.6	0.0	0.6	4.2	4.0	3.8	3.9	4.0	4.2	4.2	4.1
总计	25.5	18.9	18.6	20.2	22.7	21.8	21.9	21.3	19.2	17.6	

资料来源：格鲁吉亚经济和可持续发展部数据。

土耳其在集装箱周转量中占比最大，其次是意大利和罗马尼亚。对于南高加索地区和中亚而言，巴库—波季铁路是转移集装箱过境货物的重要路线，因为波季港的关税最具吸引力、距离最短——基于该港口在该地区的地理位置。

表3　　　　　　　　　装卸的标准集装箱数量（按海港）

海港名称	2006	2007	2008	2009	2010	2011	2012	2013	2014	2015	2016
波季港	129100	184792	209614	172800	209797	254022	284559	331324	384992	325121	273690
巴统港	0	0	44197	8813	16318	45439	73095	72123	61980	54695	56115
总计	129100	184792	253811	181613	226115	299461	357654	403447	446972	379816	329805

资料来源：格鲁吉亚经济和可持续发展部数据。

"TRACECA"国际运输走廊改变了格鲁吉亚的运输基础设施。开辟了从与阿塞拜疆接壤的红桥到巴统的东西走廊——高速公路；铁路运输投入使用，货物周转量增加，货运地理位置也发生了变化。所有这些都对该国的社会经济状况产生了积极影响。

2007年2月签订的关于巴库—第比利斯—阿哈尔卡拉基—卡尔斯铁路运营的三方协议对土耳其、格鲁吉亚和阿塞拜疆之间的区域关系至关重要。该项目旨在将南高加索纳入泛欧运输走廊。阿塞拜疆拨出3.4亿拉里的贷款（贷款年限：25年；贷款利率：1%），用于建造93公里的新铁路并重建160公里的"马拉达—阿哈尔卡拉基"铁路。初始阶段，其产能将为500万吨，之后将增至1000万吨。格鲁吉亚段的施工作业于2013年完成，铁路一直延伸到达土耳其边境。土耳其2016年才开始修建其境内铁路段，2017年5月，埃尔多安（Erdogan）在北京宣布，修建工作计划于2017年年底完工，他们对通过这条特殊的铁路参与中国"一带一路"倡议非常感兴趣。通过这条铁路，中国将格鲁吉亚与欧洲相连。首先，运往土耳其的货物将通过铁路进行运输。但最重要的是，这将是连接亚洲和欧洲的路线，该路线将沿2013年开通的"马尔马拉伊（Marmarai）"隧道穿过博斯普鲁斯海峡，而且土耳其打算在新的欧亚走廊中发挥主要作用。该隧道随后将与巴库—第比利斯—卡尔斯干线相连，并从那里与亚洲最大的货物运出国中国相连。黑海地区将建立高效的亚欧运输走廊，该走廊将与包括"TRACECA"在内的许多过境项目竞争，这必将会减少通过黑海盆地各港口的货物，波季可能不得不对货物进行重组，因为该港口强烈依赖来自阿塞拜疆、中亚和中国的集装箱货物，其中大部分将分流向铁路运输。

土耳其积极支持巴库—第比利斯—卡尔斯铁路，这源于其地缘战略利益，并暗示着该国东部地区及其运输基础设施的发展，该地区运输基础设施基本上为海港（萨姆松、特拉布宗、里泽、霍帕）。

巴库—第比利斯—卡尔斯铁路项目的实施对阿塞拜疆也很重要，通过修建连接阿塞拜疆和伊朗的阿斯塔拉—拉什特—加兹温铁路以及实施巴库—第比利斯—卡尔斯铁路项目，阿塞拜疆将拥有穿过其境内的纵向和横向两条运输路线。通过该项目，亚洲和高加索国家将有机会联通地中海，泛欧和泛亚系统的连接将更加紧密。

四 中国"一带一路"倡议

2008年国际金融危机后，中国成为推动世界经济发展的主要力量。中国提出的倡议称为"一带一路"，"一带一路"倡议旨在建立一条新的多式联运走廊，该走廊分为陆海两个流向，贯穿欧亚大陆。

这条通道连接65个国家，占世界人口的62.3%，土地面积的38.5%，全球经济产量的三分之一。"一带一路"的地理区域是伟大的"丝绸之路经济带"和"21世纪海上丝绸之路"。"一带一路"将经过以下走廊：俄罗斯的"欧亚经济走廊"、"东盟（ASEAN）"、哈萨克斯坦的"光明之路"、土耳其的"中间走廊"、蒙古的"草原之路"、越南的"两廊一圈"、波兰的"琥珀之路"、英国的"北方经济引擎"计划、"TRACECA"和俄罗斯的"南北国际运输走廊"。

2000年前，绵延7000公里的"丝绸之路"是连接欧洲、亚洲和非洲或者说连接东西方的桥梁，是中国发展的象征。对中国而言，除了经济意义外，"一带一路"还展示了中国在世界舞台上日益强大、稳定、发达的形象。

中国在该项目中的目标是：通过互利合作，在参与国之间确保安全、提高福利；建立互联的基础设施、发展开放型经济；简化投资和贸易程序，建立自由贸易区。

五 格鲁吉亚的发展前景

对格鲁吉亚而言，从社会经济角度来看，过境功能是增加财政预算收入、保持金融稳定、发展服务业和创造就业的途径。

格鲁吉亚已与中国建立了稳定的关系。中国与格鲁吉亚签署了自由贸易协定，希望深化经济合作。

然而，格鲁吉亚—中国关系有着发展的前景。2015年12月13日，第一列来自中国连云港的过境列车抵达第比利斯。随着这列火车的到来，"丝绸铁路"正式开通。这列火车将继续开往土耳其。这是"丝绸之路"的首批过境货物和已完成项目。未来，过境列车将在最短的时间内从亚洲到达欧洲，反之亦然。伊斯坦布尔的货物最多将在14—15天内到达，而走海运则需要40—45天。

对于格鲁吉亚而言，如果土耳其能够吸引中国将部分货物转移到巴库—第比利斯—卡尔斯铁路，这也非常重要。

格鲁吉亚的政治经济发展前景具有重要意义：

1. 在现代全球空间中，横贯大陆的运输走廊变得异常重要，其发展速度惊人，联结了经济和政治两极，并创造了沟通的框架。

2. 格鲁吉亚通过连接欧洲和亚洲的TRACECA运输走廊与泛欧运输基础设施相连。TRACECA是促进区域合作、增加货物流、确保安全和可持续发展的保障。

3. 格鲁吉亚的过境职能是其实现政治、经济和社会发展、参与全球空间、促进就业和民生改善的一个因素。国际社会也在推动这一职能的发展。

4. 中国"一带一路"倡议是一个伟大的倡议，已成为一项全球倡议。

5. 格鲁吉亚拥有参与中国走廊的运输和物流潜力，但无疑需要配备现代化的海运、铁路、高速公路基础设施，提高现有道路的通行能力，并确保这些道路的安全与稳定性。

6. 格鲁吉亚坚持正确的对外政治取向，积极参与到世界进程中。格鲁吉亚是世界贸易组织（WTO）等多达40个国际组织的成员国。格鲁吉亚可持续发展的未来取决于格对外政治和经济的方向。

历史和当代背景下的格鲁吉亚与中国关系

纳娜·格拉什维利[*]

当今,在格鲁吉亚和整个世界政治、社会、经济和其他进程的背景下,扩展知识领域变得日益重要——不管是在地理位置方面,还是主题方面。这首先意指那些领土远离格鲁吉亚的国家。从这个观点来看,考虑到所有既有决定因素(文明成果、从古至今所取得的科技成就、高水平的经济发展,等等),我们应该对中国予以特别关注。这不仅因为我们对这个国家抱有极大的兴趣,而且还因为中国在解决全球问题方面的潜力和作用与日俱增。众所周知,中国是世界政治版图上的核心角色之一,中国发展势头迅猛,并且勇于应对新的挑战。此外,中国拥有五千多年的悠久历史,中国人民也非常注重对其古代文明成果与传统的传承。在这种情况下,我想引用中国的一句老话:"饮水思源",意思是"一切现在皆源自于过去"。这是中国伟大的思想家、哲学家孔子(公元前551—前479年)所宣讲的道义。孔子有一句名言,其意思是说:"必须到历史中以及被遗忘的古老智慧中去寻找解决当前问题的关键"。事实上,如果不去全面地研究和考虑过去的历史,就不可能充分理解和正确评价当前的事件或事实。

众所周知,中国是世界上最古老的文明发源地之一,中国文明源远流长,博大精深。几个世纪以来,中国作为一个具有独特和自足文明的

---

[*] 纳娜·格拉什维利,格鲁吉亚第比利斯国立大学教授、人文学院远东地区研究及汉学系主任。

国家而完全独立地发展。而且，中国本身也是所有东亚及东南亚国家中的典范和榜样。[1] 正是在中国的影响下，各种物质和精神文化元素、各个工艺美术领域、各种哲学宗教教义（儒家和道家）、国家管理机构、城市规划原则等得以在各个邻国广泛传播。古代中国人同样意识到了他们在世界范围内的特殊作用和意义，而非局限在该地区。因而，他们认定中国是宇宙的中心，所以宣称"普天之下，莫非王土"。甚至就连其国名"中国"（即中央国家）显然也佐证了这一看待问题的方法。[2] 中国历史兴衰交替，既有政治团结与和平时期，也有战争和改朝换代的时期。

谈及格鲁吉亚和中国之间的关系，首先要简短地回顾一下历史。首先应该指出的是，从打通"伟大的丝绸之路（Great Silk Road）"这一国际商队贸易公路的古代晚期开始，中国就与中亚和东亚、波斯（西南亚国家，现称伊朗）、地中海和黑海盆地以及高加索国家建立了密切的贸易经济关系。"伟大的丝绸之路"的历史起源于公元前 2 世纪，中国外交家和旅行家张骞奉汉武帝（公元前 141—前 187 年）之命，前往中亚各国执行一项特殊使命。公元前 120 年，张骞回到中国，向朝廷上报了西域各国政治经济相关的有趣而重要的信息，均为前所未闻之事。张骞概述了与西域各国建立贸易和交往关系的必要性。然而，还应该注意的是，在此之前，中国已经通过"玉石路"（连接中国北部和中部与波斯）与外部世界建立了联系。丝绸之路便是在此基础上开始建立的。"伟大的丝绸之路"一词由德国历史学家和地理学家费迪南·冯·李希霍芬（1833—1905 年）首次提出，他在 1868—1872 年组织了七次对中国的考察，切实研究了与丝绸之路有关的问题。最初，中国丝绸的主要消费者是罗马帝国的贵族。后来，经过帕提亚（亚洲西部古国，在伊朗东北部）和波斯的中转，中国丝绸出口至拜占庭[3]。

---

[1] *The Cambridge history of ancient China*: *from the origins of civilization to 221BC*, ed. by M. Loewe and E. L. Shaugnessy, Cambridge University Press, 1999, pp. 232 – 241.

[2] Harrison L. J., *The Chinese Empire*, *a short history of China from Neolithic times to the end of the 18th century*, New York, 1972, p. 14.

[3] Zviadadze G., *The Great Silk road Passed Through Georgia*, Tbilisi (in Georgian); Xinru Liu (2010). The Silk road in the world history, New York: Oxford University Press, 1989.

除了丝绸这一主要的贸易产品，各种金属、宝石、手工艺品、瓷器和奢侈品也是从中国进口的。应该强调的是，除了贸易目的，丝绸之路还充当了远东、欧洲、北非和亚洲其他地区之间的跨文化桥梁之功能。因此，通行于丝绸之路的商人和旅人有意无意地将本地和外国的文化元素从一个地方带到了另一个地方。通过他们，文化对话以及思想、精神价值、传统和各种技术的交流和分享得以实现。格鲁吉亚在一定程度上也参与到了这些过程中①。因此，在古代格鲁吉亚——科克禾迪（西部）和伊比利亚（东部），人们已经对中国和中国人有了一定的了解。由于其便利的地缘政治位置，格鲁吉亚自古以来便是连接西方和东方的桥梁。格鲁吉亚的这一功能在政治、社会和经济领域展露无遗。就这一点而言，格鲁吉亚作为国际贸易关系中的一个过境国，其重要性尤其显著。根据历史记载，自古以来就有贸易通道从格鲁吉亚经过，有关信息见于希罗多德、斯特拉博等希腊作家的作品中②。在上述通道中，最重要的一条是横跨大陆的丝绸贸易商队之路，它将遥远的中国与地中海和黑海盆地的国家连接起来。但是也应该注意，在原始地图和资料中，格鲁吉亚并没有出现在古老的"丝绸之路"的路线之上。事实是，在历史上，丝绸之路从格鲁吉亚以南（相距较远）经过，仅其外围分支进入了南高加索地区。

在公元三、四世纪之交，前亚（Anterior-Asian）地区的政治局势致使这一世界贸易路线的线路发生了重大的变化。拜占庭帝国建立（公元395年）后，该贸易路线立即朝向帝国的首都——君士坦丁堡（土耳其港市，现称伊斯坦布尔）改道，君士坦丁堡成为欧亚边界最重要的贸易和文化中心③。

---

① Gelashvili N., "Intercultural impact in the Near East in middle ages", *Byzantine studies in Georgia* -3, Vol. I, Tbilisi (in Georgian), 2011, pp. 104 – 105.

② Gablishvili L., "Georgia and the Great Silk Road in late antiquity and the middle ages", *Proceedings of the Georgian national academy of sciences (series of history)*, #2, Tbilisi (in Georgian), 2021.

③ Uturashvili M., "Historical aspect of the 'Great Silk Road'", *The Silk Road and Caucasus*, Tbilisi (in Georgian), 2017.

后来，这条高加索路线变得特别重要，6世纪，主要的商队干道得以扩大，并增加了一些旁路。自那时起，格鲁吉亚就积极参与到丝绸之路中。当时的事实是，由于拜占庭和波斯之间的冲突，通过波斯向拜占庭和地中海国家运输丝绸变得危险重重。由于6世纪的相应政治局势，萨珊朝时期的伊朗禁止通过其领土向西方出口丝绸，并禁止了丝绸的自由贸易[1]。正因为如此，人们开始寻找新的贸易路线，这与丝绸之路上的军事政治局势变化直接相关。这就是为什么那些向拜占庭供应中国丝绸和其他产品的亚洲商人（包括中国人）开发了一条新的路线。也就是说，这条通道从里海一路向北——穿越高加索山脉，通往拜占庭。

　　伊朗和拜占庭长期为争夺来自北高加索的贸易通道的主导权而战。在五、六世纪之交，北高加索人控制了这片领土范围内的达里阿利（Dariali）峡谷部分，他们游刃有余地在拜占庭和伊朗之间周旋，时而支持一方，时而又支持另一方，取决于哪一方更有利可图。应该注意的是，当地人除了相应的税款外，还从贸易商队得到实物报酬——各种珠宝、珠子、贝壳等。从6世纪下半叶开始，丝绸之路的高加索段（北高加索方向）成为了一条常规的贸易通道[2]。丝织品、珠子、餐具、不同种类的木制品、瓷器和其他产品通过这种方式运输，这些产品在丝绸之路上的需求更大[3]。应该注意的是，考古学家在库班河支流博尔沙亚拉巴河（Bolshaia Laba）的上游发现了一个中国商人的墓葬，墓葬中有着各种物品，包括带有刺绣的丝绸面料以及这位商人的个人记录。研究结果表明，该墓葬可追溯至中国唐朝统治时期（618—907年）。

　　自中世纪以来，格鲁吉亚还有更多关于中国的信息，这些均在考古文物和格鲁吉亚书面记录中得到了证实。在格鲁吉亚各地发现的考古材料中，有中国丝织品、瓷器、刻有中文的铜币等的碎片。人们在公元前2

---

[1] Gelashvili N., Georgia in the light of Iran-Byzantine wars (6th century), *Pro Georgia, Journal of Kartvelological studies*, #26, Warsaw, 2016, pp. 77–78.

[2] Goiladze V., Great Silk Road and Georgia, Tbilisi (in Georgian), 1997, pp. 80–81.

[3] Ierusalimskaia A. A., *An Unusual Archaeological Monument*, St. Peterburg (in Russian), 2012.

世纪和随后时代的墓葬中发现了中国丝织品的残余①。还应注意的是，在格鲁吉亚境内发现的众多外国钱币中，也有一枚中国钱币，这表明伊比利亚—卡特里（格鲁吉亚东部）与外部世界有着密切的贸易和经济往来。特别是1993年，在阿里城堡（Ali castle）附近哈舒里区（Khashuri district）姆茨赫季瓦里村（village of Mtskhetijvari）进行的考古工作中，发现了一枚刻有中文的铜币，铜币中间有一个方形的孔。根据专家们的研究，确定这是南宋统治时期（1127—1279年）铸造的钱币，具体来说是1200年②。这枚中国钱币对于研究12—13世纪格鲁吉亚的贸易和经济历史具有重要意义。这并非偶然，根据科学研究，古代有一条重要的贸易商队道路经过该钱币发现地点③。因此，毫无疑问，我们将会发现更多有趣的材料，从而进一步揭示古代格鲁吉亚和中国之间的关系。

许多格鲁吉亚中世纪的书面资料中都提到了关于中国和中国人的有趣信息。现在我们仅列举其中的几个：11世纪波斯诗歌《微史拉密安》（*Visramiani*）的格鲁吉亚语版本、约阿内·夏夫特里（Ioane Shavteli）的 *Abdulmesiani*、绍塔·鲁斯塔韦利（Shota Rustaveli）的著名诗歌《披着豹皮的骑士（*The Knight in the Panther's Skin*）》（由格鲁吉亚语翻译成中文）。特别值得关注的是旅行者、塔玛拉国王（1184—1213年）的赞颂诗人查赫鲁哈泽（Chakhrukhadze）的 *Tamariani*。诗人描述了他在1193—1203年间在中东和远东国家的旅行，其中包括波斯、印度和中国④。此后的书面作品中，特别值得一提的是由格鲁吉亚著名地理学家、历史学家瓦胡什蒂·巴格拉季亚尼（Vakhushti Bagrationi）（1696—1757年）所翻译的《世界政治地理》。该作品中有对中国政治地理的描述以及彩色中国地图（格鲁吉亚语）。

---

① Goiladze V., Great Silk Road and Georgia, Tbilisi (in Georgian), 1997.
② Bragvadze Z., Davitashvili A., Chinese coin from Mcxetijvari, *Dzeglis Megobari*, #1, Tbilisi (in Georgian), 1993.
③ Gablishvili L., Georgia and the Great Silk Road in late antiquity and the middle ages, *Proceedings of the Georgian national academy of sciences (series of history)*, #2, Tbilisi (in Georgian), 2021.
④ Kharadze K., China seen through the eyes of medieval Georgian travelers and geographers, *The Silk Road and Caucasus*, Tbilisi (in Georgian), 2017.

拉菲尔·达尼贝加什维利（Rafiel Danibegashvili）是公认的世界级旅行家，他在1795—1827年前往亚洲国家旅行，特别是，他曾在1813—1814年、1815年和1820年三次前往中国。他的作品中描写了很多有趣的信息——中国人的生活方式、传统、宗教问题以及当地显著的生态和地理特征。应该注意的是，中国在格鲁吉亚的书面资料中有多种称呼，包括Chini、Chin-Machini、Khataeti、Kitayuri和Machineti[1]。当前的中国国名（英文）"China"起源于古英语的"Chin（在不同的文献中也写成Cin、Cine）"这一词根。11世纪波斯诗歌《微史拉密安》的翻译版是格鲁吉亚第一部含有"Chin"一词的书面作品。

自19世纪末以来，格鲁吉亚与中国的关系变得更加具体和紧密。

举例来说，由刘峻周为首的中国人在格鲁吉亚，即阿扎尔（Adjara），积极进行茶叶种植和茶叶产业发展，取得了丰硕的成果。刘峻周于1893年与其他中国茶叶专家一起到达巴统，并带来了数千茶苗和茶树种子。他领导建立了茶苗大棚和格鲁吉亚第一家茶叶加工厂。应该注意的是，刘峻周的伟大成就为格鲁吉亚学者所熟知和研究[2]。

提及"格鲁吉亚聚居群体（Georgian colony）"在中国哈尔滨市的活动是非常有趣和重要的。根据历史记载，在20世纪初，有大量格鲁吉亚人在哈尔滨定居，形成很多格鲁吉亚社区。在格鲁吉亚社区的努力下，由伊芙莲恩·凯恩达瓦（Ivliane Khaindrava）领导的"全国格鲁吉亚人协会"于1908年成立。应该注意的是，身处哈尔滨的格鲁吉亚人积极参与了该地区的政治、经济和文化生活。同时，他们又与格鲁吉亚民主共和国相连[3]。在此背景下，值得注意的是，格鲁吉亚在远东的第一个外交使团——领事馆在哈尔滨成立，第一任领事尼科洛兹·吉什卡里亚尼（Nikoloz Jishkariani）是一位专业的医生。领事馆的活动范围不局限于满洲里，还包括西伯利亚东部。在20世纪20年代和30年代，许多格鲁吉亚人在哈

---

[1] Kharadze K., "China seen through the eyes of medieval Georgian travelers and geographers", *The Silk Road and Caucasus*, Tbilisi (in Georgian), 2017.

[2] Daghundaridze N., *At the Origins of Tea Culture in Georgia*, Tbilisi (in Georgian), 2003.

[3] Chikhladze Sh., Chigladze O, *Georgians in China in the first half of 20th century*, *Herald of oriental studies*, #Batumi：Batumi State University (in Georgian), 2021.

尔滨积极工作。其中值得一提的是 G. 西达莫尼泽（G. Sidamonidze）、B. 罗米纳泽（B. Lominadze）、A. 斯瓦尼泽（A. Svanidze）等人。从寄自哈尔滨的格鲁吉亚人的信件中可以看出，到1921年，约有3000名格鲁吉亚人居住在哈尔滨及其周边地区，而且这个数字后来还在不断增加。然而，在日本人侵占哈尔滨后，包括格鲁吉亚人在内的外国居民的数量急剧减少。因此，到1941年，格鲁吉亚社区的人数约为400人[1]。

格鲁吉亚—中国关系史上一个特别重要且成果丰硕的时期始于20世纪90年代初。在格鲁吉亚恢复独立并于1992年6月9日与中国建交之后，两国建立了高质量的新型多边关系。此后，双边关系逐步推进，尤其是在经济合作方面。

关于丝绸之路的后续，应该注意的是，西方和东方之间仍定期开展物质和智力价值层面的交流，直至15世纪初。后来，古代丝绸之路失去了其在全球的重要地位。16世纪末，由于中亚地区的持续战争和变迁，并且欧洲人开发了非洲周边海运路线，古代丝绸之路不再发挥作用。

伴随着经济增长，中国开始大力投资于道路基础设施。众所周知，当今世界面临诸多挑战。一些地区的热点问题成倍增加，极端主义、分裂主义和其他问题不断出现。在历史上，古代丝绸之路实际上是被无休止的战争和冲突所摧毁的。中国关于共建丝绸之路经济走廊的倡议将有助于更合理地利用不同国家的人力、市场、技术和资源能力，未来可期。

如前所述，格鲁吉亚和中国之间已经建立稳定的外交、贸易经济和科学文化关系。应该强调的是，中国是最早承认格鲁吉亚独立的国家之一，2022年是两国建交30周年。我们第比利斯国立大学远东地区研究—汉学系里，学术水平较高的学生会学习中国的语言、文学和文化、中国从古至今的历史、经济、历史名城、中国古代哲学宗教学说（儒家、道家）以及其他学科。

中国驻格鲁吉亚大使馆对第比利斯国立大学汉学方向的高度关注特别值得一提。尤其是，"中国语言和文化研究室"配备最新的计算机技

---

[1] Chikhladze Sh., Chigladze O, *Georgians in China in the first half of 20th century*, Herald of oriental studies, #Batumi: Batumi State University (in Georgian), 2021.

术、教育和科学文献以及对我校 2015 年教育过程所需的各种物品，对我们这些老师和学生而言，该研究室的开放着实令人振奋。所有这些都是在中国驻格鲁吉亚大使馆和"华为"公司的支持下实现的。

这里需要指出的是，关于中国的格鲁吉亚语文献相对较少，而其需求却在增加。因此我们在这方面开展了大量的工作：出版了汉语教科书、格鲁吉亚语—汉语词典，将各种文学作品从中文翻译成格鲁吉亚语以及从格鲁吉亚语翻译成中文。不久前，我们的集体作品《中国历史》已出版，书中涵盖中国从古代到现代的历史、社会经济和文化问题。此外，我的专著《中国历代首都》也即将出版。同样令人高兴的是，我校已有众多学生完成在中国重点大学的长期实习，他们目前已参加工作，活跃在格鲁吉亚和中国的各类公司、旅行社、大使馆、大学、科学领域以及其他领域。即使是在当前的后疫情时期，我们也已派出新的一批学生参加交流学习项目。基于上述所有情况可以明确的是，格鲁吉亚和中国之间的关系正在不断深化和多面化。2022 年 12 月 9 日在北京举行的"'一带一路'：中国式现代化与社会发展经验"国际研讨会便是其中一项证明。

当今，密切的贸易和经济合作是格鲁吉亚—中国关系（包括政治—外交对话）的主要支柱。在这方面，尤其值得注意的是，格鲁吉亚凭借独特的地缘战略位置成为连接欧亚大陆的运输和过境枢纽，积极参与大规模的"一带一路"项目。然而，应该注意的是，在现阶段，基于主客观的原因，丝绸之路的外高加索走廊，以及格鲁吉亚被视为欧洲和中国之间货物运输走廊中具有竞争力的替代方案，在一定程度上有所疑虑。由于这属于另一个独立的话题，我们将仅限于指出，就目前而言，格鲁吉亚仍是区域性的运输走廊，因为它在运输时间和成本方面的竞争力相对较低。另一方面，格鲁吉亚坐拥非常有利的地缘政治机会，可以成为东西方之间的贸易过境国，以及里海地区与中亚和欧洲之间的能源过境走廊。此外，分析人士认为，如格鲁吉亚能与其他走廊成员国协调交通法规和立法，并简化操作，则将能打造一条更具竞争力的过境路线。考虑到上述因素，格鲁吉亚参与丝绸之路这一大型项目变得愈发重要，可使其在全球范围内展示自身在各个领域的能力。

从古至今:格鲁吉亚人眼中的中国

奥 塔[*]

本文以书面资料为基础,讨论了格鲁吉亚从古代到现代数百年来所形成的对中国的认识。研究结果表明,在格鲁吉亚人看来,中国始终在不断变化,这种变化有时是进步,有时是倒退。在古代和中古时期,格鲁吉亚人主要通过商人和外国文学翻译来了解中国。直到17世纪,格鲁吉亚的资料才有记载有关中国的信息,但是这种信息非常有限和稀缺。从18世纪开始,格鲁吉亚读者才可以通过系统而可靠的第一手信息了解中国。在19—20世纪,格鲁吉亚社会首次出现了对中国的综合看法。公众逐渐有兴趣更详细、更深入地了解中国的政治、经济和文化。在过去三十年里,由于建立了直接联系,中格关系迅速发展。在格鲁吉亚人眼中,中国已成为格鲁吉亚最密切的经济伙伴和超级大国,在世界政治舞台上的影响力日益增大。

近十年来,中格在多个领域的合作迅猛发展。两国之间建立了密切的政治和经济关系。基于这种情况,格鲁吉亚科学界和普通民众对中国文化的兴趣也愈发浓厚。然而,科学界和普通大众对中国的认识均处于早期阶段。格鲁吉亚人对中国的兴趣日益浓厚,为了加强这一趋势并提高公众意识,我们需要研究数百年来在格鲁吉亚人的认知中,中国是如何一步步发展的,我们认为这种研究会让我们受益匪浅。这种研究不仅

---

[*] 奥塔,格鲁吉亚青年汉学家,毕业于北京大学中国史专业。

第五编　中国式现代化与中格丝路发展新机遇　◀◀　187

会为历史学家和文化工作者在将来继续开展这一方向的研究提供宝贵资料，还会引起社会各阶层人士的关注。

由于缺乏相关资料，实际上不可能准确地确定有关中国的信息最早是何时出现在格鲁吉亚的。最早的有关中国的格鲁吉亚语文字资料可以追溯到12世纪。这是否意味着我们只能从12世纪开始研究格鲁吉亚社会对中国的认识？我对这个问题的回答是否定的。虽然没有直接的文字资料证实这一点，但其他一些情况表明，格鲁吉亚人肯定更早就对中国有所了解了。

首先，"伟大的丝绸之路"的存在为我们做出这一假设提供了依据。"丝绸之路"是一个庞大的贸易网络，历经数百年的时间，将欧洲和亚洲相距遥远的地方连接起来，在古代和中古时期是信息流动的主要手段之一。"丝绸之路"起源于中国，在向西方传播对中国的认识方面发挥了举足轻重的作用。虽然"丝绸之路"的主要路线并不经过格鲁吉亚，但古希腊地理学家斯特拉博（Strabo）（公元前63年到公元24年）依然指出，格鲁吉亚凭借其优越的地理位置成为东西方贸易和南北方贸易路线的主要过境站之一[1]，这表明格鲁吉亚是"大丝路"贸易网络的一部分。"丝绸之路"上运输的商品大量进入格鲁吉亚，这一事实也能证明上述说法。考古学家在格鲁吉亚境内发现了2—3世纪的丝绸残留物[2]。据文字资料显示，早在5世纪，制作丝绸手工艺品就已经是格鲁吉亚贵族女性一项司空见惯的活动[3]。

除此之外，由于种种原因，"丝绸之路"的中心路线也多次发生改变。例如，在6世纪和7世纪之交，波斯与拜占庭的关系再次变得紧张，

---

[1] Emili Avdaliani, *Sakartvelo da abreshumis savach'ro gzebi* (Ⅵ－ⅩⅢ ss.) (*Georgia and Silk Roads* (Ⅵ－ⅩⅢ centuries)), Tbilisi: Meridiani, 2019, gv. 61－62. Irak'li Shikhiashvili, "*Abreshumis gza" da Sakartvelo* (*Arkeologiuri da Ist'oriuli ts'q'aroebis mikhedvit*) ("Silk Road" and Georgia (According to archeological and historical sources)), Tbilisi, 2019, gv. 34－36.

[2] L. Lursmanashvili, M. Datuashvili, N. Dolidze, Dzvel Sakartveloshi gavrtselebuli abreshumis ksovilis sakheebi (Kind of silk materials spread in old Georgia), *Saist'orio vert'ik'ali*, Nomeri 19, Tbilisi: Basiani, 2009, gv. 100－101.

[3] Presbyter Iakob, *The martyrdom of Shushanik*, Translated by Maia Akhvlediani, Tbilisi: Nekeri, 2019, gv. 48.

由于经济和政治上的限制,贸易商开辟了一条通往北方的新路线①。他们从中亚经过俄罗斯大草原到达北高加索,翻过高加索山脉,从格鲁吉亚西部的港口进入拜占庭②。文字资料和考古资料均可证实这一点。在格鲁吉亚西部山区的斯瓦涅蒂(Svaneti)地区,发现了7世纪从中亚进口的丝绸残留物③。在"丝绸之路"上,中亚商人是东西方之间的主要中间商。然而,除了他们,还有少数中国商人也经过这条路。能够证实这一点的证据是:在北高加索地区发掘出一座属于7世纪中国商人的古墓。除了中国商品,在古墓中还发现了用中国象形文字书写在丝绸织物上的题字④。

除了经贸因素,我们还必须考虑政治局势。特别值得一提的是,格鲁吉亚国王和贵族与波斯和亚美尼亚皇家宫廷的关系十分密切。早在公元前2世纪,波斯和中国就建立了外交关系,随着时间的推移,两国之间的交流日渐频繁⑤。因此,格鲁吉亚人可以通过与波斯皇家宫廷或贵族的接触获得有关中国的信息。在这方面,与亚美尼亚的关系更为重要。早在5世纪,在格鲁吉亚邻国亚美尼亚的文字资料中就记载了中国的情况⑥。格鲁吉亚与亚美尼亚之间的文学交流从一开始就颇为频繁。在6世

---

① Vakht'ang Goiladze, *Abreshumis didi savach'ro gza da Sakartvelo* (*Silk Road and Georgia*), Tbilisi, 1997, gv. 31.

② Олеся Жданович, Менандр Протектор, История : О посольствах тЮрков к Персам и Византийцам в 568 году, *Золотоордынское обозрение*, No 1 (3), 2014, ст. 27.

③ T'ariel K'vitsiani, Adreuli shua sauk'uneebis (Ⅵ – Ⅷ ss.) abreshumis dek'orat'iuli ksovilebi K'avk'asiidan (Deocrative textiles of silk in early Middle Ages (Ⅵ – Ⅷ centuries) Caucasia), *Arkeologiuri k'rebuli*, Ⅳ, Tbilisi: Tbilisis sakhelmtsipo universit'et'is gamomtsemloba, 2004, gv. 73 – 75.

④ А. А. Иерусалимская, Кавказ на шелковом пути, Санкт – Петербург, 1992, ст. 7.

⑤ عوامل مؤثر بر روابط ایران و چین و تأثیر آن بر مبادلاتمحصولات طبی دارویی در عصر باستان, حمیدکاویانی پویا ,بزشکي تاريخ فصلنامه,1974, ۳۵ بررسی; 丘进,《中国与罗马,汉代中西关系研究》,黄山书社2008年版,第176页。

⑥ P'awstos Buzandac'i', *History of the Armenians*, Translated from classical Armenian by Robert Bedrosian, New York 1985, p. 89.

纪到 9 世纪，大量的亚美尼亚语作品被翻译成格鲁吉亚语①。格鲁吉亚贵族与马米科尼扬家族（Mamikonians）的亚美尼亚大贵族血统之间有着密切的血缘关系和政治关系，这让我们有更充分的理由认定：格鲁吉亚人可以从亚美尼亚获得有关中国的信息②，因为马米科尼扬家族声称其祖先是中国血统，亚美尼亚历史资料首次提到中国时也涉及马米科尼扬家族的名字③。

因此，我们可以合理地假定，在 12 世纪之前，格鲁吉亚人就对中国有了一定的认知。遗憾的是，由于缺乏相关资料来源，我们无法查明有关中国的信息究竟是何时进入格鲁吉亚的、这些信息是哪方面的。另一方面，如果我们接受以下假设：格鲁吉亚人早在 12 世纪之前就了解中国，那么我们就必须回答以下问题：在格鲁吉亚当代文字资料中为什么没有相关记载。应该注意的是，格鲁吉亚和亚美尼亚文学是在 4 世纪和 5 世纪之交同时问世的。亚美尼亚文字资料首次提到中国可以追溯到 5 世纪，而格鲁吉亚文学在七个多世纪以后才首次记载中国的情况。如果格鲁吉亚人在中古时期初就了解中国，那么为什么格鲁吉亚和亚美尼亚文学在记载中国情况方面有近七百年的时间差？

依本人之见，这一问题的原因应该在于格鲁吉亚和亚美尼亚文学的发展具有特殊性。关键是在亚美尼亚文学的早期，世俗著作和宗教著作实际上是齐头并进的④，而在格鲁吉亚最初只发展了宗教文学。世俗文学

---

① Ilia Abuladze, *Kartuli da Somkhuri lit'erat'uruli urtiertoba IX–X sauk'uneebshi* (*Georgian and Armenian literary relations in IX–X centuries*), Tbilisi: Sakartvelos ssr metsnierebata ak'ademiis gamomtsemloba, 1944, gv. 12–13.

② Presbyter Iakob, *The martyrdom of Shushanik*, gv. 3.

③ P'awstos Buzandac'i', *History of the Armenians*, p. 89; Movses Khorenatsi, *Somkhetis ist'oria* (*History of Armenia*), Dzveli Somkhuridan targmna, shesavali da shenishvnebi daurto Aleksandre Abdaladzem, Tbilisi: Metsniereba, 1984, gv. 165; История епископа Себеоса, Перевод с четвертого исправленного армянского издания Ст. Малхасянц, Ереван: Армфан – А, 1939, ст. 17–18.

④ Leon Melikset-Begi, *Dzveli Somkhuri lit'erat'uris ist'oria* (*History of old Armenian literature*), Tbilisi: St'alinis sakhelobis Tbilisis sakhelmts'ipo universit'et'is gamomtsemloba, 1941, gv. 69.

在 11 世纪和 12 世纪之交才初见端倪[1]。世俗文学是后起之秀，因此早些时候的格鲁吉亚关资料没有提到过中国。提到中国的亚美尼亚资料都属于世俗著作，这一事实以及后期的格鲁吉亚资料证实了以上假设。这一时期其他国家的神学著作也没有提到过中国。这或许是因为中古时期基督教的地理或历史世界观完全以《圣经》为基础，而《圣经》没有提到中国。基督教使徒也没有在中国讲道。事实上，聂斯托留派基督教（Nestorian Christianity）的代表早在 7 世纪就进入中国了[2]，但该教派在 5 世纪的加采东大公会议（Council of Chalcedon）上遭到驱逐，格鲁吉亚和拜占庭教会断绝了与该教派的关系。因此，中国不在格鲁吉亚文学和一般基督教文学的地理世界观范围之内。

根据当今现有资料，首次记载中国的格鲁吉亚文学作品是 12 世纪中叶的，也就是译自波斯语的小说《微史拉密安》（Visramian）和一项同样译自波斯语的占星协定[3]。在获得有关中国的信息方面，一直到 18 世纪波斯都是格鲁吉亚社会的主要信息来源。在 12 世纪末，格鲁吉亚作者的作品提到了中国。应该注意的是，其中有史诗《虎皮武士》（Knight in the panther's skin），这是公认的最伟大的格鲁吉亚文学杰作[4]。由于《虎皮武士》在社会各阶层中极受欢迎，因此我们可以说这部史诗在树立格鲁吉亚民众的中国意识方面发挥了重要作用。这一时期格鲁吉亚资料中有关中国的信息非常稀缺和粗浅，提到中国时大多只是将其作为地名。在波斯语和阿拉伯语著作中使用的表示中国的地名也几乎全都很快在格鲁吉亚传播开来。在 13 世纪中叶以前，格鲁吉亚人对中国的认识一直很肤

---

[1] А. Барамидзе, Ш. Радиани, В. Жгенти, *История Грузинской литературы краткий очерк*, Тбилиси: Заря Востока, 1958, ст. 16.

[2] Pier Giorgio Borbone, Les églises d'Asie centrale et de Chine: état de la question à partir des textes etdesdécouvertes archéologiques: *essai de synthèse*, *études syriaques* 10 - Les églises en monde syriaque, Paris, 2013, pp. 458–459.

[3] *Visramiani*, Kartuli mts'erloba, T'omi 3, Tbilisi: Nak'aduli, 1988, gv. 118, 185; *Et'lta da shvidta mnatobtatus* (*Treaty on constellations and seven stars*), Gamostsa, ts'inasit'q'vaoba da enobrivi mimokhilva daurto Akaki Shanidzem, Tbilisi: Tbilisis universit'et'is gamomtsemloba, 1975, gv. 29.

[4] [格] 鲁斯塔维利,《虎皮武士》, 严永兴译, 译林出版社 2002 年版, 第 181 页; Shota Rustaveli, Vepkhistq'aosani (*Knight in the panther's skin*), Redakt'ori: Dali Germanishvili, gv. 177.

浅。格鲁吉亚人把中国想象成半传说中远东地区一个强大的大国，人口众多，以高品质的产品著称。

在13世纪，格鲁吉亚社会对中国的认知发生了重大变化。其原因是新的信息大量流入格鲁吉亚社会。在13世纪40—50年代，蒙古人征服了格鲁吉亚之后，格鲁吉亚成为大蒙古帝国的一部分，加入了该帝国内的信息流动。众多格鲁吉亚人纷纷前往远东地区。例如，在1245—1248年，两位格鲁吉亚王位继承人前往当时蒙古帝国的首都哈拉和林（Karakorum）。除了他们，许多格鲁吉亚高官显贵、神职人员和勇士也纷纷前往那里[1]。伊尔汗国建立之后，格鲁吉亚国王和贵族经常拜访蒙古帝国的皇家宫廷，许多中国学者也在那里现身[2]。除此之外，格鲁吉亚与波斯之间的文学关系也进一步发展。格鲁吉亚学者对波斯的当代历史作品谙熟于心[3]。

基于上述所有因素，格鲁吉亚对中国的全新报道更加可靠。事实上，在13—14世纪的格鲁吉亚作品中，只有一篇提到了中国，但这些作品在质量和数量上均好于前一时期。无名作者将这些记载保存在历史作品《百年编年史》中。该编年史描述了蒙古人征服格鲁吉亚的过程，并在此背景下也谈到了蒙古人在中国的活动[4]。《百年编年史》"是一部历史作

---

[1] Jaba Samushia, *Davit Ulu*（*David VII*）, Tbilisi：Palitra L, 2019, gv. 77；*The journey of William of Rubruck to the eastern parts of the world as narrated by himself*, with two accounts of the earlier journey of John of Pian de Carpine, Translated from Latin, edited with an introductory notice by William Woodvile Rockhill, London：Haklyut society, 1900, p. 32.

[2] History of the Nation of the Archers（The Mongols）by Grigor of Akanc Hitherto Ascribedto Matakia The Monk, The Armenian Text Edited with an English Translation and Notes by Robert P. Blake andRichard N. Frye, *Harvard Journal of Asiatic Studies*, Vol. 12, No. 3/4, 1949, p 309；Bayarsaikhan Dashdondog, *The Mongols and the Armenians*（1220–1335）, Leiden, Boston：Brill, 2011, p. 196；Jean Richard, *La papauté et les missions d'Orient au Moyen–Âge*（XIII–XIVème siècle）, Rome：École Française de Rome, 1977, p. 85；J. A. Boyle, *Cambridge history of Iran*, Volume 5, the Saljuq and Mongol period, Cambridge-Cambridge history university press, 1968, p. 395；

[3] Juveinis tsnobebi Sakartvelos shesakheb（*Juvaini's records on Georgia*）, Sp'arsul t'ekst's shesavali ts'aumdzghvara, Kartuli targmani da shenishvnebi daurto Revaz K'ik'nadzem, Tbilisi：Metsniereba, 1974, gv. 16.

[4] Zhamtaagmts'ereli, Asts'lovani mat'iane（*Hundred years chronicle*）, t'ekst'i gamosatsemad moamzada, gamok'vleva, shenishvnebi da leksik'oni daurto Revaz K'ik'nadzem, Tbilisi, 1987, gv. 221.

品",根据这一事实,我们认为该作品所记载的信息比散文或诗歌作品更可靠"。格鲁吉亚读者第一次有机会在历史背景下了解中国,对中国的地理位置有一个大致了解。因此,格鲁吉亚人开始认识到,中国并不是传说中一个神秘莫测的王国,而是一个真实存在、有具体边界的地方。

在15—17世纪,格鲁吉亚社会对中国的了解发生倒退。这是由诸多外部因素引起的。特别是由于中亚局势持续动荡不安,贸易变得危险,"丝绸之路"上的交通流量逐渐减少[①]。因此,在波斯,来自东方的新信息也停止了流动,而波斯提供的有关中国的知识滋养了格鲁吉亚文学。由于缺少新信息,作者们开始对传统的旧知识进行再处理。在这一时期的波斯语和格鲁吉亚语著作中,中国再次被呈现为一个传说中的东方国家。

在18世纪,格鲁吉亚人对中国的认知发生了显著变化。主要原因是有关中国的信息来源发生了改变。特别值得一提的是,如上文所述,在18世纪以前,格鲁吉亚人是通过波斯认识中国的。自18世纪之后,欧洲在这方面占据了领先地位。信息来源的变化使得格鲁吉亚对中国认知上的发展产生了重大影响。虽然数百年来波斯一直是中东地区的文化和教育中心,但应该注意的是,中古时期的波斯资料为我们提供的有关中国的信息依然非常粗浅,这些信息主要是以口头方式通过商人传播到波斯的。波斯文学对中国最真实的描述出现于13世纪和14世纪,当时中国学者在历史上第一次亲自向波斯历史学家提供了一些信息[②]。然而,在随后的几个世纪里,随着"丝绸之路"的消失,新的信息交流也停止了,学者们不得不再次对旧知识进行再处理。因此,在16—17世纪,波斯文献中有关中国的信息已经延迟了几个世纪。

与波斯相反,欧洲对中国的认识在16世纪和17世纪迅速发展,耶稣会士对此做出了主要贡献。基督教传教士学习中文,并在中文资料和个

---

① Christopher I. Beckwith, *Empires of the Silk Road*, *A history of Central Eurasia from the Bronze Age to the present*, Princeton, Oxford: Princeton university press, 2009, p. 262.

② J. A. Boyle, *Cambridge history of Iran*, Volume 5, p. 510.

人经历的基础之上研究中国的历史、地理、宗教和哲学[①]。他们提供的信息以第一手资料为基础，因而真实可信。由于18世纪20年代在莫斯科建立了格鲁吉亚文化中心，这些欧洲资料被翻译为格鲁吉亚语[②]。因此，格鲁吉亚社会得以全方位了解中国的方方面面。

19世纪初，格鲁吉亚被俄罗斯帝国征服，格鲁吉亚贵族得以通过俄国接受欧洲教育，这对格鲁吉亚许多方面的社会生活产生了影响。其中值得注意的影响是，从19世纪中叶开始，格鲁吉亚新闻界迅速发展。除了国内时事，格鲁吉亚宣传人员还积极报道国际时事。格鲁吉亚宣传人员通过订阅外国杂志和报纸以及收发电报信息，密切关注时事发展动态。从19世纪90年代开始，格鲁吉亚新闻界开始定期积极报道中国事件。除了中国历史和文化的一般描述，读者还可以了解到义和团起义、欧洲国家在中国的行动、辛亥革命的进展情况以及中国的国内政治情况[③]。最重要的是，格鲁吉亚作者的文章不仅叙事清晰，而且注重分析。特别值得一提的是，作者没有忽略欧洲国家入侵中国的真实意图。尽管事实上当时的格鲁吉亚知识分子深受欧洲教育和价值观的影响，但他们依然向世人揭示了以下真相：欧洲人试图让中国沦为半殖民地国家，以给中国人民带来教育和新文化为借口来满足自身利益[④]。格鲁吉亚宣传人员也很快指出袁世凯有做皇帝的野心[⑤]。总之，他们尊重中国悠久的历史和深厚的文化底蕴，并且同情中国人民抵抗内敌外寇的革命运动。

1918年，格鲁吉亚趁俄罗斯帝国动乱之机重获独立。虽然仅维持了

[①] Mo Dongyin, *History of the development of Sinology*, Zhengzhou: Daxiang chubanshe, 2006, pp. 43 – 59.

[②] Pridon Sikharulidze, *Mosk'ovis kartuli k'ult'uris tsent'ris ist'oriidan* (*history of the Georgian Cultural Center in Moscow*), Tbilisi, 1990, gv. 16.

[③] Maia Machavariani, Chineti 1914 W'lis kartuli gazetebis furc'lebze (China on the pages of Georgian newspapers in 1914), *K'avk'asiis mac'ne*, nomeri 17, Tbilisi, 2008, gv. 162; *Kvali* (*Trace*), Nomeri 27, Tbilisi, 1900, gv. 428 – 430; *Sakhalkho Gazeti* (*People's News*), Nomeri 1155, Tbilisi, 1914, gv. 4; Ilia Tchavtchavadze, Akhlo da shoreuli aghosavletis p'olit'ik'is sak'itkhebi (Political issues of Near and Far East), *Iveria*, nomeri 18, T'filisi, 1898, gv. 1 – 2.

[④] *Kvali* (*Trace*), nomeri 35, Tbilisi, 1900, gv. 555 – 556.

[⑤] Nik'oloz Abesadze, Revoluciis molodinshi (Waiting for the Revolution), *Sakhalkho gazeti*, nomeri 1181 – 1185, Tbilisi, 1914.

三年，但在格鲁吉亚民主共和国短暂存在期间（1918—1921年），公众生活发生了诸多变化。其中，格鲁吉亚人对中国的关注主题也发生了变化。如果说以前格鲁吉亚人主要是关注中国的政治，那么此时他们的主要关注对象则是中国的经济。格鲁吉亚当时的报刊杂志纷纷发表有关中国经济形势和发展的文章①。这种关注主题的改变绝非偶然，很大程度上与哈尔滨格鲁吉亚人社区息息相关。

在讨论格鲁吉亚人的中国意识形成史时，哈尔滨格鲁吉亚人社区是一个需要单独谈论的问题。哈尔滨市成立于19世纪和20世纪之交。在这座城市里，格鲁吉亚人有史以来第一次在中国领土上建立了一个定居点。在哈尔滨成立之初的几十年里，吸引着俄罗斯帝国的流亡人员和探险人员纷至沓来。在20世纪10年代末，有三四千格鲁吉亚人居住在哈尔滨及其周边地区②。哈尔滨格鲁吉亚人社区并非脱离于格鲁吉亚而孤立发展，而是与祖国有着密切接触。后来，格鲁吉亚民主共和国甚至在哈尔滨设立了领事馆③。在此之前，在格鲁吉亚恢复独立之后，哈尔滨格鲁吉亚人社区派出代表向格鲁吉亚民主共和国国会递交了经济计划④。该计划旨在积极建立格鲁吉亚与远东地区（包括中国）的经贸关系，并提出格鲁吉亚进出口产品的总体计划⑤。这是格鲁吉亚首次提出与中国开展直接经济合作的想法。其结果是，格鲁吉亚民主共和国对中国经济的兴趣日益浓厚。遗憾的是，上述经济计划未能付诸履行，1921年，格鲁吉亚成为苏联的一员。

在作为苏联加盟国期间，中国在格鲁吉亚人认知中的发展可以分为

---

① E. Nodia, *Chineti（China）*, K'avshiri, nomeri 17 – 18, Tbilisi, 1920, gv. 14 – 17.

② Sakartvelos evornuli cent'raluri saist'orio arkivi (National Central historical archives of Georgia), pondi 1864, anaw'eri 2, sakme 512, f. 4.

③ Irak'li Giorgadze, *Erovnuli modzraobis taviseburebani sakartveloshi XX sauk'unis 20 – 90 – ian w'lebshi（Characteristics of national movement in Georgia between 1920 – 1990s）*, Telavi – Iak'ob gogebashvilis sakhelobis telavis sakhelmw'ifo universit'et'i, 2016, gv. 155.

④ Irak'li Giorgadze, *Erovnuli modzraobis taviseburebani sakartveloshi XX sauk'unis 20 – 90 – ian w'lebshi（Characteristics of national movement in Georgia between 1920 – 1990s）*, გვ. 59.

⑤ Sakartvelos evornuli cent'raluri saist'orio arkivi (National Central historical archives of Georgia), pondi 1864, anaw'eri 2, sakme 512, f. 7.

两个阶段。第一阶段持续到20世纪50年代。在第一阶段,中国的政治形势再次成为格鲁吉亚人关注的主要主题。20世纪20—30年代,格鲁吉亚新闻界积极报道中国的政治形势[1]。中华人民共和国成立之后,格鲁吉亚人将中国视为最亲密的盟友和友好国家之一。

自20世纪60年代以来,格鲁吉亚人对中国的关注焦点再次发生转变。这一次,格鲁吉亚人关注的对象从政治转向了文化,彰显中国是一个有着伟大文化的国度。格鲁吉亚科学家对中国这一遥远国度的文学和哲学兴趣盎然。中国诗歌和散文、哲学论文纷纷被翻译成格鲁吉亚语[2]。然而,这里应该注意的是,这一时期格鲁吉亚科学家对中国文化的关注和认知具有一定的特殊性,在后来的一段时间里一些科学家仍然保持着这些特殊性。在苏联时期,尽管格鲁吉亚与中国保持着密切的政治关系,但尚未建立汉学研究机构。因此,那些研究中国文化和翻译中国文献的学者,实际上并不会讲中文,也看不懂中文,而是通过俄语这一媒介来了解中国文化。缺少资料来源,不懂中文,对中国只有肤浅的认识,这些因素最终导致上述学者尝试在西方哲学的框架下了解中国哲学和文化[3]。因此,在许多情况下,他们误解了中国古代哲学的概念。尽管如此,这是格鲁吉亚研究中国文化的一个重要时期,因为这是朝着对中国进行科学研究的方向努力的首要步骤。

在格鲁吉亚恢复独立的近三十年里,格鲁吉亚社会上的中国现象和公众对中国的认知愈加复杂和深刻。与以往各个时期不同的是,对中国的关注并不局限于一个方面。早在20世纪90年代,格鲁吉亚总统爱德华·谢瓦尔德纳泽(Eduard Shevardnadze)就在积极推动 TRASECA 项目,

---

[1] P'. Saq'varelidze, *Dzveli da akhali chineti* (*Old and new China*), Tbilisi: sakhelmw'ipo gamomtsemloba, 1926; *Musha* (*Worker*), nomeri 1564, Tbilisi, 1928, gv. 2; I. Morozovi, Chineti dghes (*China now*), *Remedas*, nomeri 1, Tbilisi, 1930, gv. 2.

[2] Rem Davidovi, Chineti kartul lit'erat'urashi (China in the Georgian literature), *Lit'erat'uruli sakartvelo*, nomeri 23, Tbilisi, 1993, gv. 4; Jarji fkhoveli, *Dzveli chinuri poezia* (*Ancient Chinese poetry*), Tbilisi: Merani, 1985; 1952 *Chinuri motkhrobebis k'rebuli*, Shesavali Sh. Alkhazishvili, Tbilisi: sabavshvo da akhalgazrdobis lit'erat'uris sakhelmw'ifo gamomtsemloba, 1952.

[3] Mosia T'it'e, *Dzveli chinuri p'oezia* (*Ancient Chinese poetry*), Tbilisi: Inovatsia, 2010.

即欧洲—高加索—亚洲运输走廊项目①。从这一时期开始，格鲁吉亚就已经将中国视为未来的经济伙伴。近十年来，由于格鲁吉亚积极参与习近平主席发起的"一带一路"倡议，两国的经济伙伴关系取得了长足进展。如今，中国是格鲁吉亚最大的经济伙伴之一②。可以说，哈尔滨格鲁吉亚人社区的代表在1919年向格鲁吉亚国会递交的经济计划在一个世纪之后终于实现了。

自1991年重获独立以来，格鲁吉亚做出了巨大努力，以提高公众和科学界对中国的认识。1991年，格鲁吉亚有史以来第一次在第比利斯建立了汉学科研所——亚非国家学院，为格鲁吉亚培养了第一批汉学家。如今，多所大学和其他教育机构设有汉学研究师资或研究所。格鲁吉亚每年翻译大量的中文文献和科技作品，举办汉学研究会议，出版有关中国的书籍。格鲁吉亚科学界不再完全依赖英语或俄语等中间语言来获得有关中国的信息，而是可以直接获取中文资料，因此对中国的认知更加真实。然而，同样应该注意的是，在两国关系中，文化与科学交流是最需要努力的方面。在现代格鲁吉亚人的眼中，中国主要是最密切的经济伙伴之一和世界超级大国。换言之，格鲁吉亚人现在主要将经济和政治因素放到了前面，再次将文化因素移到了后台。

总之，格鲁吉亚人对中国的认识和关注点随着时代的变化而不断转变。早在"丝绸之路"存在的最初几个世纪里，格鲁吉亚社会就开始知道中国了。在中古时期，一直到18世纪，格鲁吉亚人对中国的认知都是通过贸易路线上传来的信息、在想象中形成的。然而，在这一时期，中国在格鲁吉亚主要被视为一个遥远的、近乎传说中的国家。从18世纪开始，欧洲资料进入格鲁吉亚，格鲁吉亚人才大致知道中国是一个真实存在的国家。在19世纪和20世纪，格鲁吉亚人进一步细化和深化了对中国的认知，对中国的政治、经济和文化也有了大致的了解。在恢复独立后，格鲁吉亚社会开始在复杂背景下认识中国。与20世纪不同的是，如今格

---

① Eduard Shevardnadze, *Didi abreshumis gza（Silk road）*, Tbilisi: Metsniereba, 1999, gv. 60.
② Joseph Larsen, *Georgia-China relations: The geopolitics of the Belt and Road*, Tbilisi, 2017, pp. 6–8.

鲁吉亚人不再只关注中国的政治经济或任何一个特定方面，而是开始综合利用不同来源的信息，从多个视角认识中国。这一进程仍处于初始阶段。不过，相关总体进展情况表明，与政治和经济领域相比，格鲁吉亚人对中国文化的认识存在一定程度的滞后，需要再接再厉。

中国式现代化和社会发展对格鲁吉亚的影响

塔玛尔·巴达舒里[*]

近年来，中格合作取得了巨大成就，两国之间的双边关系更加稳固，合作更加富有成效。毫不夸张地说，作为世界大国的中国与格鲁吉亚之间的友谊、特别是近几年来不断增进的合作关系，已成为世界上国与国关系发展的典范。

毋庸置疑，中国是21世纪引领世界经济发展的重要国家之一。自独立以来，随着其角色的回归，格鲁吉亚重新焕发出巨大的发展潜力，成为连接欧洲和亚洲的重要门户。我们为格鲁吉亚近年来经济和社会发展所取得的成就感到自豪，这在一定程度上得益于不断深化的中格合作关系。

近年来，中国一直是格鲁吉亚非常重要的合作伙伴，这主要体现在中国对格鲁吉亚经济的投资大幅增长，对推动格鲁吉亚国内经济发展发挥了重要作用。尽管新冠疫情仍在全球蔓延，但是与上年同期相比，格鲁吉亚与中国之间的贸易仍在增长，这是一个非常有说服力的事例。

格鲁吉亚是本地区第一个与中国签署自由贸易协议的国家，这保证了格鲁吉亚产品和服务进入世界上最大的消费市场。与此同时，该协议

---

[*] 塔玛尔·巴达舒里，格鲁吉亚青年汉学家，格鲁吉亚第比利斯阿尔特大学和国民大学讲师。

对格鲁吉亚新增的投资合作项目具有非常重要的激励作用。格鲁吉亚还与欧洲和独联体建立了自由贸易关系，这将促进中国和格鲁吉亚周边国家的开放，推动格鲁吉亚向西进入欧洲，使格鲁吉亚成为独联体和欧洲与中国连接的桥梁与纽带。

众所周知，中国和格鲁吉亚的传统友谊源远流长。古"丝绸之路"对两国之间的友谊与合作产生了重要影响。对于格鲁吉亚来说，成为"一带一路"倡议的积极参与者，对发展本国经济具有重要意义。

甘肃省对与格鲁吉亚开展合作表现出了极大的热情。武威保税物流中心运营管理有限公司与格鲁吉亚国家主权基金会"格鲁吉亚伙伴基金会"签署了框架合作协议，该协议将成为加强两国务实合作、落实"一带一路"倡议的重要依据。特别值得一提的是，该协议为中欧货运班列的开通提供了便利条件。

中国是格鲁吉亚可信赖的战略合作伙伴，是世界上最早承认格鲁吉亚主权和领土完整并同格鲁吉亚建交的国家之一。目前，格中关系正处于最佳时期，两国之间的政治互信不断增强，经贸合作亮点频出，人文交流日益密切。

习近平主席指出，中格是传统友好合作伙伴。建交30年来，双方扎实推进各领域合作，在国际事务中有效沟通协调，推动中格关系健康稳定发展。新冠疫情暴发后，两国人民真诚互助，共克时艰，谱写了团结抗疫的佳话。

中国的现代化和社会发展对格鲁吉亚的影响

毫不谦虚地说，过去7年来，中国作为世界上最大的国家之一，同格鲁吉亚这个只有400万人口的小国之间发生的事情，为其他国家树立了榜样。

在21世纪的世界经济中，中国是领先的国家之一，这一点无可辩驳。格鲁吉亚对中华人民共和国主席习近平发起的"一带一路"这个全球重大项目的兴趣和作用相当大。该倡议于2013年发起，令人自豪的是，格鲁吉亚是最早响应并加入这一倡议的国家之一。格鲁吉亚在第比利斯举办了第三届"一带一路"论坛，其间多次强调格鲁吉亚是古丝绸之路和新丝绸之路的中心，这不仅归因于格鲁吉亚的地理位置，还归因于数百年来我们国家向世界展示的历史、文化和宽容。

在战略职能不断扩大的同时，格鲁吉亚正在成为具有巨大潜力的通往欧洲和亚洲的门户。

格鲁吉亚非常重视与世界贸易组织的合作。加入该组织是格鲁吉亚在融入世界经济体系方面取得的一项重要成就：格鲁吉亚在国际经济体系中的地位得到了加强，格鲁吉亚作为贸易伙伴的影响力和吸引力增大；格鲁吉亚显著改善了吸引外商投资的条件，为投资者提供了长期的贸易政策，外国市场对格鲁吉亚产品开放；另一方面，向国际市场出口格鲁吉亚产品的条件得到了改善，格鲁吉亚企业家通过世贸组织多边协定在国际市场上得到保护，不受歧视。

格鲁吉亚积极参与世贸组织的多边贸易谈判，旨在最大程度地减少贸易壁垒，从而进一步实现世界贸易自由化。另外，在与世贸组织的合作中，格鲁吉亚的法律框架与欧洲的法律框架更加协调，这是实现欧盟一体化战略目标的先决条件。

格鲁吉亚正在成为区域内和全世界的一个贸易、运输和物流枢纽。其中一个重要原因是与世界上的主要国家建立了自由贸易体制。2014年发生了一件重要的历史事件：格鲁吉亚与欧盟签署了《联合协定》，随后又签署了《深入全面自由贸易协定》，使得格鲁吉亚可以将其货物、服务和资本自由流通到欧盟市场。从经济角度来看，这意味着货物和服务可以在拥有5亿消费者的欧洲市场上自由流动。随着签证自由化进程的推进，格鲁吉亚公民可以在欧盟国家内自由行动。

而且，格鲁吉亚还与土耳其、独联体和欧洲自由贸易联盟签署了自由贸易协定，这是格鲁吉亚投资环境的明显优势。另外，格鲁吉亚还提高了开办企业和财产登记的办事效率，简化了税制，降低了税率。

作为格鲁吉亚与中国的自由贸易协定的一部分，格鲁吉亚最大的商品和服务自由贸易市场于2017年开放了。根据与中国的自由贸易协定，约有94%的格鲁吉亚出口商品被免除关税。该协定有力推动了新增投资项目在格鲁吉亚的实施、企业家精神的培养和格鲁吉亚产品出口的扩大。反过来，中国公司也有机会通过格鲁吉亚将其产品销往欧洲市场。

正如我前面提到的，"丝绸之路"的发展是格鲁吉亚政府非常重视的一件事。因此，目前全国各地正在建设的东西公路、巴库—第比利斯—卡尔斯铁路现代化、阿纳克里亚（Anaklia）深水港等重要基础设施项目也是丝绸之路的一部分。对于扩大跨地区交通流量、推动里海大铁路的建设来说，贯穿格鲁吉亚的"丝绸之路"的开通是一个重要事件。里海大铁路通过欧洲国家将中国、哈萨克斯坦、阿塞拜疆、亚美尼亚和格鲁吉亚连接起来。这些庞大的国际市场不仅为格鲁吉亚，而且为伙伴国家和潜在投资者提供了新的机遇。

在鼓励投资方面，我想强调的是格鲁吉亚最大的金融机构——完全国有的 JSC 伙伴基金。通过与该基金合作，合作伙伴可以利用格鲁吉亚的投资潜力，并享受与世界其他国家和地区开展自由贸易的好处。我们感到自豪的是，JSC 伙伴基金已成为投资者发家致富的保证。

英国广播公司一位爱尔兰裔知名分析师指出，在第比利斯论坛框架内，20 年前爱尔兰是欧洲最贫穷的国家之一，如今爱尔兰已成为欧洲第二富国，仅次于卢森堡。作为一个格鲁吉亚人，我非常希望在 20 年后格鲁吉亚能够在大伙伴和"一带一路"这一世纪工程的帮助下，成为本地区和全世界最发达、最繁荣的国家之一。

众所周知，中国和格鲁吉亚的传统友谊源远流长。古"丝绸之路"对两国之间的友谊与合作产生了重要影响。对于格鲁吉亚来说，成为"一带一路"倡议的积极参与者，对发展本国经济具有重要意义。

中国是格鲁吉亚可信赖的战略合作伙伴，是世界上最早承认格鲁吉亚主权和领土完整并同格鲁吉亚建交的国家之一。目前，格中关系正处于最佳时期，两国之间的政治互信不断增强，经贸合作亮点频出。

值得强调的是，近年来，中国在格鲁吉亚的伙伴中独领风骚，中国对格鲁吉亚经济的投资大幅增长。尽管新冠疫情仍在，但格鲁吉亚对华贸易额较 2021 年同期有所增长。

此外，许多格鲁吉亚公司纷纷扩大在中国的业务，格鲁吉亚在中国设立的商务办事处和文化中心不断增多，格鲁吉亚葡萄酒、烈酒、矿泉水和格鲁吉亚茶在中国的销量不断增长。

我想强调的是，中格传统友谊源远流长。古"丝绸之路"对两国友谊与合作产生了重要影响。重要的是，格鲁吉亚成为新"丝绸之路"上"一带一路"倡议的重要参与者。

应当注意的是，格鲁吉亚是本地区第一个与中国签署自由贸易协议的国家。该协议为格鲁吉亚产品和服务打开了世界上最大的市场。另外，该协议对格鲁吉亚新增的投资合作项目具有非常重要的激励作用。格鲁吉亚还与欧洲和独联体建立了自由贸易关系。我们的目标是将格鲁吉亚打造成欧洲和独联体国家与中国连接的桥梁与纽带。

据我所知，甘肃是中国铁路网的重要枢纽，为全国各大铁路货运公司提供服务。因此，我相信，随着中格自由贸易协定的实施以及目前双方合作协议的签署，在我们的共同努力下，贯穿格鲁吉亚的中欧走廊会在短时间内开通。

"丝绸之路经济带"（SREB）最初是一个全球性项目，规划了新欧亚大陆桥、中蒙俄经济走廊、中亚—西亚经济走廊、中南半岛经济走廊、中巴经济走廊、孟中印缅经济走廊等多条经济走廊，其中穿越高加索地区的经济走廊没有明确规划；然而，这当然并不妨碍中国企业在高加索地区开展经济活动。应当指出的是，格鲁吉亚走廊（以及阿塞拜疆走廊）位于中亚—西亚经济走廊上。

从 20 世纪 90 年代初开始，格鲁吉亚及其邻国和战略盟友阿塞拜疆就被纳入古代"大丝路"的背景。这一想法产生的实际影响包括：1993 年欧盟发起了 TRACEC（欧洲—高加索—亚洲交通走廊）项目，1996 年启动了 INOGATE 项目（向欧洲输送石油和天然气国家间项目），该项目后来得到了美国国会 1999 年通过的《丝绸之路战略法案》的支持。事实上，几乎所有为"丝绸之路"运输走廊而规划的项目目前都在成功运作。这些项目有一个缺陷：其目的是打造运输走廊和能源走廊，通过高加索地区连接欧洲与中亚；然而，欧盟并没有想到要把这些走廊一直延伸到中国。

"丝绸之路运输走廊"（SRTC）项目已经实施，促进了阿塞拜疆和格鲁吉亚（作为高加索地区联合体）加入"丝绸之路经济带"项目。巴库—第比利斯—卡尔斯铁路是"丝绸之路运输走廊"项目的一个重要组成部分，不仅通过铁路连接阿塞拜疆、格鲁吉亚和土耳其，而且还通过高加索地区连接东西方。上述铁路不仅是"钢铁丝绸之路"项目的重要组成部分，也是"一带一路"倡议的合理组成部分。

中国与欧盟正在积极讨论建立自由贸易体制，这对格鲁吉亚非常重要。就这一点而言，"丝绸之路经济带"开创了中国与欧盟经济合作的新局面。

中国和格鲁吉亚都是世贸组织的成员。两国签署了自由贸易协定，这对发展两国贸易关系非常重要。格鲁吉亚还与欧盟签署了深入全面自由贸易区（DCFTA）协定，与欧洲自由贸易联盟（EFTA）签署了自由贸易协定。因此，扩大欧盟与中国之间的贸易将推动格鲁吉亚成为连接中国与欧洲的物流枢纽（巴库—第比利斯—卡尔斯铁路以及阿纳克里亚黑海深水港项目的实施将非常重要），同时提高格鲁吉亚的安全水平。

更值得注意的是，由于里海石油和天然气输送到土耳其，格鲁吉亚已经扮演着能源运输枢纽的角色。如果我们还考虑到阿塞拜疆也设法树立区域交通枢纽的形象，我们可以说这两个国家（格鲁吉亚和阿塞拜疆）联合起来共同打造了高加索中部的一个运输和能源枢纽。

对于格鲁吉亚来说，"丝绸之路经济带"项目为其从能源运输枢纽转变为区域经济枢纽创造了机会。在这方面，应当强调的是，由于欧盟与格鲁吉亚签署了深入全面自由贸易区协定，从格鲁吉亚出口到欧盟的产品必须是在格鲁吉亚生产的。因此，格鲁吉亚可以吸引所有与没有与欧盟签署自由贸易协定的国家到格鲁吉亚投资，然后将在格鲁吉亚生产的产品出口到欧盟市场。中国就在这些国家之列，目前已经在格鲁吉亚投资了。

因此，格鲁吉亚实际上可以成为本地区的经济枢纽，这将完全符合穿越格鲁吉亚的中亚—西亚经济走廊项目的建设内容。

格鲁吉亚在其中一个走廊（即："丝绸之路运输走廊"项目的中亚—西亚经济走廊）上占有一席之地，该走廊主要为格鲁吉亚的经济发展开辟了新的途径。

格鲁吉亚和邻国阿塞拜疆一起，积极参与"丝绸之路运输走廊"的建立和发展。目前该走廊已在顺利运作。

"丝绸之路经济带"堪称"丝绸之路运输走廊"的进一步发展，因为该运输走廊正在转变成一个更具复合性的经济走廊。

格鲁吉亚已经与欧盟和中国签署了自由贸易协定，因此可以在"丝绸之路经济带"项目中发挥经济枢纽的作用。

格鲁吉亚可以利用"丝绸之路经济带"项目带来的契机，由能源运输枢纽变身为区域经济枢纽。就这一点而言，应当强调的是，根据欧盟与格鲁吉亚签署的深入全面自由贸易区（DCFTA）协定，从格鲁吉亚出口到欧盟的产品必须是在格鲁吉亚生产的。因此，格鲁吉亚可以吸引所有与没有与欧盟签署自由贸易协定的国家到格鲁吉亚投资，然后将在格鲁吉亚生产的产品出口到欧盟市场。中国就在这些国家之列，目前已经在格鲁吉亚投资了。

鉴于当今世界发生恐怖袭击和其他工业灾害的风险增加，有必要建立互补的运输和能源走廊，确保运输流的最大连续性。技术灾害、运输灾害或其他人为灾难的风险增加，彰显了发展运输走廊或经济走廊的重要性，这些走廊能够确保在危急情况下可以相互替代。

因此，要实现各经济走廊的互补与协调，必须基于这样一种办法：不根据路线的替代性，而是根据其互补性，检查亚洲能源输送到欧洲的路线。

应当指出的是，转为经济走廊互补范式最终会确保在双赢合作关系的背景下实施"一带一路"倡议，这对于该倡议最终取得成功至关重要。

阿塞拜疆和格鲁吉亚在中国"一带一路"倡议的框架内扮演着重要角色。华凌自由工业园区位于格鲁吉亚库塔伊西，是连接第比利斯（格鲁吉亚首都）与格鲁吉亚黑海港口波季（Poti）和巴塔米（Batumi）的重要枢纽。

华凌自由工业园区是由中国投资、由华凌集团建设的，2015年投入运营。尽管新冠疫情肆虐，但2021年华凌自由工业园区的投资客户群仍有所扩大，年内新增25家注册公司。

"2021年最重要的举措之一是由加拿大和中国的投资者共同开发一个

与木材加工和家具生产有关的项目。该项目为华凌自由工业园区的生产和进一步出口做准备。"

该项目初步预算为150万美元，按照计划，预算总额将增加到700万美元。

预计不久将有更多投资投入该园区，一家中国公司将开始在华凌自由工业园区生产和出口铁合金和金属硅。投资总额达500万美元，预计随着业务的发展，投资总额还会增长。2021年在华凌自由工业园区还启动了一个塑料回收项目。该项目投资总额约为200万美元。

华凌自由工业园区主要与轻工业领域的制造商洽谈业务。其中有一家从事纺织品生产和出口的德国投资者。

"该项目启动后大约将雇用2000人，投资总额约为300万欧元。"在绿色能源领域的项目中，华凌自由工业园区吸引了太阳能电池板生产项目入驻园区——这是欧洲—高加索地区该领域最大的项目。该项目的投资总额已达1000万美元，出口主要面向北美市场。

华凌自由工业园区现有90家企业入驻，其中贸易企业占70%，制造业企业占25%，服务业企业占5%。凭借这一成就，预计华凌自由工业园区将与格鲁吉亚政府签署协议，将园区占地面积由现有的36公顷扩大到58公顷，未来有望扩大到200公顷。

在华凌自由工业园区生产或交易的商品主要出口到南高加索地区和中亚、欧盟、北美和墨西哥。华凌自由工业园区与阿塞拜疆投资者密切合作，东部是阿塞拜疆的巴库港，位于里海沿岸，连接中亚、伊朗和通往印度的INSTC（国际南北运输走廊）路线。

货运服务里程达800多公里，从卡尔斯经格鲁吉亚到巴库，全程大约需要三天时间，这意味着这不是最初所宣传的高速铁路线。由于巴库—第比利斯—卡尔斯铁路穿过格鲁吉亚时火车轨距发生改变，增加了额外的成本。

撇开巴库—第比利斯—卡尔斯铁路在里海—欧洲过境问题不谈，"一带一路"倡议要从基础设施投资项目转变为初始投资基础之上的现金流生成器，首先要在"一带一路"沿线发展由中国和当地投资的自由贸易和产业园区。"一带一路"沿线的投资者——比如华凌自由工业园区——

现在能够创造利润，并帮助自己所投资的客户进行生产和贸易。"一带一路"基础设施投资所展现出的最终结果是，贸易额和出口额增加，而衡量"一带一路"基础设施投资是否成功的最终标准正是这种能力的提高，而不是项目融资。

Chapter 1 Chinese Modernization and the Chinese Experience of Modernization Development

Chinese Modernization and the Formation of its Modernization Discourse System

Zhang Yi[*]

I. Modernization, Western-centrism, as well as European and American Modernization Discourses

Modernization[①] refers to the process of human development since it took the turn to an industrial society from an agricultural society, which is embodied mainly by a range of evolution in modes of production, distribution, exchange, consumption, and social organization triggered by technological innovation, as

---

[*] Zhang Yi, Professor, Director of National Institute of Social Development, CASS.

[①] What is modernization theory? It has been a controversial issue for a long time in academic circles. Since the 1950s, research on modernization has gone through three phases: "classic modernization theory", "post-modernization theory", and "new modernization theory". The focus of academic discussion has been different in these phases. The first period focused on the modernization of developing countries that gradually became independent after World War II, the second period focused on reflecting the first period's modernization theory, and the third period focused on scientific and technological progress and social risk control. Refer to *How to Become a Modernized Country* by He Chuanqi, which was published in *WORLD SCI-TECH R&D*, No. 1, 2018, pages 5 – 16.

well as the process of transformation of the entire social structure[1]. In general, it can be divided into two stages: stage 1, when it transformed into an industrial society from an agricultural society and is featured by the transformation of social structure brought about by the industrial revolution caused by the invention of big machines; stage 2, when it transformed to a post-industrial society from an industrial society and is featured by the social structure transformation brought by the AI revolution caused by IT[2]. Of course, if we refine the latest transformation trend of human society, we can also construct the third or fourth stage of the theoretical hypothesis[3] of modernization. As a result of the constant evolution of post-industrialization, the focus of current social practice and theoretical research has gradually shifted to the transformation of human beings to a digital society or a human-robot coexistence society contributed by the Internet, AI, big data, blockchain, and metaverse[4].

Modernization originated in Britain and France. Therefore, from the perspective of a frame of reference, Western academic circles often refer to this evolution of Western Europe as "modernization from within", while that of other countries and regions influenced by Western Europe as "modernization from

---

[1] Modernization is closely tied to development when it is explained as a process. Refer to *The Modernization of China* by Gilbert Rozman, which was translated by the "Comparative Modernization" Research Group under the National Social Science Fund, published by Nanjing: Jiangsu People's Publishing House in 1995, page 4.

[2] In his book *China's Megatrends*, Naisbitt fully affirmed Daniel Bell's judgment in his book *The Coming of Post-Industrial Society*, and called the society following the industrial society the "information society", and believed that the former totally disrupted the social structure.

[3] Luo Rongqu summed modernization up as "three modernization waves" in discussions regarding its periods. The first period is between 1780 – 1860, which was driven by the industrial revolution; the second is from the second half of the 19th century to the beginning of the 20th century, which was mainly driven by "electricity and steel"; and the third started from the second half of the 20th century, which was mainly driven by petroleum energy, synthetic materials, microelectronics technology, and AI. Refer to A New Theory to Modernization by Luo Rongqu, Shanghai: East China Normal University Press, 2013, pages 108 – 113.

[4] Against the backdrop of the Internet of everything, the development in the future will also feature a tri-world of people, computers, and things.

without". In the early stage of evolution, "modernization from within" is mingled with the preemptive (early occurrence), while "modernization from without" is closely related to the secondary nature. With that said, Western academic circles constructed the concepts of "preemptive modernization from within" and "secondary modernization from without" by combining preemptive occurrence with "modernization from within". Driven by globalization, countries worldwide strengthened all-around exchanges in politics, economy, society, culture, and ecological civilization after World War II. It makes the modernization of countries/regions interwoven with exogenous factors in endogenous factors and endogenous factors nested in exogenous factors. However, in the sense of path dependence and discourse hegemony, most developing countries are endowed with strong characteristics of "secondary modernization from without".

As "modernity" features changes in contrast to "tradition", modernization carries the "well-developed" industrial characteristics of early modernization claimed by the West if the agricultural society is regarded as the reference of modern society. With that said, the so-called classical modernization theory for the purpose of studying modernization constructed the "tradition-modernity" theoretical analysis framework based on the origin and development course of Western capitalism. By virtue of the disclosure hegemony they possess, they classify countries around the world, such as Western Europe and North America, as "modern", "advanced", "rational", "democratic", and "secular", while the vast number of developing countries as "traditional", "backward" and "uncivilized". Thus, what Western scholars called "Western-centrism" or "Eurocentrism" formed. It not only laid a practical foundation for Western intellectuals to construct "Western Orientalism", but laid the theoretical foundation for modernization as referred to by the West in discourse. "The East in the eyes of the West" was systematized by ways of asymmetric dissemination of education and knowledge as well as follow-up study over oriental society by various disciplines. It was then fitted into the academic system of developing countries, forming a Western-centered explanatory power over the Eastern society. Not only did this "discourse hegemony" strengthen the "explanatory power" of the West over the East during the colonial and semi-colonial periods, but it also strengthened the ideological control of Western developed countries over developing countries during the post-colonial period[1]. The modern knowledge system based on "American centralism", i. e. , the so-called Anglo-Saxon modern knowledge system, came into being gradually at the end of World War II when the economic center shifted to the United States from Europe. As the British Royal Family has the gene from Norman, some would add Norman to enrich the connotation of the system. The modernization is endowed with the color of "development and progress" in the Western sense. Therefore, modern philosophy and social science that is characterized by modernization feature Western-Originated "start-up-maturity" path dependence.

The West also gave birth to capitalist production relations while it quickly promoted the productivity revolution in modern times. In every stage of its development, the bourgeoisie transformed its political superstructure accordingly. The *Magna Carta*, enforced in the 13th century, restricted the feudal monarchy. The Tudor dynasty formed an autocratic monarchy dominated by Protestantism. In this sense, the development of productive forces has also fueled the reform of autocratic monarchy and religious superstructures. The British bourgeois revolution, which began in 1640, finally led Cromwell to be guillotined by King Charles I. The Glorious Revolution from 1688 to 1689 established the constitutional monarchy whereby capitalist rule stabilized the achievements of the industrial revolution, forming the basic pattern in which the King "reigns but does not govern" . The parliamentary reform of 1832 guaranteed the voting rights of the industrial bourgeoisie. The People's Charter Movement in 1837 abolished the restrictions on property qualifications of parliamentary candidates and gave urban men who reached the age of 21 the right to elect and vote anonymously. The par-

---

[1] Edward W. Said: Orientalism, translated by Wang Yugen, Beijing, SDX Joint Publishing Company, 1999, page 16.

liamentary reform of 1884 finally gave all adult men the right to vote.

Louis XV's belligerence, persistent inflation, and successive natural disasters in France have aroused contradictions among the first, second, and third classes. The Enlightenment mobilized the revolutionary zeal of the bourgeoisie, which had already achieved a dominant position in the economy. The bourgeoisie initiated the world-famous "Great Revolution" in 1789 by combining and making use of the working class and the peasant class. As a result, the *Declaration of the Rights of Man and the Citizen* (declaring that men are born, and always continue, free and equal in respect of their rights) was adopted, the first Republic of France was established, and Louis XVI was guillotined. In the end, the revolutionary achievements were consolidated by the "Brumaire Coup". The *Napoleonic Code* was promulgated, which spread the idea that "all male citizens are equal, separation of the three powers, social contract, inviolability of private property, and all people are equal before the law". According to explanations of Tocqueville, the Great Revolution was not only a revolution of the religious power of the old system but also a revolution of the kingship. From the perspective of violent direction, the Great Revolution directly broke the kingship. The feudal autocratic government, i. e. , the centralized government, believed that "There is only one administrative entity, which shall be placed in the center of the Kingdom of France, and national administrative management systems are to be formulated by it; almost all domestic affairs are to be headed by only one minister; all specific affairs of all provinces are also in charge of an agent; There are no affiliated administrative agencies or agencies that can act with prior approval; The special court hears all cases related to the government and shelters all government officials. "[1] The preceding explains why people vented all their anger on the central government when the government's actions went farther and farther away from people's expectations. In consequence, revolutions

---

[1] Tocqueville: *The Old Regime and the Revolution*, Section 5, Chapter 2, translated by Li Yanming, Yilin Press, 2018 Edition.

broke out one after another, continuously and fiercely, until the feudal autocratic rule was completely overthrown.

As suggested by the whole history of modernization, it also forced superstructures to change along with economic bases as it changed the traditional social productive forces and production relations. Thus, governments, religions, and societies were pushed constantly to transform: a government was pushed to transform to bourgeois rule from feudal aristocratic landlord autocracy, and a religion was put permanently under the state's authority. Consequently, a prosperous industrial society became stepwise in the course of capitalist economic development. To sum up, modernization, as a part of Western history, was not the result of peaceful development but the superstructure reconstruction built through the baptism of the rubble of old systems. Either Britain or France established a bourgeois country different from the feudal era only through a series of protracted violent or non-violent revolutions (Glorious Revolution). They began to expand continuously to the outside world after completing theallocation of the domestic economic base and superstructure. In consequence, America, Asia, and Africa were colonized. Since then, they have also constructed the disclosure relationship between the suzerain state and its colonial states in the discourse system of western modernization. They even inhumanely promoted the "slave trade"[1]. The development of capitalist modernization triggered World War I and World War II, which finally started its next journey by taking the lives of millions of innocent people.

As Marx and Engels said in the *Communist Manifesto*, "The discovery of America and the voyage around Africa helped open up a new world for the emerging bourgeoisie. The discovered markets in East India and China, the colonization of America, the trade with colonies, means of exchange, and the in-

---

[1] Just as Marx once said, the extreme hypocrisy of bourgeois civilization and its barbaric nature shows up naked in front of us when we turn our eyes to colonies from the hometown of bourgeois civilization. It still pretends to be decent in its hometown. However, in the colony, it makes no disguise at all.

crease of general commodities have led to an unprecedented upsurge in commerce, navigation, and industry. As a result, revolutionary factors within the collapsing feudal society developed rapidly. " This implies that capital using its modern logic (even if it promoted capitalism in a colonial way) to modify modifies the logic of social development and transformation of places wherever it sweeps.

In a word, the practice of modernization in the West, from its germination to fruition, is strung together by such disclosures as the Renaissance, Great Navigation and Discovery of the New World, Enlightenment and Humanism, attaching importance to science and technology, and promoting religious reform. They laid the foundation of modern science and modern philosophy and social science of the West[1]. In the construction of countries, systems like "equality of human rights", "inviolability of private property", and "separation of powers" were designed to build a capitalist superstructure, and a civil society was developed, thereby promoting humankind to enter the industrial and post-industrial societies. Religious reforms liberated people from the Vatican, the spokesman of God, and transformed them into "diligent" workers who accepted their "destinies" to accumulate wealth and invest for profits reasonably. Therefore, the adaptability between the religious superstructure and the capitalist system was constructed[2]. Revolutions of the political superstructure broke the blood inheritance of the divine right of monarchies. A representative government was established based on the modern political party system, which limited power abuse and encouraged market competition. The emergence of civil society has

---

[1] Europe gradually implanted these "laws" into social ideology and daily life in the late 17th and early 18th centuries after the classical mechanics of Newton were published. As a result, people accept scientific explanations instead of relying on God to find an explanation for a natural phenomenon.

[2] In the opinion of Tocqueville, anti-religion was not a feature of the Great Revolution itself, but anti-religion movements ran through the French Revolution from beginning to end. "One of the early steps of the French Revolution was to attack churches. Among passions that originated from the Great Revolution, anti-religion fanaticism was first ignited and finally extinguished. " — Refer to *The Old Regime and the Revolution*, Chapter 3, translated by Li Yanming, Yilin Press, 2018 Edition.

not only established pubs, cafes, clubs, museums, theaters and other public areas in the broad area of government and family but also guaranteed the expression of public opinion through books and newspapers. All these have expanded the individual's space for social activities and liberated the productive forces, labeled cumulatively as the "modernity" of the West. Therefore, in the eyes of Marx and Engels, though the bourgeoisie has created more productive forces than all previous generations in its less than one hundred years of class rule, capital comes dripping from head to foot, from every pore with blood and dirt.

II. Modernization and Reflective Discourses Regarding Modernization

As we all know, sociology, like other philosophical and social sciences, constructed a discourse system regarding modernization with the West as its backdrop since its initial stage. Main figures who laid the foundation of Western sociology basically followed the narrative mode of "tradition-modernity" to describe the macro process of social development. Comte constructed the theory of "military period-legal period-industrial period" based on "the theological stage-metaphysical stage-empirical stage"; Maine constructed the theory of "identity society-contract society"; Spencer constructed the theory of "the Militant Type of Society-industrial society"; Tönnies constructed the theory of "community-society"; Tocqueville constructed the theory of "aristocracy-democracy"; Durkheim constructed the theory of "mechanical unity-organic solidarity"; Simmel constructed the theory of "natural economic society and monetary economic society"; Scheler constructed the theory of "solidarity and common society and competitive society"; Weber not only constructed "traditional capitalism-ration-

Chapter 1 Chinese Modernization and the Chinese Experience of Modernization Development

al capitalist economy"①, but also the theory of "traditional rule-Charisma rule-Legal-rational rule" ②; Parsons constructed the theory of "particularism-universalism" and the model variable theory of "traditional society-modern society"; Economist Lewis constructed the theory of traditional and modern economic sectors, which was widely adopted by sociology. Rostow's "take-off theory" also became the basic discourse for sociologists to discuss the process of social and economic development. Almost all of the theories mentioned above took the practice of Western modernization as a reference and discussed in-depth Western modernization. They were also involved non-western modernization.

In particular, the basic paradigm of sociology since Comte naturally had the characteristics of Western modernity, as claimed by Parsons③. Weber's sociology of religion, which is widely quoted, constructed its theoretical framework with European-American Centrism. To theoretically answer the question of why rational (or modern) capitalism was developed in the West but not in the East despite the latter's brilliant achievements in an agricultural society, he defined varlous kinds of capital production and business phenomena that have existed throughout history as traditional capitalism. However, he defined the capitalist

---

① Or traditional capitalism and rational capitalism. In Weber's view, Protestant ethics, rationalism, private property, the separation of church and state, and the market combined to promote the substitution of European capitalism for feudalism. Nevertheless his understanding was at odds with the secularization of religion and the emergence of individualism. Weber believes that Calvinism formed its spirit of capitalism by strengthening its religious teachings and religious organization life. Rational capitalism can be explained to control by Calvinists using religious asceticism over secular behaviors. Besides abstinence, it regarded economic behavior and professional life as results of vocation. Here comes the question: did Calvinism solve the conflict between rationalism and religionism?

② Peter Burke once pointed out in his book *History and Social Theory* that the concept of "charisma" (charisma) originated from discussions on early churches "Charisma organization" by Rudolf Som, an expert in church history. Weber secularized it in his discourse and endowed it with more universal applicability. Peter Burke: *History and Social Theory*, translated by Li Kang, Shanghai People's Publishing House, 2019 Edition.

③ Parsons believed that the development of modern Western society (that is, modernization) was of universal significance in human history. It was not random but oriented, although it did not rule out the fact that modernization actually includes different social forms.

spirit promoted by Calvinism as rational capitalism. Weber tried to prove that some affinity existed between Protestant ethics and rational capitalism. As various religions in the East could not foster the spirit of rational capitalism, the East repeated the tradition and struggled on the road to development. It could be understood that without the rational capitalist spirit, it was hard for the East to form a rich soil of modern capitalism[1]. Thus, Western Orientalism drew a conclusion of "rationalization", carrying the implication of Weber: modernization of Eastern society (or modernization of other societies except for Europe and America) could only be realized with the help of Western culture. Weber himself was not a monistic sociologist, but his narrative style was sometimes "paradoxical"[2] in his Eurocentric theory[3] and there were indeed many misunderstandings of "others" (including China)[4]. Put the above misreading aside, it is no doubt that in the eyes of Weber, the series of Christian reforms since Luther, as well as the localization movement of religions in Western European countries, promoted the modernization process of religious ideology and solved the problem of adaptation between religion and the development of capitalism. Religious ethics were used to endow believers with the moral rationale for accumulating

---

[1] "Confucian Capitalism" or "Neo-Confucian Capitalism", discussed by some scholars in China since the 1940s, has responded to this.

[2] Weber said in his *Concluding Remarks regarding Counter-criticism on the Spirit of Capitalism* that, it is "absurd" to think that the capitalist economic system and the capitalist "spirit" only originated from religious reform. "Religious-psychological factors can directly promote the development of capitalism only in the context of many others, particular natural-geographical "conditions". My research is only the development of a moral "lifestyle" that adapts to the emerging modern capitalism" he added. Hence, it's not my fault if any "overestimating the scope of my discussion". Refer to, "the Protestant Ethic and the Spirit of Capitalism", pages 467 – 468, translated by Yan Kewen, Shanghai People's Publishing House, 2018 edition.

[3] Su Guoxun, Rethinking on Weber's Exposition on China Culture, published in *Sociological Study*, 2011, Journal 4.

[4] Both Chinese and foreign sociologists have reflected on this. An article by Robert M. Marsh, who teaches in the Department of Sociology at Brown University, published in the American Journal of Sociology, is entitled Weber's Misunderstanding of Chinese Traditional Law". In fact, to fully understand Weber's insights, we need to go back to Weber himself. He claimed himself to be an "economic nationalist."

wealth. A self-consistent theoretical discourse was constructed regarding the relevance between modernization and religious activities.

In addition, it should be pointed out that Weber was not the only Western scholar who misunderstood Eastern society, and that other social sciences were also full of discrimination against non-Western societies. Hence, modern discourse newly built through transplantation by developing countries that moved towards independence after World War II was inevitably characterized by explanations of the East by the West. In practice, what developing countries desired most was to catch up with or outpace the world's level of development by learning from the West. What Western modernization theory provided for developing countries maintained, without exception, that "modernization is Westernization" and "Westernization is Americanization". Some writings even deliberately constructed modernization as merely a study of the development theory of developing countries. The practice of "total westernization" in most developing countries has suffered great setbacks because of "acclimatization"[1]. The main contributing reasons were often interpreted by the West as "incomplete or halfway modernization". The logic behind this kind of discourse was that only through the transformation of the superstructure of Western-style liberal democracy or through a long-term colonial process can developing countries successfully enter the right path of modernization. However, developing countries that westernized didn't welcome the expected prosperity. On the contrary, the political and economic penetration of suzerain countries into the former colonial countries was strengthened. The "real" inequality was constructed under the disguise of the so-called concept of "freedom". A new "comprador class" formed, deconstructing the economic and academic nationalism of developing countries. This inspired academic circles to think critically about the "dichotomy

---

[1] Huntington: *Political Order in Changing Societies*, translated by Wang Guanhua, et al, Shanghai People's Publishing House, 2021 Edition. He discussed in detail such problems under "Political Gap" in Chapter One "Political Order and Political Decay".

model" and "westernization model" of classical modernization theory. As a result, the famous "dependency theory" and "world system theory" were developed[①].

According to the dependency theory[②], main reasons that developing countries were blocked on their path to modernization were not that they didn't work hard, nor that their national conditions did not conform to the political and economic logic of Western capitalism. The contributing reasons were the dependent structure that the suzerain turned the former colonial country into a supplier of energy or raw materials, and the trade and international division of labor systems built accordingly. It put developing countries in a dependent position for resource export and helped form an unequal exchange relationship in the capitalist system, which made the suzerain country take most of the profits and left dependent countries trapped in poverty[③]. In a word, developed countries established an unequal "negotiation" mechanism through their world trade rules, which kept colonial or former colonial countries in a "dependent" state for a long time. The phenomenon triggered a wide-ranging discussion on Frank's "The Development of Underdevelopment". Though most scholars only use dependency theory to study Africa and America, if we look at the develop-

---

① The fact of modernization precedes research on modernization. Theoretical research on modernization originated in the 1950s and 1960s. The concept of "modernization" was put forward after World War II when the development of former colonial and semi-colonial countries after independence was discussed. At first, modernization was simply interpreted as "Westernization", and "Westernization" as "Americanization". Therefore, later modernization theories critically examined the original ones and focused on discussions centered on "dependency theory" and "world system theory".

② With regards to the development course of dependency theory, although there were "radical dependence theory", "reformist dependence theory" and "orthodox mainstream dependence theory", the theme reflected fell on the relationship between developing countries and developed countries. The theoretical basis of this relationship is the combination of Marxism and economic nationalism.

③ Amin of Egypt even refused to classify all countries in the world as "developed countries" and "underdeveloped countries". In his view, the logic of this classification implies such a setting: "There is only one form of development and only one road leading to progress and universal welfare." *Dependent Development* by Amin, *Re-discussion on Modernization Theories and Historical Experience* by Huntington, et al., page 77, Shanghai Translation Publishing House, 1993 edition.

ment history of Western Europe and Eastern Europe in the 16th – 17th century, it is found that during the rapid development of urbanization and the decline of serfdom in Western Europe, there was not only a decline of cities, but also a return of serfdom in Eastern Europe or "Central and Eastern Europe". To some extent, it also signals that the development of central countries was dependent on the actual "underdevelopment" of marginal countries.

It is adequate to say that world-system theory is an upgraded version of dependency theory. In the structural system of "the central country", "semi-marginal country" or "marginal country" created by the world capitalist system, capital flowed towards "the central country" for a long time. The development of "central countries" often coincided with the decline of "marginal countries". When the "central country" changed as a result of competition, financial capital also moved to the new "central country". This continuously widened the development gap between "central countries" and "semi-marginal countries" or "marginal countries"[1]. If the economic and political layout of the global village is understood as a spatial structure formed based on geographical relations, Wallerstein's theory has strong explanatory power. For this reason, Desai of India said, "The value bias and ideological tone of modern Western scholars when they used the concept of modernization have caused some dangerous consequences for correctly understanding the transformation process that has taken place in human society for decades."[2] Amin of Egypt also raised the question of

---

[1] Tominaga Kenichi: *Today's topic on "Modernization Theory" -A Discussion on Development Theories of Non-Western Post-Development Societies*, in *Re-discussion on Modernization Theories and Historical Experience* by Samuel Huntington, et al., page 133, Shanghai Translation Publishing House, 1993 edition.

[2] Desai: *Re-evaluation on the Concept of Modernization*: *Re-discussion on Modernization Theories and Historical Experience* by Samuel Huntington, et al., page 27, Shanghai Translation Publishing House, 1993 edition.

whether we were developing or westernizing. ① The gap in economic and social development between "central countries", "semi-marginal countries", and "marginal countries" often leads to the a in academic development. This gap has formed the hegemony of suzerain countries over former colonial countries and regions, as claimed by Gramsci, and has also formed symbolic violence, as claimed by Bourdieu. Countries in a dominant position often imposed their own culture on subordinate countries by forcing people of subordinate countries to think that imported cultures were so-called "legitimate cultures" and their own culture was an "illegal culture".

In fact, modernization is different even in Western countries, like France and Britain. Modernization of Germany is totally different from that of Britain and France. Modernization of the United States only stepped onto the right path after the War of Independence and the Civil War, forming a trend of catching up. Modes to construct superstructures in Western countries were also different. There were superstructures like constitutional monarchy, democratic republic, and federalism. In the process of modernization, catch-up is widespread in the West. E. g., America and Germany overtook Britain and France. Japan and South Korea have overtaken other countries in Western Europe. Another example is the rise of the Four Little Dragons in Asia in the middle and late 20th century. Modernization of different models has been created at different times. This makes the vast number of developing countries realize that, regardless of the "should be" of modernization, in the "real" case of modernization, there are neither examples that have succeeded in "total westernization" nor examples that have succeeded in modernization by putting aside their own culture and adopting a new one totally.

While developing countries reflect on Western modernization discourse system, Western academic circles critically also reflect on their own "moderniza-

---

① Amin: *Dependent Development, Re-discussion on Modernization Theories and Historical Experience* by Samuel Huntington, et al., page 99, Shanghai Translation Publishing House, 1993 Edition.

tion" as Western society evolves deeply from an industrial society to a post-industrial society. Thus, "post-modernity" discourse is developed. Discussions on "post-modernity" start at the moment when industrial modernity is coming to an end, and the door of post-modernity is slowly opening. Research objects have shifted from "things in modern society" . to "things in post-modern society" In terms of theoretical construction, irrationalism is adopted instead of rationalism, and relativism is adopted instead of grand narrative. "A complete man" is redefined by the unity of rationalism and irrationalism, highlighting what Marx said: "Man is the highest essence of man" . The existentialism claimed by Sartre is adopted instead of rationalism[①], and the extreme development of "the ideal post-industrial society" is raised instead of the "ideal industrial society", and the risk society is envisioned instead of the industrial society. In Beck's view, it might imply the interruption of modernization and imbalance of modern risk distribution, as well as the disintegration of the family model of industrial society. The post-modern cognitive system interprets things through the uncertainty of postmodern scientific discovery, instead of the so-called certainty of modern scientific discovery.

With regards to the construction of human social order, postmodernity in the West also starts to deconstruct various "authoritative" discourses and their explanatory powers. The continuous new scientific and technological revolutions cause reflections on the original disciplinary system constructed based on industrial society and its standards. Doubts about the industrial system arise. The discipline system of post-industrial society is used to replace that of industrial society. In consequence, a series of in-depth reflections regarding "scientific discoveries", "disciplinary boundaries", "laws governing the operation of things" and "objectivity beyond subjectivity" come off. Of course, there are

---

[①] William Barrett once said in *Irrational Man*, technology is a material embodiment rationalism because it comes from science, while bureaucracy is another embodiment of rationalism as it aims at rational control and arrangement of social life. *Irrational Man* by William Barrett, Chapter 11, translated by Duan Dezhi, Shanghai Translation Publishing House, 2012 edition.

also constructive explorations of new social forms and systems. It is adequate to say that postmodemity has not yet fully formed the so-called "postmodernity" yet. No "social norm" like industrial society has been constructed yet, and no post-modern research method with a consensus significance has been found yet.

III. Modernization and Localization of China's Modernization Discourses

Most scholars tend to think that since the Opium War in 1840, China's original logic of social evolution has been rewritten by foreign invasion. Impacted by Western industrial civilization from the ocean, the ancient agricultural civilization fell apart and gradually became a colony and semi-colony. To save the country from peril and realize national rejuvenation, the Chinese people rose up to resist. People with lofty ideals ran around shouting, trying to find a new way through changes in utensils, systems and culture. From the Movement of the Taiping Heavenly Kingdom to the Self-strengthening Movement, the Boxer Uprising, Hundred Days' Reform, the Revolution of 1911 and the Second Revolution, a series of doctrines and thoughts were introduced, and every attempt has been made to adopt a democratic republic, constitutional monarchy, parliamentary system, and presidential system. These national salvation plans, introduced in turn, ended in failure. Though industrial development was realized, it was limited to sporadic cities. The country was divided, and people endured impoverishment and long-standing debility, though the monarchy had been overthrown. History has repeatedly proven that it is impossible for a ruling class to adapt to the challenges of a new era just by mending the loopholes of its superstructure. A superstructure that has not undergone an in-depth transformation and is still feudal in essence, is difficult to integrate with the power of the whole country to promote its modernization and transformation[①].

While looking out into the world, China's intellectual circle tried to "learn from foreigners to control them" (learn from foreigners to strengthen themselves) in a bid to form an academic framework with "Chinese culture as the core and western culture for use" and construct its own practice and knowledge systems. However, the shackles of the old system deeply restricted the economic base and theoretical ideology of modernization. Also, it is hard for a modern social structure to grow out of the economic base of a feudal society. A modern social structure can only be established by spreading modern ideas and breaking old shackles. The Communist Party of China (CPC), founded at the baptism of the October Revolution, finally successfully led China's revolution towards modernization. After a long and arduous struggle, the Party led the people to the great victory of the new democratic revolution. It put an end to the fragmented political situation and organized all the people of China, thus forming the most magnificent modernization thrust in history. The founding of the PRC achieved a great leap from the feudal autocracy that had lasted for thousands of years to people's democracy, which created fundamental social conditions for the great rejuvenation of the Chinese nation and laid a fundamental political premise and institutional foundation for Chinese modernization.

---

① In his later years, Li Hongzhang said, "throughout my life, weither training troops or naval forces, they were all paper tigers. All of them are painted, and are superficial. If they are not laid bare, they can still be perfunctory for a while. Just like a broken house, apaperhanger patched it up and turned it into a clean room. Though knowing that it is pasted with paper, it can still withstand small storms if any holes are mended in time. It can be seen that the Self-strengthening Movement is only an economic one. Without the essential transformation of the decadent feudal dynasty, it is hard to internalize external Western learning into the internal modernization practice. If the failure of the Self-strengthening Movement only awakened the elite, then the collapse of the North-Ocean Navy awakened the people of the whole country. Zheng Guanying, once in his *Warning in a Prosperous Age* quoted comments of German Chancellor Bismarck as saying, "In the early years of Tongzhi Dynasty, German Bismarck speaker said 'thirty years later, Japan will prosper, will China become weak? Japanese people who travel to Europe discuss the control of academic lectures and return to practice it. Chinese people who travel to Europe ask about the advantages of ship guns and the low prices of factory, and buy and use them. Is it the source of becoming strong and weak?' "

The founding of the PRC quickly healed the wounds of war during the recovery of the national economy. Meanwhile, it abolished the feudal land system and completed the rural land reform. Urban and rural grassroot political power was established. Equality between men and women was advocated. The *Marriage Law* was promulgated to ensure the autonomy of marriage. The people's zeal for political participation was revived. All in all, a new economic base and social structure, totally different from the old China, was established along with the founding of the PRC. The subsequent industrialization and the "socialist transformation of agricultural, handicraft industry and capitalist industry and commerce" completed the transition from the new-democratic revolution to socialism, laying the industrial foundation of China. We can say that China's industrialization warded off the colonial road of Western countries. It initiated an independent modernization practice process, abandoned the strategic model of "dependent development", and set an Eastern example of government-driven development. During the period of socialist construction, an independent and relatively complete industrial system and national economic system were formed in the process of "Four Modernizations", namely, the construction of modern agriculture, modern industry, modern national defense and modern science and technology.

Since 1978, China has continuously improved its relations of production to meet the needs of the rapid development of productive forces. The advancement of the national governance system and capacity in a modernized way, as well as the smooth development of its economic base realized through the reform of the superstructure, created two miracles: rapid economic development that is rare in the world and long-term social stability. China's society has undergone a transition from a planned economy to a market economy, from an agricultural society to an industrial society, and from building a well-off society in an all-around way to finishing building a moderately prosperous society in all respects and further building a socialist modern country in an all-around way. Taking part in person in the whole practice of China's peaceful rise, sociologists in China added more Chinese colors to sociology and modernized it. Focusing on the reconstruction of social form, sociologists in China studied the transformation process of social structure, social relations, social changes, social behavior patterns and social psychology. They gradually built up a modernization discourse system of socialist sociology with China characteristics[1].

As a result of the vigorous advance of Chinese modernization, labor productivity has increased. social mobility channels have become unblocked, and labor forces are continuously entering the industrial and service sectors from the agricultural sector. The structure of employees in the tertiary industry is optimized. It causes the proportion of employees in the tertiary industry to greatly exceed that of the secondary and primary industries. According to the seventh census, the floating population has reached 490 million, signaling that China has changed from a settled society to a migratory one. The Sociology of China has once used the term "migrant workers", an innovative concept with a complex local contert, to develop theories on social mobility and population migration within the field of the sociology. It enriched the hypothesis of the urban-rural relationship caused by changes in social structure promoted by urbanization. Migrant workers not only represent the working and business groups who have moved from rural areas to cities, but also reflect the social transformation process in which farmers in China are transformed into workers and urban citizens. Most importantly, it represents the era's characteristics of the rise of industrial workers in China. By the end of 2021, China had guided more than 900 million people into urban society, accounting for 64.7% of the total population, which accelerated the process of modern urban civilization.

For thousands of years, China was a typical farmer's, agricultural, rural, and farmland society. In just a few decades of catch-up development after the founding of the PRC, China has embarked on the road to modernization that

---

[1] Zhang Yi: *Taking Root in China's Practice to Construct Socialist Sociology with Chinese Characteristics*, published on Guangming Daily on Sept. 14, 2021.

Western developed countries have been on for hundreds of years. Driven by urbanization, the tide of social mobility in China, after entering the new era, has entered the stage when migrant workers are becoming urban citizens, moving away from the stage when farmers become migrant workers. Except for a few metropolises, most big, small and medium-sized cities have liberalized their settlement restrictions. On one hand, farmers are liberated from farmland. On the other hand, the foundation for mechanized agriculture's agricultural land aggregation is formed through voluntary land transfer. A modern group of professional farmers is emerging, creating a new development pattern of simultaneous modernization of farmers, agriculture, rural areas, and farmland.

Onthe one hand, migrant workers flow into cities on a large scale. The great driving forces of industrialization and post-industrialization have also enabled China to rapidly expand its middle-income group, to more than 400 – 500 million people. The social structure foundation for the "double cycle" strategy on the consumption side is put into place on the other hand. The precise poverty alleviation strategy vigorously promoted in the new era has eliminated absolute poverty in rural areas in China for the first time, greatly improving the basic appearance of village society. In the new journey of building a socialist modern country in an all-around way, China will surely transform from the second-largest economy in the world to the largest one, and will also transform from a middle—and high-income country to a high-income country step by step. In the process of promoting common prosperity, China's income structure, urban and rural structure, human resources structure, and social stratum structure will be further optimized. As the most populous country in the world, China's modernization process will not only increase the proportion of modern civilization for the 1.4 billion people in China, but also completely change the proportion structure of the world population sharing the fruits of modernization. China will continue to create a more brilliant plan for the modernization of developing countries and contribute more effective Chinese wisdom.

The successful advancement of Chinese modernization lays a practical foun-

Chapter 1 Chinese Modernization and the Chinese Experience of Modernization Development   229

dation for innovating discourses on modernization China's sociology. The theoretical construction of sociology refines core concepts of identification and specialization. A series of research has greatly enriched the modern discourse of socialist sociology with Chinese characteristics, from research on changes in rural and urban social structure to those on occupations and industries of migrant workers, problems regarding citizenization, migration and staying-behind, good governance of a vibrant and well-ordered society, integration of urban and rural development and rural revitalization, family miniaturization and family structure change, the transformation of urban grassroot society, expanding middle-income groups and the middle class, occupational segregation and income distribution, social psychology and positive social mentality construction, and social transformation and consumption upgrading. They contribute to the theoretical innovations of Chinese sociologists for world sociology and arouse the interest of world sociologists in studying the social development of China[①].

From "Four Modernizations" to a well-off society, further to the practice of building a well-off society in an all-around way and finishing building a well-off society in an all-around way, the robust development trend of modernization in China since the reform and opening up is well written. It can be said that the concept "common prosperity" society and its related theoretical system will surely become a symbol of sociology in the next 30 years if discourses about a "well-off society" and its theoretical system constitute the development theme of socialism with Chinese characteristics in the previous period. The grand narrative from a well-off society to a common prosperity society not only guides the historical path of socialism sociology with Chinese characteristics, but also includes the future direction of socialist sociology with Chinese characteristics. Theories explaining the modernization transformation of developing countries, whether they are the world market theory, the dependency theory or the postmodern the-

---

① For details about this part, refer to Zhang Yi: *Taking Root in China's Practice to Construct Socialist Sociology with Chinese Characteristics*, published on Guangming Daily on Sept. 14, 2021.

ory, are born with major defects and cannot fully explain the rise of China. Only theories of a well-off society and common prosperity that are based on China's history and practice are the products of the organic combination of basic sociological principles and China's social practice. Therefore, the development theory of sociology, extracted from well-off and common prosperity societies, is both an in-depth summary of China's social development experience and the meta-narrative and meta-discourse of China's sociological theory innovation.

The modernization of the Chinese style was well summarized in the report to the 20th CPC National Congress of the Party. Chinese modernization is led by the Communist Party of China (CPC), which shares common features of modernization in all countries, such as science and technology, industrialization, urbanization, and secularization of religion, etc. It also has unique China characteristics that inherent to China's own national conditions. In essence, the modernization of the Chinese style requires adherence to the leadership of the Communist Party of China, which means adherence to socialism with Chinese characteristics. This includes achieving high-quality development, developing people's democracy throughout the whole process, enriching people's spiritual world, realizing the common prosperity of all people, promoting harmonious coexistence between humans and nature, humans constructing the Community of Shared Future for Mankind, and creating a new form of human civilization. Major principles of Chinese modernization are to uphold and strengthen the overall leadership of the Party, which means to adhere to the socialist road with Chinese characteristics and the people-centered development thought, deepen reform and opening up, and carry forward the spirit of struggle. All in all, China plans to realize its modernization strategy in two steps. That is, the forthcoming five years are conceived as a "critical period" for laying a solid foundation, which is necessary for realizing basic modernization by 2035, namely, the "first-step". Then, to build a prosperous, strong, democratic, civilized, harmonious and beautiful socialist modern power by the middle of the century, namely the "second step" will be completed. At the same time, we will push

Chapter 1 Chinese Modernization and the Chinese Experience of Modernization Development

forward the great rejuvenation of the Chinese nation by the modernization of the Chinese style. Modernization of the Chinese style is different from Western modernization. Modernization of China based on its actual national conditions features the following: first, modernization of a huge population; second, the common prosperity of all people; third, coordination between material and spiritual civilization; fourth, harmonious coexistence between man and nature; and fifth, modernization along the road of peaceful development. These expressions further enrich the discourse system of Chinese modernization.

After a well-off society is built in an all-around way, modernization of the Chinese style has become the focus of the whole country's work. In order for all people to share in the fruits of economic and social development, it is necessary to solidly promote common prosperity, making it a dynamic development process. Common prosperity in modernization of the Chinese style is by no means the so-called "simultaneous, synchronized and equal prosperity", nor is it uniform egalitarianism, a big pot of rice, or a new way of robbing the rich to help the poor. It is to be advanced in line with the development logic: from parts to whole and from quantitative change to qualitative change. To construct a common and prosperous society, efforts must be made to both stimulate social vitality and prevent the widening of the income gap. An important experience gained from more than 40 years of reform and opening up is that we must adhere to the principle of public ownership as the mainstay and promote the common development of diversified ownership economies. Three basic economic systems must be adhered to: the principle of distribution according to work, the coexistence of various modes of distribution, and the socialist market economic system. The potential of tertiary distribution should be developed, while hard work is encouraged and high values is attached to primary and secondary distribution. With an aging population, it is certain that a multi-level social security system will be built up and improved, playing a role in maintaining intra-generational and intergenerational equity. The strong social influence will show only when these iconic concepts and common prosperity come together to form a series of discourses. They will conthbute to the construction of a modern socialist country when they are applied to develop social policies.

In a word, the social transformation forged by Chinese modernization is a great transformation. It is a great transformation of the world's most populous country from an agricultural society to an industrial society. It is a great transformation of government-drivendevelopment closely combined with the folk initiative. It is a great social transformation to eliminate absolute poverty in rural areas and prevent urban slums from tearing apart society. In the process of social transformation, China has formed a better pattern of social integration by smoothing channels of social circulation, dispelling social tension, and uniting people's hearts. If China has successfully composed a modern ballad of industrialization, urbanization, rationalization and secularization of a populous country, in the process of rapid transformation from an industrial society to a network society and digital society, sociologists need to keep up with changes in the situation to keep abreast of the trend of scientific and technological progress. They should, continue to take root in the rule of law to unblock channels of social mobility and answer the questions of the times, and continue building the discourse of "sociology for modernization" as advocated by Mr. Fei Xiaotong. We can proudly say that the Chinese modernization discourse under construction is not only based on China's modernization practice, but also draws lessons from the achievements of human civilization (including the outstanding achievements of Western modernization practice and theory), and also absorbs the excellent traditional Chinese culture with a long history of 5,000 years. It will surely continue to make a new contributions to the innovation of new forms of human civilization.

Enhancing the Belt and Road Cooperation and the Eurasian Governance from the Perspective of Modernization

Sun Zhuangzhi[*]

In 2013, Chinese President Xi Jinping proposed a significant an important initiative to collaboratively construct Belt and Road, with the objective of advancing the shared development of countries within the region. It is an innovative concept and model of cooperation in contemporary international relations. With China's social and economic development entering a new stage, the country is advocating for innovative and green development, attaches importance to social stability and security, and aims to achieve the modernization of the national governance system and governance capacity, which also has an impact on the key direction of its foreign cooperation. Chinese modernization has attracted attention and earned the admiration of the whole world, especially Eurasian countries. It advocates learning from each other and achieving common development and has provided a realistic path choice for the cooperation between China and Eurasian countries. As President Xi Jinping stressed in his speech at the CPC in Dialogue with World Political Parties High-Level Meeting in March 2023, we

---

[*] Sun Zhuangzhi, Professor, Director of Institute of Russian, Eastern European & Central Asian Studies, CASS

should work together to reform and develop the global governance system and make the international order more just and equitable as we advance humanity's modernization in an environment of equal rights, equal opportunities and fair rules for all. [1] With the advancement of the Belt and Road Initiative (the BRI), the above-mentioned idea and practice have demonstrated special importance and appeal in Eurasia.

I. The Path Choice of Modernization Reform in Eurasian Countries

For more than 30 years, the Eurasian countries, which gained independence after the disintegration of the Soviet Union in 1991, have actively promoted modernization reform, explored the development path in line with their actual conditions, and strived to achieve economic and social progress in the process of building a new political and economic system. They have made great achievements, and also experienced many difficulties and setbacks and made a detour. Modernization is a new topic for these young countries, and they have shown some common characteristics in path choice.

1. Basic Characteristics of Modernization in Eurasian Countries

Politically, Eurasian countries have realized "Westernization" in form and "nationalization" in content. On the one hand, they are imitating the Western system, establish parliaments and implementing multi-party systems. On the other hand, they improve the status of their majority nations, emphasize the construction of a unitary democratic country, and strive to enhance the cohesion and sense of pride as a new nation-state. In fact, these are two contradictory policy orientations. And in the end, they can only accept the Western system in

---

[1] Xi Jinping: "Join Hands on the Path Towards Modernization — Keynote Address at the CPC in Dialogue with World Political Parties High-Level Meeting", *People's Daily*, March 16, 2023.

form, but largely retain or restore their traditional ruling styles.

Economically, these countries have promoted large-scale "privatization" and the "marketization" for society. According to a series of indicators, they achieved industrialization and urbanization during the Soviet era, and established relatively sound social security systems. They were more developed than neighboring developing countries and among the "first world" countries. After gaining independence, with the interruption of their traditional economic ties, a huge crisis took place, and a trend of de-industrialization and counter-urbanization emerged in these countries, leading to a difficult economic transition. However, they are still making unremitting efforts amid difficulties.

In the social field, the phenomena of "re-urbanization" and the rejuvenation of the population have appeared. After gaining independence, most Eurasian countries witnessed large-scale emigration. The urban population decreased in some countries while the proportion of the rural population increased. The great employment pressure led to more export of labor services, increasing social mobility, and the prominent problem of poverty. Central Asian and Transcaucasia countries have high birth rates, giving rise to rapid population growth and great changes in population structure. Due to weakened primary-level management, they rely more on non-governmental organizations and residents' self-governance, thus resulting in the disengagement between society and government.

In the cultural sphere, Eurasian countries stress "localization" and "secularization". While gradually achieving "de-russification" and opening to the West, Eurasian countries are trying to fill the ideological "vacuum". However, promoting the return of traditional culture and encouraging the spread of religions have brought a new challenge of extremism, thus affecting the secular systems of these countries.

2. Modernization Problems and the Construction of a Nation-State

It is obvious that in the process of pursuing modernization, Eurasian countries have seen a relatively contradictory phenomenon in the same time period, leading to the conflict between "modernization" and "modernity". Modernization is a process of progress and also a necessary step for any country, especially in the context of globalization. Nevertheless, it is likely to trigger structural adjustments. Escalating struggles between different interest groups needs to be constantly adjusted and balanced, and the superstructure should be suited to the economic base, otherwise unrest may occur. In Huntington's view, modernity is stable, while modernization is unstable. Eurasian countries already have some kind of "modernity", and may also be integrated into the world economy and learn from more advanced cultures, but both their system transformation and the development patterns they selected are unstable.

In the field of social politics, these countries are confronting more difficulties, which bring more uncertain factors to their modernization. First, the unstable foundation of a unitary nation-state. Eurasian countries are all multi-ethnic countries. They tried to change the ethnic autonomous entities established during the Soviet era and thus triggered ethnic and even inter-state conflicts. Second, religious and cultural traditions are hard to be compatible with a secular political system. In order to enhance national identity and the legitimacy of political power, the revival of religious cultures has been encouraged, which gave birth to religious-political organizations and even the politicization of Islam in Central Asia, threatening the political stability of these countries.[①] Third, the risk of power transition brought by the super presidential system. A majority of the countries have chosen a strong presidential system. Most of the leaders have been in power for a long time after consolidating their political power, and some of

---

① Виктория Панфилова: Ташкент снижает риск исламизации ——Узбекистан по новой Конституции становится светским государством, 12. 03. 2023, https: //www. ng. ru/cis/2023 - 03 - 12/5_8677_uzbekistan. html.

them even passed down the power, causing unique political conflicts. Fourth, the "disorder" of rules is due to political pluralism. In order to solve the problem of over-centralization of power and also balance the political appeal of different interest groups, some countries have adopt the parliamentary system, which often results from the influence of European political culture. Fifth, the reconstruction of a social management system. The social security system and primary-level management patterns formed in the Soviet era can no longer be continued, and grass-roots "autonomy" has been implemented. However, some countries rely on powerful departments or traditional ways to continuously strengthen their control over society. Sixth, sovereignty security and regime security under external pressure. Eurasian countries are inextricably linked with Russia, and Russia also wants to maintain its all-round influence. At the same time, the West is also trying to promote "democratization" in Eurasia and constantly putting pressure on these countries.

3. Choosing the Path to Modernization is a Great Test

At present, the international standards for modernization generally refer to economic and social standards, such as per capita output value, urban population ratio, education level and average life expectancy. To achieve these targets, efforts should be made to improve the governance capacity. During the Soviet times, Eurasian countries had reached or approached these targets. Unfortunately, with the disintegration of the Soviet Union, they witnessed a process of returning to the "starting point". Their economic and social situations have fallen to the level of developing countries, and also showed characteristics similar to other developing countries. In such circumstances, these countries need to build a nation-state on the one hand, and realize modernization rooted in specific national conditions and cultural conflicts on the other. The simple "transplantation" in the Soviet period was often not suitable for local conditions, causing prominent imbalance and inequality. After gaining independence, more and more factors against "modernity" emerged during the process of building a nation-state. This hindered these countries' opening up and integration into the international system, and resulted in relatively lagging economic and social development. However, the governing authorities are concerned about the ownership of political power, so political issues are often a priority. This "disjointed" development has led to increasingly sharp social contradictions and mounting social discontent.

The ethnicissues in newly independent countries are very complicated, including those left over from the past and new ones arising from the development of a modern nation-state. Moreover, in the special background, social issues are becoming increasingly acute and social differentiation is worsening, resulting in frequent contradictions and conflicts. Ethnic issues, which involve political rights, economic treatment, culture and education, social support and other related aspects, are difficult for developed countries to cope with successfully. For these young republics, which have only been independent for more than 30 years and even have no specific direction of national development, ethnic issues are absolutely a huge challenge. For the integration mechanism in Eurasia, in addition to solving the problems of economic and trade cooperation, it is necessary to coordinate the policies of modernization[①], because modernization is a very urgent task for these countries, and they have made different choices in state building and economic reform.

II. The Belt and Road Cooperation and Solutions for Governance Problems

The BRI can not only promote transnational and cross-regional cooperation, but also contribute to the improvement of regional and national governance. In

---

[①] На городском завтраке РСМД обсудили перспективы развития ЕАЭС, 2 марта 2023, https://russiancouncil.ru/news/na-gorodskom-zavtrake-rsmd-obsudili-perspektivy-razvitiya-eaes/?sphrase_id=96866744.

June 2016, President Xi Jinping delivered a speech at the Parliament of Uzbekistan and put forward suggestions for further enhancing the Belt and Road cooperation. He stressed that China is willing to work together with partner countries to promote various forms of win-win cooperation among governments, enterprises, social institutions and non-governmental organizations, enhance the willingness of enterprises to participate, and absorb social capital to participate in cooperative projects, which is conducive to addressing governance problems and governance deficits. [1] President Xi also proposed a cooperative idea featuring "four key points" as an important supplement and support for economic and trade cooperation. This idea plays an important role in improving the regional governance system and helping countries enhance their governance capacity.

(1) The Green Silk Road mainly means that countries along Belt and Road should deepen environmental protection cooperation, practice the concept of green development, and strengthen ecological environment protection. The areas along Belt and Road, especially the hinterland of Eurasia, have a fragile ecological environment with frequent natural disasters. Coordinated efforts are needed to prevent environmental deterioration and climate risks. China will also help Eurasian countries actively develop green industries and new energy sources, explore new types of green products, technologies and services, and improve their economic efficiency and comprehensive competitiveness.

(2) The Healthy Silk Road is to promote countries along Belt and Road to deepen cooperation in medical and health services, and strengthen win-win cooperation in the alert of infectious diseases, disease prevention and control, medical rescue and traditional medicine. The health of residents in Eurasian countries is threatened by lower coverage rate of health care, prominent poverty problems and frequent epidemic diseases. After the outbreak of the COVID-19 pandemic, China's Initiative has played a leading role in the efforts of regional

---

[1] Xi Jinping: *Join Hands to Create a New Glory of the Silk Road — Speech at the Legislative Chamber of the Uzbek Supreme Assembly*, Guangming Daily, June 23, 2016.

countries to conduct anti-pandemic cooperation and build a community of health. Besides, China also provided anti-pandemic supplies and vaccines to many Eurasian countries, and cooperated with Central Asian countries in drug development within the framework of the Shanghai Cooperation Organization.

(3) The Intelligent Silk Road is to deepen the cooperation in talent training among the countries along Belt and Road. China proposed to establish a vocational and technical cooperation alliance under the BRI to facilitate the training of all kinds of professionals. Talent training and reserve are the key to and a guarantee for promoting the BRI. On the one hand, these countries differ in talent teams and scientific and technological capacity building, and face different degrees of talent shortage. On the other hand, their education is characterized by distinctive features, rich resources and strong complementarity, indicating huge space for cooperation.

(4) The Peaceful Silk Road means that countries along Belt and Road should deepen security cooperation, practice the common, comprehensive, cooperative and sustainable Asian security concept, build a security governance model with Asian features, and cope with the risks and challenges in enhancing the Belt and Road cooperation. The Eurasian region faces not only traditional security threats, such as military conflicts and border disputes, but also a wider range of non-traditional security challenges, such as terrorism, extremism, separatism and transnational crime, as well as urgent security in energy, finance, food and network information.

For developing countries, modernization is a difficult "catching-up" process rather than a natural outcome, and can't be achieved by charity from developed countries. Instead, it requires a country to form synergy from top to bottom, formulate a systematic plan and make long-term efforts. Modernization does not mean the only ready-made Western model. Modernization should not only focus on economic growth, but also give consideration to social development and fairness. This is also a valuable experience of Chinese modernization. President Xi Jinping stressed that to achieve modernization, a country needs to follow universal laws governing the process, and more importantly, to consider its own national conditions and unique features. Chinese modernization contains elements that are common to the modernization of all countries, and also distinctive Chinese features that reflect its unique national conditions. It is the modernization of a huge population, of common prosperity for all, of material and cultural-ethical advancement, of harmony between humanity and nature, and of peaceful development. ① This is of great enlightenment and reference significance to the participating countries of the BRI, especially those Eurasian countries that have close political, economic and cultural ties with China. By enhancing together the Belt and Road cooperation, countries can share the experience of modernization, make clear the key direction of modernization, work together to promote development in all areas, and embrace bright prospects for modernization with broad, long-term cooperation.

In the process of modernization, Eurasian countries imitated the Western practices in form. Particularly, their political and economic transitions in the 1990s were basically planned under the guidance of the West, and failed in the end, especially in economy, they paid a heavy price. In recent years, most Eurasian countries have begun to redesign their systems of administrative control based on their national conditions. They hope to give full play to their own advantages in economy and attach importance to the governance experience of developing countries other than the West. Both the "New Kazakhstan" strategy put forward by Kazakhstan President Kassym-Jomart Tokayev and the constitutional reform promoted by Uzbek President Shavkat Mirziyoyev aims at achieving political and social modernization according to their own national conditions and by extensively learning from successful experiences around the world. Just as the ancient Silk Road was a road of trade and of culture, the current Belt and Road

---

① Xi Jinping delivers an important speech at the opening ceremony of a study session on studying and implementing the spirit of the 20th National Congress of the Communist Party of China, stressing the importance of correctly understanding and vigorously advancing Chinese modernization, People's Daily, February 8, 2023.

Initiative also bears a new mission of exchanges and mutual learning in governance concepts and models, and offers support and help for the modernization of other countries. The unique demonstration significance of Chinese modernization will help "latecomers" like Eurasian countries avoid more detours.

III. Promoting the Improvement of Regional Governance System Through Connectivity

One of the key features for enhancing the Belt and Road cooperation is multiple levels and players, which can promote coordination and cooperation among different countries and regions based on multilateral cooperation mechanisms. At the same time, with the bilateral and multilateral mechanisms, countries can complement each other to improve the overall regional governance capacity. In his keynote speech at the opening ceremony of the Boao Forum for Asia Annual Conference 2021, President Xi Jinping clearly stated that China would continue to work with other parties in high-quality Belt and Road cooperation, follow the principles of extensive consultation, joint contribution and shared benefits, and championing the philosophy of open, green and clean cooperation, in a bid to make the Belt and Road cooperation high-standard, people-centered and sustainable. China will work with all sides to promote "hard connectivity" of infrastructure and "soft connectivity" of rules and standards. A World Bank report suggests that by 2030, the Belt and Road projects could help lift 7.6 million people from extreme poverty and 32 million people from moderate poverty across the world. China will act in the spirit of openness and inclusiveness as it works with all willing participants to build the BRI into a pathway to poverty alleviation and growth. ①

---

① Xi Jinping: *Pulling Together Through Adversity and Toward a Shared Future for All — Keynote Speech via Video Link at the Opening Ceremony of the Boao Forum for Asia Annual Conference 2021*, Guangming Daily, April 21, 2021.

1. The BRI opens a window of opportunity for the development of regional countries

With a focus on the connectivity of economy and culture, the BRI aims to promote the smooth flow of production factors and friendly exchanges between the people, achieve mutual benefits and win-win results, and add new dimensions to the revival of the Silk Road. The new concepts proposed by Chinese leaders, such as the Clean Silk Road and the Digital Silk Road, constantly enrich the connotation of cooperation and are actually related to improving the political and economic governance of regional countries. Improving the modern management system will help Eurasian countries change unreasonable industrial structures and build a government of integrity, so as to improve their business environment and enhance their international competitiveness. More importantly, it is in line with the common needs of regional development and opens a new window of opportunity for regional countries to tap into their strengths.

Kazakhstan, located in Eurasia, is the place where the BRI was initiated, and the countries in this region are also active participants in the BRI. The Eurasian countries also have close social ties. Despite the cultural diversity, there are multiple cross-border ethnic groups in the region, which provides geographical and institutional advantages for regional cooperation. To improve the regional governance system, various multilateral mechanisms should cooperate with each other and coexist harmoniously. To improve the governance in Eurasia, first, we should enhance mutual trust and respect institutional and cultural differences. Second, we should forge a stable relationship featuring interdependence and common development, and raise the level of cooperation among regional countries through strategic bilateral and multilateral cooperation. Third, we should establish recognized rules, institutional frameworks and effective mechanisms to promote multilateral cooperation. Chinese leaders have proposed to build an SCO (Shanghai Cooperation Organization) community with a shared future, calling for efforts to reinforce the foundation of people-to-people friendship among member countries, establish multilateral cooperation mechanisms and partnership networks in all key directions, and substantiate the cooperation agenda, so as to play a leading and exemplary role in building a new type of international relations featuring mutual respect, equality, mutual benefit, openness and inclusiveness. One of the important symbols of successful regional governance lies in whether multilateral cooperation can really benefit the people of all countries and achieve the common prosperity of regional countries.

2. The BRI contributes to the benign interaction between modernization and regional governance

Regional governance includes several elements: first, the integrity of the region, which is essential for giving play to geographic advantages; second, interdependence, which means regional countries are complementary in economy and face common threats in security; third, affinity between the peoples, indicating that they can respect each other's cultural traditions; and fourth, the role of mechanisms and platforms, which means multilateral mechanisms play the role of guarantee and coordination. The high-quality Belt and Road cooperation in Eurasia is obviously conducive to developing a regional partnership in the above aspects and facilitating the process of regionalization. Regional governance is different from general multilateral cooperation. Besides the cooperation in politics and security, it also focuses on the long-term stability and common development of the region. This requires the joint participation of government departments, non-governmental organizations and social groups, especially the interaction between the social field and local level, so as to form a "three-dimensional" cooperation model. The regional governance in the hinterland of Eurasia has unique characteristics. Although the regional countries aim to be close to each other and even integrated at all levels in politics, economy and culture, the integration between these countries faces very complicated problems.

The BRI is the most important product of public diplomacy offered by China to the rest of the world. At present, the most important task is to break man-made barriers in economic and humanistic exchanges and achieve connectivity, including "hard connectivity" of infrastructure and "soft connectivity" of rules and standards. As President Xi Jinping emphasized in his important speech at the Dialogue on Strengthening Connectivity Partnership in November 2014, the connectivity we want to build should focus on infrastructure, rules and institutions and personnel movement, and calls for progress in policy communication, infrastructure linkage, trade flow, financing arrangements and friendly exchanges between the peoples. It is an all-round, three-dimensional, network-like connectivity, and a vibrant, open system that pools the wisdom and efforts of everyone. If "Belt and Road" is likened to the two wings of a soaring Asia, then connectivity is like their arteries and veins. ① In his proposal, President Xi expressed that all countries are welcome to get on board the express train of China's development. All parties may work together to establish a basic framework of connectivity based on economic corridors, and take transportation infrastructure as a breakthrough to achieve the early harvest of connectivity. Priority will be given to the railway and highway projects between China and its neighboring countries. Economic corridors such as the New Eurasian Continental Bridge are under construction by China and Eurasian countries, and the China-Kyrgyzstan-Uzbekistan railway is under planning, all of which are conducive to the connectivity of regional countries.

3. The BRI contributes to the well-being of people in every BRI country

According to the Western modernization theory, modernization is a historical process, including the transformation from traditional economy to modern economy, from a traditional society to a modern society, from a traditional politics to a modern politics, and from a traditional civilization to a modern civiliza-

---

① *Xi Jinping presides over the Dialogue on Strengthening Connectivity Partnership and delivers an important speech*, *advocating deepening connectivity partnership and strengthening pragmatic cooperation under the Belt and Road Initiative*, Guangming Daily, November 9, 2014.

tion. The modernization development model based on the development experience of major Western developed countries is called "early endogenous modernization development model" by academia, and its counterpart in late-industrializing economies is the "late exogenous modernization development model". Although Western scholars also acknowledge that the modernization of some societies is not successful, and conditions in countries moving towards modernization vary greatly, they generally believe that the unsuccessful modernization and the differences are only temporary phenomena, and all types of differences in modernization will disappear when modernization is completed. Therefore, a country that has achieved modernization will certainly have the characteristics of some Western developed countries, such as market economy, economic growth, democratic politics and urbanization. The values purported in the Western modernization model are actually centered on capital and the interests of developed countries, while developing countries can only be in a subordinate position.

Chinese modernization is completely different from Western modernization. It puts the people first and ensures that modernization is people-centered. For a modernization path to work and work well, it must put the people first. Statistics show that from 2013 to 2019, the BRI created more than 200,000 jobs for relevant countries, and China signed economic and trade agreements with more than 30 countries, contributing to the economic development and improvement of people's livelihoods in participating countries. With the escalating Ukrainian crisis, global economic development has entered a very difficult period. The broken supply and industrial chains, the shortage or even crisis of energy and food, and the rising inflation have made the regional economic governance increasingly important. In Eurasia, the Shanghai Cooperation Organization, Eurasian Economic Union and other regional organizations are paying more and more attention to trade and investment cooperation. Issues such as promoting the economic modernization of member countries, increasing local currency settlements and fending off external threats have been put on the agenda. The proportion of local currency settlements in the trade among member countries of the Eurasian Economic Union has reached 75%, indicating that remarkable changes are underway in the direction of governance in Eurasia in the new context.[①]

---

① Сара Шаймерденова: Итоги саммита ВЕЭС и председательство России в ЕАЭС в 2023 году, 21 декабря 2022, https: //russiancouncil. ru/blogs/CIS – NSO – MGIMO/itogi – sammita – vees – i – predsedatelstvo – rossii – v – eaes – v – 2023 – godu/? sphrase_id = 96866744.

Creating a New Form of Human Civilization in the Profound World Changes Unseen in a Century

Zhang Zhiqiang[*]

The great rejuvenation of the Chinese nation has not only led the profound world changes unseen in a century, but also demonstrated to mankind a new form ofcivilization. This new form of civilization is the new form of Chinese civilization, which is a new path that China has taken in overcoming the inherent contradictions and fundamental crises of modern capitalist civilization. It has revealed to mankind a possibility of a new form of human civilization. The world's unprecedented change in a century means, in a certain sense, a change in the principle of civilization, and the subjective empowerment of any specific society and ancient civilization to choose its own path to modernization. The profound changes show a future prospect of human civilization. This prospect is a new form of human civilization with a general pattern shown by the new form of Chinese civilization, a community with a shared future for mankind composed of different modern social formations created in the soil of different civilizations, and a new human civilization with beauty and difference-based unity.

---

[*] Zhang Zhiqiang, Professor, Director of the Institute of Philosophy, CASS

Chapter 1 Chinese Modernization and the Chinese Experience of Modernization Development

As General Secretary Xi Jinping pointed out at the Fifth Plenary Session of the 19th Central Committee of the Communist Party of China (CPC), the whole Party should plan as a whole the overall landscape of strategies for the great rejuvenation of the Chinese nation and the profound world changes unseen in a century, which is the basic starting point for our Party to plan the work.

To fully grasp and plan as a whole for these two overall situations, we need to deeply understand the internal connection between them. As for the profound world changes unseen in a century, their outstanding features are the great changes in the pattern of modern world civilization driven by the great rejuvenation of the Chinese nation. The great rejuvenation of the Chinese nation happens to be in sync with the great adjustments in the pattern of world history, the great adjustments in the pattern of world civilization, and the great adjustments in principles about the modern world structure and civilization values they represent.

The great rejuvenation of the Chinese nation serves not only as a force to fuel the profound world changes unseen in a century, but also as the result of the internal changes in world history in the past century. Modern China endured intense humiliation, the Chinese people were subjected to untold misery, and Chinese civilization was plunged into darkness. After a hundred years of struggle, China moved step-by-step towards national rejuvenation, gradually recasting the new glories of Chinese civilization. In a sense, the evolution, on the one hand, mirrors the path that CPC has taken in line with the basic principles of Marxism to overcome the inner contradictions and fundamental crises brought along by capitalism in a socialist way. On the other hand, it shows the progressive journey of China to realize modernization and the great rejuvenation of the Chinese nation, unleash the inner power of Chinese civilization, and complete the modern transformation of Chinese civilization. In this sense, the great rejuvenation of the Chinese nation has not only fueled the profound world changes unseen in a century, but also shown the world a new form of human civilization, a form for an ancient civilization to modernize itself. This new civilization is the new form of Chinese civilization. It is a new way for mankind to overcome the inherent contradictions and fundamental crisis of capitalist modern civilization and shows mankind the possibilities of a new civilization and a new form of human civilization.

I. The Chinese path to modernization pioneered in the profound world changes unseen in a century has demonstrated a new form of human civilization

In his "July 1st" speech, General Secretary Xi Jinping declared to the world that "As we have upheld and developed socialism with Chinese characteristics and driven coordinated progress in material, political, cultural-ethical, social, and ecological terms, we have pioneered a new and uniquely Chinese path to modernization, and created a new model for human advancement."[①]

To deeply understand the "two creations" assertion of General Secretary Xi Jinping, it is necessary to have a deeper understanding of the subject who creates the "two creations", and fully understand that "two creations" are the results achieved by all Chinese people through a hundred years of struggle under the leadership of CPC.

To deeply understand the "two creations" assertion of General Secretary Xi Jinping, it is essential to gain a deeper insight into the relationship between the two creations. We should fully realize that the Chinese path to modernization is a road taken by CPC to realize the comprehensive modernization of an ancient civilization after a hundred years of struggle and hard exploration. It is a road for colonies and semi-colonies to achieve independence and liberation. Also, it is a road for developing countries to achieve prosperity and progress and a road to overcome and surpass the inherent crises and contradictions of capitalism. We

---

[①] *Speech at a Ceremony Marking the Centenary of the Communist Party of China*, Beijing: People's Publishing House, 2021, Pages 13 – 14.

should also realize that the Chinese path to modernization created by Chinese people under the leadership of CPC has opened up a new road for mankind to transcend and overcome the internal crisis of Western modern civilization, and also provided a new form of human civilization, also a new form for modern civilization that can be used as a reference for the sustainable development of human civilization.

The wording "the Chinese path to modernization" focuses on the summary of the experience in the historical exploration of CPC, while the wording "a new form of human civilization" focuses on the future of mankind and shows the world the significance of the Chinese path to modernization in world history and human civilization. "The Chinese path to modernization" explains the specific content of "a new form of human civilization" that takes root in China, as compared to the "new form of human civilization" that is based on the future of all mankind and declares the common value of the Chinese path to modernization to all mankind.

The Chinese path to modernization created by CPC after a hundred years of struggle has helped the Chinese people accounting for nearly one-fifth of the world's population shake off absolute poverty in a historic feat, achieve a moderately prosperous society in all respects and further build China into a great modern socialist power. It creates a great miracle in the history of human civilization. As a new form of human civilization and a new form of modern civilization, it will have a profound impact on the development of world history and the direction of human civilization development.

1. As a new form of human civilization, the great significance of the Chinese path to modernization lies in the fact that it has changed the modernization logic by which the modern world dominated by Western powers has taken shape and evolved over the past 1500 years.

As Karl Marx said, "The more the original isolation of the separate nationalities is destroyed by the developed mode of production and intercourse and the division of labor between various nations naturally brought forth by these, the *more history becomes world history.*"① The "historic existence in the world" claimed by capitalism is the prerequisite for a nation's history to be a part of world history. It is the capitalist mode of production that breaks the natural division of labor among nations, gradually forming a world system featuring the peripheral societies attached to the core through the expansion of capital. In other words, the expansion of capitalism works as the driving force for a nation's history to be a part of world history. However, as Marx pointed out, though a unified world in which human beings are interdependent takes shape as a result of its expansion, capitalism has not brought about the true and complete liberation of human beings while breaking the geographical limitations and personal shackles. Instead, it has covered up the slavery relationship between people by the superficial equality of commodity exchange, and covered up the power domination between the core and the peripheral societies by the integration of world markets. It covered up the polarization within society with the illusion of development and prosperity, and covered up the excessive oppression of nature with extremely liberated productive forces. What is more important, the modernization that comes along with the expansion of capitalism puts ancient civilizations outside the West in a paradoxical situation, in which they have to choose between having their roots pulled out of their civilization and tradition by conforming to this modernization or falling behind the times by sticking to their civilization and tradition. Civilization and traditions have come to stand in opposition to this modernization, which has reduced people to isolated individuals uprooted from their soil of civilization.

The Chinese path to modernization is a new logic of modernization created by Chinese people through hard exploration under the leadership of CPC and a new form of modern civilization. Firstly, it must be able to liberate the productive forces as strong as the modernization of the Western world. CPC led Chinese people to learn all kinds of modernization experiences creatively and sum up and

---

① *Marx & Engels Collected Works*, V.1, Beijing: People's Publishing House, 2009, Page 540.

transform all kinds of modernization lessons, building up an independent and relatively complete industrial system and national economic system during the period of socialist revolution and construction. A foundation is laid for industrialization. In the new era of reform, opening up and socialist modernization, the mechanism of a socialist market economy was established, which allowed the market to play a decisive role in resource allocation, promote scientific and technological innovations and improve labor productivity. The Chinese path to modernization makes full use of socialized mass production to achieve a great development of social productive forces in China. Secondly, the Chinese path to modernization has not only brought about long-term economic development by liberating social productive forces, but also brought about long-term social stability. The simultaneous occurrence of these "two miracles (long-term economic development and long-term social stability)" fundamentally refutes the development paradox predicted for developing countries that they can't have both of these "two miracles" together. The road that Western modernization has taken for hundreds of years to shape was overrun in decades. Thirdly, the Chinese path to modernization is one modernization that overcomes the inherent contradiction between private ownership of capitalist means of production and socialized mass production. The modernization of capitalism doesn't use the greatly liberated productive forces to create social well-being shared by all the people. Instead, it further divides society. The Chinese path to modernization is a socialist modernization aimed at the common prosperity of all the people. It takes into account efficiency and fairness. Fourthly, the Chinese path to modernization has evolved from the stage where Man would conquer nature to the present mode of harmony between Man and nature. The concept of sustainable development is adopted, which is to take sustainable development of mankind as the goal and the harmonious coexistence between man and nature as the principle. What the Chinese path to modernization ultimately achieves is the overall improvement of human civilization. Fifthly, while respecting individual values, the Chinese path to modernization pays more attention to harmony between individual interests and collective interests and adheres to the values of considering individuals as a part of the world and realizing the values of individuals without imparting those of the whole. Thus, the all-round development of people is tied to the all-round progress of society. It overcomes, from the root, the individualistic values enclosed in a narrow self-centered mindset and transcends the relationship between people in capitalist society, thus building up the cultural ideals of Chinese modernization.

The key to the success of the Chinese path to modernization lies in CPC's leadership, the most essential feature of Socialism with Chinese characteristics. The combination of CPC's centralized and unified leadership and people-centered values is the exact reason that makes it able to guide the development of economic, social, cultural and ecological fields in line with people-oriented values. CPC's leadership is the exact reason that has given birth to the Chinese path to modernization, a political model distinct from Western modernization. The Chinese path to modernization with coordinated development in politics, economy, society, culture and ecology can only be attributed to CPC's leadership. Just because of CPC's leadership, China has the ability to gain economic independence through socialist construction and reform and opening up on the premise of political independence through revolution, breaking away from its dependence on the Western-led world system. What's more, the Chinese path to modernization will win complete cultural independence, ushering in the great rejuvenation of the Chinese nation and finally building up a socialist modern power in an all-round way. The Chinese path to modernization has not only demonstrated a new road to modernization for developing countries, but also changed the logic of the Western path to modernization. More importantly, it reshapes world history and provides a new form of human civilization for human beings to learn and choose.

2. The great significance of the Chinese path to modernization, a new form of human civilization, lies in the fact that it has re-injected vitality and provided direction for the world socialist movement with the path, theory, system and

Chapter 1 Chinese Modernization and the Chinese Experience of Modernization Development

culture of Socialism with Chinese characteristics.

Marx and Engels revealed the internal contradictions underpinning capitalist society using historical materialism, and pointed out that the "historical existence in the world" of capitalism would not completely liberate people. It isalong with the historical process of capitalist expansion worldwide that the global socialist movement came into being, another global historical movement that criticizes, avoids and transcends the inherent crisis of capitalism. The global socialist movement aims to provide a path to modernization that transcends capitalism, create a modern civilization form that reflects the basic value concerns of a community of human civilization, and establish a modern social formation different from capitalism. To overcome contradictions between private ownership of the means of production and modern socialized mass production that can help avoid radically from the anarchy in social production and solve the contradiction between fairness and efficiency, it is necessary to establish a value goal for social production. Socialism that is based on the people's stance stipulates, adjusts and guides socialized mass production per the needs of all people for survival and development to make production aligned with demand, realizing control of socialist values on socialized mass production. To conclude, nothing but socialism is the social formation that is compatible with modern socialized mass production. The alignment between purpose and means will be ultimately realized by socialism and modern socialized mass production. If modernization liberates greatly productive forces, then socialist value ideals can make the liberated productive forces benefit all mankind to a greater extent and eliminate inequality, while capitalism makes them follow the motive of profit seeking, deepening social differentiation. This is the fundamental difference between socialist modernization and capitalist modernization.

The global socialist movement has gone through a tortuous and arduous exploration process, offering many historical experiences and lessons in the process of exploring socialist modernization. With a clear understanding of the relationship between market mechanisms and capitalism, Socialism with Chinese characteristics gives full play to the decisive role of the market in resource allocation to get rid of the rigid drawbacks of the highly centralized planning system, and also continues to give full play to the role of the government. Benign interaction takes shape among socialist value goals, institutional mechanisms and market economy, and a unique and effective socialist market economic system is established. As a model guided by socialist value ideals to realize modern socialized mass production and then modernization, the Chinese path to modernization has opened up a new road for the global socialist movement. The path to Chinese modernization is the road to success for socialist modernization, and its fundamental features lie in its ability to include a market economy in its socialist system and mechanisms, achieve common prosperity without sacrificing development efficiency, fully liberate the productive forces on the premise of adherence to the ideal of socialist fairness, and always maintain national sovereignty and independence in the process of integrating into the international economic system. The key to the success of the Chinese path to modernization lies in the adherence to the all-round leadership of CPC. It also lies in the value guidance and political governance of CPC for economic and social development and its continued representation of the fundamental interests of the overwhelming majority of the people. CPC has neither any special interests of its own, nor represents the interests of any interest group, power group or privileged class. It has always insisted on serving the people. Only under the leadership of CPC, the development of modernization will have produced the effect of overall development of the country and society and will benefit all the people.

3. The great significance of the Chinese path to modernization, a new form of human civilization, lies in the fact that it activates the inner power of Chinese civilization, fully realizes the modernization of Chinese civilization and creates a new form of Chinese civilization.

Mr. Qian Mu once said "Greece sows the Western history, and China plants the eastern history. Old seeds wither away when sowers spread new seeds,

Chapter 1 Chinese Modernization and the Chinese Experience of Modernization Development

but those who plant roots have flourishing foliage and growing roots."① The Western civilization, though continuous as a civilization, does not present itself as a unified political subject as its main body of civilization has dispersed long ago. In contrast, the main body of Chinese civilization has always been the unified political system, with inseparable foliage and deep roots. Chinese civilization is characterized by its more than 5,000 years of continuous development and uninterrupted history, a large-scale political body condensed by the vast territory and the people, a unified order of pluralism and integration, and a unified but different order of harmony. The continuity, scale and unity are the great achievements of Chinese civilization. The reason why Chinese civilization keeps growing is that it takes historical initiative to constantly adapt to the environment and embrace internal and external challenges. Thanks to this historical initiative, Chinese civilization is able to be "open to changes", "accommodate to circumstances", and "inherit the trend of generations to adapt to changes of today". This historical initiative spirit is exactly the "general history" spirit explained by the integration of classics and history. Just because of this spirit, Chinese civilization can get out of the predicament again and again, and open up a new realm of Chinese civilization by starting from reality and creating in response to the current situation. And the mystery of the long-term existence of Chinese civilization is to be found in the DNA that gives birth to this historical initiative. It is just this spirit that enables Chinese civilization to gradually overcome bottlenecks restricting its development when it encounters difficulties and challenges in modern times, and lets Chinese civilization regain its vitality.

The successful Chinese path to modernization and the new form of human civilization created have reflected the inner vitality of Chinese civilization in a most profound and vivid way. With a profound understanding of the historical initiative of Chinese civilization, CPC employs the methodology of seeking truth from facts and creatively applies Marxism. It combines Marxism with China's his-

---

① Qian Mu, *Political Science Private Speech*, Beijing Jiuzhou Press, 2011, P256.

torical reality and civilization reality to fully activate the inner power of Chinese civilization, leading Chinese people to create a Chinese path to modernization and a new form of human civilization.

The Chinese path to modernization has far-reaching significance for the history of China. On one hand, it makes clear to all the profound Chinese civilization that it is based on; enhances the centralized and unified political authority; guides the structural functions that facilitate the development of economic and social fields using the core value of people first; builds up the awareness of Chinese nation community; puts forward the concept of coexistence of man and nature in harmony and the community of shared future for mankind; and establishes the world order concept of peaceful development and harmonious sharing featuring "unity without uniformity" and "difference-based unity". On the other hand, the Chinese path to modernization helps creatively solve a host of issues, including the lofty people-oriented ideals constrained by the imperial family world, the lack of a broad foundation for a highly concentrated power, the fragmented and unorganized people of a vast country, and the involution of a developed small-peasant economy. It has created people's democratic politics with a deep foundation, building the Party's leadership on a broad social basis in a democratic and centralized way. It introduces positive group activities like socialized mass production to ease the involution of the small-peasant economy. The historical significance of the Chinese path to modernization lies also in the truth it reveals to us, i. e. combining it with concrete reality. The development of the road must be based on a realistic understanding of the national conditions and respect for objective historical conditions. In fact, as "national character", "the soil of civilization" is a more fundamental and basic "national condition", and combining it with "reality of civilization" is a further act to deepen the combination with concrete reality.

The Chinese path to modernization has far-reaching significance for the history of the world. It shows the world a form of modern civilization, which is no longer a new civilization that is broken from its tradition and uprooted from its soil of civilization, but a new civilization that is progressively created from ancient civilizations and is consistent from ancient times to modern times. In this sense, the Chinese path to modernization, as a new form of Chinese civilization, shows the world the rebirth path of an ancient civilization, and a new form of human civilization that keeps improving instead of abandoning its origin. In this sense, the trend of "The Rise of the East and Decline of the West" in the world today reflects, in essence, the trend of the revival of ancient civilization. The profound world changes unseen in a century that we are confronted with are final changes ushered in to the world by the ancient oriental civilization on the basis of studying the achievements of modern civilization in an all-round way, carrying forward the rich accumulation of the ancient civilization in an all-round way, and continuous and arduous struggle.

Taking Chinese civilization as its foundation, modernization as its historical mission and socialism as its value ideal, the Chinese path to modernization forges a new road to modernization for the world and creates a new form of human civilization through CPC's century-long struggle. This road was explored by Chinese people under the leadership of CPC through a lot of hardships. Moving forward, we will firmly grasp the historical initiative and go along this road independently.

II. The new form of human civilization initiated by the Chinese path to modernization reveals the essence and goal of the profound world changes unseen in a century

The world history that is mainly labeled by the global expansion of capitalism is the fundamental driving force for the formation of the modern world. "Modernization" has become a normative concept with a specific historical connotation, marking a social state that is completely different from times before modernization. It is to portray the modernization that classical social theorists began to use the word "society". Only in modern times has the "society" that is different from the "community" before modernization emerged. "Society" means a state of human organization integrated by abstracted functional systems, which is different from the "community" organically integrated by concrete value norms. "Society" is the product of rationalization and the result of the rational expansion of instruments. As it has a series of operational modes of value rationalization matching the instrument rationalization, it collapses the "community" that is integrated by specific value norms. The "modern society", being the product of rationalization, is a "society" that is totally against tradition and community from the root and is against the integration of unified values and norms. "Modernization", in general, refers to the period in world history when the mode of production of capitalism is combined with a society abstracted by rationality. Wherever it goes, it will surely disintegrate any inherent civilization community to create a "universal" human civilization. What deserves more attention is that an antagonistic relationship comes into being between an abstracted society and concrete society because of the abstract nature of modern society. The abstracted society characterized by the integration of rational systems is a modern society, while the community that is organically integrated by traditional values is a society before modernization. The process of modernization is both the process of popularizing a universally abstracted society and the process of disintegrating any specific society. However, as a product of rationalization, the formation of abstracted society is the product of complex operations of programmed functions and abstract values and self-ethical practices. This complex operation lies in the historical conditions of a specific society. As Max Weber pointed out, Western Europe, as the birthplace of modern society, creates exactly the ethical conditions for Protestant ethics to constitute a capitalist spirit. This shows that rational modernization is a unique product of Western European civilization. Therefore, its universality is actually just the promotion of imperialist violence. Most non-Western European countries are unsuccessful in imitating rationalization. The reason for that is that they ignored the specific historical conditions of modernization.

The exemplary significance of theChinese path to modernization lies in its zero abstract imitation of modern society from the root. Starting from the specific civilization and historical conditions of itself, the Chinese path to modernization achieves a modernization that unleashes greatly productive forces, and facilitates the development of human beings and the harmony of society in an all-round way. The new form of human civilization created by the Chinese path to modernization is different from the so-called modern form of civilization created by Western European civilization. The fundamental difference lies in that the former is rooted in the soil of civilization of a specific society where it can take advantage of the civilization and historical conditions accumulated by a specific society for a long time, actively draw on and absorb all beneficial achievements of human civilization, and actively create a new civilization. As a new civilization of mankind, the Chinese path to modernization grows from but does not deny an old civilization. It is the result of the continued growth of the combination of old and new civilizations, but not the result of breaking away from the old civilization. The Chinese path to modernization is to modernize but not destroy an ancient civilization. In our opinion, it is the unique value of the Chinese path to modernization. It explains exactly why the new form of human civilization initiated by the Chinese path to modernization will have important exemplary significance for any other ancient civilization to modernize them based on their concrete societies.

The new form of human civilization initiated by the Chinese path to modernization is a new human civilization created under the specific historical conditions of China. It is the creative transformation and innovative development of the excellent traditional Chinese culture. This new civilization will not abstract itself into a universal value to form civilization hegemony. Instead, it shows mankind a model of successfully creating and transforming its own modern society from its soil of civilization and concrete society by its unique road. In a certain sense, the profound world changes unseen in a century mean such a change in the principle of civilization and empowerment of subjects of any specific society and ancient civilization to choose their path to modernization. Those countries, nations and other civilizations that want to achieve modernization and maintain their subjectivity, i. e. , their independence, come to deeply realize that they can truly do so only by combining the historical and civilization conditions of their specific societies and that only in this way can they fundamentally change the subjectless state of following Western modernization blindly. The profound world changes unseen in a century show all mankind a prospect of human civilization, i. e. , a big landscape of a new form of human civilization presented by the new form of Chinese civilization. It will be a community of shared future for all mankind that is composed of different forms of modern society created by different civilizations and traditions, and will be a new human civilization with beauty and difference-based unity.

In a certain sense, the new form of human civilization initiated by the Chinese path to modernization has also made clear an important truth. That is, a social formation must evolve with roots in the civilization and historical conditions of its specific society. Specifically, the role of subject played by people is manifested by their efforts to closely combine the needs of the times with the historical conditions of specific civilization to promote the evolution of their own society. In this sense, the so-called evolution of a social formation is fundamentally the evolution of a civilization and refers to the process by which civilization itself keeps activating its inner power and core values in line with the new conditions of the times. The evolution of a civilization is the growth of itself to keep growing amid evolution to prosper. The evolution of a social formation is nothing other than the concrete content of the evolution of a civilization. The modernization evolution of China's society achieved by the Chinese path to modernization implies updating of the Chinese civilization. It is therefore of great significance to demonstrate a new form for human civilization.

The century-long struggle of CPC is a fundamental manifestation of the inner vitality of theChinese civilization. Thanks to the great struggle of CPC, Chinese civilization finally evolves into its own modern form. The great struggle of CPC to create a new form of Chinese civilization is to show mankind the possibility of new human civilization and the direction and goal that a new world historical process can endeavor to achieve. As General Secretary Xi Jinping solemnly declared in his July 1st speech, "The Chinese nation has fostered a splendid civilization over more than 5,000 years of history. The Party has also acquired a wealth of experience through its endeavors over the past 100 years and during more than 70 years of governance. At the same time, we are also eager to learn what lessons we can from the achievements of other cultures, and welcome helpful suggestions and constructive criticism. We will not, however, accept sanctimonious preaching from those who feel they have the right to lecture us. The Party and the Chinese people will keep moving confidently forward in broad strides along the path that we have chosen for ourselves, and we will make sure the destiny of China's development and progress remains firmly in our own hands."[1] What we have learned from the century-old party history is precisely this kind of power to master our own destiny and historical initiative, this kind of vision to focus on all mankind and change the course of world history, and this mindset to create new values and new civilization from the foundation of human civilization!

---

[1] *Speech at a Ceremony Marking the Centenary of the Communist Party of China*, Beijing: People's Publishing House, 2021, Pages 13 – 14.

Chapter 2 Chinese Modernization and New Initiative for China's Development

Chinese Modernization and China's New Proposition for Global Governance

Ouyang Xiangying[*]

At the just-concluded 20th National Congress of the Communist Party of China (CPC), Chinese President Xi Jinping appealed to all countries in the world, "China has put forward the Global Development Initiative and the Global Security Initiative, and it stands ready to work with the international community to put these two initiatives into action." The two initiatives refer to the new global development proposition proposed by China as the world's largest developing country and the new global security initiative proposed by China as a responsible major country, which reflects China's new ideas and new measures in handling the "four major deficits (i.e., the deficits in peace, development, governance, and trust)" in the world.

I. Time Background of the Two Initiatives

Safeguarding world peace and promoting joint development are the aims of China's foreign policy, and pursuing a strategy of national rejuvenation amid global changes of a magnitude not seen in a century is the strategic focus of the

---

[*] Ouyang Xiangying, Professor, Institute of World Economics and Politics, CASS

Party in the new era. Internationally, the COVID-19 pandemic has accelerated the evolution of global changes of a magnitude not seen in a century. On the one hand, a significant shift is taking place in the international balance of power, and the concept of a Community of Shared Future for Mankind has been deeply rooted in the hearts of the people; on the other hand, economic globalization is facing headwinds, unilateralism, protectionism and hegemonism are posing a threat to world peace and development, the deficits in peace, development, security and governance are still expanding, and Ukrainian Crisis has pushed up the inflation risk and uncertainty in the global economy. In China, it is a critical period to comprehensively promote the great rejuvenation of the Chinese nation through Chinese-style modernization. On the one hand, China has made efforts to apply the new development philosophy on all fronts, promote high-quality development, create a new pattern of development, carry out supply-side structural reforms, and formulate a series of major regional strategies with overall significance, which led to a historic leap in China's economic strength; on the other hand, the country still faces the problem of imbalanced and insufficient development, and more work should be done to optimize the harmonious coexistence between human and nature and to solidly promote shared prosperity. In general, changes in the world, the times and history are unfolding in unprecedented ways. This essential judgment is absolutely right.

In the post-pandemic era, due to complicating economic and security situations, the world is facing more and more uncertainties. The main risk tipping points are as follows:

First, there is a logical conflict between the high-interest rate to curb inflation and the high debt in developed countries. The debt of developed countries in the West, headed by the United States, remains high. In the past, it was diluted by various forms of monetary easing policies, including QE (quantitative easing) and OT (operation twist) of the Federal Reserve and OMT (outright monetary transactions) of the European Central Bank, aiming at enhancing the liquidity of the economy, encouraging enterprises to invest, boosting consumption desire, stimulating economic growth and creating jobs. However, when the Russia-Ukraine conflict pushed up global inflation, the United States raised interest rates to curb the inflation. Unfortunately, high-interest rates increased the cost of debt, and the accelerated reflow of international capital has further fueled inflation. ① The reason behind America's imbalanced economic policy is that being diverted out of the real economy has become a malady, so monetary policy alone can only postpone the crisis and cannot reverse the risk of entering a recession after 2023.

Second, the violent fluctuations in the commodity market have contributed to the turbulent changes in the world. After the outbreak of the Ukrainian Crisis, energy prices fluctuated violently, and the prices of rare metals and raw materials skyrocketed around the world, which may lead to a partial adjustment of the global supply chains and industrial chains. Since Russia and Ukraine account for more than one-third of the world's grain exports, the stagnation of grain exports due to the Crisis resulted in short supply of grain in the world. The United Nations has established the Global Crisis Response Group on Food, Energy and Finance to deal with possible global food shortage. Since the implementation of the Black Sea Grain Initiative, by October 15, 2022, a total of 341 cargo vessels have left the southern ports of Ukraine with 7.5 million tons of agricultural products. Due to extreme weather and the COVID-19 pandemic, about 345 million people are affected by hunger, while about 924 million people around the world are facing serere food insecurity. ②

Third, trade protectionism has becomea point of convergence of political

---

① By October 2022, the US federal debt has surpassed 31 trillion USD, only 250 billion USD below the debt "red line" of 31.4 trillion USD. At the same time, the cumulative net inflow of overseas investment into the United States has exceeded a total inflow of 1,111.4 billion USD in 2021, setting a new high since the data were available in 1978.

② Liu Yanchunzi: *The Future of Energy and Food Security amid Mounting Global Climate Change Risks*. Source: Financial News, https://www.financialnews.com.cn/hq/cj/202210/t20221025_257863.html, [2022-10-25].

and economic struggles among major countries. At present, the international trade imbalance persists, and the global pattern of current account imbalance has not improved markedly. The introduction of *the CHIPS and Science Act of 2022* in the United States could all give rise to a new round of trade protectionism, which may break up the global value chain. It is worth noting that the US CHIPS Act authorized a number of funds as high as 280 billion USD to develop the semiconductor manufacturing industry in the United States, a practice of giving high subsidies to a single industry, while it complained to the WTO that China giving subsidies to its export enterprises in sectors like advanced materials, metal industry, textiles, light industry, special chemicals, medical products, computer hardware and building materials. This indicates that the United States obviously adopted double standards. In fact, since China joined the WTO, it has strictly abided by the obligations of the WTO *Agreement on Subsidies and Countervailing Measures*, and completely abolished the prohibited subsidies under the Agreement, which is well documented. However, the United States has replaced international law with domestic law and undermined international trade relations and basic norms through protectionism and hegemonism.

Fourth, regional security crises have a negative impact on the world situation. In his speech at the emergency special session of the UN General Assembly on Ukraine, Ambassador Geng Shuang pointed out that it has been eight months since the crisis in Ukraine broke out, the crisis is getting increasingly protracted, expanded and complicated, and its spillover effects are further penetrating to and affecting the economy and people's livelihood, which has brought about more instability and uncertainty to an already turbulent world and caused deep concerns. In addition, changes in the situations situation in Afghanistan, Libya, Central Asia and other countries have also led to instability in many regions.

II. The Impact of Changes in the Times on China

The increasing uncertainty of the external environment is both a challenge and an opportunity for the development of China.

First, with the shift of the global growth focus, the balance of power between developed and developing countries has changed significantly, which is one of the most important changes in the global economic environment. Today, more than half of the global GDP comes from emerging economies and low-income countries. In the next five years, entire emerging economies will continue to increase their share in global trade, and their contribution to global GDP growth is estimated to reach around 2/3. This will result in a great change in the global demand structure, which will substantially drive the growth from quantitative change to qualitative change. Compared with the fiscal vigilance of developed countries, emerging economies have larger fiscal space. Their relatively low overall debt and deficit levels give them plenty of space to implement fiscal and monetary policies. With the great changes in the balance of power in the global economy, the game between developing and developed countries on the right to make rules will become more intense. By formulating higher-level and stricter international rules, China can work with other emerging economies and developing countries to seek mutual benefits and win-win results. China is capable of promoting inclusive global development to share the fruits of China's development with more developing countries.

Second, long-term economic growth depends on the improvement of labor productivity, and there are three main ways to improve labor productivity, namely, technological progress, trade expansion, and institutional innovation. At this stage, institutional innovation and technological progress are particularly important, because proper institutional arrangements and technological progress are closely related to the flow of factors and will release space for the improvement of labor productivity. After a hundred years of struggle and accumulation, the Party and the people have finally explored a socialist road with Chinese characteristics, which is the most remarkable greatest consensus of Chinese society and the biggest institutional advantage of China. Currently, the fundamentals of China's economic and social development are improving, its domestic market has great potential, its ability of scientific and technological innovation has been enhanced, and its human resources are abundant, suggesting remarkable comprehensive advantages of production factors. However, China still faces urgent tasks to implement the new development philosophy and create a new pattern of development. Institutional innovation is, on the premise of adhering to the leadership of the Communist Party of China (CPC) and the socialist system with Chinese characteristics, to constantly improve the theoretical system of socialism with Chinese characteristics, resolutely get rid of all institutional mechanisms that constrain the development of productive forces, and establish institutional mechanisms that meet the requirements of the new stage of economic and social development. It is necessary to fully and faithfully apply the new development philosophy on all fronts, continue reforms to develop the socialist market economy, promote high-standard opening up, and accelerate efforts to foster a new pattern of development that is focused on the domestic economy and features positive interplay between domestic and international economic flows. In order to build a high-standard socialist market economy, China must uphold and improve its basic socialist economic systems, unswervingly consolidate and develop the public sector and unswervingly encourage, support, and guide the development of the non-public sector. The market should play a decisive role in resource allocation, and the government should better play its role. This is the institutional guarantee for China to win the economic competition.

Finally, the fundamental issue facing China is the national construction and domestic development, aiming at comprehensively promoting the great rejuvenation of the Chinese nation through Chinese-style modernization. The symbol of the great rejuvenation of the Chinese nation is the rejuvenation on all fronts, so Chinese-style modernization should be the modernization of the national governance system, including economy, science and technology, politics, law, culture, society, security and national defense. In the final stage of the 14th Five-Year Plan and on the way to achieving the long-term goal of 2035, the most important tasks include, in the aspect of economy, accelerating the creation of a new development pattern and pursuing high-quality development; in the aspect of science and technology, invigorating China through science and education and developing a strong workforce for the modernization drive; in the aspect of politics, advancing whole-process people's democracy and ensuring that the people run the country; in the aspect of rule of law, exercising law-based governance on all fronts and advancing the rule of law in China; in the aspect of culture, building cultural confidence and strength, and securing new successes in developing socialist culture; in the aspect of society, improving the people's wellbeing and raising quality of life; in the aspect of security, modernizing China's national security system and capacity, and safeguarding national security and social stability; and in the aspect of national defense, achieving the centenary goal of the People's Liberation Army and further modernize national defense and the military. What needs to be emphasized is, "Upholding the Party's overall leadership is the path we must take to uphold and develop socialism with Chinese characteristics; building socialism with Chinese characteristics is the path we must take to realize the rejuvenation of the Chinese nation; striving in unity is the path the Chinese people must take to create great historic achievements; implementing the new development philosophy is the path China must take to grow stronger in the new era; and exercising full and rigorous self-governance is the path the Party must take to maintain its vigor and pass new tests on the road ahead."[1] This is a crucial understanding that we have come to through many years of practice, and also the fundamental reason for China's strategic victory.

The development of the world cannot be achieved without contributions from China, while China cannot develop itself in isolation from the world. The

---

[1] Xi Jinping: "Hold High the Great Banner of Socialism with Chinese Characteristics and Strive in Unity to Build a Modern Socialist Country in All Respects — Report to the 20th National Congress of the Communist Party of China", Xinhua News Agency, http://www.news.cn/politics/cpc20/2022-10/25/c_1129079429.htm, [2022-10-25].

new development pattern requires us not only to make concerted efforts to build our homeland, but also to brave the wind and the waves to explore wider development space in the international community.

III. The Ideas and Connotations of the Two Initiatives

Today, human society is facing unprecedented challenges, mainly because the three prominent contradictions in the international community have not been effectively solved. These three prominent contradictions are imbalanced global development, the absence of global governance, and structural tension in international security. The Western developed countries take advantage of their leading position in global development to obtain unequal trade treaties, and through commercial, political, scientific, technological and cultural activities. They continue to gain more economic benefits and resources from backward countries, which aggravates the polarization of world economic development. The rich get richer, and the poor get poorer, resulting in a widening development gap. Ethnic contradictions, racial contradictions and social contradictions coexist. Particularly, the game of interests among major countries may intensify their contradictions and even lead to fierce conflicts. Many economically backward countries are partially blocked and isolated from the global market to a certain extent. They lack competitive advantages in import and export trade and international economic cooperation, and face substantial balance of payments deficits. They suffer from backward infrastructure and seriously inadequate public services such as education, medical care and sports. Their economy relies too much on agriculture and mining, and their national income is low. At the same time, developed economies are increasingly shift toward servitization, virtualization and hollowing out, leading to weak and unsustainable growth. The imbalanced development of the global economy has brought about the imbalanced development among different social classes around the world. In some backward regions, poverty and hunger still threaten people, and more than 700 million people in the world still live in extreme poverty. For many families, having a warm house, enough food and a stable job is still a luxury. This is the biggest challenge facing the world today, and also an important reason behind social turmoil in some countries. Since the 21st century, with the growing polarization between the rich and the poor in different classes, ethnic groups and countries, income inequality has become one of the core issues concerned by global economic governance.

In today's global governance mechanism, developed countries hold a dominant position. President Xi Jinping has pointed out, "Over the past few decades, profound changes have taken place in international economic competition, but the governance system has failed to reflect the new pattern, falling short of equal representation and inclusion."[①] In recent decades, the pattern of international economic power has changed significantly, and the contribution rate of emerging market countries and developing countries to global economic growth reached 80%. However, this change has not been reflected in time in the current global governance mechanism, so the global governance structure cannot well represent the interests and demands of developing countries. The rise of a group of developing countries will inevitably demand corresponding adjustments and changes in the global governance system, so they can earn a better position in the international benefit distribution pattern. In the post-pandemic era, amidse a slowing global economy, various economies are divided into four levels. The first level is emerging market countries and developing countries that maintain medium and high-speed growth, such as China and India; the second level is developed economies with slow or negative growth, represented by Britain and Japan, whose economic slowdown trend is more obvious; the third level is some countries and regions caught in the "middle-income trap", such as Ma-

---

① Xi Jinping: "Jointly Shoulder Responsibility of Our Times, Promoting Global Growth — Keynote Speech at the Opening Session of the World Economic Forum Annual Meeting 2017", Xinhua News Agency https: //epaper. gmw. cn/gmrb/html/2017 - 01/18/nw. D110000gmrb_20170118_1 - 03. htm, [2017 - 01 - 18].

laysia and Brazil; and the fourth level is economically backward countries and regions, which have entered a recession due to a bunch of factors including the COVID-19 pandemic. The imbalanced development and unequal international status of these countries are the root causes of the threat to international security. In recent years, on many international occasions, Chinese leaders have proposed a new concept of global governance, aiming at changing the original pattern and approach of global governance and offering a solution to economic development and world peace.

China's concept of global governance features strong "problem consciousness" and has evolved with the times, which is completely in line with Marxist materialist dialectics. On October 12, 2015, the Political Bureau of the Communist Party of China (CPC) Central Committee held a collective study on "Global Governance Structure and Global Governance System". President Xi Jinping delivered an important speech, which he systematically expounded China's new concept of leading the reform of the global governance system. He stressed that the fundamental purpose of China's participation in global governance is to obey and serve the realization of the goal of "two hundred years" and the Chinese dream of the great rejuvenation of the Chinese nation. It is necessary to make a correct assessment of the situation, seize opportunities, properly respond to challenges, take both domestic and international situations into consideration, make the global governance system "more just and reasonable", and create a better environment for China's development and world peace. In 2017, President Xi attended the opening session of the World Economic Forum in Davos and delivered a keynote speech, in which the new proposition on global governance attracted great attention internationally. He proposed, "First, we should develop a dynamic, innovation-driven growth model; second, we should pursue a well-coordinated and inter-connected approach to develop a model of open and win-win cooperation; third, we should develop a model of fair and equitable governance in keeping with the trend of the times; and fourth, we should develop a balanced, equitable and inclusive development model."① In 2019, during the closing ceremony of the China-France Global Governance Forum, President Xi pointed out that we should adhere to a vision of global governance featuring shared growth through discussion and collaboration, insisted that global affairs need to be handled by all countries through consultations, and actively advance the democratization of global governance rules. In January 2022, in his speech at the virtual session of the World Economic Forum, President Xi emphasized, "We should guide reforms of the global governance system with the principle of fairness and justice, and uphold the multilateral trading system with the World Trade Organization at its center. We should make generally acceptable and effective rules for artificial intelligence and digital economy on the basis of full consultation, and create an open, just and non-discriminatory environment for scientific and technological innovation. This is the way to make economic globalization more open, inclusive, balanced and beneficial for all, and to fully unleash the vitality of the world economy."② In the Report to the 20th National Congress of the CPC, President Xi once again stressed, "China plays an active part in the reform and development of the global governance system. It upholds true multilateralism, promotes greater democracy in international relations, and works to make global governance fairer and more equitable." He called on the international community to jointly implement the Global Development Initiative and the Global Security Initiative, and hold dear humanity's shared values of peace, development, fairness, justice, democracy, and freedom. The Chinese people are ready to work hand in hand with people from around the world to create an even brighter future for humanity. President Xi's ex-

---

① Xi Jinping: "Jointly Shoulder Responsibility of Our Times, Promote Global Growth — Keynote Speech at the Opening Session of the World Economic Forum Annual Meeting 2017", Xinhua News Agency https: //epaper. gmw. cn/gmrb/html/2017 – 01/18/nw. D110000gmrb _ 20170118 _ 1 – 03. htm, [2017 – 01 – 18].

② Xi Jinping: *The Governance of China* (Volume IV), the Foreign Languages Press, 2022 edition, page 485.

position on global governance is an integral part of the Thought on Socialism with Chinese Characteristics for a New Era, which plays an important guiding role in China's foreign exchanges.

Independence, self-reliance, openness and win-win cooperation are the basic norms in international economic relations. The former two emphasize the independence and integrity of economic sovereignty, while the latter two are operational-level strategies. They are not contradictory. Marx and Engels have long said that competition is the actual trade freedom, and the protective tariff is only a temporary solution in competition and a means of defense within the scope of trade freedom. To grow and develop, we must actively conform to the trend of economic globalization. Upholding the democratization of international relations and non-interference in other countries' internal affairs are the basic norms of international political relations. The core of the democratization of international relations is that all countries, large or small, are equal, but this is far from being realized in today's international political practice. Most international organizations are clubs of great powers. Non-interference in other countries' internal affairs has two meanings. One is that we do not interfere in other countries' internal affairs, and the other is that we do not allow any foreign countries to interfere in our internal affairs. This is the key to the peaceful coexistence of all countries in the world. There is no reason for foreign countries to interfere in our internal affairs. When handling international relations, China does not consider the social system, but proceeds from its own strategic interests. It not only looks at its own long-term strategic interests, but also respects others' interests, regardless of historical grievances and differences in social systems and ideologies. And it advocates mutual respect and equality for all countries, big or small, strong or weak. These should become the basic norms of international political relations. Defending world peace and opposing hegemonism are the basic norms of international security relations. World peace is inseparable, and the struggle to stop war and maintain peace is also interrelated and inseparable. This is a characteristic of international security relations. It is necessary to build a community of shared future for mankind, establish a new security concept with mutual trust, mutual benefit, equality and cooperation as its core, achieve effective disarmament and arms control, strengthen coordination and cooperation in international and regional affairs, and emphasize the maintenance of the authority of the United Nations and recognized international norms. These are reliable prerequisites for preventing conflicts and wars. President Xi's concept of national security emphasizes forging friendships and partnerships with its neighbors, and advocates for seeking common ground while reserving differences, rather than bullying each other into submission. More and more countries have this consensus. Only by seeking peace and promoting security through cooperation can we achieve world peace and stability and China's long-term stability. In terms of international security, China will shoulder more international responsibilities, and work with other countries to safeguard human conscience and international justice. China will seek and uphold justice and equality in international and regional affairs, play an even more active and productive role in resolving hotspot issues, and deal with contradictions and differences through consultation on an equal footing. We are ready to show our utmost sincerity and patience and remain committed to resolving any differences through dialogue.

As a responsiblemajor country, China strives to contribute more public goods to maintain world development and peace, as represented by its two initiatives. The Global Development Initiative, proposed by President Xi Jinping at the 76th session of the UN General Assembly on September 21, 2021, mainly includes six contents. First, staying committed to development as a priority. We need to put development high on the global macro policy agenda, strengthen policy coordination among major economies, and ensure policy continuity, consistency and sustainability. We need to cultivate global development partnerships that are more equal and balanced. Second, staying committed to a people-centered approach. We should safeguard and improve people's livelihoods and protect and promote human rights through development, and make sure that development is for the people and by the people, and that its fruits are shared among the people. We should continue our work so that people will have a greater sense of happiness, benefit and security, and achieve well-rounded development. Third, staying committed to benefits for all. We should care about the special needs of developing countries. We may employ such means as debt suspension and development aid to help developing countries, particularly vulnerable ones facing exceptional difficulties, with emphasis on addressing imbalanced and inadequate development among and within countries. Fourth, staying committed to innovation-driven development. We need to seize the historic opportunities created by the latest round of technological revolution and industrial transformation, redouble our efforts to harness technological achievements to boost productivity, and foster an open, fair, equitable and non-discriminatory environment for the development of science and technology. We should foster new growth drivers in the post-COVID era and jointly achieve leapfrog development. Fifth, staying committed to achieving harmony between human and nature. We need to improve global environmental governance, actively respond to climate change, and create a harmonious community of life for human and nature. Sixth, staying committed to results-oriented actions. We need to increase input in development, advance on a priority basis cooperation on poverty alleviation, food security, COVID-19 response and vaccines, development financing, climate change and green development, industrialization, digital economy and connectivity, among other areas, and accelerate the implementation of the UN 2030 Agenda for Sustainable Development, so as to build a global community of development with a shared future. The Global Security Initiative was first put forward by President Xi Jinping during the opening ceremony of the Boao Forum for Asia Annual Conference on April 21, 2022, aiming at making China's voice of building a community of human security heard amid the turbulent and changing international situation. It mainly includes six contents: first, staying committed to the vision of common, comprehensive, cooperative and sustainable security, and working together to maintain world peace and security; second, staying committed to respecting the sovereignty and territorial integrity of all countries, upholding non-interference in internal affairs, and respecting the independent choices of development paths and social systems made by people in different countries; third, staying committed to abiding by the purposes and principles of the UN Charter, rejecting the Cold War mentality, opposing unilateralism, and saying no to group politics and bloc confrontation; fourth, staying committed to taking the legitimate security concerns of all countries seriously, upholding the principle of indivisible security, building a balanced, effective and sustainable security architecture, and opposing the pursuit of one's own security at the cost of others' security; fifth, staying committed to peacefully resolving differences and disputes between countries through dialogue and consultation, supporting all efforts conducive to the peaceful settlement of crises, rejecting double standards, and opposing the wanton use of unilateral sanctions and long-arm jurisdiction; and sixth, staying committed to maintaining security in both traditional and non-traditional domains, and working together on regional disputes and global challenges such as terrorism, climate change, cybersecurity and biosecurity.

The two initiatives reflect China's latest and deepest thoughts on peace and development, and answer the questions of China, the world, the people and the times. These are important principles for China in handling international affairs in the new era. It is hoped that these two initiatives will be recognized and supported by other countries, and China is ready to work together with them to create a better future for mankind.

IV. Global Significance of the Two Initiatives

The new development philosophy tells us that growth and development are two related but not identical concepts. In the economic field, growth usually refers to the increase of a country's economic aggregate and output per capita, while development includes not only the increase of quantity, but also the overall progress of the economic process. Economic growth is not equal to economic development, and economic development is not equal to development. All productive and social activities should serve human beings, and human development is mainly manifested in the improvement of various abilities of human beings, so development should include all-around development and liberation of human beings.

Human development is mainly restricted by the imbalancebetween population, resources and environment. At present, about 1 billion people around the world have an average daily income of less than 1.25 USD, and 1 billion people are malnourished. According to the prediction of the National Intelligence Council of the United States, by 2030, the number of people living in extreme poverty will drop by about 50% thanks to economic development and personal income increase. However, if a long-term economic depression occurs in the world, by 2030, only half of the above goal would be accomplished. By 2030, the number of deaths from communicable diseases is expected to decrease by 30%, while the number from non-communicable diseases will increase. Demographers and sociologists predicted that, by the middle of this century, the world population might exceed 8 billion, mainly from developing countries in Asia and Africa, and human beings will face the threat of the spread of traditional diseases and their variations, the depletion of non-renewable energy resources and the environmental carrying capacity being close to its limit. The international community urgently needs to realize the comprehensive, coordinated and sustainable development of population, resources and environment, which depends on the new development model created by mankind to liberate itself from the traditional development concept with nature as an object of conquest.

The issues of resources and environment involve poverty in developing countries that is closely related to the unjust and unreasonable international political and economic order. Most of the current international order was established by Western countries after World War II. After developing countries gained independence from the Western colonial system, the old system of vertical international division of labor and economic structure did not change accordingly, which worsened the conditions for developing countries to seek development and has restricted their efforts to protect their resources and the environment. In order to pursue the sustainable development of mankind, the international community must first figure out solutions to the poverty problem of developing countries and help them get rid of dependence on environmental resources as much as possible. Thus is, efforts must be made to change the unjust and unreasonable old international political and economic order. At present, unilateralism, protectionism and bullying practices are on the rise, and the deficits in peace, development, security and governance continue to grow. The international system, which is not neutral, is being pushed by Western developed countries led by the United States, continues to favor vested interests. China works to promote top-level designs such as the Belt and Road Initiative, AIIB and BRICS Bank, aiming at coordinating the markets and resources at home and abroad, and at the same time, developing a dynamic growth model, a model of open and win-win cooperation, a model of fair and equitable governance, and a balanced, equitable and inclusive development model, so as to solve the problems of lack of impetus for global economic growth and uneven distribution. This should be widely recognized by the international community. By force of high-tech monoplolies and control over international systems, Western countries will not decline rapidly. Developing countries promote power equality, while developed countries strive to defend hegemony, so games and struggles are inevitable. China needs to unite with most developing countries in the world, and work with them to seek common interests and take concerted action to promote the innovation in international political and economic order.

The Global Development Initiative is not only the guiding ideology summarized by China based on the laws of economic operation in the new era, but also China's response to the UN's 2030 Agenda for Sustainable Development. This is a contribution to the world development model. As a member of the global village, when pursuing its own development, a country should take account of the development of other countries, and cannot harm the interests of other countries. Developing and underdeveloped countries should take a holistic approach to coordinate the development of all aspects and strive to meet the multi-level needs of the people. With the deepening of the practice of Socialism with Chinese characteristics, China's development model will surely lead the Chinese nation towards its great rejuvenation. By that time, China's concept of development will certainly make more significant contributions to all countries' exploration of more scientific and civilized development paths, to human exploration of the general law of social development, and even to the revival of the global socialist movement, which will highlight its more significant and far-reaching influence on the world.

The Global Security Initiative should be a bond and consensus for solving regional armed conflicts. Since the 21st century, many local wars and armed conflicts have taken place around the world. According to statistics, there are dozens of them on average every year. But no one has caused an overall influence across the world like the Ukrainian Crisis.

As an international currency, the US dollar works as a tool to support American hegemony, while its foundation is national credit. Now it seems that we can't overestimate the national credit of the United States, especially in the context of political and military opposition, when credit is no longer the first choice of the country. Rajan, former governor of India's central bank, pointed out in the column of Project Syndicate that after the foreign exchange reserves of the Russian central bank have been frozen, China, India and many other countries will be worried about their foreign exchange reserves. He added that because only a few reserve currencies have liquidity, like the euro and the US dollar, many governments will have to restrict activities such as cross-border lending of companies. The damaging credit of the US dollar will come back to bite the United States itself, and it may not be able to afford the consequences of the disillusionment of the myth.

The Ukrainian crisis is getting increasingly dangerous, so we cannot underestimate its impact on world peace and development. It once again indicates that clinging to the cold war mentality, promoting group politics, creating camp confrontation, and pursuing absolute security will not bring peace and are not in anyone's interest. With the growing negative impact of the COVID-19 pandemic in the United States and other countries, the world must unite and work together to overcome the difficulties. A behavior is irresponsible if it stresses the absolute security of one's own country, highlights ideological differences, coerces other countries into taking sides, creates isolation and repression, and promotes decoupling and chain-breaking. We should draw profound lessons from history, respect each other's sovereignty and territorial integrity, jointly safeguard the international system with the United Nations at its core, as well as the international order based on international law, and jointly promote world peace and development.

Today, the global issues we are facing include the control of regional wars and conflicts, the reconstruction of international economic and political order, and the diversity of religions and cultures. These issues which are complicated and feature intertwined interests and values. The Belt and Road Initiative is a great initiative. It is not limited to one country or one place, but aims at building an economic community and a community with a shared future for mankind. Over time, China's development model will definitely arouse people's attention and thinking of all countries, radiating with even greater vitality. By then, these two initiatives will certainly make greater contributions to all countries' exploration of more scientific and civilized development paths, and to the peace and happiness of mankind. This will demonstrate their more significant and far-reaching influence on the world.

New Process of Chinese Modernization and Initiative of Development Strategy

Jing Xianghui[*]

Strategies are of utmost importance. They are the top priority in the governance of all countries at all times. As a matter of life and death and the road either to survival or to ruin, the strategic initiative should never be overlooked because it determines the success or failure of the military struggle and the security of the state power.[①] Directly concerning autonomy, strategic initiative is the core of strategic thinking. To a certain extent, the ability of strategic thinking is also a major yard stick to measure the development of human civilization. Throughout the history of social development, the Chinese nation has made an ongoing and in-depth exploration and summary of strategic issues in its long history and culture, and has, on this basis, formed a highly developed, extensive and profound strategic thoughts and strategic thinking of unique charm, which has effectively created, preserved, continued and developed the Chinese civilization and the lineage of the Chinese nation. Drawing vast resources from the fine traditional culture of China, especially from the military thinking, the

---

[*] Jing Xianghui, Associate Professor, Institute of Information Studies, Chinese Academy of Social Sciences.
[①] *Sun Tzu*, Shanghai: Shanghai Ancient Books Publishing House, 2013, page 1.

strategic thoughts and strategic thinking of the Chinese nation have become the fertile soil and important theoretical source of the CPC's century of struggle and more than 70 years of experience and wisdom in governing and rejuvenating the country; the important ideological source of the great spirit of building the Party; and more importantly, the cultural and psychological source of the ambition, integrity, and confidence of the Chinese people. The strategic thoughts and strategic thinking of the Chinese nation have a lasting and far-reaching academic influence and ideological penetration in the world, of which the enduring popularization of Sun Tzu culture in countries of all continents including Europe and Americas is a strong proof. As we consider both domestic and external situations in a coordinative way, it is of special significance to reflect on and study the history of the CPC of the last century, especially the thinking and practice of the CPC on the strategic initiative since the beginning of the new era.

"Strategy" is a high-frequency word in the report to the 20th National Congress of the Communist Party of China convened recently. To "firmly hold the strategic initiative" is also a principal line of thinking throughout the report. When talking about the extremely unusual and extraordinary work in the five years since the 19th National Congress of the CPC, the report to the 20th National Congress of the CPC clearly pointed out, "In response to separatist activities aimed at "Taiwan independence" and gross provocations of external interference in Taiwan affairs, we have resolutely fought against separatism and countered interference, demonstrating our resolve and ability to safeguard China's sovereignty and territorial integrity and to oppose "Taiwan independence." We have strengthened our strategic initiative for China's complete reunification and consolidated commitment to the one-China principle within the international community."[1] "Confronted with drastic changes in the in-

---

[1] Xi Jinping: "Hold High the Great Banner of Socialism with Chinese Characteristics and Strive in Unity to Build a Modern Socialist Country in All Respects — Report to the 20th National Congress of the CPC (October 16, 2022)", *People's Daily*, October 26, 2022.

ternational landscape, especially external attempts to blackmail, contain, blockade, and exert maximum pressure on China, we have put our national interests first, focused on internal political concerns, and maintained firm strategic resolve. We have shown a fighting spirit and a firm determination to never yield to coercive power. Throughout these endeavors, we have safeguarded China's dignity and core interests and kept ourselves well-positioned for pursuing development and ensuring security." ① It is precise because we have kept ourselves well-positioned for pursuing development and ensuring security. In the past decade of the new era, we have experienced and accomplished "three major events of great immediate importance and profound historical significance for the cause of the Party and the people: we embraced the centenary of the Communist Party of China; we ushered in a new era of socialism with Chinese characteristics; and we eradicated absolute poverty and finished building a moderately prosperous society in all respects, thus completing the First Centenary Goal. These were historic feats — feats accomplished by the Communist Party of China and the Chinese people striving in unity, feats that will be forever recorded in the Chinese nation's history, and feats that will profoundly influence the world. ② The great transformation over the past ten years of the new era "marks a milestone in the history of the Party, of the People's Republic of China, of reform and opening up, of the development of socialism, and of the development of the Chinese nation." ③ It is pointed out in section XIII — "Adhering to and improving 'one country, two systems' and promoting the reunification of

---

① Xi Jinping: "Hold High the Great Banner of Socialism with Chinese Characteristics and Strive in Unity to Build a Modern Socialist Country in All Respects — Report to the 20th National Congress of the CPC (October 16, 2022)", *People's Daily*, October 26, 2022.

② Xi Jinping: "Hold High the Great Banner of Socialism with Chinese Characteristics and Strive in Unity to Build a Modern Socialist Country in All Respects — Report to the 20th National Congress of the CPC (October 16, 2022)", *People's Daily*, October 26, 2022.

③ Xi Jinping: "Hold High the Great Banner of Socialism with Chinese Characteristics and Strive in Unity to Build a Modern Socialist Country in All Respects — Report to the 20th National Congress of the CPC (October 16, 2022)", *People's Daily*, October 26, 2022.

the motherland" that "resolving the Taiwan question and realizing China's complete reunification is, for the Party, a historic mission and an unshakable commitment. It is also a shared aspiration of all the sons and daughters of the Chinese nation and a natural requirement for realizing the rejuvenation of the Chinese nation. We will implement our Party's overall policy for resolving the Taiwan issue in the new era, maintain the initiative and the ability to steer in cross-Strait relations, and unswervingly advance the cause of national reunification." [1]

Ⅰ. To "firmly hold the strategic initiative" is the essence of the CPC's strategic thinking

To "firmly hold the strategic initiative" is also a principal line of thinking that runs through the centennial history of the Party, and an important line through the *Resolution of the Central Committee of the Communist Party of China on the Major Achievements and Historical Experience of the Party over the Past Century* adopted at the Sixth Plenary Session of the 19th Central Committee of the Communist Party of China. In his important speech delivered at the special seminar on the study and implementation of the guiding principles of the sixth plenary session of the 19th Central Committee of the Communist Party of China attended by officials at the provincial and ministerial levels, President Xi Jinping emphasized that "the issue of strategy is a fundamental issue for a political party and a nation. Accurate judgement, scientific planning and initiative in strategy are where the hope of the cause of the Party and the people lies. Over the past 100 years, at key junctures in history, the CPC has always managed to understand, analyze and judge the major historical issues it has faced from a

---

[1] Xi Jinping: "Hold High the Great Banner of Socialism with Chinese Characteristics and Strive in Unity to Build a Modern Socialist Country in All Respects — Report to the 20th National Congress of the CPC (October 16, 2022)", *People's Daily*, October 26, 2022.

strategic perspective before coming up with the correct political strategies and tactics. This offers a strong guarantee for the Party to overcome numerous risks and challenges and constantly move from victory to victory. "[1] "The resolution of this plenary session has made a comprehensive summary of the Party's high attention to strategies and tactics and the scientific strategies and tactics proposed during its centennial struggle. Focusing on the analysis and summary of the Party's study and understanding of strategies and tactics in the course of its struggle over the past century is an important part running through the resolution of the plenary session that requires in-depth study and full understanding." [2] President Xi has made multiple explanations on the *Resolution of the Central Committee of the Communist Party of China on the Major Achievements and Historical Experience of the Party over the Past Century* adopted at the Sixth Plenary Session of the 19th CPC Central Committee, each of which takes a different perspective and drives deeper. One is on the drafting of the *Resolution of the Central Committee of the Communist Party of China on the Major Achievements and Historical Experience of the Party over the Past Century*, in which President Xi expresses three considerations on the topics of the Sixth Plenary Session of the 19th CPC Central Committee. The second is the important speech made by Prseident Xi at the second plenary session of the Sixth Plenary Session of the 19th CPC Central Committee, which expressed explicitly that the Central Committee's convening of the Sixth Plenary Session of the 19th CPC Central

---

[1] "Xi Jinping delivered an important speech at the opening ceremony of the special seminar on learning and applying the guiding principles of the Sixth Plenary Session of the 19th CPC Central Committee, stressing to drive deeper the Party history summary, study, education and publicity and better understand and apply the Party's historical experience of over the past century", *People's Daily*, January 12, 2022.

[2] "Xi Jinping delivered an important speech at the opening ceremony of the special seminar on learning and applying the guiding principles of the Sixth Plenary Session of the 19th CPC Central Committee, stressing to drive deeper the Party history summary, study, education and publicity and better understand and apply the Party's historical experience of over the past century", *People's Daily*, January 12, 2022.

Committee is a solemn strategic decision, and that the *Resolution of the Central Committee of the Communist Party of China on the Major Achievements and Historical Experience of the Party over the Past Century* is of high political, theoretical, strategic and instructive significance. The third is the important speech made by Prseident Xi at the special seminar for officials at the provincial and ministerial levels to learn and implement the guiding principles of the Sixth Plenary Session of the 19th CPC Central Committee. This speech systematically sorts out the major historical experience over the last century in the *Resolution of the Central Committee of the Communist Party of China on the Major Achievements and Historical Experience of the Party over the Past Century* from five aspects, one of which is strategies and tactics. This important speech is consistent with Prseident Xi's important discourse on learning Deng Xiaoping's far-sighted strategic thinking in his speech at the symposium commemorating the 110th anniversary of Deng Xiaoping's birthday in 2014, making a series of important discussions on strategic issues, strategic initiatives, and how to study and grasp strategies and tactics. How to theoretically summarize and explain this important historical experience in the Party's history over the past century is a major theoretical subject for the theorists.

The profound insight andunderstanding of the strategic initiative is the essence of the strategic thinking of the CPC and reflects the extraordinary boldness, wisdom and courage of the CPC members. As Mao Zedong remarked, "The initiative is an extremely important thing. Holding the initiative is like sweeping down irresistibly from a commanding height. This is realized by seeking truth from facts..." [1] Reviewing the bloody struggle and hard exploration in the Party's century-long history, we find that holding the strategic initiative firmly is an important weapon the CPC uses to unite and lead the Chinese people to fight and win, to be invincible and remain so. It is also an important methodology for the CPC to firmly hold the future of China's development and progress

---

[1] *Collected Works of Mao Zedong*, Vol. 8, Beijing: People's Publishing House, 1999, p. 197.

in its own hands and unite and lead the Chinese people to forge ahead. Firmly holding the strategic initiative is a distinctive feature of Mao Zedong Thought. Mao Zedong is universally recognized as a great strategist and military theorist. In different historical periods of revolution and construction, in different fields such as the CPC leading military struggle, leading socialist revolution and construction, leading ideological and cultural promotion, and observing and analyzing domestic and international situations, Mao Zedong systematically explained strategic issues, especially strategic initiatives. His ideas are mainly reflected in classic masterpieces made during the War of Resistance Against Japanese Aggression, such as *Strategic Problems in the Anti-Japanese Guerrilla War*, *On the Protracted War*, *The Question of Independence and Initiative Within the United Front*, and *The Question of Wars and Strategies*. The strategic offensive thought in Mao Zedong's military thoughts and important strategic guiding thoughts such as "You fight your way and we fight ours" are fundamentally all about how to seize the strategic initiative. His planning and application of this issue has become a valuable asset for the Chinese people and even human civilization. In his important speech delivered at the special seminar for officials at the provincial and ministerial levels to learn and apply the guiding principles of the Sixth Plenary Session of the 19th CPC Central Committee, President Xi emphatically quoted Mao Zedong to explain what the art of strategic leadership means. He pointed out that "Strategy is to make overall and long-term judgments and decisions according to the general trend Mao Zedong interpreted this concept vividly, 'If you sit on the podium but cannot see anything, you are not a leader. Sitting on the podium and seeing only a large number of common things that have appeared on the horizon doesn't make you a leader either because it's not unusual. Only those who can recognize things that have the potential to grow into a large number of common things in the early stage, like when the top of the mask has just shown itself, can be counted as leaders. What Mao Zedong described is strategic leadership."① He gave two examples in detail. First, after Japan launched the all-out war of aggression against China, Mao Zedong scientifically answered the question "Can this war be won? How can we win?" in *On the Protracted War* published in 1938, giving all the Chinese a clear understanding of the progress and prospect of the war of resistance, and significantly strengthening the confidence of the army and the people to hold on. Second, when discussing the future of the Party after the victory of the War of Resistance Against Japanese Aggression during the Seventh National Congress of the Communist Party of China in 1945, Mao Zedong highlighted the strategic significance of Northeast China for the prospect of the Chinese revolution in the near future. "Even if we lose all the existing base areas, as long as we get the Northeast, the Chinese revolution will be on a solid foundation. Of course, with other base areas still in our hands, the addition of the Northeast will further consolidate the foundation of the Chinese revolution. President Xi remarked, "What a far-sighted strategic decision this is! Later development has also proved what a significant role this strategic decision has played in the victory of the War of Liberation." ②

Firmly holding the strategic initiative is a principal line that runs through Xi Jinping Thought on Socialism with Chinese Characteristics for a New Era. In all aspects related to the Party's overall governance of the country, whether it is the major issues concerning systemic and deep reform that matter to the overall situation, or the bottom-line thinking of preventing and defusing major risks, President Xi attaches great importance to the key issue of firmly holding the strategic initiative. It is fair to say that since the 18th CPC National Congress, the reason why the CPC has united and led the people of the whole country to make great achievements in a new era, and why the great cause of the rejuvenation of

---

① Xi Jinping: "Better understand and apply the historical experience of the Party over the past century", *Qiushi*, Issue 13, 2022.

② Xi Jinping: "Better understand and apply the historical experience of the Party over the past century", *Qiushi*, Issue 13, 2022.

the Chinese nation has entered an irreversible historical process, lies in the fact that our Party has kept the key issue of strategic initiative firmly in our hands. In his important speech delivered at the special seminar for officials at the provincial and ministerial levels to learn and apply the guiding principles of the Sixth Plenary Session of the 19th CPC Central Committee, President Xi pointed out, "We are a big party that leads a big country and pursues a great cause. This means we cannot afford to make strategic mistakes. Some mistakes are too minor to be noticed and cannot be avoided completely, but with limited impact, they are relatively easy to correct. Nevertheless, a deviation in the strategy carries severe consequences and takes high cost. The Party learned bitter lessons in its early days... Therefore, I have always stressed that leading officials should have strategic thinking and be good at seeing and considering problems strategically." [1] When talking about the dialectical relationship between strategies and tactics, President Xi stressed, "The right strategies cannot be implemented without the right tactics. A victory in all aspects requires not only strategic planning and resolute fighting spirit, but also statics, wisdom and methods. Statics serve the strategy under its guidance. They are dialectical and unified. Firm strategies should be combined with flexible tactics. Having the big picture in mind, we should be down to earth in practice. While we steer the direction, address major issues, and plan for the long term, we should also map out plans with a focus on priorities. Both the general ledger and the sub-ledger should be checked. Without a determined strategy and vigorous statics, we may worry about gains and losses and vacillate in dilemma, missing development opportunities." [2]

We should firmlyhold the strategic initiative in the major strategic tasks related to the overall development. Xi said, "In order to remain invincible, a

---

[1] Xi Jinping: "Better understand and apply the historical experience of the Party over the past century", *Qiushi*, Issue 13, 2022.

[2] Xi Jinping: "Better understand and apply the historical experience of the Party over the past century", *Qiushi*, Issue 13, 2022.

party must remain at the forefront of the times, keep abreast of the new historical characteristics, make the overall plan scientifically, firmly hold the strategic initiative, and unswervingly pursue our strategic objectives."① "On the new Long March, we should base ourselves on the circumstances of the world, of the country and of the Party, adopt a holistic approach to both the domestic and international situations, plan the overall development of the Party and the state, promote the development of various undertakings in a coordinative way, seize the strategic focus, achieve key breakthroughs, win the strategic initiative, prevent systemic risks, avoid subversive crises, and maintain the overall development."② "The need to pursue innovative development is a conclusion drawn from the world's development process in modern times and from China's practice in reform and opening up since 1978. Pursuing innovative development is fundamental to our strategy in adapting to the changing environment of development, enhancing the impetus of development, seizing the initiative in development, and leading the new normal." ③ When talking about comprehensively strengthening the Party's governing ability in the report to the 19th National Congress of the Communist Party of China, President Xi stressed, "We should be good at managing risks. We will improve risk prevention and control mechanisms in all areas, skillfully handle various complex issues, overcome all difficulties and obstacles that we meet on our way, and keep a firm hold on the initiative in our work." ④ With regard to national security, national defense and military construction, he stressed, "Since the establishment of the National Security Commission four years ago... the work of national security has been strength-

---

① "Xi Jinping's speech at a gathering to commemorate the 80th anniversary of the victory of the Long March of the Red Army", *People's Daily*, October 22, 2016.

② "Xi Jinping's speech at a gathering to commemorate the 80th anniversary of the victory of the Long March of the Red Army", *People's Daily*, October 22, 2016.

③ Xi Jinping: "A Deeper Understanding of the New Development Philosophy", *Qiushi*, Issue 10, 2019.

④ *Collection of Documents of the 19th National Congress of the CPC*, Beijing: People's Publishing House, 2017, page 55.

ened on all fronts and the holistic initiative of safeguarding national security has been firmly grasped. " ① "To solve the deep-seated contradictions and problems in the military policy system, fully release and deepen the effectiveness of reform of national defense and the military, break the new ground in the cause of building a strong military and seize the initiative in the military competition and war, there is an urgent need to adapt to the development requirements of the situation and tasks and carry out systematic and in-depth reform of the military policy system. " ②

President Xi attaches great importance to accelerating the construction of a new developmentdynamic. He stressed on many occasions that "accelerating the construction of a new development dynamic is a strategic measure for us to seize the initiative of future development. "③ With regard to this issue, on January 11, 2021, President Xi quoted Mao Zedong's remark on guiding the military struggle delivered in 1936, which he considered still holding true for us even today, "No matter how complicated, grave, and harsh the circumstances, what a military leader needs most of all is the ability to function independently in organizing and employing the forces under his command. He may often be forced into a passive position by the enemy, but the important thing is to regain the initiative quickly. Failure to do so spells defeat. The initiative is not something imaginary but is concrete and material. " ④ His quote shows the deep insight of the leader of a major country into the time and situation based on the "domestic and external situations", and reflects the deep sense of crisis — "to ensure that the great rejuvenation of the Chinese nation will not be delayed or e-

---

① Xi Jinping: *The Governance of China Ⅲ*, Beijing: Foreign Language Press, 2020, p. 217.

② "President Xi Jinping Attended and Delivered an Important Speech at the Working Conference on Policy and System Reform of the Central Military Commission", *People's Daily*, November 15, 2018.

③ "Overall Guidance to Create a New Development Dynamic, Promote the Revitalization of Seed Industry, and the Ecological Environment Protection and Sustainable Development of the Qinghai-Tibet Plateau", *People's Daily*, July 10, 2021.

④ Xi Jinping: "Understanding the New Development Stage, Applying the New Development Philosophy, and Creating a New Development Dynamic", *Qiushi*, Issue 9, 2021.

ven disrupted", and at the same time, strongly demonstrated the tenacious revolutionary will and vibrant fighting spirit against all the difficulties — "no one can beat us or block us!"

We should firmly grasp the strategic initiative in the ideological work of the Party and prevent and resolve major risks. President Xi made a profound argument, "An important platform for publicity and theoretical work is the stressing of unity, stability and encouragement, and putting the focus on positive publicity... When it comes to major issues, including those of political principle, we must take the initiative in helping officials and the people draw a line between right and wrong and acquire a clear understanding in this regard."① "In the current situation, I think we should focus on the work of online public opinion as the top priority of publicity and theoretical work... We must face up to this fact, increase our investment, and seize the initiative in the field of public opinion as soon as possible. We can't afford to be marginalized." ② "We must seize the initiative in guiding public opinion, and make the internet a fast-growing space in building a cultural home shared by all ethnic groups and in consolidating the sense of national identity." ③ On adhering to the bottom line thinking and preventing and resolving major risks, President Xi stressed that we must always remain highly alert. "We must seize the initiative to prevent risks from arising while adopting effective measures to address and resolve those that do arise. We must be fully prepared and make proactive strategic moves to convert danger into safety and adversity into opportunity." ④ On accelerating the implementation of the innovation-driven development strategy and the transformation of the economic development model, he stressed the need to strengthen the sense of urgency, "seize the opportunity, establish the development strategy in

---

① Xi Jinping: *The Governance of China I*, Beijing: Foreign Language Press, 2018, p. 155.
② *Extract of Xi Jinping's Statement on a Holistic Approach to National Security*, Beijing: Central Party Literature Press, 2018, p. 103 and p. 104.
③ Xi Jinping: *The Governance of China III*, Beijing: Foreign Language Press, 2020, p. 301.
④ Xi Jinping: *The Governance of China III*, Beijing: Foreign Language Press, 2020, p. 73.

time, enhance the ability of independent innovation in all respects, and grasp the strategic initiative in the new round of global scientific and technological competition"[1]. In his important speech delivered at the special seminar on the study and application of the guiding principles of the sixth plenary session of the 19th Central Committee of the Communist Party of China, attended by officials at the provincial and ministerial levels, President Xi said, "All regions and departments must cross-check their ideas and arrangements of work as well as policies and measures with the Party's theories, lines, principles and policies and correct deviations in time. The strategic decisions made by the CPC Central Committee must be implemented unconditionally without being distorted or bent. When implementing the strategic decisions of the Party Central Committee, all regions and departments must formulate tactics based on their own reality. At the same time, it should be noted that some of the tactics proposed may be in line with the strategy of the central committee, while others may deviate from it. It is necessary to make a timely summary and evaluation and adjust any deviation as soon as possible."[2]

II. To firmly hold the strategic initiative means to firmly hold the historical initiative

History is a mirror that tells us what is going to happen today. Learning the history makes one wise. In logic and nature, history, present and future are mutually prescribed and interconnected. Only by keeping a clear understanding and accurate grasp of major historical issues can the historical initiative be formed. Holding the historical initiative is the basic precondition to winning initiative at present and in the future. President Xi said, "The Communist Party of

---

[1] "Xi Jinping Presided over the Seventh Meeting of the Central Financial Leading Group", *People's Daily*, August 19, 2014.

[2] Xi Jinping: "Better understand and apply the historical experience of the Party over the past century", *Qiushi*, Issue 13, 2022.

China upholds the basic tenets of Marxism and the principle of seeking truth from facts. Based on China's realities, we have developed keen insights into the trends of the day, seized the initiative in history, and made painstaking explorations. We have thus been able to keep adapting Marxism to the Chinese context and the needs of our times, and to guide the Chinese people in advancing our great social revolution."① In his important speech when greeting people participating in CPC centenary celebration preparation, he stressed, "We should thoroughly summarize the positive and negative experiences of the Party's history over the past century, and enhance historical consciousness and seize historical initiative through the study and application of historical wisdom". ② The important argument of President Xi on seizing the historical initiative provides a fundamental basis for us to deeply understand and grasp the centennial history of the CPC.

To seize the initiative of history, we must clearly understand and grasp the laws and trends of historical development. "A battle should be fought based on the situation." ③ Grasping the historical trend and seizing the historical initiative is an important experience for the CPC to create a century of glory④. President Xi stressed, "Over the past hundred years, the CPC has always believed that the Chinese people and other peoples of the world have a shared future. Respecting international trends and flowing with international currents, it has steered the course of China's development and supported the development and prosperity of all countries." ⑤ "Historical development follows its laws,

---

① *Xi Jinping's Speech at the Conference to Celebrate the 100th Anniversary of the Founding of the CPC*, Beijing: People's Publishing House, 2021, pp. 12 – 13.

② "Xi Jinping Met with Representatives of All Who had Participated in the Preparations for the Centenary Celebrations of the Communist Party of China (CPC)", *People's Daily*, July 14, 2021.

③ *Sun Tzu*, Shanghai: Shanghai Ancient Books Publishing House, 2013, p. 57.

④ See Qu Qingshan: "Grasp the Historical Trend and Take the Historical Initiative", *Qiushi*, Issue 11, 2021.

⑤ Xi Jinping: "Strengthening Inter-Party Cooperation in Pursuit of People's Wellbeing — Keynote Speech at the CPC and World Political Parties Summit", *People's Daily*, July 7, 2021.

but people are not completely passive in it. As long as we grasp the general trend of historical development, seize the opportunity of historical changes, work hard and forge ahead, the human society can advance better."① In his important speech at the Party History Learning and Education Mobilization Conference, President Xi stressed, "We should "further grasp the laws and trends of historical development, and always hold the historical initiative of the development of the Party and the country" ②, and "We must draw on the lessons of our past in order to forge our future. On the new journey of building a modern socialist country in all respects, we will carry forward our historic mission and seize the historical initiative so as to keep driving the great cause of national rejuvenation forward." ③

When talking about economic globalization, scientific and technological innovation in the new era, and the capacity-building of officials, Xi stressed that "economic globalization, a surging historical trend, has greatly facilitated trade, investment, the flow of people, and technological advances"④; "We should follow the general trend, proceed from our respective national conditions and embark on the right pathway of integrating into economic globalization with the right pace." ⑤; "Since the 18th CPC National Congress, we have summarized the development of China's science and technology undertakings, observed the general trend, made overall planning, deepened reform, and made full efforts to promote historical changes and achievements in China's science and

---

① "Xi Jinping Delivered an Important Speech at A Grand Gathering to Celebrate the 40th Anniversary of China's Reform and Opening-up", *People's Daily*, December 19, 2018.

② "Xi Jinping's Speech at the Party History Learning and Education Mobilization Conference", *Qiushi*, Issue 7, 2021.

③ "Xi Jinping's Speech at the Conference to Commemorate the 110th Anniversary of the 1911 Revolution", *People's Daily*, October 10, 2021.

④ Xi Jinping: "Jointly Build A Community With A Shared Future for Mankind", *Qiushi*, Issue 1, 2021.

⑤ Xi Jinping: "Sharing the Responsibility of the Times and Promoting Global Development", *Qiushi*, Issue 24, 2020.

technology undertakings."①; "Since the 19th CPC National Congress... we have ensured the Party's overall leadership in science and technology, reviewed the general trend and formed an efficient organization and mobilization system and an integrated and coordinated allocation model of scientific and technological resources."②; "They need to improve their political abilities, particularly the ability to set the direction, to grasp the general trend, to manage the overall situation, to maintain their political resolve, to cope with political issues, and to prevent political risks." ③ ; "To reform our Party, we must have a clear picture and be resolute in removing all theoretical and institutional barriers." ④ When talking about preventing and resolving major risks as the political responsibility of the Party committees, governments and leading officials at all levels, he stressed that we should strengthen risk awareness, keep an eye on the overall situation and trend, scientifically predict the development trend and the hidden risks and challenges, and take precautions⑤.

When talking about breaking new ground in China's major-country diplomacy, President Xi stressed, "We need to adopt a historical and holistic approach to assessing international developments and choose the right approach to China's role. A historical approach is to observe the unfolding international developments from a historical perspective. We need to review the past and learn lessons from history so as to gain a keen understanding of the underlying trends

---

① "Xi attended and delivered an important speech at the opening meeting of the 19th Academician Conference of the Chinese Academy of Sciences and the 14th Academician Conference of the Chinese Academy of Engineering", *People's Daily*, May 29, 2018.

② "Xi attended and delivered an important speech at the opening meeting of the 19th Academician Conference of the Chinese Academy of Sciences and the 14th Academician Conference of the Chinese Academy of Engineering", *People's Daily*, May 29, 2018.

③ Xi Jinping: *The Governance of China* Ⅲ, Beijing: Foreign Language Press, 2020, page 97.

④ Xi Jinping: "Stay True to the Party's Original Aspiration and Founding Mission and Carry Out Self-Reform", *Qiushi*, Issue 15, 2019.

⑤ See Xi Jinping Delivered an Important Speech at the Opening Ceremony of the Special Seminar on Adhering to the Bottom Line Thinking and Focusing on Preventing and Resolving Major Risks, *People's Daily*, January 22, 2019.

of the future. " ① When talking about building a community with a shared future for mankind, he stressed, "Today, with the world landscape and development dynamic changing, all political parties should follow the trend of the times, grasp the trend of human progress, meet the shared expectations of the people, and closely integrate their own development with the development of the country, nation and human beings. " ② "The BRICS countries should follow the historical trend, seize the development opportunities, work together to overcome challenges, and play a constructive role in building a new type of international relations and a community with a shared future for mankind. " ③ "We need to gain a keen appreciation of this underlying trend of our times and view the changing world for what it is and, on that basis, respond to new developments and meet new challenges in a responsible and rules-based way. " ④ "Going forward, we need to see where the world is going, ride on the trend of the times and turn our people's longing for a better life into reality. " ⑤ In terms of the Party's theoretical work, it is more important to grasp the general trend and take the initiative. President Xi has made important statements on this critical issue on many occasions. " Our publicity and theoretical work must help us accomplish the central task of economic development and serve the overall interests of the country. Therefore, we must bear the big picture in mind and keep in line with the trends. We should map out plans with a focus on priorities and carry them out in accordance with the situation. " ⑥ "We should increase the international influ-

---

① Xi Jinping: *The Governance of China* Ⅲ, Beijing: Foreign Language Press, 2020, page 427.

② "Xi Jinping Attended and Delivered a speech at the Opening Ceremony of CPC in Dialogue with World Political Parties High-Level Meeting", *People's Daily*, December 2, 2017.

③ "Xi Jinping attended and Delivered an Important Speech at the 10th BRICS Leaders' Meeting", *People's Daily*, July 27, 2018.

④ "Xi Jinping Attended the APEC Business Leaders Meeting and Delivered a Keynote Speech", *People's Daily*, November 11, 2017.

⑤ "Xi Attended the Opening Ceremony of the Conference on Dialogue of Asian Civilizations and Delivered a Keynote Speech", *People's Daily*, May 16, 2019.

⑥ Xi Jinping: *The Governance of China I*, Beijing: Foreign Language Press, 2018, p. 153.

ence of Chinese culture. We need to take stock of the global landscape and take targeted measures when we present the Thought on Socialism with Chinese Characteristics for a New Era to the international community. We should find better ways to tell stories about the CPC's governance of China, about our people's hard work to realize the Chinese Dream, and about China's peaceful development through mutually beneficial cooperation, helping the international community to know more about our country." [1]

To master the initiative of history, we must establish a grand view of history. Thegrand view of history focuses on historical vision, historical thinking and historical consciousness. President Xi has explained the major issue of the grand view of history on many occasions. Different from the Western grand view of history, his grand view of history is guided by historical materialism. From the perspective of the dialectical unity of historical stages and continuity, national and cosmopolitan, progressive and tortuous, it applies an integral and all-round approach towards history and reality, realizing innovative development of historical materialism. [2]

Xi stressed, "Throughout thousands of years of history, reform and open up is generally the historical norm in China. The Chinese nation's approach to reform and open-up in its march towards the future has a profound historical origin and cultural foundation." [3] "We should educate and guide the whole party to bear in mind the overall strategy of the great rejuvenation of the Chinese nation and the great changes that have not occurred in the world for a hundred years, establish a grand view of history, analyze the evolution mechanism, explore the historical laws from the long river of history, the tide of the times, and the global dynamics, propose corresponding strategies and statics and make

---

[1] Xi Jinping: *The Governance of China* Ⅲ, Beijing: Foreign Language Press, 2018, p. 314.

[2] Jin Meng and Zhou Liangshu: "The Innovative Development of Historical Materialism by Xi Jinping's Grand View of History", *Theoretical Vision*, Issue 6, 2020.

[3] "Xi Jinping Delivered an Important Speech at A Grand Gathering to Celebrate the 40th Anniversary of China's Reform and Opening-up", *People's Daily* December 19, 2018.

work more systematic, predictable and creative. "① " We should understand and grasp the Party's basic line according to the major trend of human development, the major pattern of world's changes, and the great history of China's development, thus appreciating the necessity of adhering to the basic line for a long time"② . "The excellent traditional Chinese culture nurtured in the development of more than 5,000 years of civilization, the revolutionary culture nurtured in the great struggle of the Party and the people and, the advanced socialist culture reflect the deepest spiritual pursuit of the Chinese nation and represent the unique spiritual identity of the Chinese nation. " ③ "Chinese socialism did not drop from the sky, but has stemmed from 40 years of reform and opening up and nearly 70 years of exploration since the founding of the PRC in 1949. It is the result of the Chinese people's experiences during 97 years of great social revolutions under the leadership of the CPC, founded in 1921. It is the result of more than 170 years of historical progress since 1840, during which the Chinese nation has evolved from decline to prosperity. It is the bequest and development of the Chinese civilization in the past 5,000 years or more. It is a valuable result of the painstaking efforts made by our Party and the people at great cost. It is a hard-won achievement. "④ Xi said, "The 5,000-year history of the civilization of the Chinese nation, the 170-year history of the struggle of the Chinese people since modern times, the 90-year history of the struggle of the CPC, and the 60-year history of the development of the People's Republic of

---

① Xi Jinping's Speech at the Party History Learning and Education Mobilization Conference, *Qiushi*, Issue 7, 2021.

② The Political Bureau of the CPC Central Committee Held a Meeting on Democratic Life, Stressing to Strengthening "Four Consciousnesses", Bolster "Four Confidences", Ensure the "Two Upholds" and Have the Courage to Take Responsibility and Act, and to Implement the Decisions and Arrangements of the CPC Central Committee with A Realistic and Holistic Approach, *People's Daily*, December 27, 2018.

③ Xi Jinping's Speech at the Conference to Celebrate the 95th Anniversary of the Founding of the CPC, *Qiushi*, Issue 8, 2021.

④ Xi Jinping: *The Governance of China* Ⅲ, Beijing: Foreign Language Press, 2020, p. 70.

Chapter 2 Chinese Modernization and New Initiative for China's Development   305

China are all written by the people. "① "History is the best teacher. In the historical vision of theoretical and political teachers, there should be a 5,000-year history of the Chinese civilization, a 500-year history of world socialism, a 170-year history of the Chinese people's struggle since modern times, a 100-year history of the CPC's hard work, a 70-year history of the development of the PRC, a 40-year history of reform and opening up, and historical achievements and transformation of socialism with Chinese characteristics in the new era. Some problems can be explained through vivid, in-depth and specific vertical and horizontal comparison." ② He stressed, "The great victory achieved by the Chinese people under the leadership of the CPC has enabled the Chinese nation, which has a civilization of more than 5,000 years, to move towards modernization on all fronts so that the Chinese civilization glows with new vitality in the process of modernization; it enables the socialist proposition with a history of 500 years to successfully open up a right path with high practicality and feasibility in the world's most populous country so that scientific socialism glows with new vitality in the 21 st century; and it enables the People's Republic of China with a history of more than 60 years to make remarkable achievements in its development. As a result, China, the largest developing country in the world, has lifted itself out of poverty and become the world's second-largest economy in just over 30 years. It has completely shaken off the danger of being expelled from the world and created an earthshaking development miracle in the history of social development, making the Chinese nation glow with new vitality." ③

President Xi's thorough reflection on such major issues as how to jump out of the historical cycle rate and consciously correct misconceptions beyond the

---

① "Xi Jinping Delivered an Important Speech at the Symposium to Commemorate the 120th Anniversary of Mao Zedong's Birth", *People's Daily*, December 27, 2013.

② Xi Jinping: "Take History as the Mirror to Shape Ideals, Know the History and Love the Party and the Country", *Qiushi*, Issue 12, 2021.

③ "Xi Jinping's Speech at the Conference to Celebrate the 95th Anniversary of the Founding of the CPC", *Qiushi*, Issue 8, 2021.

historical stage reflects the profound vision of the grand view of history. He has systematically reviewed the inescapable destiny of the rise and fall of feudal dynasties in China's history and drawn both positive and negative aspects of our party's experience in governance and the lessons in the evolution of some socialist countries and political parties in the world. He believes that as long as the ruling party of Marxism does not run into problems, the socialist countries will not have major problems, and we can jump out of the historical cycle rate of "rapid rise and fall"[1] . He quoted Deng Xiaoping, "To consolidate and develop socialism will take a very long historical stage. It requires unremitted efforts of several, a dozen and even dozens of generations. How long will that be! From Confucius to the present, there are only more than seventy generations. Such a judgment fully demonstrates our political sobriety of the CPC." [2]

III. To firmly grasp the strategic initiative is to firmly grasp the strategic initiative of theoretical innovation

The lasting and in-depth theoretical innovationcapacity is an important symbol to measure whether a political party or a system has vitality, and whether it has the progressiveness of the times and strong leadership. For Marxist political parties, theoretical construction and innovation are the important magic weapon for them to maintain their vigorous fighting strength and remain invincible. One important reason why the CPC, as a century-old party, can always maintain its vigor and vitality is that it constantly makes theoretical innovation, and actively guide and promote the Party's undertakings to break new ground and secure new victories. Since the 18th CPC National Congress, the CPC Central Committee

---

[1] See Xi Jinping: "The New Great Project of Party Building Must Be Consistent", *Qiushi*, Issue 19, 2019.

[2] Xi Jinping: "Several Issues on Upholding and Developing Socialism with Chinese Characteristics", *Qiushi*, Issue 7, 2019.

has attached great importance to theoretical innovation during the construction of socialism with Chinese characteristics. Considering the characteristics and practical requirements of the new era, the CPC Central Committee has constantly deepened its understanding of the laws of the Communist Party's governance, socialist construction, and social development. It has made unremitting theoretical explorations and put forward original theoretical ideas. Thus, it has effectively promoted the theoretical innovation of the Party and the progress of adapting Marxism to the Chinese context, making major theoretical innovation achievements. [1] Xi said, "One of the most important reasons why the CPC has been able to continue to develop and grow despite difficulties and hardships is that our party has always attached importance to party building through theoretical work so that the whole party has always maintained unified thoughts, firm will, coordinated actions, and strong combat effectiveness." [2] "The thought and basic strategy of socialism with Chinese characteristics for a new era are not falling from the sky or being imagined subjectively. They are the results of the painstaking theoretical exploration of the whole Party and the people of all ethnic groups throughout the country since the 18th CPC National Congress, based on our Party's promotion of theoretical and practical innovation since the founding of the People's Republic of China, especially since the reform and opening up, and the collective wisdom of innovation and creation of the whole Party and the people of all ethnic groups throughout the country." [3] "The history of our Party is a history of continuous adoption of Marxism to China's context, and a history of constant theoretical innovation and creation." [4] We should take initiative in

---

[1] See the "Four Situations" investigation group of the Central Party School Newspapers and Periodicals: "Injecting the Strength of Truth into Contemporary Chinese Marxism -Leading Officials Reviewing the Theoretical Innovation Achievements of the Party in the New Era", *Theoretical Vision*, 2018, Issue 1.

[2] "Xi Jinping Delivered an Important Speech at the Conference Commemorating the 200th Anniversary of Marx's Birth Held in Beijing", *People's Daily*, May 5, 2018.

[3] Xi Jinping: *The Governance of China III*, Beijing: Foreign Language Press, 2020, p. 63.

[4] "Xi Jinping's Speech at the Party History Learning and Education Mobilization Conference", *Qiushi*, Issue 7, 2021.

theoretical summaries, be skillful in refining symbolic concepts, and be able to make timely and accurate theoretical summary of some major theoretical and practical issues. This is an important way to seize strategic initiative in theoretical innovation. President Xi stresses, "If we want to seize the initiative in the era of rapid change, and win the victory in the new great struggle, we must continue to expand new horizons and make new summary theoretically on the basis of adhering to the basic principles of Marxism..."① "We should be able to refine symbolic concepts, create new concepts, new categories and new expressions that are easily understood and accepted by the international community, thus guiding research and discussions in the international academic community."② Since the 18th National Congress of the Communist Party of China, Xi has firmly grasped the strategic initiative. On managing the "domestic and international situations", he has put forward such original theoretical plans and China's solutions as building a community with a shared future for mankind and the Belt and Road Initiative, generating enthusiastic response from the international community and bringing tangible benefits to people around the world; on Party building, he has proposed major theoretical propositions such as the original mission, self-revolution, and the "three political forces", namely, "political judgment, political insight, and political execution", which constitute an important part of Xi Jinping Thought on Socialism with Chinese Characteristics for a New Era; on state governance, he has proposed and made comprehensive and systematic elaboration on such theoretical ideas and major principles as "the top priorities of the country", important strategic op-

---

① "Xi Jinping Delivered an Important Speech at the Opening Ceremony of the Special Seminar on 'Learning the Spirit of General Secretary Xi Jinping's Important Speeches and Welcoming the 19th National Congress of the Communist Party of China' Attended by Leading Officials at the Provincial and Ministerial Levels, Stressing the Importance of Holding High the Great Banner of Socialism with Chinese Characteristics and Striving for a Decisive Victory in an All-round Well-off Society and Realizing the Chinese Dream", *People's Daily*, July 28, 2017.

② Xi Jinping: "Speech at the Symposium on Philosophy and Social Sciences", *People's Daily*, May 19, 2016.

portunity period, strategic focus, overall development and security and "three new and one high", namely "understanding the new development stage, applying the new development philosophy, creating a new development dynamic and achieving high-quality development".

These theoretical generalizations and major judgments with symbolic concepts are connected and consistent with each other. They are ofsymbolic significance in the scientific system of Xi Jinping Thought on Socialism with Chinese Characteristics for a New Era and play an effective role in theoretical guidance. Xi has summarized many important theoretical generalizations and assertions in the history of the Party, especially since the 18th CPC National Congress. He said, "Theory originates from practice and is used to guide practice. Since the reform and opening up, we have timely summarized new and vivid practices, constantly promoted theoretical innovation, and put forward many important conclusions on major issues such as development philosophy, ownership, distribution system, government functions, market mechanism, macro-control, industrial structure, corporate governance structure, livelihood guarantee, social governance... These theoretical outcomes have not only effectively guided China's economic development, but also opened up a new realm of Marxist political economics."[1] He systematically summarized and reviewed that since the 18th National Congress of the Communist Party of China, our Party has made scientific judgments on the economic situation and made timely adjustments to the development philosophy and ideas. 13 major theories and concepts for economic and social development have been proposed including the vision of people-centered development, not taking GDP growth rate as the sole barometer of success and the judgment that China's economy has entered a period defined by three overlapping phases.[2] He also highlighted the new develop-

---

[1] Xi Jinping: "Correctly Understanding and Grasping the Major Issues Concerning Medium and Long-term Economic and Social Development", *Qiushi*, Issue 2, 2021.

[2] See Xi Jinping: "Understanding the New Development Stage, Applying the New Development Philosophy, and Creating a New Development Dynamic", *Qiushi*, Issue 9, 2021.

ment philosophy as the most important and principal one among the 13 and called upon the entire party to apply the new development philosophy fully, correctly and comprehensively.

We should firmly grasp the initiative in theoretical equipment. The Party's innovative theory can only become a truly powerful weapon of struggle if it truly equips the mind and grips the mass. There is a famous remark of Marx in the Introduction of Critique of Hegel's Philosophy of Right, "Theory is capable of gripping the masses as soon as it demonstrates *ad hominem*, and it demonstrates *ad hominem* as soon as it becomes radical. To be radical is to grasp the root of the matter. But, for man, the root is man himself." [1] President Xi stressed that in order to "make the body as indestructible as the diamond, "we must arm our minds with scientific theories and constantly cultivate our spiritual home. We should take the systematic understanding of the basic theories of Marxism as our essential ability"[2]. "Theoretical accomplishment is the core of officials' comprehensive quality. Theoretical maturity is the basis of political maturity. Political firmness stems from theoretical sobriety. In a sense, the depth of understanding of Marxist theory determines the degree of political sensitivity, the breadth of vision, and the height of ideological realm." [3] "We should deepen the study and education of the Party's innovative theories, promote the normalization and institutionalization of the education of ideals and beliefs... and promote the theoretical and spiritual unity of all people." [4] "We should further study the

---

[1] *Collected Works of Marx and Engels*, Volume 1, Beijing: People's Publishing House, 2009, page 11.

[2] Xi Jinping: "Keep the Overall Situation in Mind, Grasp the Overall Trend, Focus on Major Issues and Strive to Improve Publicity and Ideological work", *People's Daily*, August 21, 2013.

[3] "The Political Bureau of the CPC Central Committee Held a Special Meeting on Democratic Life. General Secretary Xi Jinping of the CPC Central Committee Presided over the Meeting and Delivered an Important Speech", *People's Daily*, December 27, 2015.

[4] "Xi Jinping Presided over the Symposium of Expert Representatives in the Field of Education, Culture, Health and Sports, Emphasizing the Comprehensive Promotion of the Development of Education, Culture, Health and Sports, and Constantly Enhancing the People's Sense of Gain, Happiness and Security", *People's Daily*, September 23, 2020.

Party's innovative theories, strengthen the study and education of the Party's history, and at the same time study the history of the PRC, reform and opening up, and the history of socialist development, and constantly improve political judgment, political understanding, and political execution."[1] To uphold and develop socialism with Chinese characteristics, we must attach great importance to the role of theory. "Whenever theoretical innovation makes a step forward, theoretical equipment must follow... We should take learning and applying the Party's innovative theories as the top priority of theoretical equipment."[2]

We should firmly grasp the initiative in strengthening the institutional construction of ideological work. President Xi stressed, "The collapse of a political power often begins with ideology. Political turbulence and regime change may occur overnight, but ideological evolution is a long-term process. When the ideological defense line is broken, other defense lines are difficult to hold. We must firmly hold the leadership, management and discourse power of ideological work in our hands and never lose them, or we will make irreparable historical mistakes."[3] The Decision of the Central Committee of the Communist Party of China on Several Major Issues Concerning Upholding and Developing the Socialist System with Chinese Characteristics and Promoting the Modernization of the National Governance System and Governance Capacity, which was deliberated and adopted at the Fourth Plenary Session of the 19th CPC Central Committee, emphasized the fundamental system of securing the guiding position of Marxism in the ideological work and made a series of major arrangements. This is the first time that our Party has explicitly expressed the guiding position of Marxism in the ideological work as a fundamental system. It is a major institutional innova-

---

[1] "Xi Jinping Traveled to Guizhou to Visit Officials and the Mass of All Ethnic Groups on the Eve of the Spring Festival", *People's Daily*, February 6, 2021.

[2] Xi Jinping: "Speech at the Conference on Education of 'Remaining True to Our Original Aspiration and Keeping Our Mission Firmly in Mind'", *Qiushi*, Issue 13, 2020.

[3] *Extract of Xi Jinping's Statements on the Holistic Approach to National Security*, Beijing: Central Party Literature Press, 2013, p. 100.

tion that concerns the long-term development of the Party and the country's cause, and the direction and development path of the Chinese culture. It embodies the successful experience and principles that our Party has formed in its years of efforts to lead cultural development, and fully reflects that the Party Central Committee has entered a new realm in its understanding of the laws governing socialist cultural development. [1]

President Xi highlighted institutional advantage as the greatest advantage of a party and a country. [2] "Compared with the past, the reform and opening up in the new era has many new connotations and characteristics, of which one very important is the greater weight of institutional construction... and correspondingly, the greater weight of establishing regulations and systems." [3] On this major issue, since the 18th CPC National Congress, the Party Central Committee has attached great importance to the institutional governance of the Party in accordance with the rules. It has taken strengthening the regulation and system building within the Party as the long-term and fundamental policy of full and strict governance over the Party. As a major strategic task concerning the long-term governance of the Party and the lasting stability of the country, it has been placed in a prominent position for deployment and historic achievements have been made. [4]

In the face of new situations and tasks, the Sixth Plenary Session of the

---

[1] See Huang Kunming: "Upholding the Fundamental System of Securing Marxism's Guiding Position in the Field of Ideology", *People's Daily*, November 20, 2019.

[2] Xi Jinping: "Speech at the Conference on Education of 'Remaining True to Our Original Aspiration and Keeping Our Mission Firmly in Mind'", *Qiushi*, Issue 13, 2020.

[3] *Decision of the Central Committee of the Communist Party of China on Major Issues Concerning Upholding and Improving the Socialist System with Chinese Characteristics and Promoting the Modernization of the National Governance System and Governance Capacity*, Beijing: People's Publishing House, 2019, p. 49.

[4] See the Bureau of Laws and Regulations of the General Office of the CPC Central Committee: "Opening up a New Realm of Governing the Party by Rules and Regulations in the New Era — Summary of the Achievements of the Construction of the Party's Internal Laws and Regulations since the 18th CPC National Congress", *People's Daily*, June 17, 2021.

18th CPC Central Committee analyzed the situation of the full and strict governance over the party, deliberated and passed the *Several Guidelines on Intra-Party Political Life in the New Situation* and the *Regulations of the CPC on Intra-Party Supervision*.① It is pointed out in *Several Guidelines on Intra-Party Political Life in the New Situation* that "we should improve the system of analysis, research and circulation of major ideological and theoretical issues within the Party, strengthen the ideological and theoretical guidance via the Internet, clarify the underlying ideological and theoretical issues, help party members and officials maintain their political standing, distinguish between right and wrong, and resolutely resist the erosion of wrong ideas."② This is an important part of implementing the Party's overall leadership of publicity and ideological work at the level of system building. The establishment of the responsibility system for ideological work is a major measure to strengthen the Party's overall leadership of ideological work, and also an important embodiment of the fundamental system of securing the guiding position of Marxism in ideological work. Since the 18th National Congress of the Communist Party of China, the Party's responsibility system for ideological work has been further implemented, and the special inspection tour for ideological work has taken effect. It is pointed out in *Implementation Measures of the Responsibility System of Party Committee (Party Group)'s Ideological Work* issued by the General Office of the Central Committee of the Communist Party of China that the Party should strengthen its control over publicity and ideology, and firmly grasp the leadership and initiative of ideological work. In addition, the *Learning Rules of the Theoretical Learning Center Group of the Party Committee (Party Group) of the CPC* clearly stipulates the principles of nature positioning, requirements on content and form, organization, management and assessment of the theoretical learning

---

① See Xi Jinping: "Speech at the Second Plenary Session of the Sixth Plenary Session of the 18th CPC Central Committee (Excerpt)", *Qiushi*, Issue 1, 2017.

② *Collection of Important Laws and Regulations within the CPC*, Beijing: Party Building Reading Press, 2019, page 43.

center group of the Party Committee (Party Group). This special intra-party regulation is of great significance for promoting the in-depth development of theoretical equipment, improving the theoretical and practical capability of leading officials, and strengthening the ideological and political construction of the leading group. ①

The main peak rises above the water's surface, resembling a pillar in the midst of the waves. In his report to the 19th National Congress of the Communist Party of China, Xi stressed that since the Communist Party of China was born in 1921, from that moment on, the Chinese people have had in the Party a backbone for their pursuit of national independence and liberation, of a stronger and more prosperous country, and of their own happiness; and the mindset of the Chinese people has changed, from passivity to taking the initiative." ② "The governance of a country relies on the elite and the people." "Heroes are the backbone of the country; the common people are the foundation of the country. When you put them both into good use, the country can be governed well without any complaint." ③President Xi stressed, "This country is its people; the people are the country. As we have fought to establish and consolidate our leadership over the country, we have in fact been fighting to earn and keep the people's support. The Party has in the people its roots, its lifeblood, and its source of strength."④ "I will work selflessly and live up to the expectations of the people." ⑤ Fundamentally, serving the people wholeheartedly and practi-

---

① "The Office of the Central Committee of the CPC issued the Learning Rules for the Theoretical Learning Center Group of the Party Committee (Party Group) of the CPC", *People's Daily*, March 31, 2017.

② Xi Jinping: *The Governance of China Ⅲ*, Beijing: Foreign Language Press, 2020, pp. 10 – 11.

③ *Translation and Annotation of Six Secret Strategic Teachings and Three Strategies of Huang Shigong*, Shanghai: Shanghai Ancient Books Publishing House, 2012, pp. 117 and 118.

④ *Xi Jinping's Speech at the Conference to Celebrate the 100th Anniversary of the Founding of the CPC*, Beijing: People's Publishing House, 2021, p. 11.

⑤ Xi Jinping: *The Governance of China Ⅲ*, Beijing: Foreign Language Press, 2020, p. 144.

cing people-centered development is the greatest strategic initiative of the CPC. This is also what some Western politicians and various hostile forces fear most, and the biggest reason why their despicable attempts to separate the CPC from the Chinese people and oppose them cannot succeed. "Sometimes we decide not to fight and at other times, fighting is necessary. The reason not to fight lies in us while the reason to fight lies in our enemy." [1] The CPC members always have the courage, integrity and boldness not to believe in heresies, be afraid of ghosts or succumb to pressure. [2] As long as the CPC firmly relies on the people and holds the strategic initiative, socialism with Chinese characteristics will be able to succeed in the historical journey of the great rejuvenation of the Chinese nation.

---

[1] *Questions and Replies between Tang Taizong and Li Weigong*, and *Seven Books of the Martial Arts Classic* (Part 2), Beijing: Zhonghua Book Company, 2007, p. 611.

[2] "Xi Jinping Delivered an Important Speech at the Opening Ceremony of the Training Class for Young and Middle-aged Officials at the Central Party School (National Academy of Administration), stressing Conviction, Loyalty to the Party, Seeking Truth from Facts, Having a Sense of Responsibility, and Trying to Become A Pillar of the Party Who can Make Major Contributions and Shoulder Heavy Responsibilities", *People's Daily*, September 2, 2021.

Chapter 3 Chinese Modernization and Chinese Experience of Social Development

Chinese Modernization and China's Efforts to Build a Strong Education System

Sun Zhaoyang*

A thriving education makes a thriving country, while a powerful education makes a powerful country. Education plays an important role in developing socialism with Chinese characteristics, which features rapid economic growth and social development, prosperity of the people and the country, stability and unity. In the Report to the 20th National Congress of the Communist Party of China (CPC), President Xi Jinping said, "We will continue to give high priority to the development of education, build China's self-reliance and strength in science and technology, and rely on talent to pioneer and to propel development. We will speed up work to build a strong educational system, greater scientific and technological strength, and a quality workforce. We will continue efforts to cultivate talent for the Party and the country and comprehensively improve our ability to nurture talent at home. All this will see us producing first-class innovators and attracting the brightest minds from all over."[①] Since the 18th CPC National Congress, the CPC Central Committee has, with its broad

---

* Sun Zhaoyang, Associate professor, University of Chinese Academy of Social Sciences

① Xi Jinping, "Hold High the Great Banner of Socialism with Chinese Characteristics and Strive in Unity to Build a Modern Socialist Country in All Respects — Report to the 20th National Congress of the Communist Party of China", *People's Daily*, October 26, 2022.

and far-sighted vision, courageously endeavoured to deepen reform across the board and improve education fairness, structure and quality, making great new achievements in education. Keeping in mind both domestic and international imperatives, Xi has answered, from a strategic perspective of the cause of the Party and the country, a series of major theoretical and practical questions concerning the modernization and innovative development of education and implemented major decisions and plans. He has put forward and implemented the strategy of reinvigorating China through science and education, the strategy of developing a quality workforce and the innovation-driven development strategy while giving strategic priority to education development so as to remove institutional barriers to education. China is in the process of leading the world in education, and is building a solid education system through a Chinese path to modernization.

I. Build a Strong Education System and Make New Education Achievements in the New Era

Since the 18th CPC National Congress, Xi has answered the fundamental issue of "what kind of people we should cultivate, how, and for whom" from a strategic perspective of the cause of the Party and the country, and presented a series of important proposals on education development while balancing both domestic and international situations. Education authorities have fully implemented Xi Jinping Thought on Socialism with Chinese Characteristics for a New Era, unwaveringly taken as their guide President Xi's important proposals on education development, and steadily advanced reform and innovation in ideological and political education, making a series of immense achievements.

1. Management System Fully under the Leadership of the CPC

In long-term practice, China has gradually establish a system with administration at different levels, under which the central government exercises leadership and local authorities perform their respective duties. Education reform has basically adopted a top-down approach compatible with our political system and governance structure. In terms of the management system, the government has coordinated management system, development scale and speed, regional layout, schooling models, curricula, etc. , of education authorities at all levels through avenues of legal policies, personnel organizations and appropriations based on evaluation, forming a government-dominated administrative mode (Zhao Junfang, 2009) .[1] Besides, in the education reforms of each period, the government puts forward reform objectives and assumptions, which will then be implemented by governments at all levels, according to core tasks and determines the reform contents and process. Instructions on policy formulation and implementation, effect evaluation, safeguard mechanisms and so on are passed from central governments to local ones, to schools, and then to teachers (Shi Zhongying, Zhang Xiaqing, 2008) .[2] Government-dominated and campaign-style policies facilitate the rapid expansion of education.

Government-dominated education model helps create a synergy within a short period to facilitate the rapid growth of education. However, without the guidance of the Party, market regulation and the participation of social forces, this model will likely to lead to excessive administrative management and subjective decision-making, and the absence of experts and social supervision. To overcome drawbacks of the education management system, the central government constantly promotes comprehensive reform in education with an emphasis on the Party's overall leadership over education, gradually abolishes direct administration over schools, encourages and guides social forces to invest in running schools, expands social resources input, and conducts macro-management through legislation, appropriations, planning, information services, policy

---

[1] Zhao Junfang, "The History and Experience of China's Higher Education Reform and Development over the Past 60 Years", *China Higher Education Research*, 2009 (10): 3 – 10.

[2] Shi Zhongying, Zhang Xiaqing, "China's Experience in 30 Years of Education Reform", *Journal of Beijing Normal University (Social Sciences)*, 2008 (5): 22 – 32.

guidance and necessary administrative means. A financial sharing mechanism has been established at central, provincial, municipal and county levels, and funds are reasonably shared based on economic development and affiliations of schools.

In terms of education input, China's government budgetary spending on education has accounted for more than 4% of GDP for ten consecutive years since 2012, with the cumulative amount over the past ten years reaching 33.5 trillion yuan. The average annual growth rate was 9.4%, higher than the average annual nominal GDP growth rate of 8.9% and the average annual growth rate of revenue from the national general public budget of 6.9% in the same period. From 2011 to 2021, China's total spending on education, government budgetary spending on education, revenue from the national general public budget and non-fiscal investment in education all doubled. China's total spending on education increased from 2.4 trillion yuan to 5.8 trillion yuan; government budgetary spending on education increased from less than 2 trillion yuan to 4.6 trillion yuan; revenue from the national general public budget increased from 1.6 trillion yuan to 3.7 trillion yuan; and non-fiscal investment in education increased from less than 600 billion yuan to 1.2 trillion yuan. Over 80% of the central government transfer payments to local governments were used in the central and western regions. Budgetary spending on education allocated to regions like "three regions and three prefectures" that were once deeply impoverished increased at an annual average rate of 12.2%, 2.8% above the national average. China offered more than two trillion yuan in financial aid to students across the country while giving priority to students from registered poor households at all stages of schooling, ensuring that no child is denied schooling due to financial difficulties. [1] Massive investment in education has improved the income of

---

[1] Ministry of Education: The 15th Conference of the "Education over the Past Decade" "1 + 1" Series: An Introduction to the Results of China's Education Reform and Development since the 18th CPC National Congress Based on Data, September 27, 2022. Received on October 23, 2022 from Http: // www. moe. gov. cn/fbh/live/2022/54875/twwd/202209/t20220927_665276. html.

teachers, especially grassroots teachers, improved school running conditions and promoted the overall education level.

2. Higher Education Transitioning from Mass Access to Universal Access

As China's economic and social development is faced with multiple adverse factors, such as vanishing demographic dividend, slower economic growth and contradictions in social development transition, traditional economic growth mode cannot be sustained and higher education evolves into the biggest dividend and the most important driver for high-quality development. "The development level of higher education is an important indicator of a country's development progress and potential. All countries in the world regard running universities and cultivating talents as strategic measures for national development and comprehensive national strength." [1] The expansion of higher education in 1999 played an important part in making China a major country of higher education and realizing mass access to higher education in China. According to modern higher education theory, in elite education, the gross enrolment ratio of higher education is less than 15%, in mass education more than 15% and less than 50%, and in universal education more than 50%. [2] In 2019, the gross enrolment ratio of higher education reached 51.6%. Higher education in China began to transition from mass access to universal access.

Higher education should focus on large-scale and high quality. "When the education scale is large, efforts should be made to improve education quality. We should strive to improve the quality of education by conducting in-depth

---

[1] Xi Jinping. "Speech at Forums on Ideological and Political Work at Institutions of Higher Education" on December 7, 2016, from *A Selection of Xi Jinping's Discussion on the Construction of Socialist Society*. Beijing: Central Party Literature Press, 2017 Edition: 60.

[2] Martin Trow, "Problems in the Transition from Elite to Mass Higher Education", translated by Wang Xiangli, *Foreign Higher Education Materials*, 1999 (1): 1-22.

studies on the education system, teaching system and teacher management."① China has taken a series of measures to accelerate the construction of a powerful country of higher education in an effort to enhance the comprehensive strength and international competitiveness of higher education and realize the transition from a major country of human resources to a powerhouse in terms of talent. "Deep reform" leadership groups of the Central Committee of the CPC passed the "Coordinate Development of World-class Universities and First-class Disciplines Construction Overall Plan" on August 18, 2015, in which new arrangements for the development of higher education in the new era were put forward. On June 23, 2016, the Ministry of Education announced the invalidity of 382 normative documents, including Opinions on Continuing to Implement the "985 Project" Construction Project, which officially announced the suspension of "211 Project" and "985 Project" as well as the project of building key and strong disciplines. Ministry of Education, Ministry of Finance and National Development and Reform Commission released the Implementation Measures for Coordinating Construction of World-class Universities and First-class Disciplines (for interim implementation) in January 2017, and announced the first 42 universities to be designated as world-class universities, 95 with first-class disciplines and 465 with disciplines included in the "double world-class project" in September. Xi said in his Report to the 19th CPC National Congress, "We will move faster to build Chinese universities into world-class universities and develop world-class disciplines as we work to bring out the full potential of higher education", which suggests that higher education China is on a new journey. On the basis of further improving the evaluation criteria of "double world-class project", a list of 147 universities and disciplines included in the project was published in 2022.

---

① Xi Jinping. "Speech at the 13th Meeting of the Central Finance and Economy Leading Group" on May 16, 2016, from *A Selection of Xi Jinping's Discussion on the Construction of Socialist Society*. Beijing: Central Party Literature Press, 2017 Edition: 55.

Xi attaches great importance to the development of higher education. In the past ten years, he has visited universities more than 20 times and delivered important speeches, and has written back to teachers and students from higher education institutions over 20 times, indicating direction for the reform and development of higher education and providing fundamental guidelines. Higher education has seen outstanding achievements in institutionalinnovation, talent cultivation and discipline construction. The CPC Central Committee and the State Council released a series of policy documents so as to implement plans proposed at the 18th CPC National Congress and 19th CPC National Congress, namely "promote the development of substance in higher education" and "realize the development of substance in higher education" respectively. China has built the world's largest higher education system, with 44.3 million students in total. From 2012 to 2021, the gross enrolment ratio increased by 27.8% from 30% to 57.8%. The population receiving higher education reached 240 million. The new additions to the workforce had an average education of 13.8 years. The quality and skills of the workforce changed significantly. China has formed a paradigm in terms of MOOCs (Massive Open Online Courses) and online education. By the end of February 2022, there were over 52,500 online courses and 370 million registered users as for MOOCs in China. More than 330 million college students received MOOCs credits. China ranks first in the world in the number of courses and application scale of MOOCs. It has formed a set of Chinese paradigms for the development of MOOCs, including ideas, technologies, standards, methods and evaluation. China has continued to deepen the reform of innovation and entrepreneurship education in colleges and universities, and successfully held seven sessions of the China International "Internet +" College Students Innovation and Entrepreneurship Competition, attracting a total of 25.33 million college students from 6.03 million teams from more than 120 countries and regions on five continents. The competition has directly created 750,000 jobs and indirectly provided 5.16 million jobs. All-round reform has been carried out in the construction of new engineering, new medical science, new agricultural science and new liberal arts from the aspects of education thought, development philosophy, quality and standards, techniques, quality evaluation etc. Besides, China has incorporated higher education into national strategies and industrial development and optimized the layout of disciplines and specialities to align with new development patterns. A total of 265 new specialities were added to undergraduate programmes; 17,000 new undergraduate programmes were added; and 10,000 undergraduate programmes were withdrawn or suspended, which reflects that talents cultivation is more adaptable to new technologies, new industries and new forms of business. [1]

3. Acceleration of the Opening up and Internationalization of Education

International cooperation and exchanges in education have always been an integral part of China's education system. From the early days of Chinese students studying in the Soviet Union, to studying in the UK and the US after the reform and opening up, to attracting students from developing countries to study in our country, China has gradually become the largest exporter of overseas students in the world and the largest destination of overseas students in Asia and the third in the world. At the ceremony celebrating the 100th anniversary of the founding of the Western Returned Scholars Association in October 2013, Xi Jinping put forward the policy of studying abroad in the new era "Support studying abroad, encourage returning to China, give them the freedom to come and go, and expect them to play a role in the future", thus promoting the rapid development of studying abroad in the new era. Taking into account both domestic and international situations, he has called for building a community with a shared future for mankind and the global development initiative and pointed out

---

[1] Ministry of Education: The second Conference of the "Education over the Past Decade" "1 + 1" Series: An Introduction to the Results of China's Higher Education Reform and Development since the 18th CPC National Congress, May 17, 2022. Received on October 24, 2022 from http://www.moe.gov.cn/fbh/live/2022/54453/twwd/202205/t20220517_628181.html.

that "We should unswervingly uphold the policy of opening up and strengthen inclusion, mutual learning and connectivity with other countries to promote the modernization of education".[①] The general offices of the CPC Central Committee and the State Council issued the "Opinions on the Work of the Opening-up of Education in the New Era" in April 2016, the first founding document that provided comprehensive guidance for education opening-up since the founding of the Republic of China in 1949. The document wrote that "promoting cultural exchanges and enhancing people-to-people connectivity" could accelerate the opening-up of China's education.

Since the 18th CPC National Congress, Xi Jinping has declared to expand education opening up in important instructions on a series of major international and domestic occasions. He has sincerely written back to international students, returnees from overseas studies, foreign students in China, and foreign primary and secondary school students. Such actions helped indicate the direction for the reform and development of higher education and provided fundamental guidelines. Over the past decade, China has conducted educational cooperation and exchanges with 181 countries having diplomatic ties with China, established Confucius Institutes (Confucius Classrooms) in cooperation with 159 countries and regions, and signed agreements with 58 countries and regions on mutual recognition of academic qualifications and degrees. More than 80% of overseas students chose to return to China for career development. In the 2020 – 2021 academic year, registered international students came from 195 countries and regions and 76% of them were with degrees, 35% higher than that of 2012. The Ministry of Education held 37 international High-Level People-to-People Exchange Mechanism meetings, in which more than 300 cooperation agreements were signed and nearly 3,000 concrete cooperation outcomes were achieved. China has guided universities to promote the "double world-class pro-

---

① Xi Jinping, *The Governance of China* (Vol. Ⅲ), Beijing: Foreign Languages Press, 2020: 351.

ject" through international cooperation and exchanges. Since the launch of the International Conference on the Cooperation and Integration of Industry, Education, Research and Application in 2018, the conference has attracted over 14,000 experts and scholars from more than 70 countries, facilitated more than 2,300 "one-to-one" scientific research cooperation projects between departments and experts, and cultivated more than 4,000 graduate students under the guidance of both Chinese and foreign tutors. Besides, China has carried out the Belt and Road education initiative to strengthen connectivity with other countries in terms of education, and set up 23 "Luban Workshops". The China-ASEAN Vocational Education Association has been established; the China-SCO Business and Trade Institute has been opened (SCO, Shanghai Cooperation Organization); and the Future of Africa — a project for China-Africa cooperation on vocational education has been launched, deepening educational exchanges and cooperation between China and Central and Eastern Europe. Moreover, China has built a global platform for high-end education cooperation by successfully holding the World Conference on Vocational Education Development and actively organizing the World Digital Education Conference, contributing its own wisdom and strength to global education governance. [1]

II. Build a Strong Education System and Strive to Blaze a Chinese Path to Modernization

Xi Jinping pointed out, "The role of function is essential for China to shift from a populous country to one with powerful human resources and to realize the

---

[1] Ministry of Education: The 13th Conference of the "Education over the Past Decade" "1 + 1" Series: An Introduction to International Educational Cooperation and Exchanges since the 18th CPC National Congress, September 20, 2022. Received on October 24, 2022 from http: //www. moe. gov. cn/ fbh/live/2022/54849/twwd/202209/t20220920_663141. html.

great rejuvenation of the Chinese nation". ① In order to gain an advantage in the competition in the 21st century and realize the great rejuvenation of the Chinese nation, China must value education development and accelerate the construction of a strong education system. While strengthening school education and formal education, we should also focus on the construction of a lifelong learning society to improve the quality of human resources in a comprehensive, systematic and sustainable way, which will provide a solid foundation and powerful impetus for building a great modern socialist country in all respects.

1. Give High Priority to Education Development

Xi Jinping systematically analysed the nature, value and purpose of education by making use of the stances, viewpoints, and methods of Marxism, and put forward a series of new views and opinions on giving priority to education development, which became the political declaration, powerful tools and action programs for education reform and development. ② The strategic orientation of giving priority to education development indicates the development direction for China's education work. The guiding principle is that "We will continue to follow a people-centred approach to developing education, move faster to build a high-quality educational system, advance students' well-rounded development, and promote fairness in education". ③

First, education is of critical importance to the future of our country and our Party. Since the reform and opening up, the strategic status of education in

---

① Xi Jinping, "Speech at Forums on Ideological and Political Work at Institutions of Higher Education" on December 7, 2016, from *A Selection of Xi Jinping's Discussion on the Construction of Socialist Society*. Beijing: Central Party Literature Press, 2017 Edition: p. 60.

② Ma Xiaoqiang et al., "Prioritize the Development of Education—Study and Research on Important Proposals on Education by General Secretary Xi Jinping (9)". *Educational Research*, 2021 (9): 11 – 12.

③ Xi Jinping, "Hold High the Great Banner of Socialism with Chinese Characteristics and Strive in Unity to Build a Modern Socialist Country in All Respects — Report to the 20th National Congress of the Communist Party of China", *People's Daily*, October 26, 2022, p. 2.

China has been described in many ways, such as "education is in a primary position", "we should give priority to education development", "we should reinvigorate China through science and education", and "education is essential to social stability and people's wellbeing". After giving full consideration to the nature, connotation and denotation of education, Xi Jinping creatively summarized that education was of critical importance to the future of our country and our Party. [1] The development of education has been linked with the strategic needs of the Party and the country for the first time, signalling that our Party's understanding of the law of education development has reached a new historical height. This summary is a top-level design of education development, which requires us to carry out the Party's educational policy through the whole process of educational work from the perspective of the overall development of the cause of the Party and the country. We must enhance cohesion by instilling in them the Party's ideals and convictions, inspiring them with the historic mission of national rejuvenation, and educating our people with Xi Jinping Thought on Socialism with Chinese Characteristics for a New Era so as to guide the youth to pass on the great spirit of the Party and promote the Core Socialist Values.

Second, the education focus should shift from investment to the overall situation. We have long misunderstood giving priority to the development of education as increasing investment in it, and the requirements of improving the quality and fairness of education are not fully satisfied. Also, the connotation of education development strategies could be richer. At the National Education Conference, Xi Jinping said that "We must give priority to the development of education and make it a driver for the development of the cause of the Party and the country, and ensure that education meets the requirements of the development

---

[1] Xi Jinping, "Keep to the Path of Socialist Educational Advancement with Chinese Characteristics and Nurture a New Generation of Capable Young People with Sound Moral Grounding, Intellectual Ability, Physical Vigour, Aesthetic Sensibility, and Work Skills Who Will Fully Develop Socialism and Carry Forward the Socialist Cause — Speech at the National Education Conference", *People's Daily*, September 11, 2018. p. 1.

of the cause of the Party and the country, lives up to the expectations of the people, and matches China's overall national strength and international standing".① That is, the strategy of giving priority to education development does not mean a one-sided and static consideration of its ranking among various causes of the Party and the country. Instead, it requires us to regard education as a determining factor in the overall situation so as to achieve overall victory while adopting systematic and strategic thinking.

Third, education lays a solid foundation for people's wellbeing. The 12th CPC National Congress listed education as a national development strategy for the first time to make people attach importance to education. The main purpose is to cultivate more well-educated workers so as to boost labour productivity and economic growth. Forty years of reform and opening up witnessed the miracle of a high-quality labour force bringing demographic dividends and promoting economic growth. With the development of the economy and society, people's needs have changed, and education is not simply to serve the economy. Xi Jinping declared in his Report to the 19th CPC National Congress, "The principal challenge facing Chinese society is the gap between unbalanced and inadequate development and the people's growing expectation for a better life." This transformation requires that we should not only focus on the larger quantity and scale of education, but on better education fairness and quality so as to ensure that all people will constantly benefit from education development.

Fourth, education should be developed from an international perspective. President Xi's important proposals on the priority of education development have a global vision and aim to serve the whole world and promote common prosperity, which fully reflects the confidence and responsibility of a major coun-

---

① Xi Jinping, "Keep to the Path of Socialist Educational Advancement with Chinese Characteristics and Nurture a New Generation of Capable Young People with Sound Moral Grounding, Intellectual Ability, Physical Vigour, Aesthetic Sensibility, and Work Skills Who Will Fully Develop Socialism and Carry Forward the Socialist Cause — Speech at the National Education Conference", *People's Daily*, September 11, 2018. p. 1.

try. He pointed out, "Today, the fates of people of all countries in the world are interconnected. The young of all countries should receive education to cultivate a global vision and enhance their sense of cooperation so as to jointly create a bright future for mankind."[1] The initiative to build a community with a shared future for mankind and the global development initiative proposed by Xi Jinping has enhanced China's ties with the world in terms of education. China has taken an active part in the Global Education First Initiative by the United Nations, led countries along Belt and Road in carrying out international educational exchanges and cooperation, and provided quality services, intellectual support and human resources for the implementation of the Belt and Road Initiative. In this process, it has provided more quality educational opportunities for people in developing countries. This demonstrates its responsibility and broad-mindedness as a major country.

2. Accelerate the Building of a High-quality Educational System

Basic education is a foundational project to improve the quality of the nation and to foster virtue through education. It plays a fundamental and leading role in the national education system. From the political stance of realizing the great rejuvenation of the Chinese nation, Xi Jinping formulated the strategic positioning, missions, tasks and development strategies of basic education in the new era.[2] He said, "We will accelerate high-quality, balanced development and urban-rural integration in compulsory education. We will better allocate educational resources across regions, strengthen public-benefit preschool education and special needs education, ensure the diversified development of senior secondary schools, and improve the financial aid system so it covers students at all

---

[1] Xi Jinping, "A Congratulatory Letter to the First Opening Ceremony of the Schwarzman Scholars, Tsinghua University", *People's Daily*, September 11, 2016.

[2] Niu Nansen, Li Hongen. "Basic Education is a Cause for the Whole Society — Study and Research on Important Proposals on Education by General Secretary Xi Jinping (8)". *Educational Research*, 2022 (8): 4–19.

stages of schooling."①

First, nurture a new generation of capable young people who will fully develop socialism and carry forward the socialist cause. President Xi has repeatedly emphasized and interpreted "Chinese characteristics" and "Chinese spirit" and constantly highlighted the "Chinese" consciousness to develop socialism and carry forward the socialist cause fully. Our country is in the critical period of building a modern socialist country in all respects and advancing the great rejuvenation of the Chinese nation on all fronts. Highlighting the "Chinese" consciousness of the new generation will help strengthen the psychological foundation for children's confidence in culture and values, forge a strong sense of community for the Chinese nation, and effectively establish cultural identity. He stressed that primary and secondary school students should understand the fine traditional Chinese culture and Chinese history, which "is a solid foundation for us to gain a firm footing amidst global cultural interaction". ② We should learn more about Chinese culture and history, especially the history of the Party, the country, reform and opening up, and socialism development, by reciting excellent classic poems, practising Chinese calligraphy and reading history books. We should strengthen our "Chinese" consciousness and take the initiative to develop socialism and carry forward the socialist cause fully.

Second, cultivate well-rounded people to meet the requirements of the new era. The fundamental solution to the problem of "how to cultivate people" is to build an education system that nurtures capable people with sound moral grounding, intellectual ability, physical vigour, aesthetic sensibility, and work skills. Such a cultivation model is not only the CPC's interpretation of Marx's "all-round development" theory, but also the crystallization of China's educational wisdom. According to the requirements of modern production for all-

---

① Xi Jinping, "Hold High the Great Banner of Socialism with Chinese Characteristics and Strive in Unity to Build a Modern Socialist Country in All Respects — Report to the 20th National Congress of the Communist Party of China", *People's Daily*, October 26, 2022, p. 2.

② Xi Jinping, Speech at the Art Work Conference, *People's Daily*, October 15, 2015, p. 1.

round development, Xi Jinping said that we should "foster an ethos of work among students" and "build an education system that ensures the well-rounded development of students in terms of moral grounding, intellectual and physical ability, aesthetic sensibility, and work skills". ① Young people in the new era shoulder the mission of promoting national rejuvenation through a Chinese path to modernization. Only with moral grounding, intellectual and physical ability, aesthetic sensibility, and work skills can they meet the requirements of the times. "Only in this way can our children grow into pillars in the new era with rich knowledge, sound personalities, renewed vigour and all-round abilities to shoulder the historic task of national rejuvenation."②

Third, treat basic education as a matter of public welfare. Since the 18th CPC National Congress, basic education has focused more on serving public interests. Xi Jinping said that "We should uphold overall Party leadership over compulsory education and stick to the socialist orientation in running schools" and that "Party committees and governments at all levels should insist that compulsory education be provided by the government, ensure its non-profit nature, and make compulsory education better and stronger". ③ The nature of China, a socialist country, determines that the country is the main investor of schools, and that it undertakes the main responsibility for the establishment of schools. This ensures the non-profit nature of the school system and determines

---

① Xi Jinping, "Keep to the Path of Socialist Educational Advancement with Chinese Characteristics and Nurture a New Generation of Capable Young People with Sound Moral Grounding, Intellectual Ability, Physical Vigour, Aesthetic Sensibility, and Work Skills Who Will Fully Develop Socialism and Carry Forward the Socialist Cause — Speech at the National Education Conference", *People's Daily*, September 11, 2018. p. 1.

② Xi Jinping, "Promote Well-rounded Development of Students in Terms of Moral Grounding, Intellectual and Physical Ability, Aesthetic Sensibility, and Work Skills", In-Depth under Xinhua News Agency. September 15, 2021. From http://www.xinhuanet.com/video/2021 - 09/15/c _ 1211371286. htm.

③ Xi Jinping, "Carry out Reform and Opening up at a Higher Level to Foster a New Pattern of Development — Speech at the 15th Conference of the Deep Reform Leadership Groups of CPC Central Committee", *People's Daily*, September 2, 2020. p. 1.

that schools shoulder the main responsibility. Schools should not only promote the development of each student, but also play a role in providing guidance and regulation so as to prevent utilitarianism and egoism tendencies, and encourage and empower students to take on the great responsibility of national rejuvenation.① As a socialist country, China should continue to emphasize the non-profit nature of basic education and the primary responsibility of schools therein. This can help us to respond to changes in family structure and way of life, and accelerate efforts to ensure that all people can equally benefit from the fruits of education.

Fourth, clarify that basic education is the shared responsibility of the whole society. The coordination of family, school and society is the principle of our basic education policy, which reflects our deep understanding of the law of talents cultivation. The new concept of "the whole process of talents cultivation" proposed by Xi Jinping and the cultivation of a new generation of capable young people who will fully develop socialism and carry forward the socialist cause can only be realized through joint efforts of the whole society. Families and society should actively cooperate with schools with fine family traditions and social conduct so as to consolidate school education results.② "We will advance comprehensive reform in education, strengthen the creation and management of teaching materials, refine the systems for school management and educational assessments, and improve mechanisms for school-family-society collaboration in education."③ The school-family-society education pattern requires the cooperation of all walks of life, groups and organizations. The implementation and application of comprehensive education featuring the all-round development of students

---

① Shi Zhongying, *Public Pedagogy*, Beijing: Beijing Normal University Publishing Group, 2008: 12 – 21.

② *General Secretary Xi's Important Proposals on Education*, Beijing: Higher Education Press, 2020: 51.

③ Xi Jinping, "Hold High the Great Banner of Socialism with Chinese Characteristics and Strive in Unity to Build a Modern Socialist Country in All Respects — Report to the 20th National Congress of the Communist Party of China", *People's Daily*, October 26, 2022, p. 2.

need the cooperation of several parties at different levels on all fronts.

3. Build World-class Universities with Chinese Characteristics at a Faster Pace

Through a comprehensive analysis of higher education development trends in the world and the essential requirements of China's socialist higher education development, Xi Jinping accurately analysed the difficulties, bottlenecks and pains existing in the higher education reform and development and observed the law of running a school of higher education and cultivating high-level talents, consolidating the theoretical foundation of higher education reform and development in the new era. [1] In the Report to the 20th CPC National Congress, Xi Jinping said, "We will do more to develop basic disciplines, emerging disciplines, and interdisciplinary subjects and speed up the development of world-class universities and strong disciplines with Chinese features" [2] to provide guidance for the high-quality development of higher education.

First, uphold Party's overall leadership over education. The Party is the leadership core of the higher education cause development in the new era and the fundamental political guarantee to ensure the implementation of the Party's educational policies and realize the modernization of higher education. The socialist nature of China decides that we must uphold and strengthen the Party's overall leadership over the cause of higher education. Xi Jinping said, "For quality higher education, we must uphold the Party's leadership, especially that over institutions of higher education so as to make them primary platforms to up-

---

[1] Luo Jianping, Gui Qingping, "Speed up the Building of a Socialist University with Chinese Characteristics — Study and Research on Important Proposals on Education by General Secretary Xi Jinping (6)", *Educational Research*, 2022 (6): 4 – 18.

[2] Xi Jinping, "Hold High the Great Banner of Socialism with Chinese Characteristics and Strive in Unity to Build a Modern Socialist Country in All Respects — Report to the 20th National Congress of the Communist Party of China", *People's Daily*, October 26, 2022, p. 2.

hold the Party's leadership."① To uphold the Party's overall leadership over higher education, we should improve the Party's leadership system and working mechanism over education and accurately understand and implement the president accountability system under the leadership of the Party Committee. Besides, we should promote the deep integration of Party building and cause development in universities and colleges, and ensure that the Party's political principles, standards and requirements are implemented in all links, procedures and steps involved in running schools and teaching.

Second, follow a path with Chinese characteristics in developing higher education. President Xi's expectation for China's higher education development is that we can run institutions of higher education by following a path with Chinese characteristics. The core feature of higher education with Chinese characteristics is "carrying forward the revolutionary traditions and heritage and blazing a new path to building world-class universities with Chinese characteristics". ② Following the path with Chinese characteristics in developing higher education requires us to dialectically look at China's relations with the world, continue high-level educational opening up and adhere to the development strategies of "bringing in" and "going global". In addition, we will intensify efforts to carry out high-level people-to-people exchanges, project cooperation and platform building in higher education, actively participate in global education governance, offer Chinese solutions, voice and wisdom as for common problems in higher education reform and development, and provide new ideas for developing countries to realize the modernization of higher education.

Third, speed up the building of a strong education system. Xi Jinping

---

① Xi Jinping, *The Governance of China* (Vol. Ⅱ), Beijing: Foreign Languages Press, 2017: 379.

② Xi Jinping, "Pass on Revolutionary Traditions and Heritage under Leadership of the Party and Blaze a New Path to Build World-class Universities with Chinese Characteristics — Speech at the Meeting of Teacher and Student Representatives of Renmin University of China", *People's Daily*, May 26, 2022. p. 1.

reckoned that we should properly balance the development of higher education, national rejuvenation and national prosperity, and make overall plans accordingly. We should highlight the important position of higher education in the strategy of making China a country with a strong education system, and entrust higher education with new responsibilities and historical missions. Higher education should serve the great mission of national rejuvenation and national prosperity, and should "serve the people and the governance of the Communist Party of China, advance the consolidation and development of the socialist system with Chinese characteristics, and facilitate the reform, opening up and socialist modernization."[①] Only by adhering to the building of socialism can higher education truly become the driving force for the great rejuvenation of the Chinese nation. The higher education system is an organic whole. Therefore, we should adhere to systematic thinking in running universities, launch the construction of the "double world-class project", and build high-quality colleges and universities. At the same time, we should support the differentiated development of colleges and universities in different regions at various levels and of diverse types for the overall development of higher education. We should take talents cultivation as the core work of colleges and universities, alleviate the imbalance in education and resource allocation, step up the construction of a theory to develop world-class higher education with Chinese characteristics, and improve our ability to serve national strategies and regional development.

Fourth, stick to the development of substance in higher education. The 18th CPC National Congress proposed that "We should promote the development of substance in higher education". The 19th CPC National Congress clarified that "We should realize the development of substance in higher education". Our determination to achieve the goal can be reflected in the transition from "promote" to "achieve". The essential requirement of the development of sub-

---

[①] Xi Jinping, *The Governance of China* (Vol. II), Beijing: Foreign Languages Press, 2017: 377.

stance is to provide fair and quality education. Efforts should be made to give more policy support to central and western regions, old revolutionary areas, ethnic minority areas and border areas to narrow the gap between schools, regions and groups in terms of higher education resources so that everyone can enjoy higher education in a more equitable manner. Improving the quality of undergraduate education is the route we must take to realize the development of substance. Undergraduate education is the foundation for higher education. We should give priority to talents cultivation in the work of colleges and universities, and adhere to the people-oriented principle. Institutions of higher education should stimulate students' learning potential and encourage them to study hard with the help of teachers devoted to teaching, endeavour to cultivate a new generation of capable young people who will fully develop socialism and carry forward the socialist cause so as to play a partin realizing the great rejuvenation of the Chinese nation. ①

The Report to the 20th CPC National Congress made an overall plan for education, science and technology and talents and emphasized the strategy of reinvigorating China through science and education, which reflected President Xi's strategic thought that "Education is of critical importance to the future of our country and our Party". It highlighted the strategic supporting role of education in socialist modernization and the fundamental and strategic position of education in rejuvenating China through science and education. We should adopt President Xi's important proposals on education and adhere to the strategy of rejuvenating China through science and education and give priority to education development while following the guiding principles put forward in the 20th CPC National Congress. We should optimize the allocation of education resources and promote fairness in education, cultivate high-quality talents urgently needed by the economy and society based on the needs of economic and social develop-

---

① Chen Baosheng, "Develop World-class Undergraduate Education with Chinese Characteristics", *Current Affairs* (For Study Purpose of the Party Committee Central Group), 2018 (5).

ment, and improve the education structure and focus more on education development. Besides, we should deepen reform in curricula setting and teaching, and change training models, promote education by applying digitization and information technology, and coordinate school, family and social efforts in education to form a school-family-society education pattern. We should give better play to the function of education in training basic talents and adhere to the people-centred education philosophy. Efforts should also be made to nurture a new generation of capable young people with sound moral grounding, intellectual ability, physical vigour, aesthetic sensibility, and work skills who will fully develop socialism and carry forward the socialist cause so as to make a greater contribution to build a modern socialist country and promote the great rejuvenation of the Chinese nation in all respects.

Chinese Modernization and People's Better Life

Ma Feng[*]

President Xi Jinping drew up a grand blueprint for comprehensively building a modern socialist country in the Report to the 20th CPC National Congress so as to advance the rejuvenation of the Chinese nation on all fronts through a Chinese path to modernization. President Xi stressed, "The Report to the 20th CPC National Congress clarifies that Chinese modernization is the modernization of a huge population, the modernization of common prosperity for all, the modernization of material and cultural-ethical advancement, the modernization of harmony between humanity and nature, and the modernization of peaceful development, fully demonstrating the scientific meaning of Chinese modernization. This is both a theoretical generalization and a practical requirement, which indicates a broad road to build China into a great modern socialist country in all respects and advance the rejuvenation of the Chinese nation". [①] In the Report to the 20th CPC National Congress, one of China's overall development objectives for the year 2035 is "Ensure that the people are leading better and happier

---

[*] Ma Feng, Associate Professor, National Institute of Social Development, CASS.

[①] Xi Jinping's Speech on Emphasizing Correct Understanding and Vigorously Promoting Chinese Modernization at the Opening Ceremony of the Seminar on Studying and Implementing the Spirit of the 20th CPC National Congress. *People's Daily*, February 8, 2023.

lives; bring per capita disposable income to new heights; substantially grow the middle-income group as a share of the total population; guarantee equitable access to basic public services; ensure modern standards of living in rural areas; achieve long-term social stability; and make more notable and substantive progress in promoting the people's well-rounded development and prosperity for all". ① The people's aspiration for a better life is what we are striving for. The Report pointed out, "The immutable goal of our modernization drive is to meet the people's aspirations for a better life." in our journey to realize the great rejuvenation of the Chinese nation. ②

I. Improve People's Wellbeing and Raise Life Quality

The Report to the 20th CPC National Congress wrote, "We should improve the people's wellbeing and raise their life quality". "We must ensure and improve the people's wellbeing in the course of pursuing development and encourage everyone to work hard together to meet the people's aspirations for a better life." ③

A country should not only follow the general rules of modernization, but also foster its own characteristics in the context of the national conditions while pursuing modernization. Since the founding of the Republic of China in 1949, especially since the reform and opening up, China has completed a process of industrialization that took developed countries several centuries in the space of

---

① Xi Jinping, "Hold High the Great Banner of Socialism with Chinese Characteristics and Strive in Unity to Build a Modern Socialist Country in All Respects — Report to the 20th National Congress of the Communist Party of China", *People's Daily*, October 28, 2022.

② Xi Jinping, "Hold High the Great Banner of Socialism with Chinese Characteristics and Strive in Unity to Build a Modern Socialist Country in All Respects — Report to the 20th National Congress of the Communist Party of China", *People's Daily*, October 28, 2022.

③ Xi Jinping, "Hold High the Great Banner of Socialism with Chinese Characteristics and Strive in Unity to Build a Modern Socialist Country in All Respects — Report to the 20th National Congress of the Communist Party of China", *People's Daily*, October 28, 2022.

mere decades, bringing about the two miracles of rapid economic growth and enduring social stability. This opens up broad prospects for the great rejuvenation of the Chinese nation. The 18th CPC National Congress heralded a new era in building socialism with Chinese characteristics. The overarching task of upholding and developing socialism with Chinese characteristics is to realize socialist modernization and national rejuvenation, and on the basis of completing the goal of building a moderately prosperous society in all respects, a two-step approach should be taken to build China into a great modern socialist country that is prosperous, strong, democratic, culturally advanced, harmonious, and beautiful by the middle of the 21st century. Long-term exploration and practice have been conducted since the founding of the Republic of China in 1949, especially since the reform and opening up. Then based on that, breakthroughs have been made in terms of theories and practice since the 18th CPC National Congress. It has been shown that only the Chinese Path to Modernization can improve people's lives in an all-around way, make their lives better, and fundamentally guarantee their happiness.

Since the 18th CPC National Congress, we have applied the new development philosophy, focused on promoting high-quality development, deepened supply-side structural reform and stepped up to foster a new pattern of development. By mobilizing the whole nation, we have successfully realized poverty eradication, brought about a historic resolution to the problem of extreme poverty in China, and built a moderately prosperous society in all respects as scheduled. Consequently, China has ushered in an era of comprehensive economic and social progress unprecedented in the history of the Chinese nation and benefited all the people, which lays a solid material foundation for realizing the Second Centenary Goal of building China into a great modern socialist country in all respects and advancing the rejuvenation of the Chinese nation on all fronts. Besides, people's wellbeing has been comprehensively improved. We have worked continuously to ensure people's access to childcare, education, employment, medical services, elderly care, housing, and social assistance, thus bringing about an all-around improvement in people's lives. China's average life expectancy has increased to 78.2 years. Its per capita disposable income has risen from 16,500 yuan to 35,100 yuan. More than 13 million urban jobs have been created each year on average. Besides, we have built the largest education, social security, and healthcare systems in the world. These achievements have allowed us to make historic strides in making education universally available, bring 1.04 billion people under the coverage of basic old-age insurance, and ensure basic medical insurance for 95 percent of the population. Timely adjustments have been made to the childbirth policy. More than 42 million housing units in run-down urban areas and more than 24 million dilapidated rural houses have been rebuilt, marking a significant improvement in housing conditions in both urban and rural areas. The number of internet users has reached 1.03 billion. We have ensured a more complete and lasting sense of fulfilment, happiness, and security for our people, and we have made further progress in achieving common prosperity for all. [1]

People's living standard and quality have achieved historic progress in all respects since the 18th CPC National Congress. China has fulfilled the First Centenary Goal of building a moderately prosperous society in all respects. The living environment of urban and rural residents has improved in all aspects: People's income and consumption level rise; household durable consumer goods continue to upgrade; equitable access to basic public services is ensured; the coverage of public facilities is expanded. Efforts are made to improve people's wellbeing and social security. At present, we are improving the multi-tiered social security system at a faster pace so as to build it into the system with the largest scale in the world. By the end of 2021, 1.03 billion people were covered by basic old-age insurance and 1.36 billion by basic medical insurance. The

---

[1] Xi Jinping, "Hold High the Great Banner of Socialism with Chinese Characteristics and Strive in Unity to Build a Modern Socialist Country in All Respects — Report to the 20th National Congress of the Communist Party of China", *People's Daily*, October 28, 2022.

number of people covered by unemployment insurance, work-related injury insurance and maternity insurance increased by 77.33 million, 92.77 million and 83.23 million, respectively, over 2012. Basic housing support has been enhanced. More than 31 million housing units in run-down urban areas were rebuilt from 2015 to 2021. 940,000 government-subsidized apartment units were being constructed or in preparation in 2021.① The social security system provides a safety net for people's livelihoods and helps ensure social stability. We will further improve the multi-tiered social security system that covers the entire population in urban and rural areas and see that it is fair, unified, reliable, well-regulated, and sustainable. We should ensure both development and security, make sure that social security funds are well regulated, and safeguard the bottom line of social fund security. We should take account of today's realities to plan for the future. Efforts should be made to ensure the balance of all social insurance funds for the lasting and steady operation of the system, which will promote the high-quality and sustainable development of social security programs and effectively respond to the challenges posed by aging to the sustainable development of the social development system.

The Healthy China strategy has been fully implemented, and public medical services available to urban and rural residents have gradually improved. The supply capacity of medical services has improved significantly. By the end of 2021, there were 9.45 million beds in medical and health institutions in China and 11.24 million health professionals, an increase of 65.0% and 68.4% over 2012, respectively. Residents' health has been significantly improved. China's average life expectancy has increased from 74.8 years in 2010 to 78.2 years in

---

① New Concepts Lead to New Development, a New Era Opens New Ground — One of the Reports on Major Social Economic Achievements since the 18th CPC National Congress, National Bureau of Statistics, http://www.stats.gov.cn/sj/sjjd/202302/t20230202_1896671.html, [2022 – 09 – 13].

2021, and the infant mortality rate decreased from 10.3‰ in 2012 to 5‰. ① People's health is a key indicator of a prosperous nation and a strong country. We must give strategic priority to ensuring people's health and improve policies on promoting public health. We will improve the population development strategy and establish a policy system to boost birth rates. Besides, we will pursue a proactive national strategy in response to population aging and develop elderly care programs and services. We will further reform the medical and healthcare systems and expand the availability of quality medical resources and ensure they are better distributed among regions. We will deepen the reform of public hospitals to see that they truly serve the public interest, further advance the Healthy China Initiative and patriotic health campaigns and promote sound, healthy lifestyles.

II. Meet the People's Aspirations for a Better Life

On the basis of economic development, constantly improving the people's living standards is the fundamental purpose of all the work of the Party and the country. Development is our Party's top priority in governing and rejuvenating China. China's development is for the development of the people. It is the people that create all material and spiritual wealth. The Party has made seeking happiness for the Chinese people and rejuvenation for the Chinese nation its mission.

Chinese modernization is the modernization of a huge population. "China is working to achieve modernization for more than 1.4 billion people, a number larger than the combined population of all developed countries in the world today. This is a task of unparalleled difficulty and complexity; it inevitably means

---

① New Concepts Lead to New Development, a New Era Opens New Ground — One of the Reports on Major Social Economic Achievements since the 18th CPC National Congress, National Bureau of Statistics, http://www.stats.gov.cn/sj/sjjd/202302/t20230202_1896671.html, [2022-09-13].

that our pathways of development and methods of advancement will be unique."① It is difficult to realize the modernization of 1.4 billion people, a number larger than the combined population of all developed countries in the world today. The demonstration effect of 1.4 billion people entering modern society is huge. Every step and strategy to achieve the modernization of 1.4 billion people is a Chinese solution for mankind's search for a better social system, a Chinese plan for modernization. Therefore, "Only by applying the people-centred development philosophy and ensuring that development is for the people and by the people and that its fruits are shared by the people can we have a correct outlook on development and modernization."② The Chinese path to modernization is a socialist one, and China's modernization is of socialist nature. As the core leadership in the process of modernization, the Party represents the interests of the Chinese people and has no special interests of its own. "It is because of selflessness that the Party can constantly reflect on itself in the spirit of materialism and get rid of corruption caused by any individual interest group, power group, or privileged stratum by severely punishing those influenced by those groups."③ The socialist system and the Party's leadership act as institutional and structural guarantees.

Since its founding a century ago, the Party has taken a remarkable journey and secured extraordinary historical achievements. Leading the people in creating a better life is the immutable goal of our Party. Our people love life and want better education, more stable jobs, higher income, more reliable social security, better medical and health services, more comfortable housing and a

---

① Xi Jinping, "Hold High the Great Banner of Socialism with Chinese Characteristics and Strive in Unity to Build a Modern Socialist Country in All Respects — Report to the 20th National Congress of the Communist Party of China", *People's, Daily*, October 28, 2022.

② Xi Jinping, "Ground Efforts in the New Development Stage, Apply the New Development Philosophy, and Create a New Development Dynamic", *Qiushi*, 2021 (9).

③ Xi Jinping, "Learn from History, Work Hard, and Forge ahead for a Better Future", *Qiushi*, 2022 (1).

better environment. They want their children to have a bright future after growing up, including having a good job and leading a better life. People's aspiration for a better life is the goal of our Party. On the basis of economic development, constantly improving the people's living standards is the fundamental purpose of all the work of the Party and the country. At present, the principal challenge facing Chinese society is the gap between unbalanced and inadequate development and the people's growing expectation for a better life, with the contradictions and problems in development mainly reflected in development quality. This requires us to make development quality a higher priority and strive to boost the quality and efficiency of development. Besides, imbalances and inadequacies in development remain a prominent problem; there are still wide gaps in development and income distribution between urban and rural areas and between regions; there is still a long way to go in terms of ecological conservation and environmental protection; there is also room for improvement in the work of government; and there are still weaknesses in social governance. The people's needs for a better life are increasingly extensive. In addition to higher requirements for material and cultural life, they also have growing demands in terms of democracy, rule of law, equity, justice, safety and the environment. Now and for some time to come, the development environment in China will face profound and complex changes. China remains in an important period of strategic opportunity for development, with new evolution and changes in opportunities and challenges. We need to pursue a strategy of national rejuvenation amid global changes of a magnitude not seen in a century, raise awareness about the new features and requirements brought about by the changing major contradictions in Chinese society, and have a deep understanding of the new contradictions and challenges brought by the complex international environment. Besides, we must base our work on this fundamental dimension of our national context — the primary stage of socialism, put the people's interests above all else, and make reform development gains benefit all our people in a more substantial and equitable way so as to ensure a more complete and lasting sense of fulfilment, happiness, and security for our people.

The people are the true heroes, for it is they who create history. In the period of socialist revolution, construction and reform and opening up, the Party has had a shared future and a common stake with the people and strived in unity with them to create great historical achievements. The people are the solid base of our republic and our greatest strength in governance. No political consideration is more important than the people. The world is undergoing profound changes of a scale unseen in a century. We will face a challenging external environment for some time to come. As the development environment in China faces profound and complex changes in the new development stage, we must rely on the people and do a good job of ensuring their well-being. Besides, we must constantly hold in our hearts the interests and concerns of the people, and regard the benefit of the people as our greatest political achievement; we must think for the people, respond to their needs, and work for the greater happiness of the people. We must do everything within our capacity to resolve the most practical problems that are of the greatest and most direct concern to the people. We will improve the quality of public services and make them better distributed and promote progress in education, employment, income, social security, medical care, elderly care, housing, and the environment, so as to improve the life quality of the people and promote social development level.

III. Achieve Solid Progress in Promoting Common Prosperity

"Chinese modernization is the modernization of common prosperity for all. Achieving common prosperity is a defining feature of socialism with Chinese characteristics and involves a long historical process. The immutable goal of our modernization drive is to meet the people's aspirations for a better life. We will endeavour to maintain and promote social fairness and justice, bring prosperity to all, and prevent polarization."① Chinese modernization is the modernization of common prosperity for all. We will make more notable and substantive progress in common prosperity for all by the end of 2035. Great achievements in development are created by the people and should be shared by them.

The nature of socialism is to release and develop productive forces, eliminate exploitation and polarization, and achieve common prosperity. It has proved that thereare no fewer problems after development than in the process of development. At present, the social structure of China is undergoing profound changes. The Internet has profoundly changed the way of human communication, social concepts, social psychology, and social behaviours. In the development process, we should unleash the enthusiasm, initiative and creativity of the people, and ensure that every one of our people has the chance to pursue a career through hard work and that the people work to promote the prosperity of the country and the rejuvenation of the nation while pursuing their own individual development.

Chinese modernization aims to promote inclusive and balanced development, and make the people strive in unity for Chinese modernization. Common prosperity is an essential requirement of socialism and a key feature of Chinese modernization. As the spine of the Chinese nation, the Party continues to consolidate the economic and political foundation for the people of all ethnic groups in China, and form the most solid unity toward a clear goal when it comes to the most practical problems that are of the greatest and most direct concern to the people. The Party has a clear understanding of common prosperity, "Some developed countries have been industrializing for hundreds of years. However, due to their social systems, common prosperity has not been realized, and the disparity between the rich and the poor has become wider". ② "China must reso-

---

① Xi Jinping, "Hold High the Great Banner of Socialism with Chinese Characteristics and Strive in Unity to Build a Modern Socialist Country in All Respects — Report to the 20th National Congress of the Communist Party of China", *People's Daily*, October 28, 2022

② Xi Jinping, "Promote Comment Prosperity", *Qiushi*, 2021 (20).

lutely prevent polarization, promote common prosperity and achieve social harmony and stability."[1] Over the past 100 years, the Chinese people have always, with the Party as the core, sought development and rejuvenation through solidarity. We can say that "All the achievements made by the Party and the Chinese people over the past 100 years are the result of unity and hard work, which are the most prominent defining symbol of the Party and the people".[2] In the process of building a moderately prosperous society in all respects, we have left no one behind and brought about a historic resolution to the problem of extreme poverty in China. We are setting out on a journey toward common prosperity. While building a modern socialist country in all respects, China will give full play to the advantages of Chinese modernization. We will take the initiative to address the regional gap, the gap between urban and rural areas and the income gap, promote all-round social advancement and well-rounded human development, and promote social equity and justice, with the fruits benefiting all our people in a more substantial and equitable way.[3]

We should promote inclusive development through common prosperity. Inclusiveness is an important part of the new development philosophy. The fundamental purpose of inclusive development is to enable people to share the fruits of development created by them. The coverage of inclusive development is for all the Chinese people. Inclusive development aims to ensure that everyone, not a few or some, can enjoy and have their rightful share. The contents of inclusive development involve all respects. Inclusive development means sharing the fruits of the country's economic, political, cultural, social and ecological development, and comprehensively protecting the legitimate rights and interests of the people in all fields. Inclusive development will be realized through joint

---

[1] Xi Jinping, "Promote Comment Prosperity", *Qiushi*, 2021 (20).
[2] Xi Jinping, "Xi Jinping's Speech at the 2023 Spring Festival Gathering", *People's Daily*, January 31, 2022.
[3] Xi Jinping, "Ground Efforts in the New Development Stage, Apply the New Development Philosophy, Create a New Development Dynamic", *Qiushi*, 2021 (9).

building and sharing. Only through the joint building can we realize joint sharing, and the process of the former is also that of the latter. Inclusive development is a gradual process, in which it is bound to go from low level to high level, and from unbalanced to balanced. Even very high-level inclusive development differs.

On the basis of building a moderately prosperous society in all respects, we must strive to realize, safeguard, and advance the fundamental interests of all our people when our people embrace inclusive development and common prosperity. We should value, ensure and improve people's wellbeing. Besides, we should unleash the enthusiasm, initiative and creativity of the people and ensure they work to promote the prosperity of the country and the rejuvenation of the nation while pursuing their own individual development. We need to stick to the people-centred development philosophy. The people-centred development philosophy reflects its fundamental purpose of wholeheartedly serving the people and embodies the historical materialism that the people are the fundamental force driving development. "We need to make sure that development is for the people and by the people, and that its fruits are shared among the people." Also, we need to take the people's well-being and common prosperity as its ultimate goal of economic development.

The cause of the Party and the Chinese people constitutes an important part of the cause of human progress. The creation and development of the Chinese path to modernization is not a simple continuation of the original version in Chinese history and culture, nor is it a simple application of the template envisioned by Marxist writers, or a copy of the socialist practices of other countries or another version of foreign modernization. Chinese modernization "originates from a profound understanding of our own history and national conditions, a profound summary of the modernization path of the West, a deep analysis of the modernization course of other developing countries, and an insight into mankind's pursuit of modernization"①. Chinese Path to Modernization has abandoned and transcended the old Western modernization paths. China's success has brought hope to mankind, made it possible for mankind to develop and create a better future, and provided a Chinese solution for mankind to explore a better social system. The world is undergoing profound changes of a scale unseen in a century. As changes of the times combined with the once-in-a-century pandemic, the world finds itself in a new period of turbulence and transformation. "The Human Development Index has declined for the first time in 30 years. The world's poor population has increased by more than 100 million. Nearly 800 million people live in hunger. Difficulties are mounting in food security, education, employment, medicine, health and other areas important to people's livelihoods. Some developing countries have fallen back into poverty and instability due to the pandemic. Many in developed countries are also living through a hard time."② The President of Eritrea Isaias Afwerki has a profound judgement and understanding of the development of China and the world amidst the profound changes unprecedented in a century. He thought that, "China has not only made remarkable achievements in its own national construction and economic development, but also committed itself to opposing hegemonism and building a just and equitable global order, thus making great contributions to human progress. China's global influence is growing, which can be attributed to the outstanding leadership of the CPC and the resilience of the Chinese people."③

President Xi once said that "The immutable goal of our modernization drive is to seek happiness for the Chinese people and rejuvenation for the Chinesena-

---

① Ma Feng, "Appreciate the Civilization of Others as Do to One's Own — Promote Common Prosperity of All Human Civilizations", *People's Daily*, November 5, 2017.

② Xi Jinping, "Forge Ahead with Confidence and Fortitude to Jointly Create a Better Post-COVID World — Speech at the virtual session of World Economic Forum", *People's Daily*, January 8, 2022.

③ The President of Eritrea Isaias Afwerki Meets Wang Yi, Ministry of Foreign Affairs. From https://www.mfa.gov.cn/web/wjbz_673089/xghd_673097/202201/t20220105_10479198.shtml, January 5, 2022.

tion". [1] This shows the spiritual essence and value orientation of Chinese modernization. It is the essential difference between the Chinese modernization path and the Western one, which focuses on capital and ignores people. Besides, it represents the essential distinction between Chinese and Western modernization in the international community in terms of the different development results they bring to human society.

---

[1] Xi Jinping, "Learn from History, Work Hard, Forge ahead for a Better Future", *Qiushi*, 2022 (1).

Chinese Modernization and China's Efforts to Build Urban Aging-friendly Communities

Ge Yanxia*

Xi Jinping said in his Report to the 20th CPC National Congress, "Chinese modernization is the modernization of a huge population. China is working to achieve modernization for more than 1.4 billion people, a number larger than the combined population of all developed countries in the world today. This is a prominent of unparalleled difficulty and complexity; it inevitably means that our pathways of development and methods of advancement will be unique."[①] Population aging is a prominent trend in the demographic development in China, and it represents the essential national condition in terms of the population while we are building a modern socialist country in all respects. Therefore, a proactive response to population aging is essential for building China into a modern socialist country in all respects. The Report to the 20th CPC National Congress also wrote that "We will pursue a proactive national strategy in response to population aging, develop elderly care programs and services, and provide better services for elderly people who live alone. By doing so can ensure that basic eld-

---

* Ge Yanxia, Associate Professor, National Institute of Social Development, CASS

① Xi Jinping, *Hold High the Great Banner of Socialism with Chinese Characteristics and Strive in Unity to Build a Modern Socialist Country in All Respects — Report to the 20th National Congress of the Communist Party of China.* People's Publishing House, October, 2022.

erly care is accessible to the entire elderly population. "① This indicates a clear direction and provides a fundamental principle for the development of elderly care in China. We should apply a people-centerd development philosophy and facilitate universal access to basic elderly care among the elderly. China's elderly care is often described as a "9073" (or "9064"): 90% of the elderly are cared for by family, 7% (6%) receive community care, and 3% (4%) live in a nursing home. So, it can be estimated that around 97% of the elderly, approximately 290 million, will spend their later years at home or in communities during the 14th Five-Year Plan (2021 - 2025) period. That is, strengthening the building of age-friendly communities is an effective practice to ensure that basic elderly care is accessible to the entire elderly population, and it is also an important measure under the national strategy and Healthy China Strategy for China to respond to population aging actively.

The aging population reflects a significant trend in social development and the progress of human civilization. Besides, it will be a basic national condition for some time to come. According to international standards, a country or region with over 7% of the population aged 65 or above steps into an aging society, and it enters a deep aging society and super-aging society when the figure reaches 14% and exceeds 20%, respectively. The seventh national census showed that the proportion of the population aged 65 and above was already up to 13.50% in 2020. Our country is on the verge of deep aging. The Party and the government attach great importance to the development of elderly care services, which can be reflected in related policies. The Report to the 19th CPC National Congress proposed that as we responded proactively to population aging, we should build a system where the elderly were provided with home care, taken care of by the community, and supported by community services and they could

---

① Xi Jinping, *Hold High the Great Banner of Socialism with Chinese Characteristics and Strive in Unity to Build a Modern Socialist Country in All Respects — Report to the 20th National Congress of the Communist Party of China*, People's Publishing House, October, 2022.

also choose nursing homes or facilities with medical care services. Besides, we should adopt policies to foster a social environment in which senior citizens are respected, cared for, and live happily in their later years. The CPCCC's Proposals for the Formulation of the 14th Five-Year Plan (2021 – 2025) for National Economic and Social Development and the Long-Range Objectives Through the Year 2035 reviewed and adopted by the fifth plenary session of the 19th CPC Central Committee further clarified the requirements to improve the home care and community services, promote the renovation of public facilities for the convenience of senior citizens and improve the service capacity and level. In December 2020, the National Health Commission and the China National Committee on Aging jointly issued the Notice on Establishing Demonstrative National Age-friendly Communities[①], which explicitly proposed exploring a working model and long-term mechanism for the establishment of age-friendly communities, to make the elderly truly feel satisfied, happy and secure. By 2025, 5,000 demonstrative age-friendly communities will be established in urban and rural areas. By 2035, such communities will cover all urban and rural areas. The Report to the 20th CPC National Congress also emphasized that we would pursue a proactive national strategy in response to population aging, develop elderly care programs and services, and provide better services for elderly people who live alone. By doing so, we can ensure that basic elderly care is accessible to the entire elderly population.

Although China has made a great leap in the construction of urban aging-friendly communities in recent years, there are still shortcomings and weaknesses in-home care and community services. For example, the convenience of senior citizens is low in terms of the living environment; commercial services for daily life and healthcare of the elderly are insufficient; and low awareness of re-

---

① Relevant documents and scholars refer to such communities as "age-friendly communities" and "aging-friendly communities", but we believe that their connotations are the same. And this paper uses the latter.

specting the elderly is prevalent in urban communities. The fourth sample survey on the living conditions of the elderly in urban and rural areas of China showed that more than 50% of the elderly in urban areas thought that their housing lacked alarm systems, handrails or good lighting. Other problems that cause inconvenience for the elderly involve toilets or bathrooms unfriendly to the elderly, high thresholds, uneven or slippery ground, etc. [1] As the diversified, multilevel, and multi-dimensional needs of the elderly grow, the problem of poor convenience in urban communities for the elderly has become increasingly prominent. As a result, it becomes an urgent task to strengthen the construction of urban aging-friendly communities, which is also an important part of the government's governance over the aging society. [2][3]

At present, domestic studies on aging-friendly communities are mainly conducted from the perspectives of sociology, economics, geography, city planning and architecture. For example, Yu Yifan et al. (2018), Zheng Ling and Zheng Hua (2021) elaborated on the conceptual connotation of aging-friendly communities[4][5]; Hu Tinghao and Shen Shan (2014) and Li Xiaoyun (2020) reviewed the research progress and actual practice of aging-friendly

---

[1] Wu Xiaolan, Qu Jiayao. Research on the Current Situation, Problems and Countermeasures of the Construction of Liveable Environment for the Elderly in China, *Scientific Research on Aging*, 2016 (8): 3 – 12.

[2] Luo Xingqi. The Structural Dilemma and Optimization Path of Home Care Services — A Case Study of Shanghai City. *Urban Problems*, 2017 (2): 83 – 89.

[3] Wu Ying, Li Aiqun. Research on Renovation and Reconstruction Policies and Flexibility Strategies of Old Residential Areas in Beijing: A Dual Aging Perspective. *Urban Development Studies*, 2022 (5): 73 – 79.

[4] Yu Yifan, Wang Liangfei, Guan Yiqun, Huang Xiaojing, Cui Zhe, Zhang LiRong, Li Kun, Jin Qingyuan, Fan Haoyang and Guo Shi. Theme Salon of "Old-Age-Friendly City-Design for Future": Third Annual Research Forum of Aging City. *Urbanism and Architecture*. 2018 (21): 6 – 13.

[5] Zheng Ling, Zheng Hua. The Theoretical Connotation and Construction Framework of "Aging-friendly City" — Analysis Based on Grounded Theory. *Social Science Front*, 2021 (10): 226 – 233.

communities[1][2]; Dou Xiaolu et al. (2015), Yu Yifan and Wang Qinqin (2018) summarized the experience of building aging-friendly communities at home and abroad and the enlightenment for China[3][4]; Yu Yifan et al. (2020) and Ge Yanxia and Sun Zhaoyang (2021) studied the evaluation system of aging-friendly communities[5][6]; and Wu Xiaolan (2022) and Ge Yanxia (2022) studied the construction of aging-friendly communities in China in terms of philosophy, policies and practices[7][8]. Some studies focused on the influence of family structure, living environment and surrounding public services on the health and happiness of the elderly, providing research basis for promoting the construction of aging-friendly communities.[9][10] Overall, more and more studies on aging-friendly communities are being conducted in China. However, the related research support is still lagging behind in comparison with rich community

---

[1] Hu Tinghao, Shen Shan. Research Progress and Construction Practice of Age-Friendly City. *Modern Urban Research*, 2014 (9): 14 – 20.

[2] Li Xiaoyun. Person-Environment Fit Theory and Its Implications for the Research on Age-Friendly Residential Environment in Rural Communities. *Urban Development Studies*, 2020 (7): 1 – 6.

[3] Dou Xiaolu, Jon Pynoos, and Feng Changchun. The City and Active Aging: International Initiatives Towards Age-friendly Urban Planning. *Urban Planning International*, 2015 (3): 117 – 123.

[4] Yu Yifan, and Wang Qinqin. International Literature Review of Old-Age-Friendly Living Environment and Its Enlightenment. *Urbanism and Architecture*. 2018 (21): 14 – 19.

[5] Yu Yifan, Zhu Feiyang, Jia Shuying, Guo Yuting, and Hu Yuting. Research on the Assessment of Age-friendly Community. *Shanghai Urban Planning Review*, 2020 (6): 1 – 6.

[6] Ge Yanxia, Sun Zhaoyang. Evaluation and Optimization of the Construction of Age-friendly Communities in Rural China — Based on the Aging-friendly Indicator System of the World Health Organization. *Journal of Nanjing University of Science and Technology (Social Sciences Edition)*, 2021 (5): 54 – 61.

[7] Wu Xiaolan. The Status Quo and Developing Trends of Age-Friendly Environment Building in China, *Scientific Research on Aging*, 2022 (03): 1 – 10.

[8] Ge Yanxia. Age-friendly Communities: A New Foothold in the National Strategy to Actively Cope with the Aging Population. *Chinese Social Sciences Today*, January 12, 2022.

[9] Zhao Lizhi, Liao Xiaoxuan, Wang Peiyu. A Study on the Allocation of Basic Medical Facilities under the Home-based Care Services Model: A Case Study of Beijing Municipal Administrative Center. *Urban Development Studies*, 2022 (8): 14 – 19.

[10] Jiang Weikang, Sun Juanjuan. Living Style, Living Environment and Mental Health of the Elderly in Urban and Rural Areas: An Analytical Framework for the Construction of an Age-friendly Community. *Urban Problems*, 2022 (1): 65 – 74.

practices and problems to be solved. In particular, the systematic quantitative evaluation of the aging-friendly community construction is nearly a research void due to insufficient evaluation indicator system and data, which greatly influences the objective, comprehensive understanding of the whole society in terms of the aging-friendly community construction. Enhancing systematic quantitative evaluation of the aging-friendly community construction is conducive to a comprehensive understanding of the construction, including shortcomings and weaknesses therein. In addition, it helps decision-makers identify the focus and timing of intervention, and provides a research basis for effectively promoting the construction of aging-friendly communities.

Against this background, we have developed an aging-friendly community measurement indicator system with good reliability and validity, which is suitable for cities of our country based on Person-Environment (P-E) Fit principles and the measurement indicators of aging-friendly communities by the World Health Organization (WHO). In addition, the aging-friendly degree of urban communities is quantitatively assessed, and the construction level, structural characteristics, and regional differences are analysed, aiming to quantitatively assess the compatibility between communities and the needs of the elderly at different levels and in varying dimensions. On this basis, suggestions for improving the shortcomings and weaknesses identified in the study are given to provide empirical evidence for efficiently facilitating high-quality construction of urban aging-friendly communities and improving the well-being of the elderly.

Ⅰ. Aging-friendly Community Construction under Person-Environment (P-E) Fit Principles

Person-Environment (P-E) research paradigm holds that later years represent an adult development stage where one is deeply influenced and shaped by *the environment*. [1] The elderly are particularly inclined to be affected by the environment because age-related poorer vision, mobility and cognition have a direct impact on the relationship between individuals and the environment. In other words, this research paradigm regards situational factors as key determinants of the daily behaviour and well-being of the elderly, and attaches great importance to focusing more on and improving the relationship between people and the environment as people age. [2][3] As early as the 1920s, the Chicago School established that man-made environments, such as run-down urban areas, were harmful to people's survival, health and well-being. [4] In the 1930s and 1940s, German social psychologist Lewin proposed a new idea that behaviour should be viewed as the combined effect of humans and the environment. [5] Murray, an American personality researcher, introduced "pressure" to indicate the influence of external environmental forces on an individual's objective and subjective perception. [6] Lawton and Nahemow further proposed the pressure-competence model, which held that as one aged, the relationship between him and the environment would be in a state of increasing tension with the aging of physiological function. [7] In people's later years, environmental stress in the living place may affects their abilities, behaviour and well-being. Such environmental stress may

---

[1] Wahl, H.-W., Scheidt, R., & Windley, P. G. (Eds.). *Aging in Context: Socio-physical Environments* (*Annual Review of Gerontology and Geriatrics*, 2003). New York: Springer, 2004.

[2] Scheidt, R. J., & Windley, P. G. (Eds.). *Environment and Aging Theory: A Focus on Housing*. Westport, CT: Greenwood Press, 1998.

[3] Wahl, H.-W. Environmental Influences on Aging and Behaviour. In J. E. Birren & K. W. Schaie (Eds.), *Handbook of the Psychology of Aging* (5th ed., pp. 215-237). San Diego: Academic Press, 2001.

[4] Park, R. E., Burgess, E. W., & McKenzie, R. D. *The City*. Chicago: Chicago University Press, 1925.

[5] Lewin, K., *Field Theory in Social Science*. New York: Harper, 1951.

[6] Murray, H. A., *Explorations in Personality: A Clinical and Experimental Study of Fifty Men of College Age*. Oxford: Oxford University Press, 1938.

[7] Lawton, M. P., & Nahemow, L. Ecology and the Aging Process. In C. Eisdorfer & M. P. Lawton (Eds.), *The Psychology of Adult Development and Aging* (pp. 619-674). Washington, DC: American Psychological Association, 1973.

come from the inadequacy of physical space and facilities due to their convenience for senior citizens, as well as the imperfection of social support and elderly care services. In 1984, Carp et al. proposed a positive and goal-oriented Person-Environment (P-E) Fit Model based on the needs of people's overall development. They believed that individual needs should be satisfied and balanced by utilizing and improving resources and supporting factors in the environment. ① Furthermore, Phillips et al. incorporated the cultural values of filial piety into the model and proposed a P-E Fit Model with cultural factors. ② This model held that environmental factors needed for people's all-around development included not only physical space and social support, but also cultural values. These models based on the P-E Fit research paradigm have jointly explained the complex interaction and adaptation between the elderly and their living environment, confirmed the necessity of an aging-friendly environment, and advocated adjusting and improving the material, social and cultural characteristics of the environment based on the needs of the elderly so as to strike an ideal balance between environmental support and the needs of the elderly.

Communities serve as the main spatial carrier for the life of the elderly, whose life quality is directly affected by the matching degree between the community environment and their ability and needs. Early studies on communities and the elderly mainly focused on the influence of the architectural environment on the elderly. However, there is a lack of attention to the interaction and match between people and the environment at the community level. Matching community living environments and community support become more and more important

---

① Carp, F. M., & Carp, A., A Complementary/Congruence Model of Well-being or Mental Health for the Community Elderly. In I. Altman, M. P. Lawton, & J. F. Wohlwill (Eds.), Human Behaviour and Environment: Vol. 7. Elderly People and the Environment (pp. 279 – 336). New York: Plenum Press, 1984.

② Phillips, D. R., K. H. C. Cheng, A. G. O. Yeh, O. – L. Siu. Person—Environment (P—E) Fit Models and Psychological Well-Being Among Older Persons in Hong Kong [J]. Environment and Behaviour, 2010, 42 (2): 221 – 242.

for the elderly, especially when they are faced with restricted mobility and limited housing choices.① In recent years, more and more scholars have applied the P-E Fit theory to the construction of aging-friendly communities. A constructive aging process model proposed by Scharlach based on the P-E Fit relationship believed that the establishment of aging-friendly communities must improve community residents' ability to cope with environmental changes throughout the life course.② Especially when the individual ability of the elderly is limited, we have to make up for their dysfunction using community environmental factors, which include not only the physical environment, but also social factors such as economic status, family and social environment, housing and community quality, as well as cultural factors that influence aging.

Based on the P-E Fit principles, major aging countries such as the United Kingdom, Canada, the United States, and the WHO have put forward aging-friendly indicators. Generally speaking, they cover multi-dimensional and multi-level indicators, such as outdoor space environment, transportation, housing environment, public services, social interaction, information exchanges, integration into society, respect and inclusiveness, survival and development, etc., which reflect the core characteristics of safety, health, convenience and comfort necessary for friendly and liveable communities. However, certain differences in terms of regional cultures and indicator selection also exist in the aging-friendly indicators of different countries.

---

① Kahana, E., L. Lovegreen, B. Kahana, M. Kahana. Person, "Environment, and Person-Environment Fit as Influences on Residential Satisfaction of Elders", *Environment and Behavior*, 2003, 35 (3): 434–453.

② Scharlach, A. E., "Aging in Context: Individual and Environmental Pathways to Aging-Friendly Communities: The 2015 Matthew A. Pollack Award Lecture", *The Gerontologist*, 2017, 57 (4): 606–618.

Table 1 Aging-friendly Indicators of WHO and Major Aging Countries

Name	Organization Name	Major Dimensions
Aging-friendly cities	WHO	Outdoor space and buildings, indoor housing, transportation, information exchanges, social participation, skills improvement and re-employment promotion, commercial services and healthcare, respect and inclusiveness, integration into society
Lifetime residences and lifetime communities	Ministry of Housing, Communities & Local Government	Architecture environment, housing, social bonds and belonging, integration into society, innovation and cross-sector planning
Liveable communities	American Association of Retired Persons	Land use, transportation and activities, housing, cooperation and communication, public education and participation in community planning and leadership
Liveable communities	National Association of Area Agencies on Aging	Spatial planning and division, transportation, housing, public safety, culture and lifelong learning
Liveable communities for the elderly	University of Calgary	Barrier-free environment, easy access to information and services, independence and participation in activities, feelings of being valued and respected, financial security, personal safety and community development
Aging-friendly communities	The American Aging Initiative Group	Maximum independence, promotion of social and civic participation and emphasis on basic needs

Continued

Name	Organization Name	Major Dimensions
Aging-friendly communities	The Hong Kong Council of Social Service	Outdoor space and buildings, transportation, housing, social participation, respect and social inclusiveness, community participation and employment, information exchanges, community support and healthcare
Principles behind the grading method for national demonstrative age-friendly communities	The National Health Commission (the China National Committee on Aging)	Living environment, travel facilities, community services, social participation, filial piety and respect for the elderly, technology designed to help the elderly, management and security, features and highlights

Data source: Collected and organized by the author.

Given that previous aging-friendly indicators were mainly developed and practiced in the developed economies in Europe and America, we should not mechanically imitate them while studying aging-friendly communities in China. In contrast, the WHO has fully considered the development differences between developed and developing countries, so its aging-friendly indicators have wider applicability. Taking into consideration the previous survey[1] and the heterogeneity of different regions in terms of population, economy, society and culture, we believe that indicators proposed by WHO may be more widely applicable in China. Besides, the aim of these indicators is consistent with China's overall goal of "active aging" and "healthy aging". They contain core elements of physical, social and cultural factors to ensure and maintain the life quality of the elderly. Moreover, the acquisition and measurement of these indicators are

---

[1] We have carried out relevant research in Guangzhou City, Nanjing City, Chengdu City, Suzhou City, Nantong City, Foshan City and other places to conduct the research better.

practicable. To some extent, all above ensures the good applicability of these indicators in China.

We have properly adjusted the weight of these indicators to make them suited to our national conditions. To be more specific, the weight of these indicators is rearranged by using the method of expert scoring and inviting relevant national functional departments, scientific research institutions, elderly workers from grassroots communities and elderly representatives. [1] The weight of each indicator ranges from 0 to 100 points. The lower the indicator weight coefficient, the less important the index is; and the higher, the more important. Finally, we received 10 complete and effective grading feedback forms, and obtained a comprehensive indicator weight after weighted average calculation. The results show that the weight coefficients of physical, social and cultural first-level indicators are 42.3 points, 33.4 points and 24.3 points, respectively. The second-level indicators include outdoor space, housing, transportation, skills improvement and re-employment promotion, information exchanges, commercial services for the daily life and healthcare of the elderly, respect and inclusiveness, and social integration, with their weight coefficients being 13.00 points, 17.80 points, 11.50 points, 8.82 points, 10.22 points, 14.36 points, 11.45 points and 12.85 points, respectively. It can be seen from the results that experts believe that the aging-friendly indicators proposed by WHO is basically suitable for China, while reckoning that the weight of each indicator should be different, that is, differences exist in terms of the focus and timing of intervention.

---

[1] Special thanks go to experts from the National Health Commission, the Ministry of Civil Affairs, the Ministry of Housing and Urban-Rural Development, the Chinese Academy of Social Sciences, Tsinghua University, etc., as well as elderly workers from grassroots communities and elderly representatives for their valuable suggestions on the design of the indicator system in this study.

Table 2   **Indicators of Urban Aging-friendly Communities in China and Their Weight**

First-level indicators	Weight	Second-level indicators	Weight	Third-level indicators	Weight
Physical environment	42.3	Outdoor space	13.00	Even and barrier-free roads	4.48
				Ideal lighting system	3.62
				Well-equipped facilities for the elderly	4.90
		Housing	17.80	Accessible rooms	5.86
				Even and barrier-free indoor floor	5.11
				Elderly friendly kitchens/toilets/bathrooms	6.83
		Transportation	11.50	Affordable transportation fees	2.91
				The convenience of transport for senior citizens	4.29
				Convenient and accessible transportation facilities	4.30
Social environment	33.4	Skills improvement and re-employment promotion	8.82	Opportunities for employment and voluntary services	4.45
				Opportunities for skills improvement	4.37
		Information exchanges	10.22	Channels to obtain information	5.52
				Open channels to obtain information	4.70
		Commercial services for the daily life and healthcare of the elderly	14.36	Access to primary health care	6.99
				Access to commercial services for the daily life	7.37

Continued

First-level indicators	Weight	Second-level indicators	Weight	Third-level indicators	Weight
Cultural environment	24.3	Respect and inclusiveness	11.45	Respect for the elderly	5.58
				Inclusiveness for the elderly	5.87
		Integration into society	12.85	Places for seniors to socialize	5.18
				Social activities for seniors	4.36
				Affordable costs of participating in activities	3.31

Data source: Organized by the author based on grading feedback forms from the experts.

Furthermore, Cronbach α coefficient and Speason correlation analysis are used to test the reliability and validity of the indicators. The results also show that the indicators have good reliability and validity, and can be used as a quantitative tool to study the status of aging-friendly communities in urban China. Next, a quantitative analysis of the construction of urban aging-friendly communities can be conducted by combining the indicators with the survey data. The measurement score ranges from 0 to 100 points. The higher the measurement score is, the closer the construction of aging-friendly communities is to the optimal state, and the more in line with the actual needs of the elderly; the lower the measurement score, the farther the construction of aging-friendly communities is from the optimal state, and the greater the gap between the construction and the actual needs of the elderly.

II. A Quantitative Analysis of the Construction of the Urban Aging-friendly Communities

1. Basic data

This paper mainly uses the 2019 annual data of the survey on population aging and elderly care in China jointly conducted by the National People's Congress Social Development Affairs Committee and the Chinese Academy of Social Sciences. Probability sampling methods like stratified random sampling were adopted, with 29 provincial-level administrative units (excluding Xinjiang Uygur Autonomous Region and Tibet Autonomous Region) as the sampling frame. The survey data were collected from more than 8800 elderly families in 800 communities in 8 provinces, including subjective and objective indicators of the community environment, family living environment, public services and cultural concepts of the elderly. [1][2] In addition, we further made a second weighting adjustment of the data from the dimensions of age, gender, provinces and cities, to reduce the structural deviation of the sample and meet the data requirements of the investigation into Chinese urban aging-friendly communities. Excluding the missing values and singular values, a city sample data set with a capacity of 2772 was obtained.

2. The reliability and validity test of the indicators

Cronbach α coefficient was used to test the reliability of the indicators. It is generally believed that Cronbach α coefficient value should better be above 0.8, and the range of 0.7 - 0.8 is acceptable. The reliability coefficient of the subscale should better be above 0.7, and the range of 0.6 - 0.7 is acceptable. [3] The results show that the overall Cronbach α coefficient is 0.93, and the Cronbach α coefficient of either first-or second-level indicators is above 0.93, indicating that this indicator system has good reliability for investigating into Chinese urban areas from all or certain aspects.

---

[1] Zhang Yi., "Study on Cohabitation of the Elderly People in China", *Chinese Journal of Population Science*, 2020 (4): 2 - 14, 126.

[2] Sun Zhaoyang, Ge Yanya, Zhang Bo. "The Impact of Home Care Service Supply on Elderly Care Satisfaction: Based on the Analysis of Survey Data in 8 Provinces and Cities", *Journal of the Party School of the Central Committee of the CPC (Chinese Academy of Governance)*, 2021: 1, 111 - 118.

[3] DeVellis, R. F., *Scale Development Theory and Applications*. London: SAGE, 1991.

Table 3   Cronbach α Coefficient Test Results of Indicators of Urban Aging-friendly Communities

Overall indicators	Cronbach α	First-level indicators	Cronbach α	Second-level indicators	Cronbach α
Aging-friendly communities	0.931	Physical environment	0.932	Outdoor space	0.934
				Housing	0.934
				Transportation	0.936
		Social environment	0.933	Skills improvement and re-employment promotion	0.939
				Information exchanges	0.934
				Commercial services for the daily life and healthcare of the elderly	0.935
		Cultural environment	0.933	Respect and inclusiveness	0.935
				Integration into society	0.934

The indicators and weight in this paper are determined according to the practical experience and theoretical basis of the WHO and relevant experts so as to ensure that the indicator system has good content validity. The test of structural validity requires Speason correlation analysis of all indicators and upper-level indicators. The results show that the scores of all-level indicators are significantly correlated with those of their upper-level indicators (0.61 – 0.94), while the correlation coefficient with the scores of other indicators is relatively small, indicating good structural validity of the indicator system. ①

---

① It is generally believed that the scores of all-level indicators are significantly correlated with those of their upper-level indicators, while the correlation coefficient with the scores of other indicators is relatively small, indicating good structural validity of the indicator system.

Table 4 **Correlation Matrix Results of Indicators of Urban Aging-friendly Communities**

	I−0	I−1	I−2	I−3	II−1	II−2	II−3	II−4	II−5	II−6	II−7	II−8
I−0	1.00											
I−1	0.88	1.00										
I−2	0.85	0.58	1.00									
I−3	0.86	0.63	0.63	1.00								
II−1	0.77	0.75	0.58	0.78	1.00							
II−2	0.70	0.89	0.41	0.43	0.33	1.00						
II−3	0.54	0.71	0.37	0.23	0.22	0.53	1.00					
II−4	0.35	0.18	0.68	0.18	0.21	0.14	0.04	1.00				
II−5	0.73	0.61	0.66	0.63	0.50	0.50	0.38	0.11	1.00			
II−6	0.65	0.42	0.80	0.48	0.47	0.22	0.33	0.20	0.30	1.00		
II−7	0.65	0.48	0.45	0.79	0.55	0.35	0.19	0.04	0.36	0.47	1.00	
II−8	0.78	0.57	0.59	0.89	0.74	0.38	0.20	0.23	0.66	0.35	0.41	1.00
III−1	0.32	0.27	0.23	0.33	0.69	0.09	0.11	0.05	0.15	0.32	0.47	0.13
III−2	0.56	0.48	0.51	0.46	0.68	0.27	0.17	0.35	0.28	0.40	0.40	0.38
III−3	0.70	0.58	0.50	0.76	0.91	0.29	0.19	0.14	0.51	0.37	0.44	0.78
III−4	0.67	0.82	0.40	0.44	0.32	0.94	0.44	0.17	0.46	0.22	0.33	0.40
III−5	0.63	0.75	0.38	0.44	0.33	0.88	0.31	0.21	0.38	0.22	0.34	0.39
III−6	0.50	0.70	0.26	0.25	0.19	0.75	0.59	0.01	0.42	0.14	0.24	0.19
III−7	0.31	0.32	0.27	0.13	0.14	0.16	0.83	0.08	0.17	0.34	0.13	0.19
III−8	0.32	0.37	0.32	0.12	0.16	0.14	0.73	0.09	0.14	0.37	0.09	0.11
III−9	0.46	0.67	0.23	0.22	0.17	0.63	0.73	0.03	0.41	0.11	0.20	0.18
III−10	0.01	0.14	−0.25	0.11	0.10	0.13	−0.07	0.78	0.10	0.06	0.17	0.03
III−11	0.58	0.47	0.61	0.43	0.46	0.40	0.16	0.65	0.32	0.40	0.28	0.42
III−12	0.63	0.46	0.55	0.66	0.55	0.31	0.21	0.08	0.83	0.26	0.33	0.72
III−13	0.54	0.52	0.51	0.33	0.24	0.50	0.42	0.11	0.77	0.21	0.25	0.31
III−14	0.29	0.23	0.40	0.12	0.20	0.06	0.38	0.01	0.11	0.61	0.22	0.01
III−15	0.62	0.38	0.75	0.52	0.46	0.24	0.17	0.25	0.30	0.87	0.45	0.43
III−16	0.40	0.33	0.21	0.50	0.31	0.27	0.15	0.09	0.23	0.24	0.72	0.21
III−17	0.63	0.45	0.48	0.75	0.55	0.31	0.17	0.10	0.35	0.49	0.91	0.33
III−18	0.70	0.58	0.50	0.76	0.91	0.29	0.19	0.14	0.51	0.37	0.44	0.78
III−19	0.37	0.19	0.35	0.44	0.23	0.13	−0.09	0.02	0.63	0.12	0.16	0.63
III−20	0.46	0.31	0.34	0.56	0.24	0.32	0.10	0.27	0.28	0.18	0.19	0.69

3. Results of quantitative investigation into the construction of urban aging – friendly communities

(1) Overview of the construction of national urban aging – friendly communities

In general, the average measurement score of Chinese urban aging – friendly communities is 64.02 points, which suggests that there is still a certain gap between the optimal state and the actual needs of the elderly. The standard deviation is 11.57, indicating that the degree of being aging – friendly varies in different communities.

Table 5   Results of quantitative investigation into urban aging-friendly communities in China

Overall indicators	Mean value (Standard deviation)	First-level indicators	Mean value (Standard deviation)	Second-level indicators	Mean value (Standard deviation)	Sample size
Aging-friendly communities	64.02 (11.57)	Physical environment	30.96 (4.98)	Outdoor space	6.03 (2.04)	2772
				Housing	15.46 (3.00)	2772
				Transportation	9.46 (1.67)	2772
		Social environment	17.98 (4.45)	Skills improvement and re-employment promotion	4.20 (1.92)	2772
				Information exchanges	4.91 (1.92)	2772
				Commercial services for the daily life and health-care of the elderly	8.86 (2.63)	2772
		Cultural environment	15.09 (4.08)	Respect and inclusiveness	7.49 (2.00)	2772
				Integration into society	7.59 (2.83)	2772

In terms of first-level indicators, obvious differences exist in the measurement scores of each indicator. Physical environment has the highest score of

30.96 points (73.19%)[①], followed by cultural environment, 15.09 points (62.10%), and social environment, 17.98 points (53.83%). Among the second-level indicators of the physical environment, housing has the highest score of 15.46 points (86.85%), followed by transportation, 9.46 points (82.26%), and outdoor space, 6.03 points (46.38%). Among the second-level indicators of the social environment, commercial services for the daily life and healthcare of the elderly have the highest score of 8.86 points (61.70%), followed by information exchanges, 4.91 points (48.04%), and skills upgrading and re-employment promotion, 4.20 points (47.62%). Among the second-level indicators of the cultural environment, respect and inclusiveness for the elderly have the highest score of 7.49 points (65.41%), followed by integration into society, 7.59 points (59.07%).

Generally speaking, the construction quality of urban aging-friendly communities is not high in China, and there is still a certain gap from the optimal state. Meanwhile, an obvious construction gap exists between different communities, which reflects the imbalance in the construction of the aging-friendly communities in China. In terms of sub-indicators, there are also significant differences in the measurement scores of each, indicating that there are structural weaknesses in the construction of aging-friendly communities. The most prominent shortcoming among first-level indicators is social environment, followed by cultural environment and physical environment. The most prominent shortcoming among second-level indicators of a physical environment is outdoor space, followed by transportation and housing. The most prominent shortcoming among second-level indicators of social environment is skills improvement and re-employment promotion, followed by information exchanges, and commercial services for the daily life and healthcare of the elderly. The relatively prominent shortcoming of the cultural environment is integration into society, followed by respect and inclusiveness.

---

① The percentage in brackets is the standardized measurement score.

(2) Heterogeneity analysis of the construction of the urban aging-friendly communities

① Uneven regional construction of the aging-friendly communities

According to the standards of the National Bureau of Statistics, this paper divides the sample into eastern, central, western and northeastern regions, aiming to investigate the construction of urban aging-friendly communities in different regions. A total of 1,745 observation samples are from the eastern region, including Shanghai City, Hebei Province, Shandong Province and Guangdong province; 234 observation samples are from the central region, including Henan Province; 513 observation samples are from the western region, including Sichuan Province and Shaanxi province; and 280 observation samples are from northeastern China, including Liaoning Province. The results show that there are significant differences in the measurement scores of aging-friendly communities in different regions. The eastern region has the highest score (66.66 points), followed by the western region (60.76 points), the central region (58.78 points) and the northeastern region (57.92 points). The results of sub-indicator measurement are basically the same as those of overall indicator measurement, with slight differences. In terms of physical environment, the eastern region has the highest score (31.88 points), followed by the central region (30.15 points), the eastern region (29.57 points) and the western region (28.92 points). In terms of social environment, the eastern region has the highest score (18.89 points), followed by the western region (16.87 points), the central region (16.43 points) and the northeastern region (15.57 points). In terms of cultural environment, the eastern region has the highest score (15.88 points), followed by the western region (14.96 points), the northeastern region (12.78 points) and the central region (12.20 points).

Table 6   **Overview of the construction of national urban aging-friendly communities in different regions**

Region	Overall indicators	Mean value (Standard deviation)	First-level indicators	Mean value (Standard deviation)	Observation sample size
Eastern region	Aging-friendly communities	66.66 (11.35)	Physical environment	31.88 (4.70)	1745
			Social environment	18.89 (4.57)	1745
			Cultural environment	15.88 (3.89)	1745
Central region	Aging-friendly communities	58.78 (8.80)	Physical environment	30.15 (4.21)	234
			Social environment	16.43 (3.52)	234
			Cultural environment	12.20 (3.23)	234
Western region	Aging-friendly communities	60.76 (11.45)	Physical environment	28.92 (5.70)	513
			Social environment	16.87 (3.47)	513
			Cultural environment	14.96 (4.25)	513
Northeastern region	Aging-friendly communities	57.92 (9.72)	Physical environment	29.57 (4.34)	280
			Social environment	15.57 (4.27)	280
			Cultural environment	12.78 (3.62)	280

Overall, there are significant regional differences in the construction of urban aging-friendly communities. Measurement results of overall indicators and sub-indicators present the spacial pattern of "relatively high in the eastern region, followed by the western region, and low in the central and northeastern region". This finding is consistent with the previous research result of "a decline in the central and northeastern regions of China" in terms of basic public services. [1][2]

② Economies of scale analysis of the construction of the urban aging-friendly communities

The sample cities are divided into megacities, supercities, type Ⅰ large

---

[1] An Husen, and Yin Guangwei. "Central Region Falling: Phenomenon and the Conjecture of Its Internal Mechanism", *Journal of Zhongnan University of Economics and Law*. 2009 (1): 3 – 8.

[2] Pan Wenxuan. "Central Region Falling Phenomenon of Public Service: Manifestations, Causes and Countermeasures", *Hubei Social Sciences*, 2012 (4): 61 – 64.

cities, type II large cities and other small and medium-sized cities according to the city size standards released by the Ministry of Housing and Urban-Rural Development of the People's Republic of China, and the construction of aging-friendly communities in cities with different population sizes is investigated.[①] It should be noted that population in this standard refers to a permanent urban population, excluding county and rural populations. This indicator can not only be used to measure city sizes, but also serve as an important threshold for the construction of subways, hospitals and other basic public facilities in a city. Besides, it is also a main factor to consider while determining whether a "zero threshold for household registration" is feasible. Therefore, this indicator is often used as a dividing standard to analyse city sizes and public service supply due to its strong correlation with basic facilities and public services. According to this standard, the research samples are divided into those in megacities, supercities, type I large cities, type II large cities, and small and medium-sized cities. A total of 971 observation samples are collected from 2 megacities, namely Shanghai City and Guangzhou City; a total of 308 observation samples are collected from 5 supercities, namely Chengdu City, Zhengzhou City, Shenyang City, Xi'an City and Jinan City; a total of 136 observation samples are collected from 2 type I large cities, namely Dalian City and Shijiazhuang City; a total of 542 observation samples are collected from 18 type II large cities, mainly developed the urban areas in provinces; a total of 815 observation samples are collected from 30 small and medium-sized cities. The results show that, at different population levels, there is a positive relationship between the size of

---

[①] According to city size dividing standards by the Ministry of Housing and Urban-Rural Development, megacities refer to those with a permanent population of more than 10 million; supercities are those with 5 to 10 million; type I large cities are with 3 to 5 million; type II large cities are those with 1 to 3 million; and small and medium-sized cities refer to those with less than 1 million. According to the Statistical Yearbook of Urban Construction 2019 released by the Ministry of Housing and Urban-Rural Development, there are currently 6 megacities, 11 supercities, 13 type I large cities, and more than 60 type II large cities in China.

urban population and the construction of aging-friendly communities, the larger the population, the higher the construction level of aging-friendly communities; and the smaller the population size, the lower the construction level of aging-friendly communities. The scores of aging-friendly communities are 72.23, 64.01, 68.46, 58.25 and 57.33 points in megacities, supercities, type I large cities, type II large cities, and small and medium-sized cities, respectively. As for first-level indicators, their scores are 33.82, 31.05, 32.55, 28.92 and 28.60 points, respectively in terms of the physical environment, 20.62, 17.23, 20.77, 16.06 and 15.91 in terms of social environment, and 17.79, 15.73, 15.14, 13.27 and 12.83 in terms of cultural environment.

Table 7   Construction of aging-friendly communities in cities of different sizes

City size	Overall indicators	Mean value (Standard deviation)	First-level indicators	Mean value (Standard deviation)	Sample size
Megacities	Aging-friendly communities	72.23 (8.73)	Physical environment	33.82 (3.68)	971
			Social environment	20.62 (4.07)	971
			Cultural environment	17.79 (2.73)	971
Supercities	Aging-friendly communities	64.01 (11.48)	Physical environment	31.05 (5.19)	308
			Social environment	17.23 (4.26)	308
			Cultural environment	15.73 (4.29)	308
Type I large cities	Aging-friendly communities	68.46 (8.91)	Physical environment	32.55 (4.02)	136
			Social environment	20.77 (4.02)	136
			Cultural environment	15.14 (3.27)	136
Type II large cities	Aging-friendly communities	58.25 (10.13)	Physical environment	28.92 (5.18)	542
			Social environment	16.06 (3.36)	542
			Cultural environment	13.27 (3.85)	542
Other small and medium-sized cities	Aging-friendly communities	57.33 (9.11)	Physical environment	28.6 (4.37)	815
			Social environment	15.91 (3.75)	815
			Cultural environment	12.83 (3.62)	815

In general, the overall construction level of urban aging-friendly communities basically presents an increasing trend with the increase of urban population size. On the contrary, it decreases as the urban population size dwindles. The changes of each sub-indicator are the same as those of the overall one. On the one hand, this change rule is basically consistent with the fact that the pension support system in megacities is relatively sound due to its earlier construction. On the other, it also reflects the possibility of urban economies of scale in the construction of aging-friendly communities. That is, the input-output efficiency may go higher with a higher degree of population agglomeration in cities. It should be noted that the measurement score of aging-friendly communities in supercities is lower than that in type I large cities, which may result from the large influx of youth into supercities, the relatively slow aging speed, and the suppressed demand for the construction of pension systems. Although most type-I large cities, similar to supercities, are provincial capitals, they have a much smaller youth population and a faster aging process. Therefore, they build pension systems at a faster pace than supercities.

III. Conclusions

"Getting old before getting rich" is an important objective fact in the process of population aging in China, leading to insufficient ideological preparation for aging, poor service supply, andan unbalanced supporting structure. [1] The construction of aging-friendly communities can help improve flexibility and functionality in response to aging, and it is a prerequisite for the elderly to "spend their later years at home". This paper puts forward measurement indicators of aging-friendly communities with good reliability and validity, which is suitable for Chinese cities based on the aging-friendly indicator system by

---

[1] Zhou Lingling. *Get Old before Getting Rich: The Path of Chinese Elderly Care*, Reform and Development before Sailing. Beijing: National Academy of Governance Press, 2013.

WHO. Quantitative analysis of urban aging-friendly communities is further conducted using the large national survey data. It is found that the overall construction level of urban aging-friendly communities is not high, and there is still considerable room for improvement to reach the optimal status. Structural shortcomings are outstanding, among which the most prominent one is the social environment, followed by the cultural environment and physical environment. The most prominent shortcoming in a social environment is skills improvement and re-employment promotion, followed by information exchanges, and commercial services for the daily life and healthcare of the elderly. The relatively prominent shortcoming in the cultural environment is the integration of the elderly into society, followed by respect and inclusiveness, and the most prominent shortcoming in the physical environment is outdoor space, followed by transportation and housing. Besides, obvious regional imbalance and urban heterogeneity exist in the construction of aging-friendly communities. Overall, regional imbalance presents the spacial pattern of "relatively high in the eastern region, followed by the western region, and low in the central and northeastern regions", which suggests that the construction level of the aging-friendly communities in the central and northeastern regions is relatively low. The urban heterogeneity shows that the larger the urban population is, the higher the level of aging-friendly community construction is. On the contrary, the smaller the urban population, the lower the level of aging-friendly community construction.

This paper suggests pushing forward related work from the following four aspects so as to overcome the structural shortcomings and weaknesses of the construction of urban aging-friendly communities.

First, we should enhance social and environmental support for the elderly. The focus should be placed on skills upgrading and re-employment promotion for the elderly and addressing such problems in re-employment as lack of skills, age discrimination, lack of channels, and difficulties in protecting their rights and interests. Efforts should also be made to strengthen barrier-free renovation of information exchanges among the elderly, narrow the digital divide, and provide convenient information services for them. Besides, we should improve the commercial services for the daily life and healthcare of the elderly, focus on creating more convenient, higher quality, comprehensive, and continuous commercial services, strengthen the construction of the elderly healthcare service network, promote the optimal allocation of resources and improve the service quality.

Second, we should foster a cultural environment where the elderly are cared for and respected. Efforts should be made to create a cultural environment with respect and inclusiveness for the elderly, actively create opportunities to guide the elderly to participate in social activities and facilitate their integration into society. We should also promote the fine tradition of respecting, caring for, and helping the elderly in the whole society and bring warmth to them by taking concrete measures and helping them solve difficulties, so as to increase their well-being and happiness.

Third, we should enhance physical and environmental support for the elderly. Efforts should be made to strengthen the renovation of outdoor public space, housing, and transportation for the convenience of senior citizens and conduct barrier-free construction. In the outdoor public space, the mobility and safety of the elderly should be taken into account. Targeted renovation for the convenience of senior citizens should be carried out to create a safe, comfortable and convenient living environment for them. Barrier-free renovation of urban roads, public transport vehicles, passenger depots and expressway service areas should be strengthened. For example, clear and obvious service guidance signs for the elderly should be set up, and health codes suitable for the elderly shall be introduced to improve convenience and safety in transportation.

In addition, in view of the problems of regional and urban imbalance, it is suggested toincrease further the support for the construction of aging-friendly communities in central and northeastern regions and small and medium-sized cities, optimize the supporting facilities and resources for the elderly, encourage and introduce the participation of social forces so as to jointly promote the continuous improvement of the construction level and quality of aging-friendly communities and strengthen the sense of fulfilment, engagement and satisfaction of the elderly.

Chapter 4 Chinese Modernization and Chinese Experience of Economic Development

Simulation Analysis of Chinese Modernization and China's Real Estate Tax Policy

Lou Feng[*]

I. Introduction

With the prosperity of the real estate market in the past decade, China has been actively discussing the imposition of property tax or real estate tax to stabilize the real estate market. The report of the 20th National Congress of the People's Republic of China proposed that we should improve the distribution system, adhere to the principle of distribution according to work and the coexistence of multiple distribution methods, adhere to the principle of getting more for more work, encourage hard work to become rich, promote fair opportunities, increase the income of low-income people, expand middle-income groups, and standardize the order of income distribution. Among them, property income based on real estate is an indispensable channel to increase residents' income.

The property tax is quite common in many developed countries and has

---

[*] Lou Feng, Professor and Researcher, Head of Department of Economic Analysis and Forecasting, Institute of Quantitative and Technical Economics, CASS

gradually become the main tax source for the government to provide public goods (such as public schools, police systems, etc.). At present, China's economy has gradually shifted from focusing on the speed of economic growth to focusing more on the quality of economic development. As the foundation and important pillar of national governance, the fiscal and tax system has always played a fundamental, institutional and protective role in the governance of the country. How to better play the fiscal and tax policies such as real estate tax, promote the high-quality development of China's economy, improve the distribution system, regulate the income distribution mechanism and other issues have become an important topic of concern from all walks of life.

As early as 2011, the real estate tax reform began to pilot in Shanghai and Chongqing, marking the official launch of China's real estate tax reform. The Third Plenary Session of the 18th CPC Central Committee "the decision of the CPC Central Committee on several major issues of comprehensively deepening reform" proposed to "speed up the legislation of real estate tax and promote the reform in time", which provided a legal basis for China's real estate tax reform. In 2017, the 19th National Congress of the Communist Party of China clearly proposed to "deepen the reform of the tax system and improve the local tax system". At the same time, the government work report in 2018 proposed to "steadily promote the legislation of real estate tax". The 2022 government work report clearly put forward "do a good job in the legislation of real estate tax and environmental protection tax", requiring that the real estate tax reform should be carried out first, which shows that China's real estate tax reform is speeding up. At present, it is still a controversial issue whether to promote the pilot projects in Shanghai and Chongqing to the whole country and comprehensively levy real estate tax throughout the country. The experience of developed countries such as the United States and the OECD shows that real estate tax plays an important role in controlling house prices and curbing some speculation[1]. Therefore, the outstanding question is, if China implements the real estate tax, how will each family be affected under this new reform? Their out-of-pocket will increase because of the new tax. Will it make their life worse? How will China's national economy be affected? Therefore, how to design an appropriate real estate tax reform plan will be the key to the success of this policy. Using the latest Chinese input-output table and other data, this paper constructs a computable general equilibrium (CGE) model including residents' real estate tax, and simulates and analyzes the possible results of different real estate tax reform policies.

II. Journals Reviewed

At present, the research on the impact of real estate tax reform at home and abroad mainly includes the following aspects.

First, the impact of the real estate tax reform on local finance: Hu Hongshu found that the introduction of the real estate tax will not cause an unbearable gap in local finance, but also bring sustainable and stable income to the local government, so as to effectively alleviate the financial difficulties of the local government[2]; Wei Zhichao and Yi Gang conducted empirical analysis on the basis of relevant theories and found that as long as the government reform measures are appropriate, the property tax reform will contribute to the transformation of government functions[3]; The research group of the Ministry of Finance believes that with the continuous advancement of urbanization, real estate tax

---

[1] Kuang weida, Zhu Yong, Liu Jiangtao, "The impact of real estate tax on house prices: evidence from OECD countries", *Finance and Trade Economy*, 2012 (5).

[2] Hu Hongshu, "Research on local financial gap after property tax", *Finance and Trade Economy*, 2011 (10).

[3] Wei Zhichao, "Yi Gang, Property tax reform and local public finance", *Economic Research*, 2006 (3).

revenue will become an important channel to broaden the financial revenue of local governments. ①

Secondly, the impact of the real estate tax reform on house prices: Chen Changchang and Zong Jiafeng believe that the real estate tax will reduce the long-term equilibrium price of residential assets, but in the short term, it will increase the rent, reduce the housing supply, and produce efficiency loss②; Zhu Runxi believes that the collection of property tax will not significantly inhibit house prices③; Chang Junfeng believes that under the condition that China's social welfare and security system is not perfect, it is not appropriate to levy real estate tax fully. The full levy of real estate tax will only reduce people's happiness index and have little effect on curbing high house prices, but the differential levy of real estate tax will play a role in curbing speculative investment in real estate④; Bai Chongen et al. used the data of Shanghai and Chongqing to explore the impact of the real estate tax reform on house prices. The results showed that the real estate tax reform reduced the average house prices in Shanghai by 15%, but increased the average house prices in Chongqing by 11%. ⑤

Thirdly, the impact of real estate tax reform on Residents' income distribution: Zhan Peng and Li Shi found that real estate tax reform can effectively reduce residents' income inequality by using urban household survey data⑥; Hu Haisheng et al. simulated and analyzed the impact of real estate tax reform on

---

① Research Group of Resource Tax, "Real estate tax reform and impact analysis on local finance, resource tax, real estate tax reform and impact analysis on local finance", *Financial Research*, 2013 (7).

② Chen Changchang, Zong Jiafeng, "Real estate tax and housing asset price: theoretical analysis and policy evaluation", *Research on Finance and Trade*, 2004 (1).

③ Zhu Runxi, "Motivation and orientation of levying property tax", *Tax Research*, 2006 (9).

④ Chang Junfeng, "Empirical analysis and Discussion on the impact of real estate tax on house prices since the pilot", *Economic System Reform*, 2013 (5).

⑤ Chong En Bai, Qi Li, Min Ouyang, Property Taxes and Home Prices: A Tale of Two Cities [J]. *Journal of Econometrics*, 2014 (1).

⑥ Zhan Peng, Li Shi, real estate tax and income inequality in China [J]. *Economic Rrends*, 2015 (7).

Residents' income gap under different policy schemes by using computable general equilibrium model①; Huang Xiao believes that the real estate tax not only affects residents' income and wealth, but also improves the housing and public services of low-and middle-income groups through transfer payment, which has the function of adjusting income distribution②. On the contrary, Xia Shangmo believed that the real estate tax not only could not regulate unfair income distribution, but also would produce welfare losses③; Lai and David analyzed the welfare impact of property tax based on the extended Frank model. The results show that the real estate appreciation will reduce the welfare of real estate owners, but if the property tax is also reduced, the situation will become worse for permanent residents. ④

Finally, the impact of real estate tax reform on macro-economy: Li Yan⑤, Luo Yongmin and Wu Wenzhong⑥ simulated and analyzed the impact of real estate tax reform on major macroeconomic variables by constructing a DSGE model including real estate tax. Liang Yunfang et al. simulated and analyzed the impact of real estate capital tax on real estate industry and macro-economy by using the CGE model. The results show that the increase of real estate capital tax rate can stimulate the development of real estate industry, while the decrease of real estate capital tax rate is conducive to the optimization of the internal struc-

---

① Hu Haisheng, Liu Hongmei, Wang Keqiang, "Comparative study on China's real estate tax reform scheme-Based on Computable General Equilibrium (CGE) Analysis", *Financial Research*, 2012 (12).

② Huang Xiao, "Mechanism, conditions and reform direction of real estate tax regulating income distribution", *Western Forum*, 2014 (1).

③ Xia Shangmo, "Real estate tax: can it adjust the unfair income distribution and curb the rise of house prices", *Tax Research*, 2011 (4).

④ Fu-Chuan Lai, David Merriman, "Housing appreciation (depreciation) and owners welfare", *Journal of Housing Economics*, 2010 (1) .

⑤ Li Yan, "Macroeconomic effect of combined real estate tax reform-Analysis of DSGE framework considering residential and commercial housing", *Economic and Management Research*, 2019 (12).

⑥ Luo Yongmin, Wu Wenzhong, "Macroeconomic effects of real estate tax reform and house price change-numerical simulation analysis based on DSGE model", *Financial Research*, 2012 (5).

ture of real estate industry[1]; Zodrow believes that the collection of real estate tax reduces the capital income, which has a certain impact on the real estate market and macro-economy. M. Sullivan[2] used the urban general equilibrium effect model to study the efficiency effect and distribution effect of real estate tax. The results show that in the reform of tax policy, landowners benefit, while the interests of ordinary residents suffer. [3]

It can be seen from the previous research literature at home and abroad that the real estate tax reform is a systematic project, and its reform effect will not only affect a specific industrial sector, but also affect all aspects of the social and economic system. However, looking back on the previous studies, most of them analyze the impact of the real estate tax reform from a single perspective. Although there are also studies on the impact of real estate tax reform on the overall national economy, such studies lack micro analysis of the industrial sector. Therefore, based on the previous research, this paper constructs a computable general equilibrium (CGE) model including residents' real estate tax, and analyzes the impact of real estate tax reform on China's national economy from the micro, meso and macro perspectives. Compared with previous studies, the innovations of this paper mainly include: First, this paper constructs a CGE model including real estate tax based on the latest 2017 China input-output table and other data. In the model, the industrial sector is divided into 26 sectors, which can well analyze the specific impact of the real estate tax reform on the industrial level; Second, this paper divides urban residents and rural residents into five categories according to their income level, which can more accurately analyze the specific impact of real estate tax reform on residents of differ-

---

[1] Liang Yunfang, Zhang Tongbin, Gao Lingling, "Empirical study on the impact of real estate capital tax on real estate industry and national economy", *Statistical Research*, 2013 (5).

[2] Mieszkowski, PeterM, Zodrow, George B, "The New View of The Property Tax: A Reformulation", *Regional Science and Urban Economics*, 1986 (16).

[3] M. Sullivan, "The general equilibrium effects of the industrial property tax: Incidence and excess burden", *Regional Science and Urban Economics*, 1984 (4).

ent income classes. At the same time, this paper also calculates the Gini coefficient, which can be used to analyze the impact of different real estate tax reform policies on China's Gini coefficient; Thirdly, theoretically, based on the two-stage model theory, this paper expounds the theoretical mechanism of the impact of real estate tax on the national economy. Empirically, the impact effect of the possible real estate tax reform scheme is calculated, and the comprehensive effect of the real estate tax reform scheme on the national economy is obtained, which makes up for the deficiency of the existing research.

III. Theoretical Aanalysis

According to the two-stage model theory developed by Jaecheol et al. [1], it is assumed that there are only two periods for the sales of commercial houses, and all commercial houses in these two periods are homogeneous. Since the sales of commercial houses only last for two periods, the second period is the last period. Therefore, the economic life of commercial houses produced in this period is shortened to a period.

q_t is assumed to represent the output of commercial housing constructed in the t period and Q_t is the inventory of commercial housing in the t period, and $Q_t = q_t + q_{t-1}$. In this model, the manufacturer decides whether to sell or lease commercial houses at the same time of production, s_t is set as the number of commercial houses sold by the manufacturer in the t period and l_t is the number of commercial houses leased by the manufacturer in the t period, and $q_t = s_t + l_t$. The prices of commercial houses rented and sold price by manufacturers in the t period are p_{lt} and p_{st}, respectively, since The demand function of commercial housing rental is $p_{lt} = p(Q_t)$. When the number of commercial housing rent-

---

[1] Kim Jae-Cheol, Kim Min-Young, Chun Se-Hak, "Property tax and its effects on strategic behavior of leasing and selling for a durable-goods monopolist", *International Review of Economics and Finance*, 2014 (1).

al is q, then the income function is $\psi(q) = p(q)q$.

Assuming that the real estate tax is levied on the owners of commercial houses, and assuming that the real estate tax rate r ($r \geq 0$) is fixed and proportional, then

$$\hat{\Pi}_{1r} = (1+r)\Pi_1$$

$$\hat{\Pi}_{2r} = (1+r)\Pi_2$$

$$c_{1r} = (1+r)c$$

Where, Π_1 and Π_2 are the profit functions of the first period and the second period, respectively, and c are the marginal production cost of commercial housing. Since the second period is the last period, there is no arbitrage:

$$(1+r)p_{st} = p_{lt}$$

$$\begin{aligned}
\Pi_2 &= \Pi_2(q_2, s_1, l_1 : r) \\
&= (1+r)\{p_{s2}s_2 + p_{l2}(l_2 + l_1) - rp_{s2}(l_2 + l_1) - cq_2\} \\
&= (1+r)p_{s2}s_2 + (1+r)p_{l2}(l_2 + l_1) \\
&\quad - (1+r)rp_{s2}(l_2 + l_1) - (1+r)cq_2 \\
&= p_{l2}s_2 + s_2(l_2 + l_1) - c_r q_2 \\
&= \psi(Q_2) - p(Q_2)s_1 - c_r q_2
\end{aligned}$$

Since the second phase is the last phase, there is no difference₂ between l_2 and s_2, so it is assumed that $s_2 = l_2$.

In the first phase, the selling price is different from the price without tax. If consumers buy commercial houses and use two phases, they must spend $(1+r)p_{s1} + \beta r p_{s2}$; On the other hand, if it leases a commercial house for two periods, it needs to spend $p(q_1) + \beta p(Q_2)$. Therefore, in the absence of arbitrage, so,

$$(1+r)p_{s1} + \beta r p_{s2} = p(q_1) + \beta p(Q_2)$$

Further arrangements can be obtained: $(1+r)p_{s1} = p(q_1) + \dfrac{\beta p(Q_2)}{1+r}$

$$\hat{\Pi}_r = \hat{\Pi}_r(s_1, l_1 : r)$$

$$= (1 + r)(p_{s1}s_1 + p_{l1}l_1 - rp_{s1}l_1 - cq_1 + \beta \hat{\Pi}_{2r})$$

$$= \psi(q_1) + \beta p(\hat{Q}_2)(\frac{q_1}{1+r} + \hat{q}_2) - c_r(q_1 + \beta \hat{q}_2)$$

By comparing the profit function with the profit function without tax, we find that they are very similar in function form. The difference is that the production in the first period needs to be discounted $1 + r$ in the second period.

Now let's discuss the impact of property tax on production and welfare. For ease of treatment, we assume marginal production cost $c = 0$, and consider two specific conditions below. One is when the tax rate is low enough. The other is when the demand is linear. so, the Pair equation

$$\psi'(Q_2) - \frac{r}{1+r}p'(Q_2)q_1 = c_r$$

$$\psi'(q_1) - \frac{\beta r}{1+r}p(Q_2) = (1-\beta)c_r$$

For differentiation, there are:

$$D \begin{bmatrix} \dfrac{\partial q_1^*}{\partial r} \\ \dfrac{\partial Q_2^*}{\partial r} \end{bmatrix} = \frac{1}{1+r} \begin{bmatrix} \beta p(Q_2^*) \\ p'(Q_2^*)q_1^* \end{bmatrix}$$

Where, $D = \begin{bmatrix} (1+r)\psi''(q_1^*) - \beta r p'(Q_2^*) & \\ -rp'(Q_2^*) & (1+r)\psi''(Q_2^*) - rq_1^* p''(Q_2^*) \end{bmatrix}$

So:

$$\frac{\partial q_1^*}{\partial r} = \frac{1}{1+r} \frac{\begin{vmatrix} \beta p(Q_2^*) & -\beta r p'(Q_2^*) \\ p'(Q_2^*)q_1^* & (1+r)\psi''(Q_2^*) - rq_1^* p''(Q_2^*) \end{vmatrix}}{|D|}$$

$$\frac{\partial Q_2^*}{\partial r} = \frac{1}{1+r} \frac{\begin{vmatrix} (1+r)\psi''(q_1^*) - \beta r p'(Q_2^*) \\ -rp'(Q_2^*) & p'(Q_2^*)q_1^* \end{vmatrix}}{|D|}$$

Although, it is usually impossible to determine the positive and negative of $\frac{\partial q_1^*}{\partial r}$ and $\frac{\partial Q_2^*}{\partial r}$, we can predict its symbol in the following special cases. In the case of linear demand ($q(p) = a - bp$), the collection of property tax will reduce the attractiveness of output in the first period, resulting in delayed production, so, As a result, rental prices fell in two periods, namely $p_1^* > p_2^*$, and

$$\frac{\partial p_{l1}^*}{\partial r} = -a\beta \frac{(\beta r^2 + 4r + 4)}{h(r)^2} < 0$$

$$\frac{\partial p_{l2}^*}{\partial r} = -a \frac{(4-3\beta)r^2 + 4(2-\beta)r + 4}{h(r)^2} < 0$$

In addition, the sales price in both periods decreased with the increase of tax rate.

$$\frac{\partial p_{s1}^*}{\partial r} = -2a \frac{(4-\beta)r^2 + 2(4+3\beta-\beta^2)r + 4(1+2\beta)}{h(r)^2} < 0$$

$$\frac{\partial p_{s2}^*}{\partial r} = -a \frac{(4-\beta)r^2 + 4(4-\beta)r + 12}{h(r)^2} < 0$$

Where, $h(r) \equiv 4(1+r)^2 - \beta r^2 > 0$.

It can be seen that the collection of real estate tax will not only reduce the rent price, but also reduce the sales price.

When collecting property tax, consumersurplus CS^*, manufacturer profit Π^*, tax revenue Π^* and social welfare TR^* can be expressed as:

$$CS^* = \int_0^{q_1^*} p(q)dq - (p_{s1}^* s_1^* + p_{l1}^* l_1^*) - rp_{s1}^* s_1^*$$

$$+ \beta(\int_0^{Q_2^*} p(q)dq - p_{l2}^*(q_2^* + l_1^*) - rp_{s2}^* s_1^*)$$

$$\Pi^* = (p_{l1}^* q_1^* + \beta p_{l2}^* (\frac{q_1^*}{1+r} + q_2^*))/(1+r)$$

$$TR^* = rp_{s1}^* q_1^* + \beta rp_{s2}^* Q_2^*$$

$$SW^* = \int_0^{q_1^*} p(q)\,dq + \beta \int_0^{Q_2^*} p(q)\,dq$$

In the case of linear demand, the impact of real estate tax on consumer surplus, manufacturer profits, tax revenue and social welfare is as follows:

$$\frac{\partial CS^*}{\partial r} = \frac{a^2 \beta v}{b} \frac{(12 - 15\beta + 4\beta^2)r^3 + (36 - 35\beta + 5\beta^2)r^2}{h(r)^3}$$

$$+ \frac{a^2 \beta v}{b} \frac{12(3 - 2\beta)r + 4(3 - \beta)}{h(r)^3} > 0$$

$$\frac{\partial \Pi^*}{\partial r} = -\frac{a^2}{b} \frac{(4 - \beta)r^2 + 2(4 + 3\beta - \beta^2)r + 4(1 + 2\beta)}{h(r)^2} < 0$$

$$\frac{\partial TR^*}{\partial r} = \frac{a^2}{b} \frac{(16 - 16\beta + 11\beta^2 - 4\beta^3)r^4 + (64 + 4\beta^2 - 16\beta - 4\beta^3)r^3}{h(r)^3}$$

$$+ \frac{a^2}{b} \frac{24(4 + 2\beta - \beta^2)r^2 + 16(4 + 5\beta - \beta^2)r + 16(1 + 2\beta)}{h(r)^3} > 0$$

$$\frac{\partial SW^*}{\partial r} = \frac{a^2 \beta v}{b} \frac{(4 - 5\beta)r^3 + (12 - 17\beta - \beta^2)r^2 + 12(1 - 2\beta)r + 4(1 - 3\beta)}{h(r)^3}$$

It can be seen that the collection of real estate tax increases consumers' surplus and tax revenue, and reduces manufacturers' profits. Although the real estate tax increases the tax, the impact on social welfare is ambiguous. If $\beta = 1$, then $\frac{\partial SW^*}{\partial r} < 0$, and if $\beta \approx 0$, then $\frac{\partial SW^*}{\partial r} > 0$. In addition, some values of β, SW^* may decrease first and then increase.

IV. The CGE model setting of Chinese resident real estate tax

The social accounting matrix table (SAM) of residential real estate tax constructed in this paper is compiled on the basis of the latest input-output table in 2017, combined with data such as China Statistical Yearbook and China Household Survey Yearbook. In this Sam, there are 26 production activity departments, including agriculture, mining, manufacturing, power, heat, gas and water production and supply, construction, wholesale, retail, transportation, warehousing and postal services, accommodation, catering, telecommunications, radio and television and satellite transmission services, Internet and related services, software and information technology services Monetary and other financial services, capital market services, insurance, real estate, leasing, business services, scientific research and technical services, water conservancy, environment and public facilities management, resident services, repair and other services, education, health and social work, culture, sports and entertainment, public management, social security and social organizations. Residents are divided into 10 groups: urban low-income households, urban lower middle-income households, urban middle-income households, urban upper middle-income households, urban high-income households, rural low-income households, rural lower middle-income households, rural middle-income households, rural Upper middle-income households and rural high-income households. Taxes are divided into value-added tax, business tax, cultivated land occupation tax, urban maintenance and construction tax, deed tax, stamp tax, value-added land tax, urban land use tax, enterprise income tax, individual income tax, operating real estate tax, residents' non-operating real estate tax, tariff and other taxes. In addition, it also includes accounts of enterprises, governments, investment savings, changes in deposits and loans, foreign accounts, etc. , In order to simulate the specific impact of real estate tax on China's macro economy and sectoral economy, based on previous studies[1][2][3], and combined with the possibility of real estate tax implementation in

---

① Zhang Ping, Hou Yilin, tax paying capacity, tax burden distribution and redistribution effect of real estate tax [J]. economic research, 2016 (12).

② Li Wen, Quantitative calculation of China's real estate tax revenue and feasibility analysis of acting as the main tax type of local tax [J]. Finance and Trade Economy, 2014 (9).

③ Liu Jindong, Wang Shengfa, Calculation of the progressivity and sufficiency of the new real estate tax-micro simulation based on household survey data [J]. Finance and Economics, 2015 (12).

China, this paper sets up the following eight policy simulation schemes:

Policy simulation scheme (S1): Levy 2.0% real estate tax on the real estate of urban residents;

Policy simulation scheme (S2): Levy 2.0% real estate tax on the real estate of all residents;

Policy simulation scheme (S3): levy property tax on urban residents under the condition of cumulative property tax;

Policy simulation scheme (S4): levy property tax on all residents under the condition of cumulative property tax;

Policy simulation scheme (S5): levy property tax on urban residents under the condition of per capita exemption of $20m^2$;

Policy simulation scheme (S6): levy property tax on all residents under the condition of per capita exemption of $20m^2$;

Policy simulation scheme (S7): levy property tax on urban residents under the condition of per capita exemption;

Policy simulation scheme (S8): levy property tax on all residents under the condition of per capita exemption;

By setting policy simulation scheme I and scheme II, we can clearly compare the impact of levying property tax only on urban residents or all residents on the national economy without considering other factors. At the same time, considering the various difficulties that may exist in the process of China's real estate tax collection and the possible real estate tax measures, various policy simulation schemes under the conditions of cumulative real estate tax, per capita exemption area and per capita exemption amount are set up respectively, so as to simulate better and analyze the impact of different real estate tax policies on the national economy.

V Analysis of simulation results

1. Macroeconomic impact results

Table 2　　　　Impact of real estate tax reform on main macroeconomic indicators (unit: %)

Simulation scheme	GDP	output	export	import	investment	consumption of residents	government consumption
S1	-0.118	-0.620	-1.315	-1.443	-1.764	-5.693	18.048
S2	-0.130	-0.739	-1.514	-1.662	-2.380	-5.877	20.371
S3	-0.213	-1.256	-2.636	-2.894	-3.828	-11.301	37.112
S4	-0.233	-1.510	-3.057	-3.356	-5.220	-11.572	42.078
S5	-0.054	-0.279	-0.571	-0.627	-0.865	-2.408	7.990
S6	-0.061	-0.339	-0.669	-0.734	-1.198	-2.455	9.107
S7	-0.107	-0.563	-1.189	-1.305	-1.612	-5.137	16.340
S8	-0.113	-0.621	-1.282	-1.407	-1.932	-5.179	17.418

Table 2 shows: as a kind of tax directly levied on real estate holders (in this model, real estate holders are residents), real estate tax is essentially a kind of property tax. The collection of real estate tax increases the cost of residents holding real estate and reduces residents' total consumption to varying degrees. At the same time, in the real economic system, supply and demand always affect each other. The reduction of residents' total consumption will have varying degrees of negative impact on the change of total output. At the same time, the reduction of the total output makes investors worry about the expectation of future economic development, resulting in a decline in the level of investment. For total import and total export, as a large manufacturing country, China needs to import a large number of raw materials from abroad every year. On the one hand, the reduction of the total output reduces the domestic demand for imported raw materials, on the other hand, it reduces the export of domestic products. In addition, the reduction of total consumption of residents also reduces the demand for imported products to a certain extent. For government departments, the collection of real estate tax widens the government's tax channels, increases the government's fiscal revenue, and promotes the increase of the government's total consumption to a certain extent. As an important indicator of macro-economy, the collection of real estate tax reduces the real GDP in varying degrees. Comparing the results of eight policy simulation schemes, it can be found that S3 and S4 change greatly, that is, the implementation of cumulative real estate tax will have a great negative impact on the overall macro-economy. The possible reason is that with the increase of the area of real estate held by residents, At the same time, in reality, the value of residents' real estate accounts for a considerable proportion of the total assets of residents' families. The increasing pressure of residents' tax payments is bound to affect the behavior and decision-making of families and ultimately the development of the whole macro economy.

2. Impact on sectoral output results

Table 3 Impact onsectoral output (unit: %)①

	S1	S2	S3	S4	S5	S6	S7	S8
sector1	-2.122	-2.430	-4.313	-4.885	-0.935	-1.061	-1.921	-2.040
sector2	-1.676	-1.935	-3.341	-3.890	-0.721	-0.848	-1.514	-1.636
sector3	-1.633	-1.889	-3.258	-3.799	-0.703	-0.828	-1.476	-1.595

---

① In Table 3, sector1-sector26 respectively represent: agriculture, mining, manufacturing, production and supply of electricity, heat, gas and water, construction, wholesale, retail, transportation, warehousing and postal services, accommodation, catering, telecommunications, radio and television and satellite transmission services, Internet and related services, software and information technology services Monetary and other financial services, capital market services, insurance, real estate, leasing, business services, scientific research and technical services, water conservancy, environment and public facilities management, resident services, repair and other services, education, health and social work, culture, sports and entertainment, public management, social security and social organizations.

Continued

	S1	S2	S3	S4	S5	S6	S7	S8
sector4	-1.684	-1.826	-3.320	-3.618	-0.716	-0.785	-1.520	-1.586
sector5	-1.392	-2.055	-3.153	-4.662	-0.721	-1.079	-1.279	-1.625
sector6	-1.367	-1.596	-2.867	-3.359	-0.630	-0.744	-1.242	-1.352
sector7	-1.710	-1.871	-3.567	-3.897	-0.781	-0.856	-1.553	-1.624
sector8	-0.532	-0.558	-1.110	-1.164	-0.247	-0.261	-0.484	-0.497
sector9	1.781	2.246	3.646	4.638	0.780	1.004	1.611	1.826
sector10	-3.179	-3.103	-6.634	-6.456	-1.450	-1.406	-2.887	-2.844
sector11	-0.976	-0.876	-2.068	-1.855	-0.455	-0.404	-0.888	-0.839
sector12	0.236	0.270	0.408	0.469	0.076	0.088	0.209	0.220
sector13	-1.142	-1.649	-2.600	-3.762	-0.596	-0.872	-1.050	-1.317
sector14	-1.154	-1.223	-2.379	-2.528	-0.521	-0.556	-1.047	-1.081
sector15	-2.173	-2.167	-4.542	-4.496	-0.992	-0.977	-1.973	-1.958
sector16	-4.619	-4.491	-9.610	-9.331	-2.098	-2.028	-4.193	-4.127
sector17	-2.731	-2.881	-5.324	-5.610	-1.144	-1.205	-2.463	-2.520
sector18	-0.792	-1.091	-1.766	-2.448	-0.403	-0.566	-0.726	-0.884
sector19	-0.735	-0.737	-1.508	-1.516	-0.331	-0.334	-0.667	-0.669
sector20	1.903	1.826	3.725	3.493	0.778	0.715	1.712	1.650
sector21	12.061	13.693	24.973	28.525	5.309	6.089	10.911	11.669
sector22	-2.371	-2.291	-4.955	-4.759	-1.087	-1.039	-2.154	-2.108
sector23	7.808	9.052	16.471	19.167	3.580	4.191	7.091	7.681
sector24	9.314	10.715	18.637	21.657	4.009	4.700	8.414	9.080
sector25	3.907	4.817	8.467	10.437	1.853	2.298	3.558	3.987
sector26	15.816	17.860	32.559	36.924	7.017	7.999	14.322	15.271

It can be seen from Table 3 that the collection of real estate tax has affected the output of most departments to varying degrees. Among them, the Department with the greatest negative impact is the insurance industry, which has decreased by 4.619%, 4.491%, 9.610%, 9.331%, 2.098%, 2.028%, 4.193% and 4.127%, respectively, under eight different policy schemes; In addition, the collection of property tax has also increased the output of some industrial sectors, mainly including accommodation, Internet and related services, scientific research and technical services, and water conservancy. Environment and public facilities management, education, health and social work, culture, sports and entertainment, public management, social security and social organizations. Among them, the departments with the largest increase in output are public management, social security and social organizations, which increased by 15.816%, 17.860%, 32.559%, 36.924%, 7.017% and 7.999%, respectively, under eight different policies and programmes 14.322%、15.271%; For the real estate sector, under eight different policy schemes, the output of the real estate sector decreased by 2.731%, 2.881%, 5.324%, 5.610%, 1.144%, 1.205%, 2.463% and 2.520%, respectively. In view of the fact that the policy of levying real estate tax increased the cost of residents holding real estate, reduced residents' demand for real estate and reduced the real estate market price to varying degrees, Decreased by 0.284%, 0.379%, 0.629%, 0.850%, 0.142%, 0.194%, 0.260% and 0.311% respectively.

3. Impact on government revenue

Government revenue is an important guarantee for the healthy development of various public utilities. In the CGE model of Chinese resident real estate tax constructed in this paper, the sources of government revenue are mainly various tax revenue, including value-added tax, business tax, cultivated land occupation tax, urban maintenance and construction tax, deed tax, stamp tax, value-added land tax, urban land use tax, enterprise income tax. There are 14 kinds of taxes, such as individual income tax, operating real estate tax, resident non-operating real estate tax, tariff and other taxes. As an important part of government revenue, residents' non operating real estate tax levied on residential real estate owned by residents is bound to increase government revenue. Manifested as: Under eight different policy simulation schemes, government revenue increased by 16.450%, 18.538%, 33.490%, 37.851%,

7.327%, 8.341%, 14.908% and 15.877%, respectively. Among them, S3 and S4 have a large increase, that is, under the implementation of cumulative real estate tax, real estate tax will be levied on urban residents or all residents. The reason is that on the premise of keeping the tax base of real estate tax unchanged, with the continuous increase of residents' real estate value, the amount of real estate tax paid by residents is also increasing, which makes the government revenue of S3 and S4 increase greatly under the conditions of eight policy simulation schemes.

4. Impact on Residents' disposable income and Gini coefficient

Table 4　　Impact on Residents' disposable income and Gini Coefficient (%)

	S1	S2	S3	S4	S5	S6	S7	S8
Urban low-income households	-14.548	-14.228	-11.938	-11.270	0.788	0.943	-11.957	-11.808
Urban middle and lower households	-9.950	-9.610	-11.202	-10.493	-2.047	-1.882	-8.615	-8.457
Urban middle-income households	-8.196	-7.838	-11.594	-10.847	-2.896	-2.723	-7.300	-7.134
Upper middle urban households	-7.387	-7.032	-14.075	-13.334	-3.794	-3.622	-6.780	-6.615
Urban high income household	-6.725	-6.411	-22.513	-21.857	-5.085	-4.933	-6.448	-6.302
Rural low-income households	0.726	-5.182	1.481	-4.327	0.325	-0.126	0.658	0.435
Rural middle and lower households	0.691	-2.080	1.409	-1.882	0.309	-0.349	0.626	0.056
Rural middle-income households	0.617	-1.842	1.260	-2.524	0.276	-0.727	0.560	-0.382
Rural upper middle households	0.605	-1.743	1.233	-3.711	0.270	-1.060	0.548	-0.740
Rural high income household	0.547	-1.308	1.117	-4.638	0.245	-1.070	0.496	-0.797
Gini coefficient	-0.012	-0.006	-0.043	-0.033	-0.010	-0.008	-0.012	-0.010

In the CGE model of Chinese residents' real estate tax constructed in this paper, urban residents and rural residents are divided into five groups according to their income. It can be seen from Table 4 that different types of residents are affected differently by different real estate tax collection policies. Since the four policy simulation schemes S1, S3, S5 and S7 only consider levying property tax on urban residents, the disposable income of rural residents has not been negatively impacted. On the contrary, the disposable income of rural residents has increased to varying degrees. The possible reason is that the model includes the government transfer payment to rural residents. Under other conditions unchanged, the increase of government revenue drives the increase of government transfer payment to rural residents, which increases the disposable income of rural residents to varying degrees.

Comparing the policy simulation results of S1 and S2, it can be found that with the continuous improvement of residents' income levels, the impact of real estate tax is gradually reduced. The possible reason is that with the improvement of residents' income level, residents have more choices in allocating family assets, so the impact of real estate tax on their disposable income is gradually reduced.

Comparing the policy simulation results of S3 and S4, it can be found that with the improvement of residents' income level, the impact of cumulative real estate tax on their disposable income also gradually increases. Among them, the simulation results of rural low-income households in S4 are larger. The possible reason is that their own family assets are relatively small, and the collection of real estate tax increases the family burden. Therefore, the cumulative real estate tax policy has a great impact on the disposable income of rural low-income households.

Comparing the policy simulation results of S5 and S6, it can be found that the collection of real estate tax has no negative impact on the disposable income of urban low-income households. The reason is that the real estate tax is levied under the condition of per capita exemption area implemented in S5 and S6. Due to the small per capita real estate area of urban low-income households, the implementation of the per capita exemption area avoids the collection of real estate tax on urban low-income households.

Comparing the policy simulation results of S7 and S8, it can be found that the real estate tax levied under the condition of per capita exemption reduces the negative impact of direct real estate tax to a certain extent, but it does not fundamentally change the phenomenon that the impact of real estate tax on urban low-income households is greater than that of urban high-income households. For rural residents, it has achieved the expected effect. The disposable income of rural low-income households and lower middle-income households has not been negatively affected. The impact on rural middle-income households, upper middle-income households and high-income households gradually increases with the improvement of income level.

At the same time, this paper also calculates the Gini coefficient index. Under eight different policy schemes, the Gini coefficient decreases by 0.012, 0.006, 0.043, 0.033, 0.010, 0.008, 0.012 and 0.010, respectively. It can be seen that the real estate tax policy has adjusted the wealth income distribution between urban and rural areas to a certain extent, narrowed the income gap between residents, and the implementation of the cumulative real estate tax policy has an obvious promoting effect on narrowing the income gap between residents.

VI Conclusions and policy recommendations

By constructing the CGE model of Chinese residents' real estate tax, this paper simulates and analyzes the impact of real estate tax reform on China's national economy. The policy simulation results show that in the macro-economic aspect, the collection of real estate tax has a negative impact on the actual GDP, total output, total export, total import, total investment and residents' consumption. Among them, the most serious negative impact is the policy simulation scheme 4. That is, under the condition of implementing the cumulative real estate tax, the real estate tax will be levied on all residents. The real GDP, total output, total exports, total imports, total investment and household consumption, decreased by 0.233%, 1.510%, 3.057%, 3.356%, 5.220% and 11.572%, respectively. It has a positive impact on government consumption, and the impact effect shows obvious differences between different real estate tax collection schemes. Among them, the policy simulation scheme IV still has the greatest positive impact on government consumption, which shows that government consumption increases by 42.078%. Comparing the eight policy simulation schemes, it is found that the simulation schemes with less impact on macroeconomic indicators are S5 and S6, that is, under the condition of per capita exemption area, real estate tax will be levied on urban residents or all residents.

In terms of departmental output, the collection of real estate tax increases the cost of real estate holders, reduces the rigid demand of residents for real estate, reduces the output of the real estate sector, and also reduces the real estate price to varying degrees; Among them, the most serious negative impact on the output and price of the real estate sector is policy simulation scheme IV, which shows that the output and price decreased by 5.610% and 0.850% respectively. Compared with the change results of macroeconomic indicators in policy simulation scheme 4, although the scheme can effectively optimize the supply side structure of the real estate sector and reduce real estate prices, it has a great negative impact on the main macroeconomic indicators.

In terms of government revenue, as the beneficiaries of the real estate tax reform policy, the collection of real estate tax has widened the channels of government revenue and increased government revenue. The most obvious increase in government revenue is policy simulation scheme 4. The performance is that the government revenue increased by 37.851%. The substantial increase in government revenue has also led to a significant increase in government consumption, which is reflected in the 42.078% increase in government consumption in policy simulation scheme Ⅳ. At the same time, government expenditure was mostly used in social public utilities and other fields, as shown in the output of public management, social security and social organization departments in policy simulation scheme Ⅳ increased by 36.924%.

In terms of residents' disposable income. There are obvious differences in the impact of different real estate tax collection schemes on Residents' disposable income. Comparing the results of eight policy simulation schemes, it can be found that simulation schemes S6 and S8 have relatively little impact on Residents' disposable income, and reflect the protection of real estate tax policy for low-income people to a certain extent. However, the two policy simulation schemes do not fully achieve the protection of low-income people, so the optimal combination of real estate tax reform policies needs to be carried out, so as to not only effectively implement the real estate tax reform policy, but also properly protect the low-income people.

In terms of the change of the Gini coefficient, the collection of real estate tax has reduced the Gini coefficient to a certain extent and narrowed the gap between urban and rural wealth and income. Comparing the results of eight policy simulation schemes, policy simulation scheme Ⅲ (i. e. levying property tax on urban residents under the condition of cumulative property tax) can effectively reduce the Gini coefficient, which is shown as a decrease of 0.043. However, the policy is only levying property tax on urban residents and cannot reflect the characteristics of tax fairness. Policy simulation 4 (i. e. levying property tax on all residents under the condition of implementing cumulative property tax) is the policy that can effectively reduce the Gini coefficient, which is second only to policy simulation 3. The Gini coefficient decreases by 0.033. However, although the policy can effectively reduce the Gini coefficient, it has a great negative impact on the main macroeconomic indicators. Therefore, the optimal combination of real estate tax reform policies should be made in combination with the scheme design of S6 and S8.

According to the above research conclusions, the following policy suggestions are put forward:

First, orderly promote China's real estate tax reform. At present, the reform of residential real estate tax is only piloted in Shanghai and Chongqing, and has not been fully implemented in the country. Considering the different characteristics of economic and social development in various regions of China, in determining the real estate tax rate, we should adhere to the principle of "adjusting measures to local conditions and implementing policies according to local conditions" to minimize the impact of real estate tax collection on residents. At the same time, in the process of collecting real estate tax, we should adhere to the principle of "people-oriented" and give full consideration to the family's ability to pay. For example, we should give appropriate preferential treatment to the self-housing of the elderly, the disabled or low-income families who have no source of income. At this time, the policy design can learn from the "circuit breaker" credit measures of the United States to avoid affecting the normal basic living needs of residents.

Secondly, give better play to the function of real estate tax as a tool to adjust residents' income distribution. From the policy simulation results of the model, it can be found that the collection of real estate tax reduces the Gini coefficient to a certain extent, regulates the wealth and income distribution between urban and rural areas, and reduces the income gap between urban and rural areas. Although in the policy simulation scheme of this paper, each policy simulation scheme has a certain negative impact on the economic system more or less, it can not deny the value of its policy research. In the future implementation process of real estate tax, different combinations of real estate tax reform schemes can be adopted according to the actual situation and characteristics of the development stage, in order to give better play to the function of real estate tax in regulating income distribution and promote the stable and healthy development of economy and society.

Thirdly, continuously expand the real estate tax base and increase the government's real estate tax revenue. Under realistic conditions, the value of residents' real estate is closely related to the geographical location of residents' real estate. Under the assumption that the total amount of residents' real estate remains unchanged, improving the unit value of residents' real estate will effectively expand the real estate tax base. Therefore, we should take advantage of the development opportunity of "new infrastructure" vigorously implemented by the state, improve the infrastructure construction in urban suburbs and county areas, improve the infrastructure service level of the region, drive the economic and social development of the region, so as to accelerate the improvement of the real estate value in the region, and then promote the expansion of the real estate tax base and the increase of government real estate tax revenue.

Finally, accelerate the development process of technical issues such as legislative procedures related to real estate tax and real estate value evaluation. As the public's voice for the implementation of the real estate tax policy becomes stronger and stronger, relevant government departments should timely and quickly introduce laws and regulations related to the real estate tax reform, so that the real estate tax reform has laws and regulations to follow. Meanwhile, with the rapid development of Internet big data technology, a set of convenient and fast real estate value evaluation systems should be established, which can timely reflect the dynamic impact of economic and social changes on real estate value, quickly evaluate the possible impact of real estate tax reform policy on the real estate industry, and then timely adjust the trend of real estate tax reform.

Theoretical Elucidation of the Chinese Modernization as a New Model for Human Advancement

Liu Hongkui[*]

  Civilization is not only an entity that bears a spirit and a culture, but also implies a certain level, stage and process of development. The development of human society since the industrial revolution has created a worldwide modern civilization and its basic elements. In this process, the Communist Party of China has, by leading the Chinese people, established a socialist system and explored a path of modernization that is in line with China's reality and has Chinese theoretical characteristics. Remarkable achievements have been made in the Chinese modernization: industrialization and informatization have been completed in a short time and are transforming into more advanced digitization. As any civilization is born in a specific historical process, the Chinese path to modernization also constitutes a form of civilization. The uniqueness of development theory, the significance of development achievements, the certainty of the development direction of the Chinese path to modernization, and its enlightenment for other developing countries to get rid of the Western modernization path make

---

[*] Liu Hongkui, Associate professor, Institute of Economics, CASS

it a new form of world civilization.

I. Connotation of civilization and essence of modernization

In the *Speech at a Ceremony Marking the Centenary of the Communist Party of China*, Xi Jinping pointed out, "As we have upheld and developed socialism with Chinese characteristics and driven coordinated progress in material, political, cultural-ethical, social, and ecological terms, we have pioneered a new and uniquely Chinese path to modernization, and created a new model for human advancement." [1] In the final analysis, the Party leading its people creates the Chinese path to modernization in order to provide China and the world with a new model for modern civilization.

1. Connotation of civilization

According to Samuel Huntington's summary, civilization was first put forward by French thinkers in the 18th century in relation to barbarism. [2] Later, Immanuel Wallerstein, an American sociologist, deemed in his book *The Modern World-System* that civilization is a kind of historical summation, which includes the special connection of world outlook, customs, material culture and spiritual culture. [3] The famous historian Arnold Toynbee believed in his book *A Study of History* that every civilization has its particularity and historical continuity, including aspects that are not understood by other civilizations. [4] According

---

[1] Xi Jinping: "Speech at a Ceremony Marking the Centenary of the Communist Party of China, People's Daily", July 2, 2021.

[2] Samuel Huntington: *The Clash of Civilizations and the Remaking of World Order* (Revised Edition), translated by Zhou Qi et al, Beijing: Xinhua Publishing House, 2009.

[3] Emanuel Wallerstein: *The Modern World-System*, translated by Guo Fang et al, Beijing: Social Sciences Academic Press, 2013.

[4] Arnold Toynbee: *A Study of History*, translated by Guo Xiaoling et al., Shanghai: Shanghai People's Publishing House, 2010.

to the above definitions, civilization actually has rich connotations:

Firstly, civilization is an entity that carries a kind of spirit and culture (such as a nation-state), and there are many such entities in history and in the world today. Western theoretical scholars Nikolai Danilevsky, Carroll Quigley, Oswald Spengler, Arnold Toynbee and Samuel Huntington share this view. They have summarized and sorted out the types of civilizations in human history. Among them, Russian thinker Nikolai Danilevski pointed out 10 separate types of civilization earlier in his book *Russia and Europe*. While criticizing European civilization, he put forward the concept of Slavic civilization. Samuel Huntington summed up scholars' viewpoints: Carroll Quigley believed that there were 16 obvious types of civilization in human history, Arnold Toynbee listed 20 civilizations, Oswald Spengler listed 8 major civilizations, and William McNeill and Fernand Braudel analyzed 9 major civilizations in human history. At present, academic circles at home and abroad generally believe that at least 12 major civilizations have appeared in human history, but seven of them have ceased to exist, and only Chinese civilization, Japanese civilization, Indian civilization, Islamic civilization and Western civilization exist. [1] Samuel Huntington further pointed out that the future world will not be dominated by a single universal civilization, but many different civilizations will coexist. The Chinese philosopher Liang Shuming divided the world into three civilization types, namely, European civilization, Chinese civilization and Indian civilization. [2] Among them, Chinese civilization is the only single civilization that has lasted for about 5,000 years among all civilizations. The Sixth Plenary Session of the 19th CPC Central Committee clearly pointed out that besides different forms of civilization, there is also a single development mode of human civilization, by noting that With a history stretching back more than 5,000 years, the Chinese

---

[1] Samuel Huntington: *The Clash of Civilizations and the Remaking of World Order* (Revised Edition), translated by Zhou Qi et al., Beijing: Xinhua Publishing House, 2009.

[2] Liang Shuming: *Fundamentals of Chinese Culture*, Beijing: The Commercial Press, 2021.

nation is a great and ancient nation that has fostered a splendid civilization and made indelible contributions to the progress of human civilization. ①

Secondly, civilization means a certain level or stage of development. For instance, in Karl Marx and Friedrich Engels' theory, civilization is implied as a more developed social state. Friedrich Engels noted in *The Principles of Communism* that "the communist revolution will not merely be a national phenomenon but must take place simultaneously in all civilized countries— that is to say, at least in England, America, France, and Germany."② The "civilized country" here obviously means a more developed social entity. In fact, in terms of civilization form or development stage, human beings have experienced at least primitive civilization, agricultural civilization and industrial civilization, and are now moving from industrial civilization to post-industrial civilization, information civilization or digital civilization. Each civilization form has corresponding productive forces, production relations and superstructure, thus forming the differences of various civilization forms.

Finally, civilization includes many dimensions. Xi Jinping clearly pointed out that the new form of Chinese civilization is the coordinated development of material civilization, political civilization, spiritual civilization, social civilization and ecological civilization. The above aspects are the main dimensions of civilization. Of course, civilization includes other dimensions.

It should be emphasized that the core symbol of civilization is still producing, and the main symbol of civilization entering a higher development stage is also the upgrading of productivity. This also reflects Marxist historical materialism, in which productivity is the foundation and productivity determines the relations of production and superstructure.

---

① *Resolution of the Central Committee of the Communist Party of China on the Major Achievements and Historical Experience of the Party over the Past Century*, People's Daily, November 17, 2021.

② *The Complete Works of Karl Marx and Friedrich Engels*, Vol. 4, People's Publishing House, 1958, p. 369.

2. Modernization is in essence a form of civilization.

According to the above definitions of civilization, human civilization entered a new development stage, namely the stage of industrial civilization, from the industrial revolution in the 1760s. Academic circles also use the concept of modernization to describe the course of civilization since the industrial revolution, which mainly refers to industrialization and the improvement in urbanization and social culture that it has brought about. For this reason, the main content of modernization is industrialization, and it is in essence a form of civilization. Moreover, from a historical perspective, modernization represents a worldwide historical process that refers to a change experienced by human society since the Industrial Revolution, and can be regarded as a form of civilization representing this historical era. [1] In this regard, the Chinese path to modernization also represents a new form of civilization. Driven by industrialization, this civilization form has promoted the global transformation from a traditional agricultural society to a modern industrial society, and brought about profound changes in various fields such as economy, politics, culture and ideology.

The amazing expansion of science, technology and engineering knowledge since the industrial revolution has enabled human beings to transform and utilize natural resources and social environment in an unprecedented way. In industrialization or modernization, western capitalist civilization, relying on its productivity advantages, began to brutally exploit the surplus value of workers, and promoted its industrialization and modernization through overseas expansion and colonial plunder. The data show that Europe and its colonie stook up 35% of the global land in the early 19th century. This figure reached 67% in 1878, 84% in 1914, and then continued to increase. In the early 19th century, Britain had only 1.5 million square miles of land and 20 million people. By the early 20th

---

[1] Luo Rongqu: *A New Thesis on Modernization*, Beijing: Peking University Press, 1993 edition, pp. 8 – 15.

century, Britain had 11 million square miles of land and 390 million people. ①
In its expansion, Western civilization exerted a great influence on other civilizations, infiltrating and even destroying many human civilizations (such as Central American civilization). Some other civilizations were either conquered or weakened, thus occupying a subordinate position, such as Indian civilization, Islamic civilization and Chinese civilization.

Up to now, modern industrial civilization has developed for centuries, during which Western civilization has always been dominant. However, western civilization expanded not because of its cultural influence, but by its advanced technology and productivity and organized violence. Depending on the productivity from the industrial revolution, Western civilization vigorously developed the military industry, improved the first-mover advantage in weapons, transportation, logistics and medical care, and enhanced its ability to wage war, thus contributing to the expansion of the West. As Samuel Huntington pointed out, the rise and expansion of western civilization depends largely on the organized use of force, not through the superiority of its ideas, values or religions. Westerners have forgotten this fact, but non-Westerners never have. ②

As modernization is the main symbol of civilization and progress, non-Western countries are also exploring the path to industrial modernization. However, the choice of what modernization development model is still troubling many developing countries. Classical modernization theories tell them to extract the characteristics of modernization from the process and practice of Western civilization, and then take them as the standards of modernization. Some scholars even believe that modernization is almost equivalent to Westernization, and the European and American development model is the only model of modernization. However, this model have repeatedly failed non-western countries. Accord-

---

① Samuel Huntington: *The Clash of Civilizations and the Remaking of World Order* (Revised Edition), translated by Zhou Qi et al., Beijing: Xinhua Publishing House, 2009.
② Samuel Huntington: *The Clash of Civilizations and the Remaking of World Order* (Revised Edition), translated by Zhou Qi et al., Beijing: Xinhua Publishing House, 2009.

ing to the statistics of the World Bank, among the 101 middle-income economies in 1960, only 13 economies crossed the middle-income trap in 2008, including five Western countries. The only non-western economies that really crossed the middle-income trap were a few small economies or resource-based countries such as Singapore, Hong Kong (China), the Republic of Korea and Taiwan (China) .[1] For more developing countries, the Western modernization model is beyond their reach.

3. Chinese path to modernization is a form of civilization.

From the late Qing Dynasty on, countless sages in China began to explore the path to modernization for China. The Westernization Movement in the 1860s can be regarded as the beginning of China's modernization efforts. At that time, intellectuals put forward the principle of "adopting Western knowledge for its practical uses while keeping Chinese values as the core", trying to promote China's modernization by combining China's traditional culture with advanced technology from the West. Nonetheless, due to the powerful forces of feudal bureaucrats and imperialism, none of the efforts and attempts to modernize China in modern times succeeded. After the founding of the Communist Party of China (CPC), feudal bureaucrats and imperialism were overthrown through the new-democratic revolution, and a new China was established, which laid a political foundation for China's modernization. After that, the Party led the people in establishing a socialist system through socialist transformation, and finding a Chinese path to modernization based on the basic national conditions of the primary stage of socialism. This path has made it possible for China to basically realize industrialization and be on the journey to basically build modernization and build a modern socialist country in all respects. Looking back on this course, we can

---

[1] Joint Research Group of the Development Research Center of the State Council and the World Bank: *China 2030: Building a Modern, Harmonious, and Creative Society*, Beijing: China Financial & Economic Publishing House, 2013.

see that China has risen and revived peacefully. Taking the initiative to participate in the global economic system, China has achieved industrialization and people's prosperity by relying on its own people's hard work. In this process, China did not conquer, colonize or plunder other countries and civilizations as the West did. A further review of Chinese history also shows that Chinese civilization and its influence on neighboring countries never relied on military expansion, but mainly on its cultural advantages. This determines the unique attribute of the Chinese path to modernization, so it is also a new form of civilization. In addition, the process of Chinese modernization and the new model for human advancement are also in step with the development and revival of other civilizations, which happen under the overall decline of Western civilization, so it is a part of the common development of many civilizations. In the process of China's development, other civilizations have not declined but flourished, which reflects the world significance of the Chinese path to modernization.

The success of Chinese modernization has undoubtedly broken the dogmatic thinking of equating modernization with Westernization, thus providing new enlightenment and new choices for modernization in other developing countries. It illustrates that "there is more than one path to modernization, and there is neither a fixed model of modernization nor a universally applicable standard of modernization in the world."[1] "China's practice has illustrated to the world the truth that there is not only one Western model to govern a country or promote a country's modernization. Countries can, by all means, explore their own ways."[2] It is fair to say that we, depending on facts, have declared bankruptcy of the "end of history" and of the idea that the Western system model is the only choice. The Chinese path to modernization also proves that non-western countries can completely retain and carry forward their own culture in moderni-

---

[1] Editorial Board of *Qiushi*: *A Programmatic Document to Guide the Comprehensive Construction of a Modern Socialist Country*, Insight China, Vol. 15, 2021.

[2] *Excerpts from Xi Jinping's Discourse on Socialist Political Construction*, Beijing: Central Party Literature Press, 2017, p. 7.

zation without having to totally adopt Western values. As Fernand Braudel criticized, the view that "the victory of modernization or single civilization will lead to the end of the diversity of history and culture in the great civilizations of the world" is naive.

II. Theoretical characteristics of Chinese modernization as a civilization form

Most of the current modernization theories are extracts and generalizations of the experiences of Western countries, lacking summaries of the modernization path of China. The development theories, stages and dimensions of China's characteristic modernization and industrialization are important components of world modernization, so it is necessary to sum up and refine them carefully. From the common theories of modernization and the reality of China, Chinese modernization has many theoretical characteristics in its development.

1. Establishing a socialist system under the leadership of the Party and always adhering to the goal of industrialization

As stated above, the basic premise of modernization is industrialization, and new elements and dimensions have been gradually added since then. It is hard for us to imagine a modern country without industrialization. Karl Marx and Friedrich Engels also mentioned in their classic literature that great industry created modern means of transportation and modern markets and established modern large industrial cities. The great industry created world history for the first time. In fact, it also created the history of modernization. Therefore, although modernization is not equal to industrialization, its basic content is still industrialization. By analogy, the essence of modernization is the process of social change driven by industrialization. If a country wants to realize modernization, it needs to complete industrialization first. This determines that the completion of socialist industrialization is not only the primary task at the founding of the

People's Republic of China (PRC) New China, but also the primary goal since the reform and opening up. This is the core of the Chinese path to modernization and the goal that the Party and people have been pursuing since the founding of the PRC.

Industrialization is the main reason for the strength of developed countries and has been a consistent pursuit of the Party and the State. Before the founding of the PRC, Mao Zedong emphasized many times in *On Coalition Government* and *On People's Democratic Dictatorship* that after the revolutionary war the issue of industrialization must be addressed in a systematic manner, and that it is China's primary task to transform China from a backward agricultural country into an advanced industrial country. The *Common Program of the China People's Political Consultative Conference* adopted by the Political Consultative Conference in September 1949 clearly stated that it was necessary to develop a new-democratic people's economy and steadily transform an agricultural country into an industrial country. [1] But at that time, China was still a big agricultural country with a large population and a backward economy. This was the starting point of industrialization in new China. If we had followed the traditional Western model of industrialization theory, it would have been difficult for China to become an industrialized country quickly. China had to put forward its own industrialization theory and path to industrialization. Hence to form Chinese-style industrialization theory and exploring the Chinese paths to modernization and industrialization became the direction of efforts from the founding of the PRC.

Therefore, after the founding of the PRC, China first carried out a socialist transformation and established a socialist system, thus building the political foundation for industrialization and modernization. In 1953, we put forward the General Line for the Transitional Period, that is, to gradually realize the socialist industrialization of the country and gradually realize the socialist transforma-

---

[1] Huang Qunhui: *The CPC's Leadership in Socialist Industrialization and Its Historical Experience*, Social Sciences in China, Vol. 7, 2021.

tion of agriculture, handicrafts and capitalist industry and commerce over a fairly long period of time. In 1956, we basically completed the socialist transformation of private ownership of the means of production, basically realized public ownership of the means of production and distribution according to work, and established a socialist economic system. On this guiding principle, the Eighth National Congress of the Communist Party of China put forward that the main domestic contradiction was no longer the contradiction between the working class and the bourgeoisie, but the contradiction between the people's need for rapid economic and cultural development and the current situation that the economy and culture could not meet the people's needs. The main task of the people throughout the country was to concentrate on developing socially productive forces and realizing national industrialization. We therefore proposed the four modernizations: to build China into a powerful socialist country with modern agriculture, modern industry, modern national defense and modern science and technology.

2. Giving priority to the development of heavy industry, while emphasizing the coordinated development of heavy industry and light industry.

Regarding how to carry out socialist industrialization, China's policy before reform and opening up was to give priority to the development of heavy industry, which conformed not only to the objective law of Marxist political economy, but also to the requirement of the international political and economic environment at that time. On the one hand, according to Marxist viewpoint, industrialization not only includes new science and technology and corresponding material production, but also includes equipping and transforming the main sectors of the national economy with machinery and equipment, such as light industry, agriculture, transportation and service industry. It is an objective economic law that the production of Category Ⅰ is faster than that of Category Ⅱ, and it is also a common law for all societies to expand reproduction. Therefore, Mao Zedong pointed out in *On the Ten Major Relationships* in 1956 that "heavy industry is the focus of China's construction. It has been decided that priority must be given to the development of the means of production." Mao also pointed out that "the law of giving priority to the growth of the means of production is the common law of expanding reproduction in all societies. If the capitalist society had not given priority to the growth of the means of production, its social production could not have continued to grow."[1] Moreover, the idea of giving priority to the heavy industry can be traced back to Lenin's theory of giving priority to the growth of the means of production. Lenin put forward the law of giving priority to the growth of Category I very early. That is, the means of production for the production of the means of production grow the fastest, the means of production for the production of the means of consumption grow the second fastest, and the means of consumption grow the slowest.[2] On the other hand, during the period after the founding of the PRC, we also had to balance development and security. The international political situation at that time required us to develop industries rapidly, especially heavy industry and national defense industry. In the early days after the founding of the PRC, there were two options for China's industrialization: the first was to take the path of industrialization in Western countries, that is, to develop light industry according to market demand first, and then to develop heavy industry after accumulating a large amount of capital; the second was to take the path of industrialization of the Soviet Union, that is, to give priority to the development of heavy industry through state guidance to realize industrialization in a relatively short period of time, and then to develop light industry. The international political situation at that time determined that we must realize quickly industrialization, especially heavy industry. Only in this way was China able to maintain political stability and gain a foothold in the international

---

[1] *Collected Works of Mao Zedong*, Vol. 8, Beijing: People's Publishing House, 1999, p. 121.

[2] But this is only one aspect of the problem; another is that when the means of consumption do not form a reasonable ratio to the means of production, not only do people not enjoy the benefits that economic growth is supposed to bring, but it also causes a drag on the long-term development of heavy industry.

community.

Of course, we also attached importance to the coordinated development of industry and agriculture, heavy industry and light industry. For example, in 1951, Mao Zedong pointed out: "The completion of industrialization is certainly not only for heavy and defense industries, but all necessary light industries should be built up. In order to complete national industrialization, we must develop agriculture and gradually complete agricultural socialization."① In 1957, Mao stressed once again: "There is no question of giving priority to heavy industry as the center and developing it without wavering, but under this condition, industry and agriculture must be carried out simultaneously and modernized industry and modernized agriculture must be gradually established."②

3. Developing foreign economic cooperation on the basis of independence and self-reliance

Before the reform and opening up, although we always insisted on independence and self-reliance, we never refused external assistance, but tried to participate in the international economic cycle. In 1956, Mao Zedong pointed out in his speech " *Unite All Forces That Can Be United* that "China is still very backward economically and culturally, and it will take a long time to achieve real independence, national prosperity and industrial modernization, and it needs the support of comrades and people from all countries."③ Under the guidance of this ideology, we received larger foreign aid twice before the reform and opening up. For the first time, the Soviet Union and other Eastern European countries helped China build 156 major projects in the early days after the founding of the PRC, which laid the foundation for the industrialization of the PRC. The second time was the introduction of large-scale complete sets of equip-

---

① *Collected Works of Mao Zedong*, Vol. 6, Beijing: People's Publishing House, 1999, pp. 143, 207.
② *Collected Works of Mao Zedong*, Vol. 7, Beijing: People's Publishing House, 1999, p. 310.
③ *Collected Works of Mao Zedong*, Vol. 7, Beijing: People's Publishing House, 1999, p. 64.

ment mainly provided by developed countries in the second world in the 1970s, which made up for the weaknesses of China's light industry and played an important role in solving people's urgent need for daily necessities.

4. Determining and bearing in mind the fact that China is still in the primary stage of socialism

Before the reform and opening up, the Party and state leaders realized that China was in an underdeveloped socialist stage. At the meeting on intellectuals held in 1956, Mao Zedong put forward the idea that China had entered socialism, but it was not yet completed. When considering the stages of socialist construction, he pointed out that "socialism is divided into two stages: the first is underdeveloped socialism, and the second is relatively developed socialism"[1]. In the early days after the Reform and opening up, the Party and state leaders were deeply aware of China's underdeveloped socialism and realized that China's economic foundation was too weak. The *Resolution on Certain Questions in the History of Our Party since the Founding of the People's Republic of China* adopted at the sixth plenary session of its 11th Central Committee held in June 1981 formally used the concept of the primary stage of socialism for the first time, pointing out: "Although our socialist system is still in the primary stage, there is no doubt that China has established a socialist system and entered a socialist society, and any view that denies this basic fact is wrong. " "Of course, our socialist system will inevitably go through a long process from relatively imperfect to relatively perfect. " In September 1982, the Report of the 12th National Congress of the Communist Party of China once again put forward that "China's socialist society is now in the primary stage of development" and summarized the national conditions of China's primary stage of socialism with "underdeveloped material civilization" . The main task of the primary stage of socialism is to improve productivity, and its main aspect is to improve the level of industrialization.

---

[1] *Collected Works of Mao Zedong*, Vol. 8, Beijing: People's Publishing House, 1999, p. 116.

5. Pioneering construction of the socialist market economic system

Based on China's national conditions in the primary stage of socialism, we creatively built a socialist market economic system by combining socialism with the market economy. We constantly developed light industry to meet the needs of people's lives, and continued to upgrade heavy industry, thus creating a miracle of economic growth in China. As early as 1979 Deng Xiaoping proposed that "we can develop a market economy under socialism". The *Resolution on Certain Questions in the History of Our Party since the Founding of the People's Republic of China*, published in 1981, formally put forward "upholding the planned economy as primary and market regulation as supplementary". In 1984, the 3rd plenary session of the 12th CPC Central Committee proposed that "the socialist economy is a planned commodity economy based on public ownership". In 1987, the 13th National Congress of the CPC put forward that "the system of socialist planned commodity economy should be a system of internal unity of planning and market." In 1992, Deng Xiaoping further proposed to establish a socialist market economic system in his "South Tour Speeches", pointing out the important assertion that "the proportion of planning to market forces is not the essential difference between socialism and capitalism. The practice of a planned economy is not equivalent to socialism because there is planning under capitalism too; the practice of a market economy is not equivalent to capitalism because there are markets under socialism too."[1] On this basis, the Report of the 14th National Congress of the Communist Party of China stated: "The goal of China's economic system reform is to establish a socialist market economic system". After that, the 3rd plenary session of the 14th CPC Central Committee adopted the *Decision on Several Issues Concerning the Establishment of the Socialist Market Economic System*. The establishment of the socialist market economic system has released many constraints of economic development and

---

[1] *Thematic Excerpts from Deng Xiaoping's Discourses on Building Socialism with Chinese Characteristics*, Central Party Literature Press, 1992, p. 98.

played a very important role in promoting the rapid development of China's industrialization. It has effectively played the dual role of the "visible hand" of the government and the "invisible hand" of the market, which can play the regulatory role of the market mechanism on the allocation of resources, as well as the role of the government's macro-control and concentration of power to do major things, making China's industrialization advance at an unprecedented speed.

III. Achievements of the civilization of Chinese modernization

Through the Chinese path to modernization, China realized modernization, and then gradually transformed into informationization and digitalization on the basis of industrialization, thus pushing modernization to a new height.

1. Historic achievements in industrialization

Shortly after the PRC was founded, China was basically a traditional agricultural country, with extremely weak industry. In 1954, Mao Zedong described this very vividly: "What can we make now? We can make tables, chairs, tea bowls and teapots. We can grow food, grind it into flour and make paper. However we can't make a car, a plane, a tank or a tractor."[1] This was the basis of our industrialization at that time, which was close to nothing. However, after the First Five-Year Plan period (1953 – 1957), the industrial production system of the PRC was established from scratch. With the basic framework of industrialization, China was already able to produce high-tech products such as airplanes, automobiles, power generation equipment, heavy machinery, machine tools, precision instruments and alloy steel. During these five years, China added 46 billion yuan of fixed assets, 1.9 times of the national fixed assets stock in 1952. From the more systematic data, Table 1 shows that

---

[1] *Collected Works of Mao Zedong*, Vol. 6, Beijing: People's Publishing House, 1999, p. 329.

from 1952 to 1957, the added value of the secondary industry increased from 14.18 billion yuan to 31.7 billion yuan, with the added value index of the secondary industry up by 2.45 times. The industrial added value increased from 11.98 billion yuan to 27.1 billion yuan, an increase of 126.2%, with the industrial added value index up by 2.47 times. The proportions of secondary industry and industry in GDP increased from 20.9% and 17.6% in 1952 to 29.6% and 25.3% in 1957.

For major industrial products, Table 2 shows that the output of pig iron, crude steel and finished steel reached 5.94 million tons, 5.35 million tons and 4.15 million tons, respectively, in 1957. Inthese five years, the total crude steel output was 16.56 million tons, nearly four times higher than that in 1952, and was equal to 218% of the total crude steel output in old China from 1900 to 1948. The output of raw coal and crude oil reached 131 million tons and 1.46 million tons, respectively, up by 98% and 231.8%, respectively, over 1952. The power generation was 19.3 billion kWh, an increase of 164.4% over 1952. The automobile industry was established from scratch, producing 7,900 vehicles in 1957. By the end of 1957, the national railway mileage reached 29,862 kilometers, an increase of 22% over 1952. During these five years, 33 new railways were built, 3 railways were restored, and about 10,000 kilometers of railway trunk lines, double-tracking lines and branch lines were built or renovated. The industrial structure also changed greatly, with the proportion of heavy industry in the total industrial output value increasing from 26.4% to 48.4%.

After that, from 1957 to 1979, although industrial development slowed down or fluctuated, the overall development momentum basically continued well before the reform and opening up. Table 1 shows that by 1978, the added value of the secondary industry had increased to 174.52 billion yuan, up 4.5 times over 1957, and the industrial added value had increased to 160.7 billion yuan, up 4.93 times. The added value of the secondary industry and industrial added value index increased to 1,525.2 and 1,694, respectively, 5.21 times and

5.85 times higher than that in 1957. The proportions of secondary industry and industry in GDP increased to 47.9% and 44.1%, respectively, which were high levels compared with those of developed countries. Table 2 also shows that all major industrial products saw rapid growth before 1978. Compared with that in 1957, the output of cotton yarn increased by 1.82 times, reaching 2.382 million tons, and the industry of chemical fibers was established almost from scratch. The output of raw coal increased by 3.72 times to 618 million tons. Crude oil output increased by 70.27 times to 104.05 million tons. Power generation increased by 12.3 times to 256.6 billion kWh. Crude steel output increased by 4.94 times, reaching 31.78 million tons. The ethylene industry was established from scratch, with an output of 380,000 tons. The number of cars increased by 17.87 times, reaching 149,100.

After the reform and opening up in 1978, the policy constraints hindering industrial development were further released, and industry began to grow more rapidly. Table 1 shows that from 1978 to 2012,[1] the added value of the secondary industry reached 23,516.2 billion yuan, an increase of 134 times, and the industrial added value reached 19,967.1 billion yuan, an increase of 123 times. Excluding the price factor, the secondary industry and industrial added value indexes both increased by about 37 times. However, the proportion of the secondary industry and industry in GDP did not continue to increase, but declined in the 1980s. Then it began to rise again, and maintained at a high proportion. It reached a peak (47.9%) in 2006, and then began to decline. This means that after 2006, China's industrialization reached a climax and gradually entered the late stage of industrialization. This is also consistent with the above theoretical analysis. Before the reform and opening up, China gave priority to the development of heavy industry, which promoted the higher growth rates of

---

[1] Between 1978 and 2012, China experienced rapid industrialization, reaching its peak in around 2012. After that, it entered the late stage of industrialization when the trend of servitization of the economy became remarkable, so this paper mainly uses the data of industrialization between 1978 and 2012.

heavy industry and industry relative to agriculture and service industry, and made the proportion of industry increase greatly, which was divorced from the objective law and development stage of economic development to some extent. However, after the reform and opening up, by adjusting its industrial development mode, China's industrial development became more coordinated. In particular, the service industry started to develop rapidly, seeing its proportion gradually increase in the national economy. In addition, we adopted a development model that was more in line with China's comparative advantages, and paid more attention to the coordinated development of light industry and heavy industry, even valuing more the labor-intensive light industry at a certain stage. This was especially obvious in foreign trade export. In the early days of reform and opening up, a majority of processing trade exports in China belonged to light industrial products such as clothing, shoes, hats and bags.

Industrialization in this period was also reflected in the rapid advancement of urbanization. As shown in Table 1, after the reform and opening up, urbanization entered a stage of rapid development. The urbanization rate almost doubled from 1978 to 1998, increasing by 1 percentage point every year. After 1998, urbanization accelerated again, increasing by more than 1 percentage point every year, from 33.35% in 1998 to 52.57% in 2012, leading to an urbanization rate of over 50%.

In addition, from 1978 to 2012, major industrial products grew substantially (see Table 2). Among them, chemical fiber production increased greatly, by nearly 134 times, obviously higher than that of yarn and cloth, reflecting the improvement of industrialization in the light industry. Raw coal and crude oil increased by nearly 5 times and 1 time, respectively. The relatively low growth of crude oil output was mainly due to the small oil reserves in China, thus relying more on imports. The power generation increased by 18.57 times, reflecting the strong industrial production demand. Pig iron, crude steel and finished steel, which can best reflect industrial production, increased by about 18 times, 22 times and 42 times, respectively. China gradually became the world's largest steel producer. Ethylene, the most used in the chemical industry, increased by 38 times. In addition, the rapid growth of automobile production, which increased 128 times to about 19.28 million, is more reflective of the improvement of China's comprehensive industrial capacity due to the long supply chain of the automobile industry.

In a word, since the founding of New China, it has made remarkable achievements in industrialization, and established the most complete modern industrial system in the world, with 39 major categories, 191 medium categories and 525 sub-categories, making it the only country with all industrial categories in the UN industrial classification. Among more than 500 major industrial products, China ranks first in the world in terms of output of more than 220 products. Among them, the outputs of main industrial products such as raw coal, cement, crude steel, finished steel, fertilizer, power generation, TV sets and so on have ranked first in the world for many years in a row. In 2010, China became the world's largest manufacturing country, with the added value of the manufacturing industry almost the sum of that of the United States and Japan. After 2011, China gradually entered the late stage of industrialization.[①] By the 18th National Congress of the Communist Party of China, China had actually completed most of the process of industrialization. In 2018, Xi Jinping's *Speech at the Conference Celebrating the 40th Anniversary of Reform and Opening Up* more accurately summarized the historic achievements of China's industrialization: first, "in just a few decades, we have completed an industrialization process that took developed countries several hundred years"; second, "we have established the most complete modern industrial system in the world"; and third, "China is the second largest economy and the largest manufacturing country in the world".[②] The *Resolution of the Central Committee of the Com-*

[①] See Huang Qunhui: *The CPC's Leadership in Socialist Industrialization and Its Historical Experience*, Social Sciences in China, Vol. 7, 2021.

[②] Xi Jinping: *Speech at the Conference Celebrating the 40th Anniversary of Reform and Opening Up*, People's Daily, December 19, 2018.

munist Party of China on the Major Achievements and Historical Experience of the Party over the Past Century also pointed out that China "has completed a process of industrialization that took developed countries several centuries in the space of mere decades, bringing about the two miracles of rapid economic growth and enduring social stability."[①]

Table 1   Industrial Development Achievements of China from 1952 to 2018

Year	1952	1957	1966	1978	1988	1998	2008	2018
Added value of secondary industry (100 million yuan)	141.8	317.0	709.5	1745.2	6,587.2	39,004	149,003	235,162
Industrial added value (100 million yuan)	119.8	271.0	648.6	1,607	5,777.2	34,018	130,260	199,671
Index of added value of secondary industry	100.0	245.5	564.0	1,525.2	4,332.6	13,943	38,884	58,058
Industrial added value index	100.0	247.2	608.9	1,694.0	4,756.9	15,901	45,114	65,580
Proportion of secondary industry in GDP (%)	20.9	29.6	37.9	47.9	43.8	46.2	47.4	45.3
Proportion of industry in GDP (%)	17.6	25.3	34.6	44.1	38.4	40.3	41.5	38.4
Urbanization rate (%)	12.46	15.39	17.86	17.92	25.81	33.35	46.99	52.57

Source: The author got the data by calculations according to the *Compilation of Statistical Data of New China for 60 Years* and the *Statistical Yearbook of China* of previous years, and so is the table below. The secondary industry added value index and industrial added value index are calculated with 1952 = 100.

[①] *Resolution of the Central Committee of the Communist Party of China on the Major Achievements and Historical Experience of the Party over the Past Century*, People's Daily, November 17, 2021.

Table 2　　　Growth of Main Industrial Products in China from 1952 to 2018

Year	1952	1957	1966	1978	1988	1998	2008	2012
Chemical fiber (ten thousand tons)		0.02	7.58	28.46	130.12	510.00	2,415.00	3,837.37
Yarn (ten thousand tons)	65.6	84.4	156.5	238.2	465.7	542.0	2,123.3	2,984
Cloth (100m)	38.3	50.5	73.1	110.3	187.9	241.0	710.0	848.94
Raw coal (100 million tons)	0.66	1.31	2.52	6.18	9.80	12.50	27.88	36.5
Crude oil (ten thousand tons)	44	146	1,455	10,405	13,705	16,100	19,001	20,571.14
Power generation (100 million kilowatt hours)	73	193	825	2,566	5,452	11,670	34,669	50,210.41
Pig iron (ten thousand tons)	193	594	1,334	3,479	5,704	11,864	47,067	66,354.4
Crude steel (ten thousand tons)	135	535	1,532	3,178	5,943	11,559	50,092	72,388.22
Finished steel (10,000 tons)	106	415	1,035	2,208	4,689	10,737	58,488	95,577.83
Sulfuric acid (ten thousand tons)	19.0	63.2	290.9	661.0	1,111.3	2,171.0	5,132.7	7,876.63
Fertilizer (ten thousand tons)	3.9	15.1	240.9	869.3	1,740.2	3,010.0	6,012.7	6,832.1
Ethylene (ten thousand tons)			0.54	38.03	123.21	377.30	998.26	1,486.8
Cars (10,000)		0.79	5.59	14.91	64.47	163.00	934.55	1,927.62

2. Remarkable progress in integrating industrialization with informatization

Since 2001, the world has been in the information stage, when it is an important goal for all countries to transform industry and move from a post-industrial society to an information society by using information technology. In this process, information technology and corresponding industries have been growing and expanding, thus starting a new industrialization process driven by informatization. According to the *Digital Economy Report* 2019 released by UNCTAD, the global data traffic was only 100GB/day in 1992, 100GB/second in 2002, 46,600GB/second in 2017 and 150,700GB/second in 2022. The value added of the global ICT service industry reached US $ 3.2 trillion in 2015, accounting for 4.3% of global GDP. In recent years, informatization has even evolved to an advanced stage or digitization stage. This has also led to a new trend in industrialization, namely using intelligent digital technology to transform traditional industries, which is the key to laying the future international competitiveness of the world's industrial and manufacturing industries.

While rapidly advancing industrialization, China has also paid close attention to the new situation and trends of industrialization in the international community. To catch up with the trend of industrial transformation and product development in developed countries by using information technology, in 2001, China proposed to take a new road to industrialization and promote the integration of industrialization and informatization. *The Report of the 16th National Congress of the Communist Party of China* put forward for the first time that China should take a new road to industrialization: "It is necessary to persist in using IT to propel industrialization, which will, in turn, stimulate IT application, blazing a new trail to industrialization featuring high scientific and technological content, good economic returns, low resources consumption, little environmental pollution and a full display of advantages in human resources."[1] Compared with traditional industrialization, new industrialization emphasizes the integration of industrialization with informatization. Since the 16th National Congress of CPC, China has been adhering to the road to new industrialization, and its connotation has been gradually enriched in combination with the requirements of building a well-off society in an all-around way. The Reports of the

---

[1] Jiang Zemin: *Build a Well-off Society in an All-Round Way and Create a New Situation in Building Socialism with Chinese Characteristics*, *People's Daily*, November 18, 2002.

17th, 18th and 19th National Congress of CPC all emphasized that we should stick to the road to new industrialization with China characteristics and promote the deep integration of IT application and industrialization. The 5th plenary session of the 19th CPC Central Committee proposed that new industrialization, informatization, urbanization and agricultural modernization should be basically realized by 2035, which means the transformation of major sectors of the national economy by information technology achievements should be completed. And the 14th Five-Year Plan further reaffirmed this goal. It is fair to say that in the new era and new development stage, the new task of China's modernization is to transform all sectors of the national economy with informatization and digitalization, which is also the new goal and task of modernization in all countries. The goal of the Chinese path to modernization also includes these contents, but it has new attributes and tasks.

According to China's development practice, China's information technology and information industry began to develop in 2001, but lagged behind. The data from the International Telecommunication Union shows that the proportions of Internet access, mobile phone use, fixed broadband and mobile broadband use in China were all at very low levels at that time. In 2001, China was still in the middle stage of industrialization, and informatization was just in its infancy, with the proportion of Internet use of only 1.78%, that of mobile phone use of only 6.61%, and that of the use of fixed broadband and mobile broadband of almost zero. Then China put forward the development strategy of integrating informatization and industrialization, and informatization began to accelerate. In 2010, the proportion of Internet use reached 34.3%, and that of mobile phone use reached a high level of 62.76%, but those of fixed broadband and mobile broadband use were still low, 9.23% and 3.44%, respectively. After 2010, China's informatization entered a more rapid development stage. In 2020 or so, the gaps between the indicators above and those of developed countries were small. If we further consider China's population base and rural areas' constraints, there were almost no gap with those of developed countries. Especially in urban areas, China's indicators were even better than those of developed countries.

Moreover, China's information infrastructure has developed rapidly in the past 20 years. By 2019, China had basically caught up with the development levels of the United States, Japan and Germany. According to the data of the National Bureau of Statistics, in 2019, the proportion of people using computers in various industries in China was relatively high, reaching 32% in all industries, and 25%, 28% and 68% in mining, manufacturing, and the industry of electricity, heat, gas and water production and supply respectively. Except for a few industries, such as construction, the proportions of computer use in other service industries were also high, with the highest proportion in the information transmission, software and information technology industry reaching 131% and 108% in the education industry. In terms of the use of Internet websites by enterprises, the proportion of all industries reached 51%, that of the manufacturing industry 67%, and those of other industries generally high. However, except for accommodation and catering, information transmission, software and information technology, as well as culture, sports and entertainment, the proportions of other industries were still low. The proportion of the manufacturing industry was only 10.2%, with much to be improved. It can be said that China has achieved the task of the primary stage of informatization, basically completing the technical transformation of general information communication and transmission technology to all sectors of the national economy.

3. Digitalization of traditional industries has prepared the productive force foundation for Chinese path to modernization to enter a new stage.

The rapid development of digital technology and digital economy has laid material, technical and knowledge foundations for the Chinese modernization's overall transformation to digitalization. Digitalization is the advanced stage of informatization. Countries all over the world are upgrading traditional industries through the digital technology, and China is also facing this task. On the basis of the primary stage of informatization, China has begun to carry out the transformation of informatization to the advanced stage in various departments of the national economy (namely digital transformation). Despite a gap between China's digital level and that of the United States, China's digital economy has become the second largest country after the United States due to our super-large-scale market advantage. Other countries are obviously lagging behind China and the United States in terms of digital economy due to the limitation of market size. In terms of the scale of digital economy, the number of platform enterprises, the number of industrial robots used and the degree of industrial digitalization, China is almost neck and neck with the United States and has become a major country leading the development of the global digital economy.

Although China's digital infrastructure is still in the early stage of development, some achievements have been made in recent years. In terms of 5G communication, China's 5G network basically covered the main urban areas of cities above the prefecture level in 2020. In 2020, China opened more than 600,000 new 5G base stations and connected more than 200 million 5G terminal machines. In November, 2021, the 14th Five-Year Plan Period Information and Communication Industry Planning Conference held by the Ministry of Industry and Information Technology pointed out that China had built more than 1.15 million 5G base stations, accounting for more than 70% of the world, and 450 million 5G end users, accounting for more than 80% of the world. In November 2021, the Ministry of Industry and Information Technology disclosed that more than 1,800 "5G + Industrial Internet" projects had been built in China, covering 22 key industries. In January, 2022, the *Statistical Bulletin of Communication Industry* 2021 released by the Ministry of Industry and Information Technology showed that by the end of 2021, China had built and opened 1.425 million 5G base stations, accounting for more than 60% of the global total. In terms of data center construction, due to the wide application of big data and artificial intelligence, leading Internet companies have built many super-large data centers. As for the industrial internet, many large manufacturing enterprises are accelerating the construction of industrial internet platforms at the industry level and deploying edge computing networks interconnected with mechanical equipment. In artificial intelligence, China's large-scale Internet companies are building open platforms for artificial intelligence, and have made certain breakthroughs in the fields of autonomous driving, face recognition and medical film reading. On this basis, data has also become a new factor of production. In April 2020, the *Opinions of the Central Committee of the Communist Party of China and the State Council on Building a Better System and Mechanism of Factor Marketization* included data as a new factor of production for the first time, and proposed to develop various data application scenarios in fields such as agriculture, industry, transportation and education. It is foreseeable that in the near future, China's improved digital infrastructure will surely become an important driving factor for China's industrial upgrading and economic digital transformation.

The civilization form of Chinese modernization has much in common with other civilizations in the world. It has absorbed and effectively utilized the outstanding achievements of all civilizations, especially the achievements in productivity. The common ground of the civilizations also shows its world significance. However, the Chinese modernization civilization is obviously different from other civilizations, especially the Western civilization. In this regard, Xi Jinping summed up as follows: "The modernization we are building must have Chinese characteristics and conform to China's reality. Chinese modernization is the modernization of a huge population, of common prosperity for all, of material and cultural-ethical advancement, of harmony between humanity and nature and of peaceful development. This is the direction that China's modernization must adhere to."[①]

[①] Xi Jinping: *On Grasping the New Development Stage, Implementing the New Development Concept and Constructing the New Development Pattern*, Qiushi, No. 9, 2021.

The Chinese modernization civilization was formed in peaceful development, and pursues and contributes to the peaceful development of the world. Xi Jinping always emphasizes that "the road to China's modernization is peaceful development", and pointed out that "China's peaceful development is not an expedient measure, let alone diplomatic rhetoric, but a conclusion drawn from the objective judgment of history, reality and future, and an organic unity of ideological self-confidence and practical consciousness."[1] This Chinese modernization of peaceful development has made outstanding contributions to world development. For instance, China's poverty alleviation is the greatest contribution to the UN Millennium Development Goals, for this has solved the poverty problem of hundreds of millions of people. China's contribution to world economic growth has been increasing. After the international financial crisis in 2008, with rapid industrialization, China became the biggest pulling factor of global economic growth, contributing more than 30% to the world economic growth for many years. The Belt and Road Initiative promoted by China has brought more developing countries and landlocked countries into the global economic geography, promoted the development of these countries, and made a great contribution to the balanced development of the world economy. In a word, the civilization form of Chinese modernization is the product of the profound combination of Marxism and Chinese civilization. It has put an end to the uniqueness and discourse hegemony of Western modern capitalist civilization, provided new choices for developing countries who want to realize industrialization while maintaining their own independence, and provided the wisdom of Chinese civilization for solving the problems of human social development.

---

[1] Xi Jinping: *Series of Important Speeches by General Secretary Xi Jinping* (2016 edition), Beijing: People's Publishing House, 2016, p. 263.

Chapter 5 Chinese Path to Modernization and New Opportunities for the Development of the China-Georgia BRI Cooperation

International Cooperation and Exchange in Education in the Process of Chinese Modernization: Taking Georgia as an Example

Lu Yujing[*]

The Report to the 20th National Congress of the Communist Party of China (CPC) pointed out, "Chinese modernization is socialist modernization pursued under the leadership of the Communist Party of China. It contains elements that are common to the modernization processes of all countries, but it is more characterized by features that are unique to the Chinese context."[①] In the process of Chinese modernization, CPC Central Committee attaches great importance to China's education. The Report to the 20th CPC National Congress drew a blueprint for the development of China's education in an all-round way, and clearly stated that, "We should develop education that meets the people's expectations. Education is of critical importance to the future of our country and our

---

[*] Lu Yujing, Professor, School of Foreign Languages, Lanzhou University

[①] Xi Jinping: *Hold High the Great Banner of Socialism with Chinese Characteristics and Strive in Unity to Build a Modern Socialist Country in All Respects — the Report to the 20th National Congress of the Communist Party of China*, Beijing: People's Publishing House, October 2022.

Party."[1] With the advancement of Chinese modernization, the international cooperation and exchange in education of China has also thrived and become an important part of the heart-to-heart exchange and friendly cooperation under the Belt and Road Initiative. Looking forward, while building a modern socialist country in all respects and facilitating the strategy of building a powerful China through education, China's international cooperation and exchange in education will surely be broadened and deepened.

I. Chinese Modernization and the Development of China's International Cooperation in Education

Since the reform and opening up, China's higher education has developed vigorously. In 1983, Deng Xiaoping put forward that education should be geared to the needs of modernization, of the world and of the future, which pointed out the direction for education reform. The CPC Central Committee promulgated the *Decision on the Reform of Education System* in 1985, proposing that China's universities should actively learn from the school-running and reform experience of foreign universities while summing up historical and practical experience so as to speed up the internationalization of universities.[2]

Since the beginning of this century, along with economic development and increasingly frequent international exchanges, the internationalization of China's education has deepened, and many universities have a vision to strengthen international cooperation in education. National policies and top-level designs have

---

[1] Xi Jinping: *Hold High the Great Banner of Socialism with Chinese Characteristics and Strive in Unity to Build a Modern Socialist Country in All Respects — Report to the 20th National Congress of the Communist Party of China*, Beijing: People's Publishing House, October 2022.

[2] *Decision of the Central Committee of the Communist Party of China on the Reform of Education System* released by the Central Committee of the Communist Party of China on May 27, 1985, selected from the *Selection of Important Documents Since the 12th CPC National Congress* (Volume II) published by People's Publishing House.

boosted Sino-foreign exchanges among universities and academic institutions. In 2009, China and ASEAN countries reached a consensus to take the Double 100, 000 Students Mobility Plan as one of the initiatives to deepen the strategic partnership. That is, by 2020, both the number of ASEAN students studying in China and the number of Chinese students studying in ASEAN countries will reach 100, 000, so as to enhance the international cooperation in higher education. ① This includes the exchange between China and Georgia.

Building world-class universities and disciplines is an important strategic decision for China tomake itself a world-class higher education power and an innovative nation. In 2015, the State Council issued the *Overall Plan for Promoting the Construction of World-Class Universities and Disciplines*, stating that in order to improve the competitiveness of China's higher education, we should foster world-class teachers and implement open education, and more openness and cooperation are needed in higher education. ②

In 2016, the central government proposed the major initiatives of deepening the education opening up in the new era and of jointly building the Belt and Road Initiative in education circles. In the context of multi-polarization and globalization in the world, education circles should conform to cultural diversity and people-to-people exchange and pursue the vision of building a community of human civilization.

In 2020, the State issued the *Opinions of the Ministry of Education and Other Eight Departments on Accelerating and Expanding the Opening up of Education in the New Era*, aiming at promoting China's education to the world stage

---

① Goabroad. Sohu. com: *Double 100, 000 Student Mobility Plan Triggers a Wave of Studying in Southeast Asia in Working Families*, http://goabroad.sohu.com/20100902/n274661858.shtml, September 2, 2010.

② Workers' Daily: "The State Council Issues the Overall Plan for Promoting the Construction of World-Class Universities and Disciplines, *Sina* News, http://news.sina.com.cn/o/2015-11-06/doc-ifxkmrvp5159523.shtml, November 6, 2015.

in a more open, confident and proactive manner. ①

Report to the 20th CPC National Congress also emphasized that we shall continue to give high priority to the development of education, and the central government stressed the major initiatives of deepening the education opening up in the new era and of jointly building the Belt and Road Initiative in education circles, which demonstrate the unremitting pursuit of education to have a community of human civilization. ② To promote the modernization of education, we should unswervingly uphold opening up and strengthen mutual tolerance, mutual learning and communication with other countries in the world. The status and role of international cooperation and exchange in China's education are further highlighted.

The above timeline of China's policies shows that the internationalization of China's education, especially of China's higher education, always goes hand in hand with the modernization of China.

II. Changes in Educational Layout and in Foreign Students and Chinese Overseas Students

"Going global and welcoming in" is an indispensable part in the process of education internationalization. We can review it from four aspects, namely, the scale of international Chinese education, the number of international students in China and the number of Chinese overseas students, Chinese overseas students returning to China to start business, and the ratio of public-funded students to

---

① People's Daily: "The Ministry of Education and Other Eight Departments Issues Opinions on Accelerating and Expanding the Opening up of Education in the New Era", the Ministry of Education of People's Republic of China, http://www.moe.gov.cn/jyb_xwfb/s5147/202006/t20200623_467784.html, June 23, 2020.

② People's Daily: "Lively Discussion of Delegates to 20th CPC National Congress: Accelerating the Implementation of the Innovation-Driven Development Strategy", Finance.china.com.cn, http://finance.china.com.cn/news/special/esda/20221022/5890269.shtml, October 22, 2022.

self-funded students.

1) Since the world's first Confucius Institute was established in Seoul, South Korea, on November 21, 2004, Confucius Institutes have provided standardized and authoritative modern Chinese textbooks for Chinese language learners around the world, as well as the most formal and leading channel for Chinese language teaching. China's establishment of Confucius Institutes in many countries aligns with Confucius' philosophy of "All men under heaven are brothers", "Harmony without conformity" and "The superior man on the grounds of culture meets with his friends, and by their friendship helps his virtue". These Institutes contribute to the development of friendly relationships between China and other countries, enhance local people's understanding of China's language and culture, and provide suitablet and proper learning conditions for Chinese language learners in various countries. By 2022, China has conducted education cooperation and exchanges with 181 countries that have diplomatic relations with China; Chinese language teaching has been carried out in more than 180 countries and regions; China has jointly set up Confucius Institutes and Confucius Classrooms in 159 countries and regions; 81 countries have incorporated the Chinese language into their national education systems; and China has signed mutual recognition agreements for academic degrees with 58 countries and regions. Three Confucius Institutes have been established in Georgia.

2) With the development of China's economy, more international students are interested in pursuing further study in China after learning about Chinese culture. Since the reform and opening up, staying in China has entered a new era. Over the 22 years from 1979 to 2000, China accepted about 394,000 international students. China has achieved social and political stability. with its economy developing rapidly in a sustainable manner, while its comprehensive national strength and international status have significantly enhanced. It also has made great progress in the work of Study in China. The number of international students increased greatly, from 14,000 in 1992 to 41,000 in 1996, with a five-year average annual growth rate of over 30%, and the level of international

students also improved significantly. The number of self-funded international students increased so greatly that they became the mainstream of international students in China. In 2018, there were a total of 492,185 international students from 196 countries and regions pursuing their studies in 1,004 higher education institutions in China's 31 provinces, autonomous regions and municipalities,"[1] of which 295,043 were from Asia, accounting for 59.95%. And the growth trend is even more obvious when compared with that in 2004 when a total of 110,844 international students from 178 countries and regions studied in 420 higher education institutions in China's 31 provinces, autonomous regions and municipalities. Tens of thousands of students are from 15 countries, including the United States, France, Russia, Japan and South Korea. However only a few dozen student are from Georgia. Therefore, improvements are greatly needed in both the numer and proportion of Georgian students.

According to the education exchange agreements and exchange plans between China and relevant countries, the Ministry of Education has provided Chinese government scholarships to 152 countries in 2000. Every year since 2000, many international students and scholars have received special scholarships from the Ministry of Education, such as the Great Wall Scholarship (provided through UNESCO), the Excellent Student Scholarship, the Short-term Training Scholarship for Foreign Chinese-Language Teachers, the HSK Winner Scholarship and the Chinese Culture Research Scholarship, to study or to do research in China. Later, some higher education institutions set up Chancellor's Scholarships, and some enterprises like Tencent and Alibaba also provided enterprise scholarships. Students who have been awarded Chinese government scholarships account for 12.81% of the total. The development of education for international students in the world demonstrates that the economic development

---

[1] The Ministry of Education of the People's Republic of China: *Statistical Report on International Students in China for* 2018, http://www.moe.gov.cn/jyb_xwfb/gzdt_gzdt/s5987/201904/t20190412_377692.html, April 12, 2019.

of a country is one of the prerequisites for attracting a large number of international students. Economic advantages represent a country's image and have an all-around impact on the country. The speed of China's economic development and the acceleration of Chinese modernization is bound to attract more international students to study in China. ①

At present, most international students from Georgia are scholarship students, and only a few are self-financed. It can be expected that more and more Georgian students will study in China's higher education institutions in the near future.

3) Changes in the number of Chinese students studying abroad and returning to China to start businesses

Since the reform and opening up, studying abroad has always been a popular choice. Chinese students from all over the country go to all corners of the world, from Europe, the United States, Australia, and New Zealand to Southeast Asia. When choosing a destination to study abroad, students either value the natural environment of the country, or appreciate the local humanistic environment, or consider local policies for international students, such as scholarships and free medical care. However, their choices mainly depend on discipline-related factors, like whether it is a world-renowned university, or the relationship between study and employment, etc.

The number of people going abroad to study varies every year, but it has been on the rise in the past decades. According to statistics, from 1978 to 2019, there were 6,560,600 Chinese overseas students, of whom 1,656,200 were studying or doing research abroad, while 4,904,400 finished their studies and came back. Even under the COVID-19 pandemic, the total number of Chinese students studying abroad reached 662,100 in 2021. Among them, 30,200 students are sponsored by the Chinese government, 35,600 by their

---

① *Analysis on the Significance and Advantages of the Development of Education for International Students in China at Present*, Xzbu. com: https://www.xzbu.com/9/view-9561556.htm.

employers, and 596, 300 are self-financed.

In recent years, more and more Chinese overseas students returned to China to start a business, which has brought changes to China's economic and educational development. "In 2021, for the first time, the number of Chinese overseas students who returned to China for innovation and entrepreneurship exceeded 1 million!"[1] From 1978 to 2019, more than 4.2 million of the 6.5 million overseas students returned to China. During the first 30 years of reform and opening up, the total number of overseas students at public expense and their own expense reached 1.39 million, and only 390, 000 of them returned to China.[2] Factors like the COVID-19 pandemic and changes in international relations further prompt Chinese overseas students to return to China. In 2020, 777, 000 overseas students finished their studies and returned to China, and in 2021, the number of students returned to China for employment was about 1.049 million. This indirectly reflects the internationalization of education.

Although the pandemic slowed down the momentum of studying abroad, the *2021 National Report on Studying Abroad*[3] released by the 2021 International Education Summit Forum shows that 91% of people who originally planned to study abroad stick to their plans. Improving ability is the main purpose of people who want to study abroad. Expanding international horizons, learning advanced knowledge, enriching life experience, and improving foreign language ability and employment prospects are the most important factors for overseas students. "In 2021, the state fully supported studying abroad, and encouraged returning to China. We believe that overseas students are free to come and go at will, and

---

[1] The website of the Conference on International Exchange of Professionals: http://www.ciep.gov.cn/content/2022-11/30/content_25491323.htm, November 30, 2022.

[2] Beijing Morning Post: *Less Than 30% of Chinese Overseas Students at Public Expense and at Their Own Expense Return to China*, http://news.sohu.com/20090326/n263011598.shtml, March 26, 2009.

[3] Sohu.com, *2021 National Report on Studying Abroad Released*, https://www.sohu.com/a/501268719_99945202, November 15, 2021.

they will play an important role in the future development of the motherland."①

4) The ratio of self-funded to public-funded international students (both Chinese students studying abroad and international students studying in China) has increased in the past 20 years. Now the ratio is around 90% : 10%. With the development of Sino-foreign cooperation in running schools and the internationalization of China's higher education, China has become an important destination for Asian students around 2018, and most of them are self-funded students.② In 2010, Chinese students studying abroad at their own expense accounted for more than 90% of the total overseas students,③ and the proportion has remained basically stable for many years.

III. The Process of Chinese modernization and Sino-Foreign Cooperation in Running Schools, people-to-people exchange and Scientific Research Cooperation

In December 2017, the document *Several Opinions on Strengthening and Improving people-to-people exchange with Foreign Countries* was implemented. It pointed out that a working mechanism for language interoperability should be established to promote the language that between China and other countries in the world, and multi-level channels for language and cultural exchanges should be set up. China is determined to further promote the Chinese language across the world, support more countries to incorporate Chinese teaching into their nation-

---

① Sohu. com, *2021 Big Data of Studying Abroad released, Showing Growing Number of Overseas Students...*, https://www.sohu.com/a/515785582_543744, January 13, 2022.

② The Paper: *Latest Annual Report on the Development of Chinese students Studying Abroad: Self-funded Students Account for the Majority of International Students in China*, http://news.hsw.cn/system/2022/0928/1527086.shtml, HSW.CN, September 28, 2022.

③ Liuxue86. com, *Over 90% of Chinese Overseas Students are Self-funded*, https://m.liuxue86.com/a/207169.html, March 24, 2011.

al education systems, and develop Confucius Institute into a world-class language promotion institution. Efforts should be made to improve the discipline systems of foreign languages in domestic higher education institutions, to speed up the training of non-common language talents, and to continuously improve the language communication ability of the general public. ①

Looking back, "Nanjing Architecture Vocational and Technical Education Center, jointly run by China and Germany, established in 1983, and Johns Hopkins University-Nanjing University Center for Chinese and American Studies, co-founded by China and the United States, set up in 1986, respectively marked the birth of the Sino-foreign cooperative institutions of vocational education and of higher education. We started to explore cooperative education."② In 2019, Xiong Jianhui divided China's cooperative school running into four stages. First, the initial stage is at the beginning of reform and opening up. Second, the rapid development stage starting from the economic transition in the 1990s. Especially when the *Interim Provisions for Chinese-Foreign Cooperation in Running Schools* was promulgated by the State Education Commission in 1995, which provides a direct policy basis for cooperation in running schools, the scale of cooperative education witnessed rapid expansion, covering the whole education system by the end of 2002. In the tide of the market economy and in the process of Chinese modernization, Sino-foreign cooperation in running schools has played a positive role in the internationalization of education in China. Third, after China joined the WTO after in the new millennium, two important documents, the *Regulations of the People's Republic of China on Chinese-Foreign Cooperation in Running Schools* promulgated by the State Council in

---

① Sina Finance: *The General Office of the CPC Central Committee and the General Office of the State Council issues Several Opinions on Strengthening and Improving people-to-people exchange with Foreign Countries*, http://finance.sina.com.cn/roll/2017-12-22/doc-ifypxmsq9277578.shtml, December 22, 2017.

② Xiong Jianhui: *Four Development Stages of Sino-Foreign Cooperation in Running Schools*, Sohu.com, https://www.sohu.com/a/289917862_380485, January 18, 2019.

2003 and the *Implementation Measures for the Regulations of the People's Republic of China on Chinese-Foreign Cooperation in Running Schools* promulgated by the Ministry of Education in 2004, have provided the legal basis and adjusted the development of cooperation in running schools. And fourth, with the opening up of China's education shifting from "expanding the scale" to "improving the quality", Sino-foreign cooperation in running schools entered a new era of transformation, upgrading and connotative development. In the 40 years of development, cooperation in running schools broadened the ways of talent training in China and enriched resources of domestic education, especially in higher education, while acting as a window for cultural exchanges to serve people-to-people exchange between China and foreign countries and to promote all-round opening up and socialist modernization. It has become a bridge between China and the world.

In Georgia, there are for-profit schools jointly run by Georgia with countries like Germany, Britain, the United States and Finland. However there are no such schools in cooperation with China. The work of education cooperation focuses on two Confucius Institutes and one Confucius Classroom. It is expected that in the near future, the education cooperation between the two countries will make breakthroughs at the levels of primary and secondary schools as well as colleges and universities, and the cooperation intention between departments may gradually become real cooperation in teaching and scientific research.

Several Opinions on Strengthening and Improving people-to-people exchange with Foreign Countries pointed out that it is necessary to enrich and expand the connotation and fields of people-to-people exchange and build world renowned brands of people-to-people exchange. We should adhere to the two-way efforts of "going global" and "bringing in", with the focus on supporting representative projects to go abroad, such as Chinese language, Chinese medicine, Chinese martial arts, Chinese food, Chinese festivals and Chinese folk customs and other intangible cultural heritages. We should deepen Sino-foreign cooperation in aspects such as studying abroad and running schools, international collaborative innovation of higher education institutions and scientific research institutions, cultural relics and art exhibitions and music performance, large-scale sports events and the development of key sports projects. We will form a number of internationally significant brand projects in various fields of people-to-people exchange and further enrich annual themes of people-to-people exchange between China and foreign countries. [1]

Feng Zhongping, vice president and a researcher at the China Institutes of Contemporary International Relations, said, "The key to sound relations between states lies in amity between the people, and the key to amity between the people lies in heart-to-heart exchange... With the rapid development of China and its extensive contacts with the outside world, the world is increasingly eager to know about China. In just a few years, Confucius Institutes and World Forum on China Studies have become brand projects, and Chinese TV dramas have been sought after in neighboring countries, Africa and other countries and regions... The increasing number of Chinese overseas students, tourists and overseas entrepreneurs has promoted the spread of Chinese culture overseas, and has also led to an abiding interest in Chinese language, traditional Chinese medicine and martial art around the world..." [2]

In the context of China's thriving economy and the accelerated process of Chinese modernization, international cooperative education has developed together with a people-to-people exchange, the opening up of education towards neighboring countries has been expanded, and the cooperation between Chinese and overseas higher education institutions has become increasingly frequent. For example, in October 2015, the University Alliance of Belt & Road, initiated by Lanzhou University and jointly established in Dunhuang, Gansu, by 47 Chinese and foreign colleges and universities, including Fudan University, Beijing

---

[1] Sohu. com, *2021 National Report on Studying Abroad Released*, https://www.sohu.com/a/501268719_99945202, November 15, 2021.

[2] Guangming Daily: *New Directions of people-to-people exchange between China and Foreign Countries*, https://www.sohu.com/a/221573212_115423, February 8, 2018.

Normal University and Russian Ural State University of Economics, issued *Dunhuang Consensus*, advocating establishing a think tank of international alliances of higher education institutions. By adhering to the philosophy of connectivity, openness, inclusiveness, collaborative innovation and win-win cooperation, the alliance aims to jointly build a higher education community under the Belt and Road Initiative, promote all-round exchanges and cooperation in education, science and technology, culture and other fields between higher education institutions in countries and regions along the route, and serve the economic and social development of these countries and regions. Up to now, the alliance has 178 members, covering 27 countries and regions. It has developed into a new platform with strong influence for exchange and cooperation among colleges and universities along the route of Belt and Road. Year by year, Chinese and Georgian scholars have conducted more cooperation in scientific research and jointly participate in more meetings, while the number of students exchanged has been on the rise. In 2021, the Confucius Institute participated in the International Conference of "China-Europe Silk Road Aesthetic Culture Bilateral Forum" and the International Academic Conference on Research in Linguistics Frontier Issues and Chinese Education held by Lanzhou University.

An improved pattern of people-to-people exchange leads to a closer heart-to-heart exchange between China and other countries. More high-level visits and frequent non-governmental exchanges between China and Georgia have formed a new pattern of multiple interactions. Frequent exchanges between Chinese and Georgian higher education institutions, such as Communication University of China, School of Foreign Languages and Literatures, Lanzhou University, and Zhengzhou University and Georgian universities and research institutions have contributed to the development of bilateral relations. China has set up a global platform for high-end education cooperation to contribute wisdom and strength to global education governance. In the education exchange with Georgia, many universities in Georgia have expressed their willingness in cooperation with Chinese universities. Not only the universities, Georgian primary and secondary schools are also willing to establish sister-school relations with their counterparts in China to visit and learn from each other. The sister-school relationship between Tbilisi No. 98 Public School and Nanjing No. 5 Middle School is one example.

IV. The Belt and Road Initiative and Sino-Georgian Education Cooperation

The increasingly frequent interaction between China and Georgia at the middle and high levels has greatly promoted exchanges and cooperation in education, culture and humanities between the two countries.

On September 22, 2022, Ambassador of China to Georgia Zhou Qian attended an online meeting between Qian Hongshan, Vice Minister of the International Department of the CPC Central Committee and Giorgi Amilakhvari, Chairperson of the Education and Science Committee of the Parliament of Georgia and Chairperson of Georgian-Chinese Friendship Group. Georgian side expressed that the Georgian Dream-Democratic Georgia Party attaches great importance to the development of relations between the two parties and the two countries and admires the great achievements of governance of the CPC, and it is willing to work with the CPC to strengthen experience exchange in party building and state governance, and deepen bilateral cooperation in areas including politics, economy and humanities through inter-party channels. [1] On September 23, Ambassador Zhou visited Tsulukiani, Georgian Deputy Prime Minister and Minister of Culture, Sports and Youth Affairs. Both sides expressed willingness to take the 30th anniversary of the establishment of diplomatic relations between

---

[1] The Embassy of the People's Republic of China in Georgia: *Ambassador of China to Georgia Zhou Qian Attends Video Meeting between Qian Hongshan, Vice Minister of the International Department of the CPC Central Committee and Amilakhvari, Chairperson of Education and Science Committee of the Parliament of Georgia and Chairperson of Georgian-Chinese Friendship Group*, http://ge.china-embassy.gov.cn/chn/, September 23, 2022

China and Georgia as an opportunity to deepen humanity's cooperation. Ambassador Zhou reviewed the achievements of cultural exchanges between China and Georgia in recent years and welcomed Georgia to actively participate in the cultural cooperation under the framework of the Belt and Road Initiative. He expressed China's willingness to further strengthen cooperation in holding exhibitions in each other's countries, visiting performances of art troupes and film exchanges after the pandemic eases. Georgian side expressed that China is the key direction of Georgia's foreign cultural exchange and cooperation, and Georgia is willing to work with China to innovate ways of cultural cooperation and promote new progress in cultural exchanges between the two countries. ① On September 27, Ambassador Zhou Qian met with Bokvadze, President of the Culture Commission of the Parliament of Georgia. Ambassador Zhou introduced China's achievements and experiences in cultural legislation and cultural construction, reviewed the fruits of cultural exchanges between China and Georgia, and welcomed Georgia's active participation in the cultural cooperation under the framework of the Belt and Road Initiative. Georgian side expressed that in recent years, Georgia and China have maintained high-level cultural exchanges and they are willing to further promote cultural cooperation between the two countries through specific projects. After the 20th CPC National Congress, on November 7, Ambassador Zhou Qian visited Enukidze, Deputy Chairperson of the Parliament of Georgia to introduce the spirit of the 20th CPC National Congress and China's achievements and experience in modernization. Ambassador Zhou introduced the contents of the Report to the 20th CPC National Congress on China's future development tasks, Chinese modernization, whole-process people's democracy, etc. , and expressed that China will take the 20th CPC National Congress as an opportunity to further deepen pragmatic cooperation between China and Georgia in various fields. Georgian side congratulated China on the complete

---

① Relevant information in this note and below comes from the website of the Embassy of the People's Republic of China in Georgia.

success of the 20th CPC National Congress, praised China's development achievements, and expressed its willingness to conduct in-depth exchanges with the Communist Party of China on governance and learn from China's modernization experience.

Previously, Ambassador Zhou answered Georgia's concerns in a written interview with the Georgian media center on the 20th CPC National Congress. He said that China is willing to work with other countries in the world, including Georgia, to make every effort for peace and development, shoulder the responsibility for solidarity and progress, contribute wisdom to global governance, and jointly build a community of shared future for mankind and create a better world. The Chinese government attaches great importance to jointly promoting the development of the Middle Corridor Initiative with Georgia under the framework of the Belt and Road Initiative. Chinese-funded enterprises have built a large number of infrastructure projects in Georgia. At present, the key projects under construction include E60 highway and modern railways, and many projects are upon completion. When these projects are opened to traffic, the transit time will be significantly shortened and the transportation capacity of Georgia will be improved, the role of Georgia as a transportation hub will be strengthened, and stronger infrastructure support will be provided for the development of the Middle Corridor Initiative. An increasing number of Chinese enterprises are at the Georgian market and paying close attention to the development of the Middle Corridor Initiative.

Despite the favorable geopolitical environment, the geographical conditions in Georgia, featuring many gullies, canyons and almost impassable mountains, hinder the country's transportation. Building infrastructure that can overcome the geographical environment requires a lot of investment, as well as knowledge and experience. Chinese enterprises are reshaping the geographical environment of Georgia, which will put Tbilisi in a better position on various Eurasian trade routes. For example, in 2019, China Railway 23rd Bureau Group Co., Ltd. began to build a 22.7-kilometer-long highway in Georgia, with an estimated total cost of about 428. 6 million US dollars. The project is part of the International North-South Transport Corridor. The surge of Chinese enterprises in Georgia will change the country's transportation capacity. [1] In an interview with China. org. cn in September 2022, the ambassador of Georgia to China Archil Kalandia said, "From December 2021, we have direct freight train from China (Gansu) to Georgia and vice versa. And we hope that this route will play a very good role in our bilateral trade and economic cooperation, because it is the first time that the cargo train, freight train from China (Gansu) has a final destination to Tbilisi, the capital of Georgia. And we are planning to increase the number of routes as well. " He added, "Georgia is the only country outside China to organize Belt and Road forum... We have established the Tbilisi Belt and Road Forum in 2015. And we've held three forums in 2015, in 2017 and in 2019. This year, we are planning to continue to organize Tbilisi Belt and Road Forum. We sincerely invite partners and friends from China. We would like to present them the venue in Georgia to discuss the issues and discuss the possible projects under the Belt and Road Initiative in Georgia. So it's why it also reflects the importance for us. "[2]

Since the establishment of diplomatic relations 30 years ago, China and Georgia have always been good friends of mutual trust and good partners of sincere cooperation. The two countries have always respected each other, helped each other and cooperated with each other. The joint construction of the Belt and Road Initiative between China and Georgia and their pragmatic cooperation in various fields have been deepened and substantiated. The bilateral trade volume has increased by more than 400 times compared with the 3. 68 million US dollars at the beginning of the establishment of diplomatic relations. From Janu-

---

[1] Amir Avidaliani: *China is Changing the Landscape of Georgia*, Global Times, https://mil. news. sina. com. cn/2022 – 10 – 11/doc – imqqsmrp2180192. shtml, October 11, 2022

[2] China. org. cn: *Red Star Over China in the New Era | Georgian Ambassador to China Talks About the Belt and Road Initiative in His Eyes*, https://news. ycwb. com/2022 – 09/30/content _ 41079259. htm, September 30, 2022

ary to June, 2022, China was Georgia's third largest trading partner, and has become its largest export market. [1] We should prepare a cooperation plan for the next 30 years. We will uphold the spirit of mutual respect, equality and mutual benefit, and continue to deepen the healthy and stable development of bilateral relations under the framework of the Belt and Road Initiative, of which education cooperation is an integral part. It is of far-reaching significance for China and Georgia, two countries with a long history, to exchange and learn from each other and achieve mutual benefit and win-win results in the development.

Leona, a reporter from Georgian economic center network, recalled that she first came to China in 2015, and has visited various parts of China many times since then. She believes that the 20th CPC National Congress is not only a major event in China's political life, but also of great significance to the world. China is the factory of the world and the engine of the world economy. Therefore, its stability and prosperity are closely related to the political and economic climate of the international community. [2] The prospect of education cooperation between Georgia and China is promising.

---

[1] The Ministry of Commerce of the People's Republic of China: http://www.mofcom.gov.cn/article/zwjg/zwxw/zwxwoy/202207/20220703334607.shtml, July 20, 2022

[2] Sina News: "I Watch the 20th CPC National Congress in China: Georgian Reporter: China Faces the World with an Open Attitude", Sina.com.cn, https://news.sina.com.cn/gov/xlxw/2022-10-20/doc-imqqsmrp3188491.shtml, October 20, 2022.

The Belt and Road Initiative and Perspectives of Georgia

Tamar Dolbaia[*]

I. Introduction

After the dissolution of Soviet Union, the transport strategy of Europe is to widen European market by development of international transport corridors, which is considered to be one of the best ways for post-socialist states to get involved in European space. For European Union, it is also important to diversify transport flows and to create new corridors through Georgia and South Caucasus as an alternative to corridors that are passing through Russia. New reality changed Georgia's geostrategic function and due to unique transport-geographical location it became involved in transport corridor called "TRACECA", it connects Europe and Asia and provides Georgia with transit cargo, which is guarantee for Georgia's regional cooperation, security and sustainable development. For us it is important to study possibility of involving Georgia in important processes occurring in Eurasia through initiative of China's "Belt and Road" maintaining transit function and development opportunities.

---

[*] Tamar. Dolbaia, Professor, Dean of Faculty of Social and Political Sciences, Ivane Javakhishvili Tbilisi State University, Georgia

Ⅱ. Historical Review of Georgians Transit Function

Importance and role of Georgia's transit function in development of the country begins from 19th century. In 1821, Russia openedKulevi (Redut-Kale) porto-franco on the Georgia's Black Sea coast and in 1823 started regular transportation between Odessa and Redut-Kale ports. In 1828, the newspaper "Тифлисские Ведомости", in its sixth edition wrote: "The advantageous location of Tbilisi, its proximity to Iran borders brings opportunity to attract Asian merchants..., Black Sea ports, especially now when we possess estuary of river Rioni, give us favorable conditions for connection with Europe. Also, Russia will have an opportunity to sell its products to Asians". Transit route Kulevi-Tbilisi contributed to domination of European products in Iranian market, while destroying perspectives for development of Russian trade and industry, because Russian products were more expensive and less qualitative. Iranian and Georgian merchants were going to Leipzig bypassing Russian markets and bringing European products which were cheaper and of higher quality. That's why Russian manufacturers asked its government to abolish preferences established in 1821, which eventually were abolished in 1831. But French and Germans had already mastered Asian markets and they did not return to Russian market. They continued to trade through Turkey[①].

Due to 10 years of preferential tariffs and trade in the old transit route, which united Black Sea with Caspian Sea through river (Rioni-Mtkvari) and land systems, Russia gave Europe temporary way to Iranian market, by relocating to Transcaucasia the route from Turkey to Iran, strengthening its political influence in Europe and East. Transit route from Europe to Iran was relocated from Kulevi-Tbilisi to Trapezund-Erzurum. Tbilisi lost its transit importance. This

---

① Janashia, S. (1943). History of Georgia from Ancient Times to the End of 19-th Century. Tbilisi.

first attempt for Georgia and Transcaucasia to get involved in world trade turnover had failed.

In the Soviet period, Georgia was locked in frames of planned economy and its specialization was determined by common Soviet interests. Only after independence it became necessary for Georgia to determine its role in global political and economic space by itself. Georgia does not have strategic natural resources, but has transport-geographic location, which gives it a strategic transit function and which became the main factorof formation of Georgia's foreign and internal policy.

Ⅲ. Transit Function of Georgia and International Transport Corridors

In the modern world, international transport corridors are widely spread. This is complicated technological system, in which all types of transport and communications are assembled and material, financial and information flows are streaming and synchronized. Georgia through its unique transport-geographicallocation, is involved in Transport Corridor "TRACECA", which connects Europe and Asia. Europe-Caucasus-Asia transport Corridor- "TRACECA" was created with the assistance of European Union. This project is also geopolitical, because mainly, it is created to become an alternative to international transit routes passing through Russia and diversify them. "TRACECA" route is: China (Lianyungang) -Druzhba border crossing-Kazakhstan-Uzbekistan-Turkmenistan-Azerbaijan-Georgia-Poti port. Two lines go from Poti. Line 1: Poti-Ukraine (Odessa) -Chop crossing-Slovakia-Austria. Line 2: Poti-Bulgaria-Romania-Austria.

"TRACECA" is operating since 1996, when by treaty of "Sarakhs", Chevron oil started to be transported from Kazakhstan to Batumi port by railway and from there to international market by sea. Building of Baku-Supsa pipeline, in order to export Azerbaijan oil from Georgia, gave to the corridor the "energetical" aspect. Unfortunately, "TRACECA" is not equally important for participating countries. Central Asia is oriented towards Russian and Iranian corridors, West of Black Sea-towards Pan European, for Europe, Ukraine-South Caucasus corridor, which goes through Central Asia, is interesting only in extreme cases. Only in Caucasus, there is serious attitude towards it. Georgian transport infrastructure and legal base is more or less ensuring the development of transit potential.

But management is scattered and is hindering elaboration and implementation of unified transit policy. Georgia does not have attractive tariffs. Same situation is in port services. Port fees in Georgian ports is significantly higher than in other ports of Black Sea Basin. Participants of transport infrastructure are oriented towards getting momentary maximum profit. There are many participant countries. Countries of the corridor can not agree on unified tariff and customs norms. The corridor is multimodal, which makes project expensive and prolongs transportation. Due to Georgia's small internal market, a large part of import-export flows is destined for South Caucasus and Central Asia regions. All types of transport in Georgia is involved in transit operations. If we look at overall turnover by different types of transport, we will see that undisputed leader is motor transport. 87% of transit cargo is transferred by sea transport to Armenia and Azerbaijan, and the rest to Central Asia.

Table 1　　　　　Cargo Transportation by Modes (mln. tons)

Transport Mode	2006	2007	2008	2009	2010	2011	2012	2013	2014	2015	2016
Civil Aviation	0.017	0.012	0.017	0.012	0.015	0.016	0.016	0.017	0.017	0.015	0.033
Road	27.8	27.5	27.8	28.2	28.5	28.8	29.1	29.4	29.8	30.1	30.4
Railway	21.2	22.2	21.2	17.1	19.9	20.1	20.1	18.2	16.7	14.1	11.9
Sea Ports	25.5	18.9	18.6	20.2	22.7	22.1	21.8	21.9	21.3	19.2	17.6
Tolat	74.5	68.6	67.7	65.5	71.1	48.9	49.2	47.6	46.4	44.2	42.3

Source: materials of Ministry of Economy and Sustainable Development of Georgia

Share of transit operations in turnover ofPoti port is significant-in 2004-2015 it was between 55% and 48%. Share of import grew in 2004 from 20% to 36% in 2015. Export declined in 2004 from 25% to 16% in 2014. Decline of export occurred due to transfer of part of Central Asian cargo to Russia, while Georgian market is too small to make up for the loss. The port is specialized in dry cargo and accordingly, there is high share of dry and general cargo. Share of transit cargo of Batumi port was varying from 93.9% in 2009 to 85.8% in 2015. Kazakhstan was managing the port and was specialized in export of Kazakh oil. Kazakhstan closed Batumi oil terminal and new route of Kazakh oil is unknown to us. In import, the following countries have biggest share: Ukraine, Turkey, Greece, Russia, Italy, Bulgaria. In export: Bulgaria, Italy, Turkey, Ukraine, Romania, Malta.

Table 2 Handled Cargo by Sea Ports and Sea Terminals (mln. tons)

Name of Sea Port and Sea Terminal	2006	2007	2008	2009	2010	2011	2012	2013	2014	2015	2016
Poti Sea Port	6.7	7.7	8.0	6.1	7.3	7.2	7.5	7.4	8.6	6.8	6.3
Batumi Sea Port	13.2	11.2	8.7	7.8	8.0	7.9	7.9	8.3	6.3	5.7	5.6
Kulevi Sea Terminal	0.0	0.0	1.3	2.1	3.4	3.3	2.5	2.1	2.1	2.5	1.6
Supsa Sea Terminal	5.6	0.0	0.6	4.2	4.0	3.8	3.9	4.0	4.2	4.2	4.1
Total	25.5	18.9	18.6	20.2	22.7	22.1	21.8	21.9	21.3	19.2	17.6

Source: materials of Ministry of Economy and Sustainable Development of Georgia

Turkey has biggest share in container turnover, then comes Italy and Romania. Baku-Poti railway is important for South Caucasus region and Central Asia as a way to transfer container-transit cargo, because Poti port has the most attractive tariffs and the shortest distance, based on its geographic location, in the region.

Table 3:　　　　　　　Handled Containers by Sea Ports (TEU)

Name of Sea Port	2006	2007	2008	2009	2010	2011	2012	2013	2014	2015	2016
Poti Sea Port	129100	184792	209614	172800	209797	254022	284559	331324	384992	325121	273690
Batumi Sea Port	0	0	44197	8813	16318	45439	73095	72123	61980	54695	56115
Total	129100	184792	253811	181613	226115	299461	357654	403447	446972	379816	329805

Source: materials of Ministry of Economy and Sustainable Development of Georgia

"TRACECA" international transport corridor changed Georgia's transport infrastructure. east-west corridor-motorway was developed from Red bridge (border with Azerbaijan) to Batumi; railway has been loaded, cargo turnover has increased and cargo geography has changed.

Tripartite agreement about functioning of Baku-Tbilisi-Akhalkalaki-Kars railway, which was reached in February 2007, is important for regional relations between Turkey, Georgia and Azerbaijan. The goal of the project is to involve South Caucasus in Pan European transport corridor. Azerbaijan allocated 340 mln Lari as a 25 years' and 1% loan to build new 93 km railroad and to reconstruct Marabda-Akhalkalaki 160 km railroad. Capacity at the initial stage will be 5 mln tonnes, which later will be increased to 10 mln tonnes. The construction work on Georgian section was finished in 2013 and came to Turkish border. Turkey started building its section only in 2016, which is planned to be completed by the end of this year, because they have a great interest in involvement in the Initiative of China through this particular railway, this was announced by Erdogan in Beijing in May 2017. By the railroad, China will be connected to Europe through Georgia. First of all, cargo, which is destined for Turkey, will be carried through the railroad. But most importantly, this will be the route connecting Asia with Europe, which will pass under Bosporus strait in "Marmarai" tunnel, which was opened in 2013 and Turkey, according to its plans, will play the main part in new Eurasian corridor. The Tunnel will later be connected with Baku-Tbilisi-Kars mainline and from there, it will be connected with China, the largest cargo sender country in Asia. Very effective Asian-European transport corridor will be created in Black Sea region, which will compete with many transit projects, including "TRACECA", this will definitely decrease cargo going through Black Sea Basin ports and probably Poti will have to restructure cargo, because it is strongly dependent on container cargo coming from Azerbaijan, Central Asia and China, large part of which will be transferred to railroad.

Active support of Turkey for Baku-Tbilisi-Karsrailroad, derives from the geostrategic interest and implies development of eastern regions of the country and its transport infrastructure, basically sea ports (Samsun, Trabzon, Rize, Hopa).

Implementation of Baku-Tbilisi-Kars railroad project is also important for Azerbaijan, because by building the railroadAstara-Rasht-Qazvin, which connects Azerbaijan with Iran, and by Implementation of Baku-Tbilisi-Kars railroad project, longitudinal as well as latitudinal routes will pass through Azerbaijan. Through the project, Asian and Caucasian countries will have an opportunity to gain access to Mediterranean Sea and Trans-European and Trans-Asian systems will be connected stronger.

Ⅳ. INITIATIVE OF CHINA: Belt and Road

After the world economic crisis in 2008, China took obligation of developing the world economy by itself. Initiative of China is not accidentally called "The Belt and Road" and "Globalization 2.0". China's The Belt and Road Initiative is oriented towards creating of new multimodal transport corridor, which is directed through Eurasian continent in two flows-land and sea.

This road unites 65 countries, 62, 3% of world population, 38, 5% of land area, one-third of global economic production. Geographic area of "The

Belt and Road" is "Economic Belt Great Silk Road" and "21st Century Great Sea Silk Road". "Belt and Road will pass through the following corridors: Russia's "Eurasian Economic Corridor", "ASEAN", Kazakhstan's "Bright Road", Turkey's "Central Corridor", Mongolian "Steppe Road", Vietnam's "Two Corridors-One Circle", Poland's "Amber Road", Great Britain's "Northern Powerhouse", TRACECA and Russia's "North-South".

"Silk Road", stretched on 7000 km 2000 years ago, was the bridge connecting Europe, Asia and Africa or east and west and a symbol of China's strength. For China, "The Belt and Road", besides its economic meaning, is connected to its values to willingness to see strong, stable, developed China in the world arena.

China's goals in the project are: by mutually beneficial cooperation, reach security and welfare among participant countries; creation of inter-connected infrastructure and development of open type economy; simplification of investment and trade procedures and creation of free trade zones.

V. The Perspectives of Georgia

For Georgia, transit function in social-economic point of view is the way to increase budget revenues, maintain financial stability, develop services and create jobs.

Georgia already has stable relations with China. China signed free trade agreement with Georgia and wanted to deepen economic cooperation.

However, Georgia-China relations do have some developing perspective. In December 13, 2015 first transit train from Chinese port Lianyungang's terminal arrived to Tbilisi. With the arrival of the train, "Silk Railroad" was officially opened. The train will continue its way to Turkey in the future. This is the first transit cargo and fulfilled project of "Silk Road". In the future, transit train will connect Asia with Europe and vice versa in the shortest period of time. Cargo in Istanbul will arrive in 14 – 15 days maximum, while during sea transportation 40 – 45 days are necessary.

For Georgia, it will also be important if Turkey manages to interest China to transfer parts of cargo to Baku-Tbilisi-Kars railroad.

VI. Conclusion

The development perspectives of Georgia has its significance.

Literature and statistical analysis of sources lets us draw following conclusions:

1. In modern global space, transcontinentaltransport corridors gain great importance and develop at a fast pace, they unite economic and political poles and create communication carcass.

2. Georgia is connected with Trans-European transport infrastructure through TRACECA transport corridor, which is connecting Europe and Asia. TRACECA is a guarantee for regional cooperation, increase in cargo flows, security and sustainable development.

3. Transit function of Georgia is a factor of its political, economic and social development, involvement in global space, employment and improvement of living standards of population. World community is also promoting development of this function.

4. Initiative of China: "The Belt and Road Initiative" is a great geoeconomic project, which has become a global initiative.

5. Georgia has transit and logistical potential to get involved in China's corridor, but will definitely need modernized sea, railway, motorway infrastructure, increase of capacity of existing roads and creating secure and stable environment on these roads.

6. Georgia's foreign political orientation is correct and the country is involved in world processes. It is a member of up to 40 international organizations, including World Trade Organization. Future of Georgia's sustainable development depends on the country's foreign political and economic directions.

Georgia-China Relations in Historical and Contemporary Context

Nana Gelashvili[*]

In modern times, in the background of the political, socio- economic and other processes, taking place in Georgia and entire in the world, it is increasingly important to expand the knowledge area both-geographically and in subject. This implies first of all, the countries territorially distant from Georgia. From this point of view, with all existing parameters (civilization acquirements, scientific and technical achievements both-in the distant past and in the recent period, high level of economic development, etc.) the Peoples Republic of China deserves special attention. This is conditioned not only by the great interest towards this truly superpower state, but also by its ever increasing potential and role in solving global issues of the world. It is widely known, that China is one of the central players on the political map of the world, which is moving forward at a fast pace and boldly accepting new challenges. At the same time the Chinese people tenderly take care of their ancient civilization acquirements and traditions of the past, whose history exceeds more than 5,000 years. In this context I would like to invoke the old Chinese wise, saying:

---

[*] Nana. Gelashvili, Professor at Ivane Javakhishvili Tbilisi State University, Head of department of Far East Regional studies-Sinology (Georgia).

Chapter 5 Chinese Path to Modernization and New Opportunities for the Development of the China-Georgia BRI Cooperation

"While drinking water, think about its source", meaning that present comes from and originates from the historical past. This is what the great Chinese thinker and philosopher Confucius (551-479 BC) preached. Namely, one of his catchphrase was the following: "The key to solving the problems of the present, must be seek in the past, in the forgotten ancient wisdom". Indeed, without studying and taking into account any segment of the historical past, it is impossible to adequately understand and properly evaluate the current events or facts.

It is well known that China is one of the oldest and richest hearth of civilizations in the world. Over the centuries it was developing completely independently as a country with a unique and self-contained civilization. Moreover, China was itself a paragon and bright example for the entire East and South-East Asian countries,[1] It was under the influence of China that various elements of material and spiritual culture, various fields of arts and crafts, philosophical-religious doctrines (Confucianism and Taoism), institutions of state management, principles of urban planning, etc. were spread in the neighboring countries. The ancient Chinese were equally aware of their special role and significance not only in the region, but in the world. Therefore they believed that China was the center of the universe, so called country under the sky and sky was recognized as the supreme deity. Even the name of the China -Zgongguo, i. e. the middle, central state, is clear confirmation for such an approach to the issue.[2]

Chinese history has alternated between periods of political unity and peace, periods of war and failed statehood.

Speaking of relations between Georgia and China, a short historical excursion is needed. First of all it should point out that from the late antique period, when "Great silk road" -international caravan-trade highway existed, China has

---

[1] *The Cambridge history of ancient China: from the origins of civilization to 221BC* , ed. by M. Loewe and E. L. Shaugnessy, Cambridge University Press, 1999, pp. 232 – 241.

[2] Harrison L. J. , *The Chinese Empire, a short history of China from Neolithic times to the end of the 18th century*, New York, 1972, p. 14.

established close trade-economic relations with Central and East Asia, Persia, the Mediterranean and Black Sea basin, as well as with Caucasian countries. History of the "Great Silk Road" originates in the 2nd century B. C. and is associated with the name of the Chinese diplomat and traveler Zhang Qian, who was sent by Emperor Wu Ti (141 – 87 BC) on a special mission to the countries of Central Asia. In 120 year BC while returning to his homeland, Zhang Qian presented to the authorities very interesting and important information about the political and economic situation in the regions of the West. Based on his report, the necessity to establish trade and diplomatic relations with distant countries beyond China's borders was outlined. However, it should be also noted here that China before that time already had relations with the outside world through the Jade Road, which connected northern and central China with Persia. It was on its basis that the development of the Silk Road began. ①The term "Great Silk Road" itself was brought into circulation by the German historian and geographer Ferdinand von Richthofen (1833 – 1905), who organized seven expeditions to China in 1868 – 1872 and properly studied the issues related to the Silk Road. The main consumers of Chinese silk were originally the nobles of the Roman Empire. Later silk was exported already to Byzantium through the mediation of Parthia and Persia. ②

In addition to the main trade product-silk, various metals, precious stones, handicrafts, porcelain and luxury items were imported from China. It should be emphasized, that along with trade purpose, the Silk Road had the function of a transcultural bridge between the Far East, Europe, North Africa and the rest of Asia. So, the merchants and travelers, moving on the mentioned road, willingly or unwillingly, carried elements of native and foreign culture from one place to another. Through them dialogue of cultures, exchanging and

---

① Xinru Liu, *The Silk Road in the World History*, New York: Oxford University Press, 2010, p. 11.

② Zviadadze G., *The Great silk road passed through Georgia*, Tbilisi (in Georgian), p. 16, Xinru Liu (2010). The Silk road in the world history, New York: Oxford University Press, 1989, p. 21.

sharing of ideas, as well as spiritual values, traditions and various technologies took place. Georgia was also involved in these processes to a certain extend. ①. So, in ancient Georgia-Kolkheti and Iberia, they already had a certain idea of China and the Chinese. Due to its convenient geopolitical location, Georgia has been a kind of connecting bridge between the West and the East since ancient times. This function of it was clearly revealed as in political, social and economic spheres. In this regard, the outstanding importance of Georgia as a transit country in international trade relations is particularly noteworthy. It is known from history that trade highways passed through Georgia from ancient times, information about this is preserved in the works of Greek authors (Herodotus, Strabo...). ② One of the most important of the mentioned roads was the transcontinental trade-caravan road of silk, which connected distant China with the countries of the Mediterranean and Black Sea basins. However it should be also noted, that in the original maps and sources Georgia did not appear in the route of the old "Silk Road". The fact is that the mentioned road historically ran much further south from Georgia and only its peripheral branch entered the South Caucasus region.

At the turn of the 3rd-4th centuries AD, the political situation in the Anterior-Asian region caused significant changes in the itineraries of the world trade routes. Immediately after the creation of the Byzantine Empire (395 AD), the trade routes became oriented towards the capital of the empire-Constantinople, which became the most important trade and cultural center on the boundary of Europe and Asia. ③

The Caucasus route gained special importance later, namely in the VI cen-

---

① Gelashvili N., *Intercultural impact in the Near East in middle ages*, Byzantine studies in Georgia -3, Vol. I, Tbilisi (in Georgian), 2011, pp. 104 – 105.

② Gablishvili L., *Georgia and the Great Silk Road in late antiquity and the middle ages*, Proceedings of the Georgian national academy of sciences (series of history), #2, Tbilisi (in Georgian), 2021, pp. 29 – 30.

③ *History of Byzantium*, editor-in-chief Skazkin S. D., Moskow (in Russian), 1967, p. 121.

tury, when the main caravan artery was expanded and side roads were added to it. Since that time Georgia has been actively involved in the Silk Road. The fact was that due to the conflict between Byzantium and Persia during the mentioned period, the transportation of silk through Persia to Byzantium and Mediterranean countries became very dangerous and risky. Due to the created political situation in the 6th century Sasanian Iran prohibited the export of silk to the West through its territory, as well as the free trade with silk. [1] Because of this, the search for new trade routes began, which was directly related to the changes in the military-political situation on the Silk Road That's why Asian merchants, including Chinese, who supplied Byzantium with Chinese silk and other products, developed a new route. Namely it was a road leading from the Caspian Sea to the north-crossing the Caucasus mountain ranch and leading towards Byzantium.

Between Iran and Byzantium for a long time were going on wars for dominance over the roads, coming from the North Caucasus. At the turn of the 5th-6th centuries, the Dariali Valley section of this territory was controlled by the population of the North Caucasus, who conveniently maneuvered in relation to Byzantium and Iran, in particular, sometimes supporting one, and sometimes the other, depending on which of them had a more profitable offer. It should be noted that the local population, in addition to the appropriate tax, from the trade caravans also received payment in kind-various jewels, beads, shells, etc. From the second half of the 6th century on the Caucasian section of the Silk Road, it was its North Caucasian direction, which became a regular trade highway. [2] Through this way were transported silk fabrics, beads, dishes, different kinds of wooden articles, porcelain and other products, which were more in

---

[1] *History of Byzantium*, editor-in-chief Skazkin S. D., Moskow (in Russian), 1967, p. 325.

[2] Gelashvili N., Georgia in the light of Iran-Byzantine wars (6th century), Pro Georgia, Journal of Kartvelological studies, #26, Warsaw, 2016, pp. 80 – 81.

demand on the Silk Road. ① It should be noted that in the upper reaches of the River Kuban tributary-Bolshaia Laba, archaeologists discovered the burial of a Chinese merchant with various items, including embroidered silk cloth and personal records of this merchant. According to research results, the tomb belonged to the period of the Chinese Tang Dynasty rule (618 – 907).

Since the middle ages there was much more information about China in Georgia, which is confirmed by both-archaeological artifacts and Georgian written sources. Among the archaeological materials, discovered in various parts of Georgia, there are fragments of Chinese silk fabric, porcelain, bronze coin with Chinese inscriptions and so on. The remains of Chinese silk fabrics were found in the tombs of the 2nd century BC and the following era. ② It should also be noted that among the numerous foreign coins found on the territory of Georgia, there is also a Chinese coin, which indicates the intensive trade and economic relations of Iberia-Kartli (eastern Georgia) with the outside world. In particular, in 1993, during the archaeological works carried out in the village of Mtskhetijvari, Khashuri district-near the Ali castle, was found a bronze coin with Chinese inscriptions, which had a square-shaped hole in the middle. On the basis of research carried out by specialists, it was established that the mentioned coin was minted during the reign of the Southern Song Dynasty (1127 – 1279), specifically-in 1200. ③ The extracted Chinese coin is of great importance for the study of the trade and economic history of Georgia in the 12th-13th centuries. It should not be accidental, that it was discovered in the very areas where, according to scientific researches, still in ancient times a great trade-

---

① Ierusalimskaia A. A., An unusual archaeological monument, St. Peterburg (in Russian), 2012, pp. 349 – 351.

② *Goiladze V.*, Great Silk Road and Georgia, Tbilisi (in Georgian), 1997, pp. 35 – 36.

③ Bragvadze Z., Davitashvili A. *Chinese coin from Mcxetijvari*, Dzeglis Megobari, #1, Tbilisi (in Georgian), 1993, pp. 46 – 47.

caravan road passed. ① Therefore, there is no doubt that many more interesting materials will be discovered in the future, which will shed more light on the relations, existing between Georgia and China in the distant past.

Many Georgian written sources of middle ages contain interesting information about China and Chinese. This time, we'll limit ourselves to naming only a few of them. These are: the Georgian version of the 11th century Persian poem "Visramiani", "Abdulmesiani" by Ioane Shavteli, well-known poem "The Knight in the Panther's Skin" by Shota Rustaveli (which is translated from Georgian to Chinese). Special interest deserves "Tamariani" by Chakhrukhadze, a traveler and poet panegyrist of King Tamar (1184 – 1213). Author describes his travels in 1193 – 1203 – s in the Middle and Far East countries, including Persia, India and China. ② Among the later period works deserves special mention the "World Political Geography" translated by famous Georgian geographer and historian Vakhushti Bagrationi (1696 – 1757). The mentioned work contains a political-geographical description of China and a color map of China in Georgian. Rafiel Danibegashvili is recognized as a world-class traveler, who traveled to Asian countries in 1795 – 1827, specifically China he visited three times (in 1813 – 1814, 1815 and 1820). His work contains extremely interesting information about the Chinese people's way of life, traditions, and religious issues, as well as local ecological and geographical distinctive characteristics. It should be noted that China is referred to by various names in the Georgian written sources, including Chini, Chin-Machini, Khataeti, Kitayuri, and Machineti. ③ The present name of the country "China" is derived from the root "Chin". The translation of the 11th century Persian poem

---

① Gablishvili L., Georgia and the Great Silk Road in late antiquity and the middle ages, Proceedings of the Georgian national academy of sciences (series of history), #2, Tbilisi (in Georgian), 2021, p. 37.

② Katsitadze D., *History of Iran, III -XVIII centuries*, Tbilisi (in Georgian), 2009, pp. 10 – 13, 18 – 19.

③ Katsitadze D., History of Iran, III -XVIII centuries, Tbilisi (in Georgian), 2009, pp. 24 – 26.

"Visramiani" is the first Georgian written composing in which term "Chin" appears.

Georgian-Chinese relations have grown more tangible and intense since the end of the 19th century.

As an example, consider the fruitful activity of the Chinese inGeorgia, namely in Adjara (led by Liu Zunzhou, same as-Lao Jinjao) in the perspective of tea cultivation and tea industry development. Liu Zunzhou arrived in Batumi in 1893, along with other Chinese tea specialists and brought several thousand tea seedlings and seeds. The establishment of the tea seedling greenhouse and the first tea processing factory in Georgia are related to his leadership. It should be noted, that great achievements of Liu Zunzhou are well known and studied by Georgian scholars. ①

It is very interesting and important tomention activities of the "Georgian colony" in Harbin city of China. History records a large number of Georgian communities settling in the mentioned city during the first years of the 20th century. The "National Society of Georgians," led by Ivliane Khaindrava, was founded in 1908 as a result of Georgian communities' efforts. It should be noted that Georgians from Harbin were active participants in the region's political, economic, and cultural life. At the same time they were connected with the democratic republic of Georgia. ② In this context, it is worth noting that the first diplomatic mission-the consulate of Georgia in the Far East was established in Harbin, with the first consul being a doctor by specialty-Nikoloz Jishkariani. The area of activity of the consulate covered not only Manchuria, but also eastern Siberia. In the 20s and 30s of the 20th century many Georgians actively worked in Harbin. Among them it is worth mentioning G. Sidamonidze, B. Lominadze, A. Svanidze and etc. It is clear from the letters of Georgians from

---

① Daghundaridze N., *At the Origins of Tea Culture in Georgia*, Tbilisi (in Georgian), 2003, pp. 27 – 29.

② Chikhladze Sh., Chigladze O, *Georgians in China in the first half of 20th century*, Herald of oriental studies, # Batumi: Batumi State University (in Georgian), 2021, pp. 92 – 93.

Harbin, that by 1921 about 3000 Georgians lived in the city and its surroundings, and this number was increasing. But when the Japanese captured Harbin, the number of foreign residents, including Georgians, drastically decreased. As a result by 1941, the Georgian community numbered about 400 people. ①

A particularly important and fruitful period in Georgia-China relations starts in the beginning of 1990s. Following the restoration of Georgia's independence and the establishment of diplomatic relations between Georgia and China on 9 June 1992, the two friendly countries established qualitatively new, multilateral relations. Bilateral ties have advanced gradually since then and mostly focused on economic cooperation.

In terms of the Silk Road's subsequent fate, it should be noted, that the exchange of material and intellectual values between the West and the East continued at periodic intervals till the beginning of the 15th century. In later times, the ancient Silk Road lost its global importance, and at the end of the 16th century, it ceased to function due to the ongoing war vicissitudes in the Central Asian region and the exploitation of the oceanic route around Africa by Europeans. It should be noted that China was the first country to take practical steps to put the "New Silk Road" concept into action. It was given the new impetus to the Silk Road concept in 2013 by introducing the well-known concept of "Belt and Road".

Along with economic growth, China has begun to invest heavily in road infrastructure. As it is known, the modern world is facing a lot of challenges. Hot spots have multiplied in some regions, extremism, separatism and other kind problems are emerging. In the historical past, the old Silk Road was actually destroyed by endless wars and conflicts. The initiative of the government of the People's Republic of China about forming the economic corridor of the Silk Road by joint efforts, which will contribute to the more rational use of human, mar-

---

① Chikhladze Sh., Chigladze O., *Georgians in China in the first half of 20th century*, *Herald of oriental studies*, # Batumi: Batumi State University (in Georgian), 2021, p. 100.

ket, technical and resource capabilities of different countries, will appear very positive. ①

As it was mentioned, there are already stable traditions of diplomatic, trade-economic and scientific-cultural relations between Georgia and China. It should be emphasized that China was one of the first to recognize the independence of Georgia and in 2022 the 30th anniversary of the establishment of diplomatic relations between the two friendly states was fulfilled. Our department- "Far East regional studies: Sinology" at Ivane Javakhishvili Tbilisi state university's students at a high academic level study Chinese language, literature, culture, history of China from the ancient times to modern period, economics, historical cities, ancient Chinese philosophical-religious doctrines (Confucianism, Taoism) and other subjects.

The great attention of the embassy of the Peoples Republic of China in Georgia to the Sinology direction at Tbilisi State University deserves special mention. In particular, for us-teachers and students opening of the "study room of Chinese language and culture", equipped with the latest computer technology, educational and scientific literature, as well as with various items, necessary for the educational process in 2015 at university was a great stimulus. All this was implemented with the financial support of the Chinese embassy in Georgia and the company "Huawei".

It should be noted here that the literature in the Georgian language about China is relatively small and the demand for it is increasing. That is why intensive work is carried out in this direction: there are published Chinese language textbooks, Georgian-Chinese dictionary, various literary works are translated from Chinese to Georgian and from Georgian to Chinese. Not long ago we published our collective work "History of China", which covers the history, socio-economic and cultural issues from ancient times to modern period, besides my

---

① Kharadze K., *China seen through the eyes of medieval Georgian travelers and geographers*, *The Silk Road and Caucasus*, Tbilisi (in Georgian), 2017, pp. 57–59.

monograph " Historical capitals of China" will be soon published. It is also pleasant to note, that many of our students have completed long-term internships in leading Chinese universities, who currently successfully work both in Georgia and China in various companies, travel agencies, embassies, universities, scientific fields and others. Even now, in post-pandemic period a new stream of our students has already joined exchange study programs. Based on all the above, it is unequivocally clear, that the relations between Georgia and China are deepening and becoming multifaceted. One of the proofs of this is the international symposium "The Belt and Road": Experiences of Modernization and Social Development of China", which was held in Beijing on December 9 in 2022.

Today, close trade and economic cooperation is the main pillar of Georgia-China relations, including political-diplomatic dialogue. In this regard, the large-scale "Belt and Road" project is particularly noteworthy, in which Georgia is actively involved as a transport and transit hub connecting Eurasia due to its unique geostrategic location. However, it should be noted that at this stage the Transcaucasian corridor of the New Silk Road, as well as Georgia's consideration as a competitive alternative among corridors for transporting goods between Europe and China, are somewhat dubious for subjective and objective reasons. Because this is a separate topic, we will limit ourselves to noting that for the time being, Georgia remains a regional transport corridor due to its relatively low competitiveness characteristics in terms of transit time and costs. On the other hand, Georgia has a very favorable geopolitical opportunity to become a trade transit country between East and West, as well as an energy transit corridor between the Caspian region and Central Asia and Europe. Furthermore, analysts believe that if Georgia harmonizes traffic regulations and legislation with the other corridor members and simplifies operations, it will become a much more competitive transit route. Taking into account the factors above mentioned, Georgia's participation in the large-scale project of the New Silk Road becomes even more relevant, thus enabling it to globally demonstrate its capabilities in various fields.

China in the Eyes of Georgian People:
From Antiquity to the Present Times

Otari Tchigladze*

In this paper we discuss the development of knowledge about China in Georgia over the centuries from ancient times to modern times based on written sources. As a result of the research, we showed that the phenomenon of China in the Georgian people's perception was constantly changing, sometimes the change was progressive and sometimes regressive. In the ancient era and the Middle Ages, Georgians got to know China mainly through merchants and by translation of foreign literature. Until the 17th century, very limited and scarce information about China could be found in Georgian sources. Georgian readers got acquainted with the first systematic and reliable information about China only from the 18th century. In the 19th – 20th century, a complex view of China appeared in Georgian society for the first time. The public gradually became interested in getting more detailed and deeper knowledge about Chinese politics, economy and culture. In the past three decades, as a result of establishing direct contacts, China-Georgia relations have developed very rapidly.

China-Georgia multilateral cooperation saw a very rapid development in the last decade. Close political and economic ties have already been established be-

---

* Otari. Tchigladze, Georgian Young Sinologist, graduated from Peking University

tween the two countries. Based on these circumstances, the interest in Chinese culture is also growing in Georgian scientific circles and among the general masses. However, the awareness towards China both in scientific circles and in general society is in its early stage. In order to strengthen this dynamic of growing interest towards China and raise a public awareness, we think it would be beneficial to study how the phenomenon of China developed in Georgians' peoples perception over the centuries. This will not only provide valuable material for historians and culturologists to continue research in this direction in the future, but will also interest all strata of the society.

Due to the lack of sources, it is practically impossible to say precisely when the first information about China appeared in Georgia. The earliest Georgian-language written source about China belongs to the 12th century. Does this mean that only from the 12th century we can start researching the understanding of the Chinese phenomenon in the Georgian society? My answer to this question is negative. Although there are no direct written sources confirming this, a number of other circumstances indicate that Georgians must have known China much earlier.

First of all, the existence of the Great Silk Road gives us the basis for this assumption. This huge trade network, which for centuries connected the distant points of Europe and Asia, was one of the main means of information flow in antiquity and the Middle Ages. The Silk Road originated from China and played a major role in the spread of knowledge about China to the West. Although the main route of the Silk Road did not pass through Georgia, the ancient Greek geographer Strabo (63BC-24AD) still notes that Georgia, due to its geographical location, was one of the main crossing points of the West-East and South-North trade routes[1], which implicates that Georgia was a part of the Great Silk Road

---

[1] Emili Avdaliani, *Sakartvelo da abreshumis savach'ro gzebi (VI-XIIIss.)* (*Georgia and Silk Roads (VI-XIII centuries)*), Tbilisi: Meridiani, 2019, gv. 61 – 62. Irak'li Shikhiashvili, "*Abreshumis gza*" *da Sakartvelo (Arkeologiuri da Ist'oriuli ts'q'aroebis mikhedvit)* ("*Silk Road*" *and Georgia (According to archeological and historical sources)*), Tbilisi, 2019, gv. 34 – 36.

trade network. This is also evidenced by the fact that products traveling on the Silk Road entered Georgia in abundance. Remains of silk from 2nd-3rd centuries was discovered on the territory of Georgia by archeologists[1]. According to written sources, as early as 5th century, making silk handicraft was a very common activity among the women of nobility in Georgia[2].

In addition to that, the centralroute of the Silk Road also changed its location several times due to a number of reasons. For example, at the turn of the 6th and 7th centuries, when relations between Persia and Byzantium became tense again, due to economic and political restrictions, traders cut a new route to the north[3]. They came from the Central Asia to the North Caucasus through the Russian steppes, crossed the Caucasus and entered Byzantium from the ports of Western Georgia[4]. This is confirmed not only by written but also by archaeological sources. In the western mountains of Georgia, in Svaneti region, remains of silk from the 7th century, which was imported from Central Asia, were found[5]. Central Asian merchants were the main intermediaries between West and East along the Silk Road. However, apart of them, a small number of Chinese merchants also passed through this road. This was proven by unearthing a tomb belonging to a Chinese merchant dating back to the 7th century in the North Caucasus. In addition to Chinese products, inscriptions written in Chinese

---

[1] L. Lursmanashvili, M. Datuashvili, N. Dolidze, Dzvel Sakartveloshi gavrtselebuli abreshumis ksovilis sakheebi (Kind of silk materials spread in old Georgia), *Saist'orio vert'ik'ali*, Nomeri 19, Tbilisi: Basiani, 2009, gv. 100 – 101.

[2] Presbyter Iakob, *The martyrdom of Shushanik*, Translated by Maia Akhvlediani, Tbilisi: Nekeri, 2019, gv. 48.

[3] Vakht'ang Goiladze, *Abreshumis didi savach'ro gza da Sakartvelo* (*Silk Road and Georgia*), Tbilisi, 1997, gv. 31.

[4] Олеся Жданович, Менандр Протектор, История : О посольствах тЮрков к Персам и Византийцам в 568 году, *Золотоордынское обозрение*, № 1 (3), 2014, ст. 27.

[5] T'ariel K'vitsiani, Adreuli shua sauk'uneebis (Ⅵ-Ⅷ ss.) abreshumis dek'orat'iuli ksovilebi K'avk'asiidan (Deocrative textiles of silk in early Middle Ages (Ⅵ-Ⅷ centuries) Caucasia), *Arkeologiuri k'rebuli*, Ⅳ, Tbilisi: Tbilisis sakhelmtsipo universit'et'is gamomtsemloba, 2004, gv. 73 – 75.

hieroglyphs on silk fabric were also found in the tomb①.

Along with the trade-economic factor, we must also take into account the political situation. In particular, the close relationship of Georgian kings and nobility with the royal court of Persia and Armenia. Diplomatic relations between Persia and China were established as early as in the 2nd century BC and exchanges between two countries only got morefrequent as time went on②. Consequently, Georgians could have received information about China through contacts with the Persian royal court or nobles. In this regard, ties with Armenia are even more important. Already in the written sources of the 5th century in Georgia's neighboring Armenia, references to China have been recorded③. The exchange between Georgian and Armenian literature were very frequent from the very beginning. Quite a number of works were translated from Armenian into Georgian between the 6th and 9th centuries④. Close kinship and political ties between the Georgian nobles and the great Armenian noble lineage of Mamikonians give us more grounds to assume that Georgians could have received information about China from Armenia⑤, as the Mamikonians claimed that their ancestry was of Chinese origin, and the first mention of China in Armenian sources is also related to their name. ⑥

Therefore, we can reasonably assume that before the 12th century, Geor-

---

① А. А. Иерусалимская, Кавказ на шелковом пути, Санкт-Петербург, 1992, ст. 7.

② 35，83，1974，بررسی عوامل مؤثر بر روابط ایران و چین و تأثیر آن بر مبادلاتمحصولات طبی دارویی در عصر باستان，حمیدکاویانی پویا；丘进，《中国与罗马，汉代中西关系研究》，黄山出版社2008年版，第176页。

③ P'awstos Buzandac 'i', *History of the Armenians*, Translated from classical Armenian by Robert Bedrosian, New York 1985, p. 89.

④ Ilia Abuladze, *Kartuli da Somkhuri lit'erat'uruli urtiertoba IX-X sauk'uneebshi* (*Georgian and Armenian literary relations in IX-X centuries*), Tbilisi: Sakartvelos ssr metsnierebata ak'ademiis gamomtsemloba, 1944, gv. 12 - 13.

⑤ Presbyter Iakob, *The martyrdom of Shushanik*, gv. 3.

⑥ P'awstos Buzandac 'i', *History of the Armenians*, p. 89; Movses Khorenatsi, *Somkhetis ist'oria* (*History of Armenia*), Dzveli Somkhuridan targmna, shesavali da shenishvnebi daurto Aleksandre Abdaladzem, Tbilisi: Metsniereba, 1984, gv. 165; История епископа Себеоса, Перевод с четвертого исправленного армянского издания Ст. Малхасянц, Ереван: Армфан - А, 1939, ст. 17 - 18.

gians had a certain perception of China. Unfortunately, due to the lack of sources, it is impossible to find out exactly when the information about China entered Georgia and what it was about. On the other hand, if we accept the assumption that Georgians knew about China way before the 12th century, then we have to answer the question why this knowledge was not recorded in contemporary Georgian written sources. It should be noted that Georgian and Armenian literature emerged at the same time, at the turn of the 4th-5th centuries. The first mention of China in Armenian written sources could be traced back to the 5th century, while it took seven more centuries for Georgian literature to have first records on China. If the Georgians did know about China in the early Middle Ages, then why do we see a time gap of almost seven hundred years between Georgian and Armenian literature in terms of records about China?

In my opinion, the reason for this should be the peculiarities of the development of Georgian and Armenian literature. The point is that in the early period of Armenian literature, secular and religious writing actually developed simultaneously[1], while in Georgia only religious literature was developed at first. Secular literature was formed only at the turn of the 11th-12th centuries[2]. The late emergence of secular literature should be the reason why China is not found in earlier Georgian sources. This assumption is confirmed by the fact that the Armenian sources that mention China all belong to secular writings, as well as the Georgian sources of the later period. China is not found in the Christian theological writings of other countries of this period either. Probably because the medieval Christian geographical or historical worldview was based entirely on the "Holy Bible", in which China is not mentioned. Neither did the apostles preach in China. It is true that representatives of the Nestorian Christianity en-

---

[1] Leon Melikset-Begi, *Dzveli Somkhuri lit'erat'uris ist'oria* (*History of old Armenian literature*), Tbilisi: St'alinis sakhelobis Tbilisis sakhelmts'ipo universit'et'is gamomtsemloba, 1941, gv. 69.

[2] А. Барамидзе, Ш. Радиани, В. Жгенти, *История Грузинской литературы краткий очерк*, Тбилиси: Заря Востока, 1958, ст. 16.

tered China as early as the 7th century①, But this sect was banished in the 5th century at the Council of Chalcedon, and the Georgian and Byzantine Church had severed their ties with it. Accordingly, China was outside the reach of geographical worldview of Georgian and generally Christian literature.

Based on the sources available today, China first appears in Georgian literature in the writings of mid-12th century. Namely, inthe novel "Visramian" translated from Persian and in an astrological treaty also translated from Persian②. In terms of receiving information about China, Persia maintained the status of the main source of information for Georgian society until the 18th century. China was mentioned in the works of Georgian authors at the end of the 12th century. It should be noted that among them is the epic poem "Knight in the panther's skin", which is recognized as the greatest masterpiece of Georgian literature③. As the latter was immensely popular among all strata of society, we can say that "Knight in the panther's skin" played a major role in building awareness of China among the masses. Information about China in Georgian sources of this period is very scarce and superficial. Mostly mentioned only as toponyms. Almost all the toponyms denoting China used in Persian and Arabic writings soon spread in Georgia too. Until the middle of the 13th century, Georgians' knowledge of China was superficial. China was imagined as a semi-legendary large and powerful country of the Far East, with a large population, distinguished by high quality products.

In the 13th century, the phenomenon of China changed significantly in Georgian society. The reason for this was the influx of new information. After the

---

① Pier Giorgio Borbone, Les églises d'Asie centrale et de Chine: état de la question à partir des textes etdesdécouvertes archéologiques: essai de synthèse, études syriaques 10 - Les églises en monde syriaque, Paris, 2013, pp. 458 - 459.

② *Visramiani*, Kartuli mts'erloba, T'omi 3, Tbilisi: Nak'aduli, 1988, gv. 118, 185 ; *Et'lta da shvidta mnatobtatus* (*Treaty on constellations and seven stars*), Gamostsa, ts'inasit'q'vaoba da enobrivi mimokhilva daurto Akaki Shanidzem, Tbilisi: Tbilisis universit'et'is gamomtsemloba, 1975, gv. 29.

③ [格] 鲁斯塔维利:《虎皮武士》, 严永兴译, 译林出版社 2002 年版, 第 181 页; Shota Rustaveli, Vepkhistq'aosani (Knight in the panther's skin), Redakt'ori: Dali Germanishvili, gv. 177.

conquest of Georgia by the Mongols in the 40s – 50s of the 13th century, Georgia became part of the great Mongol empire and joined the flow of information within the empire. Many Georgians personally visited the Far East. For example, in 1245 – 1248, two heirs to the royal throne of Georgia traveled to Karakorum, capital city of Mongol empire at that time. In addition to them, a number of Georgian dignitaries, clerics and warriors traveled there[1]. After the establishment of the Ilkhanate, Georgian kings and aristocrats often visited their royal court, where many Chinese scholars were also present[2]. Apart from that, Georgian-Persian literary relations developed further. Georgian scholars were closely aquainted with contemporary Persian historical works[3].

Based on all the factors mentioned above, new, more reliable reports about China arrived in Georgia. It is true that only one of the Georgian writings of the 13th-14th centuries contains references about China, but these references are qualitatively and quantitatively better than those from the previous period. Theserecords are preserved in the historical work "hundried years Chronicle" by anonymous author. The chronicle describes the process of Mongol conquests and in this cotext also touches upon Mongol activities in China[4]. Based

---

[1] Jaba Samushia, *Davit Ulu* (*David VII*), Tbilisi: Palitra L, 2019, gv. 77; *The journey of William of Rubruck to the eastern parts of the world as narrated by himself, with two accounts of the earlier journey of John of Pian de Carpine*, Translated from Latin, edited with an introductory notice by William Woodvile Rockhill, London: Haklyut society, 1900, p. 32.

[2] History of the Nation of the Archers (The Mongols) by Grigor of Akanc Hitherto Ascribedto Matakia The Monk, The Armenian Text Edited with an English Translation and Notes by Robert P. Blake andRichard N. Frye, *Harvard Journal of Asiatic Studies*, Vol. 12, No. 3/4, 1949, p. 309; Bayarsaikhan Dashdondog, *The Mongols and the Armenians* (1220 – 1335), Leiden, Boston: Brill, 2011, p. 196; Jean Richard, *La papauté et les missions d'Orient au Moyen-Âge* (*XIII-XIVème siècle*), Rome : École Française de Rome, 1977, p. 85; J. A. Boyle, *Cambridge history of Iran*, Volume 5, the Saljuq and Mongol period, Cambridge-Cambridge history university press, 1968, p. 395;

[3] *Juveinis tsnobebi Sakartvelos shesakheb* (*Juvaini's records on Georgia*), Sp'arsul t'ekst's shesavali ts'aumdzghvara, Kartuli targmani da shenishvnebi daurto Revaz K'ik'nadzem, Tbilisi: Metsniereba, 1974, gv. 16.

[4] *Zhamtaagmts'ereli*, *Asts'lovani mat'iane* (*Hundred years chronicle*), t'ekst'i gamosatsemad moamzada, gamok'vleva, shenishvnebi da leksik'oni daurto Revaz K'ik'nadzem, Tbilisi, 1987, gv. 221.

on the fact that "hundried years chronicle" is historical work, the information contained in it could be considered more reliable than in works of prose or poetry. For the first time, Georgian readers were given the opportunity to learn about China in a historical context and to have a general idea about its geographical location. As a result, Georgians began to realize that China was not a legendary kingdom existence of which was shrouded in mystery, but rather a real place with concrete borders.

In the 15th-17th centuries, the Chinese phenomenon experienced a kind of regression in the Georgian society. This was caused by a number of external factors. In particular, as a result of constant unrest in Central Asia, trade became dangerous and the traffic on the Silk Road gradually decreased[1]. Due to this, in Persia, from where Georgian literature was nourished by knowledge about China, the flow of new information from the east also stopped. In the absence of new information, authors began to reprocess the old, traditional knowledge. In the Persian and Georgian writings of this period, China is presented again as a legendary country of the East.

In the 18th century, significant changes can be seen in the Georgians' perception of China. The main reason for this was altering the source of information about China. In particular, as we have already mentioned, before the 18th century, knowledge about China came to Georgians from Persia. From 18th century onward, Europe took the leading position in this regard. The change in the source of information had a great impact on the development of the Chinese phenomenon in Georgian society. Although Persia has been a kind of cultural and educational center ofthe Middle East for centuries, it should be noted that medieval Persian sources still provide us with rather superficial information about China, which was mainly spread orally through merchants to Persia. The most authentic accounts of China in Persian literature appeared in the 13th and 14th

---

[1] Christopher I. Beckwith, *Empires of the Silk Road, A history of Central Eurasia from the Bronze Age to the present*, Princeton, Oxford: Princeton university press, 2009, p. 262.

centuries, when for the first time in history Chinese scholars personally provided some information to Persian historians[1]. However, in the following centuries, with the disappearance of the Silk Road, the flow of new information stopped and the old knowledge was reprocessed again. Accordingly, in the 16th-17th centuries, the information about China in the Persian literature was several centuries out of date.

Contrary to Persia, knowledgeabout China grew rapidly in Europe in the 16th and 17th centuries, with the main contribution of the Jesuits. Jesuit Missionaries learned the Chinese language and, based on Chinese sources and their personal experience studied the history, geography, religions, philosophy of China[2]. Thus, the information they provided was authentic and based on primary sources. Thanks to the Georgian cultural center established in Moscow in the 1720s, these European materials were translated into Georgian[3]. Consequently, Georgian society got acquainted with various aspects of China.

As a result of the conquest of Georgia by the Russian Empire at the beginning of the 19th century, the Georgian aristocracy was allowed to receive European education through Russia, which influenced many aspects of the society's life. Among them, the rapid development of the Georgian press from the middle of the century isnoteworthy. Apart from the current events in the country, Georgian publicists also actively covered international affairs. Georgian publicists closely followed the development of events by subscribing to foreign magazines and newspapers and through telegrams. From the 90s of the 19th century, the Georgian press began to actively and regularly cover the events of China. In addition to the general description of Chinese history and culture, readers had the opportunity to learn about the Yihetuan Rebellion, the actions of European

---

[1] J. A. Boyle, *Cambridge history of Iran*, Volume 5, p. 510.

[2] Mo Dongyin, *History of the development of Sinology*, Zhengzhou: Daxiang chubanshe, 2006, pp. 43 – 59.

[3] Pridon Sikharulidze, *Mosk'ovis kartuli k'ult'uris tsent'ris ist'oriidan* (*history of the Georgian Cultural Center in Moscow*), Tbilisi, 1990, gv. 16.

states in China, the progress of the Qinghai Revolution, and the internal politics of China①. Most importantly, the articles of Georgian writers were not only descriptive in nature, but also had analytical roots. In particular, the authors did not miss the real intentions of European states in China. Despite the fact that the Georgian intelligentsia of that time was strongly influenced by European education and values, they still revealed that Europeans were actually trying to put China in a half-colonized state for their own benefit under the pretext of bringing education and a new culture to Chinese people②. Georgian publicists also were quite fast to note Yuan Shikai's aspirations to become an emperor③. In general, they respected China's rich history and culture and sympathized with the revolutionary movement of the Chinese people against internal or external enemies.

In 1918 Georgia took advantage of the unrest in Russian empire and regained its independence. Although the freedom was only maintained for 3 years, many changes were made in public lifeduring this short period of existence of the Democratic Republic of Georgia (1918 – 1921). Among them, the subject of interest towards China has also changed. If previously the main attention of Georgians was directed to China's politics, this time the main object of interest was China's economy. Articles on China's economic situation and development were written in Georgian magazines and newspapers of that time④. Such a change of interests was not accidental and was largely related to the Georgian community of Harbin.

The Georgian community of Harbin is one of the issues that need to be

---

① Maia Machavariani, Chineti 1914 W'lis kartuli gazetebis furc'lebze (China on the pages of Georgian newspapers in 1914), K'avk'asiis mac'ne, nomeri 17, Tbilisi, 2008, gv. 162; Kvali (Trace), Nomeri 27, Tbilisi, 1900, gv. 428 – 430; Sakhalkho Gazeti (People 's News), Nomeri 1155, Tbilisi, 1914, gv. 4; Ilia Tchavtchavadze, Akhlo da shoreuli aghosavletis p'olit'ik'is sak'itkhebi (Political issues of Near and Far East), Iveria, nomeri 18, T'filisi, 1898, gv. 1 – 2.

② Kvali (Trace), nomeri 35, Tbilisi, 1900, gv. 555 – 556.

③ Nik'oloz Abesadze, Revoluciis molodinshi (Waiting for the Revolution), Sakhalkho gazeti, nomeri 1181 – 1185, Tbilisi, 1914.

④ E. Nodia, Chineti (China), K'avshiri, nomeri 17 – 18, Tbilisi, 1920, gv. 14 – 17.

mentioned separately when talking about the history of the development of awareness of China among Georgians. In this city, founded at the turn of the 19th and 20th centuries, a settlement of Georgians was established on the territory of China for the first time in history. As in the first decades of its existence, Harbin enjoyed wide political and economic autonomy, many exiles and adventurers from the Russian Empire flocked to this city. At the end of the 1910s, about three to four thousand Georgians lived in Harbin and its surroundings[1]. The Georgian community in Harbin did not develop in isolation from Georgia, rather they had a quite close contacts to their home country. Later, even the consulate of the Democratic Republic of Georgia was opened here[2]. Before that, after the restoration of Georgia's independence, the Georgian community of Harbin sent representatives who presented the economic plan to the parliament of the Democratic Republic of Georgia[3]. This plan was aimed at establishing active trade and economic ties between Georgia and the Far East, including China, and outlined a general plan of what products could be exported and imported[4]. This was the first time when the idea of direct economic cooperation between Georgia and China was raised. As a result, interest in China's economy increased in the Democratic Republic of Georgia. Unfortunately, the abovementioned economic plan could not be fulfilled, because in 1921 Georgia became a member of the Soviet Union.

During the period of being part of the Soviet Union, thedevelopment of Chinese phenomenon in Georgians perception can be divided into two stages. In

---

[1] Sakartvelos evornuli cent'raluri saist'orio arkivi (National Central historical archives of Georgia), pondi 1864, anaw'eri 2, sakme 512, f. 4

[2] Irak'li Giorgadze, *Erovnuli modzraobis taviseburebani sakartveloshi XX sauk'unis* 20 – 90 – *ian w'lebshi* (*Characteristics of national movement in Georgia between* 1920 – 1990s), Telavi – Iak'ob gogebashvilis sakhelobis telavis sakhelmw'ifo universit'et'i, 2016, gv. 155.

[3] Irak'li Giorgadze, *Erovnuli modzraobis taviseburebani sakartveloshi XX sauk'unis* 20 – 90 – *ian w'lebshi* (*Characteristics of national movement in Georgia between* 1920 – 1990s), p. 59.

[4] Sakartvelos evornuli cent'raluri saist'orio arkivi (National Central historical archives of Georgia), pondi 1864, anaw'eri 2, sakme 512, f. 7.

the first stage, up to the 50s of the 20th century, the political situation of China once again became main subject of interest. The political situation of China was actively covered in the Georgian press during the 20s and 30s [1]. After the establishment of the People's Republic of China, China was perceived as one of the closest allies and friendly countries.

Since the 60s of the 20th century, the Georgians focus of interest towards China was shifted once again. This time, the cursor of interest shifted from politics to culture and brought China to the fore as a country with a great culture. Georgian scientists were interested in the literature and philosophy of this distant country. Pieces of Chinese poetry and prose, several philosophical treatises were translated into Georgian[2]. However, it should be noted here that the interest of Georgian scientists in this period towards Chinese culture and its perception was characterized by some peculiarities, which continued in the following period among a number of scientists. Despite the close political relations with China during the Soviet period, Chinese studies in Georgia were not yet established. Accordingly, those scholars who studied Chinese culture and translated Chinese literature, could not actually speak or read in Chinese, rather they got aquainted with Chinese culture through the medium of the Russian language. The lack of sources, ignorance of the Chinese language and having only a superficial knowledge of China finaly led those scholars to try and understand Chinese philosophy and culture in the framework of westenr philosophy[3]. As a result, in many cases, they misunderstood the concepts of ancient Chinese philosophy. Nevertheless, this was an important period in terms of the study of Chi-

---

[1] P'. Saq'varelidze, *Dzveli da akhali chineti* (*Old and new China*), Tbilisi: sakhelmw'ipo gamomtsemloba, 1926; *Musha* (*Worker*), nomeri 1564, Tbilisi, 1928, gv. 2; I. Morozovi, Chineti dghes (China now), *Remedas*, nomeri 1, Tbilisi, 1930, gv. 2.

[2] Rem Davidovi, Chineti kartul lit'erat'urashi (China in the Georgian literatura), *Lit'erat'uruli sakartvelo*, nomeri 23, Tbilisi, 1993, gv. 4; Jarji fkhoveli, *Dzveli chinuri poezia* (Ancient Chinese poetry), Tbilisi: Merani, 1985; 1952 *Chinuri motkhrobebis k'rebuli*, Shesavali Sh. Alkhazishvili, Tbilisi: sabavshvo da akhalgazrdobis lit'erat'uris sakhelmw'ifo gamomtsemloba, 1952.

[3] Mosia T'it'e, *Dzveli chinuri p'oezia* (Ancient Chinese poetry), Tbilisi: Inovatsia, 2010.

nese culture in Georgia, because it was the first steps taken in the direction of scientific study of China.

In the last three decades since the restoration of Georgia's independence, the phenomenon of China and the publicperception of China have become more complex and profound in the Georgian society. Unlike previous periods, interest in China is not limited to one aspect. Back in the 90s of the previous century, the President of Georgia, Eduard Shevardnadze, was actively promoting the project of TRASECA-Europe-Caucasus-Asia transport corridor[1]. Already from this period, China was seen in Georgia as a future economic partner. Real progress in this regard was witnessed in last decade, after Georgia got actively involved in the "One Belt One Road" project initiated by President Xi Jinping. Today, China is one of the largest economic partners of Georgia[2]. It can be said that the plan, which was presented by the representatives of the Georgian community of Harbin to the parliament of Georgian in 1919, has been realised after a century.

Since Georgia regained its independence in 1991, great efforts have been made to raise awareness towards China both in a public and in scientific circles. In 1991, for the first time in the history of Georgia, a scientific institute for the study of China-the Asia-Africa Institute was established in Tbilisi, where the first batch of Georgian sinologists was brought up. Today, a number of universities and other educational institutions have a faculty or research institute for China studies. Every year, a number of literary and scientific works are translated from Chinese, conferences are held and books on China are published. Georgian scientific circles are no longer completely dependent on an intermediary language, such as English or Russian, to receive information about China, rather they can directly access Chinese sources, Which makes the per-

---

[1] Eduard Shevardnadze, *Didi abreshumis gza (Silk road)*, Tbilisi: Metsniereba, 1999, gv. 60.
[2] Joseph Larsen, *Georgia-China relations: The geopolitics of the Belt and Road*, Tbilisi, 2017, pp. 6 – 8.

ception of the Chinesa more authentic. However, it should also be noted that cultural-scientific exchange is the direction that needs most work in the relations between the two countries. In the eyes of modern Georgians, China is mainly perceived as one of the closest economic partners and a world superpower. In other words, mainly economic and political factors are brought forward. The cultural aspect has been again moved to the background.

In conclusion, the knowledge andinterests of Georgians towards China was constantly changing according to different eras. the Georgian society got acquainted with China in the early centuries of the existence of the Silk Road. During the Middle Ages, until the 18th century, the perception of China was nurtured in the imagination of Georgians by the information that came along the trade routes. However, during this period, China was mostly viewed in Georgia as a distant, almost legendary country. Only from the 18th century, when European sources entered Georgia, did Georgians have a general idea of China as a real country. In the 19th and 20th centuries, this general idea was further detailed and deepened in the direction of politics, economy and culture. After the restoration of independence, the Georgian society began to perceive China in a complex picture. From now on, unlike the last century, attention was not paid only to China's politics, economics or any specific aspect, but The process of understanding China from the multiple perspectives by combining different sources of information has begun. The process is still in its initial stages and modern dynamics show that there is a certain lag in cultural awareness compared to the political and economic aspects, which requires further work.

The Impact of Chinese Modernization and Social Development on Georgia

Tamar Patashuri[*]

In recent years, the outstanding achievements in the cooperation between China and Georgia have made the bilateral relations more solid and the cooperation more fruitful. It is no exaggeration to say that the friendship between China, as a world power, and Georgia, especially the growing cooperative relations in the last few years, has become a model for the development of state-to-state relations in the world.

Undaubtedly, China is one of the important countries leading the world's economic development in the 21st century. Since its independence, Georgia, with its return to its role, has regained great development potential and become an important gateway between Europe and Asia. We are proud of the achievements Georgia has made in its economic and social development in recent years, which is partly due to the ever-deepening cooperative relations between China and Georgia.

In recent years, China has been a vital partner of Georgia, which is mainly reflected in the substantial growth of Chinese investment in Georgia's econo-

---

[*] Tamar. Patashuri, Young Georgian Sinologist, Lecture, Alte University & Georgian National University SEU in Tbilisi, Georgia.

my, which has played an important role in driving Georgia's domestic economic development. The increase in trade between Georgia and China compared to the same period last year is a case in point, despite the ongoing global spread of the COVID-19 pandemic.

Georgia is the first country in the region to sign a free trade agreement with China, which guarantees access to the world's largest consumer market for Georgian products and services. At the same time, the agreement is a very important incentive for new investment cooperation projects in Georgia. Georgia also has free trade relations with Europe and the Commonwealth of Independent States, which will facilitate the opening of China and neighboring countries of Georgia and the passage to Europe in the west, making Georgia a bridge and bond connecting the Commonwealth of Independent States and Europe with China.

It is well known that China and Georgia enjoy a time-honored traditional friendship. The ancient Silk Road greatly influenced the friendship and cooperation between the two nations. For Georgia, becoming an active participant in the Belt and Road Initiative[1] is of great significance to developing the country's economy.

Gansu Province has shown great enthusiasm for cooperation with Georgia. The framework cooperation agreement signed between Wuwei Bonded Logistics Center Operation and Management Co., Ltd. and Georgia Partners Foundation, the state-owned sovereign fund of Georgia, will serve as an important basis for strengthening practical cooperation between the two countries and implementing the Belt and Road Initiative. In particular, it provided convenient conditions for the launch of China-Europe freight trains.

China is a reliable strategic cooperative partner of Georgia and one of the first countries in the world to recognize Georgia's sovereignty and territorial in-

---

[1] Yan Dong (2017). "China's Strategy in the Caucasus." Foreign Policy Research Institute, April 3, www. fpr * i. org/article/2017/04/chinas-strategy-caucasus/.

tegrity and establish diplomatic relations with Georgia. At present, the bilateral relations between Georgia and China are in the best period with increasing political mutual trust, bright spots in economic and trade cooperation, and increasingly close cultural and people-to-people exchanges.

President Xi Jinping pointed out that China and Georgia are traditionally friendly and cooperative partners. Since the establishment of diplomatic relations 30 years ago, the two sides have steadily promoted cooperation in various fields, effectively communicated and coordinated in international affairs, and promoted the healthy and stable development of China-Georgia relations. After the new crown pneumonia epidemic outbreak, the people of the two countries have sincerely helped each other and overcome difficulties together, writing a good story of uniting and fighting the epidemic.

The Impact of China's Modernization and Social Development on Georgia

I shall not be humble and admit that what has happened between China, one of the largest countries in the world and Georgia, a small, 4-million country, over the past 7 years is an example for other countries.

In the twenty-first-centry world economy, indisputably, China is one of the leading countries. Georgia's interest and role in the major, global project "One Belt, One Road" initiated by the President of the People's Republic of China, Xi Jinping, is pretty big. Georgia is proud to be one of the first countries to respond to and join this initiative, launched in 2013. It hosted the third "One Belt, One Road" Forum in Tbilisi, during which it was repeatedly emphasized that Georgia is the center of the old and new Silk Road, and this is explained not only by its geographical location, but also by the history, culture and tolerance that our country has demonstrated to the world over the centuries.

While its strategic functions are expanding, Georgia is becoming a gateway to Europe and Asia with great potential.

The collaboration of Georgia with the World Trade Organization is a priority. Membership in the Organization is an important achievement in terms of the integration of our country into the world economic system: Georgia's position in the international economic system has been strengthened, and the country has become more influential and attractive as a trading partner; the country has significantly improved the conditions for attracting foreign investments, as the investor is provided with a long-term trade policy and foreign markets are opened for Georgian products; on the other hand, the conditions for exporting Georgian products to the international market have improved and Georgian entrepreneurs have been protected from discrimination in these markets through the WTO multilateral agreements.

Georgia actively participates in the World Trade Organization multilateral trade negotiations aimed at further liberalizing world trade by minimizing trade barriers. In addition, in cooperation with the World Trade Organization, the legal framework of Georgia has become more harmonized with the European one, which is a prerequisite for achieving the strategic objective of EU integration.

Georgia is becoming a hub for trade, transport and logistics, not only in the region, but worldwide. One of the important reasons for this is the establishment of a free trade regime with the world's leading countries. In 2014, an important historic event took place: Georgia and the EU signed the Association Agreement and later the Deep and Comprehensive Free Trade Agreement, allowing Georgia to freely circulate goods, services and capital to the EU market. From an economic point of view, this means the free movement of goods and services in the European market of half a billion consumers. As a result of the visa liberalization process, our citizens are able to move freely within the EU countries.

Moreover, Georgia has signed a free trade agreement with Turkey, the CIS and the European Free Trade Association, which is an obvious advantage of the country's investment climate. In addition, there are also improved rates for starting a business and registering property, as well as a simplified tax system with lower tax rates.

The largest free market for goods and services produced in Georgia was opened in 2017 as part of the Free Trade Agreement between Georgia and the People's Republic of China. However, in accordance with the Free Trade Agreement with China, about 94% of Georgian imports to China are exempt from customs duties. The agreement is a very important motivation for the implementation of new investment projects in Georgia, the development of entrepreneurship and the increase in the export of Georgian products. In turn, Chinese companies have the opportunity to sell their products to the European market through Georgia.

As I mentioned earlier, the development of the Silk Road is one of the main priorities for the Government of Georgia. Therefore, the main infrastructure being built throughout the country is a part of the Silk Road, including the East-West Highway, the modernization of the Baku-Tbilisi-Kars railway, and the deep-water port of Anaklia. The launch of the Silk Road through Georgia is an important event in terms of enhancing transregional traffic flows and the Trans-Caspian Railway, which connects China, Kazakhstan, Azerbaijan, Georgia and Georgia through European countries. These large international markets open up new opportunities not only for Georgia, but also for partner countries and potential investors.

In terms of investment encouragement, I would like to highlight Georgia's largest financial institution-the JSC Partnership Fund, which is 100% owned by the state. In partnership with the Fund, partners can use the investment potential of our country and enjoy the benefits of free trade with the rest of the world. We are proud that the JSC Partnership Fund has become a guarantee of business success for the investors.

Within the framework of Tbilisi Forum, a well-known analyst of the BBC of Irish origin stated that 20 years ago, Ireland was one of the poorest countries in Europe, and today it takes second place in Europe after Luxembourg. As a Georgian, I am very hopeful that in 20 years, Georgia will become one of the most developed and prosperous countries in the world, not only in the region, but also in the whole world, with the help of its big partner and the project of the century "One Belt, One Road", it will succeed.

It is well known that China and Georgia enjoy a time-honored traditional friendship. The ancient Silk Road greatly influenced on the friendship and cooperation between the two countries. For Georgia, becoming an active participant in the Belt and Road Initiative along the new Silk Road significant to developing the country's economy.

China is a reliable strategic cooperative partner of Georgia and one of the first countries in the world to recognize Georgia's sovereignty and territorial integrity and establish diplomatic relations with Georgia. Georgia and China are in the best period of bilateral relations with increasing political mutual trust and bright spots in economic and trade cooperation. I would like to take this opportunity to congratulate Chinese people on the 100th anniversary of the founding of the Communist Party of China[1].

It is worth emphasizing that China has been taking the lead among Georgian partners in recent years, which is mainly reflected in the substantial growth of Chinese investment in the Georgian economy. Despite the ongoing spread of COVID-19, Georgia's trade volume with China has increased compared to the same period in 2021.

In addition, many Georgian companies are also growing their business in China, as reflected in the increasing number of Georgian commercial offices and cultural centers in China, as well as increased sales of Georgian wine, spirits, mineral water and Georgian tea in China.

The traditional friendship between China and Georgia dates back to ancient times. The ancient Silk Road has exerted a great influence on the friendship and

---

[1] Meine Pieter van Dijk and Patrick Martens (2016). The Silk Road and Chinese Interests in Central Asia and the Caucasus: The Case of Georgia. Maastricht School of Management Working Paper No. 2016/12, August, p. 5, www.msm.nl/resources/uploads/2016/09/MSM-WP2016-12-1.pdf.

cooperation between the two countries. It is important for Georgia to be a major player in the Belt and Road Initiative of the new Silk Road.

It should be noted that Georgia is the first country in the region to sign a free trade agreement with China. The deal opens the world's largest market for Georgian products and services. In addition, the agreement is a very important motivator for new investment cooperation projects in Georgia. Georgia also has free trade relations with Europe and the Commonwealth of Independent States. Our goal is to make Georgia a bridge and link between Europe and the CIS countries and China.

As far as I know, Gansu is an important hub of China's railway network and provides services to major railway freight companies throughout China. Therefore, I believe that with the implementation of the free Trade Agreement between China and Georgia and the signing of the cooperation agreement between the two sides today, with our joint efforts, the China-Europe corridor through Georgia will be opened in a short time[1].

The Silk Road Economic Belt (SREB), which was a global project from the very beginning, provided for several economic corridors such as the New Eurasian Land Bridge, the China-Mongolia-Russia Economic Corridor, the Central Asia-West Asia Economic Corridor, the Indo-China Peninsula Economic Corridor, the China-Pakistan Economic Corridor and the Bangladesh-China-India-Myanmar Economic Corridor, among which the economic corridor crossing the Caucasus was not clearly outlined; however, this definitely did not prevent Chinese companies from conducting economic activities in the Caucasus. It should be pointed out that the Georgian corridor (as well as that of Azerbaijan) is located in the Central Asia-West Asia Economic Corridor.

Georgia, together with its neighbor and strategic ally, Azerbaijan, has been considered in the context of the historic Great Silk Road right from the be-

---

[1] Fabio Indeo (2017). "A Comprehensive Strategy to Strengthen China's Relations with Central Asia." In: China's Belt and Road: A Game Changer? Ed. by Alessia Amighini. Milano: Italian.

ginning of the 1990s. The practical implications of this idea have been the TRACECA project initiated by the EU in 1993, the INOGATE project starting in 1996 and somewhat later was supported by the Silk Road Strategy Act adopted by the United States Congress in 1999. In fact, practically all projects envisaged regarding the Silk Road transport corridor are functioning successfully today. One of the flaws of these projects can be considered to be the fact that they were designed to create both transports as well as energy corridors to connect Europe through the Caucasus to Central Asia; however, they did not envisage extending the corridors all the way to China[①].

The inclusion of Azerbaijan and Georgia (as the Caucasian Tandem 21) in the SREB project is facilitated by the already implemented Silk Road Transport Corridor (SRTC) project, an important part of which is the Baku-Tbilisi-Kars railway, connecting not only Azerbaijan, Georgia and Turkey with a railroad but also connecting East and West, in general, through the Caucasus. As an essential part of the Iron Silk Road project, the railroad mentioned above is a logical piece of the OBOR initiative.

The fact that the institution of a free trade regime between China and the EU is under active discussion is very important for Georgia. In this regard, the SREB creates a new stage in the economic cooperation between China and the EU[②].

China and Georgia are members of the World Trade Organization. The fact that a free trade agreement has been signed between the two countries is very important in terms of the development of trade relations. Georgia also has the Deep and Comprehensive Free Trade Area (DCFTA) agreement with the European Union as well as a free trade agreement with the European Free Trade Association (EFTA). Hence, the expansion of trade between the EU and China

---

[①] Hilary Appel and Vladimir Gel'man (2015). "Revising Russia's Economic Model: The Shift from Development to Geopolitics." PONARS Eurasia Policy Memo, No. 397, November, www.ponarseurasia.org/sites/default/files/policy-memos-pdf/Pepm397_Appel-Gelman_Nov2015.pdf.

[②] Aleksandr Knobel' (2017). "Eurasian Economic Union: Development Prospects and Possible Obstacles." Problems of Economic Transition, 59 (5): 335–360. (In Russian.)

will enable Georgia to become a logistical hub, connecting China with Europe (for which the Baku-Tbilisi-Kars railway and the implementation of the Anaklia Black Sea Deep Water Port project will have vital importance) and increase the level of its security at the same time.

Of further note is that due to the transportation of Caspian oil and gas to Turkey, Georgia already plays the role of an energy resources transportation hub. Let us also consider that Azerbaijan has managed to gain the image of a regional transport hub, too. These two countries Georgia and Azerbaijan, combined create a Central Caucasus transportation and energy hub.

For Georgia, the SREB project creates an opportunity to transform its role as an energy resources transportation hub to a regional economic hub in general. In this regard, it should be underlined that with the DCFTA agreement signed between the EU and Georgia, products exported from Georgia to the EU must be produced in Georgia. This, therefore, makes Georgia attractive to all countries without free trade agreements with the EU to invest in Georgia and export the production manufactured here to the EU market. This includes China as well, which is already investing in Georgia.

Consequently, Georgia can actually become an economic hub in the region which would be in full accordance with the content of the Central Asia-West Asia Economic Corridor project crossing Georgia.

Georgia finds its place in one of the corridors, the Central Asia-West Asia Economic Corridor of the SREC project, which creates principally new ways for the development of its economy.

Georgia and neighboring Azerbaijan have been actively participating in the creation and development of the SRTC. This corridor is already successfully operating[1].

---

[1] Richard Ghiasy and Jiayi Zhou. The Silk Road Economic Belt. Considering Security Implications and EU-China Cooperation Prospects. Solna, Sweden: Stockholm International Peace Research Institute, 2017, p. IX, www.sipri.org/sites/default/files/The-Silk-Road-Economic-Belt.pdf.

It can be said that the SREB is the further development of the SRTC as the transport corridor is being transformed into a much more complex economic corridor.

Georgia can play the role of an economic hub in the SREB project as it already has free trade agreements in place with both the EU as well as China.

For Georgia, the SREB project creates an opportunity to transform its role as an energy resources transportation hub to a regional economic hub in general. In this regard, it should be underlined that with the DCFTA agreement signed between the EU and Georgia, products exported from Georgia to the EU must be produced in Georgia. This, therefore, makes Georgia attractive to all countries without free trade agreements with the EU to invest in Georgia and export the production manufactured here to the EU market. This includes China as well, which is already investing in Georgia.

Consequently, Georgia can actually become an economic hub in the region which would be in full accordance with the content of the Central Asia-West Asia Economic Corridor project crossing Georgia[①].

Given the increased risks of terrorism and other industrial disasters in the contemporary world, it is important to have complementary transport and energy corridors, which should ensure the maximum continuity of transport flows. The increased risks of technological catastrophes, transportation disasters or other man-made disasters underline the importance of the development of transport or economic corridors, which can ensure that they can substitute one another in critical situations.

Therefore, the possibility of the complementarity and harmonization of the economic corridors must be based upon an approach that envisages inspecting the routes for transporting Asian energy resources to Europe, not according to

---

① Joseph Larsen. Georgia-China Relations: The Geopolitics of the Belt and Road, 2017, p. 19.

their alternativeness but rather in the context of their complementarity①.

It should be pointed out that transferring to the paradigm of the complementarity of the economic corridors will ultimately ensure the implementation of the OBOR initiative in the context of a win-win cooperation relationship which is vital for the ultimate success of this initiative.

This is especially important for the functioning and subsequent development of the Central Asia-West Economic Corrido②

Azerbaijan and Georgia play key roles within the framework of China's Belt & Road Initiative. The zone is based in Kutaisi and is an important connecting hub between Tbilisi (the capital of Georgia) and Georgia's Black Sea Ports of-Poti and Batumi③.

Hualing FIZ was built by Hualing Group with Chinese investments and began operating in 2015. Despite the COVID – 19 pandemic, Hualing FIZ was able to increase its investor client base in 2021, with 25 new companies registered during the past year.

"One of the most important initiatives of 2021 was a project related to wood processing and furniture production, developed together with investors from Canada and China. This project provides for production at the FIZ and further export.

The initial budget for this project was US $ 1. 5 million, and in general, it

---

① Vladimer Papava and Michael Tokmazishvili. "Pipeline Harmonization Insteadof Alternative Pipelines: Why the Pipeline "Cold War" Needs to End." Azerbaijan in the World. The Electronic Publication of Azerbaijan Diplomatic Academy, 2008, 1 (10), June 15, www. biweekly. ada. edu. az/vol_1 _no_10/Pipeline_harmonization_instead_of_alternative_pipelines. htm; Vladimer Papava and Michael Tokmazishvili (2010) . "Russian Energy Politics and the EU: How to Change the Paradigm." Caucasian Review of International Affairs, 4 (2): pp. 103-111, www. criaonline. org/Journal/11/Done_Russian_ Energy_Politics_and_EU_How_to_Change_the_Paradigm_by_Vladimer_Papava_and_Michael_Tokmazishvili. pdf.

② Ruan Zongze. "Belt and Road Initiative: A New Frontier for Win-Win Cooperation." China International Studies, 65, 2017, (July/August): pp. 78 – 85.

③ For example, Joseph Larsen. Georgia-China Relations: The Geopolitics of theBelt and Road, 2017, p. 19.

is planned to increase it to US $7 million.

Further investment into the zone is expected shortly, with a Chinese company starting the production and export of ferroalloys and silicon metal at the-Hualing FIZ. The total volume of the investments amounted to US $5 million, and it is also expected to increase this as the business develops. It is also pointed to a recycled plastic project, launched at the FIZ in 2021. Investments in this project amounted to about US $2 million.

Hualing FIZ conducts most of the negotiations with manufacturers of the light industry sector. One of these is a German investor, dealing with the production and export of textile products.

"About 2,000 people will be employed once the project is launched, and the total investment in it is about 3 million". Among the projects in the green energy field, Hualing FIZ has attracted solar panel production-and the largest project in this sector in the European-Caucasus region. The total investment for this project has reached US $10 million, with the exports mainly for the North American market.

Hualing FIZ now has 90 resident companies, of which 70% are in trading, 25% in manufacturing and 5% in the services sector. This success is expected to lead to an agreement with the Georgian government to expand the zone's territory to 58 hectares, up from the existing 36 hectares. There are additional prospects to expand the FIZ to 200 hectares[1].

The main export destinations for goods manufactured or traded at Hualing FIZ are the South Caucasus and Central Asia, the European Union, North America, and Mexico. The FIZ closely cooperates with investors from Azerbaijan, whose Baku Port to the east, on the Caspian Sea, connects with Central Asia, Iran and the INSTC route to India[2].

---

[1] For example, Joseph Larsen. Georgia-China Relations: The Geopolitics of theBelt and Road, 2017, p. 19.

[2] Agenda. ge. "Georgia Makes New European Free Trade Deal." Agenda. ge, 2017, June 6, www. agenda. ge/news/59578/eng.

Chapter 5 Chinese Path to Modernization and New Opportunities for the Development of the China-Georgia BRI Cooperation   503

Cargo services on the 800-odd kilometers from Kars to Baku via Georgia take about three days, meaning it is not the high-speed line it was initially promoted as[1]. Additional costs take place due to train gauge changing as the BTK crosses into Georgia.

The Caspian-European BTK transit issues aside, the development of Chinse and locally invested Free Trade and Industrial zones along the Belt and Road Initiative is a primary example of the BRI moving from being an infrastructure investment play to being a cashflow generator based on that initial investment[2]. This means that investors along the BRI-such as the Hualing FIZ-can now generate profits and help their own invested clients manufacture and trade[3]. The BRI infrastructure investment is now showing up, with the end result being increased trade turnover and exports[4], with the ultimate success measurement of the BRI infrastructure investments to be measured in this increased capability rather than the project financing[5].

---

[1] MESD of Georgia. "Rules of Origin." Free Trade with the EU, Ministry of Economy and Sustainable Development of Georgia, 2017, www.dcfta.gov.ge/en/dcfta-for-businness/ Rules-of-Origin-.

[2] Mariam Zabakhidze, Giorgi Bakradze and Batu Kutelia. *Georgia and China*: "*Carry Away Small Stones to Move a Big Mountain*," 2017, pp. 14 – 16.

[3] Vladimer Papava, "One Belt One Road Initiative And Georgia". GEORGIAN FOUNDATION FOR STRATEGIC AND INTERNATIONAL STUDIES, 2017.

[4] Silk Road Briefing, Georgia's Belt And Road Initiative-Accelerating Trade Between Central Asia And Europe", 2022, https://www.silkroadbriefing.com/news/2022/02/07/georgias-belt-and-road-initiative-accelerating-trade-between-central-asia-and-europe/.

[5] Bulletin of the Georgian National Academy of Sciences, Vol. 12, No. 1, 2018; China-Georgia Economic Relations in the Context of the Belt and Road Initiative.